SOCIAL PSYCHOLOGY

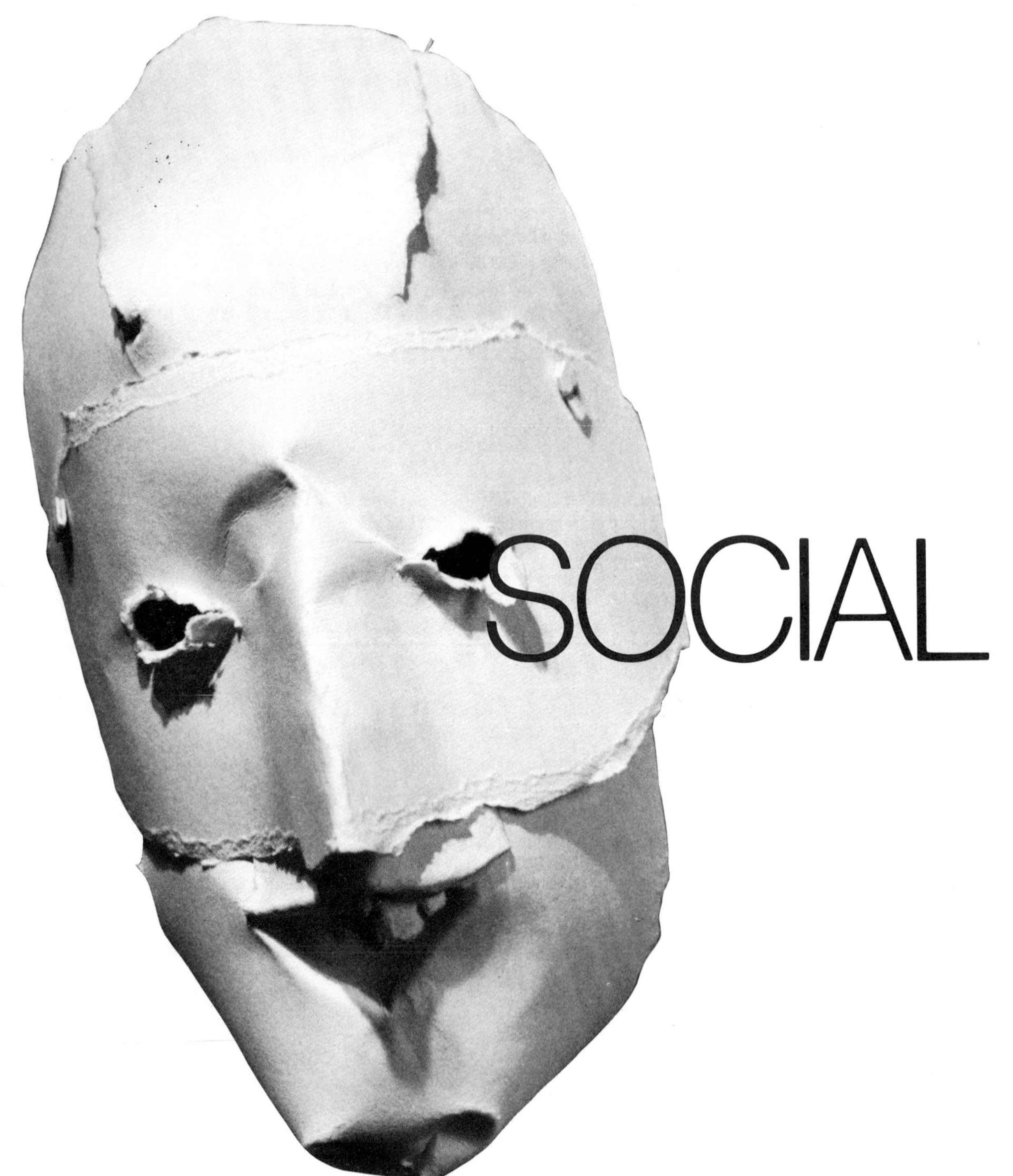
SOCIAL

Teresa E. Litten
Dorcas

David G. Myers

Hope College
Holland, Michigan

PSYCHOLOGY

McGraw-Hill Book Company

New York St. Louis San Francisco Auckland Bogotá Hamburg Johannesburg London Madrid Mexico Montreal New Delhi Panama Paris São Paulo Singapore Sydney Tokyo Toronto

To Peter,
Andrew, and Laura

SOCIAL PSYCHOLOGY

1234567890VNHVNH89876543

ISBN 0-07-044273-8

See Acknowledgments on pages 649–652.
Copyrights included on this page by reference.

This book was set in Plantin by Monotype Composition Company, Inc. The editors were Patricia S. Nave, Alison Meersschaert, and James R. Belser; the designer was Joseph Gillians; the production supervisor was Dennis J. Conroy. The photo editor was Inge King. The drawings were done by J & R Services, Inc. The masks were created by Tom Huffman; the cover and part-opening photographs were taken by Joseph Gillians.
Von Hoffmann Press, Inc., was printer and binder.

Library of Congress Cataloging in Publication Data

Myers, David G.
Social psychology.

Bibliography: p.
Includes indexes.
1. Social psychology. I. Title.
HM251.M897 1983 302 82-13069
ISBN 0-07-044273-8

CONTENTS

PREFACE

In all history human social behavior has been systematically and scientifically studied in but one century. That century is ours. Considering that we have barely begun, the results are, I believe, gratifying. Social psychologists have gleaned significant insights into belief and illusion, love and hate, conformity and independence. Although much mystery remains, we can now offer partial answers to such questions as: Will people act in new and better ways if we can first persuade them to adopt new attitudes? Do males and females differ? How? Why? When are people most likely to help another? What kindles social conflict, and what steps can be taken to transform closed fists into open arms? Learning even tentative answers to such questions can stimulate our minds. Moreover, becoming sensitive to the social forces at work upon us can help free us from susceptibility to unwanted manipulation. I hope that such will be among the benefits of studying social psychology.

When I was invited to write this book, I immediately envisioned a text that would present social psychology as an intellectual adventure. This text was to be at once solidly scientific and warmly human, factually rigorous and intellectually provocative. It would be reasonably comprehensive in its coverage of the discipline, yet it would also stimulate students' *thinking*. In short, this text would present social psychology as an investigative reporter might, providing an up-to-date summary of important phenomena of social thinking and social behavior, and of how such phenomena have been revealed and how they are being explained. And it would cultivate students' abilities to think like competent social psychologists—to inquire, to analyze, to relate principles to everyday happenings.

To stimulate thinking, one must describe selected concepts concretely enough to give students some proficiency in working with the ideas. Students should understand the ideas well enough to trigger their own thinking—by relating them to other concepts and to their own experiences and observations. The time required to stimulate such thinking prohibits an exhaustive catalog of theory and research. But for the undergraduate who is being introduced to social psychology this is no great sacrifice. The introductory text prepares one not to be a social psychologist, but to understand the field and its relation to one's life. Those who gain an enduring interest in the discipline may then go on to further study.

But how does one select material for inclusion in a "reasonably comprehensive" introduction to the discipline? I sought to present theories and findings that are neither too esoteric for the typical undergraduate nor better suited to other psychology courses. I chose instead to present material that casts social psychology in the intellectual tradition of the liberal arts. By the teaching of great literature, philosophy, and science, liberal education seeks to expand people's thinking and awareness and to help free them from the confines of their current social environment. Social psychology can significantly contribute to these goals of liberal education. Many undergraduate social psychology students are not psychology majors; virtually all will enter professions other than social psychology. By focusing on humanly significant issues, one can present much of the fundamental content that preprofessional psychology students need, but in ways that are also stimulating and useful to all liberal arts students.

The book opens with a single chapter that introduces research methods, and forewarns students of how findings can seem obvious—once you know them—and of how social psychologists' values penetrate the discipline. The intent is to give students just enough to prepare them for what follows.

The remainder of the book is organized around its definition of social psychology: the scientific study of how people think about (Part Two, Social Thinking), influence (Part Three, Social Influence), and relate (Part Four, Social Relations) to one another.

Part Two on social thinking examines how we view ourselves and others. For example, Chapter 3 introduces attribution theory and then looks in greater depth at three concepts that are both intellectually provocative and theoretically controversial: the fundamental attribution error, the self-serving bias, and the benefits of self-efficacy.

Part Three explores social influence. By appreciating the cultural sources of our attitudes, and by learning the nature of conformity, persuasion, and group influence, we can better recognize subtle social forces at work upon us.

Part Four considers both unpleasant and pleasant aspects of social relations—aggression and altruism, prejudice and attraction, conflict and peacemaking.

The concluding section (Part Five) describes the application of social psychology to environmental issues and to courtroom judgments. Not only these chapters, but nearly all the later chapters in the text apply principles discussed in earlier chapters.

Several other features are also worthy of note. Formal definitions appear in the text margin—when and where students need them and where they may easily be reviewed for study purposes. To communicate the human side of social psychology, all chapters present "Behind the Scenes" personal reflections by selected investigators. Finally, the *Teacher's Resource and Test Manual* contains a package of teaching ideas, including ready-to-use class demonstrations for each chapter. It also includes two separate categories of test questions—the usual "basic-knowledge questions" that test students' retention of chapter content, and also "application questions" that test students' ability to relate concepts to novel situations.

IN APPRECIATION

Although only one person's name appears on the cover of this book, the truth is that many people—a whole community of scholars—have invested themselves in it. None of these people agrees with everything I have written nor should any of them be held responsible. Yet their suggestions helped make this a better book than it would otherwise have been.

Mark Snyder, Elaine Hatfield, and Charles Kiesler consulted on the organization of the book and the content of selected chapters. The opportunity to meet and work with these esteemed colleagues added significantly to the pleasure of my work.

Several individuals read all or virtually all of the manuscript. Reflecting upon their comments heightened my respect for the professional competence and commitment of each of them: Martin Bolt, Calvin College; Ranald Hansen, Oakland University; William Ickes, University of Missouri at St. Louis; Edward E. Jones, Princeton University; Martin Kaplan, Northern Illinois University; Teru L. Morton, University of Hawaii; Tom Tyler, Northwestern University; and Kipling Williams, Drake University.

Other professional colleagues willingly provided expert reviews of selected chapters or sections. Their constructive criticisms and suggestions averted numerous errors. I am grateful to each of these people: Anthony Doob, University of Toronto; Bert Hodges, Gordon College; Chester A. Insko, University of North Carolina; Billy Van Jones, Abilene Christian College; Norbert Kerr, Michigan State University; David L. McMillen, Mississippi State University; Darren Newtson, University of Virginia; Paul Paulus,

University of Texas at Arlington; Garold Stasser, Miami University; Homer Stavely, Keene State College; Elizabeth Tanke, University of Santa Clara; William C. Titus, Briarcliff College; and Mary Stewart Van Leeuwen, York University.

Several other very special people deserve a special mention. Hope College provided a whole intellectual community. Friends and colleagues—Les Beach, Jane Dickie, Jack Holmes, Steven Hoogerwerf, Donald Luidens, John Shaughnessy, and Phillip Van Eyl—consulted on various chapters. Carol Myers critiqued every chapter and helped me reflect upon advice from the nearly three dozen other critics. My students Janet Swim and Dean Morier assisted in countless small ways in the development and production of the manuscript. Karen Alderink and Beverly Kindig used their professional word processing skills to produce draft after draft with amazing efficiency. For class testing and for professional reviewers, Betty Hayes cheerfully produced some 75,000 xeroxed pages.

Were it not for the initiative and encouragement of Nelson Black of McGraw-Hill, it never would have occurred to me to write this book. Alison Meersschaert, McGraw-Hill senior editor, guided me throughout the project and sustained me with her unfailing enthusiasm. She is a true pro, and now a valued friend.

Finally, my hidden coauthor is my friend and writing coach, poet-essayist Jack Ridl. His fingerprints are on nearly every paragraph.

To each one of these persons, I am in debt. Collectively, they made writing this book a stimulating, gratifying experience.

David G. Myers

SOCIAL PSYCHOLOGY

INTRODUCTION

Chapter

Introducing Social Psychology

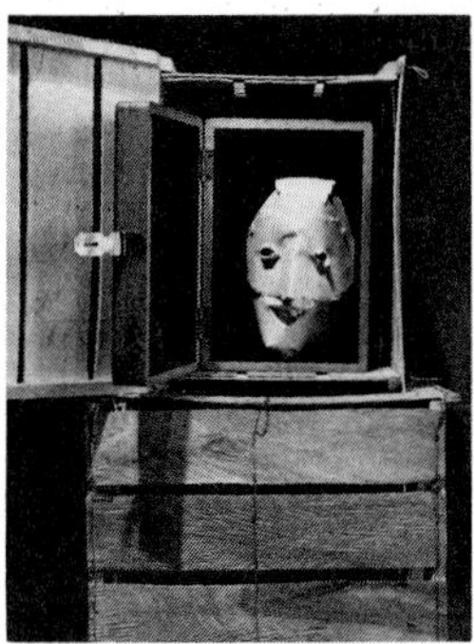

What is social psychology? Let's consider some down-to-earth examples of the kinds of occurrences and questions that fascinate social psychologists:

David Rosenhan (1973) and seven of his friends and Stanford University colleagues conducted a controversial test of some mental health workers' clinical insights. Each made an appointment with a mental hospital admissions office and complained of "hearing voices," saying "empty," "hollow," and "thud." Apart from this single complaint and giving false names and vocations, they truthfully answered all questions about their life histories and emotional states. Yet, seven of the eight were diagnosed as schizophrenic (the eighth was said to be suffering a manic-depressive psychosis). Once admitted, they exhibited no further symptoms. The clinicians nevertheless managed to "discover" the sources of the pseudopatients' problems after analyzing their life histories. One person's schizophrenia was said to be the result of childhood mixed emotions regarding his parents. Moreover, while the pseudopatients were hospitalized—for nineteen days on the average—their normal behaviors, such as note taking, were often overlooked or misinterpreted to fit the staff's preconceptions based on the diagnostic labels.

Why are mental health workers vulnerable to this type of misjudgment? More generally, what determines the impressions we form of ourselves and of others?

President John F. Kennedy, like most other American presidents, enjoyed the support of a bright and loyal group of advisers who collaborated in his decision making. One of their first major decisions was to approve a Central Intelligence Agency plan to invade Cuba. The high morale of the group fostered a sense that the plan couldn't fail. Since no one sharply disagreed with the idea, there appeared to be consensus support for the plan. After the resulting fiasco in Cuba's Bay of Pigs (the small band of U.S.-trained and U.S.-supplied Cuban refugee invaders was easily captured and soon linked to the American government), Kennedy was heard wondering aloud, "How could we have been so stupid?" Reflecting on the group's decision making, Arthur Schlesinger, a member of the Kennedy inner circle, later reproached himself in his book *A Thousand Days* "for having kept so silent in the cabinet room. I can only explain my failure to do more than raise a few timid questions by reporting that one's impulse to blow the whistle on this nonsense was simply undone by the circumstances of the discussion" (1965, p. 255).

How are we affected by our participation in groups? Or, to broaden the question, to what extent and in what ways do other people influence our attitudes and actions? And how might we as individuals resist unwanted social pressure, or even get a group to consider our point of view?

Fuzz, an ABC television movie filmed in Boston, depicted teenagers setting derelicts on fire for kicks. Two nights after the broadcast, some Boston teenagers who had viewed the movie forced Evelyn Wagler to douse herself with gasoline and then set her afire, burning her fatally.

What stimulates violent behavior? Are the media a significant force in shaping our behavior and attitudes toward other people? Beyond this, how do stereotyped impressions originate, and why, even in this "enlightened" era, does prejudice persist? On the brighter side, how do we come to help, to like, and sometimes even to love particular persons? And how can just and amiable social relations be encouraged?

What are the common threads running through these questions? As diverse as they are, they all deal with how people view and affect one another. And that is what social psychology is all about. As we shall see, social psychologists attempt to answer such questions by using the scientific method. They aim to study attitudes and beliefs, conformity and independence, love and hate. So, to put it formally, we might say that *social psychology* is *the scientific study of how people think about, influence, and relate to one another.*

Social psychology: *The scientific study of how people think about, influence, and relate to one another.*

Social psychology is still a very young science. We keep reminding people of this, partly as an excuse for our incomplete answers to some of the questions raised above. But it is true. The first social psychology experiments were not reported until the late 1800s and no book on social psychology was published before this century. Not until the 1930s did social psychology assume its current form, and not until after World War II did it begin to emerge as the vibrant field it is today. In just the last fifteen years the number of social psychology periodicals has more than doubled. More and more, social psychologists are applying their concepts and methods to social concerns such as energy conservation, health, and courtroom decision making.

But what *are* the concepts and methods of social psychology? What distinguishes social psychology from other fields that also explore human nature?

SOCIAL PSYCHOLOGY AND THE OTHER DISCIPLINES

Although social psychologists are keenly interested in how people think about, influence, and relate to one another, they are not the only people with these interests. Sociologists, personality psychologists, and even novelists and philosophers are also curious about these matters. The academic disciplines are seldom sharply defined. Where does physics leave off and chemistry begin? Such divisions are overlapping. Nevertheless, let us briefly consider the similarities and differences between social psychology and some of these related fields.

Social Psychology and Sociology

Social psychology is often confused with sociology. True, sociologists and social psychologists do share some common interests—for example, in studying how people behave in groups. Moreover, social psychology is really a subfield of both its parent disciplines, sociology and, especially, psychology (it is *not* a grand synthesis of the two fields). So the confusion is understandable.

Although there is no distinct demarcation between social psychology and the rest of sociology, their subject matters and methods do differ. Most sociologists study the structure and functioning of *groups*, from small groups to very large groups (societies). The social psychologist is usually interested in the *individual*—how a person thinks about other people, is influenced by them, relates to them. Thus while social psychologists, like other sociologists, are interested in groups, they generally want to ascertain how groups affect individual people, or, sometimes, how an individual can affect a group. For example, while many sociologists might be interested in how the racial attitudes of middle class people as a group differ from those of lower socioeconomic classes, the social psychologist would be more interested in how racial attitudes develop within the typical individual. For instance, does merely labeling people as members of some group—football players, blacks, sorority women, the aged—lead one to overestimate both the similarity of people within the groups and the differences between the groups? (The answer, by the way, turns out to be yes.)

Although sociologists and social psychologists use some of the same research methods, social psychologists rely much more heavily upon experiments in which they manipulate a factor such as social pressure to see what

The social psychologist is usually interested in the individual within the group. (Erika Stone/ Peter Arnold, Inc.)

effect it has. The complexity of the problems most sociologists deal with makes experimentation difficult, so they will often use surveys to study, say, the relationship between people's socioeconomic class and their racial attitudes. Obviously, ethical considerations also preclude sociologists' experimenting with such factors as people's economic levels. One just doesn't manipulate someone's long-term economic well-being to see its effect on racial attitudes. A social psychologist, however, might very briefly induce some people to feel frustrated to see how this experience affects their attitudes toward other people.

Social psychology also differs from two areas closely related to sociology: "social work" and "social problems." Social psychologists are eager to see their principles applied to problems such as crime and marital breakdown, but the problems themselves are not the primary focus of social psychology.

Social Psychology and Personality Psychology

Since social psychology and personality psychology both focus upon the individual person, they, too, are closely related. Indeed, the American Psychological Association has found it so difficult to separate these two areas that it has included them in the same journals (the *Journal of Personality and Social Psychology* and the *Personality and Social Psychology Bulletin*). Their difference lies, first, in the *social* character of social psychology. Personality psychologists give greater attention to our private internal functioning. Second, personality psychologists also have a special concern for *differences* between individuals—in traits such as self-esteem or aggressiveness, for example. Why are some individuals more aggressive than others? Social psychologists focus more on our common humanity, on how individuals, in general, view and affect one another. What circumstances, for example, prompt the average person to behave aggressively?

"It is easier to know mankind than any man."

La Rochefoucauld, Maxims

There are other differences between personality psychology and social psychology. Social psychology has a shorter active history. As Lee Sechrest (1976) has noted, many of the heroes of personality psychology —people like Sigmund Freud, Carl Jung, Alfred Adler, and Abraham Maslow—are dead. By contrast, all but a few of social psychology's leading contributors are alive and active. Also, social psychology has fewer famous "heroes"—people who have invented grand theories—and many more unsung heroes—creative researchers who are contributing smaller scale theories. We will meet some of these people in the autobiographical "Behind the Scenes" inserts sprinkled throughout this book.

Levels of Explanation

Sociology, social psychology, and personality psychology hardly exhaust the perspectives from which we can study human beings. There is a whole range of useful perspectives. These perspectives are organized into academic disciplines ranging from basic sciences such as physics up to integrative disciplines such as philosophy. Which perspective is most relevant all depends on what it is you want to talk about. Take love, for example. A physiologist might describe love as a state of arousal. A social psychologist would examine how various characteristics and conditions— good looks, similarity of the partners, sheer repeated exposure to one another—enhance the emotion of love. A poet would extol the sublime experience that love can sometimes be. A theologian might describe love as the goal, the God-given epitome of human relationships. Since an event, like love, can often be described simultaneously at various levels, we need not assume that one level is *causing* the other—by supposing, for example, that a brain state is causing the emotion of love or that the emotion is causing the brain state. The emotional and physiological perspectives are simply two ways of looking at the same event.

It is also important to remember that one level of explanation is not necessarily superior to another. Successful scientific explanation, for example, need not invalidate or preempt the perspectives of literature and philosophy. Thus an evolutionary explanation of the universality of incest taboos (in terms of the genetic penalty one's offspring pay for inbreeding), need not preempt a sociological explanation (which might see its function as preserving the family unit), or a theological explanation (in terms of moral truth). These various, possible explanations of the incest taboo can complement rather than contradict one another.

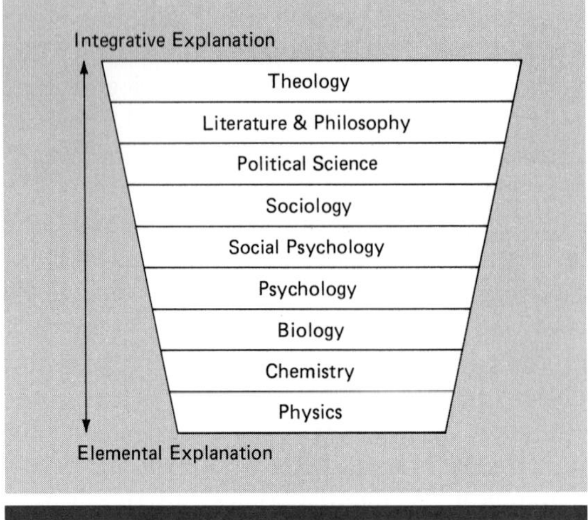

FIGURE 1-1 Partial hierarchy of disciplines. The disciplines range from basic sciences that study nature's building blocks up to more integrative disciplines that study whole complex systems. Successful explanation of human functioning at one level need not invalidate explanation at other levels.

Once we recognize the complementary nature of various levels of explanation, we are liberated from all the useless argument over whether human nature should be viewed scientifically or more subjectively. It is not an either/or matter. The scientific and subjective perspectives are both valuable for their own purposes. Although this book pays particular attention to the fruits of scientific research, we need not demean the rich insights of other approaches. Sociologist Andrew Greeley (1976) is right: "Try as it might, psychology cannot explain the purpose of human existence, the meaning of human life, the ultimate destiny of the human person." Social psychologists ask some very important questions, but these are not among them.

"Knowledge is one. Its division into subjects is a concession to human weakness."

Sir Halford John MacKinder, 1887

If "all truth is one," then all of these levels of explanation should fit together to form the whole picture, just as different two-dimensional perspectives of an object may be assembled, without contradiction, into a more complete three-dimensional picture.

In short, humans can be viewed from multiple perspectives, each of which is incapable of answering most questions raised by other perspectives. Social psychology, the scientific study of how people think about, influence, and relate to one another, is *one* perspective from which we can view and better understand ourselves.

HOW WE DO SOCIAL PSYCHOLOGY

Unlike other scientific disciplines, social psychology has 4.3 billion amateur members. While few of us have firsthand experience in nuclear physics, we are the very subject matter of social psychology. From daily observations of

(Sidney Harris/ *American Scientist*)

people, including ourselves, each of us forms many ideas concerning how people think about, influence, and relate to one another. Professional social psychologists have an edge on the amateurs because they observe human behavior more systematically, often with experiments which create miniature social dramas in which cause and effect can be pinned down more precisely. Most of what you will learn about social psychological research methods will simply be absorbed as you read the remaining chapters. But let us go backstage now and take a brief look at how social psychology is done. This glimpse behind the scenes will be just enough, I trust, for you to appreciate the nature of the evidence discussed in the remainder of this book.

Most social psychological research is conducted either in the laboratory or in the *field* (everyday situations outside the laboratory), and it is either *correlational* (asking whether two factors are naturally associated) or *experimental* (manipulating one factor to see its effect on another). Understanding the difference between correlational and experimental research is crucial if you are to be a critical reader of psychological research, especially of that which is reported in newspapers and magazines.

Field research: *Research done in natural, real-life settings outside the laboratory.*

To illustrate the advantages and disadvantages of these two procedures, consider a practical question: Is college a good financial investment? Surely you have heard claims made about the economic benefits of going to college. But these claims are sometimes nothing more than the optimistic speculations of college recruiters and administrators, so they merit scrutiny. How might we separate fact from falsehood in assessing the impact of college upon students' later earnings?

Correlational Research

Correlational research: *The study of the naturally occurring relationships among variables.*

First, we might ascertain whether any relation—or *correlation*, as we say—exists between people's educational levels and their earnings. For example, if college is a good financial investment then people who are graduated from college should, on the average, earn more than those who do not attend. We might therefore survey a representative group of graduates and of nonattenders and see whether a correlation between education and income really exists.

But how are we to conduct a well-done survey? Let's pause to see how it is done.

Survey Research

Survey researchers obtain a representative group by taking a *random sample*—in which every person in the total group has an equal chance of being chosen to participate. With this procedure any subgroup of people—red-haired disco dancers, for example—will tend to be represented in the survey to the extent they are represented in the total population.

One amazing fact is that whether the survey researcher is studying the characteristics of people in a city or in the whole country, about 1200 randomly selected participants will enable the researcher to be 95 percent confident of describing the entire population with an error margin of 3 percent or less. To visualize this, imagine a huge jar filled with beans—50 percent red and 50 percent white. Someone who randomly samples 1200 of these will be 95 percent certain to draw out between 47 percent and 53 percent red beans regardless of whether the jar contains 10,000 beans or 100 million beans. If we think of the red beans as supporters of one presidential candidate and white beans as the other candidate's supporters, we can understand why, since 1950, the Gallup polls taken just before U.S. national election days have, on the average, diverged from election results by only 1.6 percent (Gallup Opinion Index, 1978). Bear in mind that such polls do not actually predict voting, they only *describe* public opinion as of the moment they are taken. Public opinion can shift, as it did toward candidate Ronald Reagan just before the 1980 U.S. election.

Note that the representativeness of the survey sample is far more crucial than its size. In 1936, a weekly news magazine, *Literary Digest*, mailed a postcard presidential poll to 10 million Americans whose names they had obtained from telephone books and automobile registrations—thus omitting those who could not afford either (Cleghorn, 1980). Among their more than 2 million returns, Alf Landon won by a landslide over Franklin D. Roosevelt. But when the actual votes were counted a few days later, Landon carried two states.

In 1980, the ABC television network may have similarly misled the public. Following the Carter-Reagan presidential debate (after 11 P.M. in the east, 8 P.M. in the more pro-Reagan west), they invited listeners to place a 50

DOONESBURY **by Garry Trudeau**

Survey researchers must be sensitive to subtle—and not so subtle—biases. (Copyright, 1980, G.B. Trudeau. Reprinted with permission of Universal Press Syndicate. All rights reserved.)

cent long distance call, indicating who they thought won the debate (Schwartz, 1980). The result? Among the more than 700,000 callers, Mr. Reagan had a better than 2 to 1 edge, thus contributing to his winning image. Although ABC had repeatedly acknowledged that this was not a scientific sampling, survey researchers, whose more systematic polls indicated the debate outcome was a virtual draw, were nevertheless aghast. Whose supporters were more likely to care enough to place a call, they asked, to be willing to pay for it, to stay up and keep calling when the line was busy? Clearly, it is not so much the size of a survey sample that matters as how closely it represents the population being studied.

The wording of questions can also affect responses. A recent poll found that only 7 percent of Americans thought government programs should be cut back if they cut out "aid to the needy." Yet 39 percent would kill funds if the "needy" item was called "public welfare" (Marty, 1982).

To return to our question about the education-income relationship, we might wish that survey researchers would ask a representative (random) sample of adult Americans some straightforward (unbiased) questions about their income and educational attainments. Happily, it has already been done for us. Christopher Jencks (1979) recently digested data from eleven different national surveys. The conclusion: White American males who completed college had a whopping 49 percent earnings advantage over those who did not, and the percentage was even larger for black Americans.

These results illustrate one of the great advantages of survey research. It can generate lots of data from a representative sample of people in the "real world." So, did we answer our question about the impact of college on earnings? Assuming that these trends do continue, can we now agree with college recruiters that higher education is your gateway to economic success?

Before we answer yes, let us take a closer look. We know for a fact that formal education has been associated with earnings. That is indisputable. But

Box 1-1

You Get What You Ask For

Not only answers to survey questions, but also important everyday decisions are influenced by how an issue is posed. Amos Tversky and Daniel Kahneman (1981) posed the following problem to their students at Stanford University and at the University of British Columbia:

Imagine that the U.S. is preparing for the outbreak of an unusual Asian disease, which is expected to kill 600 people. Two alternative programs to combat the disease have been proposed. Assume that the exact scientific estimate of the consequences of the programs are as follows:

Those given the following two choices favored Program A by about 3 to 1:

If Program A is adopted, 200 people will be saved.

If Program B is adopted, there is 1/3 probability that 600 people will be saved, and 2/3 probability that no people will be saved.

But when the same two choices were stated differently, Program B was favored by 3 to 1:

If Program A is adopted, 400 people will die.

If Program B is adopted, there is 1/3 probability that nobody will die, and 2/3 probability that 600 people will die.

does this necessarily mean that education *causes* higher incomes? Perhaps you can identify factors other than education that might explain the education-earnings correlation. (We call these factors *variables* since people will vary on them.) What about family social status? What about a person's intellectual ability and achievement drive? Might these not already be higher in those who go to college? Perhaps some combination of these variables produces the higher earnings, and not the attaining of a college degree. Or perhaps education and earnings are correlated because those who have money in the first place can most easily afford college.

Correlation and Causation

The education-earnings question illustrates the most irresistible thinking error made by both amateur and professional social psychologists. When two factors like education and earnings go together, it is terribly tempting to conclude that one is causing the other, *if* we are predisposed to believe such a conclusion. Learning that the number of storks in various Dutch towns once correlated with the number of babies born in each probably will not convince you to repudiate your sex education. (Roofs were nesting sites. More roofs meant more storks and more people.)

Consider two examples of the correlation-causation issue from the realm of psychology. If a particular style of child-rearing is associated with the personality traits of children exposed to it, what does this tell us? For example, if as Freud believed, children who receive harsh, demanding toilet training do indeed become uptight and compulsive, does this validate what has been called Freud's "Scott Tissue theory of personality"? With every correlation, there are at least three possible explanations (see Figure 1-2). The effect of the parents on the child ($x \rightarrow y$) is only one. You might, however, be surprised at the strength of evidence for how children mold their parents ($x \leftarrow y$) (Bell & Harper, 1977). Or maybe, as explanation 3 in Figure 1-2 suggests, there is a common source to both the child-rearing style and the child's traits. Perhaps the characteristics of both parent and child are rooted in their shared genes. Or maybe the toilet-training technique and the child's personality are both the result of the whole parent-child relationship.

As a second example, consider the very real correlation between self-esteem and academic achievement. Children with high self-esteem tend also to have high academic achievement. (As with any correlation, we can also state this the other way around: High achievers tend to have high self-esteem.) Why do you suppose this is? Some believe that a "healthy self-concept" contributes to achievement. Thus, boosting a child's self-image may also boost the child's school achievement. Others argue that high achievement produces a favorable self-image. But careful recent studies of a nationwide sample of 1600 young men, by Jerald Bachman and Patrick O'Malley (1977), and of

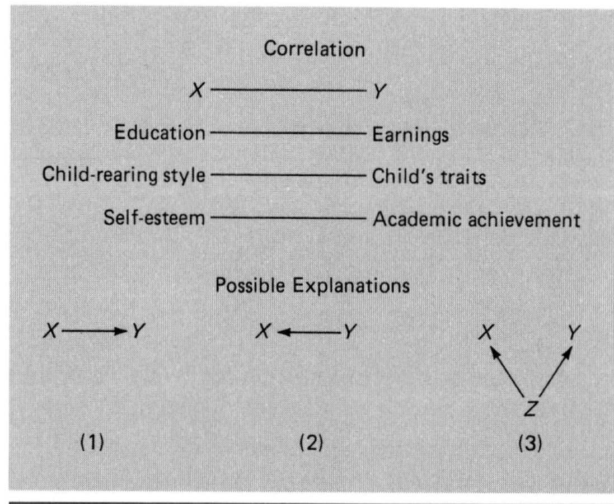

FIGURE 1-2 When two variables are correlated, any combination of at least three explanations is possible.

715 Minnesota youngsters, by Geoffrey Maruyama, Rosalyn Rubin, and Gage Kingsbury (1981), revealed a surprising result: Self-esteem and achievement were *not* causally related. Rather, they were correlated merely because they were both linked to intelligence and family social status. Extract the effect of intelligence and family status, and the correlation between self-esteem and achievement evaporates.

In short, the great strength of correlational-survey research is that it tends to occur in real-world settings where it can examine important factors like race, sex, and education that cannot be manipulated in the laboratory. Its great disadvantage lies in the ambiguity of its results. Knowing that two variables, such as education and income, go up and down together enables us to predict one, knowing the other. But this does not establish cause and effect. Fortunately, statistical techniques have now been developed which can *suggest* cause-effect relations in correlational research. They do so either by pulling apart obviously related factors (like education, family status, and aptitude) to isolate the predictive power of each when considered independently of the others, or by taking into account the sequence of events (for example, by ascertaining whether changes in achievement tend more to precede or follow changes in self-esteem). But the moral of the story remains: Correlational research cannot definitely tell us what is causing what.

So of what use is it? Astronomy is essentially a correlational science: Astronomers observe and correlate the movements of heavenly bodies. Who among us has failed to be awed by the precision with which astronomers can predict the time and location of the next solar eclipse? Psychologists likewise observe and correlate variables such as personality traits and aptitude which emerge over long periods of time. These are things you cannot easily manipulate in the laboratory. When personnel researchers ascertain how people's characteristics predict their on-the-job performance, they are conducting a very practical kind of correlational research.

To sum up, correlational science is predictive science, and prediction is one of the chief aims of every science. Knowing that two variables are associated allows us to predict one, knowing the other. But prediction is not cause-effect explanation. Thus correlations cannot tell us whether *changing* one variable (like education) will produce changes in another (like income).

Experimental Research

Control

The near impossibility of discerning cause and effect among naturally correlated events prompts most social psychologists to create laboratory simulations of real life processes whenever such are feasible and ethical. We might liken these simulations of life to what aeronautical engineers do. These engineers could begin by observing how flying objects perform in a wide variety of natural environments. But the variations in both atmospheric conditions and flying objects are so complex that they would surely find themselves perplexed about how to use such data to design better aircraft. So, instead, they construct a simulated reality, one which is under their control—a wind tunnel. Now they can manipulate the wind conditions and ascertain the precise effect of particular wind conditions on particular wing structures.

Like aeronautical engineers, social psychologists experiment by constructing social situations that simulate important features of our daily lives. By varying just one or two factors at a time—while holding all other things constant—the experimenter can pinpoint how changes in these one or two things affect us. Just as the wind tunnel helps the aeronautical engineer discover basic principles of aerodynamics, so does the experiment enable the social psychologist to discover basic principles of social thinking, social influence, and social relations. And just as the ultimate aim of wind tunnel simulations is to understand and predict the flying characteristics of complex aircraft, so also social psychologists do experiments in order to understand and predict.

The experimental method is used in about three-fourths of social psychological research studies (Higbee, Millard, & Folkman, 1982). To illustrate, consider effects of television on children's attitudes and behavior (to be discussed more fully in Chapter 10). Observations of children in natural settings have revealed that children who watch lots of violent television programs tend to be more aggressive than those who watch few. This suggests that children might be learning some of their behavior from what they see on the screen. But, as I hope you now recognize, this is a correlational finding. As Figure 1-2 reminds us, there are at least two other cause-effect interpretations which do not implicate television as the cause of the children's aggression. (What are they?) Social psychologists have therefore brought television programs into the laboratory where they can expose children to violent or nonviolent programs and then observe the effects of this viewing on their behavior. For example, Robert Liebert and Robert Baron (1972) showed young Ohio boys and girls either a violent excerpt from a gangster television show or an excerpt from an exciting track race. The children who viewed the violence were subsequently most likely to vigorously press a special red button which supposedly would transmit a burning pain to another child. (Actually, there was no other child, so no one was really harmed.) Experiments such as this one indicate that television *can* be one cause of children's aggressive behavior.

As this experiment illustrates, social psychology is fascinating partly because it is at the junction between life and the laboratory. Throughout this book we will be keeping one foot in each by drawing our data mostly from the laboratory and our illustrations mostly from life. In fact, there is in social psychology a healthy interplay between laboratory research and everyday life. Hunches gained from everyday experience have inspired much laboratory research, and such research has illuminated important facets of human nature, deepening our awareness of what is before us. This interplay is evident in the research on children's television. What people saw in everyday life suggested some experiments that would test the actual effect of watching television. Network and government policy makers are now well aware of the results of these experiments. So, what we see in life can often be scrutinized in carefully managed experiments, the results of which may then be applied to social problems.

However, generalizing from laboratory to life should be done cautiously. The laboratory, for all it may aid us in uncovering some basic secrets of human existence, is still a simplified reality. It tells us what effect to expect of variable X, all other things being equal—which in the complexity of life they never are. Moreover, as you will see, the participants in many social psychological experiments are college students. While this may help you identify with them, college students are hardly a random sample of all humanity. Would the same results be obtained with people of different ages, educational levels, and cultures? This is always an open question, though experience has taught us to distinguish between the *content* of people's thinking and acting—their attitudes and norms, for example—and the *process* by which they think and act—how their attitudes affect their actions and vice versa, for example. The content probably varies more from culture to culture than the process. People of different cultures may hold different opinions, for instance, yet form them in similar ways.

Experimental research: *Studies which seek clues to cause-effect relationships by manipulating one or more factors, while controlling others.*

So far we have seen that the logic of experimentation is very simple: By constructing and controlling a miniature reality we can vary one factor and then another and discover how these factors, separately or in combination, affect people. The laboratory experiment allows us to test ideas gleaned from life experience, and with due caution we can relate our findings to the real world. Now let us go just a little deeper and see how an experiment is done.

Every social-psychological experiment has two essential ingredients. One we have just considered—*control.* We manipulate one or two factors, while attempting to hold constant all other factors. The other ingredient is *random assignment.*

Random Assignment: The Great Equalizer

Recall that we were reluctant to credit college with the higher incomes of college graduates since graduates may benefit not only from their education but also from their social backgrounds, aptitudes, and so forth. A survey researcher might measure each of these likely other factors and then note the income advantage enjoyed by college graduates above and beyond what would be expected from them. Such statistical gymnastics are all well and good, but the researcher can never adjust for all the possible factors that might, in addition to attending college, differentiate graduates from nonattenders. The alternative explanations for the correlation are limitless. The income difference could be due to ethnic heritage, or sociability, or good looks, or any of hundreds of other factors that the researcher has never thought of.

So, let us for the moment give free reign to our imagination and see how all these complicating factors might be equalized in one fell swoop. Suppose someone gave us the power to take a group of high school graduates and *randomly assign* some to college and some to other endeavors. Each person would have an equal chance of being assigned to either the college or noncollege condition of our pretend experiment. So the people in both groups would, in every conceivable way—family status, looks, aptitude, and whatever— average about the same. Random assignment would roughly equalize all these previously complicating factors. Any later income difference between these two groups could therefore not be attributed to any of these factors. Rather, it would almost surely have *something* to do with the variable we manipulated. Similarly, if an experiment on malaria in Central America revealed that only people assigned to sleeping rooms with unscreened windows catch it, this would not mean that unscreened windows by themselves *cause* malaria; but it would indicate that the cause has something to do with lack of screens.

Random assignment: *Assigning participants to the conditions of an experiment such that each one has an equal chance of being in a given condition. This equalizes the conditions at the beginning of the experiment. Thus if participants in the different conditions later behave differently, it will rarely be due to pre-existing differences among them.*

The Ethics of Experimentation

Our college example also illustrates why some experiments are neither feasible nor ethical. Social psychologists would never manipulate people's lives in this way. In such cases we rely upon the correlational method and squeeze all the information we can out of it. In other cases, such as the issue of how children are affected by watching television, we briefly alter people's social experience and note the effects. Sometimes the experimental treatment is a harmless, perhaps even enjoyable experience to which people give their knowing consent. Sometimes, however, researchers find themselves operating in that gray area between the harmless and the risky.

Social psychologists often venture into that ethical gray area when they design experiments which really engage people's thoughts and emotions. Experiments need not have what Elliot Aronson and J. Merrill Carlsmith (1969) call *mundane realism*. That is, laboratory behavior (for example, delivering electric shocks as part of an experiment on aggression) need not be literally the same as everyday behavior. For many researchers, that sort of realism is, indeed, a not-too-important, mundane matter. But as Aronson and Carlsmith emphasize, the experiment *should* have *experimental realism*—it should absorb and involve people. Experimenters do not want their people

Mundane realism: *Degree to which an experiment is superficially similar to everyday situations.*
Experimental realism: *Degree to which an experiment absorbs and involves its participants.*

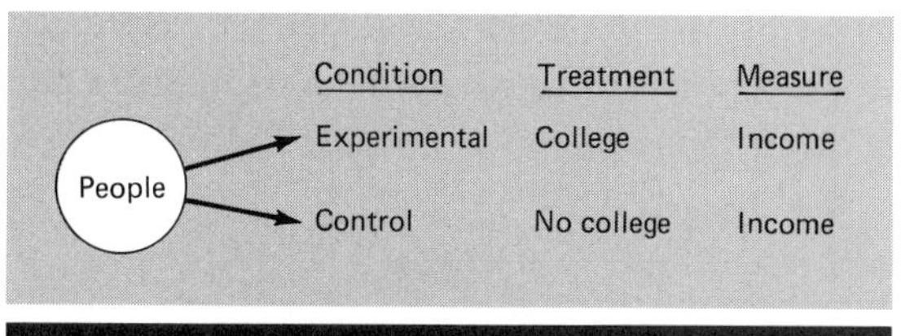

FIGURE 1-3 Randomly assigning people either to a condition which receives the experimental treatment or to a control condition, which does not, can give the researcher confidence that any later difference is somehow caused by the treatment.

consciously playacting or ho-humming it; they want to engage real psychological processes. Forcing people to choose whether to give intense or mild electric shock to someone else can, in this sense, be a realistic measure of aggression.

Achieving experimental realism often requires deceiving the participants. If the person in the next room is actually not receiving the shocks which the participants administer, the experimenter does not want the participants to know this. If they knew it, the experimental realism would be destroyed. Thus deception is sometimes a necessary part of social psychological experiments. Experimenters also seek to hide their predictions lest the participants, in their eagerness to be "good subjects," merely confirm the experimenter's expectations. In very subtle ways, the experimenter's words, tone of voice, and gestures may inadvertently "demand" desired responses. To minimize such *demand characteristics*, experimenters typically standardize their instructions or even write or tape-record them.

Demand characteristics: *Cues in an experiment that tell the participant what behavior is expected.*

Researchers often walk a difficult tightrope in designing experiments that will be involving, yet ethical. Some researchers have found it necessary to temporarily lead people to believe that they are hurting someone. Other researchers have subjected people to strong social pressure to see if they will change their opinions or their behavior. These are not pleasant experiences. As we shall see, some of these experiments raise the age old question of whether ends justify means—whether the insights gained can justify deceiving and sometimes distressing people. For right now, suffice it to say that in recent years there has developed a heightened sensitivity to the well being of those who volunteer for their experiments. Ethical principles developed by the American Psychological Association (1981) now urge investigators to:

Informed consent: *An ethical principle requiring that research participants be told enough to enable them to choose whether they wish to participate.*

Tell potential participants enough about the experiment to enable them to give their *informed consent.*

Be truthful. Deception should be used only if justified and if there is no alternative.

Protect people from harm and significant discomfort.

Treat information about the individual participants confidentially.

Fully explain the experiment afterwards, including any deception. The only limit on this rule is when the feedback would be brutal, making people realize they have been stupid or cruel. The experimenter should be sufficiently informative *and* considerate that people leave feeling at least as good about themselves as when they came in. Better yet, the participants should be repaid by having learned something about the nature of psychological inquiry.

Theories in Social Psychology

Although the examples so far in this first chapter have demonstrated the practical benefits of basic research in social psychology, practical application is not our only reason for doing social psychology. Many of us are in the profession because we have a hard time thinking of anything more intrinsically fascinating than our own human existence. If, as Socrates counseled, "The unexamined life is not worth living," then simply "knowing thyself" better is a worthy enough goal.

"Nothing has such power to broaden the mind as the ability to investigate systematically and truly all that comes under thy observation in life."

Marcus Aurelius, Meditations

As we wrestle with human nature to make it give up its secrets we usually organize our ideas and findings into *theories*. A theory is an integrated set of principles that explain and predict observed phenomena. Some people wonder why social psychologists are so preoccupied with their theories: Why don't they just gather facts? In response, our aeronautical engineering analogy is again useful. The engineers soon would be overwhelmed if, without any guiding principles, they tried to develop, merely by trial and error, an exhaustive catalog of ways in which different wind conditions affect different wing structures. So, instead, they formulate broad concepts about how air movements interact with wing structures, and use the wind tunnel to test predictions derived from these concepts. Whether in aeronautical engineering or in social psychology, theories are a scientific shorthand.

In everyday language, "theory" often means "less than fact"—a middle rung on a confidence ladder going down from fact to theory to guess. But to any kind of scientist, facts and theories are different things, not different points on a continuum. Facts are what we observe. Theories are *ideas* that explain and interpret facts. "Science is built up with facts, as a house is with stones," said Jules Henri Poincaré, "but a collection of facts is no more a science than a heap of stones is a house."

Theory: *An integrated set of principles that explain and predict observed events.*

Like the law of gravitation, theories attempt to summarize countless factual observations by capturing underlying principles in common to them all. In no way could you begin to remember all the factual results from the thousands of social psychological experiments. But if this bewildering body of facts could be condensed to a much shorter list of theoretical principles which predict most of the observed facts, then you would have a hold on something much more powerful (as well as more memorable!) than any long list of disconnected facts.

One task of each theory is to generate *hypotheses*. A hypothesis explains some observation and predicts a specific future result. These predictions serve several purposes. First, they provide the criteria by which theories are evaluated through testing of the hypotheses. By making specific predictions, a theory "puts its money where its mouth is." Second, predictions give direction to research. Any scientific field will mature much more rapidly if its researchers have a sense of direction, rather than the habit of haphazardly collecting isolated facts. Theoretical predictions suggest new areas for research; they send investigators looking for things they might never have thought of. Finally, the predictive feature of good theories can also make them very practical as well. In a world torn by strife and conflict, what would be of greater practical value than a complete theory of aggression, one that would predict the conditions under which to expect it and how to control it? As Kurt Lewin, one of the founders of modern social psychology, declared, "There is nothing so practical as a good theory."

Hypothesis: *A testable proposition that describes a relationship that may exist between events.*

For example, observing that crowds of people sometimes explode violently, we might theorize that the presence of other people sometimes makes individuals feel anonymous, thus decreasing their inhibitions against doing harm. Let's let our minds play with this theory for a moment. Perhaps we could test it by constructing a laboratory experiment similar to execution by electric chair. What if individuals in small groups were asked to simultaneously administer punishing shocks to a hapless victim, without knowing which of them were actually shocking the victim? Would these individuals administer stronger shock than individuals acting alone, as our theory predicts? Or we might manipulate anonymity: Would people hiding behind Halloween masks deliver stronger shock than people who were identifiable? If the results confirm our theory, this might suggest some practical applications. Perhaps, for instance, incidents of police brutality could be reduced by having officers wear large name tags and drive cars identified with large numbers.

But how do we conclude that one theory is better than another? A good theory does all its functions well: (1) It effectively summarizes a wide range of observations, and (2) it makes clear predictions that can be used (a) to confirm or modify the theory, (b) to generate new exploration, and (c) to suggest practical application. When theories are discarded, usually it is not because they have been falsified, but because, like an old model car, they have been displaced by newer, better models.

But do social psychology's theories provide *new* insight into the human condition? Or do they only describe the obvious?

IS SOCIAL PSYCHOLOGY SIMPLY SOPHISTICATED COMMON SENSE?

Many of the conclusions presented in this book will probably have already occurred to you, for the subject matter of social psychology is all around you. Since every human being daily observes people thinking about, influencing, and relating to one another, there is bound to be some accumulated social wisdom. For centuries, philosophers, novelists, and poets have observed and commented upon social behavior, often with keen insight. Might it therefore be said that social psychology is only common sense dressed in new jargon? Does it simply formalize what any good amateur social psychologist already intuitively knows?

The I-Knew-It-All-Along Phenomenon

One problem with commonsense explanations is that we tend to invoke them *after* we know the facts. Events are far more "obvious" and predictable in hindsight than beforehand. As Baruch Fischhoff and his colleagues (Slovic & Fischhoff, 1977; Wood, 1979) have demonstrated many times, our recollection of what outcomes we would have expected from some experiment or historical situation is instantly distorted once we know what really did happen. When people are told the outcome of an experiment, the outcome suddenly seems less surprising to them than it is to people who are simply told about the experimental procedure and its possible outcomes. In one of Fischhoff's experiments, Israeli students estimated the likelihood of various possible outcomes of President Richard Nixon's forthcoming trips to Peking and Moscow (Fischhoff & Beyth, 1975). When, after his visits, the students were asked unexpectedly to remember their predictions, they mistakenly remembered them as coinciding closely with what they now knew had happened. Finding out that something had happened made it seem more inevitable.

Likewise, in everyday life we often do not expect something to happen until it does. We then suddenly see clearly the forces which brought it to be and thus seldom feel surprised. We say we really "knew all along that he was going to act that way." As the Danish philosopher-theologian Sören Kierkegaard surmised, "Life is lived forwards, but understood backwards."

20-20 hindsight. (Reprinted from *Psychology Today* Magazine, copyright © 1975 Ziff Davis Publishing Company.)

If the I-knew-it-all-along phenomenon is pervasive, you may now be feeling that you already knew about it. Indeed, almost any conceivable result of a psychological experiment can seem like common sense—*after* you know the result. The phenomenon can be crudely demonstrated by giving half of a group some purported psychological finding and the other half the opposite result. For example:

Social psychologists have found that, whether choosing friends or falling in love, we are most attracted to people whose traits are different from our own. There seems to be wisdom in the old saying, "Opposites attract."

Social psychologists have found that, whether choosing friends or falling in love, we are most attracted to people whose traits are similar to our own. There seems to be wisdom in the old saying, "Birds of a feather flock together."

It is my experience that when fifty people are given one of these findings and fifty the opposite finding and all are asked to "explain" the result and then indicate whether it is "surprising" or "not surprising," virtually all will find whichever result they were given "not surprising."

As these examples indicate, we can draw upon the stockpile of ancient proverbs to make almost any result seem commonsensical. Nearly every possible outcome is conceivable, so there are proverbs for almost all occasions. Shall we say with John Donne, "No man is an island," or with Thomas Wolfe, "Every man is an island"? Does "haste make waste" or is "he who hesitates lost"? Is "A penny saved is a penny earned" true or is it "Pennywise, pound foolish"? If a social psychologist reports that separation intensifies romantic attraction, someone is sure to reply, "Of course, 'Absence makes the heart grow fonder'." Should it turn out the reverse, the same person may remind us, "Out of sight, out of mind." No matter what happens, there will be someone who knew it would.

"A first-rate theory predicts; a second-rate theory forbids; and a third-rate theory explains after the event."

Aleksander Isaakovich Kitaigorodskii

This hindsight bias creates a problem for many psychology students. When you read the results of experiments in your textbooks, the material often seems easy, even commonsensical. When you subsequently take a multiple choice test on which you must choose among several plausible outcomes to an experiment, the task may become surprisingly difficult. "I don't know what happened," the befuddled student later bemoans. "I thought I knew the material."

The I-knew-it-all-along phenomenon also affects our assessments of our knowledge. If what we learn does not surprise us, then we are inclined to overestimate how much we already knew. Consider this question (to which 1 is the correct answer): "Which is longer, (1) the Suez Canal, or (2) the Panama Canal?" What is the likelihood you could have answered this question correctly if I had not told you the answer? Fischhoff found that University of Oregon students who were not told the answers to such questions tended to rate them as toss-ups; those who had been told the correct answers thought they probably would have gotten most right.

Now that you and I know about this tendency to overestimate our past wisdom, will we be as vulnerable to it as these Oregon students? Fischhoff (1977) wondered about this, also. He forewarned some more Oregon students that on these questions people

> exaggerate how much they have known without being told the answer. You might call this an I-knew-it-all-along effect. . . In completing the present questionnaire, please do everything you can to avoid this bias. One reason why it happens is that people who are told the correct answer find it hard to imagine how they ever could have believed in the incorrect one. In answering, make certain that you haven't forgotten any reasons that you might have thought of in favor of the wrong answer—had you not been told it was wrong.

How much effect do you think these "debiasing instructions" had? Incredibly, they had no effect. Being fully forewarned about the hindsight bias did not reduce it at all! (Surely, though, now that you and I know the result of *this* experiment. . .)

Hindsight bias: *The tendency to exaggerate one's ability to have foreseen how something turned out,* after *learning the outcome. Also known as the I-knew-it-all-along phenomenon.*

Is there no way to reduce the hindsight bias? With Paul Slovic, Fischhoff did find one way (Slovic and Fischhoff, 1977). People were told the results of several experiments. Some were then asked "Had the study worked out the other way, how would you explain it?" These people perceived the result as much less inevitable than did those who had not imagined an opposite result.

The I-knew-it-all-along phenomenon can have pernicious social and personal consequences. It is conducive to arrogance—overestimation of our own intellectual powers and of the perceptiveness of our after-the-fact explanations. Moreover, since outcomes seem as if they should have been foreseeable, we are most likely to blame decision makers for what are, in retrospect, their "obvious" bad choices than to praise them for their good choices, since these, too, were "obvious." Thus, *after* the Japanese attack on Pearl Harbor, Monday-morning historians could read the signs and see the "inevitability" of what had happened. Likewise, we sometimes chastise ourselves for our "stupid mistakes"— for not having better handled a situation or a person, for example. Looking back now, we see how we obviously should have handled it. But sometimes we are too hard on ourselves. We forget that what is now obvious to us was not nearly so obvious at the time.

The conclusion to be drawn is *not* that common sense is usually wrong. My hunch is that most conventional wisdom likely does apply—under certain conditions. After all, both amateur and professional social psychologists observe and form theories about the same human nature. The point is that our common sense is often *after the fact*—it describes events more easily than it predicts them—and we therefore easily deceive ourselves into thinking that we know and knew more than we do and did.

"The whole of science is nothing more than refinement of everyday thinking."

Albert Einstein

BEHIND THE SCENES

Baruch Fischhoff

After completing my undergraduate education, I spent several years living on a kibbutz. During this time, my primary intellectual effort (other than pondering the meaning of personal commitment and self-actualization) was writing a guide to teaching history to adolescents. The challenges were to make kids care about their history and to help them draw useful lessons from it. When I returned to school, I wondered whether an academic approach could produce higher-quality speculations about historical understanding than I had derived from my personal experience and hunches. The writings of historians provided insights into their craft. But it was the research methods of psychology and, in particular, the work of Daniel Kahneman and Amos Tversky that helped me identify and study the role of hindsight in historical judgment. Consistent with its conclusions, the hindsight research is an attempt to explore systematically a bit of common sense. Everyone knows that hindsight is different from foresight. What psychology could offer was a more detailed description of how large and how justified that difference is—and how people might be helped to use their minds more effectively. (*Baruch Fischhoff, Decision Research, Eugene, Oregon*)

We have seen what social psychology is, how its research is done, and how it differs from common sense. There is but one other matter to which we should be sensitized before embarking on our journey into the discipline.

SOCIAL PSYCHOLOGY AND HUMAN VALUES

Social psychology has no scientific answer to questions of human values: What ends are ultimately desirable? What ought we to do? What vision of the good life is worthy of our aspirations? Although social psychologists have no privileged answer to these questions, their personal values nevertheless penetrate their work in several subtle and not-so-subtle ways.

Obvious Ways in Which Values Enter the Picture

We have seen already how values influence our ethical standards in doing research. But even before we reach this stage of a research project, our values have already entered the picture—beginning with our choice of the topic. It was not merely by accident that the 1960s saw an upsurge of interest in aggression and the 1970s a new wave of research on sex-role socialization and sex-role stereotypes. These research trends were products of the decades in which they occurred.

Value considerations may also influence the type of people attracted to various disciplines. Some have suggested that psychology and the other social sciences tend to attract people who are eager to challenge tradition, people who would rather shape the future than preserve the past (Campbell, 1975; Moynihan, 1979). If this is true, what would you guess to be the political leanings of American psychologists, sociologists, and political scientists: Republican or Democrat? Surveys of these groups indicate that Democratic party leanings have, at least in the past, outnumbered Republican leanings by nearly a 5 to 1 ratio (McClintock, Spaulding, & Turner, 1965; Scully, 1970). (I hasten to add, however, that most psychological experiments are motivated not by overt political goals, but simply by a quest to understand human functioning.)

Note that this is a correlational finding. Do you suppose the political liberalism of some social scientists is more a cause or a consequence of their being social scientists?

Finally, values obviously enter the picture in a very different sense—as the *object* of social psychological analysis. Social psychologists have investigated how values are formed, how they can be changed, and how they influence our attitudes and actions. None of this, however, tells us which values are "right."

Not-So-Obvious Ways in Which Values Enter the Picture

Less often recognized are the subtle ways in which value commitments masquerade as objective truth. The social sciences seem especially vulnerable to the expounding of values disguised as facts. Unlike workers in the physical sciences, whose analyses are more value free, and in the humanities, where

FIGURE 1-4 What do you see? (R.C. Jones from *Psychology Today*, Third Edition. Copyright © 1975 by Random House, Inc. Reprinted by permission of CRM Books, a Division of Random House, Inc.)

values are more openly discussed, psychologists and sociologists are more often blind to their implicit values. Here are three not-so-obvious ways in which values enter social psychology and related areas.

1. Science Has Subjective Aspects

There is a growing awareness among both scientists and philosophers that science is not so purely objective as commonly thought. Contrary to popular opinion, scientists do not merely read what's out there in the book of nature. Rather, they interpret nature, using their own mental categories. This is the same way you and I think in our daily lives; we, too, view the world through the spectacles of our preconceptions.

The point is easily demonstrated. For instance, what do you see in Figure 1-4? Can you see a dalmatian dog on thc right sniffing thc ground at the center of the picture? Until they are given this expectation, most people are blind to what those who have the preconception are able to see. But once your mind has the preconception, it controls your interpretation of the picture—so much so that is becomes difficult *not* to see the dog. This is the way our minds work. While reading these words you have probably been unaware, until this moment, that you have been looking at your nose. This illustrates a common phenomenon—our minds blocking from our awareness something that is there, if only we were predisposed to perceive it. This tendency to prejudge reality on the basis of our expectations is one of the most important facts about the human mind.

Another classic demonstration of how our presuppositions control our interpretations was provided by a Princeton-Dartmouth football game some years ago (Hastorf & Cantril, 1954; see also Loy & Andrews, 1981). The game lived up to its billing as a grudge match; it turned out to be one of the roughest and dirtiest games in the history of either school. A Princeton All-American was gang-tackled, piled on, and finally forced out of the game with a broken nose. Fistfights erupted, and further injuries occurred on both sides.

Not long after the game, two psychologists, one from each school, showed films of the game to students on each campus as part of a social psychology experiment. The students played the role of "objective" scientists, noting each infraction as they watched and who was responsible for it. As you might suppose, the Princeton students were much more likely than the Dartmouth students to see their Princeton players as the victims rather than the agents of illegal aggression. The Princeton students, for example, saw twice as many Dartmouth violations as the Dartmouth students saw. There is an objective reality out there, but we are always viewing it through the spectacles of our preconceived beliefs and values.

"Science does not simply describe and explain nature; it is part of the interplay between nature and ourselves; it describes nature as exposed to our method of questioning."

Werner Heisenberg, Physics and Philosophy

The point applies not only to our everyday thinking, but also to scientific theorizing. The content of social psychology is not just the sum total of facts gleaned from our objective experiments. Rather, it is the result of interactions between human minds and human nature. Our theories are never literal pictures of reality handed to us by nature. They are the products of human imagination, mental creations which attempt to simplify and impose some order on reality—just as your mind used certain assumptions to impose order on the black-and-white marks in Figure 1-4.

Since the community of scholars at work in any given area often share a common viewpoint, their assumptions may go unchallenged. But this does not mean they are inconsequential. As sociologist Louis Wirth (1977) has observed, "The most important thing . . . that we can know about a person is what he takes for granted, and the most elemental and important facts about a society are those things that are seldom debated and generally regarded as settled." Sometimes, however, someone from outside the camp will call attention to what is being taken for granted. For example, some of social psychology's previously unexamined assumptions are now being illuminated by feminists and by Marxists, both of whom stand somewhat outside the camp of traditional social psychology. Feminist critics are calling attention to subtle masculine biases, and Marxist critics to competitive, individualistic biases (for example, assuming that conformity is bad)—biases which can affect what we "see" as we design and interpret our experiments. (Of course, any such group has its biases, too.)

So what do we conclude: That since science has its subjective side we should dismiss it? Quite to the contrary. The realization that human thinking always involves interpretation is precisely why we need scientific analysis. Observation and experimentation help us clean the spectacles through which we view reality. By constantly checking our beliefs against the facts, as best as we can discern them, we restrain our biases.

2. Psychological Concepts Have Hidden Values

Values also influence psychology's specific concepts. This is most readily apparent in attempts by psychologists to specify the good life. We refer to people as mature or immature, as well-adjusted or poorly adjusted, as mentally healthy or mentally ill, as if these were statements of fact, when they are really disguised value judgments. The personality psychologist Abraham Maslow, for example, was well known for his sensitive descriptions of the characteristics of "self-actualized" people—people who, with their needs for survival, safety, "belongingness," and self-esteem satisfied, go on to fulfill their full human potential. Seldom recognized is that the initial selection of the self-actualized persons to be analyzed was done on a subjective basis by Maslow himself. Thus the resulting description of their self-actualized personalities—spontaneous, autonomous, mystical, etc.—is a statement of Maslow's personal values. Someone who is not self-actualized has simply failed to satisfy Maslow's definition. As M. Brewster Smith (1978) has noted, had Maslow begun with someone else's collection of heroic personalities—people like Napoleon, Alexander the Great, and John D. Rockefeller, Sr.—the resulting description of self-actualization would have been quite different.

Psychological advice likewise reflects the advice giver's personal values. When mental health professionals advise us how to live our lives, when child-

Psychological advice also reflects the advice-giver's personal values. Psychologists not only share their technical expertise, they also propound their own personal values. (Erika Stone/Peter Arnold, Inc.)

rearing experts tell us how to handle our children, and when humanistic psychologists counsel us to do our own thing instead of living up to others' expectations, they are usually propounding their personal values, not just sharing their technical expertise. Most people, failing to realize this, are quite willing to abdicate their own judgment to the "professional" judgment. Because value decisions should concern us all, scientists and professionals included, we had best not abdicate them to the scientists and professionals alone. Science can help us discern how better to achieve our ultimate goals, once we have settled on them. But the questions of ultimate moral obligation, of ultimate purpose and direction, and of the ultimate meaning of life are not directly addressed by a science of behavior.

"Scientists should be on tap but not on top."

Sir Winston Churchill

The pervasiveness of hidden values can also be illustrated in the research-based concepts of personality and social psychologists. Our labels reflect our judgments of what we have observed. Pretend you took a personality test and the psychologist, after scoring your answers, announced "You scored high in self-esteem. You are low in anxiety and you have exceptional ego-strength." Ah, you think, I suspected as much, but it feels good to know that. Now another psychologist gives you a similar test. For some peculiar reason this test even asks some of the same questions. Afterward, the psychologist informs you that you are apparently quite defensive, for you scored high in "repressiveness." How could this be, you wonder. The other psychologist said such nice things about me. It could be because all these labels describe the same set of responses (a tendency to say nice things about oneself and not to acknowledge problems). Shall we call it high self-esteem or defensiveness? The label reflects the researcher's value judgment about the trait.

That value judgments are often hidden within our social psychological language is no reason to malign social psychology. It is true of all human language. Whether someone engaged in guerilla warfare is labeled a "terrorist" or a "freedom fighter" depends on our sympathy with the cause. Whether someone involved in an extramarital affair is practicing "open marriage" or "adultery" depends on one's personal values. "Brainwashing" is social influence we do not approve of. "Perversions" are sex acts we do not practice. Remarks about "ambitious" men and "aggressive" women, or about "cautious" boys and "timid" girls, convey a hidden message, do they not?

Throughout this book I will call your attention to additional examples of hidden values. The point of these examples will, I trust, never be that the implicit values are necessarily bad and that we should get rid of them. It is simply that scientific interpretation, even at the level of our labeling of phenomena, is a very human activity. It is therefore quite natural and inevitable that social psychologists' prior beliefs and values will influence what they think and write. For example, when I picked postcollege income as a way to measure the effect of college, did this convey a subtle message (which in this case I don't really believe) that the primary purpose of a college education is to maximize your potential earnings?

3. There Is No Bridge from "Is" to "Ought"

One of the most seductive errors tempting those in the social sciences is converting one's description of what *is* into a prescription of what *ought* to be. Philosophers have called this the *naturalistic fallacy*. The gulf between "is" and "ought," between scientific description and ethical prescription, remains as wide today as when philosopher David Hume pointed it out 200 years ago. Thus no survey of human behavior—say, of sexual practices—logically dictates what is "right" behavior. If most people don't do something, that does not make it wrong; if most people do it, that does not make it right. You and I may welcome information about what is as we contemplate what ought to be, but ethical decisions must in the end be made on their own merits.

Naturalistic fallacy: *Defining what is good in terms of what is observable. For example: What's typical is normal; what's normal is good.*

The well-known research on moral development by developmental psychologist Lawrence Kohlberg (1981) is a case in point. Kohlberg has observed that moral thinking unfolds through a consistent series of stages, just as physical development occurs in a predictable sequence. Few people, however, ever reach the "highest" stage of moral development, the "postconventional" level of self-chosen moral principles. Experiments have therefore been undertaken to ascertain how people may be stimulated to achieve higher levels of "maturity" in their moral thinking. Notice here a subtle shift from objective *de*scription of stages of moral thinking to *pre*scription of the postconventional stage. By seeming to provide a scientific basis for our own moral thinking [which Norma Haan (1978) has found is especially characteristic "of males who live in technical, rationalized societies"], Kohlberg's scheme provides a handy rationale by which we social scientists can judge opposing moral philosophies as immature.

My purpose here is not to quarrel with the value judgments implicit in Kohlberg's very influential description of moral development. The point is simply that there is no way we can move from objective statements of fact to prescriptive statements of what ought to be without injecting our values.

SUMMING UP

Social psychology is the scientific study of how people think about, influence, and relate to one another. Sociology and psychology are social psychology's parent disciplines. Social psychology tends to be more individualistic in its content and more experimental in its method than other areas of sociology. Compared to personality psychology, social psychology focuses less attention on differences among individuals and more attention on how people, in general, view and affect one another. There are many additional perspectives on human nature, each of which asks its own set of questions. Successful explanation of human functioning by one perspective does not invalidate explanation by other perspectives.

Most social psychological research is either correlational or experimental. Correlational studies, sometimes conducted with systematic survey methods, ascertain the relationship between variables, such as between amount of education and amount of income. Knowing two things are naturally related is valuable information, but it usually does not indicate what is causing what. When possible, social psychologists therefore prefer to conduct experiments in which cause and effect can be pinned down more precisely. By constructing a miniature reality that is under their control, experimenters can vary one thing and then another and discover how these things, separately or in combination, affect people. When participants are randomly assigned to an experimental condition, which receives the experimental treatment, or a control condition, which does not, then any resulting difference between the two conditions can be attributed to the experimental treatment. Ethical problems often encountered in conducting experiments have necessitated the development of ethical standards for research.

Social psychologists organize their ideas and findings into theories. A good theory will distill a bewildering array of facts into a much shorter list of predictive principles. These predictions can be used to confirm or modify the theory, to generate new exploration, and to suggest practical application.

Social psychology's findings may sometimes seem obvious. However, experiments indicate that outcomes are generally far more "obvious" after the facts are known than they are beforehand. This hindsight bias tends to make people overconfident about the validity of their intuition.

Social psychologists' values penetrate their work in obvious ways, like their choice of research topics. Less easily recognized are subtle ways in which values permeate social psychology. There is a growing awareness of the subjectivity of scientific interpretation, of values hidden in the concepts and labels of social psychology, and of the gulf between scientific description of what is and ethical prescription of what ought to be. This penetration of values into science is not unique to social psychology, nor is it anything to be embarrassed about. That human thinking is seldom dispassionate is precisely why we need systematic observation and experimentation if we are to check our cherished conjectures against reality.

SOCIAL THINKING

The bulk of this book is organized around our definition of social psychology: the scientific study of how people think about (Chapters 2 to 5), influence (Chapters 6 to 9), and relate to (Chapters 10 to 14) one another.

This first group of chapters, on social thinking, examines some of the sources and effects of how we view ourselves and others. Chapter 2 explores the relationship between our attitudes and our behavior. Do our attitudes determine our behavior? Does our behavior determine our attitudes? Or does it work both ways? Chapter 3 analyzes how we attribute responsibility to other people and to ourselves. For example, when do we attribute people's actions to their circumstances, and when to their own dispositions? Do we explain our own actions similarly? Chapter 4 looks at the amazing and sometimes rather amusing ways in which we form false beliefs about our social worlds, and Chapter 5 considers how such tendencies could lead us to believe in extrasensory perception and to err in our judgments of one another. Perhaps studying how errors distort our social thinking can serve a constructive purpose—by helping us improve our thinking, making it more accurate, more in touch with reality.

Chapter

Behavior and Attitudes

Among the fifty-two Americans held hostage in Iran were several who, before television cameras, expressed sympathy with their captors' demands for the return of the deposed Shah of Iran. In the United States, Americans were suspicious about this. We wondered: Did these hostages' statements reflect their real attitudes? Or just the coercive pressures they faced? More generally, do people's actions usually mirror their actual feelings?

When we question the hostages' *attitudes* toward the Shah, we refer to their beliefs about what he did, their liking or disliking him, and their consequent inclinations to support or oppose him. Taken together, these reactions—these beliefs, feelings, and inclinations to act—define a person's attitude toward something. They are the ABCs of attitudes: *a*ffect (feelings), *b*ehavior tendency, and *c*ognition (thought). For example, the Gallup Organization predicts whether people will actually vote by ascertaining their feelings of involvement in an upcoming election (affect), their intentions to vote or not vote (behavior tendency), and whether they know where to go to vote (cognition) (Crespi, 1977). Generally, we assume there is some logical relationship among the components. For example, a person who *believes* that a particular ethnic group is lazy and aggressive, may *feel* dislike for such people and therefore tend to *act* in a discriminatory manner. Any of these three dimensions can be tapped when assessing people's attitudes, but usually we ask them for their feelings, positive or negative.

Attitude: *A predisposition towards some object; includes one's beliefs, feelings, and behavior tendencies concerning the object. People's attitudes are often assessed by asking for their feelings.*

Social psychologists study how our attitudes change and how they affect our actions. In one recent three year period, over 1000 new articles and books appeared on attitudes (Eagly & Himmelfarb, 1978). This abundance of research is not surprising. The ways people view and influence one another is an important part of what defines social psychology. It seems fitting, therefore, to begin our journey into social psychology with a close look at how our attitudes affect our actions.

DO OUR ATTITUDES DETERMINE OUR BEHAVIOR?

"The ancestor of every action is a thought."

Ralph Waldo Emerson, Essays, First Series

"Thought is the child of Action."

Benjamin Disraeli, Vivian Grey

To ask whether our attitudes determine our behavior is to ask a fundamental question about human nature: What is the relationship between what we *are* (on the inside) and what we *do* (on the outside)? Philosophers, theologians, and educators have long speculated about the connection between thought and action, character and conduct, private word and public deed. The prevailing assumption, an assumption that underlies most teaching, counseling, and child rearing, has been that our beliefs and feelings determine our public behavior. So, if we want to alter the way people act, we had best change their hearts and minds.

Are We All Hypocrites?

"In the beginning," social psychologists wholeheartedly shared the assumption that to know a person's attitudes is to predict that person's actions. However, during the 1960s, new research findings led social psychologists to question this view. In 1964, Leon Festinger concluded that research had in fact not supported the assumption that changing people's attitudes will change their behavior. Festinger also advanced the radical notion that the attitude-behavior relation actually works the other way around, with our behavior as the horse and our attitudes as the cart. As Robert Abelson (1972) put it, we are, apparently, "very well trained and very good at finding reasons for what we do, but not very good at doing what we find reasons for."

But the most damaging blow to the supposed potency of our attitudes was still to come. In 1969, social psychologist Allan Wicker reviewed several dozen research studies covering a wide variety of people, attitudes, and behaviors, and offered the shocking conclusion that the expressed attitudes of a group of people usually predict less than 10 percent of the variation in their behaviors. For instance, students' attitudes toward cheating bear little relation to the likelihood of their cheating. People's expressed convictions regarding the church have but a modest relationship to church attendance on any given Sunday. Self-described racial attitudes predict little of the variation in behavior that occurs when people confront an actual interracial situation.

If people don't play the same game that they talk, it's little wonder that attempts to change behavior by changing attitudes have so often failed.

Warnings about the dangers of smoking have only minimally affected smoking among those who already smoke. Increasing the public's awareness of the desensitizing and brutalizing effects of a prolonged diet of television violence has stimulated many Americans to voice a desire for less violent programming—but ironically, they still watch media murder as much as ever. Appeals for safe driving habits have had far less effect on accident rates than have lower speed limits and divided highways (Etzioni, 1972).

"Between the idea
And the reality
Between the motion
And the act
Falls the Shadow"

T. S. Eliot, The Hollow Men

At about the time that Wicker and others were offering their dismal assessment of the potency of attitudes, some personality psychologists began to suggest that personality traits—at least those measured by our best-known personality tests—also fail to predict our behavior (Mischel, 1968). If we want to know how helpful people are going to be, for example, we usually won't learn much by giving them tests for self-esteem, anxiety, etc. If the situation makes clear-cut demands, we are much better off knowing how most people act, or so many studies seemed to suggest. Likewise, many psychotherapists began to argue that talking therapies such as psychoanalysis seldom "cure" people's problems, so therapists should instead work directly on modifying the problem behavior and stop analyzing personality defects that hypothetically underlie the problem. All in all, the developing picture of what controls our behavior seemed to focus on factors outside us—external social influences, for example—and to play down internal factors such as attitudes and personality traits. The emerging human image was that of little billiard balls, which have different stripes and colors to be sure, but which are all similarly buffeted by the forces upon them.

In short, the original thesis that our attitudes do indeed determine our actions was countered during the 1960s by the antithesis that our attitudes determine virtually nothing. If the philosopher Hegel had then looked over our shoulders, he would likely have said, "Aha! Thesis. Antithesis. Now for the synthesis." And so it happened. The surprising finding that what people say often fails to correspond to what they do sent social psychologists scurrying to find out why. Surely, we reasoned, our convictions and feelings make a difference sometimes. After all, is it not true that "a man's best friend is his dogma?" As always, the luxury of hindsight enabled us to impose order on the findings. In fact, what I am about to explain seems so obvious now that I find it hard to imagine why most social psychologists (myself included) were not thinking this way before the early 1970s. However, I remind myself that the truth is obvious only once it is known, and that today's "obvious" synthesis sometimes becomes tomorrow's controversial thesis.

"It may be desirable to abandon the attitude concept."

Allan Wicker (1971)

When Do Attitudes Predict Behavior?

The apparent reason why we so often act contrary to our expressed attitudes is that, as Figure 2-1 suggests, our behavior and our expressions of our attitudes are both subject to other influences. Hence we should never have expected our attitude statements to predict our actions in every situation. If we could just neutralize the "other influences" noted in Figure 2-1—making all other things equal—our attitudes might predict our behaviors very well.

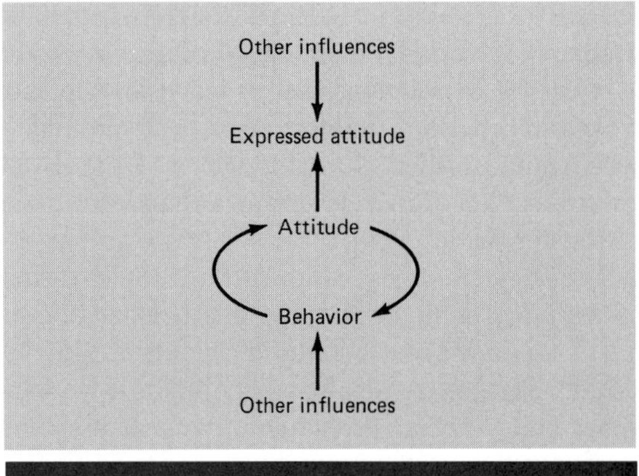

FIGURE 2-1 Our expressed attitudes may imperfectly predict our behavior because both are subject to other influences.

Other Influences on Expressed Attitudes

Unlike a physician measuring heart rate, we social psychologists never get a direct reading on people's true attitudes (if there is such a thing as a "true attitude"). Rather, we measure their *expressed* attitudes. And expressions are behaviors, which, like other behaviors, are subject to outside influences. For example, in Chapter 1 we saw that the way one poses a survey question can affect the answer given. So also can the conditions under which the person responds. This was vividly demonstrated when the United States House of Representatives once overwhelmingly passed a salary increase for itself in an off-the-record vote, then moments later overwhelmingly defeated the same bill on a roll-call vote. Potential constituent criticism had distorted the true congressional sentiment on the roll-call vote. We often tend to express what we think others want to hear.

Since people often don't wear their hearts on their sleeves, social psychologists have longed for a "pipeline to the heart" that would enable them to know people's concealed attitudes. Edward Jones and Harold Sigall (1971) therefore invented the *bogus pipeline* method for measuring people's attitudes. It's not a real pipeline, but it is the closest thing we have to one. In one experiment, conducted with Richard Page, Sigall (1971) had University of Rochester students hold a locked wheel, which if unlocked could turn a pointer to the left, indicating disagreement, or to the right, indicating agreement. When electrodes were attached to their arms, the fake machine supposedly measured miniature muscular responses that were said to gauge their suppressed tendency to turn the wheel left (disagree) or right (agree). To demonstrate this amazing new machine, the researchers asked the students a few questions, on which the experimenter had already secretly ascertained their attitudes. After a few moments of impressive flashing lights and whirring sounds, a meter on the machine announced the student's attitude—which was nothing more than the attitude position the student had earlier indicated. The procedure convinced everyone.

Note the deception here, and recall from Chapter 1 that professional ethics approve such deception only when necessary and justified.

People's expressed attitudes are sometimes not their real attitudes. (© 1961 United Feature Syndicate, Inc.)

Once the students were convinced, the attitude meter was then hidden and they were asked questions concerning their attitudes toward blacks and requested to guess what the meter revealed. How do you suppose these white collegians responded in comparison to other students responding on a typical paper-and-pencil measure? Those responding with the bogus pipeline admitted more negative beliefs than did those using the standard attitude scale. It was as if they were thinking "I'd better reveal my opinions lest the experimenter think I'm out of touch with myself." For example, those responding to the standard scale rated blacks as being more sensitive than Americans in general; those responding with the bogus pipeline reversed these judgments. Since displays of racial prejudice are generally considered gauche among today's sophisticated collegians, it seemed that the bogus pipeline was able to cut through the feigned attitudes.

Bogus pipeline: *A procedure for detecting people's true attitudes. Participants are first convinced that a new machine can use their physiological responses to measure their private attitudes. Then they are asked to predict the machine's reading, thus revealing their attitudes.*

Experiments with the bogus pipeline have produced additional interesting results. For example, Joseph Faranda, Joseph Kaminski, and Barbara Giza (1979) found that men and women students at the University of Delaware expressed similar attitudes about women's rights and roles when questions were asked with a paper-and-pencil test. But when using the bogus pipeline, men expressed much less sympathy toward women's rights than did women. (I suspect some of us are now thinking we knew-it-all-along that "most college men are closet chauvinists.") Such studies suggest that people's real attitudes are sometimes distorted when expressed.

"Quiet! Daddy voted his conscience today!"

Public actions cost more than private convictions. (Al Ross/ *Saturday Review*, 9/6/75)

Other Influences on Behavior

If people's attitude expressions are affected by outside influences, their other behaviors are probably even more so. As Chapters 6 to 9 will illustrate again and again, social influences can be enormous—enormous enough sometimes to induce people to violate their deepest convictions. Thus, before Jesus' crucifixion his disciple Peter denies knowing him; hostages may concede to their captors' demands; presidential aides may go along with actions they know are wrong. Recent research offers another vivid example: high school students' decisions to smoke or not to smoke marijuana are apparently less predictable from their prior attitudes toward marijuana than from the number of their friends who smoke it (Andrews & Kandel, 1979).

Since on any given occasion we are affected not only by our inner attitudes but also by the situation we face, should not *averaging* many occasions enable us to detect more clearly the impact of our attitudes? Predicting people's behavior is like predicting a baseball player's hitting. The outcome of any particular time at bat is nearly impossible to predict, because it is affected not only by what the batter brings to the plate, but also by what the pitcher throws and by unmeasurable chance factors. By averaging many times at bat we neutralize these complicating factors. Thus, knowing the players, we can predict their approximate batting *averages*. Or to use an example from research, people's general attitude toward religion poorly predicts whether they will go to church next Sunday (since church attendance is also influenced by the weather, the preacher, how one is feeling, etc.). But people's religious attitudes predict quite well the total quantity of their religious behaviors over a period of time (Fishbein & Ajzen, 1974; Kahle & Berman, 1979).

Attitude-Behavior Correspondence

Other conditions further improve the predictive potency of attitudes. As Icek Ajzen and Martin Fishbein (1977) have been pointing out for several years, when the attitude measured is general—say, an attitude toward ethnic minorities—and the behavior is very specific—say, a decision whether to help a particular black person in a particular situation—we should not expect a close correspondence between our words and our actions. Indeed, report Fishbein and Ajzen, in twenty-six out of twenty-seven such research studies, attitudes did not predict behavior. But attitudes *did* predict behavior in all twenty-six studies they could find in which the measured attitude corresponded closely to the situation being considered. For example, we can expect that attitudes toward the general concept of "health fitness" will poorly predict specific exercise and dietary practices. The likelihood of people's jogging more likely depends on their opinions about the costs and benefits of *jogging*. Thus to change people's health habits through persuasion, one should alter their attitudes toward *specific* health-related practices (Olson & Zanna, 1981).

So far we have seen two conditions under which our attitudes will predict our behavior: (1) when the "other influences" upon our attitude statements and our behavior are minimized, and (2) when the measured attitude is specific to the observed behavior. One other condition is suggested by Figure 2-1: An attitude should better predict behavior when the attitude becomes more potent.

Attitude Potency

Our attitudes are impotent when we act automatically, without pausing to consider them. Often we act out well-learned "scripts," not stopping to reflect on what we're doing. In the hallway, we may respond similarly to friends and to strangers with an automatic "Hi." Such mindless action is often adaptive. Since we normally concentrate on only one thing at a time, acting without premeditation frees our minds to work on new problems. As the philosopher Alfred North Whitehead argued, "Civilization advances by extending the number of operations which we can perform without thinking about them." In novel situations our behavior is less automatic; when there is no well-learned script we usually do think before we act.

If people were prompted to think about their attitudes before acting, might they then be truer to themselves? Mark Snyder and William Swann (1976) wanted to find out. So two weeks after 120 of their University of Minnesota men students indicated their attitudes toward affirmative-action employment policies, Snyder and Swann invited them to act as jurors in a sex-discrimination court case. Only if the men were first induced to remember their attitudes—by being given "a few minutes to organize your thoughts and views on the affirmative action issue"—did their attitudes predict their verdicts. Similarly, people who take a few moments to review their past behavior tend

"Your wife says you left your briefcase on the front lawn."

Often we act without thinking. (Bill Levine/*Saturday Review*, 2/2/80)

"Only individuals who know what they believe and who know the implications of what they believe for what they do are in a position to put their beliefs into practice."

Mark Snyder (1982)

to express attitudes that better predict their future behavior (Zanna, Olson, & Fazio, 1981). In an experiment with Deborah Kendzierski, Snyder (1982) also discovered that most students who had favorable attitudes toward psychological research were willing to volunteer for an experiment—*if* they had earlier heard someone offhandedly remark that whether you volunteer or not "is really a question of how worthwhile you think experiments are." Students who had not received this subtle reminder of the relevance of their attitudes seldom volunteered.

Another way experimenters have induced people to focus on their inner convictions is to make them self-conscious: for example, to have them act in front of a mirror (Carver & Scheier, 1981). Perhaps you can recall suddenly being acutely aware of yourself upon entering a room having a large mirror. Making people self-aware in this way promotes consistency between words and deeds (Gibbons, 1978; Froming, Walker, & Lopyan, 1982). For example, Edward Diener and Mark Wallbom (1976) noted that nearly all college students *say* that cheating is morally wrong. But will they follow the advice of Shakespeare's Polonius, "To thine own self be true"? Diener and Wallbom set University of Washington (Seattle) students to work on an anagram-solving task (said to predict IQ) and told them to stop when a bell in the room sounded. Left alone, 71 percent cheated by working past the bell. Other students, made self-aware by working in front of a mirror while hearing their tape-recorded voices, were truer to themselves—only 7 percent cheated. It makes one wonder: Would eye-level mirrors in stores decrease shoplifting by making people more conscious of their attitudes against stealing?

"Without doubt it is a delightful harmony when doing and saying go together."

Montaigne, Essays

Finally, we acquire our attitudes in a manner that sometimes makes them potent and sometimes not. An extensive series of experiments by Russell Fazio and Mark Zanna (1981) indicates that when our attitudes are rooted in our experience—not just in hearsay—they are far more likely to endure and to predict our subsequent actions. One of their studies was conducted with the unwitting assistance of Cornell University. A housing shortage forced the university to assign some first-year students to several weeks on cots in dormitory lounges while others basked in the relative luxury of their permanent rooms. When questioned by Dennis Regan and Fazio (1977), students in both groups espoused equivalently negative attitudes regarding the housing situation and how the administration was dealing with it. But when given opportunities to act upon their attitudes—to sign a petition and solicit other signatures, to join a committee being formed to investigate the situation, to write a letter on the matter—only those whose attitudes were rooted in direct experience with the temporary housing acted upon their attitudes. [As this experiment also hints, people are especially likely to act in accord with their attitudes when it is in their self-interest (Borgida & Campbell, 1982; Sivacek & Crano, 1982).] Other research by Fazio and Zanna, Charles Kiesler (1971), William Watts (1967), and Steven Sherman and colleagues (1983) indicates that, compared to attitudes formed passively, those which are forged in the hot fire of actual experience are also more clearly defined, more certain, more stable over time, more readily remembered, and more resistant to attack.

I have been reporting what, for most of us, is generally true. To be sure, we differ from one another. Some people, more than others, consistently act according to their inner convictions. For example, people who report themselves as strongly inner-directed are indeed more likely to actually exhibit attitude-behavior consistency than are "self-monitoring" people who say they readily adjust their behavior in response to external circumstances (M. Snyder, 1981; 1982; in press; Snyder & Campbell, 1982; Scheier, 1980; Zanna, Olson & Fazio, 1980). Nevertheless, it seems clear that, for most of us, our attitudes predict our actions (1) if other influences are minimized, (2) if the attitude is specific to the action, and (3) if, as we act, we are conscious of our attitudes, either because something reminds us of them or because we acquired them in a manner that makes them strong. When these conditions are not met, our attitudes seem disconnected from our actions.

So it is now plain that, depending on the conditions, the relationship between our attitude statements and our behavior can range from no relationship to a substantial one. La Rochefoucauld, the seventeenth-century French writer, was correct: "It is easier to preach virtue than to practice it." Yet we can breathe a sigh of relief that our attitudes are, after all, *one* determinant

"The view that attitudes have essentially no effect on behavior can be rejected with a high degree of confidence."

Peter Bentler & George Speckart (1981)

of our actions. This conclusion is reinforced by the recent findings of Lynn Kahle and others that people's attitudes can indeed predict their actions two weeks, two months, or even two years later (Kahle, 1983; Kahle & Berman, 1979). To return to the philosophical question with which we began, there *is* a connection between what we are and what we do, even if that connection is often looser than most of us would like to believe.

Now we turn our attention to the less commonsensical idea that our behavior determines our attitudes. It is true that we sometimes stand up for what we believe, but it is also true that we will believe in what we stand up for. If social psychology has taught us anything during the last twenty-five years, it is that *we are likely not only to think ourselves into a way of acting but also to act ourselves into a way of thinking.*

Much of the research which documents this conclusion has been inspired by social psychological theories. However, instead of beginning with these theories, I think it more interesting to reverse the order and first marshal the evidence for the effects of behavior on attitude, because this principle synthesizes a wide range of seemingly unrelated phenomena. I invite you to play theorist as you read this evidence. Speculate *why* actions affect attitudes, and then compare your ideas with the theoretical explanations proposed by social psychologists.

DOES OUR BEHAVIOR DETERMINE OUR ATTITUDES?

How do we learn to bicycle, type, play a musical instrument, or swim? As with much we learn, we must *do* it to know it. We can read books on bicycling, but we cannot *know* bicycling until we have done it. In these instances our action's effect upon our knowing is recognized easily. But is this effect limited to knowing physical skills? Consider the following incidents, each based on actual happenings:

Sarah is hypnotized and told to take off her shoes when a book drops on the floor. Fifteen minutes later a book drops and Sarah quietly slips out of her loafers. "Hey Sarah," asks the hypnotist, "why did you take off your shoes?" "Well . . . my feet are hot and tired," Sarah replies. "It has been a long day." The act produces the idea.

George has electrodes temporarily implanted in the region of his brain that controls his head movements. When the electrode is stimulated by remote control, George always turns his head. Unaware of the remote stimulation, he thinks this activity is spontaneous and when questioned always offers a reasonable explanation for it: "I'm looking for my slipper," "I heard a noise," "I'm restless," or "I was looking under the bed" (Delgado, 1973).

Carol's severe seizures were relieved by surgically separating her two brain hemispheres. Now, in an experiment, a picture of a nude woman is flashed to the left half of Carol's field of vision and thus to the nonverbal right side of her brain. A sheepish smile spreads over her face and she begins chuckling. Asked why, she invents—and apparently believes—a plausible explanation: "Oh—that funny machine" (Gazzaniga, 1972). Frank, another split-brain patient, has the word *smile* flashed to his nonverbal right hemisphere. He obliges and forces a smile. Asked why, he explains that "this experiment is very funny."

Such illustrations hint that the effect of what we do on what we "know" is not limited to physical skills. Indeed, the mental aftereffects of our behavior are evident in so rich a variety of experimental and social situations that we can but sample from the smorgasbord. I trust that the following examples will, nonetheless, indicate the power of self-persuasion. Each of the topics below illustrates that our attitudes can follow behavior.

Role Playing

The word *role* is borrowed from the theatre and, as in the theatre, refers to prescribed actions—actions expected of those who occupy a particular social position. When stepping into a new social role we must perform its actions, even if we feel somewhat inauthentic. But generally our sense of "phoniness" does not last long.

Recall a time when you stepped into some new role—perhaps your first days on a job, or in a sorority or fraternity, or at college. That first week on campus, for example, you may have been supersensitive to the new social prescriptions and tried valiantly to meet them, to root out your "Harry High School" behavior. At such times we often feel artificial; self-consciously we observe our new talk and actions, because they aren't naturally ours. Then one day an amazing thing happens: We notice that our insincere sorority enthusiasm and our pseudointellectual college talk no longer feel forced. We have begun to absorb the role. Granted, we chose the role. Yet now it has begun to fit as comfortably as our old jeans and T-shirt.

Evidence abounds confirming these speculations about the effects of acting out a role. In one study, young women smokers who played the emotional role of lung cancer victim subsequently reduced their smoking more than those merely given factual information about the dangers of smoking (Janis & Mann, 1965; Mann & Janis, 1968). In another, researchers observed industrial workers who were promoted to foreman (a company position) or shop steward (a union position). The new roles demanded new behavior. And, sure enough, the men soon developed new attitudes. The foremen became more sympathetic to the management's positions, the stewards to the union's (Lieberman, 1956).

This study by Lieberman hints at the tremendous importance of our vocational role. The career you choose will affect not only what you do on

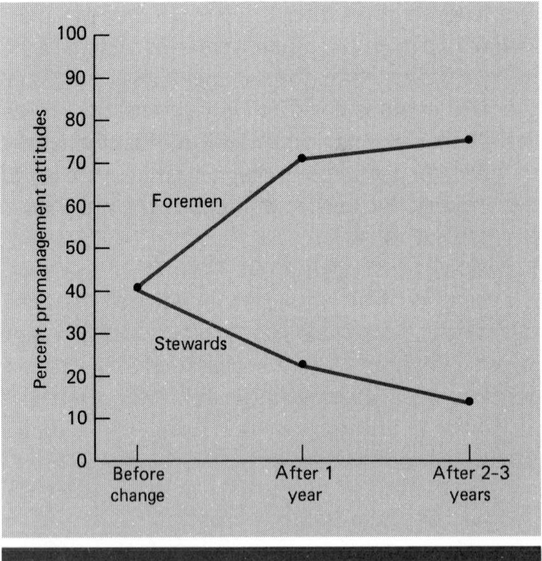

FIGURE 2-2 Workers promoted to the role of union steward or company foreman developed attitudes compatible with their new role. (Data from Lieberman, 1956.)

the job, but also the attitudes and values you are likely to develop. New teachers, police officers, soldiers, and managers usually internalize their roles with significant effects on their attitudes and personalities. The marines "make a man out of you"—not by intellectual indoctrination, but by having you act out the new role requirements. A recent study of 1600 young men revealed that the status of their occupations affected their attitudes toward themselves; those who acted out higher-status roles developed higher self-esteem (Bachman & O'Malley, 1977).

The effect of behavior on attitude is evident even in the theatre. Self-conscious playacting may diminish as the actor becomes absorbed into the role and experiences genuine emotion. For instance, children's creative dramatic activity can be an effective means of enlarging their understandings. Fantasy becomes reality as each child acts within the rules of an imaginary reality. For example, in William Golding's novel *Lord of the Flies*, a group of shipwrecked English boys descend to uncivilized, brutal behavior. When a movie version of the book was made, the youngsters who acted it out became the creatures prescribed by their roles. The movie's director, Peter Brook (1964), reported that "Many of their off-screen relationships completely paralleled the story, and one of our main problems was to encourage them to be uninhibited within the shots but disciplined in between them" (p. 163).

The Foot-in-the-Door Phenomenon

Can we not all recall times when, after agreeing to help out with a project or to join an organization, we eventually ended up far more involved than we ever intended, vowing that in the future we would say no to such requests?

How does this happen? Experiments suggest that if you want people to do a big favor for you, a good technique is to get them to do a small favor first. In the best-known demonstration of this *foot-in-the-door* principle, Jonathan Freedman and Scott Fraser (1966) found that after complying with a small request (for example, to sign a safe-driving petition), California homemakers were three times more likely to comply later with a bigger request to place an ugly "Drive Carefully" sign in their front yards than were women who had not first been approached for the small favor.

Other researchers have confirmed Freedman and Fraser's finding (DeJong, 1979). Several of these studies have tried to elicit altruistic acts, such as contributing to a charity. For example, Patricia Pliner and her collaborators (1974) found 46 percent of Toronto suburbanites willing to contribute to the Cancer Society when approached directly. Others, asked a day ahead to wear a lapel pin publicizing the drive (which all agreed to do), were nearly twice as likely to donate when the Cancer Society came calling.

However, the seductive power of the foot-in-the-door phenomenon has limits. When the behavior is costly to us, such as giving blood when we have never before done so, our simply agreeing to display a publicity poster for the upcoming blood drive seems not to markedly increase our later willingness to donate (Cialdini & Ascani, 1976; Foss & Dempsey, 1979). But when we agree to a series of escalating commitments, we will sometimes consent to a very substantial request. Shalom Schwartz (1970) of the University of Wisconsin was pleasantly surprised to find that of 144 blood donors he invited to be on call as bone marrow donors (requiring an extraction procedure under general anesthesia with subsequent soreness), 59 percent agreed. Schwartz surmised that his procedure of escalating commitments had produced a "momentum of compliance." All 144 had first agreed to give blood and, when approached in the canteen after donating, had further agreed to leave their seats and talk with the interviewer. After the interviewer explained the procedure and the need, he simply asked the people to permit their already donated blood to be tested to determine whether their type of bone marrow was currently needed. Ninety-five percent of them agreed to the test. Then the interviewer explained, "Carrying out these tests is a pretty complicated and expensive business for us in the lab, so we don't want to go ahead with them unless we know there is at least a 50/50 chance you will consider donating marrow if you turn out to be compatible." Eighty-three percent of the initial group now indicated there was a 50-50 chance that they would donate. Only after making these commitments were they asked if they would join "a pool of people willing to be on call should they be needed to donate marrow."

Foot-in-the-door phenomenon: *The tendency for people who have first agreed to a small request to comply later with a larger request.*

Note that in all these experiments the initial compliance—signing a petition, wearing a lapel pin, agreeing to a blood test—was voluntary, never coerced by threat or bribe. We will see again and again that when people bind themselves to public behaviors *and* perceive these acts to be their own doing, they come to believe more strongly in what they have done. Why does this happen? The answer is not entirely clear. What, for instance, produces the foot-in-the-door effect? One possibility is that the initial act affects the person's *attitude* toward such action. If this occurs, then shouldn't we expect the greatest compliance when the small request corresponds closely to the large request?

Robert Cialdini and his collaborators (1978) demonstrated the powerful effects of a commitment that is similar to the desired action. They experimented with the *low-ball technique*, a tactic reportedly used by some new-car dealers. After the customer agrees to buy a new car because of its extremely good price and begins completing the sales forms, the salesperson removes the price advantage by charging for options the customer thought were included, or by checking with the boss who disallows the deal because "we'd be losing money." Folklore has it that more customers will stick with their purchase, even at the higher price, than would have agreed if the full price had been revealed at the outset. Cialdini and his collaborators found that this technique does indeed work. For example, when introductory psychology students were invited to participate in an experiment at 7:00 A.M., only 24 percent showed up. But if they first agreed to participate without knowing the time and only then were asked if they would participate at 7:00 A.M., 53 percent came. New experiments with University of Missouri-Columbia students by Jerry Burger and Richard Petty (1981) indicate that the low-ball technique is effective partly because once a commitment has been made, one feels obligated to the requester.

Low-ball technique: *A technique for getting people to agree to do something. People who have agreed to (but have not yet performed) an initial request are more likely to comply when the requester makes the request more costly than are people who are approached only with the costly request.*

An even more popular explanation for the foot-in-the-door phenomenon presumes a change not in the person's attitudes, but in the person's self-image (DeJong, 1981; Rittle, 1981). To paraphrase Freedman and Fraser, after Melinda signs the safe-driving petition, she may become, in her own eyes, a person who agrees to requests made by strangers, who takes action on things she believes in, who helps a good cause. If this "self-perception" explanation is correct, then shouldn't people who *refuse* an initial request be *less* likely to comply with a subsequent request, assuming they now feel more like *non*doers? Such is precisely what Mark Snyder and Michael Cunningham (1975) found. When Minneapolis residents were asked if they would be willing to participate in a thirty-question survey, 33 percent agreed to do so. Others first received a preliminary call from someone else, asking if they would participate in an eight-question survey. Nearly all said yes, and when later the actual survey taker called and indicated the survey would be *thirty* questions, 52 percent were still willing to participate. A third group of people were initially asked if they would be willing to answer a fifty-question survey. Most *refused*, and thus, when a survey taker called with the thirty-question survey, only 22 percent were willing to participate.

The foot-in-the-door phenomenon is well worth being aware of so that we won't be naively vulnerable to it. Someone trying to seduce us, financially, politically, or sexually, usually will try to create a momentum of compliance.

As we shall see, great evils sometimes result from the corrupting effects of gradually escalating commitments. Doing a small evil act makes the next evil act easier. To paraphrase another of La Rochefoucauld's *Maxims* (1665), it is not so difficult to find one who has never succumbed to a given temptation as to find one who has succumbed only once.

Marketing researchers have found that this principle works even when we are aware of a profit motive; hence, salespeople are often trained to use it (Reingen & Kernam, 1977; Varela, 1971). Our harmless initial commitment—returning a card for more information and a free gift, simply agreeing to attend a meeting just to hear about an investment possibility—often starts us toward a larger commitment.

The day after I wrote the last sentence above, a life insurance salesperson came to my office and offered a thorough analysis of our family's financial situation. After finishing his presentation, he did not ask whether I wished to buy his life insurance, or even whether I wished to engage his free service. His question was instead a small foot-in-the-door, one carefully calculated to elicit my agreement: Did I think people should have such information about their financial situation?

The foot-in-the-door is not always so harmless. This process of step-by-step commitment, of spiraling action and attitude, contributed to the escalation of the Vietnam war. Once difficult decisions were made and defended, our leaders seemed blind to information incompatible with their acts. They noticed and remembered comments that harmonized with their actions, but ignored or dismissed information that undermined their assumptions. As Ralph White (1971) put it, "There was a tendency, when actions were out of line with ideas, for decision-makers to align their ideas with their actions."

Effects of Moral and Immoral Acts

The wartime examples, above, suggest the interesting possibility that acting in violation of our moral standards does not heighten conscience, but rather sets in motion a process of self-justification that may ultimately lead us to believe in what we have done. Thomas Jefferson recognized this possibility in 1785:

> He who permits himself to tell a lie once finds it much easier to do it a second and third time, till at length it becomes habitual; he tells lies without attending to it, and truths without the world's believing him. This falsehood of the tongue leads to that of the heart, and in time depraves all its good dispositions.

Experiments bear out this point. People induced to give spoken or written witness to something about which they have real doubts will often feel bad about their deceit. Nevertheless, they begin to believe what they are saying, *provided* they were not excessively bribed or coerced into doing so. Especially when there is no compelling external explanation for one's words, saying becomes believing (Klaas, 1978).

Box 2-1

Acting Oneself into Belief: Saying Is Believing

University of Oregon psychologist Ray Hyman (1981) describes how by acting the role of a psychic he convinced himself of his own psychic powers.

> I started reading palms when I was in my teens as a way to supplement my income from doing magic and mental shows. When I started I did not believe in palmistry. But I knew that to "sell" it I had to act as if I did. After a few years I became a firm believer in palmistry. One day the late Stanley Jaks, who was a professional mentalist and a man I respected, tactfully suggested that it would make an interesting experiment if I deliberately gave readings opposite to what the lines indicated. I tried this out with a few clients. To my surprise and horror my readings were just as successful as ever. Ever since then I have been interested in the powerful forces that convince us, [palm] reader and client alike, that something is so when it really isn't. (p. 86)

Does the "saying is believing" effect occur in everyday life as well as in the laboratory? Apparently it does. First, there is clear evidence that most of us—politicians included—adapt what we say to please our listeners. Social psychologist Philip Tetlock (1981b) has found that the policy statements of American presidents tend to be quite simplistic during the political campaign (for example, "To control inflation, we need major cuts in government spending"). Immediately after the election their statements become more complex—until the next election year—suggesting that the simplistic statements are part of an *impression-management* strategy (Baumeister, 1982; Schlenker, 1980; Tedeschi, 1981). Similarly, we are readier to tell people good news than bad, and we adjust our message toward our listener's position (e.g., Manis, Cornell, & Moore, 1974; Newtson & Czerlinsky, 1974; Tesser, Rosen, & Conlee, 1972). These aren't really lies, mind you; we just shade our views this way or that, depending on whether it is a pacifist we are talking to or someone from the Veterans of Foreign Wars.

Impression management: *Presenting oneself in ways calculated to gain others' approval. Synonym: self-presentation.*

Second, once we have uttered our modified message, we tend to believe it. Tory Higgins and William Rholes (1978) confirmed that "saying is believing" by having Princeton University students read a personality description of someone and then summarize it for another who either liked or disliked this person. Sure enough, these Princetonians not only gave a more positive description when the recipient liked the person, they also then liked the person more themselves. And when asked to recall what they had read, they remembered the description as being more positive than it was. In short, it seems that we are prone to adjust our messages to our listeners, and, having done so, to believe the altered message.

"I had thought I was humoring [my captors] by parroting their cliches and buzz words without personally believing in them. . . . In trying to convince them I convinced myself."

Patricia Campbell Hearst,
Every Secret Thing

"And for those of you who may disagree with my public stance on Salt II, remember, privately I'm saying quite the opposite."

Impression management: We sometimes express what we think others want to hear. (Drawing by Dana Fradon; © 1979 *The New Yorker* Magazine, Inc.)

The action → attitude sequence occurs not just with shading the truth but with more immoral acts as well. Cruel acts corrode the consciences of those who perform them. Harming an innocent victim—by uttering hurtful comments or delivering electric shocks—typically leads aggressors to disparage their victims, thus helping to justify the hurtful behavior (Berscheid, Boye, & Walster, 1968; Davis & Jones, 1960; Glass, 1964). In all the studies that have established this, people were most likely to justify their action if they were coaxed, not coerced into it, if they felt some responsibility because they agreed to do the deed.

In everyday life, oppressors similarly disparage their victims. We tend not only to hurt those we dislike, but to dislike those we have hurt. In times of war, soldiers will generally denigrate their victims, as in American soldiers' dehumanizing references to Vietnamese people as "gooks." This is yet another instance of the spiraling effects of action and attitude: The more one commits atrocities, the easier it becomes. The same holds for prejudice. If a group holds others in slavery, it is likely to perceive the slaves as having traits that justify continuing the oppression. Our actions and attitudes feed one another, sometimes to the point of moral numbness.

"Our self-definitions are not constructed in our heads; they are forged by our deeds."

Robert McAfee Brown, Creative Dislocation—The Movement of Grace

These observations suggest that evil acts not only reflect the self, they shape the self. Situations which elicit evil acts therefore gnaw at the moral sensitivity of the actor. The following depicts what happened to one man who was but a small cog in the Nazi machine.

Cruel acts often beget cruel attitudes. (© J. Ross Baughman/Visions)

Q: Did you kill people in the camp?

A: Yes.

Q: Did you poison them with gas?

A: Yes.

Q: Did you bury them alive?

A: It sometimes happened. . . .

Q: Did you personally help kill people?

A: Absolutely not, I was only paymaster in the camp.

Q: What did you think of what was going on?

A: It was bad at first but we got used to it.

Q: Do you know the Russians will hang you?

A: (Bursting into tears) Why should they? *What have I done?* (Arendt, 1971, p. 262)

Fortunately, the principle works in the other direction as well. Moral action has positive effects on the actor. Experiments demonstrate that when children resist temptation, they tend to internalize their conscientious behavior if the deterrent is strong enough to elicit the desired behavior, but mild enough to leave them with a sense of choice. In a dramatic experiment, Jonathan Freedman (1965) introduced elementary school children to an enticing battery-controlled robot, but instructed them not to play with it while he was out of the room. Freedman used a severe threat with half the children and a mild threat with the others. Both were sufficient to deter the children. Several weeks later, a different researcher, with no apparent relation to the earlier events, left each child to play in the same room with the same toys. Fourteen of the eighteen children who were given the severe threat now freely played with the robot; but two-thirds of those given the mild deterrent still resisted playing with it. Having made the conscious choice not to play with the toy, they apparently internalized their decision, and this newly acquired attitude controlled their subsequent action. Here, then, is more evidence suggesting that attitudes and actions affect each other.

The effect of moral action on moral thinking is also apparent in other experiments. For example, children who are actively engaged in enforcing rules or in teaching moral norms to younger children subsequently follow the moral code better than children who are not given the opportunity to be teachers or enforcers (e.g., Parke, 1974). This indicates that the exercise of discipline has an effect on the one who disciplines as well as on the one disciplined. Perhaps, then, providing opportunities for responsibility, such as firstborn children often have, may be one way to enhance self-control. Jean Piaget (1948) likewise suggested that children's spontaneous enforcement of rules during their play develops their moral thinking.

Interracial Behavior and Racial Attitudes

If moral action helps create moral attitudes, might not more positive interracial behavior lead to the reduction of racial prejudice? Such was part of social scientists' testimony prior to the Supreme Court's 1954 decision to desegregate schools. The argument ran like this: If we wait for the heart to change—through preaching and teaching—we will wait a long time for racial justice. But if we legislate moral action, we can, under the appropriate conditions, indirectly affect heartfelt attitudes. Although this idea runs counter to the popular notion that "you can't legislate morality"—which is right in that one cannot *directly* legislate moral attitudes—the evidence (see Chapter 12) suggests

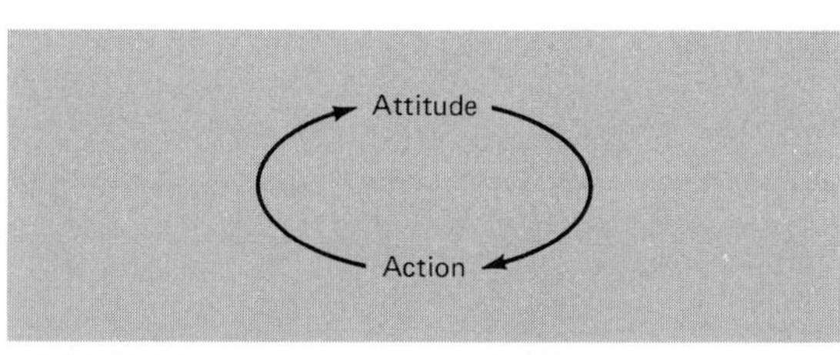

FIGURE 2-3 Attitudes and actions generate one another, like chicken and egg.

that substantial cognitive change has, in fact, followed on the heels of desegregation. For example:

Since the Supreme Court decision the percentage of white Americans favoring integrated schools has more than doubled.

In the ten years after the Civil Rights Act of 1964 the percentage of white Americans who described their neighborhoods, friends, co-workers, or fellow students as all-white declined by about 20 percent for each of these measures—a significant increase in interracial behavior. During the same period, the percentage of white Americans who said that blacks should be allowed to live in any neighborhood increased from 65 percent to 87 percent (ISR Newsletter, 1975).

More uniform national standards against discrimination have been followed by decreasing differences in racial attitudes among people of differing religion, class and geographic region. As we have come to act more alike, we have come to think more alike (Greeley & Sheatsley, 1971; Taylor, Sheatsley, & Greeley, 1978).

This evidence does not prove the point, for there are other ways to account for these altered attitudes. But it is consistent with the contention that our attitudes follow our behavior.

"We do not love people so much for the good they have done us, as for the good we have done them."

Leo Tolstoy, War and Peace

Experiments support the contention that positive behavior toward someone fosters one's liking for that person. Doing a favor for an experimenter or another subject, or tutoring a student, generally increases one's attraction to the person helped (Blanchard & Cook, 1976). Note that these experiments complement those which demonstrate that *harming* another leads people to denigrate their victims.

In 1793, Benjamin Franklin tested this idea that doing a favor engenders liking. As clerk of the Pennsylvania General Assembly, he was disturbed by opposition from another important legislator. So Franklin set out to win him over:

I did not . . . aim at gaining his favour by paying any servile respect to him but, after some time, took this other method. Having heard that he had in his library a certain very scarce and curious book I wrote a note to him expressing my desire of perusing that book and requesting he would do me the favour of lending it to me for a few days. He sent it immediately and I return'd it in about a week, expressing strongly my sense of the favour. When we next met in the House he spoke to me (which he had never done before), and with great civility; and he ever after manifested a readiness to serve me on all occasions, so that we became great friends and our friendship continued to his death. This is another instance of the truth of an old maxim I had learned, which says, "He that has once done you a kindness will be more ready to do you another than he whom you yourself have obliged." (Rosenzweig, 1972, p. 769)

People tend to believe what they hear themselves saying. (Culver Pictures)

Social Movements

The effect of a society's racial behavior on its racial attitudes suggests the possibility, and the danger, of employing the same idea for political socialization on a mass scale. Such was clearly evident in Nazi Germany, where participation in mass meetings, wearing uniforms, demonstrating, and especially the public greeting "Heil Hitler" established for many a profound inconsistency between behavior and belief. Historian Richard Grunberger (1971) reports:

> The "German greeting" was a powerful conditioning device. Having once decided to intone it as an outward token of conformity, many experienced schizophrenic discomfort at the contradiction between their words and their feelings. Prevented from saying what they believed, they tried to establish their psychic equilibrium by consciously making themselves believe what they said. (p. 27)

However, the practice is not limited to totalitarian regimes. Our own political rituals—the daily flag salute by schoolchildren, singing the national anthem—use public conformity to build a private conformity to patriotism. I recall participating in air-raid drills in my elementary school not far from the Boeing Company in Seattle. I remember my own fears of the Russians after we repeatedly acted as if we were the objects of Soviet aggression. In another case, several observers have noted that the civil rights marches and demonstrations of the 1960s were as important for their contributions to the identity and commitment of the demonstrators as for their direct effects on legislation. These actions were initiated as a result of an *idea* whose time had come. Yet the public actions helped drive the idea more deeply into the hearts of the participants.

The historic 1965 civil rights march to Selma, Alabama. Such political acts can amplify the idea lying behind them. (James H. Karales/ Peter Arnold, Inc.)

Brainwashing

For many, the most dramatic human influence is *brainwashing*, a term first used to describe what happened to American prisoners of war (POWs) during the Korean War. Actually, the Chinese "thought-control" program was not nearly as irresistible as this term suggests. Still it was disconcerting that several hundred prisoners cooperated with their captors and that twenty-one chose to remain after being granted permission to return to America. Edgar Schein (1956) interviewed many of the POWs during their journey home. Schein recorded that the captors' methods included a

> *pacing of demands*. In the various kinds of responses that were demanded of the prisoners, the Chinese always started with trivial, innocuous ones and, as the habit of responding became established, gradually worked up to more important ones. Thus after a prisoner had once been "trained" to speak or write out trivia, statements on more important issues were demanded of him. This was particularly effective in eliciting confessions, self-criticism, and information during interrogation.
>
> Closely connected with the principle of pacing was the principle of constant *participation* from the prisoner. It was never enough for the prisoner to listen and absorb; some kind of verbal or written response was always demanded. Thus if a man would not give original material in question-and-answer sessions, he was asked to copy something. Likewise, group discussions, autobiographical statements, self-criticisms, and public confession were all demanded as active participation by the prisoner.

Thus compliance with a small request was followed by a larger request, a practical application of the foot-in-the-door technique. Threats of torture were generally not used to elicit the prisoners' compliance. Instead, the Chinese offered inducements and rewards, evidently cultivating in the captives some sense of responsibility for their behavior.

Action Therapies

Let us consider, last, the professionals who help people change. Many new psychotherapies emphasize the client's chosen actions. These, in contrast to older therapies such as psychoanalysis, agree that clients' insights into why they behave as they do often is not enough to alter how they behave. So reality therapy induces people to act more responsibly. Behavior therapists attempt to shape behavior and, if they care about inner dispositions at all, assume that these will tag along after the behavior. Assertion training employs the same foot-in-the-door procedure we have seen to be effective in changing attitudes: The individual first role-plays small assertions in a supportive context and then gradually bigger assertions in everyday life. Rational-emotive therapy assumes that we generate our own emotions; its clients are given "homework" assignments to act in new ways that will generate new emotions. Encounter groups subtly induce participants to behave in novel ways in front of the group: to express anger, cry, act with high self-esteem, express positive feelings.

Research indicates that regardless of their methods, treatments which elicit specific behaviors achieve results superior to those from purely verbal therapies (Bandura, 1977). The experiments we have reviewed in this chapter suggest that people's inner changes will be most significant when they are encouraged to "own responsibility" for their new actions (rather than to attribute the responsibility for their acts to the therapist or to group pressure). For example, in three experiments Edward Jones and his associates (1981) influenced Duke and Princeton University students to present themselves to an interviewer in either self-enhancing or self-deprecating ways. Remarkably, their public displays of self-approval or disapproval carried over to their later private responses on a test of actual self-esteem. Saying is believing, even when one is talking positively or negatively about oneself. Jones and his colleagues found that this was especially true when the students had been made to feel responsible for how they presented themselves to the interviewer.

Is there not here a practical moral? If we want to change ourselves in some important way, perhaps we'd best not depend exclusively on introspection and intellectual insight. Sometimes we need to act—to begin writing that paper, to make those phone calls, to go see that person—even if we don't feel like acting. Jacques Barzun (1975) recognized the energizing power of action in advising aspiring writers to engage in the act of writing even if passive contemplation has left them feeling uncertain about their ideas:

> If you are too modest about yourself or too plain indifferent about the possible reader and yet are required to write, then you have to pretend. Make believe that you want to bring somebody around to your opinion; in other words, adopt a thesis and start expounding it. . . . With a slight effort of the kind at the start—a challenge

to utterance—you will find your pretense disappearing and a real concern creeping in. The subject will have taken hold of you as it does in the work of all habitual writers. (pp. 173–174)

WHY DO OUR ACTIONS AFFECT OUR ATTITUDES?

We have seen that several independent streams of observation—laboratory experiments, social history, and therapeutic interventions—merge to form one river: the effect of our overt actions on our inner attitudes. This conclusion is more clearly established than its explanation. Do these diverse observations contain any clues to *why* action affects attitude? Social psychologists are like detectives. In the case of "attitudes follow actions," two theoretical culprits are suspect. Let's examine each.

Self-Justification

Cognitive dissonance: *Feelings of tension that arise when one is simultaneously aware of two inconsistent cognitions. For example, dissonance may occur when we realize that we have, with little justification, acted contrary to our attitudes, or made a decision favoring one alternative despite reasons favoring another.*

One explanation is that we are motivated to rationalize our behavior. Such is the implication of Leon Festinger's *cognitive dissonance theory* (Wicklund & Brehm, 1976). The theory is very simple, but its range of application is enormous. It assumes we feel tension ("dissonance") when two of our thoughts or beliefs ("cognitions") are psychologically inconsistent—when we recognize that they don't fit together. Festinger furthermore argued that we adjust our thinking to reduce this tension. For example, Steven Sherman and Larry Gorkin (1980) aroused dissonance in their Indiana University students by giving them the following riddle:

A father and his son are out driving. They are involved in an accident. The father is killed, and the son is in critical condition. The son is rushed to the hospital and prepared for the operation. The doctor comes in, sees the patient, and exclaims, "I can't operate, it's my son!" How could this be?

Although virtually all the students had previously indicated they strongly favored sexual equality and other feminist ideals, most failed to solve the riddle (by identifying the doctor as the son's mother). Believing that "I am nonsexist" yet now realizing that "I perceived this riddle with sexist assumptions" thus evoked dissonance. When later the students judged a case of alleged sex discrimination, how do you suppose those who had failed the riddle reacted? They reacted with exceptionally strong support for the female complainant, thus reducing their dissonance and reaffirming their nonsexist self-image.

Applications of dissonance theory pertain mostly to discrepancies between our behavior and our attitudes. We are aware of both. Thus if we sense that they are inconsistent we feel pressure for change. So if you can persuade

BEHIND THE SCENES

Leon Festinger

Dissonance theory arose as I pondered a perplexing report of rumors after a 1934 earthquake in India. In the area outside the disaster zone, many of the rumors predicted that even worse disasters would soon follow. I wondered: Why would people spread and believe such frightening, anxiety-provoking ideas? Then it occurred to me that perhaps these rumors were not "anxiety-provoking" but rather "anxiety-justifying." Perhaps since people were already frightened by the earthquake, even though they lived outside the area of destruction, they needed something to justify their fear. And that's how my ideas about cognitive change and dissonance reduction—making your view of the world fit with how you feel or what you've done—were born. (*Leon Festinger, New School for Social Research*)

people to adopt a new attitude, their behavior should adjust accordingly; that's common sense. Or if you can induce a person to behave differently, dissonance may be reduced by attitude change; that's the self-persuasion effect we have been reviewing.

Insufficient Justification

Cognitive dissonance theory is noted for several surprising predictions. Perhaps you can reason them out. Imagine you are a subject in a famous experiment conducted by Festinger and J. Merrill Carlsmith (1959). For an hour the study requires you to perform dull tasks such as turning wooden knobs again and again. After you finish, the experimenter explains that the study concerns the effect of people's expectations upon their performance. The next subject, who is waiting outside, must be led to expect that this is going to be an interesting experiment. The experimenter then informs you that the assistant who usually creates this expectation was unable to attend this session: "So could you fill in and do this?" Since it's for science and you are being paid, you agree to tell the next subject (who is actually the experimenter's real assistant), what a delightful experience you have just had. "Really?" responds the supposed subject. "A friend of mine was in this experiment a week ago and she said it was boring." "Oh no," you respond, "it's really very interesting. You get good exercise while turning some slinky knobs. I'm sure you'll enjoy it." Finally, before you leave the lab, someone else who is doing a study of how people react to experiments asks you to complete a questionnaire indicating how much you actually enjoyed your knob-turning experience.

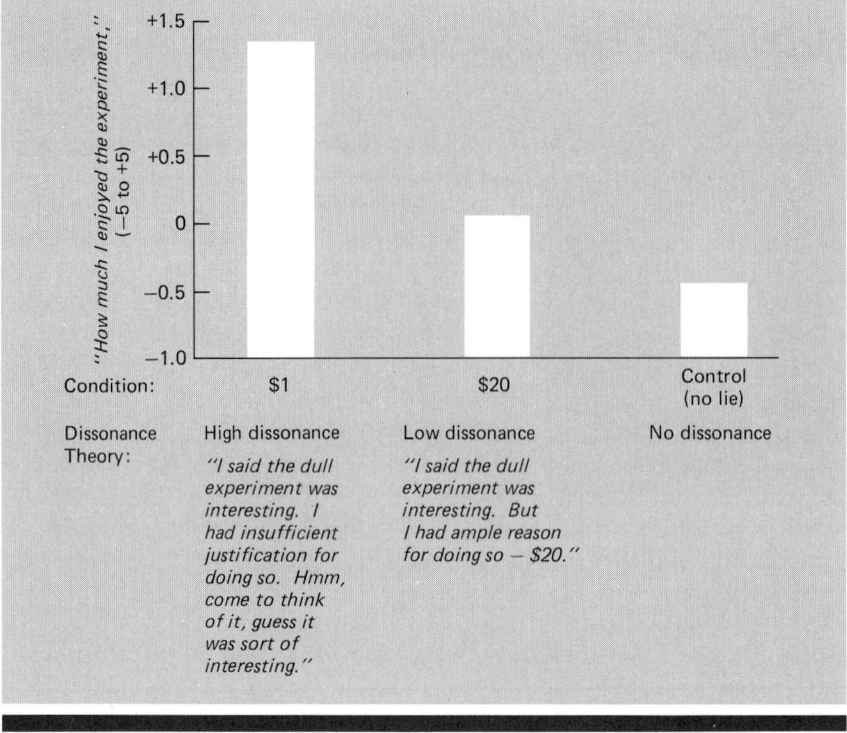

FIGURE 2-4
Insufficient justification: Dissonance theory predicts that when our actions are not fully explained by external rewards or coercion, we will experience dissonance, which can be reduced by coming to believe in what we have done. (Data from Festinger & Carlsmith, 1959.)

Insufficient justification effect: *Reduction of dissonance by internally justifying one's behavior, when external inducements are "insufficient" to fully justify it.*

Now for the prediction: Under which condition would you be most likely to believe your little lie and say the experiment was indeed interesting—when paid $1 for doing so, as some of Festinger and Carlsmith's subjects were, or when paid a generous $20, as others were? Contrary to the common notion that big rewards produce big effects, Festinger and Carlsmith reasoned that those paid just $1 would be most likely to adjust their attitudes to their actions. Having *insufficient justification* for their action, they would experience more discomfort (dissonance) and thus be more motivated to believe in what they had done. Those paid $20 had sufficient justification for what they did and hence should have experienced less dissonance. As Figure 2-4 indicates, their results fit this intriguing prediction.*

*There is a seldom-reported final aspect of this 1950s experiment which illustrates the more lax research ethics prevailing back then. Imagine yourself finally back with the experimenter, who is truthfully explaining the whole study. Not only do you learn that you've been duped, but the experimenter asks for the $20 bill back. Do you comply? Festinger and Carlsmith note that all of their Stanford student subjects willingly reached into their pockets and gave back the money. This is a foretaste of some quite amazing observations of compliance and conformity to be discussed in Chapter 7. As we shall see, when the social situation makes clear demands, people are usually very responsive.

Many other experimenters have obtained similar results. In general, people are most likely to persuade themselves of the validity of an act when they feel some choice about doing it and when it has foreseeable consequences. Imagine yourself as one of the UCLA students in an illustrative experiment by Barry Collins and Michael Hoyt (1972). You agree, for a measly 50 cents, to write an essay against dorm visitation rights for the opposite sex (it is hardly sufficient justification and it's contrary to your real feelings, but the researcher needs some arguments for the unpopular position). Furthermore, you sign a form taking responsibility for the essay, and you think your college administrators will use your essay to help determine college policy. Under these circumstances you may, like the UCLA students, find it difficult to resist feeling increased sympathy for the antivisitation position.

Earlier we noted the insufficient-justification principle working with punishments as well as rewards. Recall, for example, that children who were severely threatened to deter them from playing with an attractive toy devalued the toy less than those who, having received only a mild threat, had to struggle with themselves a bit. When a parent says, "Clean up your room, Johnny, or I'll knock your block off," Johnny won't need to search inside himself for a justification for his cleaning his room. The severe threat is a fully adequate justification. Note that the theory of cognitive dissonance is concerned with what *induces* a desired action, rather than with the relative effectiveness of rewards and punishments administered *after* the act. It aims, for example, to have Johnny say, "I am cleaning up my room because I want a clean room," rather than "I am cleaning up my room only because my parents are making me." In managing businesses and colleges, people may therefore be more likely to support rules if they have a sense of being responsible for the rules under which they behave.

Such implications of dissonance theory have led some to view it as an integration of humanistic and scientific perspectives. Authoritarian management will be effective, the theory predicts, only so long as the authority is present; behavior is not so likely to be internalized when there is little sense of choice. As Bree, a formerly enslaved talking horse in C. S. Lewis's *The Horse and His Boy* (1974), observes, "One of the worst results of being a slave and being forced to do things is that when there is no one to force you any more you find you have almost lost the power of forcing yourself" (p. 193). Similarly, prisoners coerced into participating in "rehabilitation" activities in order to secure their release can easily justify their cooperation by what it gains them; hence there may be little need to justify their good behavior with new attitudes. Perhaps this is one reason why prisoner rehabilitation programs have apparently had so little effect. Dissonance theory is hardly permissive in its implications, for it insists that encouragements and inducements be enough to elicit desired action. But it does suggest that managers, teachers, and parents use only enough incentive to elicit desired behavior, thus encouraging people to attribute their actions to themselves.

Dissonance after Decisions

The emphasis on perceived choice and responsibility implies that making *decisions* will produce dissonance. When faced with an important decision—what college to attend, whom to date, which job to accept—we are sometimes torn between two equally attractive alternatives. Perhaps you can recall a time when, having committed yourself to one course of action, you become painfully aware of dissonant cognitions—the desirable features of what you had rejected and the undesirable features of what you had chosen. If you decided to live on campus, you may have realized you were forgoing the greater spaciousness and freedom of an apartment in favor of the cramped, noisy quarters and restrictive house rules of the dorm. If you elected to live off campus, you perhaps pondered that your decision entailed physical separation from campus and friends, as well as the necessity of cooking.

Recently my wife and I decided the time had come to replace our gas-slurping 1972 Ford with a more fuel-efficient car. We waffled between a Honda Civic (a cute little car with high mileage rating, but one hardly big enough to accommodate our family) and a Ford Fairmont (roomier, gas mileage good, but not so good as the Honda's). Whatever we were to decide, some dissonance was sure to be aroused.

Our new Honda was delivered last week. Splendid little car. Quiet motor. Now that I think about it, its front-wheel drive is perfect for this town where it snows 100 inches a year. And, yes, we're helping with the war on energy waste.

Experiments indicate that after making an important decision we usually reduce dissonance in the way this example suggests—by upgrading the chosen alternative and denigrating the option passed over. In the first published dissonance experiment (1956), Jack Brehm had University of Minnesota women rate eight products, such as a toaster, a radio, and a hair dryer. They were then shown two objects they had rated closely and told they could have whichever they chose. Later, when rerating the eight objects, the women increased their evaluation of the item they had chosen, and decreased their evaluation of the rejected item. It seems that when we've chosen our fate, the grass does *not* then grow greener on the other side of the fence. The fence is more likely to be entwined with sour grapes.

"Every time you make a choice you are turning the central part of you, the part of you that chooses, into something a little different from what it was before."

C. S. Lewis,
Mere Christianity

Other experiments indicate that making a decision can affect our thinking even before we learn the consequences of our decision. Robert Knox and James Inkster (1968) found that racetrack bettors felt more confidence in their chosen horse if they had just bet on it than if they were about to bet on it. Likewise, contestants in carnival games of chance feel more confident of winning right after agreeing to play, than right before, and voters indicate more esteem and confidence in their candidate just after voting than just before (Younger, Walker, and Arrowood, 1977). Three days after President Carter's energy package was finished and committed to print he confessed to his cabinet that he once had doubts about the program, but that "now I'm feeling better and better about it" (NBC News, 1977a). There may sometimes be but a slight difference between the two options, as I can recall in helping

"Monday is out for the break because I have to see my social worker; Tuesday they're showing a film I wouldn't want to miss; Wednesday's my pottery lesson . . ."

Choosing between two attractive alternatives. (*Cartoons From Punch*, edited by William Hewison, Copyright © 1979 Punch Publications Ltd.)

make faculty tenure decisions. The competence of one faculty member who barely makes it and that of another who barely loses out seem not very different—until after the decision is made and announced.

Self-Perception

Although dissonance theory has inspired a tremendous amount of research, its phenomena have also been explained by an even simpler theory. Consider how we make inferences about other people's attitudes. We observe a person's behavior and the situation in which it occurs, and then we attribute the behavior either to the person's traits and attitudes or to environmental forces. If we see Mr. and Mrs. Jones coercing their little Sally into saying "I'm sorry," we attribute Sally's behavior to the constraints of the situation, not to her personal regret. If we see Sally apologizing with no apparent inducement, we are more likely to attribute the apology to Sally herself.

Self-perception theory: *The theory that when we are unsure of our attitudes we infer them much as would someone observing us—by looking at our behavior and the circumstances under which it occurs.*

Self-perception theory (proposed by Daryl Bem, 1972) assumes that we make similar inferences when we observe our own behavior. When our attitudes are weak or ambiguous, we are in the same position as someone observing us from the outside. Hearing myself talk informs me of my attitudes;

observing my actions provides clues to how strong my beliefs are, especially if my behavior is not easily attributable to external constraints. The acts we freely commit are sometimes quite self-revealing.

The philosopher-psychologist William James proposed a similar explanation for emotion a century ago. We infer our emotions, he suggested, by observing our bodies and our behaviors. A stimulus such as a growling bear confronts a woman in the forest. She tenses, her heartbeat increases, adrenalin is secreted, and she runs away. Observing all this, she then experiences fear. At a college where I was to lecture, I awoke before dawn and was unable to get back to sleep. Observing my wakefulness, I concluded that I must be anxious.

"I can watch myself and my actions, just like an outsider."

Anne Frank, The Diary of a Young Girl

You may be skeptical of this idea; I was when I first heard it. However, some experiments support it. Research on the effects of facial expressions even suggests a way for you to experience the self-perception effect (Izard, 1971; Kleinke & Walton, 1982; Rhodewalt & Comer, 1979). For example, when James Laird (1974) induced college students to frown while electrodes were attached to their faces—"contract these muscles," "pull your brows together"—they reported feeling angry. However, it's more fun to try out Laird's other finding: Those induced to smile felt happier and found cartoons more humorous. We have all experienced this self-perception phenomenon. We're feeling crabby, but then the phone rings or someone comes to the door and elicits from us warm, polite behavior. "How's everything?" "Just fine, thanks. How are things with you?" "Oh, not bad. . . ." If our irritableness is not intense, this warm behavior may change our whole attitude after we hang up. It's tough to smile and feel grouchy. When Miss America parades with her styrofoam smile she may, after all, be helping herself feel happy.

"The free expression of outward signs of emotion intensifies it. On the other hand, the repression as far as possible, of all outward signs softens our emotions."

Charles Darwin, The Expression of the Emotions in Man and Animals

Recent experiments at Dartmouth College by John Lanzetta and his colleagues (e.g., 1976) confirm that people tend to perceive the emotion that their faces are displaying. For example, in one experiment Katherine Burns Vaughan and Lanzetta (1981) had students observe a person receiving electric shock. Some of the observers were asked to make an expression of pain whenever the shock came on. Compared to students not given this instruction, these grimacing students perspired more and had a faster heart rate whenever they observed the person being shocked. Acting out the person's emotion apparently enabled the observers to feel more empathy.

Our nonverbal behaviors also influence our attitudes. In a clever experiment, Gary Wells and Richard Petty (1980) had University of Alberta students "test headphone sets" by making either vertical or horizontal head movements while listening to a radio editorial. Who most agreed with the editorial? Those who had been nodding their heads up and down. Why? Wells and Petty surmised that positive thoughts are compatible with vertical nodding and incompatible with horizontal motion.

Overjustification

Perhaps you can see how self-perception theory might explain the insufficient-justification effect. If we heard someone waxing eloquent about the dangers of open dorm visitation after being paid $10 to do so, surely we would be less likely to accept the authenticity of that person's views than if we thought the person was expressing those opinions for virtually no pay. Perhaps we make similar inferences when observing ourselves.

Self-perception theory goes even a step further. Contrary to the notion that rewards always increase motivation, it suggests that unnecessary rewards sometimes have a hidden cost. Rewarding people for doing what they already enjoy may lead them to attribute their doing it to the reward, thus undermining their self-perception that they do it because they like it. Experiments by Edward Deci at the University of Rochester (e.g., Deci & Ryan, 1980) and Mark Lepper and David Greene (1979) at Stanford have confirmed this *overjustification effect*. People who are paid for playing with enjoyable puzzles subsequently play with the puzzles less than people who play without being paid; promising children a reward for doing what they intrinsically enjoy (for example, playing with magic markers) turns their play into work. As self-perception theory predicts, this is especially true when the child has no strong preexisting attitude toward the task (Fazio, 1981).

Overjustification effect: *The consequence of bribing people to do what they already like doing; they may be led to see their action as externally controlled rather than intrinsically appealing.*

As self-perception theory also implies, an *unanticipated* reward afterward does *not* diminish intrinsic interest, apparently because people can still attribute their action to their own motivation. (It's like the heroine who, having fallen in love with the woodcutter, now learns that he's really a prince.) And if compliments for a good job make us feel more competent and successful, this can *increase* our intrinsic motivation. But if an unnecessary reward is offered beforehand in an obvious effort to control behavior, the overjustification effect is likely. So what matters is what a reward implies: rewards and praise that *inform* people of their achievements (that make them feel "I'm very good at this") will likely *boost* their intrinsic motivations; rewards that seek to *control* people, that lead them to believe it was the reward that caused their effort ("I did it for the money"), will likely *diminish* the intrinsic appeal of an enjoyable task (Rosenfeld, Folger, & Adelman, 1980).

For example, Carl Benware and Deci (1975) found that being rewarded for supporting something we believe in can undermine our belief. University of Rochester students delivered a statement which tried to convince others that students should have some say about course offerings in their college—a position in which they all believed. Half were paid $7.50 to espouse this position, and half did so without pay. Those who were paid subsequently *decreased* their commitment to what they had proclaimed.

A folktale illustrates the overjustification effect. An old man lived alone on a street where boys played noisily every afternoon. The din annoyed him, so one day he called the boys to his door. He told them he loved the cheerful sound of children's voices and promised them each 50 cents if they would return the next day. Next afternoon the youngsters raced back and played more lustily than ever. The old man paid them and promised another reward the next day. Again they returned, whooping it up, and the man again paid them, this time 25 cents. The following day they got only 15 cents and the man explained that his meagre resources were being exhausted. "Please, though, would you come and play for 10 cents tomorrow?" The boys were disappointed and told the man they would not be back. It wasn't worth the effort, they said, to play all afternoon at his house for only 10 cents.

But unlike pleasant play, many important activities are not enjoyable to begin with. In some of these instances, the overjustification principle may still be useful. Timothy Wilson and Daniel Lassiter (1982) gave six-year-old children several toys to play with, but then forbade half of them from playing with an unappealing foam rubber motorcycle. Whether forbidden or not, the children preferred not to play with the motorcycle. One week later a different experimenter left each child alone with an attractive toy and the motorcycle, assuring each that "you can play with either." Those who had previously been forbidden to play with the unappealing motorcycle now played with it twice as long as those who had not been forbidden. Can you see how the overjustification principle explains this? Giving people strong extrinsic reasons for their *not* performing an unappealing activity ("because I'm not allowed to") may undermine their intrinsic reasons ("because I don't like it").

In other instances, temporarily forbidding an important activity may not sufficiently arouse intrinsic interest. Young Maria may find her first piano lessons frustrating. Tommy may not have an intrinsic love of fifth-grade science. Sandra may not look forward to making those first sales calls. In such cases, the parent, teacher, or manager should probably use some incentives to coax the desired behavior (Workman & Williams, 1980; Boggiano & Ruble, 1981). So, if we provide students with *just enough* justification to perform a learning task (and use such rewards to help them feel competent), we may help them maximize their enjoyment of it and their eagerness to pursue the subject on their own. When the justification is overly sufficient—as happens in classrooms where teachers dictate behavior and use rewards to control the children—child-driven learning may diminish (Deci, Nezlek, & Sheinman, 1981). My younger son eagerly consumed six or eight library books a week—until our library started a reading club which promised a party to those who read ten books in three months. Three weeks later he began checking out only one or two books during our weekly visit. Why? "Because you only need to read ten books, you know."

Self-Justification Versus Self-Perception

We have seen two plausible explanations of why our actions affect our attitudes: (1) the dissonance-theory assumption that we are motivated to justify our behavior in order to reduce our internal discomfort, and (2) the self-perception-theory assumption that we calmly observe our behavior and make reasonable inferences from it, just as we do when observing other people. But which explanation is right? It's difficult to find a critical test which decides between them. In most instances they make the same predictions, and each theory can be bent to accommodate most of the findings we have considered (Greenwald, 1975). Daryl Bem (1972), the self-perception theorist, has even suggested it boils down to a matter of loyalties and aesthetics. This illustrates the subjectivity of scientific theorizing (as discussed in Chapter 1). Neither dissonance theory nor self-perception theory has been handed to us by nature.

Both are products of human imagination—creative attempts to simplify and explain what we've observed.

It is not unusual in science to find that a principle (such as "attitudes follow behavior") is predictable from more than one theory. Physicist Richard Feynman (1967) marvels that "one of the amazing characteristics of nature" is the "wide range of beautiful ways" in which it can be described; "I do not understand the reason why it is that the correct laws of physics seem to be expressible in such a tremendous variety of ways" (pp. 53–55). Like different roads leading to the same place, different sets of assumptions can lead to the same principle. If anything, this *strengthens* our confidence in the principle. It becomes credible not only because of the data which support it, but also because it rests on more than one theoretical pillar.

Can we say one of our theories is more adequate than the other? On one key point strong support has emerged for dissonance theory. Recall that dissonance is, by definition, an aroused state of uncomfortable tension. To reduce this tension we supposedly change our attitudes. Self-perception theory says nothing about tension being aroused when our actions and attitudes are not harmonious. It assumes merely that when our attitudes are weak to begin with, we will use our behavior and its circumstances as a clue to our attitudes (like the person who said, "How do I know how I feel until I hear what I say?").

Are conditions that supposedly produce dissonance (for example, making decisions or acting contrary to one's attitudes) actually arousing? Studies—ranging from measures of people's heart rates while they supposedly experience dissonance to analyses of whether they react as people generally do when aroused—indicate that the answer is indeed yes (Kiesler & Pallak, 1976). In one clever study by A. Gonzalez and Joel Cooper (1975), members of Princeton eating clubs agreed to write essays advocating abolition of the clubs. Afterwards, the experimenter inquired whether the new "lighting in the room . . . made them feel tense or uneasy." Sure enough, when the subjects filled out rating scales, those led to feel responsible for their essays indicated that the lights had made them somewhat tense. Actually, the lights were not new. The students, who apparently felt some discomfort over what they had done, had readily accepted a plausible explanation for their tension. (This result hints at a conclusion discussed in Chapter 4: People often have difficulty identifying the causes of their own feelings and actions.)

So dissonance conditions do indeed arouse tension. But is this arousal necessary for the "attitudes-follow-behavior" effect? There are indications that the answer is again yes. For example, in experiments with University of Washington students, Claude Steele, Lillian Southwick, and Barbara Critchlow (1981) found that when arousal was reduced by drinking alcohol the attitudes-follow-behavior effect disappeared. Students who had been induced to write an essay favoring a big tuition increase reduced their dissonance by adjusting their attitudes—*unless* after writing the unpleasant essay they imbibed alcohol, supposedly as part of a beer- or vodka-tasting experiment. Apparently, alcohol and other drugs can be a substitute way to reduce dissonance.

"Some forms of alcohol abuse may evolve through the reinforcement of drinking as a means of reducing dissonance."

Claude Steele, Lillian Southwick, & Barbara Critchlow (1981)

Thus dissonance procedures are arousing, and arousal is an ingredient of the self-persuasive effects of acting contrary to one's attitudes. But dissonance theory cannot explain all the findings. When people argue a position that is in line with their opinion, although a step or two beyond it, procedures that usually eliminate any arousal don't seem to reduce the change in one's attitudes (Fazio, Zanna, & Cooper, 1977, 1979). Dissonance theory also does not explain the overjustification effect, since being paid to do what you like to do generally should not arouse great tension. And what about situations where the induced action really does not contradict any attitude—when, for example, people are induced to smile or grimace. Here, too, one struggles to explain why dissonance (tension) would be produced. In these cases, self-perception theory has a ready explanation.

In short, it appears that dissonance theory successfully explains what happens when we act contrary to our clearly defined attitudes (for example, regarding the draft, the presidential election, or some hot campus issue): We feel tension, so we adjust our attitudes to reduce it. In more mundane situations or in situations where our attitudes aren't well formed, self-perception theory seems superior (Chaiken & Baldwin, 1981). I am reminded of wave and particle theories of light, which coexist as complementary theories, each explaining certain phenomena that the other cannot explain. Likewise, social psychologists have found convincing evidence for both self-justification and self-perception. As often happens in science, the competing theories are both partial images of a reality that is too complex for any one theory to explain. Until someone creates a new theory which better explains these phenomena, we will remain grateful for both.

A Philosophical and Educational Footnote: How Do We Know?

Less than a century ago, psychology and epistemology (the study of the nature of knowledge) were closely related branches of philosophy. After nearly a century of going its own way, can psychology, philosophy's prodigal child, bring something home to its mother discipline? Does all this theory and research concerning the effects of our actions on our thinking say something about how we come to know things?

"There is no such thing as genuine knowledge and fruitful understanding, except as the offspring of doing."

John Dewey, School and Society

As we have seen, saying and doing are sometimes believing; what we say and do affects what we know. Other evidence confirms the point: we learn by doing. Teachers, even young children acting as tutors, learn and remember well what they teach (V. L. Allen, 1976; Staub, 1975). As developmental psychologists Jerome Bruner (1975) and Jean Piaget both stressed, children's active play, which is the work of childhood, contributes to their intellectual development.

To say that we learn by doing as well as by rational contemplation is not to say that the self-persuasive effects of action are irrational. That which prompts us to act may also prompt us to think. Writing an essay, or role-playing an opposing view, forces us to recall and think up arguments we otherwise might have ignored. Action stimulates thought. For example, research indicates that we remember information best when we have actively explained it in our own terms. Gordon Bower and Mark Masling (1979) gave Stanford students a list of bizarre correlations, such as "As the number of fire hydrants in an area decreases the crime rate increases." Students who simply studied or were given explanations for these correlations recalled only about 40 percent of them when tested later. But students who invented their own explanations recalled 73 percent of the correlations. (Take a moment to conjecture an explanation for the fire hydrant–crime correlation, and in a later chapter I will test your recall of the relationship.)

The memorability of self-produced information may be one reason why information we have reformulated in our own terms affects us more (Greenwald, 1968; Petty, Ostrum, & Brock, 1981). As one student recently wrote me, "It wasn't until I tried to verbalize my beliefs that I really understood them." As a teacher and a writer, I must therefore remind myself not always to lay out finished results. It is better to stimulate students first to think through the implications of theory X, thus making them active listeners and readers. Even taking notes deepens the impression through active expression. William James (1899/1922) made the same point eighty years ago: "No reception without *reaction*, no impression without correlative expression—this is the great maxim which the teacher ought never to forget."

SUMMING UP

What is the relationship between our inner attitudes and our external actions? Social psychologists agree that attitudes and actions have a reciprocal relationship, each feeding the other. Popular wisdom stresses the impact of attitudes on action. Surprisingly, our attitudes—usually assessed as our feelings toward some object or person—are often quite poor predictors of our actions. Moreover, changing people's attitudes typically fails to produce much change in their behavior. These findings sent social psychologists scurrying to find out why we so often fail to play the game we talk. The answer now seems clear: our attitude expressions and our behaviors are each subject to many influences. Our attitudes *will* predict our behavior (1) if these "other influences" are minimized, (2) if the attitude corresponds very closely to the predicted behavior (as in voting studies), and (3) if we are conscious of our attitudes (either because something reminds us of them or because we acquired them in a manner that makes them strong). Thus there *is* a connection between what we think and feel and what we do, even if that connection in many situations is looser than we'd like to believe.

One important lesson recent social psychology teaches is that the attitude-action relation works also in the reverse direction: we are likely not only to think ourselves into action, but also to act ourselves into a way of thinking. When we act, we amplify the idea lying behind what we have done, especially when we feel responsible for it. Many streams of evidence converge to establish this principle. The actions prescribed by social roles mold the attitudes of the role players. Research on the foot-in-the-door phenomenon indicates that committing a small act (for example, agreeing to do a small favor) later makes people more willing to do a larger one. Actions also affect our moral attitudes: We tend to justify as right that which we have done. Similarly, our racial and political behaviors help shape our social consciousness: We seem not only to stand up for what we believe, but also to believe in what we have stood up for. Many new psychotherapy methods capitalize upon the self-persuasive effects of behavior by encouraging their clients to act in new ways in order to generate new emotions.

Two competing theories explain *why* our actions affect our attitudes. *Dissonance theory* assumes that we are motivated to justify our behavior in order to reduce the tension we feel when acting contrary to our attitudes or after making a difficult decision. It further proposes that the less external justification we have for an act, the more dissonance we'll feel, and thus the more our attitudes will change. *Self-perception theory* assumes that when our attitudes are weak we simply observe our behavior and its circumstances and infer what our attitudes must be. One interesting implication of self-perception theory is the "overjustification effect": Rewarding people to do what they like doing anyway can turn their pleasure into drudgery (if the reward leads them to attribute their behavior to the reward). Evidence exists to support both dissonance and self-perception theories, suggesting wisdom in each. Often, the two theories predict similar results. For example, both theories suggest that our actions help shape our knowledge of ourselves and of the world.

Chapter

Explaining Behavior

3

The eldest of nine children, Joan Little had grown up along the dirt streets of Washington, North Carolina's shantytown. By age eighteen she was reportedly living a "fast life." In the summer of 1974 the young black woman began a seven- to ten-year sentence for breaking and entering. In the Beaufort County jail her every movement—even her taking a shower—could be monitored on the jail video system.

According to his wife, Clarence Alligood, the sixty-two-year-old night jailer, "didn't like coloreds that much." But during Joan Little's eighty-one days at the jail he did her a number of favors. Late at night he brought her sandwiches, and he let her use his office phone at odd hours.

At 4 A.M. on the 82d day, a town police officer found Joan Little gone and Alligood lying face down on her cell bunk, dead. Naked from the waist down, he held in one hand his ice pick, with which he had been stabbed eleven times. Under his body was a woman's kerchief. The county medical examiner identified sperm on his leg.

When Joan Little surrendered, one week later, she was charged with first-degree murder—for which North Carolina's mandatory penalty was death in the electric chair. Soon, advocates of civil rights, women's rights, and prisoners' rights flocked to her defense.

Joan Little admitted killing Alligood. The issue was the cause for the killing. Should it be attributed to an evil disposition in Joan Little? Was she, as the prosecution contended, basically a bad person? Did she with a premeditated plan of murder and escape entice Alligood into her cell? Or should the killing be attributed to the situation she faced? Did she (as the jury ultimately decided) kill in self-defense, resisting rape?

Earlier that same year, Patricia Hearst was kidnapped by some young revolutionaries who called themselves the Symbionese Liberation Army. Two months later she renounced her former life, her wealthy parents, and her fiancé, and announced that she had joined her captors. "Try to understand the changes I've gone through," she asked. Much to everyone's surprise, Hearst (now "Tania") apparently meant business. Twelve days later her part in a bank robbery was videotaped and shown on national television. In her eventual trial, the issue was once again the cause for the crime. Should her part in the robbery be attributed to the conditions of her captivity and intimidation by her captors? Or (as the jury ultimately decided) were her actions internally motivated? Was she sufficiently unconstrained that she could have done otherwise?

As this case illustrates, a scientific analysis of causation is different from—but related to—moral and legal judgments of responsibility. Scientists seek explanations; jurors ponder whether one could have chosen to act differently (V. L. Hamilton, 1980). The research to be considered below pertains to how we explain people's behavior. As we shall see, our explanations profoundly influence our judgments of people. Depending on one's explanation, killing someone may be judged as murder, manslaughter, self-defense, or patriotism.

ATTRIBUTING CAUSALITY: TO THE PERSON OR THE SITUATION?

The Joan Little and Patricia Hearst cases are dramatic examples of a question we face daily. In trying to understand people, we are constantly wondering *why* they have acted as they have. When a salesperson says, "That outfit really looks nice on you," does this reflect a genuine feeling, or is it a ploy the salesperson is trained to use in such situations? If worker productivity declines, shall we presume it is because workers are getting lazier or because of changes in their work situation (for example, inefficiencies resulting from new regulations)? Does a young boy's lashing out at his school classmates mean he has a hostile personality or he is responding to stressful circumstances?

How Do We Explain Others' Behavior?

We spend an enormous amount of time analyzing and discussing why things happen as they do. Our conclusions about why people act as they do are profoundly important. They help determine our feelings and reactions to people and our decisions regarding them. For example, Antonia Abbey (1982) reports that a man is more likely than a woman to attribute the woman's friendliness to sexual interest, and thus to respond in ways that women deem inappropriate.

Attribution theory analyzes how we make judgments about people. There are several distinct varieties of attribution theory. But they do share some common assumptions: that we seek to make sense of our world, that we often attribute people's actions either to internal or external causes, that we do so in fairly logical ways. Let us consider these assumptions.

Attribution theory: *The theory of how people explain others' behavior—for example, by attributing it either to internal* dispositions *(enduring traits, motives, and attitudes) or to external* circumstances.

Fritz Heider (1980), widely regarded as the originator of attribution theory, analyzed the "common-sense psychology" by which people explain everyday events. He concluded that people tend to attribute someone's behavior either to *internal* causes (for example, the person's disposition) or *external* causes (for example, something about the person's situation). Thus, a teacher may wonder whether Johnny's underachievement is due to lack of motivation and ability (a "dispositional attribution") or to his physical and social circumstances, such as poor nutrition and family difficulties (a "situational attribution"). This distinction between internal (dispositional) and external (situational) causes can become blurred (Ross, 1977; F. D. Miller, Smith, & Uleman, 1981). To say a schoolchild "is fearful" may differ only in semantics from saying, "School frightens the child." Moreover, situational influences operate through the person. In George Bernard Shaw's *Pygmalion*, Professor Higgins transforms his student, Eliza Doolittle, from a coarse flower girl into a woman of genteel speech. After she successfully survives a society ball with her origins undetected, the question arises: Who did it? Is her triumph explained only by the professor's external influence or also by her internal efforts? Clearly, both deserve credit. So we shouldn't think that external and internal influences are separate factors that sum to 100 percent. Nevertheless, we shall see in this and later chapters that social psychologists have found the internal-external distinction to be useful.

In Chapter 2 we considered the self-perception theory of how we make internal or external attributions about ourselves. For example, if we observe ourselves doing a pleasurable activity for pay, we may begin to attribute our doing the activity to the external reward (the overjustification effect). Attribution researchers study how we explain others' behavior, as well as our own. They seek to predict when we will attribute others' behavior to their dispositions and when to the external situation. Using common sense, how do we make attributions?

Edward Jones and Keith Davis (1965) noted that under certain conditions, people have a strong tendency to *infer* that people's intentions and dispositions *correspond* to their actions. If I observe Rick making a hurtful, sarcastic comment to Linda, I may infer that Rick is a hostile person. Jones and Davis's "theory of correspondent inferences" specifies the conditions under which such inferences are likely. For example, behavior that is normal or expected tells us less about the person than behavior that is unusual for a situation. If Rick is sarcastic in a job interview, where one would normally be pleasant, this tells us more about Rick than were he to make the same sarcastic remark just after his new car was dented.

As this analysis suggests, people often make quite rational attributions. In further testimony to the reasonable ways in which we explain someone's behavior, attribution theorist Harold Kelley (1973) of UCLA has noted how people use information about "consistency," "distinctiveness," and "consensus." For example, when explaining someone's behavior (why Bob just tripped over the feet of his dancing partner, Lisa), most people appropriately use information concerning *consistency* (Does Bob often trip over Lisa's feet?), *distinctiveness* (Does Bob trip over the feet of his other dance partners?), and *consensus* (Do others trip over Lisa's feet?) (McArthur, 1972). If we learn that Bob and Bob alone usually stumbles over Lisa's feet—and, in fact, over the feet of all his dance partners—we will likely attribute the incident to Bob, as logically we should. So our commonsense psychology often explains behavior much as would a professional scientist. (Kelley does, however, find that in everyday explanation people often discount a contributing cause of someone's behavior if other plausible causes are already known. If I can specify one or two reasons why a student did poorly on an exam, I may ignore or discount other possible reasons.)

Further evidence of the reasonable manner in which we form judgments of one another comes from research by Norman Anderson (1968; 1974) on "information integration." Anderson and his collaborators have discerned some logical rules by which we combine different pieces of information about a person into an overall impression. For example, suppose that you have an upcoming blind date with someone who is said to be intelligent, daring, lazy, and sincere. Research on how people combine such information suggests that you would likely weigh each item of information according to its importance. If sincerity is especially important to you, you will give it more weight. If you are like the participants in experiments by Solomon Asch (1946), David Hamilton and Mark Zanna (1972), and Bert Hodges (1974), you may also give extra weight to information that comes first, and you may be more sensitive to negative than positive information. First impressions can color your interpretation of later information. Having first learned that someone is "intelligent," you may then interpret the person's being "daring" as meaning courageous rather than reckless. Negative information, such as "she is dishonest," also has extra potency, perhaps because it is more unusual. Once you have interpreted and weighed each piece of information, you then use your mental algebra to integrate information. The result is your overall impression of your date.

So far, so good. We form impressions of others and explain their behavior in some ways that are eminently rational. More fascinating, though, are the predictable errors that distort our commonsense judgments. This chapter and the two that follow present new research on the foibles and fallacies of our social thinking. Reading these chapters may make it seem, as one student put it, that "social psychologists get their kicks out of playing tricks on people." However, the experiments are not an intellectual magic show designed to demonstrate "what fools these mortals be" (although some of the experiments are indeed amusing). Their purpose rather is to reveal *how* we think about ourselves and others. For the same reason other psychologists study visual illusions—not just as mind-teasing demonstrations, but for what they reveal about how our visual system processes information. Since it may be shocking to discover that one of the ironic facts of human nature is our capacity for illusion and self-deception, we should also remember that our modes of thought are generally adaptive. Our erroneous thinking is often simply a by-product of our mind's strategies for simplifying the complex information it receives. This parallels our perceptual mechanisms, which generally give us a useful image of the world, but will sometimes produce visual illusions.

A second reason for focusing upon the biases that penetrate our thinking is that we are generally unaware of them. My hunch is that you will find more surprises, more challenges, and more personal benefit in an analysis of our errors and biases than you would in a string of testimonies to what you are already aware of: our capacity for logical thought and intellectual achievement. It is not out of wicked pleasure that social psychologists study human deficiencies as well as topics like love and altruism. Rather, it is because these are the lessons we are most prone to overlook—which is also why classic epics of world literature so often portray pride and other human failings. Perhaps our becoming aware of and sensitive to the most common fallacies of our social thinking can help us improve it, making it more accurate, more in touch with reality.

The Fundamental Attribution Error

As later chapters will reveal, social psychology's most important lesson concerns how much we are affected by our social environments. At any given time, what we say and do depends substantially on the situation, as well as on what we bring to the situation. In experiments, a slight difference between two situations sometimes produces great differences in the way people respond. I see this when I teach classes at both 8:30 A.M and 7:00 P.M. Silent stares greet me at 8:30; at 7:00 o'clock it almost takes a bullhorn to break up the party. In each situation, some individuals are more talkative than others, but the difference between the two situations exceeds the individual differences.

Attribution researchers have found that people fail to appreciate this important lesson of social psychology. When explaining someone's behavior, they often underestimate the impact of the situation and overestimate the extent to which it reflects the person's characteristic traits and attitudes. Thus, even knowing the effect of the time of day on classroom conversation, I may assume that the people in the 7:00 P.M. class are more extroverted than the "silent types" who enroll at 8:30 A.M.

Fundamental attribution error: *The tendency for observers to underestimate situational influences and overestimate dispositional influences upon others' behavior.*

This discounting of situational effects, dubbed the *fundamental attribution error* by Lee Ross (1977), has been evident in many experiments. In the first such study, Edward Jones and Victor Harris (1967) had Duke University students read debaters' speeches supporting or attacking Fidel Castro. When the position taken was said to have been chosen by the debater, the students

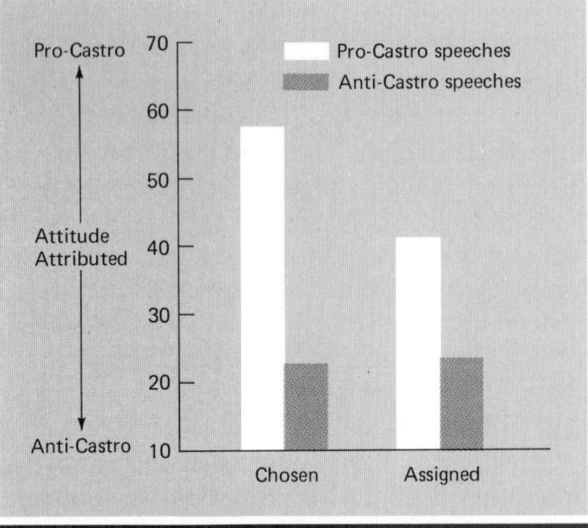

FIGURE 3-1 The fundamental attribution error. When people read a debate speech supporting or attacking Fidel Castro, they attributed corresponding attitudes to the speech writer, even when its position was assigned by the debate coach. (Data from Jones & Harris, 1967.)

logically enough assumed it reflected the debater's attitude. But what happened when the students were told that the position had been assigned by the debate coach? Remarkably, even knowing that the debater was assigned a pro-Castro position did not prevent their inferring that the debater had some pro-Castro attitudes (see Figure 3-1; also, A. G. Miller, Jones, & Hinkle, 1981). More recent research conducted by Jones with Janet Morgan Riggs and George Quattrone (1979) reveals that when people first read an essay and *then* learn whether its position was chosen or assigned, the choice versus no-choice information is virtually ignored; people assume an assigned essay reflects its writer's attitude as much as does a freely chosen essay.

Does the fundamental attribution error also occur in everyday life? If we know the checkout cashier is programmed to say, "Thank you and have a nice day," will we nevertheless automatically conclude that the cashier is a friendly, grateful person? David Napolitan and George Goethals (1979) explored this question by having Williams College students talk with a supposed clinical psychology graduate student who acted either warm and friendly or aloof and critical. Half the students were told beforehand that her behavior would be spontaneous. The other half were told that for purposes of the experiment she had been instructed to feign friendly (or unfriendly) behavior. The effect of this information? The students totally disregarded it. If she was friendly, they inferred she was really a friendly person, and if she was unfriendly, they assumed she was an unfriendly person, regardless of why she acted as she did. As when viewing a dummy on the ventriloquist's lap, or a movie actor playing a scripted "good-guy" or "bad-guy" role, it is difficult to escape the illusion that the programmed behavior reflects an inner disposition. Perhaps this is why Leonard Nimoy, who played Spock on *Star Trek*, entitled his book, *I Am Not Spock*.

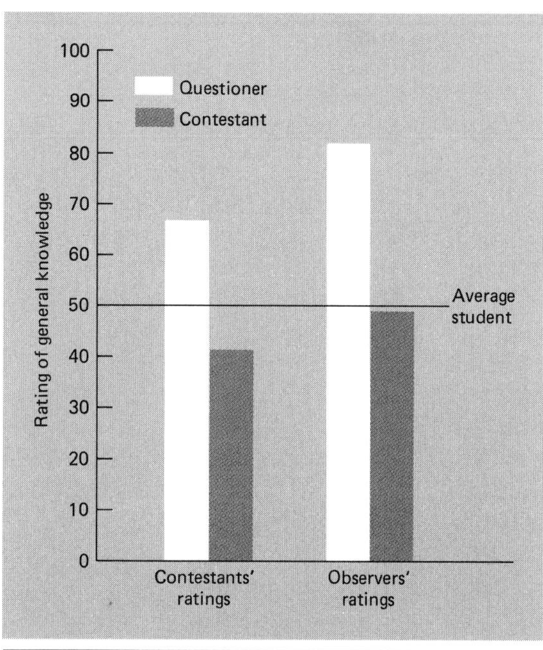

FIGURE 3-2 Both contestants and observers of a simulated quiz game assumed that a person who had been randomly assigned the role of questioner was actually far more knowledgeable than the contestant. This failure to appreciate the extent to which the assigned roles of questioner and contestant simply made the questioner *seem* more knowledgeable illustrates the fundamental attribution error. (Data from Ross, Amabile, & Steinmetz, 1977.)

The discounting of social constraints is also evident in a fascinating experiment by Lee Ross, Teresa Amabile, and Julia Steinmetz (1977). They randomly assigned some Stanford University students to play the role of questioner and others to play the role of contestant in a simulated quiz game. They invited the questioners to make up difficult questions that would demonstrate their general wealth of knowledge. It's fun to imagine such questions: "Where is Bainbridge Island?" "What is the seventh book in the Old Testament?" "Who is the current editor of *Psychology Today*?" If even these few questions have you feeling a little uninformed, then you will appreciate the results of this experiment. Despite being fully aware that the roles randomly assigned to questioner and contestant guaranteed that the questioner would have the advantage, both the contestants and observers of the experiment succumbed to the erroneous impression that the questioners *really were* more knowledgeable than the contestants. (See Figure 3-2.)

In real life, those with social power usually initiate and control conversation, often leading underlings to overestimate their superiors' knowledge and intelligence. Medical doctors, for example, are often presumed to be experts on all sorts of questions unrelated to medicine. Similarly, it has been my experience that students often overestimate the brilliance of their teachers. (Teachers are, as in the experiment, questioners on subjects of their special expertise.) When some of these students later become teachers, they are usually amazed to discover that teachers are not so brilliant after all.

BEHIND THE SCENES

Lee Ross

The story of the "questioner-contestant" study really began during my transition from graduate student to assistant professor. I had noticed that shy people often felt themselves to be less bright, interesting, or well-informed than their more outgoing companions who so willingly "held forth" about their favorite topics. I suspected strongly that these feelings of relative inferiority were often unwarranted, and were at least partially a *result* of their social reticence. Nevertheless, it took some firsthand experience for these impressions to become shaped into a specific research idea.

This firsthand experience was provided by a pair of Ph.D. oral examinations: my own thesis defense, and the Ph.D. oral examination of my first advisee about seven months later. My orals began with one distinguished professor asking me the wavelength, in angstroms, of red light—a rather shocking question for me to face, given that my dissertation dealt with the external control of overeating in obese versus normal subjects. The experience did not improve much as each professor confronted me with questions that revealed potential oversights in my research design and conceptual analysis, and gaps in my overall knowledge about social psychology. I came away from the experience feeling quite shaken and rather in awe of my examiners, whose questions seemed to reveal the type of insight, confidence, and familiarity with the field that I feared I would be unable to match in performing my own new academic duties. The inevitable lurking fear of the first-year professor, "Now, *at last,* they are going to find me out," had never been more intense.

Fortunately, my next experience of participating in a Ph.D. oral examination, a few months later—this time as one of the *examiners*—proved to be highly therapeutic. Given the opportunity to *ask* penetrating questions instead of answer them, and to focus on whichever aspects of the candidate's dissertation or other relevant research that *I chose*, I found my own contribution quite indistinguishable from that of my fellow professors on the examining committee. Indeed, the hapless candidate seemed to agree—for, as he later confided to me, he left his Ph.D. oral examination feeling much as I had felt six months before, dissatisfied with his performance and unduly impressed with the incisiveness and command of his examiners (including the most junior of them!). Fortunately, I was under no illusion that I had become any wiser in the period between these two examinations. Instead, I recognized that the impressions of relative wisdom that both of us had formed in the role of candidate had failed to "discount" sufficiently for the tremendous self-presentational advantage enjoyed by the questioner.

The phenomenon just begged to be "bottled" in the form of an experiment manipulating "questioner versus candidate" roles. But at the time I could not think of any satisfactory theoretical rationale for undertaking such an experiment, and I gradually forgot about the idea. Five years later, however, my research interests had shifted from obesity to problems of attribution theory and intuitive psychology. I was preparing a series of lectures on biases in the attribution process, and was thinking in particular about a "fundamental" attribution error identified by Fritz Heider long before. This error involves our tendency to make inappropriate inferences about actors because we fail to make adequate allowance for the impact of situational forces and constraints on their performances. Suddenly, I recalled my "questioner versus candidate" experience and recognized its relevance as a special case of this more fundamental error.

During my lecture the next day I instructed a couple of randomly chosen student volunteers to ask the class as a whole some difficult general-knowledge questions to which they personally knew the answers. They did so, and the class en masse laughed and/or groaned at the difficult, esoteric nature of the questions. More important, however, the class was virtually unanimous in concluding that my two randomly selected students were trivia hotshots (indeed, that they had probably been selected *because* they were hotshots). The strength of the phenomena convinced me to do the formal experiment (with Teresa Amabile and Julia Steinmetz) in which we compared randomly assigned questioner, contestant, and observer roles, and added some necessary control groups. (*Lee Ross, Stanford University*)

We are most likely to commit the fundamental attribution error when explaining *other people's* behavior. For example, experimenters have had someone perform an act while someone else observes. Typically, the actor will explain his or her own behavior in terms of the situation, while the observer holds the actor responsible. Put differently, people tend to attribute others' actions to their personal dispositions ("John was hostile because he is an angry person") even when they would attribute a similar act on their own part to environmental factors ("I was angry because everything was going wrong").

We have all experienced the attribution error in moments of conflict with someone close to us. At such times we generally see our own feelings as a just response to the situation but attribute the other's feelings to a nasty disposition. Of course, the other person's perception is just the reverse. As this example suggests, attribution theory can be applied to many situations in everyday life (Frieze, Bar-Tal, & Carroll, 1979; Harvey & Weary, 1981). Later chapters will indicate some of these applications. For right now, let us consider three illustrations.

One is the "Peter Principle": that people who do well on a job are promoted until they reach a position in which they are incompetent (Peter & Hull, 1969). When this happens, the managers who made the promotions likely made an attribution error. They attributed the employee's previous success to personal traits that are expected to produce the same success in the next situation. Actually, the previous success may have reflected a happy fit between the person and that particular situation.

Second, consider the differing perceptions of Watergate-related activities by persons inside and outside President Nixon's administration. The principal actors in the Watergate drama portrayed their own acts as morally justifiable. But most outside observers thought the same acts reprehensible. Were the President and his aides coldly calculating when they claimed good motives? Or did the actors and observers of the Watergate episode sincerely differ in their attributing causes? To find out, Stephen West, Steven Gunn, and Paul Chernicky (1975) induced people to commit a crime similar to the Watergate burglary. Florida State University students were approached by a private investigator and asked to assist in burglarizing a local advertising firm on behalf of the Internal Revenue Service. After the investigator gave an elaborate justification for this activity and guaranteed immunity from prosecution (strong situational pressure!), approximately one-half agreed to participate. At this point, the experiment was explained and the students were asked why they had decided as they did. Others were first told about the experiment in great detail, and were then asked to explain the behavior of those who had agreed to participate. Can you guess the result? While the "actors" tended to attribute their participation to environmental factors ("The plan was foolproof"), the observers were more likely to attribute the actors' decisions to personal dispositions ("He likes taking risks"). The experiment demonstrated that an actor's interpretations can differ greatly from those of an outside observer, even when both have identical information. (*Note:* After this experiment, participants were carefully debriefed and no one appeared to be upset.)

Attributions of responsibility are at the heart of many judicial decisions (Fincham & Jaspers, 1980). Joan Little's jury attributed her behavior to the situation, and found her not guilty. Patricia Hearst's jury attributed her behavior to herself, and found her guilty. In 1980, when the FBI enticed eight members of the U.S. Congress into taking bribe money from a supposed Arab sheik, a controversy immediately erupted: Were the representatives corrupt politicians who were caught green-handed? Or had they been entrapped by a unique situation into committing a crime they otherwise never would have? Such cases exemplify many judicial controversies: The prosecution argues, "You are to blame, for you could have done otherwise"; the defendant replies, "It wasn't my fault; I was a victim of the situation."

Why the Attribution Error?

The evidence sampled above points to a fundamental error in the way we explain other people's behavior: We attribute it so much to their inner dispositions that we often ignore powerful situational determinants. Why is there this tendency to underestimate situational determinants of others' behavior, but not our own?

Attribution theorists point out, first, that we have a different perspective when observing than when acting (Jones & Nisbett, 1971; Jones, 1976). When we watch another person act, that *person* occupies the center of our attention and so seems to cause whatever happens. When we act, the environment commands our attention. If this is true, what might we expect if the perspectives were reversed—if somehow we could see ourselves as others see us and if we saw the world through their eyes? Should this not eliminate or even reverse the typical attribution error?

Using this reasoning, see if you can predict the result of a clever experiment conducted by Michael Storms (1973) with Yale University students. If you were a subject in Storms' experiment you might have found yourself seated facing another student with whom you were to talk for a few minutes. Beside you is a TV camera that shares your view of the other student. Facing you from alongside the other student are an observer and another TV camera. Afterward, both you and the observer who faced you judge whether your behavior was caused more by your personal characteristics or by the situation you were reacting to.

Question: Which of you will attribute the least importance to the situation? Storms found it was the observer (another demonstration of the fundamental attribution error). Now what if we reverse your and the observer's points of view by having you each watch the videotape recorded from the other's perspective? (You now view yourself while the observer views what you saw.) This reverses the attributions: You now tend to see your behavior as emanating more from your person, while the observer now attributes it mostly to the situation you faced. So it seems that one reason we normally underestimate the impact of others' situations is that our attention is on *them*, more than on their situation.

This experiment brings to mind the response of Patricia Hearst's jury. They were shown the videotape of her brandishing the gun during the bank robbery. This surely directed the jury members' attention to the person of

Patricia Hearst during bank robbery. Did the videotape focus the jury's attention upon her person and away from her situation? (United Press International)

Patricia Hearst and away from any pressures in the situation. Perhaps after observing her own behavior even Patricia Hearst herself felt more personally responsible. Arthur Miller and his associates (1977) analyzed how people attributed blame in the Hearst case and noted, "One can only speculate how the trial would have been affected by a similar filmed record of her kidnapping."

Seeing ourselves on television is just one means of redirecting our attention to ourselves. Seeing ourselves in a mirror, hearing our tape-recorded voices, having our pictures taken, filling out a biographical questionnaire—such experiences similarly focus our attention inward, making us *self*-conscious instead of *situation*-conscious.

Robert Wicklund, Shelley Duval, and their collaborators have explored the consequences of so focusing upon oneself (Duval & Wicklund, 1972; Wicklund, 1979). Recall from the last chapter that inner attitudes often lie dormant unless attention is drawn to them; people who are made self-conscious by looking in a mirror act more in line with their attitudes (for example, they are less likely to cheat). When people's attention is focused upon themselves they also attribute more responsibility to themselves. Allan Fenigstein and Charles Carver (1978) demonstrated this by having their students at Kenyon College and the University of Miami (Florida) imagine themselves in some hypothetical situations. Those made self-conscious, by thinking they were hearing their heartbeats while pondering the situation, saw themselves as more responsible for the outcome than did those who thought they were just hearing extraneous noises. These investigators, along with Michael Scheier, have also found that some people are consistently more self-conscious than others. In experiments, people who report themselves as privately self-conscious (for example, who agree with statements such as "I'm generally attentive to my inner feelings") behave similarly to people whose attention has been self-focused with a mirror (Carver & Scheier, 1978). In short, people whose attention is focused on themselves—either briefly during an experiment or because they are self-conscious persons—view themselves more as observers typically do; they attribute their behavior more to internal factors and less to the situation.

Other evidence confirms that we usually attribute causation to whatever our attention is focused upon. Shelley Taylor and Susan Fiske (1978) have found that when someone in a group is made salient (conspicuous), we tend to see that person as causing whatever happens. If we are positioned to look at Joe, an average member of a group, Joe will seem to have a greater than average influence upon the group. Similarly, the only black person in a white group, or the only female in a male group, is viewed as a stronger personality than when that same person is less salient.

So far, we have seen one good reason for the fundamental attribution error: Causality is found where we are looking, or where our attention is drawn. Several other explanations have also been suggested (Ickes, 1980). For example, perhaps our whole western world view inclines us to assume that people, not situations, are the source of what happens. Jerald Jellison and Jane Green (1981) report that, among University of Southern California students, internal explanations are more socially approved. "You can do it," we are assured by the pop psychology of our positive-thinking culture. The

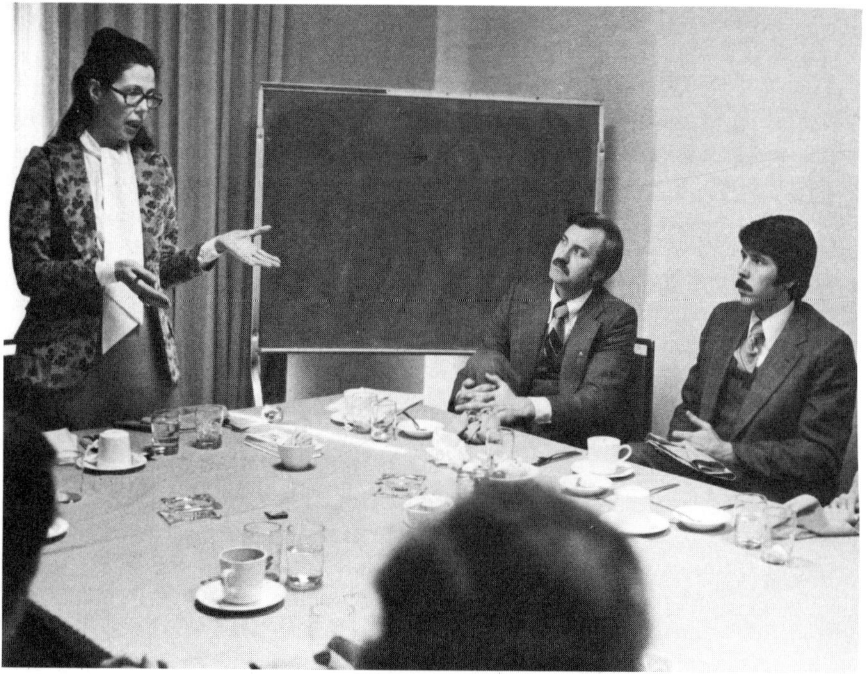

A salient person in a group is often perceived as disproportionately causing whatever happens in the group. (Mimi Forsyth/ Monkmeyer)

popular assumption is that, with the right disposition and attitude, anyone can surmount almost any problem; that you get what you deserve and deserve what you get. Thus bad behavior is often explained by labeling the person who does it as "sick," "lazy," or "sadistic." It is therefore not surprising that as children grow up in western culture they increasingly explain people's behavior in terms of their personal characteristics (Ross et al., 1978; Ross, 1981; Ruble et al., 1979). As a first grader, one of my sons brought home an example of how this occurs. When he unscrambled the words "gate the sleeve caught Tom on his" into "The gate caught Tom on his sleeve," his teacher, applying the western cultural assumptions of the curriculum materials, marked this wrong. The "right" answer located cause within Tom, not the gate: "Tom caught his sleeve on the gate." Some languages enable more external attributions. Instead of "I was late," Spanish idiom allows one to say "The clock caused me to be late."

"The fundamental attribution error is a replicated, [strong] tendency."

Edward E. Jones (1979)

"The fundamental attribution error has been accorded stature in much contemporary work on social perception without having been adequately or critically analyzed."

John Harvey, Jerri Town, & Kerry Yarkin (1981)

Like most provocative ideas, the presumption that we're all prone to a fundamental attribution error has its critics. Granted, say some, there may be an attribution *bias*, but in any given instance this may or may not produce an "error," just as parents who are biased to believe their child is a virgin may or may not be in error (Harvey, Town, & Yarkin, 1981). Moreover, some everyday circumstances, such as in church or on a job interview, are like the experiments we have been considering: They involve clear constraints which actors can detect more easily than observers. Hence the attribution error. But other settings—in one's room, at a park—allow people to exhibit their own individuality. In settings such as these, people may see their own behavior as *less* constrained, and as more internally directed, than do observers (Monson & Snyder, 1977; Price & Bouffard, 1974; Quattrone, 1982). So it is probably an overstatement to suggest that in all settings observers underestimate situational influences (Ajzen, Dalto, & Blyth, 1979; Small & Peterson, 1981; Monson, Tanke, & Lund, 1980).

Future research will surely clarify how "fundamental" (pervasive) the attribution "error" is. For the moment, it seems safe to presume that the bias does occur in many circumstances. Remembering that our analysis of thinking errors has a constructive goal, how then might we benefit from being aware of the bias? Perhaps being sensitive to it can help us assess our reactions to people. Recently, I assisted with the interviewing of two candidates for a faculty position. The first candidate was interviewed by six of us at once, each of us having the opportunity to ask two or three questions. I came away thinking, "What a stiff, awkward person he is." The second candidate I met privately over coffee and we immediately discovered we had a close friend in common. As we talked, I became increasingly impressed by what a "warm, engaging, stimulating person she is." Only later did I remember the fundamental attribution error and reassess my confident analysis. I had attributed his stiffness and her warmth to their dispositions; in fact, I later realized, such behavior may have resulted partly from the formality versus informality of their interview situations.

PERCEIVING OURSELVES

We have considered how we explain others' behavior, paying special attention to the fundamental attribution error. When we explain our own behavior, a second powerful bias enters. Although we readily blame the situation for our difficulties and failures (as the fundamental attribution error would predict), we are more likely to take credit for our successes.

The Self-Serving Bias: "How Do I Love Me? Let Me Count the Ways"

It is widely believed that most of us suffer the "I'm not OK—you're OK" problem of low self-esteem. For example, counseling psychologist Carl Rogers (1958) concluded that most people he has known "despise themselves, regard themselves as worthless and unlovable." As comedian Groucho Marx put it, "I'd never join any club that would accept a person like me." The evidence, however, indicates that writer William Saroyan was closer to the truth: "Every man is a good man in a bad world—as he himself knows." Although social psychologists are debating the reason for this "*self-serving bias*," there is general agreement regarding its reality, its prevalence, and its potency.

Self-serving bias: *The tendency to perceive oneself favorably.*

Attributions for Positive and Negative Events

Time and again, experiments have found that people readily accept credit when told they have succeeded (attributing the success to their ability and effort), yet often attribute failure to such external factors as bad luck or the problem's inherent "impossibility" (Zuckerman, 1979). Similarly, in explaining their victories, athletes commonly credit themselves, but are more likely to attribute losses to something else: bad breaks, bad officiating, the other team's super effort (Lau & Russell, 1980; Peterson, 1980; Ross & Lumsden, in press; Scanlan & Passer, 1980). And how much responsibility do you suppose car drivers tend to accept for their accidents? On insurance forms, drivers have described their accidents in words such as these: "An invisible car came out of nowhere, struck my car and vanished." "As I reached an intersection, a hedge sprang up, obscuring my vision and I did not see the other car." "A pedestrian hit me and went under my car." (*Toronto News*, 1977) Situations that combine skill and chance (for example, games, exams, job applications) are especially prone to the phenomenon: Winners can easily attribute their successes to their skill, while losers can attribute their losses to chance. When I win at Scrabble, it's because of my verbal dexterity; when I lose, it's because "Who could get anywhere with a Q but no U?"

In experiments that require two people to cooperate in order to make money, most individuals blame their partner for failure (Myers & Bach, 1976). This follows a tradition established in the most ancient example of self-serving bias: Adam's excuse, "The woman whom thou gave to be with me, she gave me fruit of the tree, and I ate." When other people are blamed for their bad deeds while one's own are excused, open hostility is not far away. It happens in aggressive confrontations between police and citizens. It happens in parent-child relations. It happens in marriage. Each party sees its own "firmness" as reasonable, but attributes the other's actions to a cruel disposition. After a quarrel, husband John attributes the biting words of wife Mary to her nastiness, but sees his own anger as justified.

Michael Ross and Fiore Sicoly (1979; see also Thompson & Kelley, 1981) observed another marital version of the self-serving bias. They found that married people usually felt they took more responsibility for such activities as cleaning the house and caring for the children than their spouses were willing to give them credit for. Every night, my wife and I pitch our laundry at the foot of our bedroom clothes hamper. In the morning, one of us puts it in. Recently she suggested that I take more responsibility for this. Thinking that I already did so 75 percent of the time, I asked her how often she thought she picked up the clothes. "Oh," she replied, "about 75 percent of the time."

Students exhibit this self-serving bias. In a half dozen recent studies, researchers Walter Stephan, Robert Arkin, Mark Davis, William Bernstein, and others have consistently found that after receiving an examination grade, those who do well tend to accept personal credit by judging the exam a valid measure of their competence (for example, Arkin & Maruyama, 1979; Davis & Stephan, 1980; Gilmor & Reid, 1979). Those who do poorly are much more likely to criticize the exam as a poor indicator. Reading about these experiments, I cannot resist a satisfied "knew-it-all-along" feeling. But we college professors are not immune to the self-serving bias. Mary Glenn Wiley, Kathleen Crittenden, and Laura Birg (1979) asked 230 scholars who had submitted articles to sociology journals why their papers had been accepted or rejected. The scholars attributed their rejections mostly to factors beyond their control (for example, bad luck in the editor's choice of critic for the paper). As you can by now imagine, they did not equally attribute their acceptances to *good* luck in the editor's choice of critics, but rather to controllable factors like the quality of their article and the effort they put into it.

The experiments dealing with students' means of explaining their good and bad performances are complemented by experiments on teachers' ways of explaining their students' good and bad performances. Here, however, the evidence is not as clear. Such is perhaps to be expected, since teachers have less at stake in a student's exam performance than does the student. As you might suspect, though, people assigned the role of teacher tended to take credit for positive outcomes, and blame failure on the student (Arkin, Cooper, & Kolditz, 1980; Davis, 1979; Tetlock, 1980). (At least this seems to be true when the student's performance reflects upon the teacher and when the teacher is given no reason to feign modesty.) Teachers, it seems, are likely to think, "I helped Maria to be graduated with honors. But, despite all my help, Melinda flunked out."

Other experiments have asked people to explain what someone has done to them. For example, Susan Green and Alan Gross (1979) had George Washington University students read paragraphs describing something that happened either to them or to someone named "David." For example:

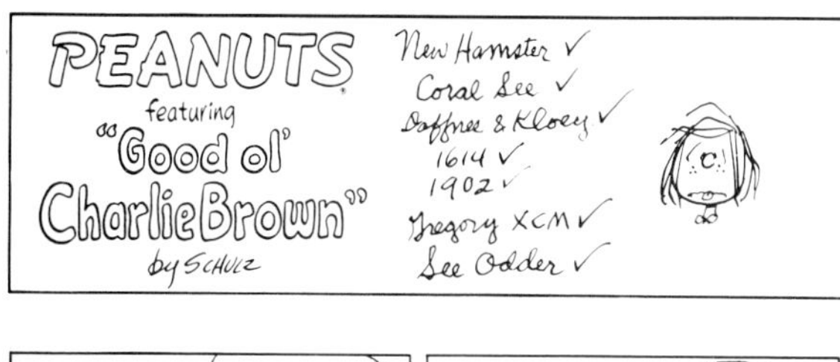

Peppermint Patty attributes her failure to external circumstances.

Assume that David attended a party last week. At this party David met and had a 15-minute conversation with Roger, whom David found to be a very interesting person. Roger has just moved to this area and doesn't yet have a telephone. Near the end of the conversation Roger obtained David's phone number but said it would not be possible to call him during that week. However, Roger called David only two days later and arranged to have lunch with him. Why did Roger phone David sooner than he said he would?

When asked how much they would attribute the sooner-than-expected call to "something about Roger," "something about David," or "something about the situation," the students gave little credit to David. (When I gave this paragraph to my students they speculated, for example, that "Roger may have needed to know something important that he hadn't anticipated," or that "Roger wanted to make new friends, and may have had a change of plans which allowed him to call David sooner.") Other students were given the same paragraph, except with the word "you" substituted for "David." How do you suppose they explained Roger's early call? Green and Gross found these students claiming twice as much credit as that given David. My students do the same, some offering such heartwarming explanations as "Roger decided, after the conversation, that he liked me better than he thought he would" or "Roger really wanted to have lunch with me because he found me so fascinating he didn't want to wait a week."

Can We All Be Better Than Average?

These indications of a self-serving bias are reinforced by research studies that invite people to compare themselves to others: On nearly any dimension that is both subjective (Felson, 1981) and socially desirable, most people see themselves as better than average. For example, most business people see themselves as more ethical than the average business person (Baumhart, 1968; Brenner & Molander, 1977). Most community residents see themselves as less prejudiced than others in their communities (Fields & Schuman, 1976; Lenihan, 1965; O'Gorman & Garry, 1976). Most drivers—even most drivers who have been hospitalized for accidents—believe themselves to be safer and more skillful than the average driver (Svenson, 1981). Most Americans perceive themselves as more intelligent than their average peer (Wylie, 1979). Most French people perceive themselves as superior to their peers in a variety of socially desirable ways (Codol, 1976). Even smog-breathing Los Angeles residents view themselves as healthier than most of their neighbors, and most college students believe they will outlive their actuarially predicted age of death by about ten years (Larwood, 1978; C. R. Snyder, 1978). (This calls to mind Freud's joke about the man who told his wife, "If one of us should die, I think I would go live in Paris.")

Recently, the College Board (1976–1977) invited the nearly 1 million high school seniors taking its aptitude test to indicate "how you feel you compare with other people your own age in certain areas of ability." Judging from the students' responses, it appears that America's high school seniors are not

"I'm drawing up a list of all my good points and all my flaws, and so far my good points are running way, way ahead of my flaws."

The self-serving bias. (Reprinted from *Better Homes and Gardens* Magazine.)

wracked with inferiority feelings. In "leadership ability," 70 percent rated themselves as above average, 2 percent as below average. Sixty percent reported themselves as better than average in "athletic ability," only 6 percent as below average. In "ability to get along with others," *zero* percent of the 829,000 students who responded rated themselves below average, 60 percent rated themselves in the top 10 percent, and 25 percent saw themselves among the top 1 percent!

These tendencies toward self-serving attributions and self-congratulatory comparisons are not the only indications of favorably biased self-perception. We shall see in the next two chapters that: (1) we more readily believe flattering than self-deflating information; (2) most of us overestimate how desirably we would act in a given situation; (3) we evidence a "cognitive conceit" by overestimating the accuracy of our beliefs and judgments; (4) we misremember our own past in self-enhancing ways; (5) if an undesirable act cannot be misremembered or undone, then, as we noted in Chapter 2, we may justify it. To top it off, (6) judging from photos, we guess that attractive people have personalities more like our own than do unattractive people (Marks, Miller, & Maruyama, 1981), and (7) we apparently have what researcher Neil Weinstein (1980; Weinstein & Lachendro, 1982) terms "an unrealistic optimism about future life events." At Rutgers University, at least, students perceive themselves as far more likely than their classmates to experience positive events such as getting a good job, drawing a good salary, and owning a home, and as far less likely to experience negative events such as getting divorced, having lung cancer, being fired.

No doubt many readers are finding all this either depressing or contrary to their own occasional feelings of inadequacy. To be sure, those of us who exhibit the self-serving bias—and apparently that's most of us—may still feel inferior to certain specific individuals, especially when we compare ourselves to someone who is a step or two higher on the ladder of success, attractiveness, or whatever.

And not everyone has a self-serving bias. Some people *do* suffer from unreasonably low self-esteem. Are such people hungering for esteem and therefore more likely than people with high self-esteem to exhibit the self-serving bias? Is the self-serving bias just a boastful cover used by those plagued with low self-esteem? This is what some theorists, such as Erich Fromm, have proposed (Shrauger, 1975). But to the contrary, those who explain their successes and failures with the greatest self-serving bias tend also to score *high* on tests of self-esteem (Ickes & Layden, 1978; Ickes, in press; Levine & Uleman, 1979; Rosenfeld, 1979).

"Narcissism, like selfishness, is an overcompensation for the basic lack of self-love."

Erich Fromm,
Escape from Freedom

On the other hand, those who do not exhibit self-serving bias may tend toward depression. Several recent studies by Lauren Alloy and Lyn Abramson (1980; 1982; Abramson, Alloy, & Rosoff, 1981; Alloy, Abramson, & Viscusi, 1981; Kuiper, 1978) have found that while most people shuck off responsibility for their failures on a laboratory task, or perceive themselves as having been more in control than they were, depressed people are more accurate in their self-appraisal. Sadder but wiser, they seem to be. Perhaps, then, depressed people suffer because they lack the ability of nondepressed people to distort reality in their own favor. Thus they may find it harder to maintain a positive mood and self-esteem. There is also evidence that while most people see themselves more favorably than other people see them (thus providing yet another demonstration of the "normal" self-serving bias), depressed people see themselves *as* other people see them (Lewinsohn et al., 1980). This prompts the unsettling thought that Pascal may have been right: "I lay it down as a fact that, if all men knew what others say of them, there would not be four friends in the world." And that truly is a depressing thought.

Given that depressed people exhibit little self-serving bias, one wonders: Are there other groups who are similarly free of the bias? On the types of tasks we have been considering, would historically oppressed groups be less inclined to inflated self-perceptions? Chapter 12 describes some situations in which people have tended to attribute a man's success to his ability, but a woman's success to luck. When explaining their *own* successes and failures, are women less likely than men to take credit for success and shuck the blame for failure? Women *are* more prone to depression, which is what we would expect if they are less prone to self-serving bias.

Self-serving perceptions are not lies; they are self-deceptions. In fact, as the new research on depression suggests, there may be some practical wisdom in such pride: Self-deceptions may be adaptive and have survival value. Cheaters, for example, may give a more convincing display of honesty if they believe in their honesty. Belief in our superiority can also motivate us to achieve, and can sustain our sense of hope in difficult times.

The self-serving bias is not always adaptive, however. Pride does indeed often go before a fall. People who blame others for their social difficulties are often less happy than people who accept some responsibility for their own behavior, especially if they attribute the problem to an avoidable mistake and not a permanent flaw in their own character (Newman & Langer, 1981; Peterson, Schwartz, & Seligman, 1981; C. A. Anderson, Horowitz, & French, 1982). Research by Barry Schlenker (1976; Schlenker & Miller, 1977a, 1977b) at the University of Florida has also shown how self-serving perceptions can poison a group. In nine different experiments Schlenker had people work together on some task. He then gave them false information that suggested their group had done either well or poorly. In every one of these studies the members of successful groups claimed more responsibility for their group's performance than did members of groups who supposedly failed at the task. Likewise, most presented themselves as contributing more than the others in their group when the group did well; few said they contributed less.

"Victory finds a hundred fathers but defeat is an orphan."

Count Galeazzo Ciano, The Ciano Diaries

Such self-deception can be detrimental to a group. It can lead its members to expect greater-than-average rewards when their organization does well, and less-than-average blame when it does not. If most individuals in a group believe they are underpaid and underappreciated, relative to their better-than-average contributions, disharmony and envy will likely rear their smug heads. College presidents will readily recognize the phenomenon. If, as one survey

"I admit it does look very impressive. But you see nowadays everyone graduates in the top ten per cent of his class."

Can we all be better than average? (William W. Haefeli/*Saturday Review*, 1/20/79)

revealed, 94 percent of college faculty think themselves better than their average colleague (Cross, 1977), then when merit salary raises are announced and half receive an average raise or less, many will feel an injustice has been done them.

Biased self-assessments can also distort managerial judgment. Even when groups are comparable, people tend to consider their own group superior (Codol, 1976; D. M. Taylor & Doria, 1981; Zander, 1969). Thus, most corporation presidents predict more growth for their own firms than for their competition (Larwood & Whittaker, 1977). Similarly, production managers often overpredict their production (Kidd & Morgan, 1969). As Laurie Larwood (1977) noted, such overoptimism can produce disastrous consequences. If those who deal in the stock market or in real estate perceive their business intuition to be superior to their competitors', they may be in for some severe disappointments. Even the capitalist economist Adam Smith, normally a defender of people's economic rationality, foresaw that people overestimate their chances of gain, owing to "an absurd presumption in their own good fortune," which arises from "the overweening conceit which the greater part of men have of their own abilities" (Spiegel, 1971, p. 243).

When Larwood also surveyed people in a northeastern city, she found that most thought they were more concerned than their fellow citizens about preserving clean air and water and believed they used less electricity than the other residents. These average citizens were self-proclaimed better-than-average citizens. Larwood notes that if most people "are merely the average persons that they must be statistically, but behave as though they are superior, their goals and expectations must inevitably conflict." For example, all of us will likely use more than our fair share of resources.

Self-Disparagement

Perhaps you have by now recalled times when someone was not self-boasting but self-disparaging. On such occasions, there may still have been a self-serving process at work. For example, most of us have learned that putting ourselves down is often a successful technique for eliciting "strokes" from others. We know that a remark such as "I wish I weren't so ugly" will at the very least elicit a "Come now. I know a couple of people who are uglier than you."

There is, however, yet another reason why people verbally disparage themselves and praise others. Think of the football coach who, before the big bowl game, extols the awesome strength of the upcoming opponent. Is the coach sincere? Robert Gould, Paul Brounstein, and Harold Sigall (1977; see also Bond, 1979) found that in a laboratory contest their University of Maryland students similarly aggrandized their anticipated opponent, but only when the assessment was made publicly. Those who indicated their assessments privately and anonymously credited their future opponent with much less ability. When coaches publicly exalt their opponents, they not only convey an image of modesty and good sportsmanship, they set the stage for a favorable evaluation no matter what the outcome. A win becomes a praiseworthy achievement; a loss, attributable to the opponent's "great defense."

"Humility is often but a trick whereby pride abases itself only to exalt itself later."

La Rochefoucauld, Maxims

Sometimes people go further and sabotage their chances for success with self-defeating behavior. But even this sometimes serves one's self-image. To understand why this is, recall that people eagerly protect their self-images by attributing their failures to external factors rather than to themselves. Can you see why, *fearing failure*, people might therefore handicap themselves by partying half the night before a job interview, getting a headache the day of a big date, or shrugging off studying before a big exam? When one's self-image is tied up with one's performance, it can be more self-deflating to try hard and fail than to have a ready excuse. If we fail while working under a handicap we can cling to a sense of competence; if we succeed under such conditions, it can only heighten our self-image.

Self-handicapping: *Protecting one's self-image by creating a handy excuse for failure.*

This analysis of *self-handicapping*, proposed by Edward Jones and Steven Berglas (1978; Berglas & Jones, 1978), has been confirmed in experiments. For example, might you act as their Duke University students did in an experiment that was said to concern "drugs and intellectual performance"? Imagine yourself guessing answers on some horribly difficult aptitude questions and then being told "Yours was one of the best scores seen to date!" Feeling more than a little lucky, you are then offered a choice between two drugs before answering more of these items. One drug is said to aid intellectual performance and the other to inhibit it. Which drug do you want? Most of their students wanted the drug that would supposedly disrupt their thinking, thus providing a handy excuse for their anticipated poorer performance. Similarly, Melvin Snyder and his collaborators (Frankel & Snyder, 1978; Snyder et al., 1981) found that Dartmouth College students did best answering anagrams which were alleged to be terribly difficult or when supposedly distracting music was being played. Such conditions provide an excuse for poor performance, thus enabling one to try hard without risking self-esteem.

Why the Self-Serving Bias?

The self-serving bias has been explained in two basic ways (Tetlock & Levi, 1982). These parallel the two explanations considered in Chapter 2 for the effect of actions upon attitudes. One view is akin to self-perception theory; it sees the self-serving bias as springing not from any deep emotional need to enhance oneself, but simply as a by-product of the way we process and remember information about ourselves. The other view, more like dissonance theory, attributes the bias primarily to self-serving motives. Which view is correct? Is the bias simply a perceptual error, an unemotional defect in the way we process information? Or does it result from egotistical motives? Perhaps instead of asking which view is true—assuming one is correct and the other false—we might better ask: Which view is more adequate to the facts as we now understand them? And how might the insights of the two views be integrated?

Let us look first at the explanation that deals with the way we process information. Recall the study by Michael Ross and Fiore Sicoly (1979) in which married people gave themselves more credit for household work than did their spouses. Might this not be due, as Ross and Sicoly believe, to the greater ease with which we recall things we have actively done, compared with what we've not done or what we've observed others doing? I can easily picture myself picking up the laundry, but I have difficulty picturing myself absentmindedly overlooking it.

But why do we assume more responsibility for our successes than our failures, and for the good things that happen to us than the bad? Perhaps it is because our efforts usually do bring positive results. Consider, for example, the UCLA students who were asked by John Cunningham, Philip Starr, and David Kanouse (1979) to explain some imaginary events. When asked to explain why "Ted dislikes you," they were much less likely to hold themselves responsible ("This Ted guy must have a chip on his shoulder") than when asked to explain why "Ted likes you" ("I'm easy to relate to"). Might this not be because in the past people have far more often expressed their liking than their disliking of us? Thus someone who dislikes us is distinctive, and when people act in distinctive ways we tend naturally to think their behavior says something about them, not about us.

The other view—that we are motivated to protect and enhance our self-esteem—is akin to dissonance theory, which assumes a similar self-protective motive. As one theorist put it, "Dissonance-reducing behavior is ego-defensive behavior; by reducing dissonance, we maintain a positive image of ourselves—an image that depicts us as good, or smart, or worthwhile" (Aronson, 1980, p. 109). Experiments indicate that the emotions we feel after success and failure play a role in the self-serving bias (Bradley, 1978; Zuckerman, 1979; Gollwitzer, Earle, & Stephan, 1982). We are not just cool information-processing machines. For example, after people have taken a test, those who are given information which implicates their self-esteem exhibit more self-serving bias than do less ego-involved people (D. T. Miller, 1976).

Other research confirms that most of us are strongly motivated to protect and enhance our self-esteem. Abraham Tesser (1980) at the University of

Tesser thinks the threat to self-esteem is greatest for an older child with a highly capable younger sibling. (Erika Stone/ Peter Arnold, Inc.)

Georgia found that a "self-esteem maintenance" motive predicts a variety of interesting findings, even the amount of friction among brothers and sisters. Do you have a sibling of the same sex who is close to you in age? If so, it is likely that comparisons were drawn between the two of you. Tesser presumes that if one of you is perceived as more capable than the other, the less able one will likely be motivated to act in ways that maintain his or her self-esteem. (Tesser thinks the threat to self-esteem is greatest for an older child with a highly capable younger sibling.) Tesser's data fit his theory of self-esteem maintenance. For example, men with a brother who is different in ability recall not getting along well with him; men with a brother of similar ability recall very little friction.

But what is this self-esteem motive? Is it primarily a desire to see ourselves favorably, or to have others see us favorably, or both? Did the participants in all these experiments really *perceive* themselves with a self-serving bias? Or were they *presenting* themselves in ways that would enhance their public image? (For example, do high school seniors taking the College Boards paint such a rosy picture of themselves partly to put on a good face to prospective colleges?) One point is clear: People are more modest when their self-flattery is vulnerable to being debunked—when responding to the bogus pipeline (discussed in Chapter 2), or when experts will be scrutinizing their self-evaluations (Arkin, Appelman, & Burger, 1980; Schlenker, 1976; Riess et al., 1981; Weary et al., 1982). Thus Professor Smith will likely express less confidence in the significance of her work when presenting it to faculty colleagues than when presenting it to students. Of course, expressed modesty, or even self-disparagement, is sometimes false. One's being more modest when presenting oneself to experts need not mean one is being more honest. Since modesty often creates a good impression (Forsyth, Berger, & Mitchell, 1981; Schlenker & Leary, 1982), people will sometimes present *less* self-esteem than they privately feel (Bernstein, 1979; Weary, 1980; Tetlock, 1980; Greenberg, Pyszczynski, & Solomon, 1982).

The observation that people see and present themselves with a favorable bias is hardly new. In fact, research on the self-serving bias confirms some ancient wisdom about human nature. The tragic flaw portrayed in Greek drama was *hubris*, or pride. Like the subjects of our experiments, the Greek tragic figures were not self-consciously evil; they merely thought too highly of themselves. In literature, the pitfalls of pride are portrayed again and again. And in religion, pride has long been considered first among the "seven deadly sins." The Nazi atrocities were rooted not in self-conscious feelings of inferiority, but in Aryan pride.

If pride is akin to the self-serving bias, then what is humility? Is it self-contempt? Or can we be self-affirming and self-accepting without a self-serving bias? To paraphrase the English scholar-writer C. S. Lewis, humility surely is not handsome people trying to believe they are ugly, and clever people trying to believe they are fools. False modesty can actually lead to an ironic pride in one's better-than-average humility. (Perhaps some readers have by now congratulated themselves on being unusually free of the self-serving bias.) True humility is more like self-forgetfulness than false modesty. It leaves people free to rejoice in their special talents and, with the same honesty, to recognize those of others.

Self-Efficacy

We have seen two potent biases recently uncovered by social psychologists: a tendency to ignore powerful situational forces when explaining others' behavior (the fundamental attribution error) and a tendency to perceive and present ourselves favorably (the self-serving bias). The first bias can prevent us from understanding the causes of others' problems (for example, assuming that unemployed people are necessarily lazy or incompetent, rather than victims of economic circumstance), while the self-righteous pride inherent in the second bias can fuel conflict among people or nations who all see themselves as more moral and deserving than others (Sillars, 1981).

But is there not a danger if we stop here and say no more? Do you have a feeling that although all this rings true, something else needs to be said lest people be excused for any misdeed and patronized as mere objects to be environmentally controlled? Or lest, having taken an ax to our inflated selves, we lose the self-confidence we formerly had? As Pascal taught 300 years ago, no single truth is ever sufficient, because the world is not simple.

"Half the truth is often a great lie."

Benjamin Franklin, Poor Richard

Although future research on the fundamental attribution error and on the self-serving bias will no doubt modify some aspects of the picture painted above, we can, I think, accept its basic points. Yet, an equally important

BEHIND THE SCENES

Albert Bandura

Our research on perceived self-efficacy was an unintended outgrowth of another line of study. Psychological treatments have traditionally attempted to change people through talking. In the social learning view, human behavior can be altered more fundamentally by mastery experiences than by conversation. In testing this notion with phobic disorders, we were discovering that people not only quickly overcame their phobias through mastery experiences, but they often showed striking changes in areas of functioning quite unrelated to the treated dysfunction. Thus, for example, mastering an animal phobia reduced social timidity, expanded personal endeavors, fostered self-directed triumphs over recurrent problems, and boosted venturesomeness in a variety of ways. These observations suggested that treatments produce generalized psychological benefits by strengthening people's sense of efficacy that they can master and manage events in their lives.

We refocused our research efforts to gain a deeper understanding of the sources of personal efficaciousness and how self-percepts of efficacy affect thought patterns, actions, and emotional arousal. Research conducted in our laboratory and elsewhere shows that people's perceptions of their efficacy touches most everything they do, including their stress reactions, achievement strivings, and career pursuits. (*Albert Bandura, Stanford University*)

complement to these truths has emerged from research on self-esteem. For example, high self-esteem—a sense of one's self-worth—appears to be adaptive. People with high self-esteem are not only less depressed than people with low self-esteem, but also less neurotic, less troubled by ulcers and insomnia, and less prone to drug and alcohol addictions (Brockner & Hulton, 1978). On the other hand, people whose ego is temporarily deflated—say, by being told they did miserably on an intelligence test—are more likely then to disparage other people. More generally, people who are negative about themselves tend also to be negative about others (Wills, 1981).

Self-efficacy: *A sense that one is competent and effective. Distinguished from self-esteem, a sense of one's self-worth. A bombardier might feel high self-efficacy and low self-esteem.*

Other research on topics such as "locus of control," "achievement motivation," "self-esteem," "personal causation," "learned helplessness," "illusory incompetence," and "intrinsic motivation" reveals the benefits of seeing oneself as competent and effective. Albert Bandura (1977, 1978, 1982) has integrated much of this research into a concept of *self-efficacy*, a scholarly

"Nonsense, Bentley! You can win 'em all!"

Positive thinking has its benefits—and, when unrealistic, its costs. (Drawing by Ross; © 1979 *The New Yorker* Magazine, Inc.)

version of the truth behind the old "power of positive thinking." Believing in our own possibilities—and enabling others to believe in theirs—is conducive to effective coping and to self-improvement.

Locus of Control

More than a thousand research studies have explored the consequences of people's believing that they control their own destiny (termed "internal locus of control"). These studies compare such people to those who more often assume that their fate is determined by chance or outside forces ("external locus of control"). The way people answer questions on tests of locus of control (see Box 3-1) predicts their behavior in other situations (Bar-Tal & Bar-Zohar, 1977; Gilmor, 1978; MacDonald, 1973; Phares, 1976). For example, disadvantaged children with a strong internal locus of control achieve more in school than do those with a weak sense of personal control. People who believe themselves internally controlled are also more likely to be nonsmokers (or to successfully stop smoking), to wear seat belts, and to practice birth control (instead of trusting fate). They are more independent and resistant to being manipulated, they are better able to delay instant gratification in order to achieve long-term goals, and they make more money.

"To him that will, ways are not wanting."

George Herbert, Jacula Prudentum

Box 3-1

Locus of Control

Do you more strongly believe that:

In the long run people get the respect they deserve in this world.	or	Unfortunately, an individual's worth often passes unrecognized no matter how hard he tries.
What happens to me is my own doing.	or	Sometimes I feel that I don't have enough control over the direction my life is taking.
The average person can have an influence in government decisions.	or	This world is run by the few people in power, and there is not much the little guy can do about it.

People's answers to questions such as these [drawn from Julian Rotter's Internal-External Locus of Control Scale (1973)] help predict their achievements and behaviors.

By and large, all the research converges on the same conclusion: People benefit from a strong sense of personal effectiveness.

Learned Helplessness

The benefits of a sense of personal efficacy have also been demonstrated in animal research. Dogs which learn a sense of helplessness (by being taught they cannot escape shocks) will later fail to take initiative in another situation when they *could* escape the punishment. By contrast, animals which are taught personal control (by allowing them to escape their first shocks successfully) adapt easily to a new situation. Researcher Martin Seligman (1975, 1977) notes similarities in human situations, such as when depressed or oppressed people become passive because they believe that their efforts have no effect. Helpless dogs and depressed people both suffer paralysis of the will, passive resignation, even physical immobility.

Here is a clue to how institutions—whether malevolent, like concentration camps, or benevolent, like hospitals—can unwittingly dehumanize people. In hospitals, "good patients" don't ring bells, don't ask questions, don't try to control what's happening (S. E. Taylor, 1979). Such passivity may be good for hospital efficiency, but it is bad for patients. Feelings of efficacy, of an ability to control one's life, have been linked to health and survival. Several diseases are associated with feelings of helplessness and diminished choice. So is the rapidity of decline and death in concentration camps and nursing homes. For example, research by Ellen Langer, Irving Janis, and John Wolfer (1975) indicates that hospital patients who are induced to believe in their ability to control stress require fewer pain relievers and sedatives and are seen by nurses as exhibiting less anxiety.

In a related experiment, Langer and Judith Rodin (1976; Rodin & Langer, 1977) treated elderly patients in a high-rated Connecticut nursing home in one of two ways. With one patient group the benevolent care givers stressed "our responsibility to make this a home you can be proud of and happy in." These patients were treated as passive recipients of the normal well-intentioned, sympathetic care. Three weeks later, most were rated by themselves, by interviewers, and by nurses as further debilitated. Their experience must have been similar to that of James MacKay (1980), an eighty-seven-year-old psychologist:

> I became a nonperson last summer. My wife had an arthritic knee which put her in a walker, and I chose that moment to break my leg. We went to a nursing home. It was all nursing and no home. The doctor and the head nurse made all decisions; we were merely animate objects. Thank heavens it was only two weeks. . . . The top man of the nursing home was very well trained and very compassionate; I considered it the best home in town. But we were nonpersons from the time we entered until we left.

Langer and Rodin's other treatment promoted self-efficacy. It stressed the patients' opportunities for choice, their possibilities for influencing nursing-home policy, and their responsibility "to make of your life whatever you want." These patients were also given small decisions to make and responsibilities to fulfill. Over the ensuing three weeks, 93 percent of this group showed improved alertness, activity, and happiness.

These research findings suggest that systems of governing or managing people which maximize their sense of self-efficacy will be most conducive to health and happiness (Deci, 1980; Schulz & Hanusa, 1980). If institutionalized residents are allowed choice in such matters as what to eat for breakfast, when to go to a movie, whether to sleep late or get up early, they may live longer and certainly will be happier than if these decisions are made for them.

Collective Efficacy

Although it is commonly thought that hopelessness breeds militant social action, the truth is that it more often breeds apathy. Protesting members of aggrieved groups generally have more self-pride and a stronger belief in their ability to influence events than do those who don't protest (Caplan, 1970; Forward & Williams, 1970; Lipset, 1966). In many countries, university students, not the most severely disadvantaged members of the society, spearhead political activism. Bandura (1982) writes:

> People who have a sense of collective efficacy will mobilize their efforts and resources to cope with external obstacles to the changes they seek. But those convinced of their inefficacy will cease trying even though changes are attainable through concerted effort. . . . As a society, we enjoy the benefits left by those before us who collectively resisted inhumanities and worked for social reforms that permit a better life. Our own collective efficacy will, in turn, shape how future generations will live their lives.

"Argue for your limitations, and sure enough they're yours."

Richard Bach, Illusions: Adventures of a Reluctant Messiah

Although this psychological research and comment on self-efficacy is new, the emphasis on taking charge of one's life and realizing one's potential dates way back. The you-can-do-it theme of Horatio Alger's rags-to-riches books is an enduring American idea, an idea that has surfaced recently in many popular books and courses which urge people to succeed through positive mental attitudes. Bandura believes that self-efficacy grows not so much by self-persuasion ("I think I can, I think I can") as by undertaking challenging yet realistic tasks and succeeding. Nevertheless, insofar as research on self-efficacy gives us greater confidence in traditional virtues such as perseverance and hope, it performs no small service.

"Poised somewhere between sinful vanity and self-destructive submissiveness is a golden mean of self-esteem appropriate to the human condition."

Stanford Lyman, The Seven Deadly Sins: Society and Evil

Still, let us remember the point on which we began our consideration of self-efficacy: Any truth, separated from its complementary truth, is but a half-truth. The truth embodied in the concept of self-efficacy may encourage us not to resign ourselves to bad situations, to persist despite initial failures, to exert effort without being overly distracted by self-doubts. But lest the pendulum swing too far toward *this* truth, we had best remember that it, too, is not the whole story. If positive thinking can accomplish anything, then, by implication, if we are unhappily married, poor, or depressed we have but ourselves to blame. Shame. If only we had tried harder, been more disciplined, less stupid. Failing to appreciate that people's difficulties sometimes reflect the oppressive power of social situations can tempt us to blame them for their difficulties, or even to blame ourselves too harshly for our own.

SUMMING UP

Attribution researchers study how we explain people's behavior. For example, when will we attribute someone's behavior to internal causes, such as the person's disposition, and when to the situation? By and large we make quite reasonable attributions. However, we are consistently prone to two errors. When explaining people's behavior it is difficult to resist the *fundamental attribution error*. This is a tendency to attribute their behavior so much to their inner traits and attitudes that we discount situational constraints, even when these are obvious. We make this attribution error partly because when we watch someone act, that *person* is the focus of our attention. In general, we attribute causation to whatever our attention is focused upon. When *we* act, our attention is usually on what we are reacting to. Thus we are more sensitive to the situational influences upon ourselves.

When perceiving ourselves, we are prone to another error: the *self-serving bias*. This is a tendency to blame the situation for our failures while taking credit for our successes, and to see ourselves as generally "better than average." Even self-disparaging and self-handicapping behaviors can sometimes be understood as strategies for protecting and enhancing one's self-esteem. Two explanations have been offered for the self-serving bias. One explanation sees it as simply a by-product of the way we process information. For example, if good things more often happen to us than bad things, it is not illogical to blame unusual circumstances for occasional bad outcomes. The other view explains the bias in terms of our motivation to protect and enhance our self-image. Evidence indicates that we are indeed motivated to see and to present ourselves favorably.

Research on these tendencies to ignore powerful situational forces when explaining others' behavior and to adopt an inflated view of ourselves is complemented by other research on the benefits of believing in our own potential, and encouraging others to believe in theirs. People with a strong sense of *self-efficacy* cope better and achieve more than do people who lack a sense of their own competence and effectiveness.

Chapter

How We Form and Sustain Social Beliefs

What a piece of work is man!
how noble in reason! how
infinite in faculty! . . .
in apprehension how like a
god!
William Shakespeare,
Hamlet, Prince of Denmark

We are the hollow men
We are the stuffed men
Leaning together
Headpiece filled with straw.
T. S. Eliot,
The Hollow Men

For decades social psychologists have studied human thinking. We have been fascinated by how people form their ideas and how their ideas shape their actions. Surely there is truth in the motto of the United Nations Educational, Scientific and Cultural Organization (UNESCO): "Since wars begin in the minds of men, it is in the minds of men that the defenses of peace must be constructed." What we believe about events and people underlies much of our social behavior—our reactions to situations, our loyalties and our prejudices, our decisions to help or to hurt.

In the past, social psychologists have often viewed us as "rational animals." Just as developmental psychologist Jean Piaget analyzed the mature adult's capacities for abstract logic, so have social psychologists studied the intuitive logic we so skillfully use when integrating pieces of information. Recently, though, researchers in "cognitive social psychology" have been rethinking thinking. There has been what one prominent researcher calls "an explosion of research in social cognition" (S. Fiske, 1980), and attention has now shifted to the errors of human intuition. Contrary to Hamlet's poem of praise, quoted above, many recent experiments indicate that we are not always "noble in reason" and we are certainly not "infinite in faculty." Chapter 1 described one shortcoming, the I-knew-it-all-along phenomenon. In Chapter 3 we saw two powerful errors: the fundamental attribution error and the self-serving bias. This chapter presents several more of the rather amazing and occasionally amusing ways in which we form beliefs that sometimes prove false.

Since this chapter, like the one preceding, deals largely with predictable errors in human thinking, I urge you to keep in mind that the proverbial glass is half full as well as half empty. The brain's ability to recognize patterns, handle language, and reason abstractly outstrips our largest computers (Walker, 1981). Moreover, an explanation of how we arrive at unfounded convictions no more means that all our convictions are unfounded than does explaining how people make counterfeit money mean that all money is counterfeit. But if one were to suggest that counterfeit money abounds (as I shall suggest that counterfeit beliefs abound) one would need to explain how this happens.

"People are good enough to get through life, poor enough to make predictable and consequential mistakes."

Baruch Fischhoff (1981)

Understanding the frailty of our wisdom may serve a constructive purpose—moving us to a clearer way of thinking about our thinking. It may, for example, help mute our arrogance and amplify our humility. Furthermore, understanding illusory thinking can help us scrutinize the whirlpool of conflicting ideas swirling constantly about us.

A BRIEF HISTORICAL PERSPECTIVE

Throughout this century, psychology has explored the mind's amazing ability to fabricate experiences—dreams, hallucinations, perceptual illusions, and hypnotically induced delusions. For example, Sigmund Freud was fascinated by our vulnerability to illusions. As Calvin Hall (1978) explained, "Freud unmasked our hypocrisies, our phony ideas, our rationalizations, our vanities, and our chicaneries, and not all the efforts of humanists and rationalists will restore the mask."

An artificially constructed belief about reality feels much like an objectively correct belief. Biopsychologist Jerre Levy (1978; Levy, Trevarthen, & Sperry, 1972) recounts an experiment with patients whose two brain hemispheres had been surgically separated. When the right half of a girl's face was projected to the patients' nonverbal right hemispheres and the left half of a *woman's* face was projected to their verbal left hemispheres, they confidently *pointed* (nonverbally) to a completed picture of the girl to identify the picture seen, but *said* they saw a woman. Each hemisphere invented the missing half face. Apparently, the invented image was experienced the same as an objectively correct belief.

Past studies of human problem solving provide further evidence concerning the bounds of our ability to reason clearly. Consider the classic "horse-trading" problem:

> A man bought a horse for $60 and sold it for $70. Then he bought the same horse back for $80 and again sold it, for $90. How much money did he make in the horse business?

"To err is human."
Seneca

The answer (see Box 4-1) may seem obvious, but most American college students incorrectly answer even so simple a question as this. (A German university colleague informs me that most German banking executives also miss this one.)

The most unambiguous evidence concerning the formation of false beliefs comes, however, not from the speculations of Freud or the classic experiments of early American psychology, but from the vast new research literature on how our minds process information. These new revelations are, I believe, among psychology's most important contributions to human self-understanding.

WE OFTEN DO NOT KNOW WHY WE DO WHAT WE DO

> There is one thing, and only one in the whole universe which we know more about than we could learn from external observation. That one thing is Man. We do not merely observe men, we *are* men. In this case we have, so to speak, inside information; we are in the know. (pp. 18-19)

The truth of this observation by C. S. Lewis (1960) is self-evident; some things we (men and women) know best by intuition and personal experience. The *fallibility* of our self-knowledge is, however, considerably less self-evident; sometimes we *think* we are "in the know," but our inside information is demonstrably erroneous. This is the unavoidable conclusion of some fascinating recent research.

We Easily Forget Our Previous Attitudes

If your attitudes were changed during an experiment, would you be aware of the change? Several experiments have asked people whose attitudes have been altered to recall their preexperiment attitudes. The result is unnerving: People often insist that they have always felt much as they now feel. For example Daryl Bem and Keith McConnell (1970) took a survey among Carnegie-Mellon University students. Buried in it was a question concerning student control over the university curriculum. A week later the students agreed to write an essay opposing student control. After doing so, their expressed attitudes shifted toward greater opposition to student control. When asked to recall how they had answered the question a week previous, they "remembered" holding the opinion that they *now* held and denied that the experiment had affected them.

George Goethals and Richard Reckman (1973) found that people's knowledge of their past was no better when the issue was school busing. High school students whose attitudes were shifted by an eloquent speaker from pro to con (or from con to pro) were unaware of having changed. D. R. Wixon and James Laird (1976) found their Clark University students similarly denying having changed. When reminded how they formerly felt, the students usually either denied ever feeling that way or offered persuasive excuses for their new opinion, such as political events which had transpired just before the experiment. But the fact was that control groups that had not undergone the persuasion experience were unchanged by those events outside the experiment. Concluded Wixon and Laird, "The speed, magnitude, and certainty" with which people revised their own histories "was striking."

My intuition rebels at these findings. I can identify past attitudes that *are* different from my present convictions (see also Aderman & Brehm, 1976). But for the moment, let's assume that on at least some topics we are indeed blind to the evolution of our opinions. By definition, it will be impossible for us to be aware of such blindness. Thus from our own experience we cannot recall the times our opinion has changed without our knowing it.

However, we *can* spot the phenomenon in others, such as when politicians declare themselves as having always supported the position they now espouse. Likewise, reports from Israel during the euphoric aftermath of the 1977 Begin-Sadat summit meeting indicated that many Israelis were claiming they had long felt affinity with the Egyptians, who had always been "different" from the other Arab countries. Observers of Israel say this self-perception is false: Previously, Jordan and Lebanon were regarded most favorably (Babad, 1978).

Box 4-1

Answer to Horse-Trading Question

The most frequent answer is $10. (People typically reason that when the man bought the horse back for $80 he lost the $10 made in the initial deal, putting him back to zero.) The man actually made $20, as this accounting indicates:

	Buying Price: (Money Paid Out)	Selling Price: (Money Taken In)
Deal 1	$60	$70
Deal 2	80	90
Total	$140	$160 (Profit = $20)

If this is not convincing, get out some play money, go through the transactions, and see how much they profit you.

People who adopt new attitudes often misremember their old attitudes. Vice President George Bush challenged the media to prove that he ever accused Ronald Reagan of advocating "voodoo economics." The next evening NBC news responded to the challenge by broadcasting a videotape of Bush making the accusation. (Steve Liss/Liaison)

We Readily Deny Real Influences upon Us

Why did you choose your college? Why did you lash out at your roommate? Why did you fall in love with your fiancé or spouse? Most people have ready answers to such questions. How accurate are their answers? A number of experiments have asked people why they did what they did and then compared their introspections with objective evidence indicating what *really* influenced them. People readily proclaim why in a particular situation they have felt or acted as they have. Yet, when the influences are not obvious, people are often poor judges of the sources of their behavior. Factors that have had big effects on people are sometimes reported as having little effect, and factors having little effect are sometimes perceived as having had a big effect.

Richard Nisbett and Stanley Schachter (1966) demonstrated this by asking Columbia University students to take a series of electric shocks of steadily increasing intensity. Beforehand, some of them were given a fake pill which, they were told, would produce feelings of heart palpitations, breathing irregularities, and butterflies in the stomach—the very symptoms that usually accompany being shocked. Nisbett and Schachter anticipated that the people would therefore attribute these symptoms of shock to the fake pill, rather than to the shock, and would thus be willing to tolerate more shock than people not given the pill. Indeed, the effect was enormous—people given the fake pill took four times as much shock. Afterwards, informed they had taken more shock than average, they were asked why. Not only did their answers make no reference to the pill, when pressed (and even after the experimenter explained the hypotheses of the experiment in detail) they denied any influence of the pill. They would usually say the pill likely did affect *others*, but not themselves; a typical reply was, "I didn't even think about the pill."

Other times people think they *have* been affected by something that has had no effect. For example, Nisbett and Timothy Wilson (1977) had some University of Michigan students evaluate a documentary film. While some of them watched, a power saw was run outside the room. Most people felt that this distracting noise affected their ratings. Actually, their ratings were indistinguishable from those of control subjects who viewed the film without distraction.

Perhaps most thought-provoking, though, is a study by Janet Weiss and Paula Brown (1976). They asked fifty-four Harvard University undergraduate women to record their mood each day for two months. The women also recorded factors that might affect their moods: the weather, their health, the stage of their menstrual cycles, day of the week, amount of sleep, sexual activity, etc. At the end of the two months each then judged how much each of these factors had affected her mood. Remarkably, there was no relationship between their perceptions of how important a factor was and how well the factor actually predicted mood. For example, the women believed day of the week was relatively unimportant, but among the factors studied this was actually the best predictor of mood. Such findings raise a disconcerting question: How much insight do we have into what makes us happy or unhappy?

Finally, we often poorly predict our own future behavior. When asked whether they would comply with demands to deliver cruel electric shocks, or would be hesitant to help a victim if several other people were present, people overwhelmingly deny their vulnerability to such influences. But as we shall see, experiments have shown that many of us are vulnerable.

To a striking extent, then, we often make false assertions about what we have felt in the past, what has influenced us, and what we will feel and do. Our intuitive "self-insights" are sometimes dead wrong. However, we must be careful not to overstate the matter. When the causes of behavior are conspicuous and the correct explanation fits our intuition, our self-perceptions can be accurate. For example, Peter Wright and Peter Rip (1981) recently found that California high school juniors *could* discern how their reactions to a college were influenced by such features as its size, tuition, and distance from home. It is when the causes of behavior are not obvious (even to an observer) that our self-explanations become more erroneous.

Perhaps people have better self-insight *at the moment they act*, but quickly forget what they knew, just as by the end of a good racquetball volley the players sometimes forget who served, though surely they did know at the time of the serve (White, 1980). Yet the deficiencies in our self-knowledge seem not entirely due to forgetting. How little we actualize Thales' advice, "Know thyself," is reinforced by cognitive psychologists, who contend that we are unaware of much that goes on in our minds. Studies of perception and memory show that our awareness is mostly of the *results* of our thinking and not of the process of our thinking (Hilgard, 1977). For example, asked where the letter "r" is on the keyboard, a typist will have difficulty answering verbally; the knowledge is, so to speak, "in the fingers" (Smith & Miller, 1978). We all have experienced the results of our mind's unconscious workings—when we set an unconscious mental clock to record the passage of time and to awaken us at an appointed hour, or when we achieve a seemingly spontaneous creative insight after a problem has unconsciously "incubated." Similarly, creative scientists and artists often cannot report the thought process that produced their insights.

This research on the incompleteness of our self-knowledge offers at least two practical implications. The first is for psychological inquiry. The introspections of one's clients or research subjects may provide useful clues to their psychological processes, but these self-reports are often untrustworthy. People's errors in self-understanding place limits on the scientific usefulness of their subjective personal reports (D. W. Fiske, 1980; but also Ericsson & Simon, 1980).

"The naked intellect is an extraordinarily inaccurate instrument."

Madeline L'Engle, A Wind in the Door

The second implication has ramifications for our everyday lives. The sincerity with which people report and interpret their experiences is no guarantee of the validity of these personal reports. Personal testimonies are powerfully persuasive, but they may also convey unwitting error. Perhaps keeping this potential for error in mind can help us to feel less intimidated by other people and to be less gullible.

OUR PRECONCEPTIONS CONTROL OUR INTERPRETATIONS AND MEMORIES

Schema: *A concept that directs one's apprehension of events. Loosely speaking, a preconception. Plural: schemata.*

Recent experiments indicate that one of the most significant facts about our minds is the extent to which our preconceived notions (called "schemata") bias the way we view, interpret, and remember the information that comes to us. Most of us do not need experiments to acknowledge that our existing beliefs affect how we interpret and recall events. Yet generally we fail to realize how great this effect is. Let's look at some recent experiments which suggest that the biasing power of our beliefs is indeed very great. Some of these experiments examine how *pre*judgments affect the way people perceive and interpret information they are then given. Other experiments plant a judgment in people's minds *after* they have been given information. These experiments study how after-the-fact ideas bias people's *recall.*

BEHIND THE SCENES

Richard Nisbett

When I was in college, I frequently had a great deal of trouble getting to sleep. I would lie awake for two or three hours, tossing and turning. With great reluctance, I decided to try sleeping pills. I bought a bottle of Sominex, and took a pill one night. As I lay in bed, I monitored my symptoms: Did I feel any drowsier? Was my breathing slow and relaxed? No! It was just as bad as usual! Why wasn't it working? Was I upset over something? Well, there was the exam coming up on Tuesday. The last letter from Janet was sort of distant-sounding. Yes, I was upset. Apparently I was such a nervous wreck that even a sleeping pill couldn't calm me down. Around 6 A.M. I drifted off for a fitful two hours of sleep—my worst night ever.

Years later when I met Stanley Schachter I understood what had happened that night. Sominex is a very weak sleep agent, so the actual drug effect was minimal. But since I didn't know I could expect so little effect, I assumed that I was particularly worked up. The implication is that if you give people placebos under some conditions, you will get a "reverse placebo" effect: The symptoms will be worse than usual because of the causal attributions people will make when they don't get better as promised. Mike Storms and I actually demonstrated this effect with insomniacs.

Physicians, psychiatrists, and clinical psychologists now understand that people's causal attributions (which are often in error) can worsen their illnesses or impede their responses to treatment. This new understanding can be traced directly to Schachter's pioneering work.

P.S. My own work did nothing to cure me of insomnia. That had to wait for a clipping from *Ladies' Home Journal* that my mother sent when she heard I was studying insomnia. The article said not to work right up to bedtime. I stopped doing that and sleepless nights have been rare since. And what did I learn from that? That we aren't very good at detecting cause-and-effect relationships, such as the relationship between working late and insomnia, unless we have a theory that leads us to expect the relationship. And that contributed to my work with Timothy Wilson on awareness of the causes of our behavior. (*Richard Nisbett, University of Michigan*)

Box 4-2

There Is More to Vision than Meets the Eye

Consider this phrase:

A
BIRD
IN THE
THE HAND

Do you notice something unusual about it?
Now count the F's in this sentence:

FINISHED FILES ARE THE RE-
SULTS OF YEARS OF SCIENTIF-
IC STUDY COMBINED WITH THE
EXPERIENCE OF YEARS.

Answers: Did your preconceptions prevent your seeing the "the" twice in the phrase? Did your listening for the "F" sound prevent your finding all six F's in the sentence?

How We Perceive and Interpret Events

Evidence for the biasing effects of our prejudgments and expectations is standard fare for introductory courses in psychology. Numerous demonstrations illustrate that what we see in a picture can be influenced by what we are led to expect. (See Box 4-2, and recall the dalmatian dog in Chapter 1 of this book.)

Charles Lord, Lee Ross, and Mark Lepper (1979) have documented the incredible biasing power of our beliefs. They showed Stanford University students, half of whom favored and half of whom opposed capital punishment, two purported new research studies. One study confirmed and the other disconfirmed the students' existing beliefs about the crime-deterring effectiveness of the death penalty. Both the proponents and opponents of capital punishment readily accepted the evidence which confirmed their belief, but were sharply critical of the "disconfirming" evidence. Showing the two sides an identical body of mixed evidence had therefore not narrowed their disagreement, but increased it. Each side had perceived the evidence as supporting its belief and now believed even more strongly.

"As I am, so I see."

Ralph Waldo Emerson, Essays

Is this why, in politics, religion, and science, ambiguous evidence often fuels rather than extinguishes the fires of debate among people who hold strongly opposing opinions? Recall from Chapter 1 how easy it is to underestimate the extent to which beliefs and values penetrate science. Philosophers of science have therefore been reminding us that our observations of reality are always "theory-laden." There is an objective reality out there, but we are always viewing it through the spectacles of our preconceived beliefs and values. This is one reason why our beliefs are important; they shape our interpretation of everything else.

That presuppositions affect both scientific and everyday thinking is becoming an accepted fact. Less well known are some recent experiments which systematically manipulate people's presuppositions, with astonishing effects upon how they interpret and recall what they observe. For example, Melvin Snyder and Arthur Frankel (1976) showed Dartmouth College men a silent videotape of a woman being interviewed. Those told she was being interviewed about sex perceived her as more anxious during the interview and as a generally more anxious person than did those who were told she was being interviewed about politics. Similarly, Myron Rothbart and Pamela Birrell (1977) had University of Oregon students assess the facial expression of "Kurt Walden," pictured here. Students told he was a racist leader in the Nazi Gestapo who was responsible for barbaric medical experiments on concentration camp inmates judged his expression in this picture to be cruel and frowning (can you see that barely suppressed sneer?). Those told he was a leader in the anti-Nazi underground movement whose courage saved thousands of Jewish lives judged the facial expression as more warm and kindly. (On second thought, look at those gentle eyes and that almost smiling mouth.)

Kurt Walden: Is he cruel or kindly? (Myron Rothbart)

To give you a feeling for the next set of experiments, can you remember the relationship reported near the end of Chapter 2 between fire hydrants and crime rate? Did you attempt to explain the relationship? (The point of the example was that people who actively explain something are the most likely to remember it.) Now let me clear the record by confessing that the investigators in that study actually had no information about the relationship between the number of fire hydrants in an area and its crime rate; they just made up the relationship. What do you suppose it really is? As the number of fire hydrants in an area goes up, does the crime rate tend to go up or down?

Experiments by Lee Ross and his Stanford University colleagues have similarly planted a falsehood in people's minds and then tried to discredit it. If a false idea biases people's processing of information, then, if the idea is later discredited, will its effects upon their thinking be erased? For example, imagine a baby sitter who surmises, during an evening with an infant who cries constantly, that bottle feeding produces colicky babies: "Come to think of it, cow's milk obviously is better suited to calves than babies." When, afterwards, it is discovered that the infant was suffering a high fever, will the sitter nevertheless persist in now presuming that bottle feeding causes colic (Ross & Anderson, 1982)?

The experiments indicate that it is indeed surprisingly difficult to demolish a falsehood, once the person has conjured up a rationale for it. In each experiment, first a belief was established, either by proclaiming it true (as with our fire hydrants and crime example) or else by inducing the person to conclude its truth after inspecting two sample cases. Then, people were asked to explain *why* it is true. Finally, the initial information was totally discredited—the person was told the truth, that the information was manufactured for the experiment and that half the people in the experiment were given opposing theory or data. Nevertheless, the new belief amazingly survived the discrediting about 75 percent intact, presumably because the people still retained their invented explanations for the belief.

For instance, Craig Anderson, Mark Lepper, and Ross (1980) asked people to decide whether people who take risks make good or bad fire fighters. They were given only two concrete cases to inspect; one group was shown a risk-prone person being a successful fire fighter and a cautious person an unsuccessful one. The other group was shown cases suggesting the opposite conclusion. After forming their theory that risk-prone people make better or worse fire fighters, the people wrote an explanation for it—for example, that risk-prone people are brave, or that cautious people are careful. Once formed, each explanation could exist independently of the information which initially created the belief. Thus when that information was discredited, the people still held their self-generated explanations and therefore continued to believe that risk-prone people really *do* make better or worse fire fighters. These experiments also indicate that the more closely we examine our theories and explain how they *might* be true, the more closed we become to discrediting information.

"No one denies that new evidence can change people's beliefs. Children do eventually renounce their belief in Santa Claus. Our contention is simply that such changes generally occur slowly, and that more compelling evidence is often required to alter a belief than to create it."

Lee Ross & Mark Lepper (1980)

Do people who take risks make good or bad firefighters? (© Thomas S. England 1980/Photo Researchers, Inc.)

Psychiatrist Robert Coles (1973) offers a delightful real-life parallel to these experiments. For years, Sigmund Freud sought to understand the childhood origins of Leonardo da Vinci's personality. One day he discovered that Leonardo reported a recurring memory of a vulture touching his lips while he was in the cradle. Noting that "vulture" is an ancient symbol for "mother," Freud constructed an elegant analysis of Leonardo based upon this revelation. Later, when compiling the complete edition of Freud's works, an editor discovered that the German translation of Leonardo's memory was in error—the Italian word which had been translated "vulture" actually meant "kite." With the original key to Freud's analysis discredited, did the remaining edifice come crashing down? You can guess the answer.

Our beliefs, even if false, are perpetuated in additional ways. People routinely oversimplify the explanations of complex events. Researchers have found that once people identify a cause which seems to help explain an event, other contributing causes are discounted (Shaklee & Fischhoff, 1977). This phenomenon surely occurs in everyday experience. For instance, the background of a juvenile delinquent may differ in so many ways from that of the average nondelinquent that nearly any simplistic theory of delinquency can be "verified" by casual observation, thus allowing one to discount other competing explanations. Moreover, we are inclined to "assimilate" events—to interpret and recall them in ways compatible with what we already believe. Thus we much more readily incorporate a new fact within our beliefs than revise our beliefs in light of the fact (Tversky & Kahneman, 1980), and we best remember information when it is consistent with our ideas (Craik & Tulving, 1975; Schulman, 1974).

In summary, the evidence is compelling: Our beliefs and expectations have a powerful effect upon how we notice and interpret events. On the whole, we surely benefit from our preconceptions, just as scientists benefit from creating theories that guide them in noticing and interpreting events. But the benefits sometimes entail a cost; we become prisoners of our own thought patterns. Thus the canals that were so often "seen" on Mars turned out to indeed be the product of intelligent life—an intelligence on earth's side of the telescope. Sometimes, when our theories and beliefs are strong, we fool ourselves.

"Two-thirds of what we see is behind our eyes."

Chinese proverb

How We Recall Events

Do you agree or disagree with this statement?

Memory can be likened to a storage chest in the brain into which we deposit material and from which we can withdraw it later if needed. Occasionally, something gets lost from the "chest," and then we say we have forgotten.

About 85 percent of college students agree (Lamal, 1979). But the statement is false. Our memories are not copies of our past experience which remain on deposit in a memory bank. Rather, they are reconstructed at the time of withdrawal (Loftus, 1980b; Loftus & Loftus, 1980). Like a paleontologist inferring the appearance of a dinosaur from bone fragments, we reconstruct our distant past from fragments of information. Thus we can easily (though unconsciously) revise our memories to suit our current knowledge. One of my sons recently complained, "The June issue of *Cricket* magazine never came." Moments later, when his mother found it for him, he delightedly remarked, "Oh good, I thought I'd gotten it."

Memory construction enables people to revise their own past histories. For example, Michael Ross, Cathy McFarland, and Garth Fletcher (1981) exposed some University of Waterloo students to a message convincing them of the desirability of toothbrushing. Later, in a supposedly different experiment, these students recalled brushing their teeth more often during the preceding two weeks than did other students who had not heard the message. Noting the similarity of such findings to happenings in George Orwell's *Nineteen Eighty-Four*—where it was "necessary to remember that events happened in the desired manner"—social psychologist Anthony Greenwald (1980) surmises that we all have "totalitarian egos" that continuously revise our past to suit our present views.

You can demonstrate memory reconstruction by recalling a scene from a pleasurable past experience. Do you see yourself in the scene? If so, your memory must be a reconstruction of what you experienced, for we do not in reality look at ourselves. Since people are unaware of the errors and distortions which they build into the reconstruction, they will often be sure enough of their faulty memories to stake money on them. According to one mid-1970s poll, 70 percent of Americans remember seeing the assassination of John F. Kennedy on television in 1963. The truth is that although still photos were published in magazines, the film was not shown on television until 1976 (*Saturday Review*, 1978).

Studies of conflicting eyewitness testimonies further illustrate our tendency to recall the past with great confidence but meagre accuracy. Elizabeth Loftus and John Palmer (1973) showed University of Washington students a film of a traffic accident and then asked them questions about what they saw. People who were asked "How fast were the cars going when they smashed into each other?" gave higher estimates than those asked "How fast were the cars going when they hit each other?" A week later they were also asked whether they recalled seeing any broken glass. Although there was no broken glass in the accident, people who had been asked the question with "smashed into" were more than twice as likely as those asked the question with "hit" to report seeing broken glass. This demonstrates how in constructing a memory we unconsciously use our general knowledge and beliefs to fill in the holes, thus organizing mere fragments from our actual past into a convincing memory.

Memory construction. When people who viewed a filmed automobile accident (A) were then asked a question implying a more severe accident (B), they integrated the two pieces of information and "remembered" a more serious accident than that actually witnessed (C). (From E. F. Loftus, 1979).

A

B

"About how fast were the cars going when they **SMASHED** into each other?"

C

BEHIND THE SCENES

Elizabeth Loftus

My husband and colleague, Geoff, often teases me about how my research on reconstructive memory began. It's not exactly the way I teach students how psychologists get ideas for their research. But here it is.

A former professor of mine at Stanford left to take a job with the U.S. Department of Transportation in Washington, D.C. He had been on the job a short time when our paths crossed, and he said, "You know, there's a great need for good research on traffic accidents, and there's money to support it!" Unfortunately, I was studying memory for words and didn't know much about traffic accidents (except for the few that I'd had myself as a teenager). One day, I was struck with a thought, and I announced to Geoff: "I'm going to study memory for traffic accidents." "Big deal," he said, unimpressed. His lack of enthusiasm wasn't surprising, since I had no particular scientific hypotheses, and no specific research ideas. But I started wondering about the interaction between accidents and the words people use to describe them. I talked to colleagues about the accidents they had been involved in, and noticed that different people described an event in different ways. I began wondering whether I could change the way people remembered their own accidents as a function of the words I used to describe the event. The experiments that I did showed that indeed people's memories for these sorts of events could be modified rather easily. I owe a great debt to the colleague who suggested the title for the article that described this work: "Reconstruction of automobile destruction." (*Elizabeth Loftus, University of Washington*)

As we shall see in Chapter 5, psychiatrists and clinical psychologists are not immune to these powerful, unwitting human tendencies. Indeed, we all *selectively notice, interpret, and recall events in ways which sustain our ideas*. Such are the gymnastics which our minds perform to perpetuate our beliefs.

Does knowing how our preconceptions affect the way we notice, interpret, and recall events suggest any helpful implications? Consider these: If explaining why our beliefs might be true tends to freeze our beliefs, then perhaps we could compensate for this bias by forcing ourselves also to explain why an opposing belief might be true. Or, if this is too difficult, we can ask people who hold an opposing belief to explain how the world looks from their perspective. Lee Ross and Mark Lepper (1980) further advise that we compensate for our belief-confirming bias by going out of our way to skeptically test evidence that supports our beliefs. We might even conduct crude experiments to test our beliefs. For example, if we think our child's nightmares result from television watching, then we might randomly designate TV and non-TV days and note the consequences.

WE OVERESTIMATE THE ACCURACY OF OUR JUDGMENTS

We have seen how easily we can form false impressions of (1) what we have thought and felt in the past, (2) why we do what we do, and (3) what we will do. And we have seen how our beliefs control our perceptions, interpretations, and memories. Such tendencies help create another illusion of human thought.

The Overconfidence Phenomenon

The intellectual conceit evident in our judgments of our past knowledge (the I-knew-it-all-along phenomenon described in Chapter 1) extends to estimates of our current knowledge. For example, Daniel Kahneman and Amos Tversky (1979) gave people factual questions (similar to the one in Box 4-3) asking them to fill in the blanks—for example, "I feel 98 percent certain that the air distance between New Delhi and Peking is more than ______ miles but less than ______ miles."

Box 4-3

The Overconfidence Phenomenon

Pose this factual question to a sample of people.

How many Japanese cars were imported into the U.S. in 1980?

(1) Make a high estimate such that you feel there is only a 1 percent probability the true answer would exceed your estimate.

(2) Make a low estimate such that you feel there is only a 1 percent probability the true answer would be below this estimate.

In other words, the people are asked to respond with a range of figures broad enough to make them feel 98 percent sure that the true figure will be included. Nevertheless, about 30 percent of the time, the true answer to such questions (1.9 million for this question) lies outside this range.

The people apparently failed to appreciate the extent to which errors would creep into their reasoning: About 30 percent of the time, the true answers to the questions lay outside the range in which people felt 98 percent confident. When Baruch Fischhoff, Paul Slovic, and Sarah Lichtenstein (1977) asked University of Oregon students to indicate their certainty while answering factual multiple-choice questions, the same *overconfidence phenomenon* occurred. The actual probability of their choosing the right answer was typically much less than they estimated. This finding has now been observed in several experiments; if people's answers to a question are actually only 60 percent correct, they will typically *feel* 75 percent sure.

Overconfidence phenomenon: *The tendency to be more confident than correct—to overestimate the accuracy of one's beliefs.*

Why Are We Overconfident?

Overconfidence is an accepted fact in experimental psychology (Fischhoff, 1982). The issue now is what produces it. Why, given our fallibility, are we so confident of our judgments? Why does experience not lead us to a more realistic self-appraisal? There are a number of reasons (Einhorn & Hogarth, 1978). For one thing, people are not inclined to seek out information that might disprove what they believe. P. C. Wason (1960) demonstrated this, as you can, by giving people a sequence of three numbers—2, 4, 6—which conformed to a rule he had in mind (the rule was simply three ascending numbers). To enable the people to discover the rule, Wason allowed each person to generate sets of three numbers. Each time Wason told the person whether the set did or didn't conform to the rule. When sure they had discovered the rule, the people were to stop and announce it. The result? Seldom right, but never in doubt: Twenty-three out of twenty-nine people convinced themselves of a wrong rule. They had formed some erroneous belief about what Wason's rule was (for example, counting by twos) and then searched for only *confirming* evidence (for example, 8, 10, 12) rather than attempting to *disconfirm* their hunches. Other experiments confirm that *it is hard for us to discard our ideas*. We are eager to verify our beliefs, but we are not inclined to seek evidence which might disprove our beliefs.

"When you know a thing, to hold that you know it; and when you do not know a thing, to allow that you do not know it: this is knowledge."

Confucius, Analects

This preference for confirming information helps explain why our self-images are so remarkably stable. In experiments at the University of Texas at Austin, William Swann and Stephen Read (1981a; 1981b) discovered that students rather consistently seek, elicit, and recall feedback that confirms their beliefs about themselves. Swann and Read liken their findings to how someone with a domineering self-image might behave at a party. Upon arriving, the person *seeks* those guests whom she knows acknowledge her dominance. In conversation she then presents her views in ways that *elicit* the respect she has come to expect. After the party, she has trouble recalling conversations in which her influence was minimal and more easily *recalls* her persuasiveness in the conversations that she dominated. Thus, she believes that her self-image has been strongly confirmed.

Overconfidence in Everyday Life

In everyday life, what *actually* happens more readily catches our attention than what *doesn't* happen. For example, most people do reasonably well at their jobs. Therefore managers may feel confident of their ability to identify promising applicants; as they scan their employees, they are gratified by how well most are doing. The managers cannot examine those they did not hire, so it is difficult to imagine how managers could disconfirm any overconfidence in their hiring ability (Slovic, 1972). Similarly, stock experts, armed with the lastest scoop, market their services with the confident presumption that they can beat the stock market average. But, incredible as it may seem, economist Burton Malkiel (1975) reports that "over long periods of time mutual fund portfolios [which are selected by the best investment analysts in the business] have not outperformed randomly selected groups of stocks."

Editors' assessments of manuscripts also reveal the surprising amount of error in human judgment. In psychology, for example, studies have revealed that there is usually a distressingly modest relationship between one reviewer's evaluation of a manuscript and a second reviewer's evaluation. It's not just true of psychology. Writer Chuck Ross (1979), using a pseudonym, mailed a typewritten copy of Jerzy Kosinski's novel *Steps* to twenty-eight major publishers and literary agencies. All rejected it, including Random House, which had published the book in 1968 and watched it win the National Book Award and sell more than 400,000 copies. The novel came closest to being accepted by Houghton Mifflin, publisher of three other Kosinski novels:

"The wise know too well their weakness to assume infallibility; and he who knows most, knows best how little he knows."

Thomas Jefferson, Writings

"For years I was afraid of overconfidence, but when I finally gave in to it, it wasn't bad at all."

Overconfidence has its benefits as well as its costs. (Drawing by Lorenz; © 1978 *The New Yorker* Magazine, Inc.)

"Several of us read your untitled novel here with admiration for writing and style. Jerzy Kosinski comes to mind as a point of comparison. . . . The drawback to the manuscript, as it stands, is that it doesn't add up to a satisfactory whole."

Remedies for Overconfidence

What constructive lessons can we draw from research on overconfidence? One might be to downplay other people's dogmatic statements. When people are absolutely sure that they are right, we might read it as an 85 percent chance of their being correct (Fischhoff, 1982). But the accuracy of this adjustment depends on the person and the judgment: Sometimes people who feel 100 percent sure are indeed 100 percent right; sometimes the odds of their being right are less than 85 percent.

Regarding the atomic bomb: *"That is the biggest fool thing we have ever done. The bomb will never go off, and I speak as an expert in explosives."*

Admiral William Leahy to President Truman, 1945

In experiments, two techniques have successfully reduced the overconfidence bias. Training people by giving them prompt feedback on the accuracy of their judgments seems to help (Lichtenstein & Fischhoff, 1980). In everyday life, weather forecasters and those who predict the odds in horse racing both receive clear, daily feedback on the accuracy of their predictions—and experts in both of these groups do quite well at estimating the probable accuracy of their predictions (Fischhoff, 1982). Another way to reduce the overconfidence bias is to get people to think of one good reason why their judgments might be wrong, thus forcing them to consider disconfirming information (Koriat, Lichtenstein, & Fischhoff, 1980). Perhaps managers could therefore foster more realistic judgments by insisting that all proposals and recommendations include reasons why they might not work.

Still, we should be careful lest we undermine people's self-confidence to a point where they spend too much time in self-analysis, or where self-doubts begin to cripple their decisiveness. Overconfidence can cost us, but like other biases, it has its adaptive benefits, too.

ANECDOTES ARE OFTEN MORE PERSUASIVE THAN FACTUAL DATA

A panel of psychologists interviewed a sample of thirty engineers and seventy lawyers, and summarized their impressions in thumbnail descriptions of those individuals. The following description has been drawn at random from the sample of thirty engineers and seventy lawyers:

Jack is a thirty-nine-year-old man.

Question: What is the probability that Jack is a lawyer rather than an engineer?

Given no more information than this about Jack, most people surmise that the chances of his being a lawyer are 70 percent, if indeed that is the frequency (or "base-rate") of lawyers in the sample from which he was drawn.

But what do you suppose happens if we add some irrelevant anecdotal information about Jack?

Jack is a thirty-nine-year-old man. He is married with no children. A man of high ability and high motivation, he promises to be quite successful in his field. He is well liked by his colleagues.

Many people recognize that this information contains no clues as to whether Jack is a lawyer or engineer, for they typically say that it's about 50-50 which he is—*regardless* of whether they were told his group was 70 percent lawyers or 30 percent lawyers (Kahneman & Tversky, 1973). This illustrates the extent to which we use even useless anecdotal information and ignore abstract (for example, statistical) information.

Our Use of Useless Information

Our willingness to ignore useful information and use useless information is also apparent in some amusing new experiments. Ellen Langer, Arthur Blank, and Benzion Chanowitz (1978), had an experimenter make a simple request of people about to use a copying machine. Of those approached with, "Excuse me, I have five pages. May I use the Xerox machine?," 40 percent declined the request. But only 7 percent refused when the request was accompanied by a nonsensical justification: "Excuse me, I have five pages. May I use the Xerox machine, because I have to make copies?" This request, Langer explains, fits a well-learned script: Help someone—if a reason is given.

Consider also the following two questions, adapted from an experiment by Henry Zukier (1982; Nisbett, Zukier, & Lemley, 1981).

Roberta is a university student who spends about three hours studying outside of classes in an average week. What would you guess her grade point average to be?

Judith is a university student who spends about three hours studying outside of classes in an average week. Judith has four plants in the place she's living in now. On an average weekday, she goes to sleep around midnight. She has a brother and two sisters. Two months was the longest period of time she dated one person. She describes herself as being often a cheerful person. What would you guess her grade point average to be?

The first question has but one bit of useful information. Those given it usually estimated low grades. People given questions such as the second did not believe there is any connection between how many plants one has and grade average. Yet, when such worthless information was added to the useful information about study time it diluted the impact of the useful information—so much so that it no longer made much difference whether the hypothetical student was said to study three or thirty-one hours per week!

Thomas Gilovich (1981) observed a similar use of useless information when he asked California sportswriters and football coaches to judge the professional potential of hypothetical college football players. Gilovich was disturbed to discover that judgments were affected not only by relevant information concerning the player's ability, but also by such trivia as whether the player came from the same hometown as a well-known professional player.

The Persuasive Power of Vivid Information

As this last experiment indicates, specific, anecdotal information can have great persuasive power. Researchers Richard Nisbett and Eugene Borgida (Nisbett et al., 1976), exploring the tendency to overuse anecdotal information, showed University of Michigan students videotaped interviews of people who were supposedly subjects in experiments. For instance, in one actual experiment most subjects failed to assist a seizure victim. Being told how most subjects really acted had almost no effect upon people's predictions of how the individual they observed acted. The apparent niceness of this individual was more vivid and compelling than the general truth about how most subjects really acted: "Ted seems so pleasant that I can't imagine him being unresponsive to another's plight." This illustrates the *base-rate fallacy*: Focusing upon the specific individual seemed to push into the background useful information about the population the person came from.

Base-rate fallacy: *The tendency to ignore or underuse base-rate information (information that describes most people), and instead to be influenced by distinctive features of the case being judged.*

There is, of course, a positive side to viewing other individuals as individuals and not merely as statistical units. But a problem arises when we formulate our beliefs about people in general from our observations of particular persons; preoccupation with individuals can easily distort our perception of what is generally true. Our impressions of a group, for example, tend to be overly influenced by extreme members of the group. This was clearly the case when one man's attempt to assassinate President Reagan caused people to bemoan, "It's not safe to walk the streets anymore," and that "There's a sickness in the American soul." As psychologist Gordon Allport put it, "Given a thimbleful of facts we rush to make generalizations as large as a tub."

Based on recent research we can now state the principle more formally: People are slow to deduce particular instances from a general truth, but are remarkably quick to infer general truth from a vivid instance. One University of Michigan study presented students with a vivid welfare case—a magazine article about a ne'er-do-well Puerto Rican woman who had a succession of unruly children sired by a succession of common-law husbands. When this case was set against factual statistics about welfare cases—for example, information indicating that, contrary to this case, 90 percent of welfare recipients in her age bracket "are off the welfare rolls by the end of four years"—the facts had less effect on people's opinions about the laziness and hopelessness of welfare recipients than did the single vivid case (Hamill, Wilson, & Nisbett, 1980).

"Examples work more forcibly on the mind than precepts."

Henry Fielding, Joseph Andrews

Or ponder this: Borgida and Nisbett (1977) have found that student impressions of potential teachers are influenced more by a few personal testimonies concerning the teacher than by a comprehensive statistical summary of many students' evaluations. This is not to say that people totally ignore general, statistical information (Borgida & Brekke, 1981). But what do you suppose happened when, after being told that the average rating by 112 students in a "Learning and Memory" course was between "very good" and "excellent," some students also heard two or three students from the course express their feelings directly ("I thought the course was too simplistic. . . .")? The two face-to-face testimonies should simply have increased the statistical summary by two more persons, right? To the contrary, the two or three testimonies had more impact than the statistically summarized testimonials of many more people.

Before buying my new car I consulted the *Consumer Reports* survey of car owners and found the repair record of the Dodge Colt, which for a time I considered, to be quite good. A short while later, I mentioned my interest in the Colt to a student. "Oh no," he moaned, "don't consider a Colt. I worked in a gas station last summer and serviced two Dodge Colts that kept falling apart and being brought in for one thing after another." How did I use this information—and the glowing testimonies from two friends who were Honda owners? Did I simply increment the *Consumer Reports* surveys of Colt and Honda owners by an iota of two more each? Although I knew that, logically, that is what I should have done, it was nearly impossible to downplay my consciousness of these vivid accounts.

People's individual testimonies are more compelling than general information partly because vivid information more deeply etches itself upon the mind (Reyes, Thompson, & Bower, 1980). Consider these questions:

Question 1: Does the letter k appear more often as the first letter of a word or as the third letter?

Question 2: What percent of deaths in the U.S. each year are due to:
_____ accidents
_____ cardiovascular diseases (e.g., heart attacks and strokes)?

Question 3: Pretend a stranger told you about a person who is short, slim, and likes to read poetry and then asked you to guess whether this person is a professor of classics at an Ivy League university or a truck driver. Which would be your best guess?

People's answers (see Box 4-4) usually reflect the misleading persuasive power of the vivid information contained in these questions. Researchers now believe that such anecdotal information is persuasive not only because it is usually more vivid than general information, but also because it often seems more

Box 4-4

The Persuasive Power of Vivid Instances

Answer to Question 1: The letter k is three times more likely to appear as the third letter. Yet, most people judge that k appears more often at the beginning of a word. We can more easily recall words beginning with k, surmise Amos Tversky and Daniel Kahneman (1974), and ease of recall is our basis for judging the frequency of events.

Answer to Question 2: Cardiovascular diseases cause ten times as many deaths as accidents: 50 percent versus 5 percent. Most people overestimate the relative frequency of accidents, which are more vivid and memorable.

Answer to Question 3: Most people guess the professor, thus committing the common error of giving too much weight to the vivid information and underusing their general knowledge of the number of truck drivers. There are obviously at least several thousand times as many truck drivers as Ivy League classics professors. Thus there are sure to be many times more truck drivers who fit the description, even if the description is hundreds of times more typical of classics professors.

specifically relevant (Bar-Hillel, 1980; Borgida & Brekke, 1981; Tversky & Kahneman, 1980).

After these vivid examples of the "vividness effect," some words of caution are in order. First, what we mean by "vividness" is not altogether clear. Is it emotional interest to the perceiver? Is it the concreteness of the stimulus? Second, Shelley Taylor and Suzanne Thompson (1982) report that the supposedly greater impact of vivid information is actually rather elusive in laboratory experiments. They surmise that this is because experimenters typically have the undivided attention of their subjects, whether presenting them with vivid information or with non-vivid information. In everyday life vivid and non-vivid information compete for our attention, with the vivid information usually winning. Finally, Taylor and Thompson remind us that for a vivid message to be persuasive it is the message itself that must be vivid, not its presentation. After hearing a dull message delivered by a flamboyant speaker, one may remember the medium but not the message.

A vivid, but unrepresentative, example of the value of a lottery ticket. Louis Eisenberg gets a kiss from his wife after winning $5 million on a $1 New York State Lotto ticket. (Wide World Photos)

Our predisposition to have our attention drawn by striking testimonials and anecdotes has implications for everyday life. Thus state lotteries, which return less than half of the billions of dollars they take in, exploit the impact of a few winners. Because the statistical reality always stays buried in the back of people's minds, the lottery system seduces people into perceiving a lottery ticket as having a much greater earnings potential than it actually does.

Donald Elman and Jeffrey Killebrew (1978) demonstrated a similar insensitivity to statistical reality among Ohio drivers. They observed nearly 5000 cars leaving store parking lots. When no reminder was given to use seat belts, only about 15 percent of the drivers did so. People given a leaflet as they left the store, reminding them to "SAVE A LIFE—BUCKLE YOUR SEAT BELT TODAY!!" were no more likely to buckle up. Others were given the same leaflet with an incentive added: "The Northeastern Ohio Safety Project will give a GIFT CERTIFICATE to every second driver who is wearing a seat belt when leaving this parking lot." Of these, nearly three times as many, 41 percent, were seat-belted when they reached the exit. Still others received a leaflet promising the gift certificate to every 100th driver wearing a seat belt. Did the unlikelihood of this incentive demolish its effect? Hardly. The astonishing result was that virtually as many of these people—37 percent—were belted as they drove out.

Constructive Applications

The impact of a vivid anecdote is well known to effective speakers and writers. A vivid image can bring to life the general truth that it illustrates. As William Strunk and E. B. White (1979) assert in their classic, *The Elements of Style*.

> If those who have studied the art of writing are in accord on any one point, it is on this: the surest way to arouse and hold the attention of the reader is by being specific, definite, and concrete. The greatest writers—Homer, Dante, Shakespeare—are effective largely because they deal in particulars. (p. 21)

Concrete examples are not only more attention-getting, they are also better remembered. Joanne Martin (1982) observed that even *concepts* are better remembered when concrete details are included. She had Coast Guard recruits read one of the following paragraphs and then write everything they could recall from it. Those who read an abstract description of what happens when a Coast Guard regulation is broken recalled only 27 percent of the words afterwards:

> If a new Seaman Apprentice breaks a Coast Guard regulation, and this frequently happens, then he usually gets caught. If he gives serious personal excuses for what he did, then the Executive Officer usually refers the matter to mast. Usually in these cases the defendant is found guilty. If the new Seaman Apprentice is found guilty, then he will be sentenced with a variety of punishments.

Other recruits read a concrete instance of this information:

> Robert Christensen, a new Seaman Apprentice, reported for duty on the CG Cutter Seagull two days late. His excuse for being late was that his father had become seriously ill while he was visiting home. The Executive Officer did not accept his excuse. He referred the matter to mast. Seaman Apprentice Christensen was found guilty and sentenced to one month extra duty, a $50 fine each month for two months, and one month restriction.

Can you feel the difference? Those given this anecdotal paragraph not only recalled almost twice as many words as those given the abstract paragraph, they also were about twice as likely to recall important points such as "found guilty."

Teachers have learned by experience that engaging everyday examples of basic principles help students grasp the principles. Vivid instances and testimonials have a rich, compelling quality—sometimes so rich and compelling that we are persuaded even when those instances are grossly unrepresentative of human experience. Recently, after a National Cancer Institute study showed Laetrile to be an ineffective cancer treatment, a U.S. senator objected: "I know of a person who had skin cancer, who was diagnosed as a terminal case. The person took Laetrile and she's alive two years later" (Sun, 1981).

ILLUSIONS OF CAUSATION, CORRELATION, AND PERSONAL CONTROL

Our vulnerability to error in our social thinking is further increased by three more types of illusory thinking.

Correlation and Causation

The first of these illusions was discussed in Chapter 1: the nearly irresistible temptation to assume that two events which occur together are necessarily causally connected. Recall that there is a relationship between people's educational attainments and their earnings, between certain child-rearing styles and the personalities of children thus brought up, and between self-esteem and academic achievement. But, having discerned these relationships, we too readily jump to the conclusion that education pays financial dividends, that specific child-rearing styles have predictable effects, and that achievement can be boosted by improved self-esteem.

Sometimes a mere coincidental association between two events induces a false conviction that one causes the other. Experiments with animals, children, and adults demonstrate that the power of coincidence can produce superstitious behaviors. If an act, such as a good-luck ritual, just happens to be performed before the occurrence of a rewarding event, one could easily assume that the act *caused* the reward. Such a presumption can incline an animal or person to perform that act ever more frequently, and thus increase the probability that the act will again be performed shortly before the reward comes. (This is part of the magic of experimental psychology—pulling habits out of a rat.) Of course, only very occasionally will a reward indeed follow the behavior. But this erratic, "partial reinforcement," as experimental psychologists call it, is especially conducive to persistent behavior.

In the best-known experimental study of superstitious behavior, B. F. Skinner (1948) presented food to hungry pigeons every fifteen seconds for a few minutes each day. Can you guess what happened? Remember that the food appeared at regular intervals, regardless of the bird's behavior. In Skinner's words:

> In six out of eight cases the resulting responses were so clearly defined that two observers could agree perfectly in counting instances. One bird was conditioned to turn counter-clockwise about the cage, making two or three turns between reinforcements. Another repeatedly thrust its head into one of the upper corners of the cage. A third developed a 'tossing' response, as if placing its head beneath an invisible bar and lifting it repeatedly. Two birds developed a pendulum motion of the head and body, in which the head was extended forward and swung from right to left with a sharp movement followed by a somewhat slower return. . . . Another bird was conditioned to make incomplete pecking or brushing movements directed toward but not touching the floor.

Perhaps if we had walked into the laboratory at this point, we would have diagnosed the pigeons as severely neurotic. What produced these strange behaviors? Whatever the bird was doing as the food tray appeared was, of course, strengthened, and therefore more likely than other behaviors to recur and be further reinforced fifteen seconds later.

Over time, the superstitious behavior sometimes gradually shifted to a different act. One bird added a hopping step to its sequence. When the food tray was presented once every minute, the bird would hop vigorously for the forty seconds preceding the appearance of the food. It was no small effort to convince the bird that this behavior was ineffectual. After the food mechanism was turned off, the bird hopped more than ten thousand times before quitting! Said Skinner:

> The bird behaves as if there were a causal relation between its behavior and the presentation of food, although such a relation is lacking. There are many analogies in human behavior. Rituals for changing one's luck at cards are good examples. A few accidental connections between a ritual and favorable consequences suffice to set up and maintain the behavior in spite of many unreinforced instances. The bowler who has released a ball down the alley but continues to behave as if he were controlling it by twisting and turning his arm and shoulder is another case in point. These behaviors have, of course, no real effect upon one's luck or upon a ball half way down the alley, just as in the present case the food would appear as often if the pigeon did nothing—or, more strictly speaking, did something else.

Subsequent laboratory experiments confirm that children and adults will develop superstitious behaviors in much the same way. In one study, preschool children were given a piece of candy after pressing a red button or a blue button, or both, for a combined total of thirty responses (Zeiler, 1972). Next, the rules were changed, and for a brief period of time the children were rewarded for *not pressing* the *blue* button. Most of the children then came to press the red button at a high rate, even though these responses were irrelevant. There were a few exceptions. One child dropped a piece of candy on the floor and left the apparatus to crawl around and search for it. While he was doing so, the next piece of candy was delivered on schedule. He then spent the rest of the experimental session crawling around the floor, reaching up to get the candy after each delivery.

All of us engage in harmless superstitious behaviors from time to time. If a tragedy does not occur while one wears a rabbit's foot, the "success" of that ritual may prompt its continuation. The coach wins a couple of big games while wearing red socks and thereafter continues the practice. Near Seattle, on the island where I grew up, we all had our "lucky fishing spots"—where we had once caught a good-sized salmon. There we continued fishing, eventually catching more. George Gmelch (1978) has described the superstitious behaviors of baseball pitchers and hitters. Pitching and hitting involve

Superstitious beliefs can arise when correlation is confused with causation. (© 1963 United Feature Syndicate, Inc.)

considerable chance and uncertainty and thus are much more vulnerable to the development of superstitious behavior than is fielding, where the player's personal control is much higher and the success rate is already near perfection (.975 on the average).

Illusory Correlation

Illusory correlation: *Perception of a relationship where none exists, or perception of a stronger relationship than actually exists.*

Our confusion concerning correlation-causation is often compounded by our susceptibility to perceiving correlation where none exists. When we expect to see significant relationships we easily misperceive random events as significantly related. As part of their research with the Bell Telephone Laboratories, William Ward and Herbert Jenkins (1965) showed people the results of a hypothetical fifty-day cloud seeding experiment. They told their subjects which of the fifty days the clouds had been seeded and which of the days it had rained. This information was nothing more than a random mix of results; sometimes it rained after seeding, sometimes it didn't. People nevertheless were convinced—in conformity with their intuitive supposition about the effects of cloud seeding—that they really had observed a relationship between cloud seeding and rain.

Other experiments confirm that people easily misperceive random events as confirming their beliefs (Crocker, 1981; Jennings, Amabile, & Ross, 1982). When we believe a correlation exists between two things, we are more likely to notice and recall confirming than disconfirming instances. The joint occurrence of two unusual events—say the premonition of a strange event and the subsequent occurrence of that event—is especially likely to be noticed and remembered, far more than all the times those unusual events do not coincide. Hence, we easily overestimate the frequency with which these strange

Box 4-5

Finding Order in Random Events

If someone were to flip a coin six times, would one of these sequences of heads (H) and tails (T) be more likely than the other two: HHHTTT or HTTHTH or HHHHHH?

Daniel Kahneman and Amos Tversky (1972) found that HTTHTH and its reverse seem more likely to people than the other possible sequences. Actually, all possible sequences are equally likely.

things happen. If, after we think about a friend, that friend calls us, we are far more likely to notice and remember this coincidence than all the times we think of a friend without any ensuing call, or receive a call from a friend about whom we have not been thinking.

The difficulty we have recognizing coincidental, random events for what they are predisposes us to perceive order even when we are shown a purely random series of events. (See Box 4-5.) For example, bridge players would find it extraordinary if they were dealt a hand with all cards of one suit. In reality, this is no more unlikely than any other hand they might be dealt.

A more serious example of people "discovering" order in random events comes from World War II. During Germany's bombing blitz on England, Londoners developed elaborate theories of where the Germans were aiming. However, when London was later divided up into small, geographic areas, bomb hits per area were seen to have occurred in a purely random pattern (Feller, 1968).

Illusion of Control

Illusion of control: *Perception of uncontrollable events as subject to one's control, or as more controllable than they are.*

Our tendency to perceive random events as though they were related feeds the frequent illusion that chance events are subject to our personal control. Already we have seen an example of an illusion of control—superstitious behavior. During recent droughts in England and in the United States the news media reported several instances of rain dances, a few of which were followed by rain. In some prescientific cultures rain dances have occurred frequently enough to receive occasional reinforcement. This is usually enough to maintain them, especially since the believer has ways of accounting for failures.

Ellen Langer (1977) has demonstrated the illusion of control with experiments on gambling behavior. People were easily seduced into believing they could beat chance. If they chose a lottery number for themselves they demanded four times as much money for the sale of their lottery ticket as

"The next dance you will see is for partly cloudy conditions with moderating temperatures."

The illusion of control. (Drawing by Peter Steiner © 1979, *Saturday Review*)

people whose number was assigned by the experimenter. If they played a game of chance against an awkward and nervous person, they were willing to bet significantly more than when playing against a dapper, confident opponent. In these and other ways, Langer consistently observed that people act as if they can control chance events.

Observations of real-life gamblers have confirmed these experimental findings. Dice players often behave as if they could control the outcome by throwing softly for low numbers and hard for high numbers (Henslin, 1967). Putting the experimental results to practical use, Langer suggests that state lotteries can maximize betting by giving participants maximum choice on their tickets—letting people choose their own lucky numbers. The extent to which the gambling industry thrives because gamblers are victimized by their illusion of control is strong testimony to how resistant to reason the phenomenon is. Gamblers' hopes that they can beat the laws of chance sustain their gambling. Even the gambling industry itself can suffer the illusion: Las Vegas table dealers who experience a string of losses for the house have sometimes lost their jobs (Goffman, 1967).

Another of Langer's studies indicates that if people experience some unusual early successes in a chance situation, later failures may be discounted (Langer & Roth, 1975). People predicted the outcomes of thirty coin tosses. Langer rigged the feedback so that some people experienced mostly wins during the first ten flips while others experienced either mostly losses or a random sequence of wins and losses. Across all thirty trials, however, each person accumulated the same total outcome: fifteen wins and fifteen losses.

BEHIND THE SCENES

Ellen J. Langer

Imagine the following scenario. It was the fifth hand of a poker game with colleagues at Yale. I accidentally missed a person when dealing the cards around the table. I quickly remedied the situation by dealing the next card to that individual. Despite the fact that all the cards on the table were still face down, everyone yelled "misdeal." They all clearly understood my arguments that it made no difference which card the individual was dealt. Nevertheless, they insisted that I deal the game over so that everyone got the cards that "rightfully belonged" to them. Curious about this, I started to watch for similar behavior and was surprised at how prevalent it was. I was not the only one who pressed the already lit button in the elevator! The question this provoked was: If it is so important for people to feel control that they won't even relinquish it in chance situations, then what does this say about people who characteristically are denied the opportunity to exercise control? The populations I focused on were hospital patients and the elderly. The studies were designed so as to enable these populations to develop a real sense of control. When the hand was redealt and all the cards were on the table, everyone felt this resulted in a better deal for all. (*Ellen J. Langer, Harvard University*)

Nonetheless, those who started with a fairly consistent sequence of wins made inflated estimates of how many flips they had actually predicted and how many they could predict given another hundred trials. Having experienced early success, people evidently came to perceive themselves as skilled, and therefore did not give as much weight to later failures. It appears that the motivation to see events as controllable is so strong that just one cue like early positive results can induce an illusion of control over what is obviously a mere chance task.

In my home we have occasionally flipped a coin to settle disputes. At one point my older son began arguing that he always lost coin tosses. I reminded him that each flip was a 50-50 proposition. To my dismay, he suffered several more consecutive losses. No amount of rational persuasion could then convince him that he really had a 50-50 chance on the next toss. What makes Langer's results so striking is that her subjects were not ten-year-old boys, but educated Yale University students.

Tversky and Kahneman (1974) have identified another way by which an illusion of control may arise: We fail to recognize the statistical phenomenon of *regression toward the average* even though it often occurs in real life. The phenomenon is simply illustrated: Most students who have obtained extremely high scores on an exam will obtain lower scores on the next exam. Their first scores are at the ceiling and thus each student's second score is more likely to fall back ("regress") toward his or her own average than to push the ceiling even higher. (This is why a student who does consistently good work, even if never the best, will sometimes end a course at the top of the class.) Conversely, those who do worst on the first exam are likely to improve. Thus if those who scored lowest are tutored after the first exam, the tutors are likely to be rewarded for their efforts, even if the tutoring had no effect.

Regression toward the average: *The statistical tendency for extreme scores or extreme behavior to fall back toward one's average.*

Likewise, a counselor who is visited by people at their most depressed is more likely to be gratified by their subsequent improvement than to observe further deterioration. When things are desperately bad we will try anything rather than sit passively, and whatever we try—going to a psychotherapist, starting a new diet-exercise plan, reading a self-help book—is more likely to be followed by improvement than by further deterioration. Thus it often seems effective, whether it actually had an effect or not.

Sometimes we do recognize that events can seldom continue at an unusually good or bad extreme. Experience has taught us that when everything is going great, something will go wrong, and that when life is dealing us terrible blows we can usually look forward to things getting better. Often, though, we fail to recognize this regression effect. A football coach who rewards his team with lavish praise and a light practice after their best game of the season and harrasses them after an exceptionally bad game may soon conclude that rewards lead to poorer performance in the next game while punishments improve performance. Parents and teachers may reach the same conclusion after reacting to unusually good or bad behaviors. It seems, suggest Tversky and Kahneman, that nature operates in such a way that we often feel punished for rewarding others and rewarded for punishing them.

OUR ERRONEOUS BELIEFS MAY GENERATE THEIR OWN REALITY

One additional reason why false beliefs are so resistant to disconfirmation is that our beliefs sometimes lead us to act in ways which elicit their apparent confirmation. In Chapter 3, we noted that this *self-fulfilling prophecy* effect applies to our beliefs about ourselves. People with a strong sense of self-efficacy—who believe in their competence and ability to achieve—do, in fact, achieve more than comparable people who have lower self-expectations. Our beliefs about other people can also be self-fulfilling. In his well-known studies

Self-fulfilling prophecy: *The tendency for one's expectations to evoke behavior that confirms the expectations.*

of "experimenter bias," Robert Rosenthal (1966) demonstrated that research subjects sometimes live up to what is expected of them. For example, in one experiment, subjects judged the successfulness of people in various photographs. Although all the experimenters read the same instructions, those led to expect high ratings nevertheless obtained higher ratings than did experimenters who expected their subjects to see the people as failures. Even more startling—and controversial—have been subsequent reports that teachers' beliefs about their students similarly serve as self-fulfilling prophecies.

Do Teachers' Expectations Affect Their Students?

There is little doubt that teachers do have higher expectations for some students than for others. Perhaps you have detected this after having a brother or sister precede you in school, or from having received a label such as "gifted" or "learning disabled," or when sensing that the conversation in the teachers' lounge sent your reputation ahead of you, or upon learning that the teacher had scrutinized your school file or discovered your family's social status. Do teachers' expectations formed in such ways have any effect upon students? It's clear that teachers' evaluations are *correlated* with student achievement: Teachers think well of students who do well. But are teachers' evaluations more caused *by* or the cause *of* student performance? A study of 4300 British schoolchildren by William Crano and Phyllis Mellon (1978) suggests that the teachers' beliefs are as much a cause as a consequence of their students' performance. High evaluations (especially of the child's social

Teachers' beliefs are a cause as well as a consequence of their students' performance. (© Suzanne Szasz, 1981/Photo Researchers, Inc.)

development) were more likely to be followed by high academic performance than was high performance to be followed by high evaluations.

Could we test this conclusion experimentally? For example, pretend that a teacher is given an erroneous impression that Jane, Sally, Johnny, and Manuel, four randomly selected students, are unusually capable. Will the teacher then likely give special treatment to these four, thus eliciting superior performance from them? In a now famous experiment, Rosenthal and Lenore Jacobson (1968) reported precisely that. Randomly selected children in a San Francisco elementary school who were said (on the basis of a fictitious test) to be on the verge of a dramatic intellectual spurt did then spurt ahead in IQ score. Since this dramatic result seemed to suggest that the school problems of "disadvantaged" children might merely reflect their teachers' low expectations, the findings were soon publicized in the national media as well as in many college textbooks in psychology and education. But further analysis revealed the teacher-expectations effect to be not so powerful and reliable as this initial study led many to believe. Some critics questioned the IQ measure and the statistical procedures used by Rosenthal and Jacobson (Thorndike, 1968; Elashoff & Snow, 1971). Moreover, by Rosenthal's own count, in only about 30 percent of the published experiments do teachers' expectations significantly affect students (Rosenthal & Rubin, 1978). Thus while some studies find that teachers' expectations do indeed affect students, even more find no demonstrable effect. Evidently, low expectations do not usually doom a capable child, nor do high expectations magically transform a slow learner into a valedictorian. Human nature is not so pliable.

Why do teachers' expectations sometimes affect students? Rosenthal and other investigators report that teachers look, smile, and nod more at "high-potential students." But the effect seems not entirely due to such nonverbal messages. Teachers also may teach more to their "gifted" students, set higher goals for them, call on them more, and give them more time to answer (Rosenthal, 1973; Chaikin & Derlega, 1979).

Reading the experiments on teacher expectations has always made me wonder about the effect of *students'* expectations upon their teachers. You no doubt begin many of your courses well aware of student comments that "Professor Smith is interesting" and "Professor Jones is a bore." Recently, Robert Feldman and Thomas Prohaska (1979; Feldman & Theiss, 1982) demonstrated that such expectations can affect both student and teacher. Students in a learning experiment who expected to be taught by a competent teacher perceived their teacher (who was unaware of their expectations) as more competent and interesting than did students with low expectations; furthermore, the students actually learned more. In a follow-up experiment, Feldman and Prohaska videotaped teachers and had observers later rate their performance. Teachers assigned a student who nonverbally conveyed positive expectations were judged most capable. No doubt there will soon be some actual classroom studies of the effects of students' expectations. Care to predict the results?

Box 4-6

The Self-Fulfilling Psychology of the Stock Market

On the evening of January 6, 1981, Joseph Granville, a popular Florida investment adviser, wired his clients: "Stock prices will nose-dive; sell tomorrow." Word of Granville's advice soon spread, and January 7 became the heaviest day of trading in the history of the New York Stock Exchange. The Dow Jones average dropped 23 points. All told, stock values lost $40 billion.

Nearly a half-century ago, John Maynard Keynes likened such stock market psychology to the popular beauty contests then conducted by London newspapers. To win, one had to pick the six faces out of a hundred that were, in turn, chosen most frequently by the other newspaper contestants. Thus, as Keynes wrote, "Each competitor has to pick not those faces which he himself finds prettiest, but those which he thinks likeliest to catch the fancy of the other competitors."

In like fashion, investors have to pick not simply the stocks that touch their fancy, but the stocks that will find favor among other investors. The name of the game is to predict the behavior of others. As one Wall Street fund manager explained, "You may or may not agree with Granville's view—but that's usually beside the point." If you think his advice will cause others to sell, then you want to sell quickly, before prices drop more. If you expect others to buy, you buy now to beat the rush. Such is the self-fulfilling psychology of the stock market.

NOTE: Adapted from Steve Lohr, "The Puzzling Stock Market," *The New York Times*, January 13, 1981, pp. D1, D9.

Do We Get What We Expect?

We have seen that the expectations of experimenters and teachers are occasionally self-fulfilling. Is there a similar self-confirming effect of our own beliefs about people? Do we tend to get from others what we expect of them? The answer, from studies of social interaction, is a convincing yes.

In laboratory games, hostility nearly always begets hostility: People who perceive their opponents as noncooperative will readily induce them to *be* noncooperative (Kelley & Stahelski, 1970). Self-confirming beliefs abound in times of conflict. Each party's perception of the other as attacking, resentful, and vindictive induces the other to display these behaviors in self-defense, thus creating a vicious self-perpetuating circle. For example, married persons may act in ways that induce each other to confirm their perceptions. Whether I expect my wife to be in a bad mood or in a warm, loving mood may affect how I relate to her, thereby inducing her to confirm my belief.

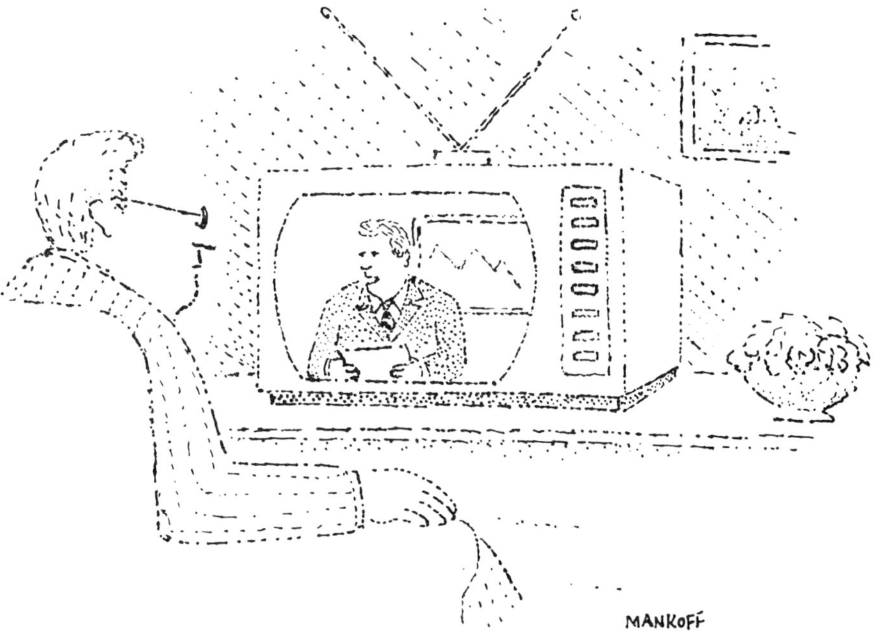

"On Wall Street today, news of lower interest rates sent the stock market up, but then the expectation that these rates would be inflationary sent the market down, until the realization that lower rates might stimulate the sluggish economy pushed the market up, before it ultimately went down on fears that an overheated economy would lead to a reimposition of higher interest rates."

(Drawing by Mankoff; © 1981 *The New Yorker* Magazine, Inc.)

Several experiments conducted by Mark Snyder at the University of Minnesota show how, once formed, erroneous beliefs about the social world can induce others to confirm those beliefs. In one study, Snyder, Elizabeth Tanke, and Ellen Berscheid (1977), had men students talk on the telephone with women they thought (from having been shown a picture) were either attractive or unattractive. Analysis of just the women's comments during the conversations revealed that the women who were presumed attractive did in fact speak in a more warm and likable way than the women who were presumed unattractive. The men's erroneous beliefs had become a self-fulfilling prophecy, leading them to act in a way that influenced the women to fulfill their stereotype that beautiful people are desirable people.

"The error of our eye directs our mind: What error leads must err."

Shakespeare, Troilus and Cressida

In another experiment, Snyder and William Swann (1978a) found that when people interacted with someone who expected them to be hostile, they responded by using a noise weapon more aggressively. When led to see this hostility as a reflection of themselves—for example, when told, "People's use of the noise weapon reflects the type of person they are"—they subsequently were also more hostile to a naive person who had no prior knowledge about them. These experiments help us understand how social beliefs, such as stereotypes about handicapped people or about people of a particular race or sex, may be self-confirming. We help construct our own social realities. How others treat us reflects how we and others have treated them.

As we noted in Chapter 3, our beliefs about *ourselves*—whether we are effective and competent or not—can be similarly self-confirming. In several recent experiments, Steven Sherman (1980) has found that people tend to fulfill predictions they make of their own behavior. For example, when Bloomington, Indiana, residents were called and asked to volunteer three hours to an American Cancer Society drive, only 4 percent agreed to do so. When a comparable group of other residents were called and asked to *predict* how they would react if they were to receive such a request, almost half predicted they would agree to help—and most of these did indeed agree to do so when later they were contacted by the Cancer Society. This not only illustrates a self-serving bias (people overestimated how desirably they would act were they to be approached unforewarned), it also illustrates the self-fulfilling consequences of predicting one's own behavior. Formulating a plan for how we would want to act in a given situation makes it more likely that we will really do it. This suggests several constructive applications. For example, might asking teenagers "What would you do if your friends pressured you to smoke?" enable them to be more self-determined when such a situation actually arises?

CONCLUSIONS

We could extend the list of thinking errors, but I trust this has been a sufficient glimpse of the ease and the manner with which people come to believe what is not true. The threat to our vanity posed by research on the limits and fallacies of human thought is amplified by the fact that most of the participants in these experiments were highly intelligent people, generally students at leading universities. Moreover, these predictable distortions and biases occurred even when they were motivated by money to think optimally. As one researcher concluded, the illusions "have a persistent quality not unlike that of perceptual illusions" (Slovic, 1972).

Research in cognitive social psychology thus mirrors the mixed review given humanity in literature, philosophy, and religion. On the one hand, many research psychologists have spent lifetimes exploring the awesome capacities of the human mind (see Manis, 1977). We are capable of great achievements and impressive insights into nature. We are smart enough to have sent people to the moon. Indeed, our very name, homo sapiens, literally means the wise species. On the other hand, our intuition is more vulnerable to error than we intuitively suspect. With rather incredible ease, we can form and sustain false beliefs.

But have these experiments just been playing intellectual tricks on their hapless participants, thus making their intuitions look worse than they are? Richard Nisbett and Lee Ross (1980) contend that, if anything, the laboratory procedures *overestimate* our intuitive powers. The experiments usually present people with clear evidence and forewarn them that their reasoning ability is being tested. Seldom does life say to us: "Here is some evidence. Now put on your intellectual Sunday best and answer these questions."

Often our everyday failings are inconsequential, but not always so. As the next chapter will illustrate, false impressions, interpretations, and beliefs can produce serious consequences. When making important social judgments—Why are so many people on welfare? Do the Russians desire peace or conquest? Does she (he) love me, or my money?—even small biases can have profound social consequences. Since we know that errors even creep into sophisticated scientific thinking, it seems safe to conclude that none of us is exempt from them. Apparently human nature has not changed since 3000 years ago when the Psalmist observed that "no one can see his own errors." As Winston Churchill wryly observed, "Man will occasionally stumble over the truth, but most of the time he will pick himself up and continue on."

"It ain't so much the things we don't know that get us in trouble. It's the things we know that ain't so."
Nineteenth-century American saying

Lest we succumb to the cynical conclusion that *all* beliefs are absurd, I hasten now to balance the picture. The elegant analyses of the imperfections of our thinking are themselves a tribute to human wisdom. Were one to argue, as an absolute truth, that *all* human thought is illusory, the assertion would be self-refuting, for it, too, would be but an illusion. It would be logically equivalent to contending that all generalizations are false, including this one.

Just as medical science has found it a useful working assumption that any given body organ exists to serve a function, so have behavioral scientists found it useful to assume that our modes of thought and behavior are generally adaptive. The rules of thought which produce so many false convictions and such striking deficiencies in our statistical intuition often serve us well. Frequently, the errors are a by-product of our minds' strategies for simplifying the complex information it receives. Herbert Simon (1957) was among the modern researchers who first described the bounds of human reason. Simon contends that to cope with reality we simplify it. Consider the awesome complexity of a chess game, for example. A game can unfold in an almost infinite variety of ways; the number of possible chess games is greater than the number of particles in the universe. How do we cope with such complexity? We adopt some simplifying rules of thumb—called *heuristics*. These heuristics are imperfect—they sometimes lead us into defeat—but they do enable us to make efficient, snap judgments.

Heuristics: *Simple, efficient thinking strategies—rules of thumb. Heuristics help us simplify and cope with complex realities, but in so doing will occasionally lead to costly errors.*

Or consider how our perceptual mechanisms produce visual illusions. For example, the clarity of an object helps determine its perceived distance. This is usually a valid rule because in any scene, distant objects *are* seen less sharply than near objects. But our reliance on this heuristic sometimes distorts our perceptions. If visibility is poor and objects become blurred, distances are overestimated, sometimes causing accidents.

Illusory thinking can likewise spring from heuristics that are generally useful and may even facilitate our survival. The belief in one's power to control events helps maintain hope and effort where despair might otherwise prevail. If things are sometimes subject to control and sometimes not, we will maximize our outcomes by "positive thinking." Optimistic thinking pays dividends, which is probably why it has been selected and retained during the history of our species.

We might even say that our beliefs are like scientific theories—sometimes in error, yet useful as generalizations. To say that a theory (or a way of thinking) is imperfect is not to say it should be discarded. Yet, just as we constantly seek to improve our theories, might we not also work to reduce error in our social thinking? In school, math teachers teach, teach, teach, until the mind is finally trained to process numerical information accurately and automatically. We assume that such ability does not come naturally, else why bother with the years of training? Research psychologist Robyn Dawes (1980)—who is dismayed that "study after study has shown [that] people have very limited abilities to process information on a conscious level, particularly social information"—suggests that we should also teach, teach, teach how to process social information.

"To be conscious that you are ignorant is a great step to knowledge."

Benjamin Disraeli, Sybil

Richard Nisbett and Lee Ross (1980) believe that such education could indeed reduce our vulnerability to certain types of error. As a beginning, they propose that people first be trained to recognize likely sources of error in their own social intuition. Such is precisely the constructive intent of this chapter. Second, they advocate statistics courses that are geared to everyday problems of logic and social judgment. Third, they suggest that such teaching will be most effective when richly illustrated with concrete, vivid anecdotes and examples from everyday life. Finally, they suggest teaching memorable and useful slogans, such as:

"It's an empirical question." In other words, hunches need to be checked against the relevant data.

"Which hat did you draw that sample out of?" In other words, vivid but unrepresentative samples are suspect. Also: "You can lie with statistics, but a well-chosen example does the job better."

"Beware the fundamental attribution error." In other words, consider the actor's situation before jumping to conclusions about his disposition. Also: "What would you have done if you were in her shoes?"

SUMMING UP

Research psychologists have for a long time explored the mind's awesome capacity for processing information. Recently, researchers in "cognitive social psychology" have turned their attention to the errors we typically make when processing information. Since we are generally unaware of how errors enter our thinking, an examination of our "illusory thinking" can be revealing and, if it helps improve our thinking, beneficial.

This chapter described six ways in which we form and sustain false beliefs—"reasons for unreason," we might call them. First, we often do not know why we do what we do. In experiments, people whose attitudes have been changed will often deny that they have been influenced; they will insist that how they feel now is how they have always felt. When powerful influences upon our behavior are not so conspicuous that any observer could spot them, we too can be oblivious to what has affected us.

Second, our preconceptions help govern our interpretations and memories. In experiments, people's prejudgments have striking effects upon how they perceive and interpret information. Other experiments have planted judgments or false ideas in people's minds *after* they have been given information. These experiments reveal that just as before-the-fact judgments bias our perceptions and interpretations, so do after-the-fact judgments bias our recall.

Third, we tend to overestimate the accuracy of our judgments. This "overconfidence phenomenon" seems partly due to the much greater ease with which we can imagine why we might be right than why we might be wrong. Moreover, people are more likely to search for information that can confirm their beliefs than information that can disconfirm them.

Fourth, vivid anecdotes and testimonies can be powerfully persuasive, often more so than factual data drawn from a much broader sample of people. This is apparently due to the attention-getting power of vivid information, and to the ease with which we later recall it.

Fifth, we are often swayed by illusions of causation, correlation, and personal control. It is tempting to perceive causal connnections among events which are merely correlated (the "correlation-causation" fallacy), to perceive correlations where none exist ("illusory correlation"), and to think we can control events which are really beyond our control (the "illusion of control").

Finally, erroneous beliefs may generate their own reality. Studies of experimenter bias and teacher expectations indicate that at least sometimes an erroneous belief that certain people are unusually capable (or incapable) can lead one to give special treatment to those people. This may elicit superior (or inferior) performance, and therefore seem to confirm an assumption that is actually false. Similarly, in everyday social affairs we often get what we expect.

These six sources of illusory thinking, plus three more considered previously (the I-knew-it-all-along phenomenon, the fundamental attribution error, and the self-serving bias), indicate our capacity for forming and sustaining false beliefs. Often these illusions of human thought are by-products of thinking strategies (called "heuristics") that usually serve us well, just as visual illusions are a by-product of perceptual mechanisms that help us organize sensory information. But they are errors nonetheless, errors that can warp our perceptions of reality and prejudice our judgments of persons.

Chapter

Illusory Thinking in Everyday Life

"Superstition, which is widespread among the nations, has taken advantage of human weakness to cast its spell over the mind of almost every man."

Cicero,
De Divinatione

College students sitting in a lecture are told they are about to be fooled—that a performer will resort to a clever set of tricks to make them believe he can read their minds. The gentleman steps to the front of the room and, true to the prediction, deftly performs his sleight of mind, startling his audience volunteers with eerie revelations about their own thoughts. When the demonstration is over, the lecture hall buzzes with the remarks of excited students who believe they have witnessed a true clairvoyant (B. Singer & Benassi, 1980–81).

How could they have been so gullible? Especially when they have been told outright that the man was a magician? Why, for that matter, are paranormal phenomena so attractive to credulous minds? As in all ages, today's pied pipers need only pipe and there will be people who follow. Our culture is fascinated with claims that defy scientific explanations. Devotees of Edgar Cayce and Jeane Dixon, and believers in dream telepathy, out-of-body experiences, psychokinesis, astrology, demonology, levitation, horoscopes, and ghosts all know that prejudice sometimes prevents scientists from recognizing unexpected truths. Just occasionally a mind-boggling claim turns out to be true.

When confronted with extraordinary claims, we are therefore vulnerable to two errors. Being totally skeptical of all extraordinary claims will sometimes lead us to reject truth. As Hamlet said, "There are more things in heaven and earth, Horatio, than are dreamt of in your philosophy." During the

An amateur magician performing psychic tricks convinced most college students of his psychic powers. (Photograph courtesy of Barry Singer and Victor Benassi.)

eighteenth century, scientists scoffed at the notion that meteorites had extraterrestrial origins. When two Yale scientists dared deviate from the conventional opinion, Thomas Jefferson responded, "Gentlemen, I would rather believe that those two Yankee Professors would lie than to believe that stones fell from heaven" (Diaconis, 1978). Twenty years ago how many of us would have believed claims for cosmic black holes and mysterious subatomic particles? On the other hand, naivete can make us gullible to all sorts of falsehoods. A completely open mind is vulnerable to having garbage thrown in. In times past, people have been convinced that bloodletting is therapeutic, that one's personality can be predicted from the bumps on one's head, that witches and fairies really exist. An open but critical stance thus seems the best posture from which to sift truth from fantasy.

"Skeptical scrutiny is the means. . . by which deep insights can be winnowed from deep nonsense."

Carl Sagan

My primary purpose in this chapter is to apply principles from the previous chapters by illustrating the seductive power of illusory thinking in everyday life. If illusory thinking is as pervasive as the research described in Chapters 3 and 4 suggests, then it will have penetrated many realms of human thought. By exploiting the ways people form and perpetuate false beliefs, falsehoods might easily be perpetrated upon credulous minds (Zusne & Jones, 1981). P. T. Barnum put it cynically: "No one has ever lost money by underestimating the intelligence of the American people." To illustrate, I

"To dismiss from the research and teaching endeavors of psychologists any portion of experience, however bizarre, is to correspondingly limit the usefulness of the discipline."

Warren H. Jones (1980b)

have chosen two domains where, in our day, illusory thinking seems especially evident: belief in extrasensory perception (ESP) and inflated beliefs in the validity of subjective psychological descriptions and explanations of people's personalities.

BELIEF IN ESP

Parapsychologists (psychologists who study "paranormal" claims) have proposed four types of ESP, each of which is said to occur without using the physical senses. *Telepathy* is one person's sending thoughts to another. For example, in an experiment, one person may look at a picture and try to "send" this picture to a "receiver" in another room. *Clairvoyance* is perceiving distant events, such as sensing that one's child has just been in a car accident. *Precognition* is "preknowing" (foretelling) future events, such as the assassination of a political leader. *Psychokinesis* is "mind over matter"—for example, levitating a table or, in an experiment, influencing the roll of a die by concentrating on a particular number.

The main reason for this look at ESP is not to indicate that such psychic phenomena do not exist, but to use belief in ESP as an example of how people form beliefs. If you are among the majority of college students who believe that psychic phenomena exist (Gallup Poll, 1978; Jones, Russell, & Nickel, 1977), you needn't renounce your belief to understand this example. Similarly, I, a psychologist, can acknowledge that clinical psychology is vulnerable to illusory thinking (as I shall elaborate later in this chapter), without forgoing my belief that clinical psychology is a worthwhile profession. As it happens, though, most research psychologists are quite skeptical about ESP. So let's first see why.

Doubts About ESP

Leaving no stone unturned in their search for the killer of some two dozen Atlanta boys in the early 1980s, the Atlanta police flew in the famed "police psychic" Dorothy Allison. Allison was but the most prominent stone in a psychic avalanche. But months after she was gone, and after hundreds of other psychic visions had been scrutinized, the murderer remained at large, until later the case was apparently solved through tireless police work.

Las Vegas casinos skim off only 1.4 percent of money bet at the craps tables. So a psychic who could beat chance by even 3 percent could make as much profit off the game as the house normally does. But casino owners, who, in a sense, perform ESP experiments every night of the week, worry little about people who can predict or influence the roll of the dice. The casinos continue to operate, showing, as always, the expected return.

Is there, in all the world, a single psychic who can discern the contents of a sealed envelope, move remote objects, or read others' minds? If so, magician James Randi will be surprised—and poorer. For nearly twenty years, he has been offering $10,000 to anyone who can perform just one such feat. To date, nearly 600 would-be psychics have inquired, 57 of whom submitted to a test. All have failed (Randi, 1981; see also Morris, 1980b; Broad, 1980; Randi, 1980).

Since "police psychics" and "stage psychics" who perform for profit have so consistently been debunked, parapsychologists are attempting to put ESP on a more solid foundation by demonstrating it in controlled laboratory experiments. Have such experiments fared better? British psychologist C. E. M. Hansel (1980) typifies the skepticism of most research psychologists:

> After a hundred years of research, not a single individual has been found who can demonstrate ESP to the satisfaction of independent investigators. . . . The aim of parapsychology should be to produce one individual who can give a reliable and repeatable demonstration of ESP. (p. 314)

Even John Beloff (1978), past president of the Parapsychological Association, acknowledges that "no experiment showing the clear existence of the paranormal has been consistently repeated by other investigators in other laboratories with the same results."

When scientists add to the foregoing considerations the fact that what we know about the dependence of mind upon the physical brain is evidence against the notion that the mind could operate apart from the brain, belief in truly extrasensory communication strikes them as fanciful, as bordering on the irrational. Perhaps, however, such arguments do not prove to your satisfaction that ESP does not exist. Such a conclusion would not surprise me; I have not proved it to myself either. How does one prove something does not exist? Discrediting a thousand ghost stories does not disprove that, somewhere, there lurks a ghost. But it would cause one to wonder why so many people believe in ghosts.

So let me try a less ambitious assertion: Regardless of whether ESP exists, the mental illusions described in Chapter 4 almost guarantee that humanity would invent such a belief. People have tendencies to make false proclamations about what has influenced them; to have difficulty assessing the workings of their minds; to notice, interpret, and recall events which confirm their expectations; to be overconfident about their intuitions; to be overly persuaded by unrepresentative anecdotes; and to miss the distinction between coincidence and causation. These tendencies are the ingredients in nature's recipe for convincing gullible minds of phenomena that may not exist. To illustrate, let us recall some of these illusory thought processes.

Why People Believe in ESP

The Persuasive Power of Vivid Anecdotes and Experiences

People's beliefs in ESP sometimes illustrate the mind's tendency to be easily persuaded by vivid experiences and amazing anecdotes which seem to defy coincidence and to have no other obvious explanation. An extraordinary personal experience—such as the "psychic performance" experienced by California State University at Long Beach students and described at the beginning of this chapter—may instantly override skepticism. The person then clings to this felt truth, even if, when the phenomenon is probed, it evaporates.

In view of how compelling such dramatic experiences are, it is not surprising that belief in the paranormal is now normal: In a 1978 Gallup Poll, 64 percent of college graduates said they believed in ESP, and in another national survey 58 percent of Americans said they had "personally experienced" ESP (Greeley, 1975).

In experiments with Southern Illinois University students, Scot Morris (1980a) used the power of a vivid experience to teach students how easily people are fooled. For example, a supposed psychic would have a student volunteer pick a card from a standard deck: the four of diamonds, let us say. Then three other volunteers—to assure there were no accomplices—were told, "Call 755-8472 and ask for David. Tell him you are in an ESP experiment with me and ask what card we have selected." During the next couple of minutes the supposed psychic would concentrate, fingers to his brow, and then the excited students would return: "He got it! He got it! The four of diamonds!" At the next class period the hoax would be revealed and some of the tricks explained. (For example, the accomplice who received the call was clued by the name David, which began with the fourth letter of the alphabet and ended with the first letter of diamonds.) This experience of being fooled, combined with a lecture that critically analyzed claims for ESP, reduced the students' beliefs in ESP to a level well below that of other students at their university. The students were also asked to recall the opinions about ESP which they had expressed just after the demonstration in the previous class period. Most students misrecalled having expressed opinions that were close to what they now believed (see Figure 5-1).

Extraordinary Explanations for Ordinary Events

Several of the other illusory thinking processes summarized in Chapter 4 also help explain why people may draw erroneous conclusions from their experiences. First, people often fail to consciously detect what has influenced them. This leaves them free to concoct false explanations for their experiences. Second, the deficiencies in people's statistical intuition lead them to see unusual events as almost impossible. What are the odds that at least two people in a group of thirty will have the same birthday? Most people grossly underestimate the correct answer—7 in 10. Our failure to recognize chance occurrences for what they are predisposes us to seek extraordinary explanations for ordinary events.

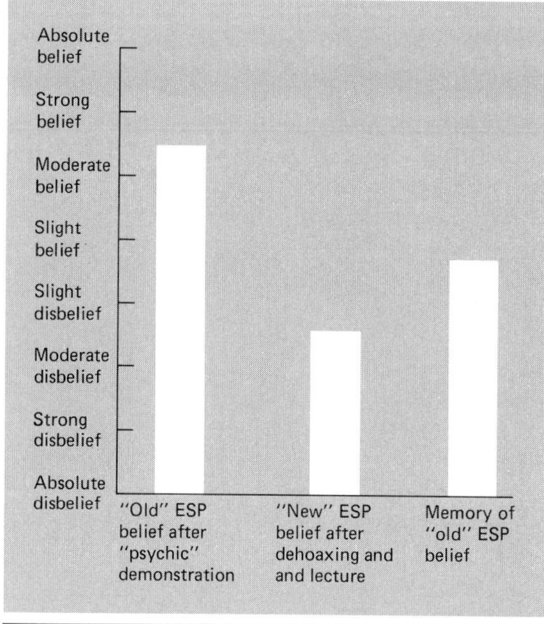

FIGURE 5-1 Belief in ESP was high after seeing "ESP demonstration" and much lower after dehoaxing and a skeptical lecture. When students tried to recall their first opinion (after the demonstration), they "pulled down" their old belief toward their new one, minimizing the change.

You can use people's failures to recognize ordinary events to demonstrate your "psychic powers." Tell a group you are going to "send" them a number between 1 and 4: "Open your minds and see what appears on your mental screen." (What number do *you* get, right now?) After "sending" the number, but before you ask what they "received," announce that you were thinking "3" (the most common response), although "2" (the second most common response) also crossed your consciousness. If someone objects that there is something predictable about responses to the "1 to 4" range, you can do it again with 1 to 10, this time "sending" a 7. (Far more than 10 percent of people will choose 7.)

The mass media, which thrive more by entertaining than by informing, exploit our susceptibility to extraordinary explanations for ordinary events. The *National Enquirer* (1978) invited readers to submit their predictions of events for an upcoming year. The 1500 resulting entries in their ESP contest were sealed in a bank vault until the end of the year, whereupon they were examined and the "amazing winner" was identified. In "a stunning display of psychic ability," Mrs. Florentine Von Rad-Keyye Kaiser scored "5 out of 5 psychic predictions" (p. 1). Setting aside the hindsight temptation to recall and interpret vague predictions—"A beautiful feeling of hope will surge through America"—in light of what one knows has actually happened, we need only consider the objective probability that among 1500 entrants there would be at least a small number who would have chanced onto some accurate

The mass media exploit our fascination with seemingly extraordinary occurrences. (Sidney Harris/*American Scientist*)

predictions. If 1500 people are set to flipping coins, nearly 50 will come up with five heads in a row. If you set a computer to randomly generating 1500 match-ups and final scores for the next Super Bowl game, the best few among these could be selected to provide a "stunning display of the computer's psychic ability."

"An idea isn't responsible for the people who believe in it."

Don Marquis, The Sun Dial

The point of this example is not just to show how easily one can demolish spectacular claims (every belief system has its exploiters) but to illustrate how deficiencies in our statistical intuition can deceive us all. Given the countless events in the world each day, some extraordinary coincidences are bound to occur. To see why, let's pretend you experienced only 100 events each day. The first event can be paired with the other 99, the second event with the remaining 98 (because it has already been paired with the first event), and so forth. All told, there are 4950 possible pairings of just 100 events. Over a ten year period, you and twenty friends would experience 38 million such pairs. And this doesn't include the many more pairs formed across days (for example, today's premonition and tomorrow's events) or across persons (for example, your thoughts being similar to a friend's). But surely among just those 38 million pairs, you and your immediate friends could recall some startling coincidences. (Similarly, if you started flipping a coin right now you would be justifiably amazed to get twenty heads in a row. But with 38 million tosses you could expect twenty heads in a row on numerous occasions.)

The Illusion of Control

The illusions of causation, correlation, and personal control compound the problem by leading people to perceive phenomena that really are not there. Fred Ayeroff and Robert Abelson (1976) used these illusions to manufacture a false belief in ESP among their Yale students. On each of 100 occasions, one student tried to transmit mentally one of five possible symbols to another student who guessed what was transmitted. Both the sender and the receiver then indicated whether they were confident or not confident that a "hit" had been scored. In all conditions of the experiment, the ESP success rate was nearly identical to the chance rate of 20 percent. Nevertheless, when students were drawn into the drama of the experiment by choosing their symbols and being given a "warm-up" period before the experiment began, they were "confident" that ESP was transpiring more than 50 percent of the time. Moreover the "senders," who were more actively involved by the experiment than were the "receivers," were also more confident of hits than were the receivers (see also Benassi, Sweeny, & Drevno, 1979).

Preconceptions Bias Interpretations and Memories

That people notice, perceive, interpret, and recall events in ways which sustain their existing ideas has clear implications for beliefs in ESP. Given our lack of insight into these tendencies, it is almost inevitable that we will trust our intuition more than we ought. Thus if a false belief in ESP emerges, there is every reason to expect its perpetuation.

"Our beliefs . . . have an active life of their own and fight tenaciously for their own survival."

David Marks & Richard Kammann,
The Psychology of the Psychic

Two New Zealand psychologists, David Marks and Richard Kammann (1980), illustrated how our preconceptions control our apprehension of the world. They used drawings made by people who tried to receive images of remote locations being viewed by ESP senders. When each drawing was laid alongside a photograph of the scene being viewed, impartial judges were often amazed at the correspondence between the two. But judges who were given no preconceptions about which drawing went with which scene were typically incapable of correctly matching drawings with scenes. The first method of analysis yielded impressive support for ESP; the second yielded no support. Can you imagine why the difference? The drawings, like most ESP prophecies, were ambiguous enough to allow a variety of later interpretations, once people knew the outcome. They were like the following poem (Dooling & Lachman, 1971):

With hocked gems financing him
Our hero bravely defied all scornful laughter
That tried to prevent his scheme
Your eyes deceive he said
An egg not a table correctly typifies
This unexplored domain.
Now three sturdy sisters sought proof
Forging along sometimes through calm vastness
Yet more often over turbulent peaks and valleys
Days became weeks

As many doubters spread fearful rumors
About the edge
At last from nowhere winged creatures appeared
Signifying momentous success.

Now reread the poem, knowing that the title is "The Voyage of Christopher Columbus."

Consider our dreams. Do they foretell the future, or do they only seem to because we are more likely to remember dreams that come true? Some years ago, when the Lindbergh baby was kidnapped but before its body was discovered, two Harvard psychologists, Henry Murray and D. R. Wheeler (1937), invited the public to send in their dream reports concerning the whereabouts of the child. (Note that these premonitions were not forced under tense laboratory conditions; rather they were spontaneously experienced and then volunteered by people who felt they might have significance.) Of the 1300 dream reports received, how many correctly perceived the child as dead? Five percent. And only 4 of the 1300, less than a seemingly chance number, correctly predicted the three basic facts: death, burial in the ground, and location among trees. For example, Mrs. J. K. recalled,

I thought I was standing or walking in a very muddy place among many trees. One spot looked as though it might be a round, shallow grave. Just then I heard a voice saying, "The baby has been murdered and buried there." I was so frightened that I immediately awoke.

"All superstition is much the same whether it be that of astrology, dreams, omens, retributive judgment, or the like, in all of which the deluded believers observe events which are fulfilled, but neglect and pass over their failure, though it be much more common."

Francis Bacon,
Novum Organum

I have always wondered about Mrs. J. K. and the writers of those other three reports. Surely, they remembered the successes of their dreams better than the other 1296 remembered their failures. Did some of the four also sell copies of their letters to newspapers and magazines, enabling others to read their glowing testimony to the clairvoyant power of dreams?

Murray and Wheeler did what our minds are generally not inclined to do—record "misses" as well as "hits." If we want to analyze the predictive abilities of psychics—or of football forecasters, psychiatrists, or investment counselors—there are actually four relevant types of information. (See Fig. 5-2.)

Our attention tends to be drawn to instances in the Yes-Yes box; logically, however, occurrences in the other three boxes are also informative. Moreover, information from any one of these logical boxes can only be interpreted when comparative information is available from the others. Knowing that four people correctly predicted the fate of the Lindbergh baby tells us little unless we also know how many predictions went awry.

Finally, recall our earlier consideration of the fragility of our memories. The ease with which unusual events can become distorted or exaggerated is demonstrated by the party game of "pass the story around the circle." Because

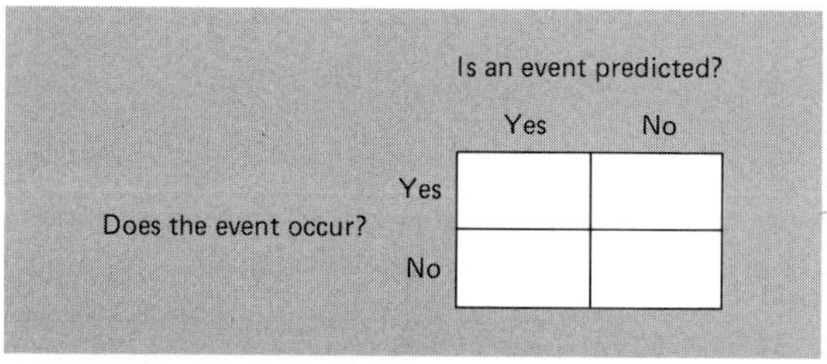

		Is an event predicted?	
		Yes	No
Does the event occur?	Yes		
	No		

FIGURE 5-2 How accurate are the predictions of psychics and other forecasters? The answer requires data on "misses" as well as "hits." Striking occurrences in the Yes-Yes box can only be evaluated in the context of data from the other boxes.

memories are malleable, stories often evolve into a more dramatic form as they are retold. Unaware of their memory reconstructions, people can even fool themselves (Russell & Jones, 1980). Ernest Hilgard (1977), no doubter of hypnotic phenomena, describes how reports of extreme age regressions under hypnosis unwittingly incorporate shreds of people's forgotten past experience. The case of Bridey Murphy received tremendous publicity during the 1950s and was the subject of a best-selling book. Under hypnosis, Virginia Tighe, a housewife, assumed the personality and Irish brogue of a girl, Bridey Murphy, who claimed to be her previous incarnation. After considerable controversy over the reincarnation evidence, two enterprising reporters in Chicago looked into Virginia's background.

With the help of Rev. Wally White, pastor of the Chicago Gospel Tabernacle where Virginia attended Sunday School, it did not take them long to locate Mrs. Anthony Corkell. Now a widow with seven children, she was living in the old frame house where she had lived when Virginia was in her teens. For five years Virginia lived in a basement apartment across the street. Mrs. Corkell's Irish background had fascinated the little girl. One of her friends recalled that Virginia even had a "mad crush" on John, one of the Corkell boys. Another Corkell boy was named Kevin, the name of one of the imaginary Bridey's friends. Note also the similarity of Corkell and Cork, the city where Bridey was supposed to have lived. And what was Mrs. Corkell's maiden name? Bridie (with an "ie") Murphy! (Gardner, 1957, p. 318)

With the aid of some forgotten childhood experiences, Mrs. Tighe had managed to construct an imaginary past and to convince herself, her hypnotist, and a worldwide following of its authenticity.

The Motivation to Believe

In addition to various deficiencies in the processing and remembering of information, people may also believe in ESP because they *want* to. We humans have always had a hard time accepting our finiteness. Today, believers in ESP

"Men freely believe that which they desire."

Julius Caesar,
De Bello Gallico

proclaim our potential for omniscience—reading others' minds and knowing the future. We also yearn for mystery in an age when religious faith has waned and science seems to be demystifying our existence (Jones, 1980a; McBurney, 1980). Some scientists argue that as an escape from humdrum life, pseudoscience offers phony mysteries instead of real mysteries, that it displaces science with science fiction.

FALLACIOUS PERSONALITY INTERPRETATION

It is easy to identify the illusory beliefs of eras and groups *other* than our own. We delight in seeing others' pretensions punctured, but we draw back with considerable defensiveness when the pin pricks our own. Many of us are already inclined to be skeptical about ESP and other occult phenomena, but we are considerably more trusting of our ability to judge people's personalities. Some people *are* quite sensitive and perceptive. Nevertheless, if illusory thinking distorts all domains of human thought, then we are probably susceptible to it as we characterize others and receive psychological analyses of ourselves.

Amateur Psychologizing

Judging Others

As Chapter 4 indicated, we often lack insight into our own thinking. Richard Nisbett and Nancy Bellows (1977) have shown that this sometimes renders us unaware of what has influenced our judgments of others. They had University of Michigan students read what was described as a woman's job application folder. While perusing the folder, the students were either informed or not informed that the woman (1) was physically attractive, (2) had an excellent academic record, (3) had spilled coffee during her interview, (4) had been in a car accident, and/or (5) would later be introduced to them. Next, they judged the woman's characteristics and assessed which of the five factors had influenced their judgments. As Nisbett and Bellows expected, the students accurately recognized that their judgments of her intelligence were strongly influenced by her academic record, an obviously relevant factor. However, when the factor was less obviously related to the trait being judged, the students inaccurately assessed what had influenced their judgments. Virtually no relationship existed between how much the five factors had influenced their judgments of her likability, empathy, and flexibility and how much they *thought* the factors had influenced them. This demonstrates that at least some of the time we are insensitive to how the qualities and actions of other people have molded our impressions of them.

There are several additional reasons why our everyday assessments of people are prone to error. We all have what in Chapter 4 were called "schemata," or what researchers also call "implicit personality theories": "Salespeople are extroverted," "Show people are egocentric," "Scholars are

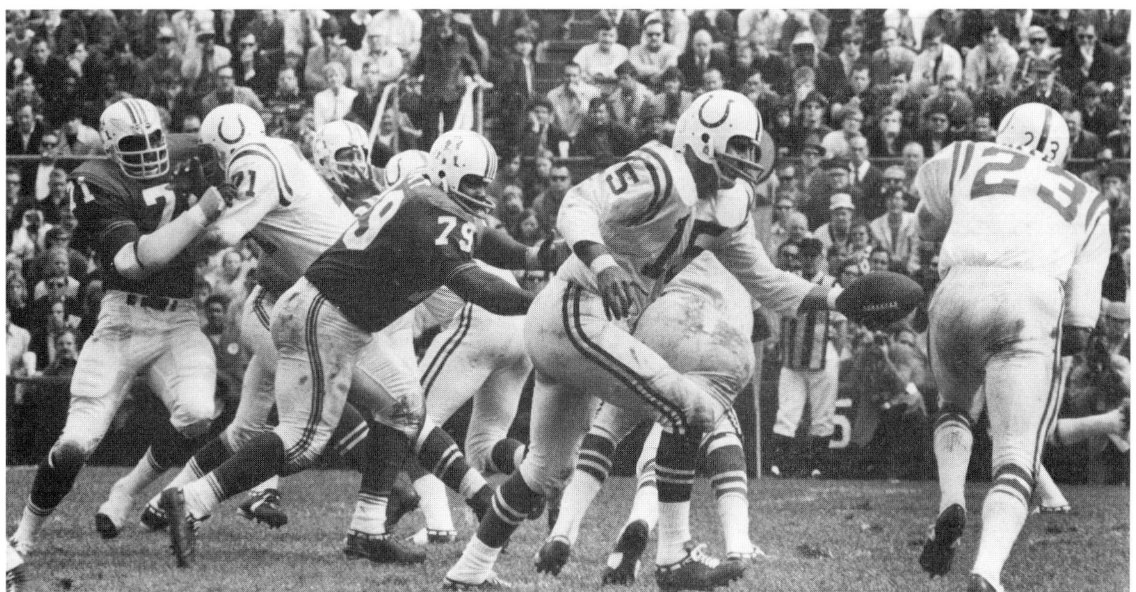

We tend to overestimate the similarities of people within categories, and also to overestimate the differences between categories. (© Michael Philip Manheim 1970/Photo Researchers, Inc.)

reclusive." Once formed, these theories and stereotypes are easily perpetuated in ways usually unnoticed. People will notice "only what they have schemata for," writes Ulric Neisser (1976), "and willy-nilly ignore the rest" (p. 80).

We stereotype partly as a simple result of our tendency to categorize. Stereotyping is a by-product of our desire to make order out of the world. Classifying things simplifies the world. But sometimes this gives us an overly simplistic picture of a complex reality. As we shall see in Chapter 12 on prejudice, studies indicate that people tend to overestimate the similarities of items *within* categories (for example, football players, janitors, old people) and also to overestimate the differences *between* the categories.

Judging Ourselves

Illusory thinking also contaminates our judgments of ourselves. Consider the "Barnum effect"—named in honor of P. T. Barnum, who said, "There's a sucker born every minute," and also remarked that a good circus had a "little something for everybody." Read the following, which is intended to be a description that fits most people. How well does it fit you?

You have a strong need for other people to like you and for them to admire you. You have a tendency to be critical of yourself. You have a great deal of unused energy which you have not turned to your advantage. While you have some personality weaknesses, you are generally able to compensate for them. Your sexual adjustment has presented some problems for you. Disciplined and controlled on the outside, you tend to be worrisome and insecure inside. At times you have serious doubts as to whether you have made the right decision or done the right thing. You prefer a certain amount of change and variety and become dissatisfied when hemmed in by restrictions and limitations. You pride yourself on being an independent thinker and do not accept other opinions without satisfactory proof. You have found it unwise to be too frank in revealing yourself to others. At times you are extroverted, affable, sociable, while at other times you are introverted, wary and reserved. Some of your aspirations tend to be pretty unrealistic. (Forer, 1949)

In many experiments, C. R. Snyder (1974) and others have shown people such descriptions (this one was constructed from a horoscope book). Told, as were you, that the information is true of most individuals, people usually indicate that it fits so-so. But if told that the description is designed specifically for them on the basis of their psychological tests or astrological data, people usually say the description is very accurate. In fact, given a choice between a fake "Barnum description" and a real personality description based on a bona fide test, people tend to say that the phony description is the more accurate (Hyman, 1981).

People also are more inclined to accept false results supposedly derived from projective tests (like the Rorschach inkblots) than from a less subjective procedure. And having accepted the phony results, they express increased confidence in psychological testing and in the skill of their clinician. Richard Petty and Timothy Brock (1979) have found that people also live up to assessments provided by a psychologist. Ohio State University students who were told, "You are an open-minded person. You have the ability to see both sides of an issue," later wrote a fairly balanced assessment of two issues. Those told that "You are not a wishy-washy person. . . . You can take a strong stand on one side and defend it," wrote one-sided assessments of the issues.

Finally people see these Barnum descriptions as more true of themselves than of people in general, especially when the description is positive. Here, then, is yet more evidence of a self-serving bias. Within reason, the more favorable a description is, the more people believe it and the more likely they are to perceive it as unique to themselves (Snyder, Shenkel, & Lowery, 1977; Shavit & Shouval, 1980; Schlenker et al., 1979).

In summary, we are often

Unaware of what has influenced our assessments of others

Prone to perceive people in line with our stereotypes

Susceptible to the "Barnum effect" (accepting worthless diagnoses)

Professional Psychologizing

These findings raise some disconcerting implications for psychiatry and clinical psychology. Regardless of whether a particular diagnosis has any validity, the recipient is likely to stand in awe of it, especially after expending effort and

Impressing One's Clients

money to receive it. The Barnum effect suggests a recipe for impressing clients: Give people a subjective test; make them think that its interpretation is unique to them; and drawing upon things true of most people, tell them something that, while positive, is somewhat ambiguous. Such an approach should increase your clients' faith in your clinical skills—even if what they have been told has no diagnostic validity. Those who offer psychological analyses—whether in capes, plain clothes, or white coats—usually seem right.

The Barnum effect demonstrates an "illusion of uniqueness." Actually, we are more alike than we realize. Edmund Bourne (1977) has shown how our similarities can inflate the seeming accuracy of our descriptions of people. When members of small, intimate groups described each other, Bourne found that their descriptions of any given individual agreed fairly well. But further analysis revealed that their agreement resulted mostly from impressions that they applied in general. For example, although two fraternity brothers might agree that John is more extroverted than introverted, they might also report this about fraternity men in general. When these stereotypes about people in general were extracted, Bourne found that the agreement about others' personalities fell nearly to the level of chance. Other investigators are more optimistic about our ability to discern others' unique personalities (Funder, 1980). However, this much can be said for sure: When clinical diagnosticians agree in their assessment of a particular patient, this is informative only to the extent that their agreement cannot be attributed to what clinicians might say about *any* patient. As clinical psychologist Paul Meehl (1956) has noted, "It is not very illuminating to say of a known psychiatric patient that he has difficulty in accepting his drives, experiences some trouble in relating emotionally to others, and may have problems with sexuality."

Illusory Correlations

Mental health professionals are vulnerable to other illusions as well. Every day they make judgments: Is Susan Smith suicidal? Should John Jones be committed to a mental hospital? If released, will Mac Aroni be a homicide risk? To help make decisions and diagnoses, psychiatrists and clinical psychologists often rely on psychological tests. The assumption is that test results are a clue to correct diagnoses. Sometimes they are. Other times they are not, but the clinician *thinks* they are. When symptoms and test performances are assessed independently, there is often much less correlation between the two than clinicians suppose.

For example, pioneering experiments by Loren Chapman and Jean Chapman (1969; 1971) at the University of Wisconsin have had people study patients' test performances and diagnoses. After doing so, both college students and professional clinicians perceived expected associations (for example, between particular responses to Rorschach inkblots and homosexuality) even when the expected associations were demonstrably absent or even contrary to what was expected. For instance, clinicians who believed that suspicious people draw peculiar eyes on the Draw-a-Person test were likely to perceive such a relationship—even when shown cases in which suspicious people drew peculiar eyes *less* often than nonsuspicious people. This illusory correlation results from biases in our processing of information. When we believe a relationship exists between two things we are more likely to notice confirming than disconfirming instances. If you were shown a series of slides in which the word pairs lion-tiger, lion-eggs, bacon-eggs, and bacon-tiger were shown equally often you would probably overestimate the co-occurrence of the familiar lion-tiger and bacon-eggs.

Consider the following court transcript in which a psychologist (Psy) is being questioned by an attorney (Att):

Att: You asked the defendant to draw a human figure?

Psy: Yes.

Att: And this is the figure he drew for you? What does it indicate to you about his personality?

Psy: You will note this is a rear view of a male. This is very rare, statistically. It indicates hiding guilt feelings, or turning away from reality.

Att: And this drawing of a female figure, does it indicate anything to you; and, if so, what?

Psy: It indicates hostility towards women on the part of the subject. The pose, the hands on the hips, the hard-looking face, the stern expression.

Att: Anything else?

Psy: The size of the ears indicates a paranoid outlook, or hallucinations. Also, the absence of feet indicates feelings of insecurity. (Jeffery, 1964)

The illusory correlation phenomenon explains why many clinicians, such as this one, continue to believe in their interpretations of projective tests even though research casts grave doubt on them. For example, in one study, twenty experts in the analysis of human figure drawings could not discriminate drawings made by schizophrenics, neurotics, homosexuals, and "normal" college students (Wanderer, 1969). Nevertheless, when the clinician knows the person who has taken the test, it is easy to find things about the person in the test, thus "confirming" the usefulness of the test.

Illusory correlation probably contaminates other aspects of clinical intuition besides test interpretation. Amos Tversky and Daniel Kahneman (1973) suggest how. A clinician hears a patient complain that he or she is tired of life. Worried about whether the patient is likely to attempt suicide, the clinician recalls not only the previous history of this patient, but also previous cases brought to mind by the present case. Several biases may affect this memory search. Tversky and Kahneman explain:

Since attempted suicide is a dramatic and salient event, suicidal patients are likely to be more memorable and easier to recall than depressive patients who did not

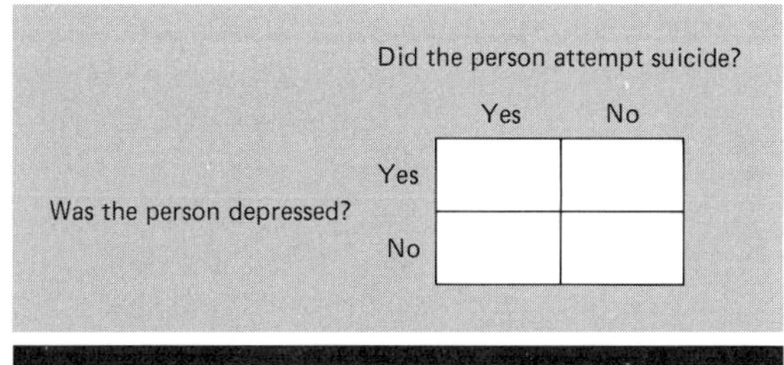

FIGURE 5-3 If past suicide victims were often depressed, does this mean that depressed people are likely to attempt suicide? To answer such a question, data for all four boxes are needed.

attempt suicide. As a consequence, the clinician may recall suicidal patients he has encountered and judge the likelihood of an attempted suicide by the degree of resemblance between these cases and the present patient.

If the clinician recalls that past suicidal patients were nearly all similarly depressed, then a serious illusory correlation may have occurred, for this may actually say little about the probability of a depressed person's attempting suicide. When predicting whether someone is suicidal or homicidal, it surely pays to err on the side of protecting people who do not need it. Still, the point to remember is that in studying the depression-suicide relationship, there are four types of data, all relevant (see Figure 5-3). Striking occurrences in the Yes-Yes box can only be evaluated in the context of data from the other boxes.

In fairness to clinicians, I hasten to add that the shortcomings we are considering could also be shown at work among political analysts, historians, sportscasters, personnel directors, stockbrokers, and many other professionals, including the research psychologists who point them out. As a researcher I have often been blind to the shortcomings of my theoretical analyses. I am so eager to presume that my idea of truth is *the* truth that no matter how hard I try, I cannot see my own error. This has been especially evident from the editorial review process that precedes any research publication. During the last fifteen years I have read several dozen reviews of my own submitted research papers and have been a reviewer for several dozen others. My experience is that it is far easier to spot someone else's sloppy thinking than to perceive my own equally sloppy thinking.

Hindsight and Overconfidence

In our psychological society a speculative psychology-of-the-gaps pops up everywhere to "explain" human behaviors not yet explainable scientifically. If we do not understand something we may invent an explanation to fill the gap in our knowledge. Oedipal interpretations of homosexuality, existential theories of the popularity of *Star Wars*, and Freudian explanations of Richard Nixon's puzzling behavior are offered to a public that can hardly be expected to discriminate psychology's hunches from its established facts. After-the-fact psychologizing is especially vulnerable to the hindsight bias. Therefore, the Freudian psychological autopsies which "psychohistorians" have performed

"Undergraduate psychology can, and I believe should, seek to liberate the student from ignorance, but also from the arrogance of believing we know more about ourselves and others than we really do."

David L. Cole (1982)

on famous personalities from Martin Luther to Richard Nixon are offered with little fear of being proved wrong (Runyan, 1981). Knowing how the person turned out, psychohistorians can easily give an after-the-fact interpretation of childhood experience that confirms their theory.

Recall from Chapter 1 how Stanford University psychologist David Rosenhan (1973) and seven colleagues demonstrated hindsight bias with mental health professionals. After giving false names and vocations, they gained admission to mental hospitals by complaining they had been hearing voices. During the clinical interviews they otherwise reported honestly their life histories and emotional states. Most got diagnosed as schizophrenic. Thus the clinicians searched for and easily found incidents in the pseudopatients' (normal) life histories and hospital behavior that "confirmed" and "explained" the diagnosis. For example, Rosenhan tells of one pseudopatient who truthfully explained to the interviewer that he

> had a close relationship with his mother but was rather remote from his father during his early childhood. During adolescence and beyond, however, his father became a close friend, while his relationship with his mother cooled. His present relationship with his wife was characteristically close and warm. Apart from occasional angry exchanges, friction was minimal. The children had rarely been spanked.

The interviewer, "knowing" the person was "schizophrenic," "explained" the problem this way:

> This white 39-year-old male . . . manifests a long history of considerable ambivalence in close relationships, which begins in early childhood. A warm relationship with his mother cools during his adolescence. A distant relationship to his father is described as becoming very intense. Affective stability is absent. His attempts to control emotionality with his wife and children are punctuated by angry outbursts and, in the case of the children, spankings. And while he says that he has several good friends, one senses considerable ambivalence embedded in those relationships also.

Rosenhan later told some mental hospital staff members (who had heard about his controversial experiment but doubted such mistakes could occur in their hospital) that during the ensuing three months one or more pseudopatients would seek admission to their hospital. After the three months, he asked the staff to guess which of the 193 patients admitted during that time were really pseudopatients. Although there were actually none, 41 of the 193 new patients were accused by at least one staff member of being normal.

Lee Ross and his collaborators (1977) have shown how creating hindsight explanations might exaggerate a clinician's self-confidence. Recall from Chapter 4 Ross's finding that the act of explaining and defending a belief enables one to understand how it *might* be true, and thus to continue to believe it even if the data which inspired it are discredited. In one experiment, people read actual clinical case histories, and then some of them were told that a particular event later occurred (for example, suicide) and were asked to use the case history to explain this event. Finally, they were informed that there actually was no available information about the patient's later life. When the people were then asked to estimate the likelihood of the occurrence of several possible events, including the one they had explained, the event they had explained now seemed quite likely. In another study, some of the Stanford University students of Ross and his collaborators were led to think they had excellent clinical intuition (based on their ability to distinguish authentic suicide notes from fictitious ones). After they explained their success, they were informed that the positive feedback was false. However, since this still left the students with the reasons they had conjured up to explain their apparent success (their empathy, their insights gained from reading a novelist who committed suicide, and so forth), the students maintained their inflated beliefs in their clinical intuition. Clearly, then, the mere activity of explaining and interpreting (in which mental health workers are engaged constantly) may itself contribute to overconfidence in one's judgments.

"To begin with it was only tentatively that I put forward the views I have developed . . . but in the course of time they have gained such a hold upon me that I can no longer think in any other way."

Sigmund Freud, Civilization and its Discontents

Self-Confirming Diagnoses

People can also be induced to give information that fulfills their clinician's expectations. In a clever series of experiments at the University of Minnesota, Mark Snyder and William Swann (1978b; see also Snyder & Campbell, 1980; Snyder & Gangestad, 1981; Snyder & Skrypnek, 1981) gave interviewers hypotheses to test concerning possible personal traits of individuals. To get a feel for their experiments, imagine yourself on a blind date with someone who has been told that you are an uninhibited, outgoing person. To see whether this is true, your date slips questions into the conversation, such as, "Have you ever done anything crazy in front of other people?" As you answer such questions, will your date meet a different "you" than if you were probed for times you were shy and retiring?

Snyder and Swann found that interviewers who were to probe people to see if they had a particular trait treated them as if they had it. For example, the questions interviewers selected to test for extroversion could hardly have been better calculated to elicit extroverted answers (for example, "What would you do if you wanted to liven things up at a party?"), and likewise if the person was to be tested for introversion (for example, "What factors make it hard for you to really open up to people?"). Targets being tested for extroversion therefore actually behaved more sociably, while people tested for introversion revealed a more shy and reserved self.

At Indiana University, Russell Fazio, Edwin Effrein, and Victoria Falender (1981) reproduced this finding and also discovered that those asked the "extroverted questions" later perceived themselves as actually more outgoing than those asked the introverted questions. Moreover, they really became noticeably more outgoing. An accomplice of the experimenter later met each subject in a waiting room, and 70 percent of the time correctly guessed from the subject's outgoingness which condition the subject had come from. Here, then, is more evidence that our erroneous beliefs may generate their own reality.

In subsequent experiments, Snyder and his colleagues attempted several techniques to induce people to search for behaviors that would *disconfirm* the trait they were testing. In one experiment, they (Snyder, Campbell, & Preston, 1982) actually told the interviewers that "it is relevant and informative to find out ways in which the person . . . may not be like the stereotype." In another experiment Snyder (1981a) even offered "$25 to the person who develops the set of questions that tell the most about . . . the interviewee." Still, people resisted asking "introverted questions" when testing for extroversion. This illustrates a principle discussed in Chapter 4: When testing our beliefs (for example, that black men are good athletes), we are more likely to seek information that would verify them (for example, athletic superstars who are black) than to seek disconfirming information (for example, poorly coordinated men who are black).

Recall, too, that this bias toward confirmation is one important reason for the "overconfidence phenomenon." Apparently, people think confirming information (the information in those Yes-Yes boxes) is more relevant than disconfirming information. Snyder and Nancy Cantor (1979; see also Cohen, 1981) had people read one week's events in the life of a woman named Jane. Equal numbers of extroverted behaviors (for example, Jane animatedly conversed with another patient in the doctor's office) and introverted behaviors (Jane spent her office coffee break by herself) were included. Two days later the people were asked to recall behaviors that were relevant to a job for which she was being considered. Those who evaluated her for a job as "research librarian" recalled twice as many instances of introverted behavior as extroverted behavior; those evaluating her for a job as "real estate salesperson" recalled twice as many extroverted behaviors as introverted behaviors. One might have thought Jane had two personalities—except that both groups had read about the very same Jane. When they were then asked how well suited they thought Jane would be for both jobs, the result was even more astonishing. Those who had evaluated her for the salesperson job thought she would make a lousy research librarian, while those who had evaluated her for the librarian position (and who had therefore recalled introverted behaviors) thought her very well suited for the position—despite the fact that both groups had read the identical description of Jane. Snyder's provocative conclusion (1978): Even if someone doubted an erroneous idea enough to go and test it, "one would nevertheless be particularly likely to find all the evidence that one needs to confirm and retain" the belief.

"As is your sort of mind,
So is your sort of search:
you'll find
What you desire."

Robert Browning,
Easter-Day

It has long been said that the behaviors of people undergoing psychotherapy come to fit the theories of their therapists (Whitman, Kramer, &

BEHIND THE SCENES

Mark Snyder

Our research on "when belief creates reality" may help us understand the effects of the social stereotypes that pervade our society. There is no denying the existence of stereotypes, stereotypes about sex, age, race, religion, bodily appearance, sexual orientation, occupation, social class, and political affiliation. Stereotypes are often highly inaccurate. It is simply not true that all women are dependent and conforming, that all physically attractive people have good personalities, that all lesbians have masculine personalities, that all Jews are materialistic, or that all professors are liberals. How is it, then, that these and so many other erroneous stereotypes continue to exist and are so stubbornly resistant to change?

Research on the impact of social beliefs suggests one answer: When people have faith in their stereotypes, they may treat other people in ways that actually elicit behaviors that support those stereotypes. And even if individuals were to develop doubts about their stereotypes, they might test them by selectively gathering evidence that appears to confirm them. Such may be the power of social stereotypes; even when they are wrong, they may create and sustain their own social reality. Now that we understand the powerful forces that work to perpetuate social stereotypes, our research goals are to discover how to help individuals learn which of their stereotypes are mistaken, and how to help the victims of false stereotypes find ways to liberate themselves from the constraints of others' stereotypes. (*Mark Snyder, University of Minnesota*)

Baldridge, 1963). Patients of Freudian therapists, for example, tend to report dreams laden with Freudian content. Based on Snyder's experiments, can you see why this might happen? Snyder (1981a) illustrates:

> The psychiatrist who believes (erroneously) that adult gay males had bad childhood relationships with their mothers may meticulously probe for recalled (or fabricated) signs of tension between their gay clients and their mothers, but neglect to so carefully interrogate their heterosexual clients about their maternal relationships. No doubt, any individual could recall some friction with his or her mother, however minor or isolated the incidents.

"Don't rely too much on labels,
For too often they are fables."

C. H. Spurgeon,
Salt-Cellars

When human intuition has been matched against statistical prediction, intuition has virtually always come in second. (Drawing by Lorenz; © 1980 *The New Yorker* Magazine, Inc.)

For example, a psychologist and a psychiatrist, Harold Renaud and Floyd Estess (1961), conducted life history interviews of 100 healthy, successful adult men and were startled to discover that the childhood experiences of these men were loaded with "traumatic events," tense relations with certain people, and less-than-optimal handling by their parents—the very factors usually invoked to explain psychiatric problems.

Given these hindsight and diagnosis-confirming tendencies, it will probably come as no surprise that most clinicians and interviewers express considerably more confidence in their intuitive assessments than in statistical data. Indeed, if they are pressed for evidence, we may expect that interviewers will readily recall examples that confirm their interviewing ability. Yet when intuitive prediction is matched against statistical prediction (for example, predicting graduate school success using a formula that includes grades and aptitude scores), the latter usually does as well or better (Meehl, 1954; L. R. Goldberg, 1968; Sawyer, 1966). Statistical predictions are indeed unreliable, very unreliable, but human intuition is even more unreliable (Cocozza & Steadman, 1978; Fersch, 1980; Szucko & Kleinmuntz, 1981).

These findings are shocking, an offense to the human ego. To see why such findings are apparently true, consider the assessment of human potential by graduate admissions interviewers. University of Oregon researcher Robyn Dawes (1976) illustrates why statistical prediction is so often superior to an interviewer's intuition when predicting certain outcomes such as graduate school success:

What makes us think that we can do a better job of selection by interviewing (students) for a half hour, than we can by adding together relevant (standardized) variables, such as undergraduate GPA, GRE score, and perhaps ratings of letters of recommendation. The most reasonable explanation to me lies in our overevaluation of our cognitive capacity. And it is really cognitive conceit. Consider, for example, what goes into a GPA. Because for most graduate applicants it is based on at least $3\frac{1}{2}$ years of undergraduate study, it is a composite measure arising from a minimum of 28 courses and possibly, with the popularity of the quarter system, as many as 50. . . . Surely, not all these evaluations are systematically biased against independence and creativity. Yet you and I, looking at a folder or interviewing someone for a half hour, are supposed to be able to form a better impression than one based on $3\frac{1}{2}$ years of the cumulative evaluations of 20–40 different professors. Moreover . . . what you and I are doing implies an ability to assess applicant characteristics that will predict future behavior differently from past behavior; otherwise, why not just use past behavior as the predictor? Those who decry the "dehumanization" of admitting people on the basis of past record are clearly implying such an ability. . . . Finally, if we do wish to ignore GPA, it appears that the only reason for doing so is believing that the candidate is particularly brilliant even though his or her record may not show it. What better evidence for such brilliance can we have than a score on a carefully devised aptitude test? Do we really think we are better equipped to assess such aptitude than is the Educational Testing Service, whatever its faults?

In summary, the evidence suggests that professional clinicians . . .

Can easily convince clients of worthless diagnoses

Are frequently the victims of illusory correlation

Are too readily convinced of their own after-the-fact analyses (hindsight bias and overconfidence)

Fail to appreciate how erroneous diagnoses can be self-confirming

CONCLUSIONS

Research on illusory thinking has significant implications for psychology and for each of us, personally. Here, briefly, is my sense of these implications. I present these thoughts not as the last word, but in the hope that they will stimulate you to formulate your own conclusions.

Implications for Psychology

The solidest piece of scientific truth I know of, the one thing about which I feel totally confident, is that we are profoundly ignorant about nature. Indeed, I regard this as the major discovery of the past 100 years of biology . . . It is this sudden confrontation with the depth and scope of ignorance that represents the most significant contribution of 20th century science to the human intellect. We are, at last, facing up to it. In earlier times, we either pretended to understand how things worked or ignored the problem, or simply made up stories to fill the gaps. (Lewis Thomas, 1978)

Psychology has crept only a little way across the edge of insight into our human condition. Ignorant of their ignorance, some psychologists are tempted to invent glib stories to fill the gaps in our understanding. If these stories are not rigorously checked against objective reality, they will be resilient to disconfirmation. More than that, intuitive observation will support them, even if they are mutually contradictory. Research on illusory thinking therefore beckons psychologists to a new humility concerning the truth of their unchecked speculation. It reminds research psychologists why, in the true spirit of science, they must test their preconceptions before propounding them as truth. To seek the hard facts, even if they threaten one's cherished illusions—that is the ideal of every science.

"One thing I have learned in a long life: that all our science, measured against reality, is primitive and childlike—and yet it is the most precious thing we have."

Albert Einstein, Albert Einstein: Creator and Rebel

Do not misunderstand: I am *not* arguing that the scientific method can answer all human questions. There are questions which it cannot address and ways of knowing which it cannot capture. But science *is* an appropriate means for examining claims about nature, human nature included. Propositions that imply observable consequences are best evaluated by systematic observation and experiment—which is the whole point of social psychology. To be sure, inventive genius is also required, lest researchers test only trivialities. Moreover, ideas gained from everyday experience feed the research process. But whatever unique and enduring insights psychology can offer will be hammered out by research psychologists sorting through competing truth claims. Science always involves an interplay between intuition and rigorous test, between creative hunches and skepticism.

Psychology will never be as exact a science as chemistry. But psychology's distinct contribution is its objective observations and experiments, even granting that the results always require interpretation. For reasons that by now are obvious, psychological investigations must not rely exclusively upon people's subjective reports of the workings of their minds or of why they acted or felt as they did. We must gather information in a way analogous to how we assess our personal health. If we are having doubts about our health we will utilize at least two sources of information about our condition: our intuitive feelings *plus* what the lab technician's microscope may detect, even if our unaided observation could not. The experimental method is the research psychologist's microscope.

"Science is the great antidote to the poison of enthusiasm and superstition."

Adam Smith, Wealth of Nations

Knowing the enormity of illusory thinking therefore points not to the cynical conclusion that all beliefs are arbitrary, but to the need for a science of human thought and behavior, to the need to restrain our imagination by subjecting our speculations to empirical scrutiny.

Personal Implications

Knowing our susceptibility to erroneous belief also has implications for our view of ourselves. First, it cautions us, "Judge not." Since our judgments of others are readily susceptible to error, we can easily wrong people when we spread our judgments. We can become too sure that Johnny Jones's troubles are caused by his "overprotective mother," or that our first impression of the new neighbor or the prospective employee is an accurate assessment.

Second, we ought not take ourselves too seriously, nor should we feel intimidated by people who are unwavering "true believers." The temptation to think more of ourselves and our wisdom than we ought is ever present. If illusory thinking taints all domains of human belief, then it is bound to contaminate my ideas and yours, and the next person's, too. The belief we can hold with greatest certainty is the humbling conviction that some of our beliefs contain error.

Is research on pride and error *too* humbling? Are the researchers who uncover our susceptibility to error the modern counterpart to Gregers Werle in Henrik Ibsen's play *The Wild Duck*? (Werle demolished people's illusions, leaving them without hope or meaning.) Surely we can acknowledge the hard truth of our human limits and still sympathize with the deeper message that people are more than machines. Our subjective experiences are a large part of the stuff of our humanity—our art and our music, our enjoyment of friendship and love, our mystical and religious experiences.

"Rob the average man of his life-illusion, and you rob him also of his happiness."

Henrik Ibsen, The Wild Duck

The cognitive and social psychologists who explore illusory thinking are not out to remake us into unfeeling, logical machines. They would grant, or even insist, that intuition and feeling not only enrich human experience, but are even an important source of creative ideas. They would add, however, the humbling reminder that our susceptibility to error also makes clear our need for disciplined training of the mind. Norman Cousins (1978) calls this "the biggest truth of all about learning: that its purpose is to unlock the human mind and to develop it into an organ capable of thought—conceptual thought, analytical thought, sequential thought."

SUMMING UP

If the predictable errors of human thinking are as pervasive as the preceding chapters suggest, then they likely penetrate our everyday beliefs and judgments. To review and apply the illusory thinking principles discussed previously, we considered two illustrations: why most people believe in ESP, and why both lay people and mental health professionals are prone to overestimate the validity of their psychological interpretations.

The point of the first illustration is not that psychic phenomena do not exist, but that, whether or not they do, illusory thinking almost guarantees that humanity would invent such a belief. As it happens, impressive stage demonstrations of ESP have been either debunked or duplicated by skeptical magicians, and laboratory ESP experiments have, at best, yielded modest results which cannot be replicated. Most research psychologists therefore assume ESP to have been amply discredited. Why, then, do people believe in ESP?

There are several reasons. The first is the mind's tendency to be more easily persuaded by vivid testimonials than by facts. Recall, also, that people tend to make false proclamations about what has influenced them; to be overconfident about their intuitive judgments; to notice, interpret, and recall events which confirm their expectations; and to miss the distinction between coincidence and causation. When added together, these tendencies may convince people of phenomena that may not exist. That such can occur has been demonstrated in laboratory experiments. College students have readily become convinced that they are experiencing ESP, even while objective results indicate they are not.

Experiments indicate that illusory thinking also distorts our psychological analyses of people. As we judge others we are sometimes unaware of what has influenced our assessments of them and we are inclined to perceive them in line with our stereotypes. For example, when judging ourselves we are susceptible to the "Barnum effect" (accepting worthless diagnoses), especially when the feedback is positive.

Psychiatrists and clinical psychologists are not immune to illusory thinking. As they diagnose and treat their clients, they are often the victims of illusory correlations. After-the-fact explanations of people's difficulties are easy, sometimes too easy. Indeed, the very act of explaining can breed overconfidence in one's clinical judgment. When interacting with clients, erroneous diagnoses are sometimes self-confirming, since interviewers tend to seek and to recall information which illustrates and verifies whatever they are looking for.

Research on the errors that so easily creep into our intuitive judgments documents the need for rigorous testing of our intuitive conclusions. The scientific method used by social psychologists cannot answer all questions, and is itself vulnerable to bias. Nevertheless, it can help us sift truth from falsehood. Finally, knowing our own susceptibility to error can reduce our vulnerability to some of these errors, can beckon us to greater humility, and can reassure us when we are feeling intimidated by people who admit no possibility of error within their judgments.

SOCIAL INFLUENCE

Chapter 1 defined social psychology as the scientific study of how people think about, influence, and relate to one another. Chapters 2 to 5 on "social thinking" examined how we view ourselves and others, and alluded to "social psychology's most important lesson": the enormous power of social influences.

Chapters 6 to 9 will explore the extent and the nature of these social influences. Research on social influence helps make the invisible visible; it reveals the unseen social forces that push and shove us. By knowing the cultural sources of our attitudes and behavior (Chapter 6), the nature of social conformity (Chapter 7), the principles of persuasion (Chapter 8), and the effects of our participation in groups (Chapter 9), we can better "see" these invisible influences. Seeing, we may better understand why people feel and act as they do, and we may ourselves be freer—less vulnerable to unwanted social manipulation.

Chapter

Cultural Influences on Attitudes and Behavior

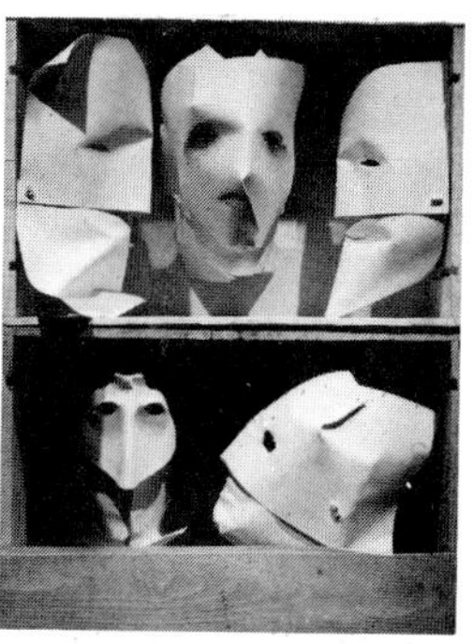

What we eat and drink, what we believe, what music we enjoy, depend largely upon our culture. We all know this. Yet, given how readily most of us accept our way as *the* way, the diversity of human cultures is remarkable. Ian Robertson (1977) notes that

> Americans eat oysters but not snails. The French eat snails but not locusts. The Zulus eat locusts but not fish. The Jews eat fish but not pork. The Hindus eat pork but not beef. The Russians eat beef but not snakes. The Chinese eat snakes but not people. The Jalé of New Guinea find people delicious. (p. 61)

The range of dress habits is just as great. If you were a traditional Muslim woman you would cover your entire body, even your face, and be thought deviant if you didn't. If you were a North American or European woman you would expose your face, arms, and legs, but you would cover your breasts and pelvic region, and be thought deviant if you didn't. If you were a Tasaday tribe woman in the Philippines you would go about your daily activities naked, and be thought deviant if you didn't.

Culture has a similarly strong impact upon our social behavior. This chapter first illustrates the fact of cultural differences, and how social norms and roles help transmit such differences. Then the chapter probes a very significant role, one's sex role. No other role has such pervasive consequences.

Analyzing this one role—asking how males and females differ, and what produces their differences—allows us to explore some fascinating new research, to appreciate the complexity of trying to disentangle biological and cultural influences upon human behavior, and to reflect on issues that pertain to our lives as men and women.

NORMS

American males may feel uncomfortable when Middle Eastern heads of state greet the U.S. president with their familiar kiss upon the cheek. A West German student at a university where "Herr Professor" is seldom talked with outside the lecture hall considers it strange that at my institution most faculty office doors are open and students freely stop by. An Iranian student in her first visit to an American McDonald's restaurant fumbles around in her paper bag looking for the eating utensils until, astonished, she notes the other customers eating their French fries with, of all things, their hands.

Norms: *Rules for accepted and expected behavior. Norms prescribe "proper" behavior.*

As these examples illustrate, all cultures—be they juvenile gangs, remote tribes, or nations—have their own accepted ideas about appropriate behavior. Often, these social expectations, or *norms*, are viewed negatively, as a force that imprisons us all in its blind effort to perpetuate tradition. Norms restrain and control us so successfully and so subtly that we hardly sense their existence. Like fish in the ocean, we are so totally immersed in the ideas and behaviors of our culture that we must leap out of it in order to understand it. There is no better way to learn the norms of our culture than to visit another culture and see that its members do things *that* way, while we do them *this* way. I tell my children that while, yes, many cultured Europeans eat meat with the fork facing down in the left hand, we Americans consider it good manners to cut the meat and then transfer the fork to the right hand: "I agree. It is inefficient. But it's the way *we* do it."

Cultural norms may seem arbitrary and confining. However, just as a play moves smoothly when the actors know their lines, so our everyday social behavior occurs smoothly to the extent that people perform expected behaviors. Consider Michael Argyle's description of five stages that transpire when a British family moves into a home and the wife is visited by the woman next door (D. Cohen, 1980). First, the greetings, after which the visitor enters. Next, the visitor admires the house. During the third stage, the newcomer serves coffee and biscuits and the women exchange information—mainly about husbands. The fourth stage smooths any feelings that may have been ruffled during stage three (such as if one woman said her husband was a labor union executive while the other said her husband was in management). Stage five is the farewells.

Argyle notes that for the social interaction to proceed smoothly both persons must recognize each of the five stages. The rare visitor who arrives at the house and says "My man's with IBM," or the householder who immediately thrusts coffee and biscuits on the visitor, reveals a lack of social skill. Indeed, many awkward, embarrassing moments are caused by our unintentionally violating social norms: walking into the wrong restroom, arriving at the party in coat and tie to find everyone else in jeans, clapping at a pause during a symphony.

Norms not only grease the social machinery, they also liberate us from preoccupation with what we are saying and doing. In strange situations, the norms may be unclear, so we carefully monitor others' behavior and adjust our own accordingly. But in familiar situations, our words and acts come effortlessly. Well-learned, ritualistic ways of interacting free us to concentrate on other matters.

Cultural norms vary greatly. Thus a person whose roots are in an expressive Mediterranean culture may be perceived by someone from a more formal northern European culture as "warm, charming, inefficient, and time-wasting," while the northern European may be perceived as "efficient, cold, and overconcerned with time" (Triandis, 1981). Yet we humans do hold some norms in common. Best known is the taboo against incest. In virtually every culture, parents are not to have sexual relations with their children, nor siblings with one another. Harvard social psychologist Roger Brown (1965) has described a less well known but equally universal norm. His description of this norm caused me to respond with: "Ah yes, I've seen-it-all-along. Why did I never notice it?"

Brown's "universal norm" concerns how people of unequal status relate to one another. Every society has its hierarchy: Based on lineage, wealth, occupation, or whatever, some people are recognized as higher and some as

"Look, everyone here loves vanilla, right? So, let's start there."

Some things are true across cultures. (Drawing by P. Steiner; © 1980 *The New Yorker* Magazine, Inc.)

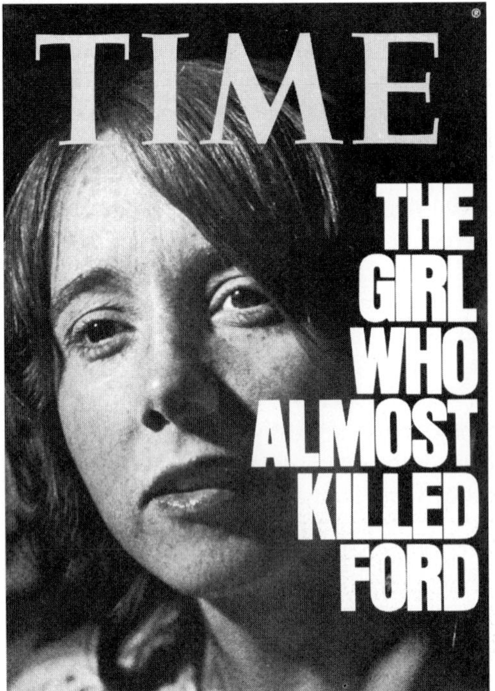

If a 27-year-old male had held the gun, would your headline have been "The Boy Who Almost Killed Ford?"

Grace Welch
Central Islip, N.Y.

Forms of address communicate status. (Copyright 1975 Time Inc. All rights reserved. Reprinted by permission.)

lower on the status ladder. One can detect this status hierarchy in the ways people address each other and initiate relationships. Have you ever noticed that people's speaking to a superior in a distant, respectful way (for example, title and last name) is also the way they speak to a stranger? And that the familiar address (for example, first name) often used in speaking to an inferior is also used in speaking to intimate friends? Our building custodian, "Steve," addresses the faculty as "Dr. So and So." A student and a professor will similarly address one another in a nonmutual way, as will doctors and patients, and other dyads occupying roles with clearly unequal status.

Most languages have two forms of the English pronoun "you": a polite, respectful form and a familiar form (for example, "Sie" and "du" in German, "vous" and "tu" in French, "usted" and "tu" in Spanish). Norms for the use of these pronouns often express the inequality of status. The familiar form is used with one's intimates and with one's inferiors (for example, not only with close friends and family members but also in speaking to children and dogs). Thus a German child's respect receives a boost when strangers begin addressing the child as "Sie" instead of "du." Nouns, too, can express assumed social inequalities. Hence we have had black "boys" and white "men," the "girls" in the secretarial pool and "women" of the faculty. Even among faculty studied by Rebecca Rubin (1981), young female professors were far more likely than young male professors to have students call them by their first names.

This first aspect of Brown's universal norm—that forms of address communicate not only social distance, but also social status—is closely correlated to the second aspect. In Europe, where most dyads begin a relationship with the polite, formal "you" and may eventually progress to the more intimate "you," someone obviously has to initiate the increased intimacy. Who do you suppose does so? Advances in intimacy are usually suggested by the higher status person. On some congenial occasion, the elder, or richer, or more distinguished of the two may say, "Why don't we say *du* to one another?" The norm extends beyond language to every type of advance in intimacy. It is more acceptable to borrow a pen from or put a hand on the shoulder of one's intimates and subordinates than to behave in such a casual way with strangers or superiors. Similarly, the president of my college invites faculty to his home before they invite him to theirs. In general, then, the superior is the pacesetter in the progression toward intimacy.

Dyad: *A group of two. In social psychology, two people interacting on a one-to-one basis.*

Universal norms are intriguing because they would seem to reflect some universal aspect of human nature or some universal requirement of human social life. If it is indeed universally true that advances in intimacy are initiated by persons of higher status, then who initiates with whom will indicate relative social status. For example, on your campus who initiates dates? When I attended college in the early 1960s, except for specially designated weeks or for sorority parties, the women never did. Since then, the women's liberation movement has affected the self-perceived status of millions of women, including many who do not consider themselves feminists. Although the male-initiated date is still far more frequent, women now feel freer to initiate a casual date. If and when women achieve total social equality with men, will they feel as free to initiate contact with men as men now do with women?

Box 6-1

Non-Role Dating: You Can Change the Script

Male Questioner: *I think it's fine for women to invite me out, but how do I tell them that? And when I suggest we do something, how do I tell them that I believe the expenses ought to be shared—without making myself look like a cheapskate?*

Answer: You're not alone. Many single, divorced, and widowed men and women are raising such questions these days. Men say it would take a lot of pressure off them if women sometimes took the initiative in dating. "You'd be surprised how often we men hesitate to make a phone call," some say. "We want to go out with somebody, but we're so afraid of being turned down!" Others point out that the expectation that men always pay the bills is another unfair custom—

especially now that so many women are earning incomes too. "If dating didn't cost me so much, I'd be able to go out a lot more often," some men complain.

Many women say they'd like to feel free to ask men out, but they worry about being thought "too forward." And they would be happy to go "Dutch treat" or share the costs of dates in some other way (such as taking turns paying). Some mention that sharing expenses would take another kind of pressure off them. "I wish I hadn't gotten into the kind of physical intimacy I got into with a guy I went out with last week," said one young woman. "But I guess I felt I *owed* it to him somehow. He had gone all out to give me a really great evening and spent a lot of money on me."

Where possible, it's a good idea for women and men to get together in a group to talk such matters over and decide upon their *own* rules rather than feeling bound by traditions that force them into game playing and insist on a dependent position for women. If you know a woman well enough as a friend, you should be free to discuss these matters on a one-to-one basis as well—and without fearing you'll be thought a cheapskate! In fact, she might feel relieved to know how you feel. You might show her this column to get the discussion started.

Last week, our son Dave (a high school senior) asked his girlfriend if she'd like to stop for a snack at a fast food drive-in. Remembering he had taken her out for a special dinner a few nights before, she replied, "We'd better not. You've spent too much money on me lately." Dave grinned and said, "Then *you* pay." And she did—gladly! I asked Dave how he felt free to say that and whether he had some advice for this column. His answer? "It goes back to a long time before dating. It has to do with our attitudes toward sex roles, seeing each other as equals, knowing how to be good *friends*."

Perhaps that's the key to all this—a stress on friendship, on treating one another as persons, not sex objects. . . . As it now stands, dating is "scripted" so that persons relate as *roles* (males do this, females do that) rather than as unique individuals who can "sharpen one another" and share their God-given gifts totally apart from sex-role stereotypes.

Note: From "Non-Role Dating: You Can Change the Script" by L. Scanzoni and J. Scanzoni, *The Other Side*, May 1978, 56-57.

The norm associated with social status is not the only commonality across cultures. Anthropologist George Murdock (1945) once compiled an extensive list of cultural common denominators. The list includes sports and games, dancing, families, feasts, funerals, music, and religion. The content of each of these categories varies from culture to culture, but all cultures have each category. Similarly, though the content of norms also varies from culture to culture, the basic process of social influence—how and why people affect other people—varies much less. For example, in all cultures, norms are frequently organized into roles.

ROLES

All the world's a stage,
And all the men and women merely players:
They have their exits and their entrances;
And one man in his time plays many parts. . . .

William Shakespeare

Role theorists presume, as did William Shakespeare, that social life is like acting on the theatrical stage, with all its scenes, masks, and prescribed scripts. Like the role of Jaques, who speaks the above lines in *As You Like It*, social roles, such as parent, student, and male and female, outlast those who play them. And, as Jaques says, these roles allow some freedom of interpretation to those who act them out; great performances are defined by the particular way the role is played. However, some aspects of any role *must* be performed. Jaques must utter the above lines. A student must at least show up for exams, turn in papers, and maintain some minimum grade point average.

When only a few norms are associated with a social category (for example, pedestrians should keep to the right and not jaywalk), it is not customary to regard the position as a social role. A role is defined by a substantial group of norms. For example, I could readily generate a long list of norms prescribing my activities as a professor or as a father. Although I may acquire my particular image by violating the least important norms (as professor I seldom wear ties), violating a role's most important norms (failing to meet my classes, abusing my children) could lead to my expulsion from it. Thus, few people fail to perform the most basic requirements of their roles.

Role: *A set of norms that defines how people in a given social position ought to behave.*

In a University of Michigan survey, Richard Kulka and Mary Ellen Colten (1980) explored people's feelings about three of life's major roles: work, marriage, and parenthood. Which do you suppose provides people with the most satisfaction? Adult Americans engaged in all three roles report that they derive more satisfaction from their family roles than from their work roles. There are also some interesting variations. Compared to women, men report finding more satisfaction in work and less in parenthood. And for both men and women, parenthood seems to become less satisfying as children grow older—until the children leave home.

Effects of Role Playing

In Chapter 2, we briefly considered evidence that we tend to absorb our roles. On a first date or on a new job, we may act the role self-consciously. However, as the role is internalized, the self-consciousness subsides. What was unreal becomes real.

Philip Brickman (1978) believed that "Nowhere is social psychology further apart from public consciousness than in its understanding of how things become real for people." Take Patricia Hearst. Had she really been a dedicated revolutionary all along or had she only pretended to cooperate with her captors, people could have more readily comprehended her actions. What they could not understand (and what therefore helped make this one of the biggest news stories of the 1970s) was, as Brickman wrote, "that she could really be an heiress, really a revolutionary, and then perhaps really an heiress again." It's mind-blowing. Surely, this could not happen to you or me—or could it?

The last section of this chapter will reassure us. People's actions not only depend on the social situation but also on their dispositions. Not everyone responds the same to intense social pressures. You and I might have handled the predicament Patricia Hearst was in differently than she. Nevertheless, some social situations can move most "normal" people to behave in "abnormal" ways. This is clear from some experiments that have put well-intentioned people in an evil situation to see whether good or evil prevails. To a dismaying extent, evil wins. Nice guys often don't finish nice.

An illustration: Consider the effect of participating in a role that necessitates destructive behavior. Role "playing" often ceases to be play as the role becomes absorbed into one's traits and attitudes. Combat soldiers typically develop degrading images of their enemy. Or picture some prisoners and prison guards. Is your image positive? Negative? Some of us are haunted still by the images of the 1971 revolt at New York State's Attica Prison, or of the 1980 rampage in the New Mexico State Penitentiary near Santa Fe. There, thirty-three prisoners died, many of them having been beaten with clubs, savagely burned with blowtorches, doused with gasoline and set on fire, or dismembered with homemade knives. Does prison brutality occur because the dispositions of those involved are cruel? Could prison reform occur by employing better people as guards and by isolating sadistic prisoners? Or do prisons dehumanize people because the institutional roles of guard and prisoner tend to embitter and harden even the most compassionate of people?

"If only it were all so simple! If only there were evil people somewhere insidiously committing evil deeds, and it were necessary only to separate them from the rest of us and destroy them. But the line dividing good and evil cuts through the heart of every human being."

Aleksandr Solzhenitsyn, The Gulag Archipelago

The debate continues between those who say the evil resides solely in the individuals (reform the guards, rehabilitate the prisoners) and those who see evil in the inherent dynamics of prison life. Debate of this kind endures because we have always started with the acknowledged problem and worked backwards, speculating causes. And so, since personality and situational factors are intertwined, we can make a case for either. Recognizing this dilemma, Philip Zimbardo (1972b; Zimbardo, Haney, & Banks, 1973) sought to disentangle the two factors. In a simulated prison constructed in the basement of the psychology department at Stanford University, he subjected some decent, intelligent college men to important features of the prison

The 1980 New Mexico State Penitentiary riot. In the prison gym, an anthropologist and other workers sift ashes for the bones and teeth of inmates. Was the savagery more the result of pre-existing evil dispositions in the prisoners or of a dehumanizing prison situation? (Steve Northrup/*TIME* Magazine)

situation. Among this volunteer group, half, by a flip of a coin, were designated guards. They were given uniforms, billy clubs, and whistles, and instructed to enforce certain rules. The other half, the prisoners, were locked in barren cells and forced to wear humiliating outfits.

After little more than a day of role "playing," the guards and prisoners, and even the experimenters, got caught up in the situation. The guards devised cruelly degrading routines; the prisoners broke down, rebelled, or became apathetic; and the experimenters worked overtime to maintain prison security. There developed, reports Zimbardo (1972b), a "growing confusion between reality and illusion, between role-playing and self-identity. . . . This prison which we had created . . . was absorbing us as creatures of its own reality." The simulation was planned to last two weeks. But:

> At the end of only six days we had to close down our mock prison because what we saw was frightening. It was no longer apparent to us or most of the subjects where they ended and their roles began. The majority had indeed become "prisoners" or "guards," no longer able to clearly differentiate between role-playing and self.

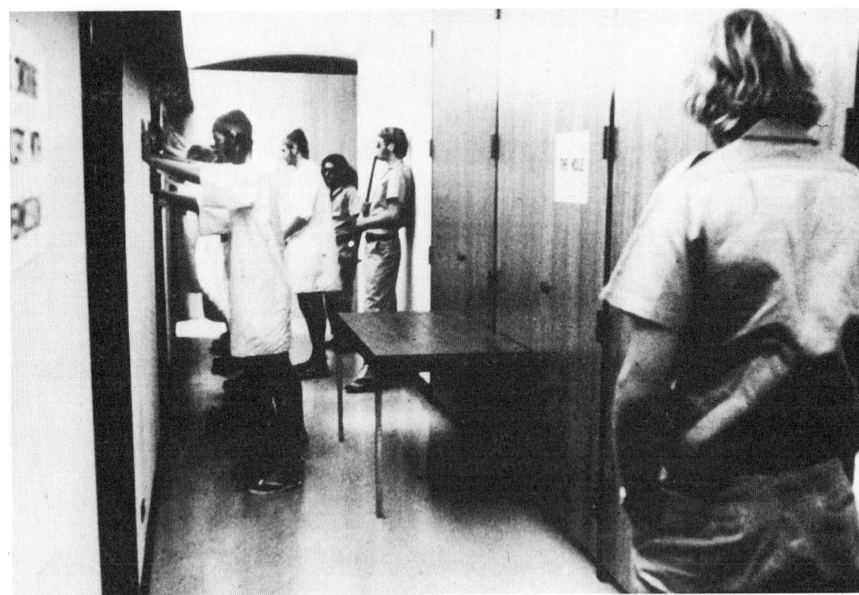

Guards and prisoners in the Stanford prison simulation quickly absorbed the roles they played. (Philip Zimbardo)

There were dramatic changes in virtually every aspect of their behavior, thinking and feeling. In less than a week, the experience of imprisonment undid (temporarily) a lifetime of learning; human values were suspended, self-concepts were challenged, and the ugliest, most base, pathological side of human nature surfaced. We were

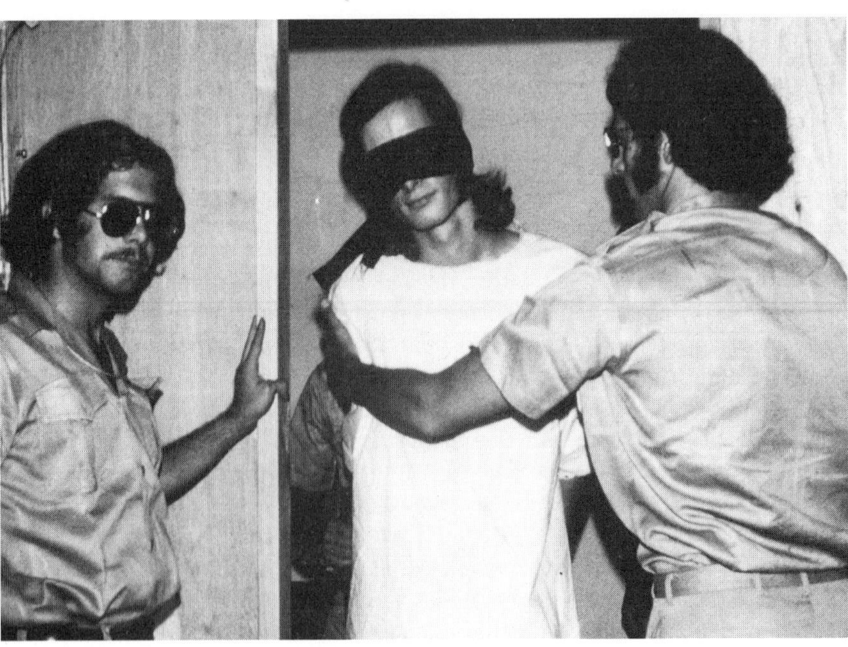

horrified because we saw some boys ("guards") treat other boys as if they were despicable animals, taking pleasure in cruelty, while other boys ("prisoners") became servile, dehumanized robots who thought only of escape, of their own individual survival, and of their mounting hatred of the guards. (Zimbardo, 1971, p. 3)

The most fundamental demonstration of this controversial simulation has not to do with real prisons, which certainly differ from the simulated one. Nor does it even have to do with the many real-life situations which may involve similarly destructive role relations. Rather, it demonstrates how that which was unreal (an artificial role) can evolve into that which is real. To make this insight concrete, consider the roles of master and slave. Imagine playing the role of slave—not just for six days, but for decades. If a few days altered the behavior of those in Zimbardo's "prison," then decades of subservient behavior is bound to have substantial corrosive effects upon the slave's traits and self-concept. The master may be even more profoundly affected, since the master's role is chosen. Frederick Douglass, a former slave, recalls his slave mistress's transformation as she absorbed her role:

"One can improvise a jail and have subjects volunteer. . . to be "prisoners." One can then report some interesting reactions of certain individuals. It's an important topic and clearly newsworthy. But it's not research, does not seriously attempt to look at relations among variables, and yields no new knowledge. It's just staging a 'happening'."

Leon Festinger (1980)

My new mistress proved to be all she appeared when I first met her at the door,—a woman of the kindest heart and finest feelings. She had never had a slave under her control previously to myself, and prior to her marriage she had been dependent upon her own industry for a living. She was by trade a weaver; and by constant application to her business, she had been in a good degree preserved from the blighting and dehumanizing effects of slavery. I was utterly astonished at her goodness. I scarcely knew how to behave towards her. She was entirely unlike any other white woman I had ever seen. I could not approach her as I was accustomed to approach other white ladies. My early instruction was all out of place. The crouching servility, usually so acceptable a quality in a slave, did not answer when manifested toward her. Her favor was not gained by it; she seemed to be disturbed by it. She did not deem it impudent or unmannerly for a slave to look her in the face. The meanest slave was put fully at ease in her presence, and none left without feeling better for having seen her. Her face was made of heavenly smiles, and her voice of tranquil music.

But, alas! this kind heart had but a short time to remain such. The fatal poison of irresponsible power was already in her hands, and soon commenced its infernal work. That cheerful eye, under the influence of slavery, soon became red with rage; that voice, made all of sweet accord, changed to one of harsh and horrid discord; and that angelic face gave place to that of a demon. (Douglass, 1960, pp. 57-58)

The transforming power of a new role is often experienced by human service professionals in the "burnout" of their initial idealism. A New York City police officer described the experience: "You change when you become a cop—you become tough and hard and cynical. You have to condition yourself to be that way in order to survive on this job. And sometimes,

BEHIND THE SCENES

Philip Zimbardo

For our simulated prison we preselected normal people, people we felt were similar to intelligent citizens, lawmakers, law enforcers, and prison staff members. When such people were randomly assigned as prisoners or guards, the power of the situation overwhelmed their prior socialization, values, and personality traits. And that's the message—the corrupting power of the prison situation—that we've taken to prison officials, judges, lawyers, and committees of the U.S. Senate and House. That "good people" could be so vulnerable to the "evil forces" in a simulated prison environment challenges us to reevaluate assumptions about the causes of social and personal pathology.

An unexpected consequence of the Stanford prison experiment was the development of the Stanford Shyness Clinic—the first facility of its kind to deal exclusively with the treatment of shyness in adults. The idea for such a shyness treatment center came from observing the parallels between shyness and the mentality of our mock guards and prisoners. Shyness is indeed a psychologically imposed prison that limits one's basic freedoms of speech, association, and movement. The "guard-self" of the shy person imposes coercive rules on the "prisoner-self"; rules that constrain his or her autonomy and make behavior easier to manage. The prisoner-self, in complying with such rules, diminishes both self-esteem and perceived competence. Starting with that metaphor, I have been able to develop strategies for preventing and overcoming shyness in children and adults (through the clinic and several "self-help" books). *(Philip Zimbardo, Stanford University)*

without realizing it, you act that way all the time, even with your wife and kids" (Maslach & Jackson, 1979). Similarly, ward attendants in institutions for the mentally retarded often start to refer to residents with derogatory labels such as "biter," "soiler," and "brat"; and the initial idealism of social workers, like that of Frederick Douglass's slave mistress, is often transformed into an impersonal, demeaning attitude (Wills, 1978).

And the clients? They often view the staff workers as cold and callous. One young man, recovering from the amputation of his leg, went with his mother to the social security office to request information about aid for the disabled. After the caseworker accused them of trying to rip off the government, they went home and cried for three hours. Of course, not all police officers, ward attendants, and caseworkers become so insensitive. Yet the wide range of personalities who experience burnout suggests we might usefully view it as being caused by bad situations rather than by inherently bad people.

Christiana Maslach (1978) has identified some ways role relations between staff and clients create burnout. The norms of the caseworker role (some of them formalized as rules and regulations) require the caseworker to ask the client very personal questions, yet restrict the caseworker's freedom to offer aid. This produces a tense relationship and induces the caseworker to keep an emotional distance. Informal norms dictate that the caseworker be assertive, the client passive and dependent. As a result, the caseworker may unknowingly come to view the clients as objects. Moreover, the situation dictates that clients bring them feedback when things go wrong, but not when things go right. And, if the casework does not bring gratifying results, to what will the professional helper likely attribute client complaints and minimal success? To the clients' dispositions, of course: "If they can't change after all I've done for them, then let's face it—there's something basically wrong with them."

Recall the fundamental attribution error from Chapter 3. When professional helpers are selectively exposed to clients' problems and negative behaviors, do they attribute these problems to the clients' dispositions rather than to their situations?

Even when a helping relationship is successful, the role of client can still breed dependency. Tom, a college freshman, is suffering the customary stresses of his new academic and social experience. One week he is unable to concentrate and so does poorly on two major exams, whereupon he begins weekly sessions with one of the college's counselors. The counseling relationship is wonderfully satisfying. Tom's concentration and grades improve. So, when Tom's counselor suggests terminating the counseling, Tom readily agrees. Then three weeks later, as he begins studying for exams in chemistry and math, Tom again feels overly anxious. Will the counseling experience now affect Tom's self-image? Did the successful help he received increase his dependence? Will it lead him to believe "I can't get through a rough time without help"? Several recent experiments suggest that those who improve after receiving help may have diminished feelings of self-efficacy. Thus, well-intentioned efforts to help can leave recipients worse off than they would have been without the help (Brickman et al., 1982).

Ellen Langer and Ann Benevento (1978) have demonstrated how dependency can be created while one experiences a subservient role. In one of their experiments, pairs of women in New York City first solved some arithmetic problems, working individually. They then solved anagrams, with one of the women serving as "boss" and the other as a subservient "assistant." Last, the women individually solved more arithmetic problems exactly as they had in the first phase. During the second phase, the "bosses" now solved more arithmetic problems than they had initially. The subservient "assistants" apparently developed a false sense of incompetence, for they now solved *fewer* problems. A demeaning role had demeaned the people who played it.

"It is the peculiar triumph of society—and its loss—that it is able to convince those people to whom it has given inferior status of the reality of this decree."

James Baldwin, Notes of a Native Son

Role Reversal

Thus far we have dealt primarily with role playing's negative effects. But role playing can also be used for good. By intentionally playing a new role, people can sometimes change themselves or empathize with people whose roles differ

"Great Spirit, grant that I may not criticize my neighbor until I have walked for a moon in his moccasins."

Old Indian Prayer

from their own. "Psychodrama," a form of psychotherapy, uses role playing for just this purpose. In George Bernard Shaw's *Pygmalion*, Eliza Doolittle, the uncouth flower vendor, discovers that if she plays the role of a lady, and is viewed by others as a lady, then she in fact is a lady. What wasn't real now is.

Role reversals can improve communication. The problem with much human conversation and argument, observed La Rochefoucauld,

> is that a man pays more attention to his own utterances than to giving an exact answer to questions put to him. Even the most charming and clever do little more than appear attentive, while in their eyes one may see a look of bewilderment as one talks, so anxious are they to return to their own ideas. (1665, No. 139)

A negotiator or group leader can therefore create better communication by having the two sides reverse roles, each arguing the other's position. Alternatively, each side can be asked to restate the other party's point (to the other's satisfaction), before replying. The next time you get into a difficult argument with someone (for example, a parent), try to stop it in the middle and have each of you restate the other's perceptions and feelings before going on with your own. The role reversal idea predicts that your mutual understanding will increase.

Role Conflict

When torrential rains immobilized army vehicles during the winter of 1944, General George S. Patton ordered all chaplains to pray for dry weather.

> **General Patton:** Chaplain, I want you to publish a prayer for good weather. I'm tired of these soldiers having to fight mud and floods as well as Germans. See if we can't get God to work on our side.
>
> **Chaplain O'Neill:** Sir, it's going to take a pretty thick rug for that kind of praying.
>
> **General Patton:** I don't care if it takes the flying carpet. I want the praying done.
>
> **Chaplain O'Neill:** Yes, sir. May I say, General, that it isn't a customary thing among men of my profession to pray for clear weather to kill fellow men.
>
> **General Patton:** Chaplain, are you teaching me theology or are you the Chaplain of the Third Army? I want a prayer.
>
> **Chaplain O'Neill:** Yes, sir. (Patton, 1949, p. 184)

The prayer, which was printed by the Army and distributed with Patton's Christmas greetings, called upon God

> to restrain these immoderate rains with which we have had to contend. Grant us fair weather for Battle. Graciously harken to us as soldiers who call upon Thee

that, armed with Thy power, we may advance from victory to victory, and crush the oppression and wickedness of our enemies, and establish Thy justice among men and nations. Amen. (pp. 184-185)

Roles are sets of norms and norms are expectations for how one ought to behave. Sometimes people's expectations conflict. In the example above, Chaplain O'Neill obviously had to struggle with the conflict between General Patton's expectations for the chaplain's role and those of the religious community, for which such prayers are not "customary." There are several types of role conflict. Each requires its own method of resolution. Consider three.

Conflict between Person and Role

Conflict between person and role: *Tension between one's personality or attitudes and the expectations of one's role.*

Surely you have sometimes found your own personality or attitudes incompatible with the expectations of an assigned role. Perhaps you were elected president of a group, but found the role a strain, given your normally unassertive nature. Or perhaps you took a job that required you to act in accord with rules that you disagreed with. The difference between the role and the real causes discomfort.

Among people new to an occupational role, such conflicts are common. Young professors frequently chafe under the expectations of the professor role and what it requires of them in order to achieve tenure. Young Massachusetts Catholic priests surveyed by sociologist Mary Ellen Reilly (1978) expressed widespread disagreement with church positions on birth control, divorce, and clerical celibacy—positions priests are expected to support. With time will their attitudes shift to become more like those of priests aged fifty-five and older, more than 90 percent of whom agreed with the church's position on these issues? If so, this would illustrate one way of resolving the conflict of person versus role: adjusting one's traits and attitudes to fit the role.

Intrarole Conflict

Have you ever been torn by conflicting expectations for how you ought to behave in a given role? The college administration may expect students serving as dormitory advisers to enforce regulations and report violations; the advisers' fellow students, however, may expect them to hold what they learn in confidence. Most professors have felt the anguish of having some of their students wish they would stick closer to the text, while others in the very same class complain that the lectures are based too much on the text. Among the young Catholic priests surveyed by Reilly, two-thirds experienced "great differences" between the expectations of the older priests and those of their younger peers.

Intrarole conflict: *Tension created by contradictory expectations about how a given role should be played.*

Intrarole conflicts can be difficult to resolve. Sometimes it is possible to have the parties with the conflicting expectations seek greater consensus. Other times the conflict can be dealt with by attaching more importance to some expectations than others. Thus the young priests indicated they were most interested in the expectations of their young peers.

Interrole Conflict

You have likely experienced conflicts between the expectations of two different roles. Perhaps you have presented one "self" to your parents as you play the role of dutiful son or daughter, and quite another "self" in your role as college student. The manners, talk, and attitudes of home and campus can be kept comfortably separate, as long as the two roles are acted on separate stages. But when the stages overlap—say, on parents' weekend or when you take friends home—you face role conflict. If two sets of expectations sharply conflict, we usually resolve the interrole conflict by keeping them separate. Thus students may breathe sighs of relief as their parents complete the campus inspections and drive home.

Interrole conflict: *Tension between the requirements of two different roles that must be played at once.*

Keeping this introduction to cultural norms and roles in mind, let us now consider, as an in-depth illustration, one cultural role on which recently there has been much research.

SEX ROLES

The power of socially prescribed roles to shape our attitudes, behavior, and even our sense of self is nowhere more evident than in society's implanting ideas about masculinity and femininity and how men and women should behave. But before considering sex-role indoctrination, let's first consider what there is to explain: How different are men and women? And to what extent do biological factors fail to explain male-female differences?

Discerning answers to these big questions requires steering through an intellectual minefield. The mines have been laid by two complicating forces. The first is ideological. Chapter 1 described how social psychologists' values penetrate their theory and research. People—research psychologists included—always view the world through the spectacles of their preconceptions. Since theories are the products of human imagination, they always incorporate the theorist's assumptions. What is more, our value judgments may blind us to the gulf between scientific description and social prescription, between what is and what ought to be.

"It is difficult, if not impossible, for most people to think otherwise than in the fashion of their own period."

George Bernard Shaw, Saint Joan: Preface

Feminist psychologists have detected psychologists' values in their writings about the differences between men and women. For example, Rhoda Unger (1979a) notes how the terminology can become subtly loaded. Take what seems to be a neutral term, "sex difference." You will soon be reading about one apparent sex difference: Males tend to act more aggressively than females. Does describing this as a "sex difference" carry a subtle connotation that the difference is a product of one's biological gender? If there is such a connotation, then labeling the aggression difference a *sex* difference can subtly preordain one's answer to the question of whether it is caused by biology or culture. Whenever discussing sex, race, or class differences we should remember that these categories are merely correlated with the behavior under study (Goldstein,

1980). Any genetic differences aside, race differences are caused by factors other than race, sex differences by factors other than sex. This important point is easy to forget when using terms such as "race differences" and "sex differences."

The second complication arises from the interweaving of biological and cultural factors. Although people are often quick to explain any observed male-female difference as either innate or socially created, things are seldom so simple. Because culture tends to amplify minor biological gender differences, the two factors are difficult to disentangle. For example, the question of whether the aggression difference is due mostly to biological factors (there *are* male-female hormone differences), to social training (girls *are* socialized to be less aggressive), or to the interaction of the two, is a scientific mine—the same one you may have previously encountered in the debate over whether people's intelligence is more a product of nature or nurture.

One can become so wary of the mines laid by ideology and by the interweaving of biology and culture as to say nothing. But if research has not settled the great questions pertaining to men's and women's natures, it has shed light on several more specific questions. Treading carefully, so as to trip as few explosions as possible, let us then venture into this minefield.

How Do Males and Females Differ?

Because experimenters have so often compared their results from male and female subjects, an extensive literature on male-female differences has evolved. What have we learned from such comparisons?

First, male-female differences are not so strong and prevalent as all the talk about them would lead one to believe. Granted, men and women differ; however, they are most assuredly not of "*opposite* sex." As researcher Lauren Harris (1979) puts it, "Neither in any physiological nor in any psychological sense are males and females 'contrary or antithetical in nature or tendency; diametrically opposed, or altogether different.' " Since the sexes' many similarities evoke less interest than their differences, we spend our time looking for and publicizing gender-related *differences*. Differences are newsworthy; similarities are not. It is more fun for a researcher to announce, "Eureka! Women are empathic; men are competitive," than to announce "I couldn't find any significant difference between men's and women's competitiveness."

Is psychology's preoccupation with differences itself a source of people's exaggerated notions of sex differences?

As we now examine a few of the commonly observed differences between men and women (at least between American men and women), bear in mind these are *average* differences. In the Boston Marathon, the average man finishes about one-half hour ahead of the average woman, but some women finish ahead of many men. Don Schollander's world-record-setting 4 minutes, 12.2 seconds, in the 400-meter freestyle swim at the 1964 Olympic Games would have placed him fifth against the women racing in the 1980 Olympics. In considering psychological rather than physical differences, the overlap

In virtually all societies, men usually fight the wars and hunt the large game, while women more often gather food and tend the children. (Bettmann Archive)

between the sexes is generally far greater. And the variation within each sex far exceeds the difference between the sexes. No wonder that when asked whether man or woman was more intelligent, the English scholar and critic Samuel Johnson is said to have replied: "Which man? Which woman?"

Are Males More Aggressive than Females?

Aggression: *Physical or verbal behavior intended to hurt someone. In laboratory experiments, this might mean delivering electric shocks or saying something likely to hurt another's feelings. By this social-psychological definition, one can be socially assertive without being aggressive.*

Here a stereotype—that males behave more aggressively—is confirmed, with evidence ranging from anthropology to social psychology. Anthropologist Margaret Mead (1935) did find societies where both men and women were characteristically hostile and aggressive or gentle and warm. But all societies have some division of labor between men and women, and inevitably hunting and fighting are primarily the men's role (Murdock, 1935). In the United States, most violent crime is committed by men. And in school and other real-life situations, girls are, as one prominent investigator has consistently found, "much less aggressive at all times regardless of how aggression [is] measured" (Eron, 1980). Boys are also far more likely than girls to engage in mock fighting (Maccoby & Jacklin, 1974, p. 237). It makes one wonder: If women were the world's political leaders, would there be fewer wars?

In real-life situations, people perceive an even larger male-female difference in aggression than found in the laboratory. When survey researchers find men admitting to more hostility and aggression, and find people perceiving males as more aggressive, might the researchers be merely collecting the biases they are trying to test? As indicated in the experiment depicted in Figure 6-1, gender differences are sometimes in the eye of the observer.

Nevertheless, when Ann Frodi, Jacqueline Macaulay, and Pauline Thome (1977) reviewed several dozen laboratory experiments on aggression, they still detected that "men were sometimes (but not always) found to be more

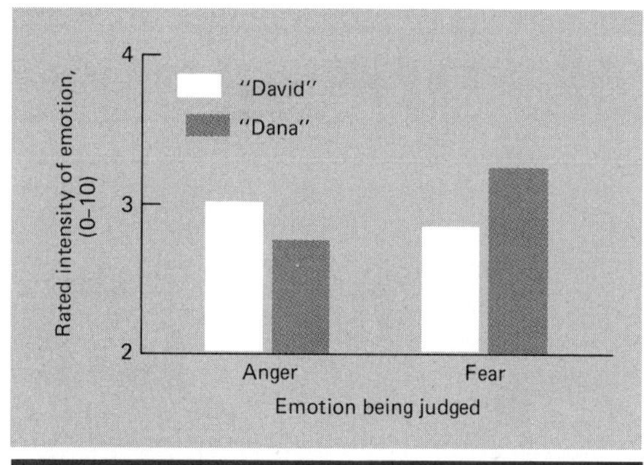

FIGURE 6-1 Are male-female differences sometimes in the eye of the beholder? Observers viewed a videotape of a nine-month old boy reacting strongly to a jack-in-the-box. Those told the child was a boy, "David," perceived "his" emotion as mostly anger. Those who thought the child was a girl, "Dana," perceived the identical reaction as mostly fear. (Data from Condry & Condry, 1976.)

aggressive than women, and women were very seldom found to be more aggressive than men." This was especially true in situations involving face-to-face physical aggression (for example, giving someone electric shocks). This difference apparently has not so much been due to women's being less easily provoked than men as to their being more anxious about aggressing (Frodi, 1978; Richardson, Bernstein, & Taylor, 1979). Remove factors that would trigger a fear of disapproval and women become less restrained.

Do Males Exert More Social Power?

"To those who think I am suggesting that we have a war between the sexes, I say: 'But we've always had one— and women have always lost it.' "

Phyllis Chesler, Woman and Madness

In power and prestige, are the two sexes "different but equal"? In every known society, men are socially dominant. In the United States, which is more egalitarian than most cultures, women comprise 51 percent of the population, but 2 percent of the 1981 U.S. Senate, 4 percent of the House of Representatives, 6 percent of the President's cabinet-level appointments, 12 percent of the state legislators, and 0 percent of the governors (Women's Campaign Fund, 1981). When a jury selects its foreman, it is indeed usually a fore*man* (Strodbeck & Mann, 1956). And even among my relatively liberated social psychology students, the emergent leader of small groups (the one who speaks for the group) is usually a male.

Men express and exert their greater social power in some fascinating subtle ways. One such way is speech (Eakins & Eakins, 1978; Haas, 1979; Kimble, Yoshikawa, & Zehr, 1980). Linguist Robin Lakoff (1975) argues that "men's speech" is straightforward, assertive. Period. However, sometimes "women's speech" seems, oh, just a bit less bold and assertive, maybe even hesitant, don't you think? "Men's speech" asserts, "It's cold in here." Maybe, though, a woman might suggest, "It's cold in here, isn't it?"

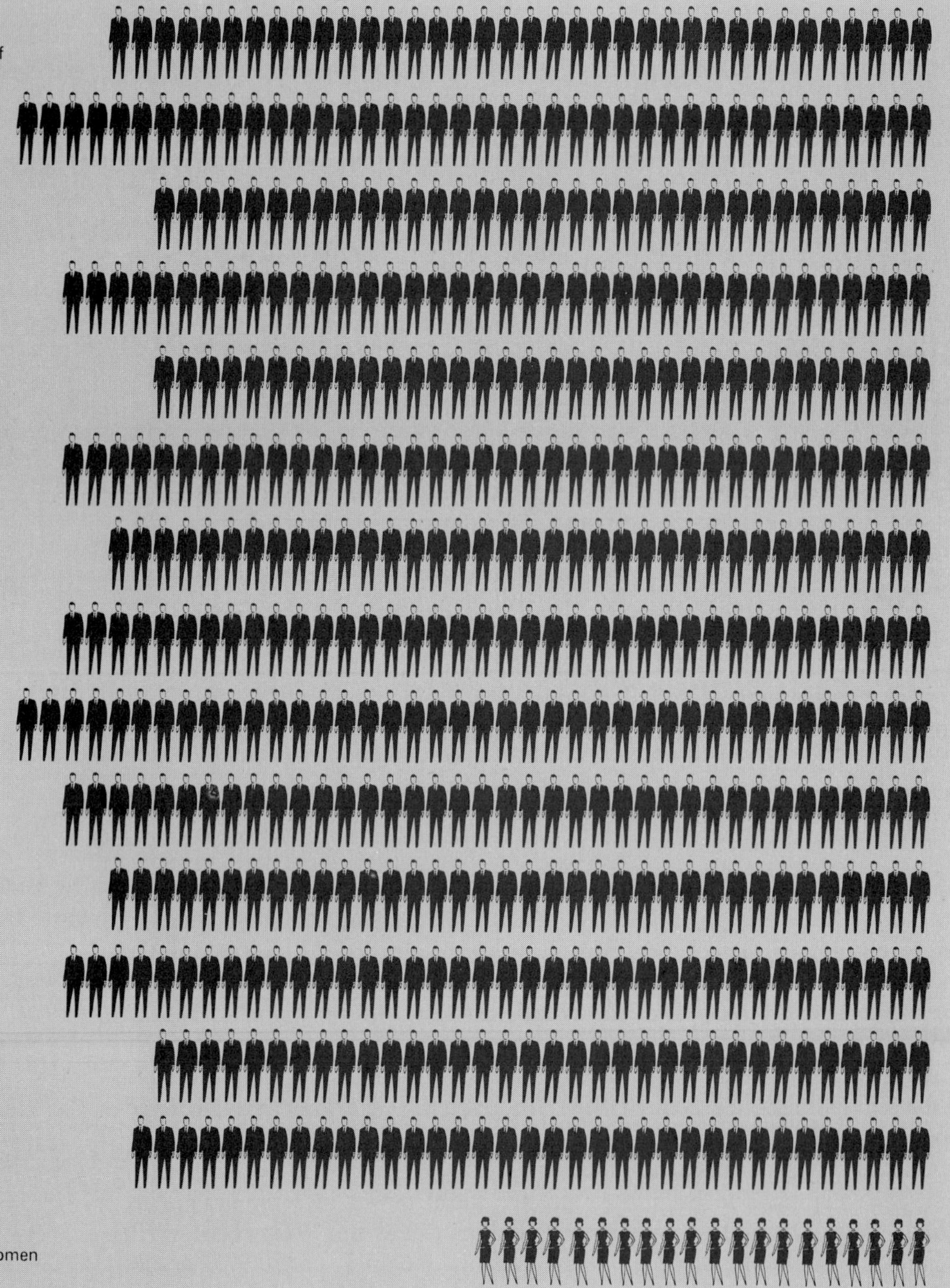
The U.S. Congress is comprised of 515 men. . .
. . .and 20 women

"Sweetheart, could you maybe include the dog?"

"Women's speech" is more hesitating and polite. (Drawing by Weber; © 1980 *The New Yorker* Magazine, Inc.)

Toni Falbo and Letitia Anne Peplau (1980) had UCLA students describe "how I get [my romantic partner] to do what I want." Consistent with Lakoff's ideas about polite and subtle feminine style, women were more likely than men to report using indirect influence ("I pout," "I am especially affectionate," "I drop hints") rather than direct influence ("I tell her what I want," "I state my needs"). Those who reported experiencing direct, straightforward communication also reported feeling most satisfied with their relationships.

"If men are always more or less deceived on the subject of women, it is because they forget that they and women do not speak altogether the same language."

Amiel, Journal, 1868

Interrupting is another expression of power. Sociologists Donald Zimmerman and Candace West (1975; West, 1982) observed that just as parents interrupt children much more than children interrupt their parents, so do men interrupt women far more than women do men. Another sociologist, Pamela Fishman (1978; also Davis, 1978), observed that in couples' naturally occurring conversations the topics that succeeded (those pursued by the listener) were usually introduced by the man. Topics that failed (those killed by an unresponsive listener) were usually introduced by the woman.

Power is also expressed and acknowledged nonverbally. Nancy Henley (1977) has documented how this power is communicated between the sexes. Men touch; women smile. Men look women in the eyes; women look away. Men are relaxed and like informality; women are more tense and likely to observe propriety. As Henley points out, intonation also can acknowledge subordination:

FIGURE 6-2 In the United States, as in every known society, men exert greater social power.

Husband: When will dinner be ready?

Wife: (*meekly*) Oh . . . around six o'clock?

These verbal and nonverbal expressions of power can be blatantly illustrated by imagining a conversation between an authoritarian boss and his submissive secretary:

Bill E. Club: Sally, get me the Struthers file.

Sally Subdued: Right here, sir. Say, uh, Mr. Club, would . . .

B.E.C.: Hey, and also get down my copy of Ringer's *Winning through Intimidation*.

S.S.: Oh dear, now where is that? . . . Here it is! . . . Uh, Mr. Club would it maybe be all right if I, ah, left for lunch ten minutes early?

B.E.C.: (*looks up after a pause*) Eh? Oh sure, Sal (patting her knee), it's okay if you take ten minutes for lunch.

Confounded: *Mixed together, not clearly distinguished.*

This boss and secretary differ in at least two ways: in sex and social status. As happens often in life, the two variables are confounded. As Table 6-1 indicates, the ways superiors relate to subordinates are also the ways men traditionally have related to women. Is "women's speech" therefore actually the "language of the powerless," or is it inherently feminine? On this issue, the jury is still out. On the one hand, social power does clearly affect speech. For example, when conversing, higher-status people (say a professor talking

TABLE 6-1 Gestures of Power and Privilege: Examples of Some Nonverbal Behaviors between People of Unequal Status and between Men and Women

Type of Behavior	Used by Superiors and by Men	Used by Subordinates and by Women
Address	Familiar	Polite
Touching	Touching OK	Don't touch
Demeanor	Informal	Guarded
Posture	Relaxed	Tense
Eye contact	Stare, ignore	Avert eyes, watch
Facial expression	Don't smile	Smile
Emotional expression	Hide	Show
Self-disclosure	Don't disclose	Disclose

Note: Adapted from *Body Politics: Power, Sex, and Nonverbal Communication* by Nancy Henley. Englewood Cliffs, N.J.: Prentice-Hall, 1977, p. 181.

to a senior student, or a senior talking to a freshman) are more likely to offer advice, interpretations, and statements of agreement or disagreement (Cansler & Stiles, 1981). Since women do have less social status and power, "women's speech" surely is, to some extent, the language of the powerless (Lamb, 1981; Thune, Manderscheid, & Silbergeld, 1980). But Robin Lakoff (1977), the linguist, believes "women's speech" is not *just* the language of the powerless. For example, powerless black Americans do not speak this way. And social psychologists Faye Crosby and Linda Nyquist (1977) found that when Boston University men and women students were given an identical laboratory role, their speech still differed.

Let's try a little experiment to get a feel for whether "women's speech" is actually just an expression of low social status. In the imaginary conversation above, switch Bill and Sally's roles. Given that Bill is now the subordinate and Sally the superior, is the conversation as plausible as before? Would you agree that Sally now sounds rather masculine and Bill atypically feminine? But, then again, some women do behave in the same way as men typically behave. And in research studies, masculine people—men and women whose attitudes, interests, or traits are more like those of the average man—are more socially dominant and less subtle in their language than are feminine men and women (Falbo, 1977; Falbo, 1982; Klein & Willerman, 1979).

Psychologists use "masculinity" and "femininity" to refer to psychological, not physical characteristics.

If power is expressed and exerted both verbally and nonverbally, then one wonders whether people could increase their social power by altering their behavior. Assertiveness training, for example, teaches women to communicate in ways more typical of people who successfully exert social power. Applying research on "sex and power," Nancy Henley (1977) offers a social prescription for both women and men:

> *Women can stop*: smiling unless they are happy; lowering or averting their eyes when stared at; getting out of men's way in public; allowing interruption; restraining their body postures; accepting unwanted touch.
> *Women can start*: staring people in the eye; addressing them by first name; being more relaxed in demeanor (seeing it's more related to status than morality); touching when it feels appropriate. . . .
> *Men can stop*: invading women's personal space; touching them excessively; interrupting; taking up extra space; sending dominance signals to each other; staring.
> *Men can start*: smiling; losing their cool, displaying emotion; confiding in other men; sending gestures of support; being honest when they are unsure of something. (pp. 202-203)

Are Females More Empathic and Sensitive?

There is little doubt that the average female is more empathic, more able to feel what another feels—to "rejoice with those who rejoice, and weep with those who weep." Martin Hoffman (1977) located sixteen studies comparing empathy in males and females. Although there was considerable overlap, the average female always slightly surpassed the average male. For example, when

Empathy: *The vicarious experience of another's feelings; putting oneself in another's shoes.*

hearing the taped sound of another infant's cry, newborn baby girls were more likely than newborn boys to cry. And when they watched someone supposedly receiving electric shocks, college women experienced more distress than men did.

Why this difference? Are women better at reading others' emotions? Or do men and women detect emotions with equal skill, but for some reason women more readily identify with others' emotions? Here, too, the jury is still out. However, in her recent analysis of seventy-five research studies, Judith Hall (1978; Rosenthal et al., 1979) discerned that women were indeed better at reading nonverbal emotional cues of both men and women. Females are especially superior at reading intentional cues, such as facial cues (Blanck et al., 1981).

"The issue is no longer in doubt; women are indeed superior to men in the decoding of nonverbal cues."

Robert Rosenthal & Bella DePaulo (1979)

Are Males Better at Visual-Spatial Tasks?

If women have a "people orientation," as evidenced by their greater empathy and sensitivity to nonverbal expressions, men may equivalently surpass women in what some psychologists have called "thing orientation." A widely agreed-upon difference is men's superiority at visual-spatial tasks. After reviewing dozens of research studies from many cultures, Lauren Harris (1978) concludes that the average man surpasses 75 to 80 percent of women on such tasks as copying geometric designs, solving mazes, detecting geometric figures embedded in complex backgrounds, and mentally rotating two- and three-dimensional shapes in order to compare them with standard figures.

Males tend to excel at visual-spatial tasks. One such task is the Rubik's Cube. Here are contestants in a timed Rubik's Cube competition. (Christian Voiujard/Gamma-Liaison)

Apparently this difference gives males an advantage in geometry, though not in algebra and arithmetic (which are more logical and less spatial). This advantage may help explain why males do better on those mathematical aptitude tests that incorporate spatial and geometric tasks. For example, among the approximately 20 million high school seniors taking the College Board's Scholastic Aptitude Test (SAT) since 1960, males' and females' average verbal aptitude scores have been nearly identical—always less than 10 points apart on the 200 to 800 scale. But in mathematical scores, males have consistently averaged 40 to 60 points higher (in 1981, 492 versus 443). Such differences may partly be due to the differing mathematics education received by males and females (Meece et al., 1982). But apparently that is not the only factor, for such differences exist even among thousands of intellectually precocious seventh graders who have been given the SAT. For example, in their recent nationwide talent search, Camilla Benbow and Julian Stanley (1980; Kolata, 1980) tested approximately equal numbers of able seventh grade boys and girls and found forty-one whiz kids who scored above 700 on the SAT mathematical test. All forty-one were boys.

"We favor the hypothesis that sex differences in achievement in and attitude toward mathematics result from superior male mathematical ability, which may in turn be related to greater male ability in spatial tasks."

Camilla Benbow & Julian Stanley (1980)

Whatever their origin, males' visual-spatial abilities may suit them better for certain tasks. Architects, for example, require a highly developed spatial sense. This may be one reason (though I suspect not the only one) why 96 percent of architects in the United States are men (Allen, 1980). Chess is a game that demands spatial ability, an ability that is highly developed in chess masters—who are virtually all male (L. J. Harris, 1979).

Conclusions

The list of male-female differences can be extended. For example, Jeanne Block has proposed a more complete list of differences suggested by recent research (see Box 6-2). Preadolescent boys are also more likely than girls to suffer various difficulties: They stutter more and are more likely to be retarded, hyperactive, or have learning disabilities. With age, these differences diminish. And in middle and older adulthood, male-female personality differences also diminish as men often become progressively less aggressive and domineering (Gutmann, 1975).

Are the known differences between men and women inherent sex differences? Perhaps. But let us not be too quick to assume so. As we shall see, although some of these differences are agreed-upon, their explanations are not. And we should remember that in many ways—in shyness, generosity, helpfulness, and overall intelligence, to name just a few—men and women do not noticeably differ (E. E. Maccoby, 1980).

Although male-female differences are small, these very differences provoke our interest. Just as detectives are interested in crimes, not in lawful behavior, so scientific detectives are intrigued by differences, not similarities. In the case of the male-female differences in aggression, power, empathy, and spatial ability, the causes for the "crimes" are still being investigated. Let us now examine the suspected culprits: biology and culture.

Box 6-2

Gender Differences in Personality

Jeanne Block (1979) identified seven areas in which researchers have found at least modest differences between the average male and the average female.

1 *Aggression*. From an early age, males are rougher, more domineering, more antisocial, more drawn to violent television programs.

2 *Activity level*. Males are more active, more exploratory, more accident-prone.

3 *Impulsivity*. Males have less impulse control, are more reactive to frustration.

4 *Susceptibility to anxiety*. Females are more fearful, more anxious, more prone to admit feelings of incompetence.

5 *Achievement*. Males are more motivated by competitive and ego-involving situations, females by social approval.

6 *Potency of the self-concept*. Males feel greater self-efficacy and power, are more defensive, describe themselves as less expressive and less sensitive.

7 *Social orientations*. Females are more empathic and more socially concerned, have fewer but more intense relationships.

Why Do Males and Females Differ? Biology

Men have penises, women have vaginas. Men produce sperm, women eggs. Men have the muscle mass to throw a spear far, women can breast-feed. Are biological sex differences limited to these obvious distinctions in reproduction and physique? Or do men's and women's genes, hormones, and brains differ in ways that also contribute to their behavioral differences? Social scientists have recently been giving increased attention to biological influences on social behavior. Consider the "biosocial" view of male-female differences.

Genetic Evolution: Doing What Comes Naturally

Virtually every cell in our bodies has in its nucleus the architectural plans for the entire body. The plans run to forty-six volumes—twenty-three acquired from our mothers, twenty-three from our fathers. These volumes are called chromosomes and their pages are our genes.

Have you ever imagined that you were the person you are, but of the other sex? Your biological gender is determined by just one of the chromosome volumes contributed by your father. That the other forty-five volumes—more than 98 percent of your genes—could be just the same and you be the other sex indicates that genetically, as well as behaviorally, men and women are far more alike than different.

Now assume, as evolutionary biologists do, that for millions of years each new organism, each new gene set, has competed with others for survival. Obviously, genes that increase the odds of an organism's survival would be most likely to be perpetuated. An organism's characteristics can therefore be analyzed for their contribution to survival. The Arctic environment, for example, selected polar bear genes programming a thick coat of warm, camouflaging, snow-white hair.

The controversial new field of sociobiology assumes that, like the polar bear's coat, social behaviors also are subject to natural selection. For example, Edward O. Wilson (1978) and David Barash (1979) contend that men and women bear the imprint of the ancestral division of labor. Men were hunters and warriors; women were food gatherers and bore and nursed the children. Thus natural selection favored the emergence of differing physical traits in males and females, and also of differing psychological traits—aggressiveness and a keen spatial sense in males, and empathy, sensitivity, and nurturance in females.

Sociobiology: *The study of the emergence of social behavior using the principles of evolutionary biology.*

Psychological differences also could be the result of a reproductive factor. Wilson reasons that aggressive males and coy females will most successfully perpetuate their genes:

> During the full period of time it takes to bring a fetus to term, from the fertilization of the egg to the birth of the infant, one male can fertilize many females but a female can be fertilized by only one male. Thus if males are able to court one female after another, some will be big winners and others will be absolute losers, while virtually all healthy females will succeed in being fertilized. It pays males to be aggressive, hasty, fickle, and undiscriminating. In theory it is more profitable for females to be coy, to hold back until they can identify males with the best genes. (p. 125)

As you can well imagine, these ideas have provoked controversy. Some assume that sociobiologists are suggesting that women are biologically suited to domestic tasks and men to work outside the home. Actually, even Wilson believes that males and females are but modestly bent by genetic predispositions. Culture, he thinks, more greatly bends the genders.

My own hunch is that a modest version of the sociobiological idea about male-female differences is plausible: It is consistent with basic principles of natural selection. But it is subject to at least two criticisms. First, much of it is speculation, not established fact. Genetic mutation and natural selection are demonstrable facts. The sociobiological edifice built upon them is thoughtful speculation. I admire sociobiologists' careful observations of organisms, from protozoa to baboons, and I am intrigued by the logical appeal of their theory. Yet when it is applied to humans, I am reminded of Mark Twain's

(1874) jest: "There is something fascinating about science. One gets such wholesale returns of conjecture out of such a trifling investment of fact."

Sociobiologists do incorporate facts in their theory. However, rather than begin with a cause and experimentally produce its effect, they sometimes start with an effect (for example, the male-female difference in aggression) and then work back to conjecture an explanation for it. This approach is reminiscent of "functionalism," psychology's dominant theory during the 1920s. "Why does that behavior occur? Because it serves such and such a function." The theorist can hardly lose at this game. Attributing behavior to social norms—after you know what behavior has occurred—is similarly sure to succeed. When one begins by knowing what there is to predict, the hindsight bias almost guarantees a successful "explanation."

Recall that the way to prevent the hindsight bias is to imagine things turning out otherwise. Let's try it. If *women* were the stronger and more aggressive sex, could we conjecture why natural selection might have made it so? I have a hunch we could. After all, since they are the primary caretakers of the young, strong and aggressive women would more successfully protect their young. Thus natural selection maximized strength and aggressiveness in women. Except, of course, it did not.

A hunch is a hunch and mine may well be wrong. Perhaps the male-female differences that exist can be more plausibly explained than their imagined opposites. Even so, as the sociobiologist would remind us, evolutionary wisdom is *past* wisdom. It tells us what behaviors were adaptive in times past. Whether such tendencies are still adaptive and commendable is quite a different question.

Hormones

The results of architectural blueprints can be seen in physical structures. The effects of genetic blueprints can be seen in bodily structures. If there are genetic sex differences, they must result in bodily sex differences. Are there bodily sex differences? Two possibilities have been much researched: sex hormones and brain organization.

Infants have built-in abilities to suck, grasp, and cry. Do mothers have a corresponding built-in predisposition to respond? Advocates of the biosocial perspective, such as sociologist Alice Rossi (1978), argue that they do. Behaviors critical to survival, such as the bonding of nursing mothers to their dependent infants, tend to be innate and culturally universal. For example, an infant's crying and nursing stimulates in the mother the secretion of oxytocin, the same sex hormone that causes the nipples to erect during lovemaking. For most of human history, the physical pleasure of breast feeding probably helped forge the mother-infant bond. Thus Rossi finds it not surprising that, while many cultures expect men to be loving fathers, *all* cultures expect women to be closely bonded to their young children. Likely, she would also not be surprised that in one study of more than 7000 passersby in a Seattle shopping mall, teenage and young adult women were more than twice as likely as

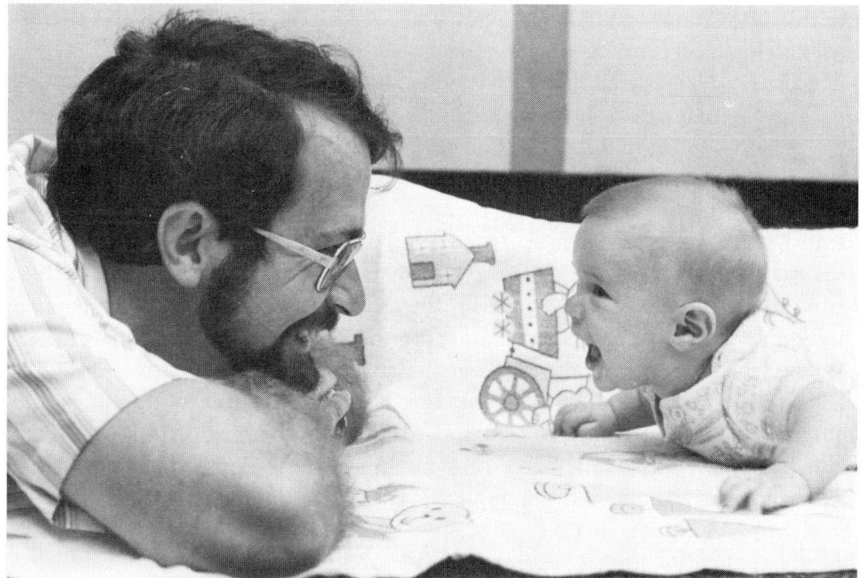

In various cultures, the "proper" role for mothers always includes a close bond with their infants. Fathers' roles range from indifference to their infants, in some cultures, to tender loving care in others. (Tom Renner)

similar-age men to pause to look at a baby (Robinson, Lockard, & Adams, 1979). Yet culture surely influences people's responses to infants, for such responses vary from culture to culture (Berman, 1980).

A universal behavior pattern—one found in every known society on earth—likely has some biological predisposition. Why else do smiles, in all cultures, signify happiness rather than unhappiness (Ekman, 1980; Keating et al., 1981)? In their influential book, *The Psychology of Sex Differences*, Eleanor Maccoby and Carol Jacklin (1974) conclude that the culturally universal male-female aggression difference does indeed have biological underpinnings. Maccoby and Jacklin say that there are other reasons to suppose the aggression difference is partly biological: It appears in subhuman primates (from an early age, male monkeys are more aggressive than females); it appears early in life (before cultural pressures could have much effect); and it can be manipulated by sex hormones (Ehrhardt & Meyer-Bahlburg, 1980; R. T. Rubin, Reinisch, & Haskett, 1980). In monkey experiments, females given male hormones become as aggressive and dominant as males. And there are cases recorded of women who received an excess of male hormones during their fetal development, either because of an injection their mother received or because of a malfunction in their own glands. In childhood, these girls reportedly acted in more aggressively "tomboyish" ways and were more interested than other girls in sports, toy guns, and playing with boys (Money & Ehrhardt, 1972). This "tomboyishness" may also have been environmentally influenced, because these girls' genitals often did not *look* normal before having corrective surgery, so the girls may have been treated differently. Nevertheless, the combined evidence seems clear: Male and female hormones do have demonstrable effects upon behavior.

Brain Organization

Male and female brains have an intriguing difference. As the two hemispheres of a person's brain mature, they become specialized. In right-handed people, verbal thinking is packaged mostly in the left hemisphere, and nonverbal thinking (for example, spatial perception) occurs predominantly in the right hemisphere. For some reason, this hemispheric specialization is more pronounced in men than in women. For instance, brain damage caused by a stroke or accident seems to produce fewer specific impairments in women, suggesting that their verbal and nonverbal skills are not so localized as men's. Among normal individuals, the average man recognizes pictures flashed in the left half of his field of vision (which are transmitted to his right hemisphere) more quickly than images flashed to the right. (This illustrates the right hemisphere's superiority at perceptual thinking.) In women, this differentiation between the right and left hemispheres is smaller (Wittig & Petersen, 1979; McGlone, 1980).

The cause of the greater asymmetry of men's brains is being debated. Could it be genetic? In some animal species there are indeed genetically determined sex differences in brain anatomy (Arnold, 1980). But could it not also be socially caused? Biology and psychology are connected by a two-way street. For example, hormones influence emotions, but emotions also influence hormone secretions. So, a correlation between biological and psychological characteristics, say between hemispheric specialization and gender, does not prove that the former is causing the latter. For example, one researcher found that, among boys, those who owned the most spatial toys (for example, construction sets) had the most hemispheric specialization. Since boys generally have more such toys than girls (Mossip, 1977), perhaps this helps account for their greater brain specialization. But then again, it could be the other way around. Maybe children's play preferences reflect their genetically determined brain organization.

Also being debated are the psychological *consequences* of the male-female difference in brain organization. Most commonly, the significance is linked to men's visual-spatial superiority. But does men's greater hemispheric specialization also provide them with a superiority in left-hemisphere verbal abilities? Clearly not. In fact, females appear to have slightly superior verbal fluency, at least during adolescence (Maccoby & Jacklin, 1974). Some researchers speculate that girls' verbal abilities develop more rapidly, making language their predominant manner of thinking; with boys, visual-spatial thinking may more fully develop in the absence of language.

No doubt further research will reveal that some of these speculations are in error (Sherman, 1978). This much, however, can be said with greater confidence: Even if male brains are better suited to certain specialized tasks, such will not signify male superiority overall. How many activities are like chess, requiring so much of one ability? Most tasks and occupations require the integration of many competencies. If more specialized brains are found better suited to specialized tasks, it likely will also be found that less specialized brains are better suited to integrative tasks (Levy, 1978).

"Some falsehood mingles with all truth."

Henry Wadsworth Longfellow,
The Golden Legend

Why Do Males and Females Differ? Culture

Does culture contribute to or just mirror male-female differences? The evidence here is clear: The impact of culture is enormous. This evidence comes from known cultural variations in sex roles, from some cases in which children have been culturally assigned the wrong sex at birth, and from recent experiments that demonstrate the social origins of male-female differences.

Cultural Differences in Sex Roles

Sex role: *A set of behavior expectations (norms) for males or females.*

We've already noted a few cultural universals: Virtually all societies are patriarchal—ruled by men. Men fight the wars and hunt large game; women gather food and tend the children (a division of labor that makes evolutionary sense to a sociobiologist). In their book, *The Longest War*, Carol Tavris and Carole Offir (1977) illustrate another universal. See if you can detect and state it:

> Among the Toda of India, men do the domestic chores; such work is too sacred for a mere female. If the women of a tribe grow sweet potatoes and men grow yams, yams will be the tribe's prestige food, the food distributed at feasts. . . . And if women take over a formerly all-male occupation, it loses status, as happened to the professions of typing and teaching in the United States, medicine in the Soviet Union, and cultivating cassavas in Nigeria. (p. 16)

The rule is this, say Tavris and Offir: Men's work, no matter what it is, is most prestigious.

So there are cross-cultural similarities. But, as Figure 6-3 illustrates, cultural differences are more numerous. In nonwesternized regions, agricultural food-accumulating societies tend to restrict women to child-related activities and men tend to regard such activities with contempt. In more nomadic hunting-gathering societies, women have greater freedom and sex-role distinctions are not so sharp (Van Leeuwen, 1978). Moreover, although every culture distinguishes masculinity from femininity, the traits and jobs assigned men in one culture are, in another, sometimes those assigned women. In some tribes, men do the weaving; in other tribes, weaving is a woman's work.

In the United States, heavy equipment operators are men, as are most physicians and dentists. In China, a woman can operate a crane without being thought masculine. In Denmark, dentistry is predominantly a woman's occupation. In Russia, 70 percent of doctors are women. A biological explanation of the American male predominance in these occupations would require human biology to be different in China, Denmark, and Russia. Plainly,

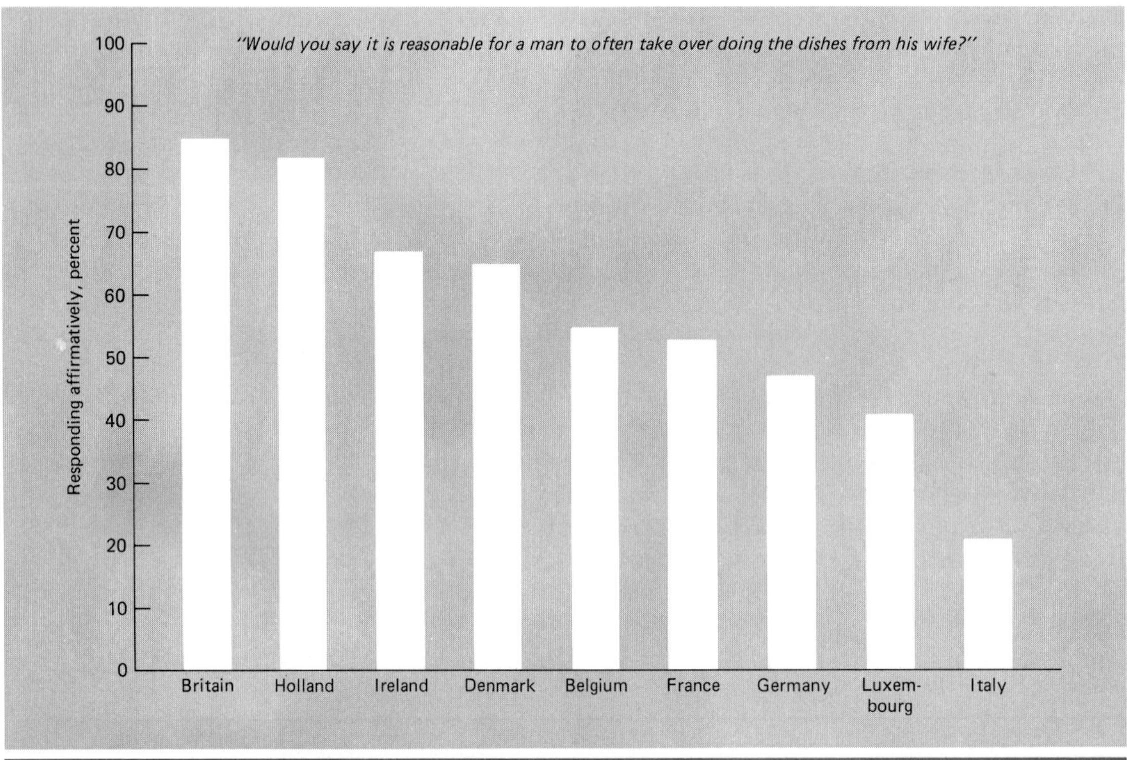

FIGURE 6-3 Cultural differences in men's willingness to do one form of "women's work"—wash dishes. In each country, men expressed even less willingness to do house cleaning, diaper changing, and ironing. (Data from a survey by the European Economic Community Commission, October–November, 1977. Reported in *Public Opinion*, February–March, 1980, p. 37.)

such is not the case. Even in the United States, secretaries, nurses, and teachers used to be mostly men. Has the biological suitability of men for these occupations somehow lessened?

Consider also traditional American sex roles. Pink and blue name tags in hospital nurseries mark the beginning of life's most pervasive social role: that of male or female. Developmental psychologist Paul Mussen (1969) observes that "no other . . . role directs more of one's overt behavior, emotional reactions, cognitive functioning, covert attitudes and general psychological and social adjustment" (p. 707). Concepts of one's sex role are developed rapidly and forcefully, even in homes where they are not consciously taught. One of my feminist colleagues was startled by her four-year-old daughter during the following recent conversation:

Sara: "I am going to be a nurse."

Mother: "Maybe you could be a doctor."

Sara: "Oh no. Only men can be doctors."

Mother: "Could you be a dentist?"

Sara: "No. Just men are dentists."

Mother: "Could you be a professor?"

Sara: "No. Professors are men."

Mother: "Sara! I'm a professor!"

Sara: "But you're really hiding a penis."

Writer Lois Gould (1980) cleverly illustrates the pervasiveness of sex-role assignment in her imaginary story of a child who was named X "so that nobody could tell whether it was a boy or a girl." From the beginning, people were befuddled, not knowing whether to say "Look at her cute little dimples!" or "Look at his husky little biceps!" X's parents took special care not to sex-type little X: "If they kept bouncing it up in the air and saying how *strong* and *active* it was, they'd be treating it more like a boy than an X. But if all they did was cuddle it and kiss it and tell it how *sweet* and *dainty* it was, they'd be treating it more like a girl than an X." School was both a problem and a joy for X: X was not fully accepted by boys or girls, yet could enjoy the activities of both. At the story's end, X's sex is revealed. When a new baby joins the family, X announces with a big, mischievous grin: "It's a Y!"

To illustrate how far American culture is from X, consider the following "predictability test" proposed by social psychologists Sandra Bem and Daryl Bem (1970):

> When a boy is born, it is difficult to predict what he will be doing 25 years later. We cannot say whether he will be an artist or a doctor or a college professor because he will be permitted to develop and to fulfill his own unique identity, particularly if he is white and middle-class. But if the newborn child is a girl, we can usually predict with confidence how she will be spending her time 25 years later. Her individuality doesn't have to be considered because it will be irrelevant. (p. 95)

Ways are changing. By 1980, 52 percent of American women were employed or looking for work (U.S. Department of Labor, 1981). And now, in at least one sense, men may actually be the *less* liberated sex: Male sex roles, some researchers believe, are the more rigidly defined. Consider some instances:

Box 6-3

Traditional Sex Roles

DEAR ANN LANDERS: My wife and I have been married for seven years. I used to think she was the most beautiful woman on earth. I was sure she'd be a terrific wife and mother.

Now it seems she can't get dinner on the table until 6:30 p.m. I come home at 6:00 and like to sit right down to a hot meal. That's the way my mother did it. No more homemade bread either. (Too much work, she says.) The laundry is always backed up. Yesterday I pulled out a shirt with a button off.

We have six children—the youngest are twins, four months old. I think a man who brings in a good paycheck every week has the right to expect a clean house, meals on time and the washing and ironing done right. Is it too much to ask her to shape up?

—ROCKFORD, ILL.

DEAR ROCK: A woman who has had six kids in seven years hasn't had much time to shape up. What have you done to help, besides getting her pregnant? If Planned Parenthood isn't forbidden by your religion, I suggest it.

Note: From a column by A. Landers in syndicated newspapers, November 18, 1979.

Parents are more tolerant of their little girls playing "like a boy" than their little boys playing "like a girl" (O'Leary & Donoghue, 1978). Better a tomboy than a sissy.

In adulthood, women are free to cry or not cry. But when Presidential candidate Edmund Muskie shed a tear over a venomous newspaper attack upon his wife, immediately he was judged by many as unfit for the office.

Women feel freer to become doctors than men to become nurses. And social norms now allow women increased freedom to choose whether or not to have a paying vocation; men who shun a job and assume the domestic role are "shiftless" and "lazy."

Eighty percent of the principal male characters on television have been "super masculine" (tough, self-reliant, domineering); women have played more diversified roles—sometimes exhibiting traditional feminine qualities, sometimes not (Peevers, 1979).

In these areas, at least, it is men who are more predictable, more locked into their role.

Gender Misassignment

Gender identity: *One's feeling of being a male or a female.*

Imagine a child assigned the wrong gender at birth, a child whose genes and internal sex organs are those of a girl, but whose parents name and treat it as a boy. What will be the child's resultant gender identity? Will its self-image be that of a girl who expects and wants to become a woman? Will it see itself as a boy? Or, given that the biological and social definitions of gender are conflicting, will it have a mixed and confused gender identity?

Such cases are not mere fantasy. Thirty years ago John Money and his colleagues found 100 children whose biological sex was ambiguous at birth—children such as genetic females who received extra male hormones while in the womb. Because the infant's genetic sex sometimes could not be determined from its genitals, the physician or the parents had to guess. Occasionally their guess was wrong. Amazingly though, nearly always the child comfortably accepted whatever gender it was assigned, whether or not it was genetically correct. "It is indeed startling," reported Money and his colleagues (1957), to see two biologically similar children

> in the company of one another in a hospital playroom, one of them entirely feminine in behavior and conduct, the other entirely masculine, each according to upbringing. As a social observer, one gets no suspicion that the two children are chromosomally and gonadally female, for psychologically they are entirely different.

There are many questions about how to explain these complex cases. But the central notion remains, that one's gender identity seems molded mostly by one's upbringing (Ehrhardt & Meyer-Bahlburg, 1980). And just as with normal children, these misassigned children's gender identity came quickly and strongly, and after age three was difficult to reverse.

Experiments on Sex Roles

The above discussions of cultural variation and gender misassignment have asked a simple question: If we hold biology constant but vary cultural expectations, what do we get? Answer: A big effect of culture. Social psychologists ask the same question when they experimentally explore the social origins of male-female differences. In the laboratory, too, social factors significantly affect how men and women behave.

Recall from Chapters 4 and 5 that our social ideas are often self-confirming. People expected to be hostile, extraverted, or gifted may actually exhibit hostility, extraversion, or high achievement. Mark Zanna and his colleagues wondered whether being stereotyped in a sex role would, similarly, lead one to fulfill the stereotype. In one experiment, Zanna and Susan Pack (1975) had Princeton University undergraduate women describe themselves to a tall, unattached, senior man they expected to meet later. Women led to believe that the man's ideal woman was "traditional" (deferent to her husband, emotional, home-oriented) presented themselves as more conventionally feminine than did women expecting to meet a man who supposedly liked independent, competitive, ambitious women. Moreover, when given a problem-solving test, those expecting to meet the nonsexist man behaved more intelligently: They solved 18 percent more problems than those expecting to meet the man with the traditional views. This adapting of themselves to fit the man's image was much less pronounced if the man was less desirable—a short, already attached, freshman.

In a follow-up experiment, Carl von Baeyer, Debbie Sherk, and Zanna (1981) had University of Waterloo women actually meet and interact with a male job interviewer who was said to have either sexist or nonsexist ideas about women's roles. Those anticipating a sexist interviewer arrived wearing more feminine makeup and accessories, were less likely to look him straight in the eye, and when asked questions such as "Do you have plans to include children and marriage with your career plans?," were more likely to give traditionally feminine answers. Other experiments confirm the point: Our sex-role beliefs, like other social beliefs, help create the reality that we presume exists (Skrypnek & Snyder, 1980).

"The more I was treated as a woman, the more woman I became."

Jan Morris's experience, after sex-change surgery from male to female

Social psychologists have also examined the effect of sex-role stereotypes in the media. It likely will not surprise you to learn that in elementary school readers, male-centered stories have outnumbered female-centered stories by more than 2 to 1, and that males in stories exhibit more competence and achievement. On television, even though men's personalities may be more rigidly stereotyped than women's, men have held three-fourths of the leading roles, and these roles are usually ones that portray responsibility. In prime-time roles, women are seldom both employed and married (Manes & Melnyk, 1974; Weigel & Loomis, 1981). In commercials, the flustered housewife agonizes over floor shine and ring around the collar, until a male authority proclaims the antidote to her worries (O'Donnell & O'Donnell, 1978; Tuchman, 1978; Welch et al., 1979). Do these images merely reflect existing sex roles? Or do they also contribute to them?

After ten years of discussing television's effects with community groups, I am convinced that most people believe television does indeed affect people—other people. Research on learning by imitation gives reason to suspect that our observing others affects us all. Although results of experiments dealing with children's imitation of sex roles are not conclusive, it appears that children are most likely to reenact behaviors performed by members of their own sex (Perry & Bussey, 1979). And some recent experiments by Florence Geis, Joyce Jennings, and their colleagues reveal that stereotyped portrayals of women can produce startling effects even with adults. The researchers had their University of Delaware students view either re-creations of four typical sex-stereotyped commercials or the same commercials with the sex roles reversed (for example, a little man proudly serves a delicious package dinner to his hungry wife, who is just home from work). When the women viewers

Children tend to imitate members of their own sex. (Drawing by Opie; © 1978 *The New Yorker* Magazine, Inc.)

then wrote essays about what they envisioned their lives to be "ten years from now," those who viewed the nontraditional commercials were more likely to express career aspirations (Geis et al., 1982).

A follow-up experiment revealed that women who viewed the nontraditional commercials were also less conforming in a laboratory test, and more self-confident when delivering a speech (Jennings, Geis, & Brown, 1980). If viewing but four vivid commercials has even a temporary effect on women's aspirations and behavior, one must wonder about the cumulative effect of the approximately 350,000 commercials commonly viewed during the growing-up years, and of the many more instances of such sex-role stereotyping in television's programs. These experiments on sex roles illustrate the central message of this chapter: that cultural norms have subtle but powerful effects upon the attitudes and behavior of each one of us.

Why Do Men and Women Differ? Biology and Culture

Thus far, I have simplified our discussion by pitting the biological explanation of male-female differences against the cultural explanation. It may seem that I wanted to see how many points each could score in this contest between scientific disciplines. Actually, there should be no contest, for two reasons: (1) the biological and social perspectives are but different levels of explanation, and (2) biological and social factors interact.

Levels of Explanation

Human nature can be examined from various perspectives—levels of explanation, we called them in Chapter 1. Somehow, we have gotten it into our heads that these levels compete: that if chemistry wins, biology loses; that if biology wins, psychology loses; or that if science wins, philosophy and religion lose. Nonsense. Different levels of explanation can make happy bedfellows. A biological explanation of male-female differences need not contradict a social-psychological explanation. Lauren Harris (1978) writes that

> the genetic-hormonal factors that create male and female children also predispose . . . activities that tend to enlarge and widen initial differences. The boy more naturally involves himself in experiences that sharpen spatial skills, the girl involves herself more in experiences that strengthen interpersonal skills. (p. 486)

If Harris is right—if biology predisposes boys to engage in the type of activity that builds spatial abilities—shall we say that the male-female difference in spatial ability is biological or cultural? Obviously it would be both: Biology initiates it and culture develops it.

The Interaction of Biology and Culture

As illustrated in the last example, biological and cultural influences are interdependent: Biological variables operate within a cultural context; and cultural effects are built upon biological foundations. Geneticists offer many examples of heredity-environment interactions. For instance, identical water buttercups have lacy leaves if growing underwater and thick waxy leaves if growing out of water.

In humans, culture tends to exaggerate small biological differences. If the wiring of men's brains enables them to be but slightly superior at spatial tasks, culture surely greatly amplifies this difference by encouraging men rather than women to perform tasks and enter occupations requiring spatial abilities. Similarly, if women's physiology bonds them more naturally with their children, culture teaches and reinforces the maternal role.

Sometimes the effect of culture depends upon what biology has endowed a person with. For example, people tend to expect those children whose bodies mature early to be verbally mature, also. Since girls usually mature earlier than boys, this expectation perhaps contributes to male-female differences. Or consider this: There is a very strong cultural norm dictating that males should be taller than their female mates. In one recent study, only 1 in 720 married couples violated this norm (Gillis & Avis, 1980). With hindsight, we can speculate a psychological explanation: Perhaps being taller (and older) helps men perpetuate their social power over women. But we can also speculate biological wisdom that might underlie the cultural norm: If people preferred partners of the same height, tall men and short women would often be without partners. As it is, biology dictates that men tend to be taller than women, and culture dictates such within couples. So it might well be biology and culture, hand in hand.

Changing Sex Roles

From the perspective of evolution, Act I of the human drama may be drawing to a close. Sex roles that were biologically adaptive in ages when women were pregnant both often and unpredictably may be less adaptive now that most women spend far more time working outside the home than mothering. Let us see how sex roles have changed in recent years and then ponder how they might change in the future.

Sex roles are converging. It is evident in people's attitudes. In 1962, only a third of the women in the metropolitan Detroit area disagreed with the statement "Most of the important decisions in the life of the family should be made by the man of the house." By 1977, more than two-thirds disagreed. And three-fourths disagreed that some work is meant for men and other work for women (Thornton & Freedman, 1979). In 1981, a Gallup poll found that 63 percent of Americans supported "the Equal Rights Amendment," and that even more—80 percent—agreed that "Equality of Rights under the law shall not be denied or abridged by the United States, or by any state on account of sex"—which *was* the ERA. In 1970, 40 percent of American women polled by the Roper organization supported most of the efforts being made to change the status of women in American society; in 1979 this figure had risen to 64 percent (*Behavior Today*, 1980). And a recent Louis Harris (1979) poll of eighteen- to forty-nine-year-old American men found them approving "the changes in women's roles" by a margin of 5 to 1. A foretaste of the future? Likely, because these increasingly liberal sex-role attitudes are especially prevalent among younger people (see Figure 6-4). Thus when America's college class of 1985 began college in 1980, 27 percent of the women said they intended to pursue careers in law, business, medicine, or engineering—a fourfold increase since 1966 (American Council on Education, 1981).

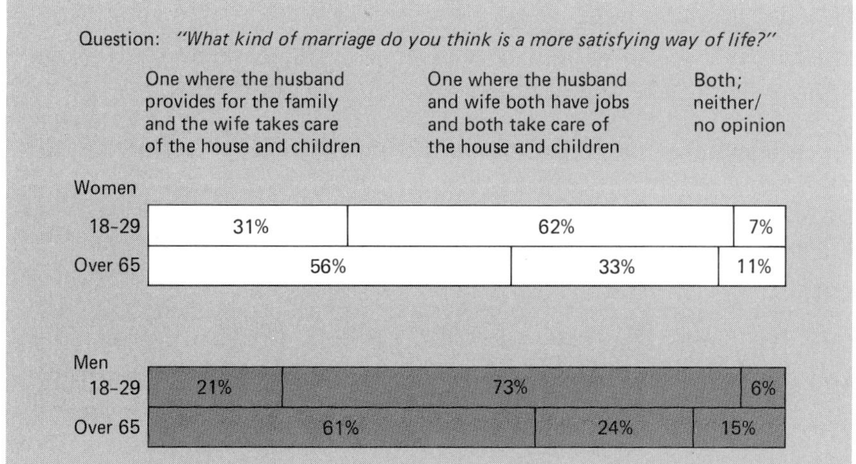

FIGURE 6-4 Sex-role norms are changing, among the young. (Data from a CBS/*New York Times* poll on sex-role norms, October, 1977. Reported in *Public Opinion*, January–February, 1979, p. 37.)

"Can man be free if woman be a slave?"

Percy Bysshe Shelley, The Revolt of Islam

But as noted in the Chapter 2 discussion of attitudes and actions, people don't always act out the attitudes they express. It's one thing for a man to say he approves "the changes in women's roles"; it's another for him to cook dinner. As one well-known actress remarked, "I've been married to a fascist and married to a Marxist, and neither one of them took out the garbage" (Tavris & Offir, 1977, p. 294).

In some ways, however, behavior *is* changing. Since 1965, American wives have been spending progressively less time in housework and child care, their husbands slightly more time (Peck, 1981). During the 1970s, the proportion of American women with full-time jobs doubled (Roper, 1979). In 1980, the U.S. labor force included 6 million married mothers with 7 million children under age six (*Newsweek*, 1980). The once-typical American family, with a husband-father who is provider and a wife-mother who is housewife, is now *a*typical. Jessie Bernard (1981) argues that this "traditional" family structure is actually a relatively recent invention that was born in the 1830s and died in 1980 when the U.S. Census Bureau ceased assuming that the male member of a household was its head (and when the number of employed women and female-headed families reached record levels for modern times).

Lois Hoffman (1977) has studied the effects of rising maternal employment. She reports that "research findings, on the whole, show that the

"They have this arrangement. He earns the money and she takes care of the house."

The traditional American family is increasingly becoming atypical. (Drawing by Weber; © 1977 *The New Yorker* Magazine, Inc.)

husbands of (employed) women help more in household tasks—including child care—than the husbands of (nonemployed) women." This, first, implies a convergence of sex roles. Second, as you might expect, Hoffman reports that children who grow up seeing both their parents holding jobs and sharing household tasks are more flexible concerning sex roles. And as sex roles converge, differences between male and female behavior are likely to shrink more. Hoffman reasons that

Does saying that men "help" with housework imply that housework is women's work?

> sex differences may be expected to diminish—some even to disappear—as socialization practices accommodate to the reality of the new adult roles. Fewer children, longer life, and working mothers—none of which are new, but all of which are now pervasive, normative, and I think here to stay—add up to new family roles, new socialization patterns, and a decrease in the differences between the sexes.

Assuming the continuation of these trends, imagine eventually reaching a point where nearly all men and women have full time jobs. If such occurs, will sex roles—for better or for worse—disappear? Carol Tavris and Carole Offir (1977) have analyzed societies where, already, nearly all women are employed. For example, based on the Marxist ideology of the equality of the sexes, the communist governments in Russia and China revolutionized the roles of women. Similarly, Israel's communal Kibbutz communities have consciously liberated women from housework. Yet each of these social experiments in equality has failed to achieve its egalitarian goals. In all three societies, women have less political and social power than men. In Russia, for example, women make up nearly half the work force but only 5 percent of the Communist Party's Central Committee. As Nikita Khrushchev once admitted, "It turns out that it is men who do the administering and women who do the work" (1980, p. 65). And when you ask, "Who works in the communal child-care nurseries?" and "Who cooks dinner?" the answers are usually as predictable as those given in the United States. Women may share increasingly in the breadwinning, but they still do most of the bread baking. Thus Tavris and Offir conclude that while

"I enjoy housework. To 'liberate' me from such is to 'enslave' me to an assigned task and call it employment."

A soon-to-be-married bachelor

> increasing numbers of women will take their place alongside men in the working world, we have less confidence that increasing numbers of men will take their place alongside women in the nursery and the kitchen. No country has given the question top priority. Until it does, the hand that rocks the cradle will be too tired to rule the world. (p. 295)

Why is it easier to prescribe than to practice the elimination of sex roles? The answer again lies with the controversy of biology versus culture. "Aha!" some say, "This feminist attempt to abolish sex roles goes against our natural state. Sure, with enough effort, some people can overcome biological dispositions for awhile, but once they slack off, they go right back to their biologically prescribed maleness or femaleness." Others point to the existence of enormous cultural variation, and suggest, "In just one or two generations you can't possibly expect political pronouncements to overturn a long history of male supremacy."

Should There Be Sex Roles?

Traditional sex roles: *"It's OK for both husband and wife to work, but only until one or the other gets pregnant."*

Sam Levenson

Describing and explaining traditional sex roles does not make them "wrong" and another set of norms "right." A scientific description of what *is* never implies a social prescription of what *ought* to be. However, many of the social scientists who study what is do have strong personal convictions about what ought to be—convictions that motivate their interest. Most sympathize with the ideology of the women's liberation movement, which argues that we should eliminate or at least modify sex roles, so that all persons can develop their own potentialities, regardless of their sex. Florence Denmark (1977), the 1980 president of the American Psychological Association, is quite candid about this: "The psychology of women is attempting to undo the sex-role stereotypes which affect expectations, self-esteem, and behavior in our society." Sandra Bem (1981) echoes this vision: "Human behaviors and personality attributes should cease to have gender."

A "Masculine" Society

There are at least three ways that a society without sex roles might be achieved. One way would be to socialize females to behave more as males are presumed to behave. For example, offer women assertiveness training to enable them to act more as men typically do.

A "Feminine" Society

However, Leonard Eron (1980), one of the researchers who has documented that "the preponderance of violence is perpetrated by males or by females who are acting like males," argues that making masculine behavior the ideal is precisely what society does *not* need. Thus the second way to achieve a society without sex roles would be to advocate the opposite:

> Rather than insisting that little girls should be treated like little boys and given exactly the same opportunities for participation in athletic events, Little League activities, and the like, as well as in all other aspects of life, it should be the other way around. Boys should be socialized the way girls have been traditionally socialized, and they should be encouraged to develop socially positive qualities such as tenderness, sensitivity to feelings, nurturance, cooperativeness, and aesthetic appreciation. The level of individual aggression in society will be reduced only when male adolescents and young adults, as a result of socialization, subscribe to the same standards of behavior as have been traditionally encouraged for women.

Androgyny

There is yet a third way to abolish sex roles: to socialize all people to develop both feminine and masculine traits so that they may draw upon whichever are appropriate in a given situation. This currently is the favored prescription among sex role researchers. It is called *androgyny*. For example, Sandra Bem contends that androgynous people combine the best of masculine and feminine qualities. Freed from sex roles, they can assert their rights one moment and be warm and tender toward a small child the next. Are people who describe themselves as both feminine and masculine (i.e., as androgynous) in fact more flexible and therefore "better adjusted"? This possibility has generated much excitement and a flood of research (see, for example, Flaherty & Dusek, 1980; Helmreich, Spence, & Holahan, 1979; Lubinski, Tellegen, & Butcher, 1981; Whitley, 1982).

Androgyny (andros, *man,* + gyne, *woman): Possession of both "masculine" and "feminine" psychological traits. The androgynous person is said to be high in both traditionally masculine qualities (for example, independence, assertiveness, competitiveness) and traditionally feminine qualities (for example, warmth, tenderness, compassion).*

Let's look at one of these androgyny experiments. First, make a guess: Given their "complementary" qualities, would a masculine man and a feminine woman be a more compatible couple than, say, a masculine man and an androgynous woman? William Ickes and Richard Barnes (1978) wondered, so they arranged laboratory blind dates by leaving pairs of University of Wisconsin men and women alone on a couch for five minutes while the experimenter supposedly went to get some questionnaires. Ten couples were composed of a masculine male and a feminine female. (These descriptions were based on their previous responses to a sex-role inventory.) One or both members of the other thirty couples were androgynous. Did "opposites attract"? Hardly. As Figure 6-5 indicates, the masculine male-feminine female couples expressed

FIGURE 6-5 Do masculine men and feminine women make the most compatible couples? After spending five minutes alone with someone of the other sex, University of Wisconsin students indicated their liking for this person whom they had just met. The masculine male–feminine female couples indicated much less attraction to one another than did other types of couples. (Data from Ickes & Barnes, 1978.)

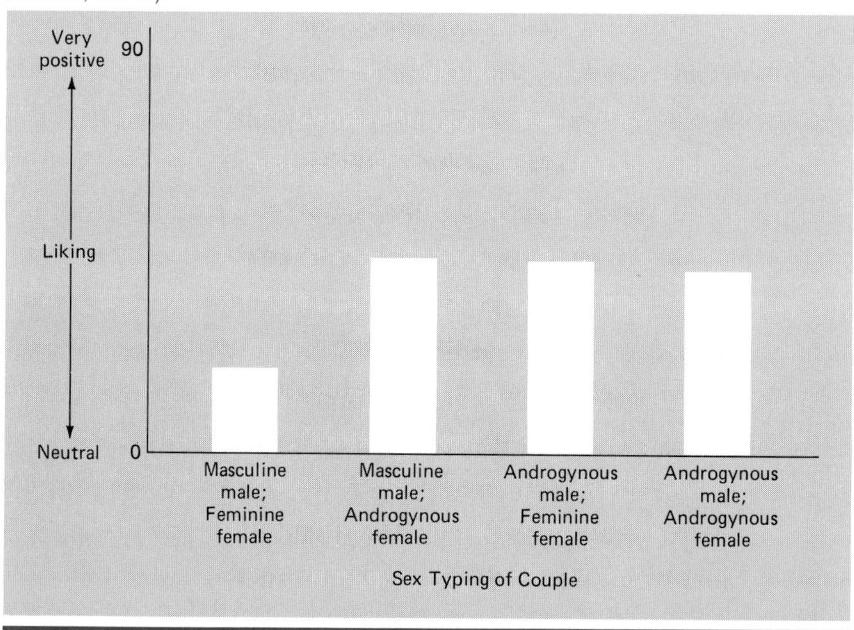

much less attraction for one another afterward than those that included an androgynous member. During the five minutes, they also talked with each other less; looked at each other less; and gestured, smiled, and laughed less. Ickes and Barnes surmised that "the behaviors prescribed by the stereotyped 'masculine' sex role were socially incompatible with those prescribed by the stereotyped 'feminine' sex role." Thus, in their initial encounters, social incompatibility between males and females may result partly from both adhering to traditional sex role orientations (Ickes, 1981). Even in marriage, couples tend to be less happy when both partners are sex-typed (Spence, Deaux, & Helmreich, in press).

Equality without Sameness?

The social ideal of androgyny is being debated, however. Is it wise to encourage everyone to incorporate and develop the best of both the masculine and feminine worlds? In her 1979 presidential address to the American Psychological Association's Division of the Psychology of Women, Barbara Strudler Wallston (1981) stated her concern about

> setting up androgyny as the new standard for mental health. This will be even more difficult to live up to than the old standards of masculinity and femininity, since androgynous people have to be able to "do it all." Isn't the real goal . . . working toward a society which allows for healthy differences?

Other scholars also question efforts to promote a unisex society. Alice Rossi (1978), who has written influential essays on behalf of sex-role equality and helped organize the Women's Caucus in the American Sociological Association, warns against minimizing the importance of our bodies:

> We cannot just toss out the physiological equipment that centuries of adaptation have created. We can live with that biological heritage or try to supersede it, but we cannot wish it away. I think we should aim for a society better attuned to its environment, more respectful of natural body processes and of the differences between individuals, more concerned for its children, and committed both to achievement in work and in personal intimacy. This version is more radical, and more human, than one of an equality between the sexes that denies differences.

Edward Sampson (1977; but see also Rianoshek, 1980, and Ickes, 1981) argues that androgyny is an excellent example of how cherished psychological ideals grow out of cultural values. He says that the androgynous ideal reflects the self-contained individualism of American culture. Each individual person is expected to contain all the esteemed qualities of the culture (for example, to embody the best of traditional male and traditional female characteristics). Sampson argues that if androgynous people have higher self-esteem and are better adjusted, it is because androgyny is well suited to American individualism. But it may be less well suited to more group-centered cultures, such as those of China or Japan. There, wholeness is sought in groups; everyone needn't be and do everything.

Sampson believes that specialized roles are not only inevitable, but also desirable. In all groups—whether cultural, occupational, or familial—specialists emerge. And each contributes to the group's well-being. For example, group dynamics expert Robert F. Bales (1958), has long argued that groups need two types of leadership—an assertive task leader who promotes ideas and a more sensitive social-emotional leader who helps keep the group together. Bales contends that it is inherently difficult for one person to act at once as both a task and a social leader. This idea that an effective group needs both types of person is contrary to the theory of leadership that maintains "One 'Great Person' can do it all." However, the point is not that women are better suited for social leadership and men for task leadership. Such abilities vary. Nor is the point even that every group should have two and only two types of leaders. The point is simply that effective groups often have role specialists.

These critics of the attempts to abolish sex roles do not argue for the retention of male supremacy. They favor equality of men and women—an equality not of sameness, but "as sides of the same coin are equal, or as partners are equal, or as components of the whole are equal" (Middleton, 1980, p. 26).

"Men and women are different. *What needs to be made equal is the value placed upon these differences."*

Diane McGuinness and Karl Pribram (1978).

In summary, whether sex roles should be preserved is obviously a point of controversy among social scientists. Some say yes. Some say no. But few argue to maintain the traditional masculine and feminine roles. Science can and does provide information useful to the debate. But, as with all matters of social prescription, science cannot decide the answer.

THE GREAT LESSON OF SOCIAL PSYCHOLOGY: PERSONS AND SITUATIONS

"There are trivial truths and great truths," declared the physicist Niels Bohr. "The opposite of a trivial truth is plainly false. The opposite of a great truth is also true" (quoted by McGuire, 1973). Each chapter in this unit on social influence teaches us about a great truth: the power of the social situation. This one great truth about the power of external pressures would sufficiently explain our behavior if we were passive, like a tumbleweed. But unlike a tumbleweed, we are not just blown here and there by the environment. We act, we react; we respond, and we get responses; we can resist the social situation, and sometimes even change it. Thus each of these "social influence" chapters concludes by calling attention to the opposite of the great truth: the power of the person.

A playful thought: *If Bohr's statement is a great truth, what is its opposite?*

Yet, even with this recognition of our own power, perhaps this chapter's stressing the power of culture leaves you somewhat uncomfortable. Most of us resent any suggestion that external forces determine our behavior. We want to think of ourselves as free beings, as the originators of our actions (well, at least of our good actions). We sense that believing in social determinism can

Emphasizing the power of the situation without a complementary emphasis upon the power of the person is conducive to "bad faith." (Drawing by Ed Arno; © 1979 *The New Yorker* Magazine, Inc.)

"Which are you—a victim of society or a crook?"

lead to what philosopher Jean-Paul Sartre called "bad faith"—evading responsibility by blaming something or someone for one's fate.

"The words of truth are always paradoxical."

Lao-Tsze, The Simple Way

Actually, social control (the power of the situation) and personal control (the power of the person) compete no more with one another than do biological and cultural explanations. Social and personal explanations of our social behavior are both valid, for at any moment we are both the creatures and the creators of our social worlds. We may well be the products of our genes and environment. But it is also true that the future is coming, and it is our job to decide where it is going. Our choices today determine our environment tomorrow.

A visual image may help us remember this great lesson of social psychology (see Figure 6-6). Social situations do profoundly influence individual persons. But individual persons also influence the social situation. The two *interact.*

This interaction occurs in at least three ways. First, a given social situation often will affect different people somewhat differently (Nisbett, 1980). Since

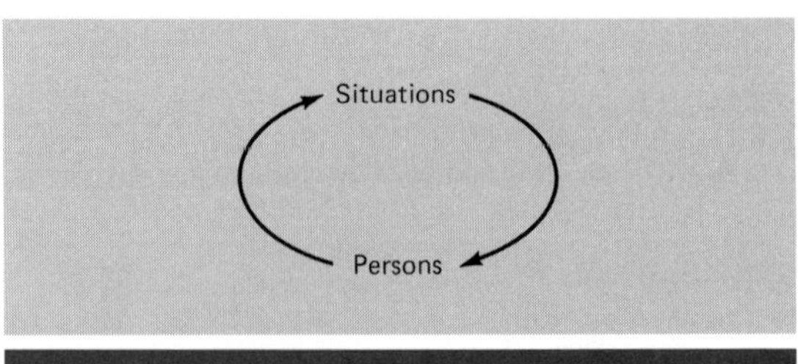

FIGURE 6-6

our minds do not see reality identically, we each respond to a situation as we perceive it. And some people are more sensitive and responsive to social situations than others (M. Snyder, 1981b). Such can also be said of cultures. Japanese people, for example, have been found more responsive to the situation than British people (Argyle, Shimoda, & Little, 1978). So asking whether people's behavior is determined by their external situations or their inner dispositions is like asking whether the area of a field is determined by its length or its width.

Interaction between persons and situations also occurs because people can choose to be part of a particular situation. When you chose your college you were also choosing to expose yourself to a specific set of social influences. Ardent political liberals are unlikely to settle in Orange County, California, join the Chamber of Commerce, or read *U.S. News and World Report.* They are more likely to live in San Francisco, join Common Cause, and read the *New Republic*—in other words, to choose a social world that reinforces their liberal inclinations.

Finally, people often create their situations. Recall again that our preconceptions can be self-fulfilling: If we expect someone to be extraverted, hostile, feminine, or sexy, our actions toward the person may induce the very behavior we expect. What, after all, composes a social situation, but the people in it? A liberal political environment is one created by political liberals. What takes place at the Elks Club bar is created by the patrons. The social

People choose their social influences. (Drawing by Vietor; © 1978 *The New Yorker* Magazine, Inc.)

environment is not like the weather—something that just happens to us. It is more like our houses—something we have made for ourselves.

This reciprocal causation (between social situations and persons) allows us to see people as either *reacting* to or *acting* upon their environment. Each perspective is correct, for we are both the products and the architects of our social worlds. However, to be practical, is one perspective wiser? Even that is complex, for in one sense, it is wise to see ourselves as the creatures of our environments—lest we become too proud of our achievements and too self-blaming for our problems—and to see others as free actors—lest we become paternalistic and manipulative.

"If we explain poverty, or emotional disorders, or crime and delinquency, or alcoholism, or even unemployment, as resulting from personal, internal, individual defects . . . then there simply is not much we can do about prevention."

George Albee (1979)

However, perhaps we would do well to assume more often the reverse—to view ourselves as free agents and to view others as influenced by their environments. Thus we would assume self-efficacy as we view ourselves, and seek always for understanding and social reform as we relate to others. (If we view others as influenced by their situations we are less likely to smugly diagnose rather than understand and empathize, less likely to pronounce unpleasant behavior as that chosen by "immoral," "sadistic," or "lazy" persons.) Interestingly, most religions similarly encourage us to take responsibility for ourselves but to refrain from judging others. Does religion teach this because our natural inclination is to excuse our own failures while blaming others for theirs?

SUMMING UP

Norms

The remarkably wide diversity of attitudes and behaviors from one culture to another indicates the extent to which we are the products of cultural norms. Norms restrain and control us, but they also lubricate the social machinery: social behavior occurs with more ease when everyone knows what is both expected and accepted.

Despite their distinct differences, cultures share some norms in common. One apparently universal norm concerns how people of unequal status relate to one another. Nonverbal behavior (for example, touching, staring) and forms of address (for example, first name basis versus last name basis) can express dominance or intimacy, depending upon whether or not they are mutually exchanged. We communicate informally with intimates, and they do with us; we often also communicate informally to those of lower status, but this tends not to be mutual. The more formal way we communicate with strangers is the same way we communicate with superiors. Moreover, increased intimacy (for example, a social invitation) is usually initiated by the person with higher status.

Roles

A role is a set of norms associated with a given social position. We tend to assimilate the roles we play. Thus our playing a destructive role can be corrupting, as illustrated in observations of students playing the role of prison guard, and in experiments that make some people subservient to or dependent upon others. Parallels to these laboratory results are found in daily life, such as in the "burnout" often experienced by police officers, ward attendants, and social workers. But role playing can also be used constructively. By reversing roles intentionally for a time, we can develop empathy for another.

The expectations associated with a role sometimes conflict. If one's personality or attitudes clash with the role one must play, the result is the conflict of person and role. Intrarole conflict arises when there is disagreement about how a given role should be played. And interrole conflict occurs when there is an incompatibility between the requirements of two different roles.

Sex Roles

These basic principles of role theory are perhaps best illustrated in the most pervasive, most heavily researched social roles: the roles of male and female. As do other sets of norms, sex roles vary widely from culture to culture. Yet some cultural norms are universal (for example, men are warriors; women care for the young children). The assimilation of particular sex roles help create male-female differences: Men commonly behave more aggressively than women; they tend to exert more social power, to have keener visual-spatial skills, and to be less empathic and less sensitive to nonverbal cues. These differences are small, and are certainly outnumbered by the ways men and women are alike. But differences, not similarities, catch the eye and provoke the mind.

Biological sex differences may contribute to behavioral differences. Sociobiologists speculate how evolution might have created a sexual division of labor. The evidence is clearer, however, that hormonal sex differences help create aggressiveness in males and a mother-infant bond in females. There is also a male-female difference in brain organization: The tendency for the left and right hemispheres to serve distinct functions is more pronounced in men than women. Both the cause and the effects of this male-female difference are currently being debated and researched.

The effect of culture on sex roles is less debatable. First, biology cannot explain the striking variations in sex roles from culture to culture. Second, although hormones can noticeably affect the masculinity or femininity of a child's interests and play behavior, the gender a child is socially assigned at birth determines its gender identity—its sense of being a male or a female. Third, laboratory experiments document that social influences affect how men and women behave. Both in day-to-day social interaction and in the media, sex-role stereotypes tend to be self-fulfilling. These three lines of research all indicate that if biology is held constant while cultural expectations are varied, the cultural effects are pronounced.

However, biological and cultural explanations need not be contradictory. They are different levels of explanation, both of which can be valid. Actually, they interact, biological factors operating within a cultural context and culture being built upon a biological foundation.

In industrialized nations such as the United States, sex roles are converging. People are beginning to accept similar roles for men and women, and women's employment rates have increased dramatically. As traditional sex roles wane, a generation of children is now being socialized to the new roles they are observing. Yet in no culture have sex roles been eliminated.

Should they be? This is an ideological, rather than a scientific question. Many social psychologists who study sex roles advocate their elimination, or at least their modification. Some advocate androgyny, the combination of feminine and masculine traits. They feel that, freed from rigid sex roles, the ideal androgynous person can, as appropriate, be "masculine" one moment and "feminine" the next. Other social psychologists question this ideal. Either they argue that it ignores biological differences, or they question the individualism of expecting each person to be all things.

Persons and Situations

The great truth about the power of social influence is but half the truth if separated from its complementary truth: the power of the person. Persons and situations interact in at least three ways. First, social situations influence individual persons, yet individuals vary in how they interpret and react to a given situation. Second, people choose many of the situations that influence them. Third, social situations are created by people. Thus power resides both in persons and in situations. We create and are created by our social worlds.

Chapter

Conformity

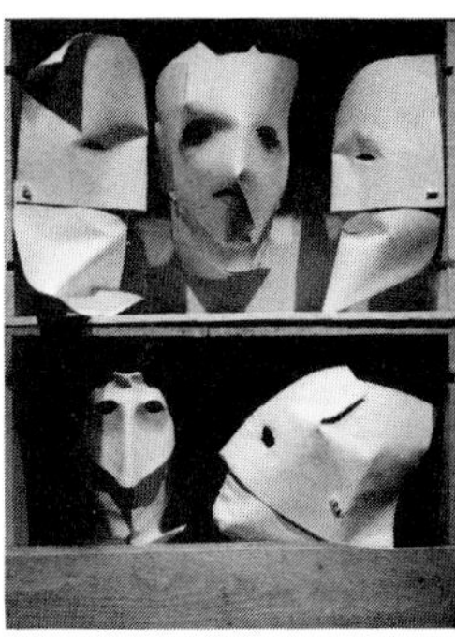

"The race of men, while sheep in credulity, are wolves for conformity."

Carl Van Doren, Why I am an Unbeliever

It was a long-awaited May afternoon. Three thousand family members and friends had gathered for the celebration. On cue, 400 Hope College seniors rose to hear the college president declare, "I hereby confer upon each of you the degree of Bachelor of Arts, with all the rights and privileges appertaining thereto." The declaration finished, the 25 new alumni in the first row began filing forward to receive their diplomas. As they did so, the other 375 eyed one another nervously, each thinking: "Weren't we instructed to sit down now and await our row's turn?" But no one sat. The seconds ticked by. Half the first row now had diplomas in hand. Outwardly, the standing herd kept its cool. But inside each head thoughts were buzzing: "We could be standing here for a half hour before it is our row's turn. . . . We're blocking the view of spectators seated behind us. . . . Why doesn't someone sit down?" Still, no one sat. Now two minutes had elapsed. The graduation marshal, whose instructions at the graduation rehearsal were being ignored, strode up to the first standing row and subtly signaled it to sit down. No one sat. So he moved to the next row and audibly ordered it to "Sit down!" Within two seconds, 375 much-relieved people were happily relaxing in their chairs.

Witnessing this scene raised in my mind three sets of questions. First, why, given the great diversity of individuals among that large group, was their behavior so uniform? Is social pressure sometimes powerful enough to obliterate individual differences? Where were the rugged individualists?

Second, 25 percent of those graduates had been my students in social psychology. Although it was the furthest thing from their minds at the moment, they knew about conformity. When studying the topic, many of them had privately assured themselves that they would be never so docile as the subjects in the famous conformity experiments. But here they were, participating in one of life's parallels to the laboratory experiments. In such situations is the heroic individualistic act always more easily fantasized than performed? Are we more susceptible to social influence than we realize? Does learning about social influence not liberate us from it? Third, is conformity as bad as my description of this docile "herd" implies? Should I have been dismayed at their "mindless conformity" or instead pleased at their "group solidarity" and "social sensitivity"?

Let us take the last question first. Is conformity good or bad? This is another of those questions that has no scientific answer. But assuming the values most of us share, two things can be said. First, conformity is at times bad (for example, when it leads someone at a party to drink too heavily before driving home), at times good (for example, when it inhibits people from cutting in front of us in a theatre line), and at times relatively inconsequential (for example, when it inclines us to wear all white when playing tennis).

Second, the very term "conformity" does nevertheless carry a negative value judgment. How would you feel if you overheard someone describing

Is conformity, such as in matters of dress, good or bad? (David Strickler/Monkmeyer)

you as a "real conformist"? I suspect you would feel hurt, because in western cultures the trait of going along with peer pressure is generally not prized. Hence American and European social psychologists more often give it negative labels (conformity, submission, compliance) than positive ones (communal sensitivity, responsiveness, cooperative team play). We choose labels to suit our judgments. In retrospect, I confess to viewing the U.S. senators who cast unpopular votes against the Vietnam war as "independent" and "inner-directed," and those who cast unpopular votes against civil rights legislation as "eccentric" and "self-centered."

"Whatever crushes individuality is despotism, by whatever name it may be called."

John Stuart Mill, On Liberty

Labels both describe and evaluate. They are, however, inescapable. We cannot discuss the phenomena of this chapter without labels. I will conform to the standard terminology, so let us be clear on the meanings of the following labels: conformity, compliance, acceptance.

When, as part of a crowd, you rise to cheer a game-winning touchdown, are you conforming? When, along with millions of others, you drink milk, are you conforming? When you and everyone else agree that men look better with combable hair than with crewcuts, are you conforming? Maybe, maybe not. The key is whether or not your behavior and beliefs would be the same apart from the group. Would you rise to cheer the touchdown if you were the only fan in the stands? Conformity is not just acting as other people act, it is being affected by how they act. It is acting differently from the way you would act if you were alone. Thus Charles Kiesler and Sara Kiesler (1969) define *conformity* as "a change in behavior or belief . . . as a result of real or imagined group pressure" (p. 2).

Conformity: *A change in behavior or belief as a result of real or imagined group pressure.*

Sometimes we conform without really believing in what we are doing. We put on the mandatory necktie, though we dislike doing so. This insincere outward conformity is called *compliance*. We comply primarily to reap a reward or avoid a punishment. If our compliance is to an explicit command, the compliance is called obedience.

Compliance: *Publicly acting in accord with social pressure while privately disagreeing.*

Other times we genuinely believe in what the group has convinced us to do. We may join millions of others in drinking milk because we have been convinced that milk is nutritious. This sincere inward conformity is called *acceptance*.

Conforming to avoid punishment more likely represents compliance than acceptance. (© 1980 United Feature Syndicate, Inc.)

Acceptance: *Both acting and believing in accord with social pressure.*

Compliance and acceptance are often related. As Chapter 2 emphasized, attitudes follow behavior. Thus compliance can breed acceptance. Unless we feel no responsibility for our behavior, we usually become sympathetic to what we have stood up for.

Researchers who study conformity have constructed some fascinating miniature social worlds—laboratory microcultures that simplify and simulate important features of everyday social influence. Let us begin our scrutiny of conformity research by examining three noted sets of these experiments, each of which has provided (1) a method that others could use to study conformity and (2) some startling findings.

CLASSIC STUDIES

Sherif's Studies of Norm Formation

The first of the three "classics" provides a bridge between the last chapter's discussion of the power of culture to create and perpetuate arbitrary norms and this chapter on conformity. Muzafer Sherif (1937) wondered whether one could observe in the laboratory the emergence of a social norm. Much like a biologist seeking to isolate a virus in the laboratory where it might then be experimented upon, Sherif wanted to isolate and then experiment with the social phenomenon of norm formation.

Were you a participant in one of Sherif's experiments, you might find yourself seated in a dark room. Fifteen feet in front of you a pinpoint of light appears. After the few seconds it remains on, you must guess how far it moves. At first nothing happens. Then it moves erratically and finally disappears. Since the dark room leaves no guide for distance you squirm before offering an uncertain "6 inches." The procedure is repeated. This time you say "10 inches." With further repetitions your estimates continue to average about 8 inches.

The next day you return, joined by two others who the day before also had the same experience. When the light goes off for the first time, the other two people offer their best guesses from the day before. "One inch" says one. The other states, "2 inches." A bit taken aback, you nevertheless guess "8 inches." Do you think that with successive repetitions of this group experience, both this day and for the next two days, your responses will change? The Columbia University men whom Sherif tested changed their estimates markedly. As Figure 7-1 illustrates, a group norm typically emerged. (The norm was false. Why? The light never moved! Sherif had taken advantage of a perceptual illusion called the autokinetic phenomenon.)

The autokinetic phenomenon: *Self* (auto) *motion* (kinetic). *The apparent movement of a stationary point of light in the dark. Perhaps you have experienced this when thinking you have spotted a moving satellite in the sky, only to realize later that it was merely an isolated star.*

Sherif and others after him used this technique to answer questions about people's suggestibility. For example, when a year later people were retested alone would their estimates again diverge or would they continue to state the group norm? Remarkably, they continued to support the group norm (Rohrer et al., 1954). (Does this suggest compliance or acceptance?)

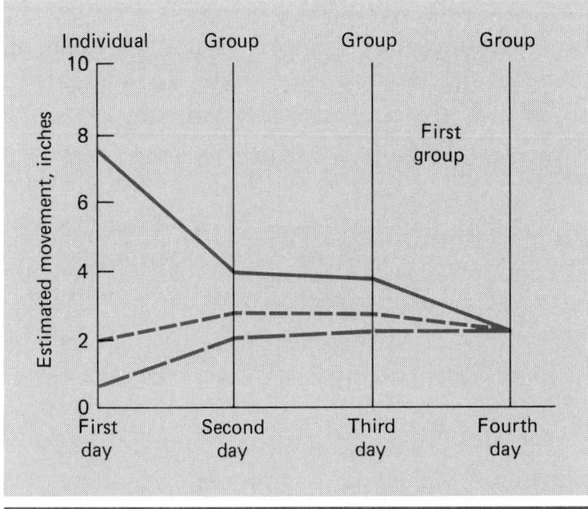

FIGURE 7-1 A sample group from Sherif's study of norm formation. Three individuals converge as they give repeated estimates of the apparent movement of a point of light. (Data from Sherif & Sherif, 1969, p. 209.)

Struck by what seems to be culture's power to perpetuate false beliefs, Robert Jacobs and Donald Campbell (1961) wondered whether such could be demonstrated and studied in their Northwestern University laboratory. Using the autokinetic phenomenon, they had a confederate plant an inflated estimate of how far the light moved. The confederate then left the experiment and was replaced by another real subject who was in turn replaced by a still newer member. The inflated illusion nevertheless persisted for five generations. These people had became "unwitting conspirators in perpetuating a cultural fraud."

Confederate: *An accomplice of the experimenter.*

In everyday life the consequences of suggestibility are sometimes amusing. In late March of 1954, Seattle newspapers reported damage to car windshields in a city 80 miles to the north. On the morning of April 14, similar windshield damage was reported 65 miles away, and later that day only 45 miles distant. By nightfall, the windshield-pitting agent had reached Seattle. Before April 15 passed, the Seattle police department received complaints of damage to over 3000 windshields (Medalia & Larsen, 1958). That evening the mayor of Seattle called on President Eisenhower for help.

"Why doth one man's yawning make another yawn?"

Robert Burton, Anatomy of Melancholy

I was an eleven-year-old Seattleite at the time. I can recall searching our windshield, having been frightened by the explanation that an H-bomb, which had recently been tested in the Pacific, was raining its fallout upon Seattle. However, on April 16 the newspapers hinted that actually the culprit might well be mass suggestibility. After April 17 there were no more complaints. A later analysis of the pitted windshields concluded that the cause was ordinary road damage. What had we been doing that we had not done before the report? Given the suggestion, we had looked carefully *at* our windshields instead of *through* them.

Suggestibility in real life is not always so amusing. Sociologist David Phillips (1974; 1977; 1979) reports that fatal auto accidents, private airplane crashes, and suicides increase after well-publicized suicides. Moreover, the increased fatalities occur in an area only after the story is publicized there. And the more newspaper inches given the story, the greater the increase in subsequent fatalities. Phillips believes that this indicates both the power of suggestion and that many car and plane fatalities may in fact also be suicides.

Asch's Studies of Group Pressure

Participants in the autokinetic experiments were faced with an ambiguous reality, one with no obviously correct answer. Social psychologist Solomon Asch (1956) suspected that intelligent people would not conform in situations where they could readily see the truth for themselves. To test his hunch and to examine factors he thought might affect conformity, Asch created a clever experimental situation.

Imagine yourself as one of Asch's volunteer subjects. You are seated at the end of a row of five people. After explaining that you will be taking part in a study of perceptual judgments, the experimenter then asks you to indicate which of the three lines in Figure 7-2 is identical to the standard line. You can easily see that it's line 2. So, you are hardly surprised when the other four people, responding before you, all say "line 2."

The next comparison proves just as easy for everyone. You think "ho hum" and settle in to endure politely a boring experiment. But on the third trial you are startled. Although the correct answer seems just as clear-cut, the first person gives what seems to you to be a wrong answer. When the second person gives the same answer, you sit up in your chair and stare at the cards. The third person agrees with the first two. Your jaw drops; you start to perspire. "What is this?" you ask yourself. "Are they blind? Or am I?" The fourth person concurs with the others. And then the experimenter looks to you. Now you are experiencing an "epistemological nightmare": "How am I to know what is true? Is it what my peers' eyes tell me or what my eyes tell me?"

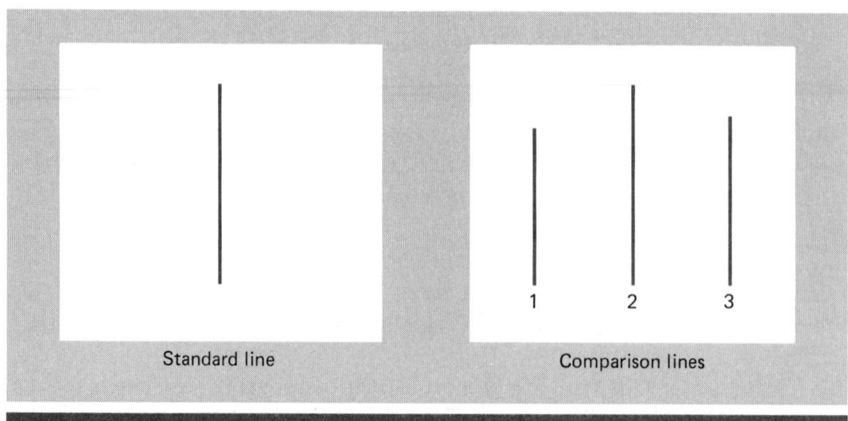

FIGURE 7-2 Sample comparison from Solomon Asch's conformity procedure. The participants were asked to judge which of three comparison lines was equal to the standard.

Hundreds of college students experienced this conflict when they participated in Asch's experiments. Those who answered alone were correct more than 99 percent of the time. Asch wondered: If several others (confederates who had been coached by the experimenter) gave identical wrong answers, would this prompt people to call true what they would otherwise have declared false? Thirty-seven percent of the time they did. Of course, that means 63 percent of the time they did not. Still, Asch was shocked; he thought the group's power would not be this great. Asch's feelings about this conformity were as clear as the correct answers to his questions:

"He who sees the truth, let him proclaim it, without asking who is for it or who is against it."

Harry George, The Land Question

> That we have found the tendency to conformity in our society so strong that reasonably intelligent and well-meaning young people are willing to call white black is a matter of concern. It raises questions about our ways of education and about the values that guide our conduct. (Asch, 1955)

Ethical note: *Professional ethics usually dictate explaining the experiment afterward (see Chapter 1). Pretend you were an experimenter who just finished a session with a fully conforming participant. Could you explain the deception without making the participant feel gullible and spineless?*

Asch's procedure became the standard for hundreds of later experiments. Such experiments lack the "mundane realism" of everyday conformity, but

One of Asch's conformity experiments. In the lower picture, the real subject, number 6, experiences conflict and tension after hearing the five persons before him respond incorrectly. (Photos by William Vandivert with permission of *Scientific American*)

they do have "experimental realism" (see Chapter 1). People do get emotionally involved in the experience. Some may even find it stressful. However, the procedure is expensive and difficult to control because it requires a troupe of confederates who must act with near-perfect consistency from subject to subject. Richard Crutchfield (1955) remedied this by automating Asch's experiment. Five participants—each a real subject—sit in adjacent booths and view questions projected on the wall across the room. Each booth has a panel of lights and switches that allows the subjects to indicate their judgments and to see how others are responding. After a few warm-up trials, all subjects find themselves responding last after observing the purported responses of the other four.

The technique also enables one to present a variety of questions. For example, Crutchfield (1955) tested military officers by presenting a circle and a star side by side. The area of the circle was one-third greater. But when each officer thought the others had judged the star as larger, 46 percent of them denied their senses and voted with the group. When a sample of the officers were tested privately, each one rejected the statement, "I doubt whether I would make a good leader." Of course, these were leaders. Yet, believing other officers all accepted the statement, almost 40 percent did so. Even ideologically objectionable positions (to people questioned individually) have been approved when the group approves. Not long before the 1960s free-speech movement surfaced at the University of California, Berkeley, Crutchfield and his colleagues found 58 percent of the students they tested there

FIGURE 7-3 Richard Crutchfield's conformity-testing procedure. People sit in adjacent booths and answer questions presented on the wall in front of them after witnessing others' purported answers. (Drawing by Anne Canevari Green.)

willing to go along with the group and agree that, "Free speech being a privilege rather than a right, it is proper for a society to suspend free speech when it feels itself threatened" (Krech, Crutchfield, & Ballachey, 1962).

The Sherif, Asch, and Crutchfield results are startling because in none of them is there any explicit pressure to conform—no promised rewards for "team play," no threatened punishments for individuality. It makes one wonder: If people are this compliant in response to such minimal pressure, how much more compliant might they be if directly coerced? Could the average American be coerced into performing the types of cruelties performed in Germany under Nazi rule? My hunch was no: Americans' democratic and individualistic values would make them resistant to such pressure. And besides, the easy verbal pronouncements of these experiments are a giant step away from compliance to pressure to harm someone. You and I would never yield to coercion to hurt another. Or would we? Stanley Milgram wondered.

Milgram's Obedience Experiments

Milgram's (1965; 1974) experiments on what happens when the demands of an authority conflict with the demands of conscience have become the most famous and controversial experiments in all of social psychology. Picture the scene: Two men, one of them responding to an ad, come to Yale's psychology laboratory to participate in a study of learning and memory. They are met by a somewhat stern experimenter in a gray technician's coat who explains that this is a pioneering study of the effect of punishment on learning. The experiment requires one of them to teach a list of word pairs to the other and to punish errors by delivering shocks of increasing intensity. To designate the roles, they draw slips out of a hat. One of the men, a mild-mannered forty-seven-year-old accountant who is the experimenter's confederate, feigns that his slip says "learner." He is ushered into an adjacent room and, while the "teacher" looks on after taking a sample shock, is strapped into a chair and has an electrode attached to his wrist.

The teacher and experimenter then return to the main room where the teacher takes his place before a "Shock Generator" with switches ranging in 15-volt increments from 15 to 450 volts. The switches are given labels such as, "Slight Shock," "Very Strong Shock," "Danger: Severe Shock," and so forth. Under the 435 and 450 volt switches is printed simply "XXX." The teacher is told to "move one level higher on the shock generator" each time the learner gives a wrong answer. With each flick of a switch, lights flash, relay switches click, and one hears an electric buzzing sound.

If the teacher complies with the experimenter's requests he hears the learner grunt at 75, 90, and 105 volts. At 120 volts the learner shouts that the shocks are painful. And at 150 volts he cries out, "Experimenter, get me out of here! I won't be in the experiment anymore! I refuse to go on!" By 270 volts his protests have become screams of agony and he continues insisting he be let out. At 300 and 315 volts he screams his refusal to answer. After

The shock generator used in Stanley Milgram's obedience experiments. (Copyright 1965 by Stanley Milgram. From the film *Obedience,* distributed by the New York University Film Library.)

330 volts he falls silent. In answer to the teacher's inquiries and pleas to terminate the experiment, the experimenter states that the learner's nonresponses should be treated as wrong answers. To keep the teacher going he uses four verbal prods:

Prod 1: Please continue (*or* Please go on).

Prod 2: The experiment requires that you continue.

Prod 3: It is absolutely essential that you continue.

Prod 4: You have no other choice, you *must* go on.

Were you a "teacher" in this experiment, how far would you go? Milgram described the experiment to 110 psychiatrists, college students, and middle-class adults. The average estimated response of all three groups was close to 135 volts; no one estimated beyond 300 volts. But, Milgram thought, these self-estimates may reflect self-serving bias. So he asked them to what voltage they thought other people would go. Virtually no one expected anyone to proceed to the end of the shock panel. (The psychiatrists guessed about one in a thousand.)

But when Milgram conducted the experiment with forty men—a vocational mix of twenty- to fifty-year-olds—twenty-five of them (63 percent) went clear to 450 volts. In fact, all who reached 450 volts complied with a command to *continue* the procedure until, after two further trials, the experimenter called it to a halt. Given this disturbing result, Milgram made the learner's protests even more compelling. As the learner was strapped into the chair, the teacher heard him mention his "slight heart condition" and heard the experimenter's reassurance that "although the shocks may be painful, they cause no permanent tissue damage." The learner's subsequent anguished protests (see Box 7-1) were to little avail; of forty new men in this experiment, twenty-six (65 percent) fully complied with the experimenter's demands (see Figure 7-4).

FIGURE 7-4 The Milgram obedience experiment. Percentage of subjects complying despite the learner's cries of protest (after 150 volts) and failure to respond (after 330 volts). (Data from Milgram, 1974, p. 35.)

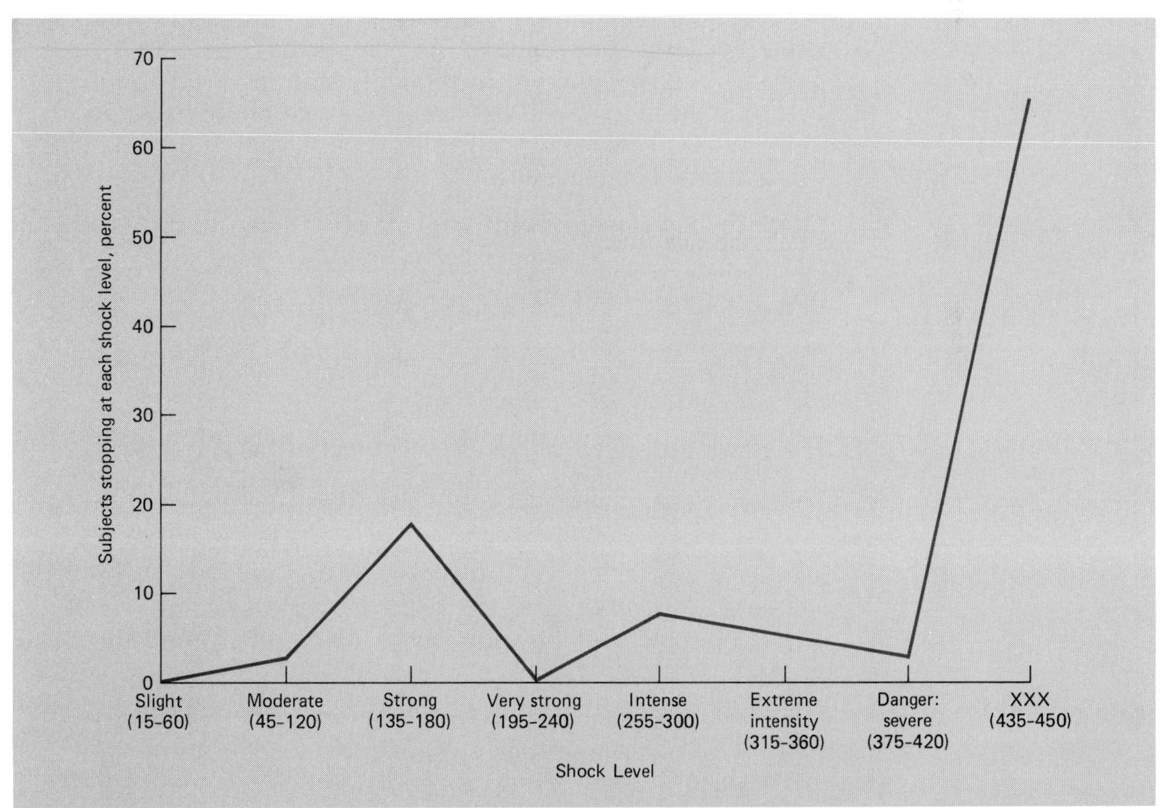

Box 7-1

The Learner's Schedule of Protests in Milgram's "Heart Disturbance" Experiments

75 volts	Ugh!
90 volts	Ugh!
105 volts	Ugh! (*louder*)
120 volts	Ugh! Hey, this really hurts.
135 volts	Ugh!!
150 volts	Ugh!!! Experimenter! That's all. Get me out of here. I told you I had heart trouble. My heart's starting to bother me now. Get me out of here, please. My heart's starting to bother me. I refuse to go on. Let me out.
165 volts	Ugh! Let me out! (*shouting*)
180 volts	Ugh! I can't stand the pain. Let me out of here! (*shouting*)
195 volts	Ugh! Let me out of here. Let me out of here. My heart's bothering me. Let me out of here! You have no right to keep me here! Let me out! Let me out of here! Let me out! Let me out of here! My heart's bothering me. Let me out! Let me out!
210 volts	Ugh!! Experimenter! Get me out of here. I've had enough. I won't be in the experiment any more.
225 volts	Ugh!
240 volts	Ugh!
255 volts	Ugh! Get me out of here.
270 volts	(*Agonized scream.*) Let me out of here. Let me out of here. Let me out of here. Let me out. Do you hear? Let me out of here.
285 volts	(*Agonized scream.*)
300 volts	(*Agonized scream.*) I absolutely refuse to answer any more. Get me out of here. You can't hold me here. Get me out. Get me out of here.
315 volts	(*Intensely agonized scream.*) I told you I refuse to answer. I'm no longer part of this experiment.

330 volts (*Intense and prolonged agonized scream.*) Let me out of here. Let me out of here. My heart's bothering me. Let me out, I tell you. (*Hysterically*) Let me out of here. Let me out of here. You have no right to hold me here. Let me out! Let me out! Let me out! Let me out of here! Let me out! Let me out!

Note: From *Obedience to Authority* by Stanley Milgram. New York: Harper & Row, 1974, pp. 56-57.

The obedience of his subjects disturbed Milgram. The procedures he used equally disturbed many social psychologists. Although the "learner" in these experiments actually received no shock (he disengaged himself from the electric chair and turned on a tape recorder that delivered his protests), some critics nevertheless said that, ironically, Milgram did to his subjects what they did to their victims: stress them against their will. Indeed, many of the teachers did experience agony. They sweated, trembled, stuttered, bit their lips, groaned, or even broke into uncontrollable nervous laughter. A *New York Times* reviewer complained that the cruelty that the experiments "inflict upon their unwitting subjects is surpassed only by the cruelty that they elicit from them" (Marcus, 1974). Critics also argued that the participants' self-concepts may have been altered. One participant's wife told him, "You can call yourself Eichmann."

"He that complies against his will,
Is of his own opinion still,
Which he may adhere to, yet disown,
For reasons to himself best known."

Samuel Butler, Hudibras

In his own defense, Milgram points not only to the lessons his nearly two dozen experiments have taught us, but also to the support he received from the participants after the deception was revealed and the experiment explained. When surveyed afterwards, 84 percent said they were glad to have participated; only 1 percent regretted volunteering. A year later, a psychiatrist interviewed forty of those who had suffered most and concluded that, despite the temporary stress, none was harmed.

Milgram did more than reveal the extent to which people will obey; he also examined the conditions that breed obedience. In further experiments he varied the social conditions and obtained compliance ranging from 0 percent fully obedient to 93 percent. Here are four of the determining factors.

Emotional Distance of the Victim

It is easiest to debase someone who is distant or depersonalized. Executioners depersonalize those being executed by placing hoods over their heads. The ethics of war allow one to bomb a helpless village from 40,000 feet, but not to shoot an equally helpless villager. Likewise, Milgram's teachers acted with least compassion when their learners could not be seen (and could not see them). When the victim was remote and no complaints were heard, nearly all participants obeyed calmly to the end. When the learner was brought into the

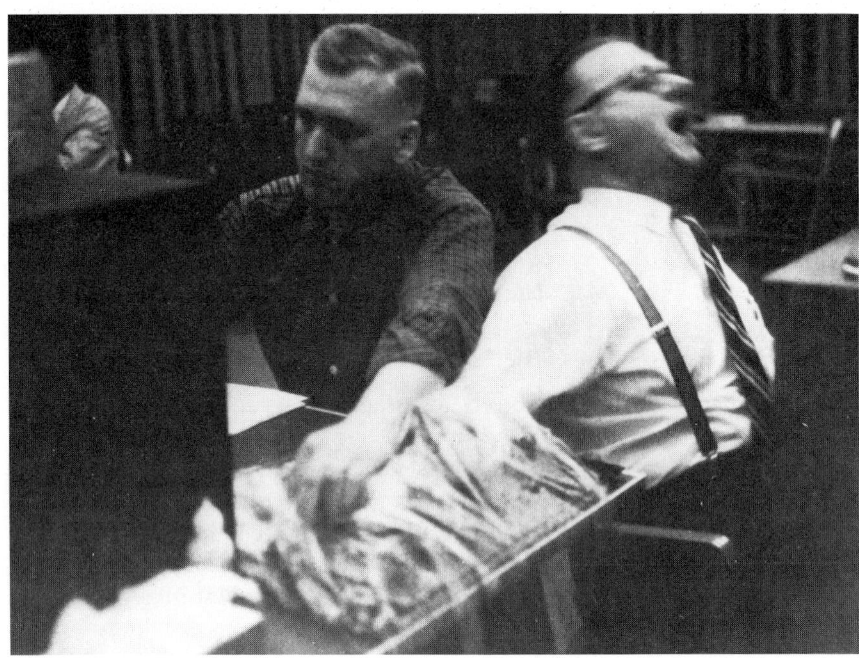

An obedient subject in the "touch" condition forces the victim's hand onto the shock plate. Usually, however, teachers were more compassionate to victims who were close at hand. (Copyright 1965 by Stanley Milgram. From the film *Obedience,* distributed by the New York University Film Library.)

same room, "only" 40 percent obeyed to 450 volts. And full compliance dropped to 30 percent when teachers were required to force the learner's hand into contact with a shock plate. Put positively, people act most compassionately toward those who are personalized. This is why those appealing on behalf of the unborn or the hungry and impoverished will nearly always personalize the target group with a compelling photograph or description.

Closeness and Legitimacy of the Authority

Milgram found that obedience was affected by the physical presence of the experimenter. When he gave the commands by telephone, full obedience dropped to 21 percent. Other studies of compliance have similarly found that when the one making the request is physically close, compliance increases. For example, if given a light touch on the arm, people are more likely to lend a dime, sign a petition, or sample a new pizza (Kleinke, 1977; Willis & Hamm, 1980; Smith, Gier, & Willis, 1982).

Moreover, the authority must be perceived as legitimate. In another twist on the basic obedience experiment, the experimenter received a rigged telephone call that required him to leave the laboratory. He said that since the equipment recorded data automatically, the teacher should just go ahead on his own. After the experimenter left, another subject who had been assigned a clerical role (actually a second confederate) assumed command. He "decided" that the shock should be increased one level for each wrong answer and commanded the teacher accordingly.

Box 7-2

Personalizing the Victims

Innocent victims trigger more compassion if personalized. In a week when a soon-forgotten earthquake in Iran kills 3000 people, a lone boy dies, trapped in a well-shaft in Italy, and the whole world grieves. The projected death statistics of a nuclear war are impersonal to the point of being incomprehensible. So international law professor Roger Fisher proposed a way to personalize the victims:

> It so happens that a young man, usually a navy officer, accompanies the President wherever he goes. This young man has a black attache case which contains the codes that are needed to fire nuclear weapons.
>
> I can see the President at a staff meeting considering nuclear war as an abstract question. He might conclude, "On SIOP Plan One, the decision is affirmative. Communicate the Alpha line XYZ." Such jargon keeps what is involved at a distance.
>
> My suggestion, then, is quite simple. Put that needed code number in a little capsule and implant that capsule right next to the heart of a volunteer. The volunteer will carry with him a big, heavy butcher knife as he accompanies the President. If ever the President wants to fire nuclear weapons, the only way he can do so is by first, with his own hands, killing one human being.
>
> "George," the President would say, "I'm sorry, but tens of millions must die." The President then would have to look at someone and realize what death is—what an *innocent* death is. Blood on the White House carpet: it's reality bought home.
>
> When I suggested this to friends in the Pentagon, they said, "My God, that's terrible. Having to kill someone would distort the President's judgment, He might never push the button."

Note: Adapted from "Preventing Nuclear War" by Roger Fisher, *Bulletin of the Atomic Scientists,* March, 1981, pp. 11–17.

With this authority of lower status, 80 percent of the teachers refused to comply fully. The confederate, feigning disgust at this defiance, then came and sat down in front of the shock generator and tried to take over the teacher's role. At this point most of the defiant participants protested. Some tried to unplug the generator. One large man lifted the zealous shocker from his chair and threw him across the room. This rebellion against an illegitimate authority contrasted sharply with the deferential politeness usually shown the experimenter.

Institutional Authority

If the prestige of the authority is this important, then perhaps the institutional prestige of Yale University had helped legitimize the experimenter's commands. In postexperimental interviews, many participants volunteered that had it not been for Yale's reputation for integrity and excellence, they would not have shocked the learner. To see whether this was true, Milgram moved the experiment to Bridgeport, Connecticut, and dissociated it from Yale. He set himself up in a somewhat run-down commercial building as the "Research Associates of Bridgeport," an organization of unknown character. When the usual "heart disturbance" experiment was run with the same personnel, what percentage of the men do you suppose fully obeyed? Though reduced, the rate remained remarkably high—48 percent.

The Liberating Effects of Group Influence

These classic experiments give us a negative view of conformity. Can conformity be constructive? Perhaps you can recall a time you felt justifiably upset with an unfair teacher, or with your peers for their inappropriate behavior, but were hesitant to object. Then one or two others objected, and you followed their example. Milgram captured this liberating effect of conformity by placing the teacher with two confederate teachers who were to collaborate in conducting the procedure. During the experiment, both defied the experimenter, who then ordered the real subject to continue by himself. Did these teachers obey? No. Ninety percent liberated themselves by conforming to the defiant confederates.

Reflections on the Classic Studies

The most common response to Milgram's results is to note their counterparts in recent history: in the "I was only following orders" defenses—of Adolph Eichmann, the chief Nazi exterminator; of Lieutenant William Calley, who directed the unprovoked slaughter of hundreds of Vietnamese villagers in My Lai; and of the participants in the Watergate break-in and cover-up. The similarities are indeed striking. As one participant in the My Lai massacre recalls,

> [Lieutenant Calley] told me to start shooting. So I started shooting, I poured about four clips into the group. . . . They were begging and saying, 'No, no.' And the mothers was hugging their children, and . . . . Well, we kept right on firing. They was waving their arms and begging. . . . (Wallace, 1969)

The obedience experiments differ from the other conformity experiments in the strength of the social pressure: Compliance is explicitly commanded, not merely the result of noncoerced imitation. Without the experimenter's coercion, people were not disposed to act cruelly. Yet all these experiments, from Sherif to Milgram, share certain commonalities. They all demonstrate how compliance can take precedence over one's moral sense. They all provoked people to abdicate their inner standards in response to group pressure. They all do more than teach us an academic lesson; they sensitize us to analogous

BEHIND THE SCENES

Stanley Milgram

While working for Solomon E. Asch, I often reflected on his conformity experiments. Some of his critics argued that the experiments involved trivial behavior, judging lines. I wondered whether this could be made into a more humanly significant experiment. Could groups induce more significant behavior from the person? First, I imagined an experiment similar to Asch's except that the group, instead of making judgments of lines, induced the person to deliver shocks to a protesting victim. But something more was needed, a control to see how much shock a person would give in the absence of group pressure. Yet how could this experimental control be set up? Someone, presumably the experimenter, would have to instruct the subject to give the shocks. But now a new question arose: Just how far *would* a person go when ordered to administer such shocks? The issue had shifted in my mind from conformity to peer pressure to a rather different matter, the willingness of people to comply with destructive orders. Immediately, I knew I would investigate this new question. It was an exciting moment for me. I realized that this simple question was both humanly important and capable of being precisely answered. *(Stanley Milgram, City University of New York)*

conflicts in our own lives. And they all illustrate and affirm certain social psychological principles discussed in earlier chapters. Let us recall some of these.

Behavior and Attitudes

In Chapter 2 we noted that one reason our attitudes often fail to determine our behavior is that, as vividly demonstrated by these classic experiments, external influences sometimes override inner convictions. When responding in the absence of others, Asch's subjects could nearly always give the correct answer. But it was another matter when they stood alone against a group. In the obedience experiments, powerful social pressure overcame deeply held values. As Milgram explains,

Some subjects were totally convinced of the wrongness of what they were doing . . . and felt that—within themselves, at least—they had been on the side of the angels. What they failed to realize is that subjective feelings are largely irrelevant to the moral issue at hand so long as they are not transformed into action. Political control is effected through action. . . . Tyrannies are perpetuated by diffident men who do not possess the courage to act out their beliefs. Time and again in the experiment people disvalued what they were doing but could not muster the inner resources to translate their values into action. (Milgram, 1974, p. 10)

But, why were the participants unable to disengage themselves? How had they become trapped? Imagine yourself as the teacher in yet another version of Milgram's experiment, one he never conducted. Assume that when the learner gives the first wrong answer the experimenter asks you to begin at 330 volts. After flicking the switch, you hear the learner agonizingly scream, complain of a heart disturbance, and plead again and again for mercy (see Box 7-1). Would you continue?

I think not. Recall the step-by-step entrapment of the foot-in-the-door phenomenon (Chapter 2) as we compare this hypothetical experiment to what Milgram's teachers experienced. The teacher's first commitment was a mild one—15 volts—and it elicited no protest. Surely you, too, would agree to do that much. By the time he had administered 75 volts and had heard the learner's first groan, he already had complied five times. On the next trial he was asked to commit an act only slightly more extreme than what he had already repeatedly committed. By the time he had administered 330 volts, the teacher, after twenty-two acts of compliance, had surely managed to reduce some of the dissonance. He was thus probably in a vastly different psychological state from that of a person who might have begun the experiment at that point. As Chapter 2 (see also Gilbert, 1981) emphasized, one's external behavior and internal disposition can feed one another, sometimes in a spiraling escalation. Compliance can breed acceptance, which in turn can enable a more extreme compliance.

"Men's actions are too strong for them. Show me a man who has acted and who has not been the victim and slave of his action."

Ralph Waldo Emerson, Representative Men: Goethe

The "blame-the-victim" mode of self-justification discussed in Chapter 2 was one such type of acceptance. Milgram reports that

Many subjects harshly devalue the victim *as a consequence* of acting against him. Such comments as "He was so stupid and stubborn he deserved to get shocked," were common. Once having acted against the victim, these subjects found it necessary to view him as an unworthy individual, whose punishment was made inevitable by his own deficiencies of intellect and character. (Milgram, 1974, p. 10)

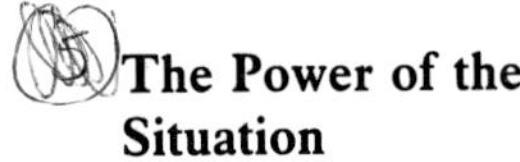

The Power of the Situation

The most important lesson of Chapter 6—that cultures powerfully shape our lives—and the most important lesson of this chapter—that current social forces are similarly powerful—point to the awesome potency of social situations. To feel such for yourself, imagine violating some less than earth shaking norms: standing up in the middle of a class; singing out loud in a restaurant; greeting some distinguished senior professors with their first names; wearing shorts to church; playing golf in a suit; munching Cracker Jack at a piano recital. In trying to break with social constraints one suddenly realizes how strong they are.

There is also a lesson here about evil. Evil is not just the result of a few bad apples that need to be replaced with good ones. It also results from social forces—from the heat, humidity, and disease that help make a whole barrel go bad. As these experiments demonstrate, powerful situations can induce people to conform to falsehoods or capitulate to cruelty. Thus, like the seductive power of the ring in J. R. R. Tolkien's *Lord of the Rings*, evil situations have enormous corrupting power. This is especially true when, as happens often in complex societies, the vilest of evils evolve from a sequence of small evils. Nazi leaders were surprised at how easily they got German civil servants to handle the paperwork of the Holocaust. They were not killing Jews, of course. They were merely pushing paper (Silver & Geller, 1978). When fragmented, evil becomes easier. Milgram studied this compartmentalization of evil by involving yet another forty men more indirectly. Rather than trigger the shock, they had only to administer the learning test. Thirty-seven of the forty fully complied.

"When you think of the long and gloomy history of man, you will find more hideous crimes have been committed in the name of obedience than in the name of rebellion."

C. P. Snow

And so it is in our everyday lives: The drift toward evil usually comes in small increments, without any conscious commitment to do evil. Procrastination involves a similar unintended drift toward self-harm (Sabini & Silver, 1982). A student knows weeks ahead the deadline for a term paper. Each diversion from work on the paper—a video game here, a TV program there—

Box 7-3

One Man's Experience of Conformity

One hundred eighty days a year I am a fifth-grade teacher. I love to think and to encourage my students to do the same. I consider myself a sensitive and gentle person. In my leisure time I enjoy literature, music, and bicycling and backpacking.

Friday nights, Saturdays, and summers I skin cattle in a rendering company, as I have done since my teens. I am one of the boys. I smoke, I drink beer, I curse. My talk is of guns, hunting, sex, and cars.

Is one of these the "real" me? No. Both are part of the real me. I really am an educated, humanitarian person in the educated, humanitarian situation and an earthy, uninhibited person in the earthy, uninhibited situation. How else can one cope with the expectations of each, but to go along with them and absorb them? People who live and work in but one type of situation may believe their social environment affects them little. Those of us who go back and forth between two radically different social worlds know better.

seems harmless enough. Yet the student gradually veers toward not doing the paper without consciously deciding not to do it.

The Fundamental Attribution Error

Why have some of us been so startled by the results of these classic experiments? It is because we expect people to act in accord with their dispositions. We are not startled when a surly person commits a heinous act, but we expect those with pleasing dispositions to be kind. Bad people do bad things; good people do good things.

When you read about Milgram's experiments, what impressions did you form of the teachers? Most people attribute negative dispositions to them. When told about one or two of the obedient subjects, people judge them aggressive, cold, and unappealing—even after being informed that most participants were similarly obedient (A. G. Miller et al., 1973). Cruelty is presumed to be inflicted by the cruel at heart.

Günter Bierbrauer (1979) tried to eliminate this underestimation of social forces (in Chapter 3 termed the fundamental attribution error). He had Stanford University students either observe a vivid reenactment of the experiment or take the role of obedient teacher themselves. Even so, they still predicted that their friends would, in a repeat of Milgram's experiment, be minimally compliant. Only if instructed to think and write about the experiment for thirty minutes did they then alter their expectation and state that the average Stanford student might flip switches up to the 260-volt mark. Bierbrauer concluded that

> While social scientists are accumulating evidence that human behavior and even human nature are products of man's environment and the prevailing social and historical conditions, the naive man remains essentially unmoved by these facts. He continues to believe that the inner qualities of his fellows ultimately reveal themselves; that only good men do good and merit praise and that only evil men do evil and deserve punishment.

> *"Eichmann did not hate Jews, and that made it worse, to have no feelings. To make Eichmann appear a monster renders him less dangerous than he was. If you kill a monster you can go to bed and sleep, for there aren't many of them. But if Eichmann was normality, then this is a far more dangerous situation."*
>
> *Hannah Arendt,* Eichmann in Jerusalem

It is tempting to presume that Eichmann and the Auschwitz camp commanders were uncivilized monsters. But after a hard day's work, the Auschwitz commanders would relax, listening to Beethoven and Schubert. Eichmann himself has been described as bland, outwardly indistinguishable from common people with ordinary jobs (Arendt, 1963). And so it was in the obedience research. Milgram's conclusion makes it harder to attribute the Holocaust to unique character traits in the German people: "The most fundamental lesson of our study," he noted, is that "ordinary people, simply doing their jobs, and without any particular hostility on their part, can become agents in a terrible destructive process" (Milgram, 1974, p. 6). As Mister Rogers often reminds his preschool television audience, "Good people sometimes do bad things." Perhaps, then, we should be more wary of political leaders whose genial and charming disposition lulls people into supposing that they would never do evil.

The classic conformity experiments answered some questions, but, as often occurs, raised others: (1) Sometimes people conform; sometimes they do not. When do they? (2) Why do people conform? Why don't people ignore the group and 'to their own selves be true'? (3) Is there a type of person who is most conforming? Let us take these questions one at a time.

WHEN DO PEOPLE CONFORM?

Social psychologists wondered: If even Asch's noncoercive, unambiguous situation could elicit a conformity rate of 37 percent, might other settings produce even more? Researchers soon discovered that conformity was indeed heightened if the judgments required were difficult to make or if the subjects were led to feel incompetent. The more insecure we are about our judgments, the more influenced we are by others' judgments. Researchers have also found that the nature of the group has an important influence. Conformity is highest under the conditions described below.

When the Group Is:

Three or More People

In laboratory experiments a group need not be large to have a large effect. Asch and other researchers found that three to five people will elicit much more conformity than just one or two. However, increasing the number of people beyond five yields diminishing returns (Rosenberg, 1961; Gerard, Wilhelmy, & Conolley, 1968). In a field experiment, Milgram, Leonard Bickman, and Lawrence Berkowitz (1969) had one, two, three, five, ten, or fifteen people pause on a busy New York City sidewalk and look up. As Figure 7-5 indicates, the percentage of passersby who also looked up increased as the number looking up increased from one to five persons.

Bibb Latané (1981) accounts for the diminishing returns of increases in group size with his "social impact theory." The theory proposes that social influence increases with the immediacy and size of the group. But as the number of influencing persons increases, the increments in social impact decrease: the second person has less effect than the first, and the nth person has less effect than the $(n-1)$th.

The way the group is "packaged" also makes a difference. Researcher David Wilder (1977) gave University of Wisconsin students a jury case. Before giving their own judgments, the students watched videotapes of four confederates giving their judgments of the case. When presented as two independent groups of two people, the participants conformed more than when the four confederates presented their judgments as a group. Similarly, two groups of three people elicited more conformity than one group of six, and three groups of two people elicited even more. Evidently, the concurrence of several small groups makes a position more credible than does a single large group.

Social impact increases with group size. (*Cartoons from Punch,* edited by William Hewison, St Martin's Press, Inc. Copyright © 1979 Punch Publications Ltd.)

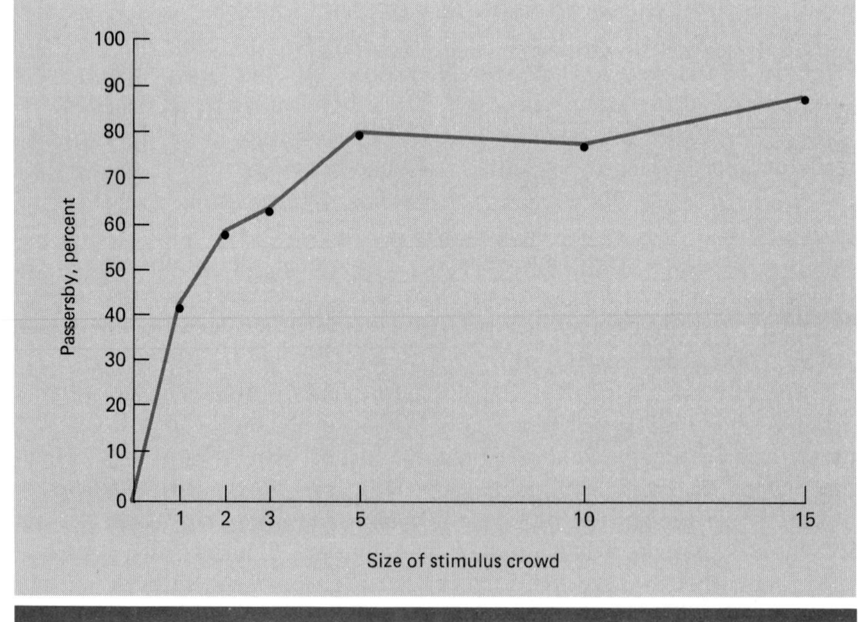

FIGURE 7-5 Group size and conformity. The percentage of passers-by who imitated a group looking upward increased as group size increased to five persons. (Data from Milgram, Bickman, & Berkowitz, 1969.)

Unanimous

Imagine yourself in a conformity experiment where all but one of the people responding before you give a wrong answer. Would the example of this one nonconforming confederate be as liberating as it was for the subjects in Milgram's obedience experiment? Several experiments have found that when a group's unanimity is punctured, so also is its social power (Asch, 1955; V. L. Allen & Levine, 1969; Morris & Miller, 1975). As Figure 7-6 illustrates, subjects will nearly always voice their convictions, if but one other person has also done so. Interestingly, the subjects in such experiments often later say they felt warm toward and close to their nonconforming ally, but deny that the ally influenced them: "I would have answered just the same if he weren't there."

"My opinion, my conviction, gains infinitely in strength and success, the moment a second mind has adopted it."

Novalis, Fragment

It is difficult to be a minority of one, to stand alone against a group. Thus, perhaps a practical lesson these experiments teach is that it is easier to stand up for something if you can find someone else to stand up with you. Many religious groups recognize this. Following the example of Jesus, who sent his disciples out in pairs, the Mormons, for example, always send two missionaries into a neighborhood together. The support of but one comrade greatly increases a person's social courage.

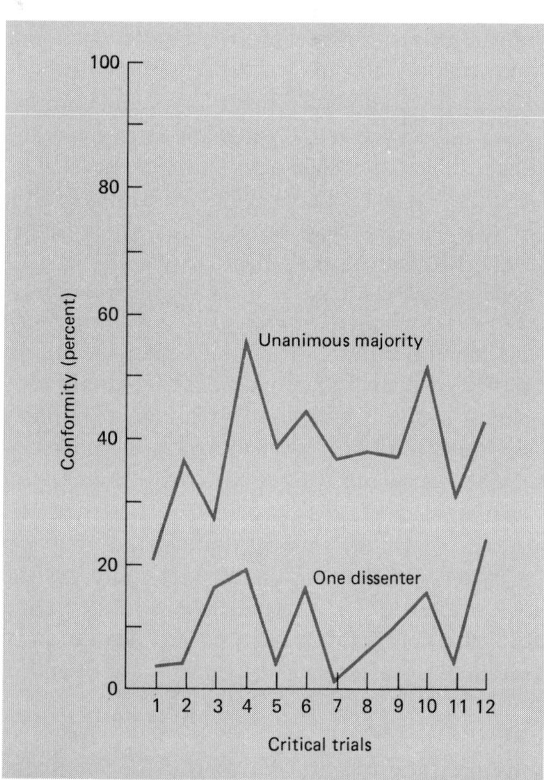

FIGURE 7-6 The effect of unanimity on conformity. When the group's unanimity was punctured by the presence of one confederate who gave correct answers, subjects conformed only one-fourth as often. (From Asch, 1955.)

The more closely knit a group is, the more power it seems to have over its members. In experiments, group members who feel or are led to feel attracted to the group are more responsive to the group's influence (Berkowitz, 1954; Lott & Lott, 1961; Sakurai, 1975). Perhaps the people we are attracted to are more credible to us. Disagreeing with such people probably disturbs us. Because we do not want to be rejected by the people we like, we may allow them to have a certain power over us.

Cohesiveness: *A "we feeling"—the extent to which members of a group are bound together, such as by attraction for one another.*

High in Status

Monroe Lefkowitz, Robert Blake, and Jane Mouton (1955) demonstrated the effect of status by having a disheveled and poorly dressed man violate the "wait" signal at street corners in Austin, Texas. His action triggered little jaywalking from the other pedestrians. But when the same confederate dressed like a bank president, his going against the "wait" prompted many more pedestrians to jaywalk with him. Clothes seem to "make the person" in Australia, too. Michael Walker, Susan Harriman, and Stuart Costello (1980) found that Sydney pedestrians were more compliant when approached by a well-dressed survey taker than one poorly dressed.

Stanley Milgram (1974) reports that in his obedience experiments people of lower status tended to accept the experimenter's commands more readily than people of higher status. For example, after administering 450 volts, one subject, a thirty-seven-year-old welder, turned to the experimenter and deferentially asked, "Where do we go from here, Professor?" (p. 46). Another subject, a divinity school professor, disobeyed at 150 volts, and after objecting, "I don't understand why the experiment is placed above this person's life," treated the experimenter as an unthinking technician, plying him with questions about "the ethics of this thing" (p. 48). As this example hints, those higher in status may also have somewhat different moral concerns.

When the Response Is:

Public

One of the first questions researchers raised was this: Would people conform more in their public responses than in their private opinions? Or would they be more readily swayed in their private opinions but unwilling to publicly conform, lest they appear wishy-washy? The answer is now clear: In experiments, people conform more when they must respond in the presence of others than when allowed to write down their answer privately. For example, Asch's subjects, after hearing others respond, were less influenced by group pressure if they could write an answer that would be seen only by the experimenter. It is much easier to stand up for what we believe in the voting booth than in front of a group whose beliefs differ from ours. These findings suggest what in Chapter 2 we called "impression management"—presenting oneself to others in ways that create a favorable impression.

"If you worry about missing the boat—remember the Titanic."

Anonymous

Made Without Prior Commitment

In 1980, Genuine Risk became only the second filly to win the Kentucky Derby. In her next race, the Preakness, she came off the last turn gaining on the leader, Codex, a colt. As they came out of the turn they were practically neck and neck. Codex then moved sideways toward Genuine Risk, causing her to hesitate and giving him a narrow victory. Had Codex brushed Genuine Risk? Had his jockey even whipped Genuine Risk in the face? The race referees huddled. After a brief deliberation they judged that no foul had occurred, confirming Codex as the winner. The decision caused an uproar. On the televised instant replays, it appeared that Genuine Risk, the sentimental favorite, had indeed been brushed. A protest was filed. In the days that followed, the decision was reconsidered. But it was not changed.

Did the race officials' commitments immediately after the race affect their openness toward reaching a different decision later? We will never know. However, we can put people through a laboratory version of this event—with and without the immediate commitment—and observe whether the commitment makes a difference. Again, imagine yourself in an Asch-type experiment. The experimenter displays the lines and asks you to respond first. After you have given your judgment and then heard everyone else disagree, the experimenter offers you an opportunity to reconsider. In the face of such group pressure do you back down? In experiments, people almost never do

The effects of prior commitment. Once they have committed themselves to a position, people seldom yield to social pressure. For example, umpires and referees rarely reverse their initial judgments. (Drawing by Mankoff; © 1980 *The New Yorker* Magazine, Inc.)

"All right! Have it your own way. It was a ball

(Deutsch & Gerard, 1955). Once having made a public commitment they stick to it. The most they will do is adjust their judgments in later situations (Saltzstein & Sandberg, 1979). Thus, for example, we may expect that judges of diving contests will seldom change their rating of a dive after observing the other judges' ratings, although they might adjust their ratings of later dives.

Charles Kiesler (1971) observed a similar effect in studies of persuasion. He found that people who state their own position on an issue before hearing others are much less susceptible to influence. Making a public commitment leads people to attribute responsibility for such action to themselves, which in turn makes them hesitant to back down (Mayer, Duval, & Duval, 1980). Smart persuaders know this. They ask questions that prompt us to make statements for rather than against what they are marketing. Textbook salespeople are more likely to ask professors what they do *not* like about their competitors' books than what they do like about them. Religious evangelists invite people "to get up out of your seat," knowing that people are more likely to hold to their newfound faith if they have made a public commitment to it.

Public commitment may reduce conformity not only because people are more accepting of what they have made a commitment to, but also because

BEHIND THE SCENES

Charles Kiesler

I was a graduate student of Leon Festinger's at Stanford and was very interested in his dissonance theory. It occurred to me that some of the manipulations in the research were confounded. Paying people only a small amount to perform an act inconsistent with their beliefs theoretically should create more dissonance. At the same time I intuitively sensed that somehow participants also would become more committed to the act by accepting the small pay, and that it would be more difficult for them to deny or distort the meaning of the act.

To study commitment separately from dissonance, I started doing studies of behavior *consistent* with beliefs. In that way dissonance could not be a factor, but commitment could be. Ultimately, I became so interested in the psychology of commitment that I began to investigate how commitment breeds resistance to conformity and attitude change. *(Charles Kiesler, Carnegie-Mellon University)* they hate to appear wishy-washy. People who "wander, waver, waffle, and wiggle," as President Gerald R. Ford said of candidate Jimmy Carter in 1976, lose respect. For example, A. R. Allgeier and his collaborators (1979) found that people whose attitudes changed over time were viewed as less decisive and reliable than those whose attitudes were stable. In the 1980 presidential campaign, all three candidates suffered from accusations of inconsistency. When President Carter, for instance, acknowledged after the Soviet invasion of Afghanistan that "my opinion of the Russians has changed most drastically in the last week, [more] than even in the previous two and one-half years," *Time* magazine (1980a) called it "a burst of candor that will haunt him through his whole campaign" (p. 30).

On the other hand: *"Those who never retract their opinions love themselves more than they love truth."*

Joubert,
Pensées

WHY CONFORM?

Here I was, a naive American attending my first lecture during an extended visit at a West German university. As the lecturer finished, I lifted my hands to join in the clapping. But rather than clap, the other people began rapping the tables with their knuckles. What did this mean? Were they disapprovingly "knocking" the speech? Surely, not everyone would so overtly rebuke the visiting dignitary. Nor did their faces indicate displeasure. No, I decided, this must be a German ovation. Whereupon, I added my knuckles to the chorus.

What prompted this conformity? Why had I not remained true to myself and clapped even while the others rapped? There are two possibilities: A person may bow to the group either to be accepted and avoid rejection, or because the group provides important information. Morton Deutsch and Harold Gerard (1955) named these two possibilities *normative* social influence and *informational* social influence.

Normative conformity is "going along with the crowd" to avoid rejection, to stay in people's good graces, or to gain their approval. In the laboratory and in everyday life, groups often reject those who consistently deviate (Schachter, 1951; C. E. Miller & Anderson, 1979). Can you recall such an experience? As most of us know, social rejection is painful. Hence when we deviate from group norms we often pay a price in anxiety, if not in rejection. Sometimes the price is high enough to compel people to support what they do not believe in. Some of the soldiers at My Lai, for example, yielded to an abhorrent act out of fear of being court-martialed for disobedience. Thus, normative influence most commonly leads to compliance. This is especially true for people seeking to climb a group's status ladder (Hollander, 1958). As John F. Kennedy (1956) recalled, " 'The way to get along,' I was told when I entered Congress, 'is to go along' " (p. 4).

Normative influence: *Conformity based on a person's desire to be accepted by the group.*

"Do as most do and men will speak well of thee."

Thomas Fuller,
Gnomologia

"*I'm awfully sorry, Dick, but we've all just had a little meeting, and we've agreed that perhaps it's best that you leave the commune.*"

Nonconformers may face rejection. (Drawing by Weber; © 1975 *The New Yorker* Magazine, Inc.)

Informational influence on the other hand, is more likely to produce acceptance. When reality is ambiguous, as it was for subjects in the autokinetic situation, other people can be a valuable source of information. The subject may reason, "I can't tell how far the light is moving. But this guy seems to know." Others' responses may also affect how we interpret ambiguous stimuli. People who witness others agreeing that "free speech should be limited," may infer a different meaning to the statement than those who witness others disagreeing (V. L. Allen & Wilder, 1980). In short, normative influence is motivated by concern for one's social image and outcomes; informational influence is motivated by the desire to be correct.

Informational influence: *Conformity that results from accepting evidence about reality provided by other people.*

In day-to-day life, normative and informational influence often occur together. I was not about to be the only person in the room clapping (normative influence), yet the others' behavior also clued me how to show my appreciation (informational influence).

Some of the experiments on "when people conform" have isolated either normative or informational influence. Consider: Conformity is greater when responses are in the presence of the group; this surely reflects normative influence (because subjects received the same information whether they responded publicly or privately). On the other hand, conformity is greater when participants feel incompetent or when the task is especially difficult; this surely reflects informational influence.

WHO CONFORMS?

Are some people generally more susceptible (or should I say, more *open*?) to social influence? Among your friends, can you identify some who are "conformists" and others who are "independent"? I suspect that most of us can. Yet there seems to be little relationship between personal characteristics and laboratory conformity. In contrast to the demonstrable power of situational factors, such as the group's unanimity versus nonunanimity, social psychologists have found only weak connections between personal characteristics and conformity. If there are compliant personality types, we do not yet know precisely how to identify them. However, researchers are exploring several areas in their search for the conformer. Let us look briefly at three.

Males Versus Females

Among Americans tested in group pressure situations during the last thirty years, there is a slight tendency for women to conform more than men. Alice Eagly and Linda Carli (1981) discerned this by using a new statistical technique to combine results from the dozens of available studies. They describe the size of the effect as "barely visible to the naked eye." Studies reporting women to be more conforming tend to be those in which participants' responses are

Are some individuals consistently more compliant than others? If so, what are their characteristics? (Drawing by Levin; © 1978 *The New Yorker* Magazine, Inc.)

witnessed by the other group members (as in the Asch experiment), and tend to have been conducted by men some years ago (Eagly, Wood, & Fishbaugh, 1981; Cooper, 1979; Sohn, 1980). Newer conformity experiments and those conducted by women have less often found females more conforming.

Although Milgram's subjects (1974) were nearly all men—some 1000 in all—forty women subjects did experience the "heart-disturbance" obedience procedure. Milgram assumed that women are generally more compliant, yet also more empathic and less aggressive. What he found was no difference: 65 percent were fully compliant.

But is labeling this small effect a "conformity difference" a negative judgment upon the women "conformers"? Remember, our label for the phenomenon is somewhat arbitrary. Perhaps we should instead use the label "greater people orientation." (Recall from Chapter 6 that women are slightly more empathic and socially sensitive.) Perhaps, then, we should say that women are slightly more flexible, more open and responsive to their social environment, more concerned with interpersonal relations. Such language carries quite different connotations from saying that women are more conforming. Recall, too, that male-female differences are not just sex differences, but also (or instead) status differences, socialization differences, and so forth. As always, it is difficult to disentangle the many factors that could help create a small behavioral difference between males and females.

Personality

Can personality tests identify the conformer? For example, since those made to feel incompetent on a task are more conforming on that task, perhaps people with chronically low self-confidence will be generally more conforming than people whose self-esteem is high. Picture a "rugged individualist": Is this person not exuding self-assurance? Surprisingly, however, people's scores on self-esteem tests correlate only modestly with their conformity scores in experiments (Wylie, 1979; Santee & Maslach, 1982).

Other personality traits are also weakly related to conformity. For example, Milgram (1974) concluded, "I am certain that there is a complex personality basis to obedience and disobedience. But I know we have not found it" (p. 205). Trait measures are reliable. (If retested, people score similarly.) But they do not predict much of the variation in people's social behavior (W. Mischel, 1968). If you want to know how conforming or aggressive or helpful someone is going to be in a specific situation, you are better off knowing the details of the situation than the person's scores on a battery of psychological tests.

This conclusion, though sometimes debated, has been demoralizing to personality researchers. It is reminiscent of how we social psychologists felt about the research that at first seemed to show that attitudes poorly predict behavior. Yet, as Chapter 2 indicated, our dismay prompted a search for the circumstances under which attitudes will predict behavior. For example, while attitudes seldom precisely predict a specific action, they better predict a person's behavior in general (across many situations). Seymour Epstein (1980) argues that the same is true of personality scores. They, too, fail to predict specific actions, but may more successfully predict a person's behavior in general. Just as your response to a single test item is essentially unpredictable, so is your behavior in a single situation. And just as your total score across many test items is more predictable, so too your total conformity or aggressiveness may be easier to predict.

Personality also better predicts behavior when the situation is unstructured. Milgram's obedience experiments created "strong" situations; they made clear-cut demands on people making it difficult for personality differences to operate. William Ickes (1982) reports that in "weak" situations—such as when two strangers are simply left alone together in a waiting room with no cues to guide their behavior—their individual personalities are freer to shine.

It is interesting to note how the pendulum of professional opinion swings. Several decades ago, most saw personality as the key determinant of a person's social behavior. Then, as new evidence pointed to the impact of situational variations and the astonishingly poor predictions of personality tests, opinion shifted toward viewing social forces, not personality, as the prime determinant of behavior. Thus, reflecting on his prison simulation and other recent experiments, Philip Zimbardo concluded that the ultimate message

> is to say what it is we have to do to break through your egocentricism, to say you're not different, anything any human being has ever done cannot be alien to you, you can't divorce it! We must break through this "we-they" idea that our dispositional orientation promotes and understand that the situational forces operating on a person at any given moment could be so powerful as to override everything prior—values, history, biology, family, church. (Bruck, 1976)

Without discounting the undeniable power of social forces, the pendulum does, however, now seem to be swinging back toward a recognition of the consequences of an individual's personality. By using ideas such as Epstein's (about predicting behavior in general) and by exploring how personality *interacts* with the situation (a given situation may affect some types one way and other types another), personality researchers are following the path of attitude researchers in clarifying the connection between who we are and what we do.

Interaction: *The effect of one factor (for example, the situation) depends on another (for example, the type of person).*

Cultural Difference

Does knowing people's cultural background help us predict how conforming they are? Here, finally, we can answer with a confident yes. When Milgram (1961) used a common conformity procedure to compare Norwegian and French students, he consistently found the Norwegian students to be the more conforming. When the obedience experiments were repeated by researchers in Munich, Rome, South Africa, and Australia, how do you suppose the results compared to those obtained with American subjects? If anything, obedience was even higher; for example, in Munich it was 85 percent (Mantell, 1971; Milgram, 1974). James Whittaker and Robert Meade (1967) repeated Asch's conformity experiment in several countries and found similar conformity

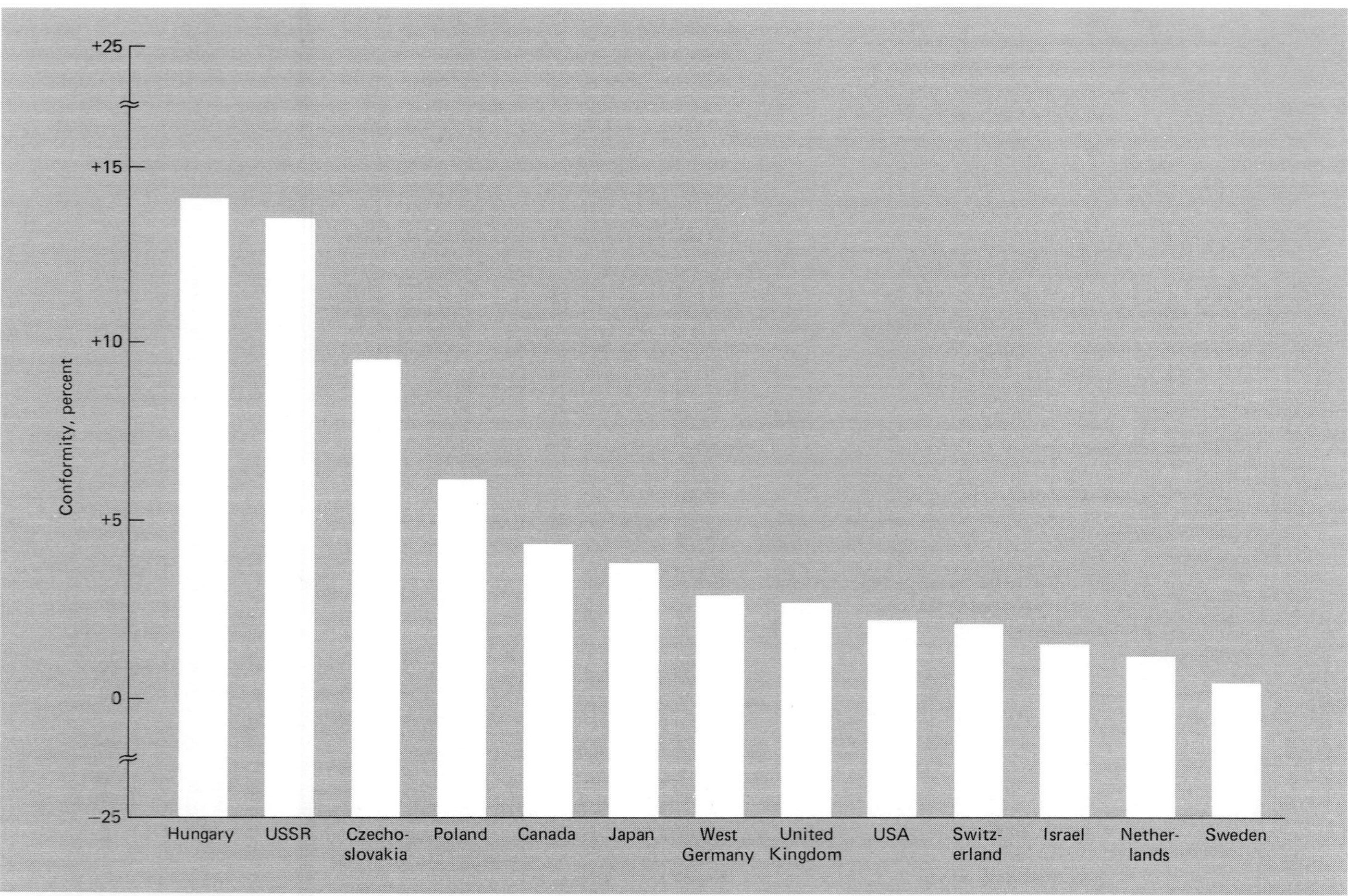

FIGURE 7-7 Conformity of twelve-year-olds to moral standards of adult authorities. (Data from Garbarino & Bronfenbrenner, 1976.)

rates in most—31 percent in Lebanon, 32 percent in Hong Kong, 34 percent in Brazil—but 51 percent conformity among Rhodesian Bantu, a tribe with strong punishments for nonconformity. However, cultures may change. Recent replications of Asch's experiment in Britain and the U.S. triggered less conformity among university students than Asch had observed two decades previous (Perrin & Spencer, 1980; Larsen, 1974).

An international team of researchers led by James Garbarino and Urie Bronfenbrenner (1976; Shouval et al., 1975) at Cornell University assessed twelve-year-olds' conformity to conventional moral standards by having them predict their behavior in a variety of situations. As Figure 7-7 indicates, children from more individualistic western nations were considerably more likely to admit to disobedient, mischievous tendencies than children from more collectivist countries, such as the U.S.S.R., where both home and school emphasize "obedience and propriety." The children in the collectivist countries described themselves as more compliant with adult expectations and less likely to join their peers in defying adult expectations.

RESISTING SOCIAL PRESSURE

This chapter, like the one preceding, has emphasized the power of social forces. It is therefore fitting that we conclude by again reminding ourselves of the power of the person. Unlike passive billiard balls, we act in response to the forces upon us. Knowing that someone is trying to coerce us may even prompt us to react in the *opposite* direction.

People value their sense of freedom and like to project an image of self-efficacy (Baer et al., 1980). Consequently, when social pressure becomes so blatant that it threatens their sense of freedom, they often rebel. Think of Romeo and Juliet. Their love for one another was intensified by their parents' opposition. Or think of a child asserting its freedom and independence by doing the opposite of what its parents ask. Savvy parents therefore often phrase requests so as to allow their children to maintain a sense of freedom: "It's time to clean up: Do you want a bath or a shower?"

The theory of psychological *reactance*—that people do indeed act to protect their sense of freedom—is supported by experiments showing that attempts to restrict a person's freedom often produce a reactive "boomerang effect" (Brehm & Brehm, 1981). Suppose someone stops you on the street and asks you to sign a petition that advocates something you mildly support. While considering the petition you are told that someone else believes "people absolutely should not be allowed to distribute or sign such petitions." Reactance

Reactance: *A motive to protect or restore one's sense of freedom. Reactance is aroused when freedom of action is threatened.*

theory predicts that such obvious attempts to limit people's freedom would actually increase the likelihood of their signing. When Madeline Heilman (1976) staged this experiment on the streets of New York City, that is precisely what she found.

Reactance can escalate into social rebellion. Like obedience, rebellion can be produced and observed in experiments. William Gamson, Bruce Fireman, and Steven Rytina (1982) have done so. Posing as a commercial research firm, they recruited people from towns near the University of Michigan to come to a hotel conference room for "a group discussion of community standards." Once there, the people learned that the discussions were to be videotaped on behalf of a large oil company seeking to win a legal case against a local station manager who had spoken out against high gas prices. In the first discussion, virtually everyone sided with the station manager. So the company could convince the court that people in the local community were on its side, the supposed company representative then began to tell more and more of the group members to defend the company. In the end, everyone was instructed to attack the manager and asked to sign an affadavit giving the company permission to edit the tapes and use them in court.

By leaving the room from time to time, the experimenter gave the group members repeated opportunities to interpret and react to the injustice they were being asked to comply with. Most groups rebelled, objecting to and resisting the demand that they misrepresent their opinions in order to help the oil company. Some groups even mobilized themselves to stop the whole effort. They made plans to go to a newspaper, the Better Business Bureau, a lawyer, or the court.

By creating and observing the unfolding of small social rebellions, the researchers gained some glimpses into how a revolt occurs. They found, for example, that successful resistance often begins soon. The more a group unquestioningly complies with the unjust demands, the more trouble it later has breaking free. And someone must be willing to seed the process by expressing the reservations which others are feeling.

These demonstrations of reactance reassure us that people are not puppets. Sociologist Peter Berger (1963) expresses the point vividly:

> We see the puppets dancing in their miniature stage, moving up and down as the strings pull them around, following the prescribed course of their various little parts. We learn to understand the logic of this theater and we find ourselves in its motions. We locate ourselves in society and thus recognize our own position as we hang from its subtle strings. For a moment we see ourselves as puppets indeed. But then we grasp a decisive difference between the puppet theater and our own drama. Unlike the puppets, we have the possibility of stopping in our movements, looking up and perceiving the machinery by which we have been moved. In this act lies the first step towards freedom. (p. 176)

Box 7-4

Is Happiness Being Just Like Everyone Else?

Three earthlings, Meg, Calvin, and Charles Wallace, have just arrived on Camazotz, a planet where "individuals have been done away with."

Below them the town was laid out in harsh angular patterns. The houses in the outskirts were all exactly alike, small square boxes painted gray. Each had a small, rectangular plot of lawn in front, with a straight line of dull-looking flowers edging the path to the door. Meg had a feeling that if she could count the flowers there would be exactly the same number for each house. In front of all the houses children were playing. Some were skipping rope, some were bouncing balls. Meg felt vaguely that something was wrong with their play. It seemed exactly like children playing around any housing development at home, and yet there was something different about it. She looked at Calvin, and saw that he, too, was puzzled.

"Look!" Charles Wallace said suddenly. "They're skipping and bouncing in rhythm! Everyone's doing it at exactly the same moment."

This was so. As the skipping rope hit the pavement, so did the ball. As the rope curved over the head of the jumping child, the child with the ball caught the ball. Down came the ropes. Down came the balls. Over and over again. Up. Down. All in rhythm. All identical. Like the houses. Like the paths. Like the flowers.

Then the doors of all the houses opened simultaneously, and out came women like a row of paper dolls. The print of their dresses was different, but they all gave the appearance of being the same. Each woman stood on the steps of her house. Each clapped. Each child with the ball caught the ball. Each child with the skipping rope folded the rope. Each child turned and walked into the house. The doors clicked behind them.

Note: From *A Wrinkle in Time* by Madeline L'Engle, New York: Dell, 1962, pp. 103-104.

Asserting Our Uniqueness

Imagine a world of complete conformity, where there were no human differences. (See Box 7-4 for one such world.) Would there be happiness in such a world? If nonconformity can create discomfort, can sameness create comfort?

People feel uncomfortable when they appear too different from others. But they are also discomfited by appearing exactly like everyone else. As experiments by C. R. Snyder and Howard Fromkin (1980; see also Duval, 1976) have shown, people feel better when they see themselves as unique, and will act in ways that set them apart and maintain their sense of individuality.

In one experiment (Snyder, 1980), Purdue University students were led to believe that their "10 most important attitudes" were either distinct from or nearly identical to the attitudes of 10,000 other students. When they then participated in a conformity experiment, those who had been deprived of their feeling of uniqueness were most likely to assert their individuality by nonconformity. In another experiment, people who heard others express attitudes that were identical to their own actually altered their positions in order to maintain their sense of uniqueness.

"There are no exceptions to the rule that everybody likes to be an exception to the rule."

Malcolm Forbes, Forbes Magazine

So it seems that while we do not like being greatly deviant, we do like to feel distinctive. But as research on self-serving bias (Chapter 3) makes clear, it is not just any kind of distinctiveness we seek, but distinctiveness in the right direction. Our quest is not merely to be different from the average, but better than average.

The tendency to see oneself as unique is also evident in people's "spontaneous self-concepts." William McGuire and his Yale University colleagues (McGuire & Padawer-Singer, 1978; McGuire, McGuire, & Winton, 1979) report that when children are invited, "Tell us about yourself," they are most likely to mention their distinctive attributes. Foreign-born children are more likely than others to mention their birthplace; redheads are more likely than black- and brown-haired children to volunteer their hair color; light and heavy children are the most likely to refer to their body weight; minority children are the most likely to mention their race. The principle, says McGuire, is that "one is conscious of oneself insofar as, and in the ways that, one is different." Thus "If I am a black woman in a group of white women, I tend to think of myself as a black; if I move to a group of black men, my blackness loses salience and I become more conscious of being a woman" (McGuire et al., 1978). This insight can help us understand why any type of minority group tends to be conscious of its distinctiveness and how the culture is relating to it, and also why the majority group is sometimes bewildered by what they perceive as the "hypersensitivity" of the minority group.

"Every person is in certain respects like all other people, like some other people, like no other people."

Clyde Kluckhohn & Henry Murray, Personality in Nature, Society, and Culture

SUMMING UP

Conformity—changing one's behavior or belief as a result of group pressure—comes in two forms. *Compliance* is outwardly going along with the group while inwardly disagreeing. *Acceptance* is believing as well as acting in accord with social pressure. Both types have been explored in laboratory experiments that ask: (1) To what extent do people conform? (2) When do people conform? (3) Why do people conform? (4) Who conforms most?

Three classic sets of experiments illustrate how conformity is studied and how conforming people can be. Muzafer Sherif observed that people's estimates of the illusory movement of a point of light were easily influenced by the judgments of others. Norms for "proper" answers emerged and were perpetuated over both long periods of time and succeeding generations of subjects. This laboratory demonstration of suggestibility parallels suggestibility in real life.

Solomon Asch used a task that was as clear-cut as Muzafer Sherif's was ambiguous. Asch had people listen to others judge which of three comparison lines was equal to a standard line and then make the same judgment themselves. When the others unanimously gave a wrong answer, the subjects conformed 37 percent of the time. Richard Crutchfield automated Asch's procedure in a way that enables testing several real subjects at once and asking them a variety of questions. Like Asch, Crutchfield was startled at the extent of conformity he observed.

Sherif's procedure elicited acceptance; Stanley Milgram's obedience experiments, on the other hand, elicited an extreme form of compliance. Under optimum conditions—a legitimate, close-at-hand commander, a remote victim, and no one else to exemplify disobedience—65 percent of his adult male subjects fully obeyed instructions to deliver what were supposedly traumatizing electric shocks to a screaming innocent victim in an adjacent room.

These classic experiments demonstrate the potency of social forces and the ease with which compliance can begin to breed acceptance. Evil is not just the product of bad people in a nice world, but also the product of powerful situations that induce people to conform to falsehoods or capitulate to cruelty.

Using conformity testing procedures such as these, many subsequent experiments explored the circumstances that are conducive to conformity. Conformity is affected by the characteristics of the group: People conform most when confronted by the unanimous reports of three or more attractive, high-status people. People also conform most when their responses are public (in the presence of the group) and when they are made without prior commitment.

These experiments reveal two reasons why people conform at all. *Normative influence* results from a person's desire to be accepted by the group. *Informational influence* results from others' providing evidence about reality. For example, the tendency to conform more when responding publicly reflects normative influence, and the tendency to conform more on difficult tasks reflects informational influence.

Who conforms? This question has produced fewer definitive answers. In experiments, females have, on the average, been slightly more conforming than males. (If this sounds negative it is because labels such as "conformity" evaluate as well as describe behavior. Call the trait "openness" or "communal sensitivity" and it takes on a more positive connotation.) Personality test scores correlate only weakly with conformity. Perhaps, however, new methods for exploring the relationship between personality and social behavior will eventually reveal stronger relationships. Variations in conformity among cultures suggest that people can be socialized to be more or less conforming.

The chapter's emphasis on the power of social pressure must not be separated from a complementary emphasis on the power of the person. We are not puppets. When attempts at social coercion become blatant, people often experience *reactance*—a motivation to defy the coercion in order to maintain their sense of freedom. When group members simultaneously experience reactance the result may be rebellion. People are not comfortable being too different from a group, but neither do they want to appear the same as everyone else. Thus, they will act in ways that preserve their sense of uniqueness and individuality. And in a group, they tend to be most conscious of their differences from the others.

Finally, a comment on the experimental method used in conformity research. Conformity situations in the laboratory differ from those in everyday life: How often are we asked to judge lines or administer shock? Much as combustion is similar for a burning match and a forest fire, the psychological processes engaged in the laboratory and everyday life are assumed to be similar (Milgram, 1974). One must be careful in generalizing from the simplicity of a burning match to the complexity of a forest fire. Yet, just as controlled experiments on burning matches can give us insights into combustion that we cannot gain by observing forest fires, so also can the social-psychological experiment offer insights into behavior not readily revealed in everyday life. The experimental situation is unique, but so too is every social situation. By testing with a variety of unique tasks, and by repeating experiments in different times and places, researchers probe for the common principles that lie beneath the surface diversity.

Chapter

Persuasion

Joseph Goebbels was Nazi Germany's minister of "popular enlightenment" and propaganda. Given the control of Germany's publications, radio programs, motion pictures, and the arts, he undertook to persuade Germans to accept Nazi ideology. Julius Streicher published *Der Stürmer*, a weekly anti-Semitic (anti-Jewish) newspaper with a circulation of 500,000 and the only paper said to have been read cover to cover by Streicher's intimate friend, Adolf Hitler. Streicher also published anti-Semitic children's books and spoke at rallies attended by hundreds of thousands. How effective were Goebbels, Streicher, and other Nazi propagandists? Did they, as the Allies alleged at Streicher's Nuremberg trial, "inject poison into the minds of millions and millions"? (Bytwerk, 1976). Most Germans were not persuaded to feel raging hatred for the Jews. But some were, others became sympathetic to anti-Semitic measures, and most of the rest became either sufficiently uncertain or intimidated to permit the Holocaust.

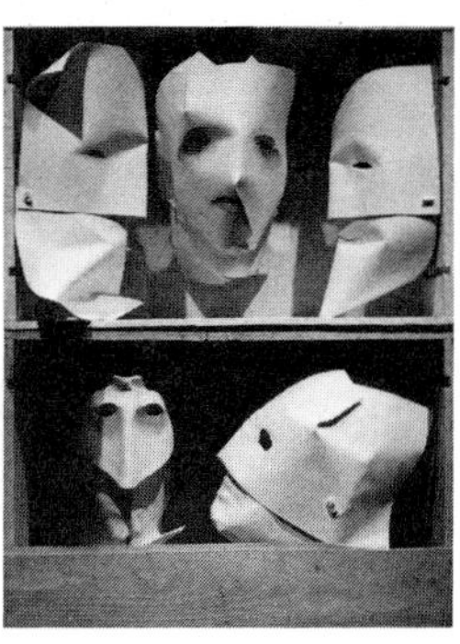

"Remember that to change thy mind and to follow him that sets thee right, is to be none the less a free agent."

Marcus Aurelius Antoninus, Meditations

Powerful persuasive forces are at work also in the United States. In the wake of numerous magazine articles and books testifying to its benefits, the number of U.S. mothers breast-feeding their newborn infants rose from 25 percent in 1971 to 55 percent in 1981 (Young, 1982). (Meanwhile, some infant-formula manufacturers are persuading mothers in Third World countries to bottle-feed their babies.) After years of antismoking ads and reams of antismoking legislation, the number of Americans who tell George Gallup

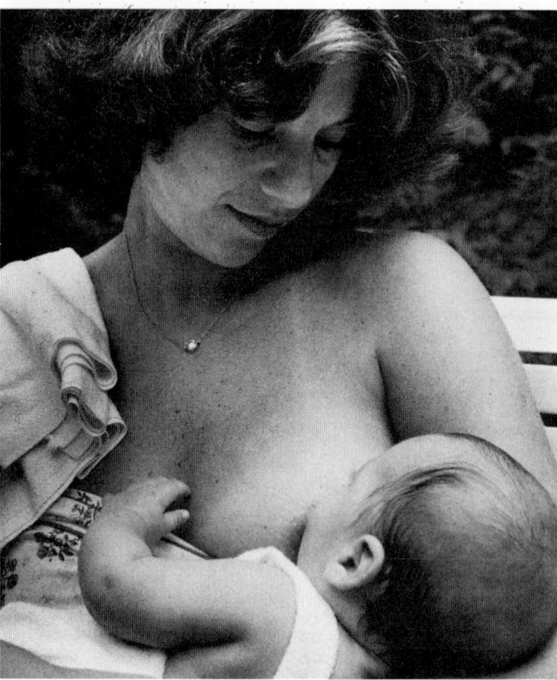

In the wake of numerous magazine articles and books testifying to its benefits, the number of U.S. mothers breast feeding their newborn infants increased dramatically in the 1970's. (Erika Stone/Peter Arnold, Inc.)

(1978b) they smoke is now steadily dropping, from 43 percent in 1972 to 36 percent in 1978. And as we saw in Chapter 6, attitudes concerning women's roles have shifted dramatically.

But then again, not all persuasive efforts succeed. Shortly after taking office, President Carter declared that the energy crisis was "the moral equivalent of war." The following summer Americans consumed more gas than ever before. Two years later, after repeated warnings by the President and after massive energy conservation publicity by both government and private business, the number of Americans who believed the energy crisis was actually "not as bad" as the President said had *risen*, from 57 percent to 69 percent (Richman, 1979).

"To swallow and follow, whether old doctrine or new propaganda, is a weakness still dominating the human mind."

Charlotte Perkins Gilman,
Human Work

As these examples show, efforts to persuade are sometimes diabolical, sometimes salutary; sometimes effective, sometimes futile. Persuasion is neither inherently good nor bad. It is usually the persuasive message's content that elicits our judgments of good or bad. The bad we call "propaganda." The good we call "education." Of course, some messages are, in fact, true, some false. True education is more factually based and less coercive than mere propaganda. Yet, generally, we call it "education" when we believe it, "propaganda" when we don't. The Boy Scouts promoting American virtues, that is education. The Red Guard promoting Communist virtues—that is propaganda.

Our opinions have to come from somewhere. So, as long as we have opinions, persuasion—whether it be education or propaganda—is inevitable. Social psychologists have therefore sought to understand what makes a message effective: What factors effectively influence us? And how, as persuaders, can we most effectively "educate" others?

Social psychologists usually study persuasion the way some geologists study erosion—by observing in brief controlled experiments the effects of various determining factors. The effects produced are on a small scale. Yet, they enable one to better understand how, given enough time, such factors could produce big effects.

Thus far, four factors have received the most study: (1) the communicator, (2) the message, (3) how the message is communicated, and (4) the audience. In other words, *who* says *what* by *what means* to *whom*?

EFFECTIVE PERSUASION

Who Says? The Effect of the Communicator

Imagine the following scene: I. M. Wright, a middle-aged American, is watching the evening news. In the first segment, a small group of radicals is shown tearing down an American flag. As they do, one shouts through a bullhorn that whenever any government becomes oppressive "it is the Right of the People to alter or to abolish it. . . . It is their right, it is their duty, to throw off such government!" Angered, Mr. Wright mutters to his wife, "It's sickening to hear them spouting that Communist line." In the next segment, a presidential candidate speaking before an antitax rally declares, "Thrift should be the guiding principle in our government expenditure. It should be made clear to all government workers that corruption and waste are very great crimes." An obviously pleased Mr. Wright relaxes and smiles: "Now that's the kind of good sense we need. It's about time someone stood up and said right out what the real problem is. That's my kinda guy."

Now switch the scene. Imagine Mr. Wright hearing the same revolutionary line at a July 4 oration of the Declaration of Independence (from which the line comes), and hearing a Communist speaker read the thrift lines from *Quotations from Chairman Mao Tsetung* (from which they come). Would the two speeches now affect Mr. Wright differently? Social psychologists have found that who says something makes a big difference in how it is perceived. But precisely what is it that makes one communicator more persuasive than another? It is to this question that researchers have directed their attention.

Credibility

All of us, I suspect, would find a statement about the benefits of exercise more believable if attributed to the National Academy of Sciences rather than to a testimonial in the *National Enquirer*. Such effects of a source's credibility may diminish after a month or so. If a message is persuasive, but with time its source is forgotten or dissociated from the message, then the impact of a high-credibility communicator may decrease as time passes, and the impact of a low-credibility communicator may actually *increase* over time—a phenomenon called the *sleeper effect* (Cook & Flay, 1978; Gruder et al., 1978).

"Believe an expert."

Vergil, Aeneid

Credible communicators are both *expert* and *trustworthy*. How does one become "expert?" One way, obviously, is to be viewed as *knowledgeable* on the topic. Praise for a poem from Agnes Stearns, "a student at Mississippi State Teachers College," is less convincing than the same praise from an acknowledged expert such as T. S. Eliot (Aronson, Turner, & Carlsmith, 1963). Another way is to *speak confidently*. Bonnie Erickson and her collaborators (1978; also Lee & Ofshe, 1981) had University of North Carolina students evaluate courtroom testimony given either in the straightforward manner said to be characteristic of "men's speech" (see Chapter 6) or in the hesitating manner of "women's speech." For example:

Question: "Approximately how long did you stay there before the ambulance arrived?"

Answer: (*Straightforward*) "Twenty minutes. Long enough to help get Mrs. David straightened out."
(*Hesitating*) "Oh, it seems like it was about uh, twenty minutes. Just long enough to help my friend Mrs. David, you know, get straightened out."

Witnesses who were straightforward were rated as considerably more competent and credible than those whose speech was hesitant.

Speech style affects a speaker's apparent trustworthiness, too. Gordon Hemsley and Anthony Doob (1978) found that if, while testifying, videotaped witnesses looked their questioner straight in the eye instead of gazing downward, they impressed people as more believable.

Norman Miller and his colleagues (1976) at the University of Southern California have found that both trustworthiness and credibility are increased by talking fast. People in the Los Angeles area who listened to tape-recorded messages on topics such as "the danger of coffee drinking" rated fast speakers (about 190 words per minute) as more objective, intelligent, and knowledgeable than slow speakers (about 110 words per minute). It is not surprising, then, that they also found the more rapid speakers more persuasive.

But is it speed alone that makes rapid speakers more persuasive? Or is it something that accompanies rapid speech, like higher intensity or pitch? Marketing researcher James MacLachlan (1979; MacLachlan & La Barbera, 1978; MacLachlan & Siegel, 1980) electronically compressed radio and television commercials without altering the speaker's pitch, inflection, and intensity. (This is done by deleting minute segments, about 1/50th of a second in length, from all parts of the speech.) He found that speed itself does seem to be a factor. When the commercials were speeded up by 25 percent, listeners comprehended just as well, rated the speakers as more knowledgeable, intelligent, and sincere, and found the messages more interesting. In fact, the normal 140- to 150-word-per-minute speech rate can be almost doubled before comprehension begins to drop abruptly (Foulke & Sticht, 1969). Interestingly, John F. Kennedy, who was regarded as an exceptionally effective public speaker, sometimes spoke in bursts approaching 300 words per minute.

Trustworthiness is also higher if the audience believes the communicator is not trying to persuade them. In an experimental version of what has since become the "hidden-camera" method of television advertising, Elaine Hatfield and Leon Festinger (Walster and Festinger, 1962) had some Stanford University undergraduates eavesdrop on the conversation of graduate students (what they actually heard was a tape recording). When the conversational topic was relevant to the eavesdroppers (for example, having to do with campus regulations), they were more influenced when the speakers were supposedly unsuspecting than when the speakers were said to be aware that someone was listening. After all, if people do not know they are being overheard, why would they be less than fully honest?

Similarly, people who argue against their own self-interest or who argue a position that is bound to cost them popularity are perceived as more sincere than those who offer self-serving arguments. Alice Eagly, Wendy Wood, and Shelly Chaiken (1978) presented University of Massachusetts students with a speech attacking a company's pollution of a river. When the speech was said to have been given either by a political candidate with a business background or to an audience of company supporters, it seemed more unbiased and was in fact more persuasive than when the same antibusiness speech was said to have been given by a proenvironment politician to a group of environmentalists. In the latter case, one could attribute the politician's arguments to personal bias or to the effect of the audience.

As if aware of this study, candidate Jimmy Carter in 1976 announced his support of amnesty for Vietnam draft resisters before, of all places, the American Legion convention. It was like advocating lower wages to a convention of labor leaders, but it did help convince the larger public of his sincerity. Being willing also to suffer on behalf of one's beliefs—which many great leaders have done—has a similar effect (Knight & Weiss, 1980).

These experiments all point to the importance of attribution: To what do we attribute a speaker's position—to the speaker's bias and selfish motives or to the factual evidence? Wood and Eagly (1981) report that when a speaker argues an *unexpected* position we are more likely to attribute the message to compelling evidence, and thus to be persuaded by it. Similarly, Joel Wachtler and Elizabeth Counselman (1981) found that students at Hobart and William Smith Colleges were most persuaded by arguments for generous compensation in a personal-injury case when the arguments came from a stingy, Scrooge-type person. Arguments for stingy compensation were most persuasive when they came from a normally warm, generous person. We might speculate, therefore, that a given arms-limitation treaty between the U.S. and the Soviet Union would be most quickly accepted and trusted by Americans if negotiated by a conservative, promilitary President.

Some television ads are obviously constructed to make the communicator appear both expert and trustworthy. Robert Young, who used to play a competent and fatherly doctor named Marcus Welby, M.D., diagnoses his friends' jitters as a caffeine problem and prescribes Sanka. Drug companies peddle pain relievers using an unhesitating white-coated speaker who declares that most doctors recommend their ingredient (the ingredient, of course, is aspirin). Yet there are other ads that do not seem to use the credibility principle. Is O. J. Simpson really a trustworthy expert on rental cars? And are you and I more likely to rent Hertz cars because Simpson recommends them?

Credibility: *Believability. A credible communicator is perceived as both expert and trustworthy.*

Attractiveness

Most people deny that endorsements by star athletes and entertainers affect them. Everyone knows that these stars are seldom if ever really knowledgeable about the products. Besides, we know the intent is to persuade us; we don't just accidentally eavesdrop on O. J. Simpson's joyful leaping through airports. But such ads are predicated upon another characteristic of an effective communicator: attractiveness. We may think that we are not influenced by

We may think a person's attractiveness does not influence how we receive their message, but researchers have found it to be otherwise. (United Press International)

how attractive or likeable the person is, but researchers have found otherwise.

Attractiveness varies in several ways. Physical appeal is one. Experimenters have sometimes found that good arguments are more influential when they come from beautiful people (for example, Chaiken, 1979; Dion & Stein, 1978). Similarity is another. As Chapter 13 will emphasize, we tend to like people who are similar to us; contrary to the old proverb, opposites generally do *not* attract. Not only do we like people who are similar to us, we are also influenced by them. For example, Theodore Dembroski, Thomas Lasater, and Albert Ramirez (1978) gave black junior high students in St. Petersburg, Florida, and Birmingham, Alabama, a taped appeal for proper dental care. When a dentist assessed the cleanliness of their teeth the next day, those who had heard the appeal from a black dentist had cleaner teeth than those who had heard the same appeal from the white dentist.

Is similarity more important than credibility? Sometimes yes; sometimes no. For example, Timothy Brock (1965) found paint store customers more influenced by the testimony of an inexpert person who had recently bought the same amount of paint they planned to buy than by an expert who had recently purchased twenty times as much. But recall that T. S. Eliot, a dissimilar but credible source, was more persuasive on the topic of poetry than Agnes Stearns, a similar but inexpert source.

Seemingly contradictory findings such as this bring out the detective in the scientist. They suggest that an undiscovered factor is at work—that similarity is more important given factor X and credibility is more important given not-X. But what is factor X? George Goethals and Eric Nelson (1973) suggest that it is whether the topic is one of *subjective preference* or *objective reality*. When the choice concerns matters of personal value, taste, or way of life, similar communicators will be most influential. But on judgments of fact—Does Seattle have more rainfall than London?—confirmation of our belief by a *dissimilar* person does more to boost our confidence. After all, a dissimilar person provides a more independent judgment. In a laboratory test, Goethals and Nelson confirmed this idea that similar communicators are much more effective on matters of value and preference than on judgments of fact.

Attractiveness: *Having qualities which appeal to an audience. An appealing communicator (often someone similar to the audience) is most persuasive on matters of subjective preference.*

There is, however, one known circumstance under which attractive communicators are less effective even on matters of preference. When an attractive source gets you to *do* something that is rather unpleasant you can justify your action by your liking for the person. When a nasty, unattractive source gets you to do the same thing, you cannot so easily attribute your compliance to your liking for the person. (This fits both self-perception and dissonance theories, as discussed in Chapter 2.) For example, Army reservists who ate fried grasshoppers at the request of a stern, unfriendly experimenter ended up liking the insects *more* than those asked by a warm, polite experimenter (E. E. Smith, 1961). It was as if they thought, "I'm not eating them because I like the experimenter, so I must be eating them because I like them."

What Is Said? The Content of the Message

Persuasion is affected not only by who says a thing, but also by *what* that person says. If you were to help organize an appeal to get people to vote for school taxes, or to stop smoking, or to contribute money to world hunger relief, you might grapple with several practical questions concerning the content of your appeal. Common sense can be made to argue on either side of these questions: (1) Is a message more persuasive if it is carefully reasoned, or if it arouses emotion? (2) How discrepant (different) should the message be from the audience's existing opinions: Do you get more opinion change by advocating a position only slightly discrepant from the listeners' existing opinions? Or by advocating a more extreme point of view? (3) Should the message express your side only, or should it acknowledge and attempt to refute opposing views? (4) If both sides are to be presented, say in successive talks at a community meeting, is there an advantage to going first or last? Let's take these questions one at a time.

Reason versus Emotion

"The truth is always the strongest argument."

Sophocles, Phaedra

"Opinion is ultimately determined by the feelings and not by the intellect."

Herbert Spencer, Social Statics

Suppose you were campaigning in support of world hunger relief. Would you best itemize your arguments and cite an array of impressive statistics? Or would you be more effective with an emotional approach, say by presenting the compelling story of one starving child? Of course, an argument need not be unreasonable to arouse emotion. Still, which is more influential—reason or emotion? Was Shakespeare's Lysander right when he said, "The will of man is by his reason sway'd"? Or was Lord Chesterfield's advice, "Address yourself generally to the senses, to the heart, and to the weaknesses of mankind, but rarely to their reason" wiser? The answer seems to depend on whom you are speaking to. Well-educated audiences, for example, are more responsive to rational appeals than are less educated audiences (Hovland, Lumsdaine, & Sheffield, 1949). Similarly, highly involved audiences are more responsive to reasoned arguments; audiences that care little are more affected by simply how much they like the communicator (Chaiken, 1980; Petty, Cacioppo, & Goldman, 1981). But generally, emotional appeals are more effective than might be implied by the view that human beings are preeminently "rational animals."

For example, messages are more persuasive when associated with good feelings. Irving Janis and his colleagues (1965; Dabbs & Janis, 1965) found that Yale students were more convinced by persuasive messages if allowed to enjoy peanuts and Pepsi while reading them (see Figure 8-1). Similarly, Mark Galizio and Clyde Hendrick (1972) found Kent State University students more persuaded by folk-song lyrics that were accompanied by pleasant guitar music than by lyrics that were sung or spoken without the accompaniment. Those who like conducting business over sumptuous lunches with soft background music can celebrate these results.

Messages also can be effective by evoking negative emotions. In trying to convince people to cut down on smoking, brush their teeth more often, get a tetanus shot, or drive carefully, a fear-arousing message can be potent. Showing cigarette smokers the horrible things that sometimes happen to

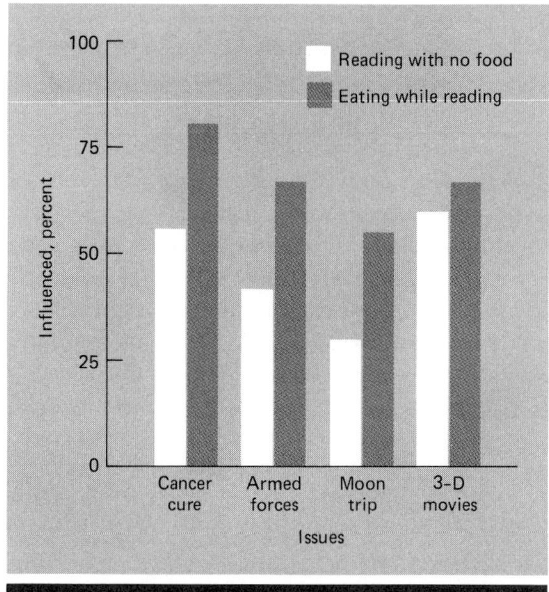

FIGURE 8-1 People who read while snacking were more persuaded than those who read without eating. (Data from Janis, Kaye, & Kirschner, 1965.)

people who smoke too much adds to the persuasiveness of a message. But how much fear should be aroused? Should you evoke just a little fear, lest people become so frightened that they tune out your painful message? Or should you try to scare the daylights out of them? Several experiments by Howard Leventhal (1970) and his University of Wisconsin collaborators have found that, generally, the more frightening a communication is, the more potent it is. For example, in a campaign to convince Ontario drivers to use their seat belts, the most influential ad depicted the risks of being thrown clear of a crash (Rochon, 1977). The ad showed a pumpkin rolling along the highway and getting run over by a car.

This general finding that fear-arousing messages are effective is being applied in ads for seat belts and against the use of cigarettes, alchohol, and drugs. But increasing listeners' fear does not always increase a message's potency. If instructions are not given on precisely how to avoid the danger—as the hellfire-and-brimstone preacher typically does—frightening messages can be too much to cope with (Leventhal, 1970; Rogers & Mewborn, 1976). Moreover, some researchers now believe that it is not fear per se that makes fear-arousing messages effective (Mewborn & Rogers, 1979). Leventhal, for example, argues that "the communication produces both persuasion *and* fear; fear does not cause persuasion."

If fear is not the key causal agent in a fear-arousing communication, then what is? I have a hunch, which I present not so much for its substantive value as for the opportunity it provides to illustrate again how social psychologists act as detectives. One possible source of the persuasiveness of frightening messages is their *vividness*. As Chapter 4 indicated, vivid anecdotes are more attention-getting and thus often more persuasive than "dry facts." So, perhaps it is significant that the messages used to arouse high fear (for example, a gory film of a lung-cancer operation) are usually not only more fear-arousing but also more vivid than the less arousing communications (for example, a film presenting facts about the smoking-cancer connection). Might it be the vivid images that have the impact? Is fear only a by-product?

Likewise, effective political propaganda often arouses fear with vivid appeals. Julius Streicher's anti-Semitic *Der Stürmer* newspaper aroused fear of the Jews not with cool statistics but with hundreds upon hundreds of unsubstantiated, yet vivid, anecdotes about Jews who were said to have ground rats to make hash, seduced and corrupted non-Jewish women, and cheated families out of their life savings. Streicher's appeals, like most Nazi propaganda, were emotional, not logical. The appeals also gave clear, specific instructions on how to combat "the danger": They listed Jewish businesses so readers would avoid them, encouraged readers to submit for publication the names of Germans who patronized Jewish shops and professionals, and directed readers to compile lists of Jews in their area (Bytwerk & Brooks, 1980). This was vivid propaganda, hard to forget. Do you think that readers of *Der Stürmer*'s vicious propaganda in Figure 8-2 might have been persuaded, not necessarily to hate Jews, but to play it safe by buying their hash from a non-Jewish butcher?

FIGURE 8-2 Fear-arousing anti-Semitic Nazi propaganda viciously suggested that Jewish butchers ground rats to make hash. (From *Der Stürmer*, No.7, February 1935, courtesy of Randall Bytwerk. Reprinted with permission of the Wiener Library.)

Joachim Winkler and Shelley Taylor (1979) demonstrated the persuasive power of vivid, fear-arousing information at the time of the 1979 nuclear accident at Pennsylvania's now infamous Three Mile Island power plant. Ten days *before* the accident, the fortunate researchers had people read an editorial that warned about possible accidents at nuclear power plants and described an accident that occurred in an Idaho Falls nuclear reactor. The nonvivid portrayal of the Idaho Falls accident stated that "an equipment failure near the reactor core resulted in the death of three workmen who responded. The level of toxic radiation was so great that special shielding measures were required during the burial of the victims." The vivid portrayal truthfully stated, "Three men, responding to an equipment failure, burnt to death from radiation while working near the reactor core. The level of radiation exposure was so great that when they were buried, their heads had to be removed and buried separately in lead lined caskets." The vivid information had no immediate added persuasive impact. But when the people were recontacted after the Three Mile Island incident, those who had read the vivid account were more likely than those who had read the nonvivid account to expect future nuclear accidents and to feel anxious about the incident. They also remembered more of what they had read, and this memory apparently led them to interpret the subsequent event as a serious incident. Could this be how the vivid anti-Semitic anecdotes worked, not just by persuading people that Jews had a diabolical nature, but by biasing their interpretation of later experiences with Jews?

How might we test this hunch that vividness rather than fear makes frightening communications persuasive? Perhaps we could create four communications, two that arouse fear and two that don't. One of each set would be vivid, one not. If we could construct each type of message (including the possibly tough job of creating a message that is not vivid but arouses fear), this would help us determine whether the key factor is vividness, or fear, or a combination of both. Note that designing such an experiment would force us to clearly define our concepts. It is one thing to speculate loosely about "vividness," and quite another to specify exactly what it is and is not. If "vividness" is taken to mean "emotional interest," then it will be difficult to distinguish it from fear-arousal.

Discrepancy

Picture the following scene: Wanda arrives home on spring vacation, hoping to convert her portly middle-aged father to her new "health-fitness lifestyle." She runs 5 miles a day, while her father chuckles that his idea of exercise is "pushing the button on my garage door opener and turning pages of the Wall Street Journal." Wanda ponders: "Would I be more likely to get Dad off his duff by urging him to try a modest exercise program, say a daily walk, or by trying to get him involved in something strenuous, say a program of calisthenics and running? Maybe if I asked him to take up a rigorous exercise program he would compromise and at least take up something worthwhile. But then again maybe he'd think I'm crazy and do nothing."

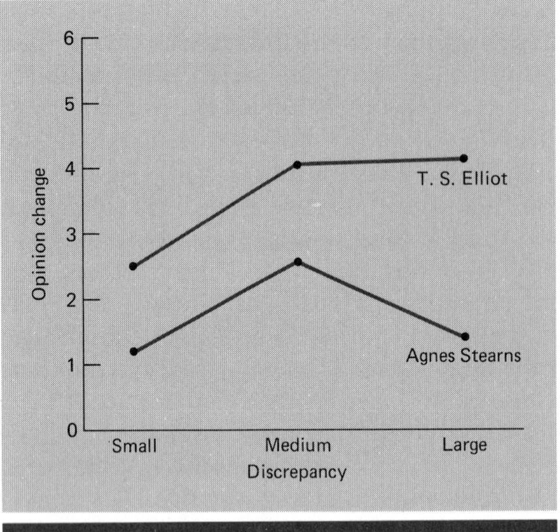

FIGURE 8-3
Discrepancy interacts with communicator credibility. A communicator with little credibility loses effectiveness when arguing an extreme position. A highly credible communicator does not lose effectiveness when arguing an extreme position. (Data from Aronson, Turner, & Carlsmith, 1963.)

Like Wanda, social psychologists have been able to reason either way. Disagreement produces discomfort, and discomfort prompts people to change their opinions (recall the discussion of dissonance in Chapter 2). So perhaps wider disagreement will produce more change. But then again, a communicator who proclaims a discomfiting message may get discredited. [One study found that the more people disagreed with conclusions drawn by a newscaster, the more biased, inaccurate, and untrustworthy they believed the newscaster to be (Zanna, Klosson, & Darley, 1976).] So perhaps wider disagreement will produce *less* change.

Given these considerations, Elliot Aronson, Judith Turner, and Merrill Carlsmith (1963) reasoned that a highly credible source would elicit most opinion change by advocating a position greatly discrepant from the position held by the recipient; a communicator with little credibility probably would be dismissed for doing so. Sure enough, when T. S. Eliot was said to have offered high praise for a poem that people initially disliked, they changed their opinion more than when he offered faint praise for the same poem. But when Agnes Stearns evaluated a disliked poem, faint praise was more persuasive than high praise. Thus, as Figure 8-3 portrays, discrepancy and credibility *interact*: the effect of large versus small discrepancy depends upon whether the communicator is credible or not (see also Bergin, 1962).

So the answer to Wanda's question—"Should I argue an extreme position?"—is, "It depends." Is Wanda in her adoring father's eyes a highly prestigious, authoritative source? If so, Wanda should push for the most complete fitness program. If not, Wanda would be wise to make a more modest appeal.

The answer also depends on how involved her father is in the issue.

Those highly involved in an issue tend to accept a narrow range of views. Thus a moderately discrepant message may seem foolishly radical to one who is highly involved, especially if the message is contrary to one's opinion rather than just a more extreme view of what one already agrees with (Rhine & Severance, 1970; Pallak et al., 1972; Petty & Cacioppo, 1979). So if Wanda's father has not yet thought or cared much about the exercise question, she can profitably take a more extreme position than if he is strongly committed to not exercising.

One-Sided versus Two-Sided Communications

Another practical issue faced by persuaders is whether to acknowledge and refute opposing arguments. Once again, common sense offers no clear answer. Acknowledging the opposing arguments might confuse the audience, thus weakening the case. On the other hand, a message might seem fairer, might be more disarming, if it anticipated the opposition's arguments.

After Germany's defeat in World War II, the U.S. Army did not want soldiers to be overconfident by thinking that Japan now would be easily vanquished. So, Carl Hovland and his colleagues (1949) in the Army's "Information and Education Division" designed two radio broadcasts arguing that the war in the Pacific would last at least two more years. One broadcast was one-sided; it failed to acknowledge the existence of such contradictory arguments as the advantage of fighting only one enemy instead of two. The other broadcast was two-sided; it mentioned and responded to the opposing arguments. As Figure 8-4 illustrates, which message was most effective depended on the listener. Those who already agreed were strengthened more by a one-sided appeal; those disagreeing were more likely to be persuaded by an appeal that acknowledged opposing arguments.

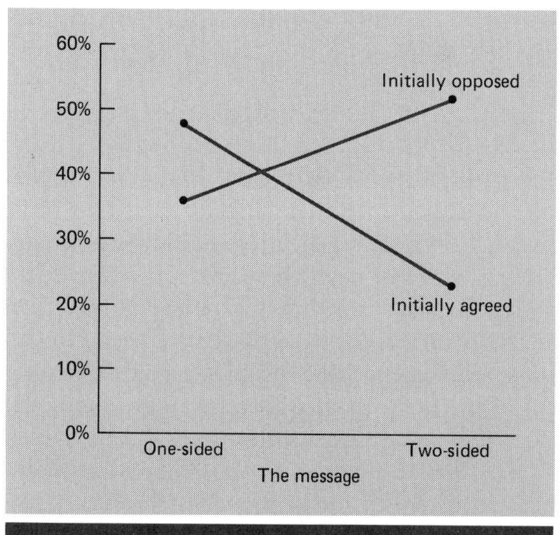

FIGURE 8-4 The interaction of initial opinion with one- versus two-sidedness. American World War II soldiers initially opposed to a message suggesting that Japanese would not be easily defeated were more persuaded by a two-sided communication. Soldiers initially agreeing with the message were strengthened more by a one-sided message. (Data from Hovland, Lumsdaine, & Sheffield, 1949.)

Subsequent experiments revealed that if people are aware of opposing arguments (as well-informed people are likely to be) or are likely later to hear the other side, then a two-sided presentation is more persuasive and enduring (Lumsdaine & Janis, 1953; R. A. Jones & J. W. Brehm, 1970). Apparently, a one-sided message stimulates an informed audience to think of counterarguments and to view the communicator as biased. Thus, a political candidate speaking to a politically informed group would be wise to compose a speech that includes a response to the opposition.

Primacy versus Recency

Imagine yourself a consultant to a prominent politician who must soon debate another prominent politician on the issue of a proposed nuclear arms limitation treaty. Three weeks before the treaty is voted upon, each politician is to appear on the nightly news and present a five-minute statement (previously prepared so that the second speaker will not be able to directly rebut the first). By the flip of a coin, your side has been given the choice whether to speak first or last. Knowing that you are a former social psychology student, everyone looks to you for advice.

Quickly, you mentally scan the psychological literature. Would going first be best? Since people's preconceptions control their interpretations and since a belief, once formed, is difficult to discredit (Chapter 4), going first could give people ideas that would bias in your favor how they would perceive and interpret the second speech. And besides, people may pay most attention to what comes first. But then again, since people remember recent things best, it would perhaps be more effective to speak last.

Your first line of reasoning predicts what is most commonly found, a *primacy effect*: Information presented early strongly affects people's judgments. First impressions *are* important. For example, can you feel a difference between these two descriptions?

Primacy effect: *Other things being equal, information presented first usually has the most influence.*

John is intelligent, industrious, impulsive, critical, stubborn, and envious.

John is envious, stubborn, critical, impulsive, industrious, and intelligent.

When Solomon Asch (1946) gave these sentences to college students in New York City, those who read the adjectives in the intelligent → envious order rated the person more positively (for example, as more sociable, humorous, and happy) than those given the envious → intelligent order. Evidently, the early-encountered information governed their interpretation of the later information, thus producing the primacy effect. Similarly, in experiments involving a task on which people must guess, when people succeed 50 percent of the time and fail 50 percent of the time, those whose successes come early are ultimately perceived as more able than those whose successes come mostly after early failures (Jones et al., 1968; Langer & Roth, 1975; McAndrew, 1981).

Does this indicate that primacy is also the rule in persuasion? Norman

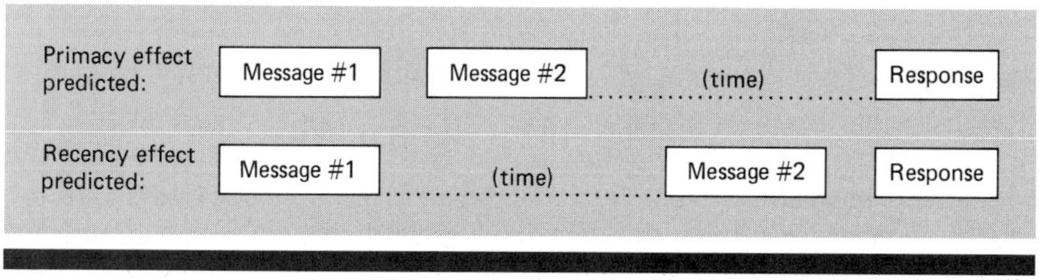

FIGURE 8-5 Primacy effect versus recency effect. When two persuasive messages are heard back-to-back and the audience then responds at some later time, the first message tends to have the advantage (primacy effect). When the two messages are separated in time and the audience responds soon after the second message, the second message tends to have the advantage (recency effect).

Miller and Donald Campbell (1959) gave Northwestern University students a condensed transcript from an actual trial of a civil suit. The testimony and arguments for the plaintiff were placed in one block, those for the defense in another. The students read both blocks. When they returned a week later to indicate their opinions, most sided with the block they had read first—another demonstration of the primacy effect.

What about the opposite possibility? Will our better memory for things most recent ever create a *recency effect*? We know from our experience (as well as from memory experiments) that today's events can temporarily outweigh more significant events of the past. To test this, Miller and Campbell gave another group of students one block of testimony to read. A week later the researchers had them read the second block, immediately after which they were to indicate their opinions. Now the results were just the reverse of those from before—a recency effect. Apparently the first block of arguments, being a week old, had largely faded from memory. In general, then, it seems that forgetting creates the recency effect (1) when sufficient time separates the two messages, and (2) when the audience does not make a commitment after the first message but must decide soon after the second message. When the two messages are back-to-back, followed by a time gap, the primacy effect will likely occur (see Figure 8-5). So, what advice would you give to the political debater?

Recency effect: *Sometimes information presented last has the most influence. Recency effects are less common than primacy effects.*

How Is It Said? The Channel of Communication

Active Experience versus Passive Reception

In Chapter 2 we noted that our actions powerfully shape who we are. When we act, we amplify the idea lying behind what we've done, especially when we feel responsible for having committed the act. We also noted that attitudes rooted in our own direct experience—rather than learned secondhand—are more likely to endure and to affect our subsequent behavior. Compared to attitudes based on experience, those formed passively are held with less certainty, are unstable, and are vulnerable to attack.

Lest we mistakenly conclude that our minds are easily molded and manipulated, it is well that we be again reminded of the limited potency of passively received messages. Commonsense psychology places enormous faith in the power of words. How do we try to get people out to a campus event? Post notices. How do we get drivers to slow down and keep their eyes on the road? Put "Drive Carefully" messages on billboards. How do we try to prevent trash from being dropped on campus? Litter the campus bulletin boards and mailboxes with antilitter messages.

"Without knowing the force of words, it is impossible to know men."

Confucius, Analects

Are people that easy to persuade? Consider two well-intentioned efforts that suggest not. At Scripps College in California, a week-long antilitter campaign urged students, "Keep Scripps' campus beautiful," "Let's clean up our trash," and so forth. Such slogans were placed in students' mailboxes each morning and displayed in prominent posters across the campus. On the day before the campaign began, social psychologist Raymond Paloutzian (1979) placed litter near a trash can along a well-traveled sidewalk and then stepped back to record the behavior of 180 passersby. Not one picked up anything. On the last day of the campaign the test was repeated with 180 more passersby. Did the pedestrians now race one another in their zeal to comply with the appeals? Hardly. Only two of the 180 picked up trash.

Channel of communication: *How the message is delivered—whether face to face, in writing, on film, or in some other way.*

Are spoken appeals any more persuasive? Not necessarily. Those of us who do public speaking, as teachers or persuaders, become so easily enamored of our spoken words that we are tempted to overestimate their power. Ask college students what aspect of their college experience has been most valuable or what they remember from their freshman year, and few, I am sad to say, recall the brilliant lectures that we faculty remember giving. Thomas Crawford (1974) and his associates evaluated the impact of the spoken word by going to the homes of people from twelve churches shortly before and after they heard sermons opposing racial bigotry and injustice. When asked during the second interview whether they had heard or read anything about racial prejudice or discrimination since the previous interview, only 10 percent spontaneously recalled the sermons. When the remaining 90 percent were asked directly whether their priest "talked about prejudice or discrimination in the last couple of weeks," more than 30 percent denied hearing such a sermon. It is therefore hardly suprising that the sermons had no impact on racial attitudes.

When you stop to think about it, the preacher has so many hurdles to surmount it's a wonder that preaching affects as many people as it does. As Figure 8-6 indicates, speakers attempting to change people's actions must deliver a message which not only gets their attention but is also understandable, convincing, memorable, and compelling. A carefully thought-out appeal must consider each of these steps in the persuasion process.

However, passively received appeals are not always ineffective. When Ultra-Brite toothpaste was introduced with a massive "boost your sex appeal" advertising campaign, it quickly became the third leading seller. My drugstore sells two brands of aspirin, one heavily advertised and one unadvertised.

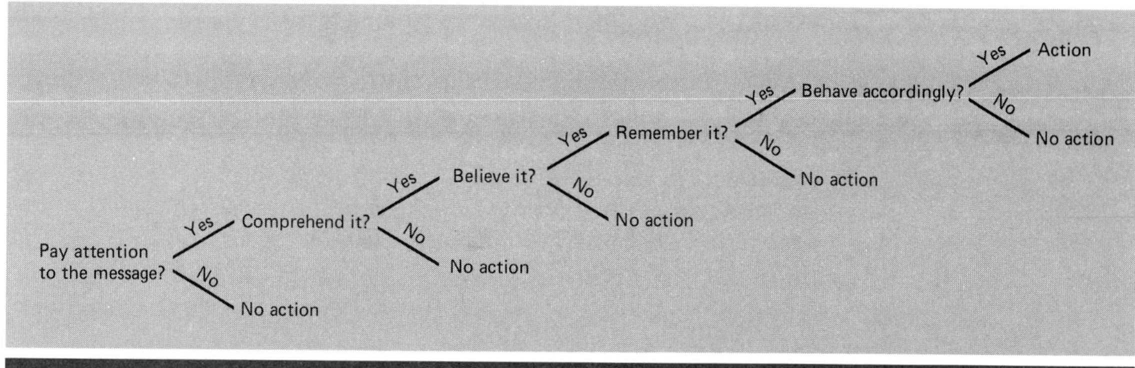

FIGURE 8-6 To elicit action, a persuasive message must clear several hurdles. As we shall see, what is crucial is not so much remembering the message itself as remembering one's own thoughts in response. (Adapted from McGuire, 1978.)

Apart from slight differences in how fast each tablet crumbles in your mouth, any pharmacist will tell you the two brands are identical. Aspirin is aspirin. Our bodies cannot tell the difference between them. But our pocketbooks can. The advertised brand sells for three times the price of the unadvertised brand. And sell it does, to millions of people. Such is the power of the media.

With such power, can the media enable a wealthy political candidate to buy an election? Was John Anderson's 1980 presidential candidacy doomed from the beginning because he had only half as much money for advertising as the two major-party candidates? With equal money for media exposure might he have won? Joseph Grush (1980) analyzed candidate expenditures in all the 1976 Democratic presidential primaries and found that those who spent the most in any election usually got the most votes. As Grush notes, the effect of this exposure was often to make an unfamiliar candidate into a familiar one. (This parallels laboratory experiments in which mere exposure to unfamiliar stimuli breeds liking; see Chapter 13.) Would the media be as potent with familiar candidates and issues? Likely not. Researchers have time and again found little effect of political advertising on voters' attitudes in the general presidential election (although, of course, even a small effect could swing a close election).

Since passively received appeals are sometimes effective and sometimes not, can we specify in advance the types of topics on which a persuasive appeal is most likely to be successful? One general rule seems to be that persuasion decreases as the significance and familiarity of the issue increases. Thus on minor issues, such as which brand of aspirin to buy, it is easy to demonstrate the media's power. On more familiar and important issues, such as racial attitudes in racially tense cities, persuading people is like trying to push a piano uphill. It is not impossible, but one "shove" won't do it.

Personal versus Media Influence

Studies of persuasion have demonstrated that the major influence upon our most important beliefs and attitudes is not the media but our direct contact with people. Two field experiments illustrate the strength of personal influence. Some years ago, Samuel Eldersveld and Richard Dodge (1954) studied political persuasion in Ann Arbor, Michigan. Citizens intending not to vote for a revision of the city charter were divided into three groups. Of those exposed only to what they saw and heard in the mass media, 19 percent voted for the revision on election day. A second group received four mailings in support of the revision. Forty-five percent voted for it. People in a third group were personally visited and given the appeal face to face. Seventy-five percent of these people cast their votes for it.

In a more recent field experiment, a research team led by John Farquhar and Nathan Maccoby (1977; Maccoby & Alexander, 1980; Maccoby, 1980) tried to reduce the frequency of heart disease among middle-aged adults in three small California cities. To ascertain the relative effectiveness of personal and media influence, they interviewed and medically examined some 1200 people both before the project began and at the end of each of the following three years. Residents of Tracy, California, received no persuasive appeals other than those usually occurring in their media. In Gilroy, California, a two-year multimedia campaign used TV, radio, newspapers, and direct mail to teach people about coronary risk and what they could do to reduce it. In Watsonville, California, this media campaign was supplemented by personal contacts with two-thirds of those whose blood pressure, weight, age, and so forth put them in a high-risk category. These contacts, in small groups or individually, used behavior-modification principles (for example, setting specific objectives, reinforcing success). As Figure 8-7 indicates, after one, two, and three years the high-risk people in Tracy (the control town) were about as much at risk as before. High-risk people in Gilroy, which was deluged with media appeals, improved their health habits and were now somewhat less at risk. Those in Watsonville, who also received the personal contacts, changed most of all.

Similar results were obtained in evaluating the impact of *Freestyle*, a 1978–1979 public television series designed to alter children's sex-role stereotypes, to convince them, for example, that it is all right for females to do mechanical, scientific, and athletic things and for males to be nurturant and do housework. Jerome Johnston, James Ettema, and Terrance Davidson (1980) studied over 7000 children, some of whom had not seen the programs, some of whom had seen the series, and some of whom had seen the series and discussed it with their teacher. The attitudes of those who simply viewed the programs changed somewhat, but attitudes changed much more among those who had both seen and discussed the program.

Would you say that Freestyle *sounds like education or propaganda?*

I suspect college students will have little trouble recognizing in their own experience the potency of personal influence. Ask those who live on campus whether during their college years they have learned and profited most from their contact with "books," or "professors," or "friends and fellow students."

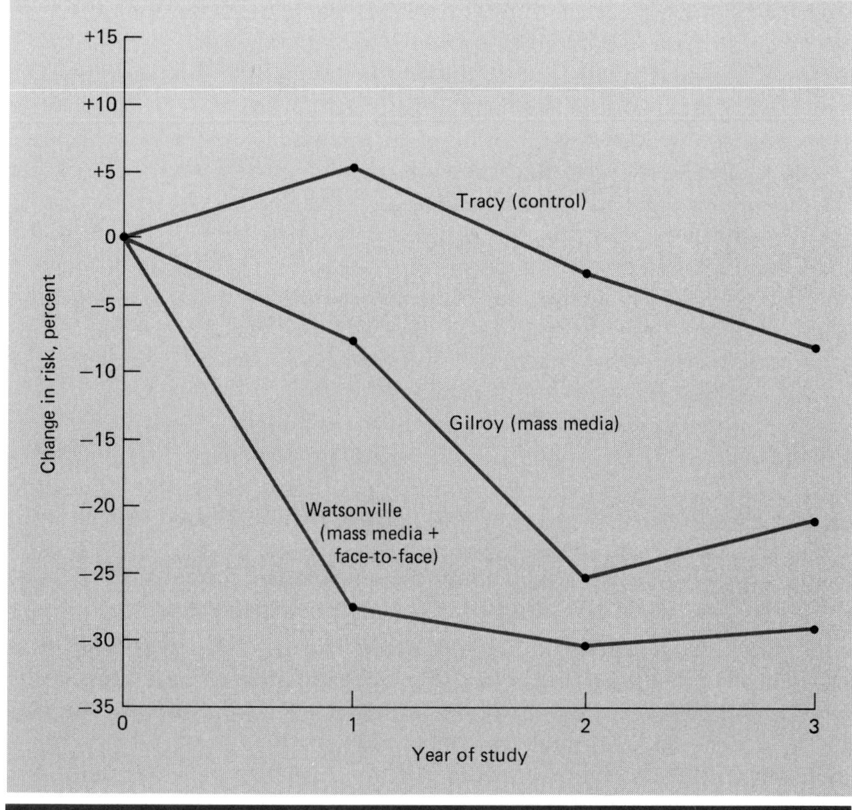

FIGURE 8-7 Percentage change from baseline (0) in coronary risk after one, two, or three years of health education. (Data from Maccoby, 1980.)

An overwhelming number usually choose the last. Educational researchers have confirmed the students' intuition: out-of-class personal relationships powerfully determine how students change during college (Astin, 1972; Wilson et al., 1975).

Face-to-face persuasion is also demonstrated by rumors. In the late 1970s, without being blown up at all by the media, the rumor that an ingredient of Bubble Yum bubble gum was spider eggs burst across the country. Another popular rumor was that the 1979 gas shortage was created by the oil companies dumping oil in the Arizona desert in order to drive up prices. Yet others concerned McDonald's supposed use of red worm meat in its hamburgers, and Jack in the Box's use of kangaroo meat in its hamburgers. All of these rumors were widespread enough that the media eventually felt it necessary to discount them.

However, even though face-to-face influence is usually greater than that of the media, we should not underestimate the media's power. Those whose personal influence on our opinions is considerable must get their ideas somewhere. Oftentimes their sources are the media. Elihu Katz (1957) observed that much of the media's effects operate in a "two-step flow of communication"—from media to opinion leaders to those of us in the rank and file. For example, if I want to evaluate stereo equipment, I defer to the opinions of my teenage son, who gets some of his ideas from radio and the printed page.

By itself, the two-step flow model is an oversimplification. (The media also communicate directly to mass audiences.) But the model does remind us that the influences of media can penetrate the culture subtly. Even if the media had little direct effect upon people's attitudes, they could still have a big effect, indirectly. Those rare children who grow up without watching television do not grow up apart from television's influence. Unless they live as hermits, they will likely join in TV-imitative play on the school ground and ask their parents for the TV-related toys that their friends have.

Our lumping together all media from mass mailings to television is surely also an oversimplification. Studies comparing different media generally find that the more vivid the medium, the more persuasive its message. Thus the order of persuasiveness seems to be: live, videotaped, audiotaped, and written. But to add to the complexity, Shelly Chaiken and Alice Eagly (1978) note that researchers have found that messages are best *comprehended* when written. Since comprehension is one of the first steps in the persuasion process (see Figure 8-6), Chaiken and Eagly reasoned that if a message is difficult to comprehend, persuasion might actually be greatest when the message is written. They gave University of Massachusetts students easy or difficult messages in writing, on audiotape, or videotape. Figure 8-8 displays their results: Difficult messages were indeed most persuasive when written, easy messages when videotaped.

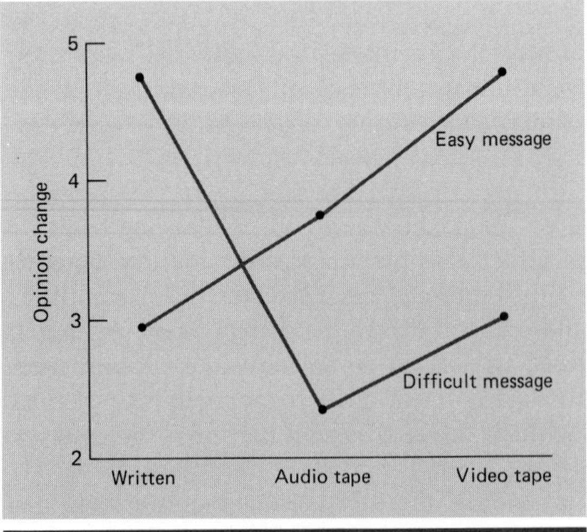

FIGURE 8-8 Easy-to-understand messages were most persuasive when videotaped. Difficult messages were most persuasive when written. Thus the difficulty of the message interacted with the medium to determine persuasiveness. (Data from Chaiken & Eagly, 1978.)

To Whom Is It Said? The Audience

As we saw in Chapter 7, there are several reasons why people's measurable traits seem to bear no strong, straightforward relation to their responsiveness to social influence. Regarding one's susceptibility to persuasion, such is true for an additional reason: A particular trait may contribute to one step in the persuasion process (Figure 8-6), but work against another. For example, if intelligent people quickly comprehend but slowly yield to a message, then we cannot state a simple relationship between intelligence and persuasibility. Instead, we might expect personality to interact with particular aspects of the communication. For example, a difficult message is often most persuasive with intelligent people (who apparently understand it better). Less intelligent people are more persuaded by a simple message; once they understand the message, they more readily yield to it without counterarguing (McGuire, 1968).

What the Audience Is Thinking

Much of the research we have so far considered can be faulted for ignoring the individuals to whom the message is addressed. Actually, as this last example indicates, what's crucial is not the message itself—or even what gets remembered from it—but what responses the message evokes in the recipient's mind (Petty, Ostrom, & Brock, 1981). Thoughtful, involved people are rarely passive listeners. They are not mere sponges, waiting to soak up any message. While listening, they are either internally agreeing or counterarguing. Thus, as counterarguing decreases, persuasion generally increases.

What circumstances breed counterarguing? One, obviously, is a communicator of low credibility propounding a disagreeable message (Perloff & Brock, 1980). Another is a *forewarning* that someone is going to try to persuade you. If you had to tell your parents that you wanted to drop out of school, you would likely anticipate their trying to persuade you to stay. So, you might develop a list of arguments to counter every conceivable argument they might make. Jonathan Freedman and David Sears (1965) demonstrated the difficulty of trying to persuade someone under such circumstances. They forewarned one of two large groups of California high school seniors that they were going to hear a talk entitled "Why Teenagers Should Not Be Allowed to Drive." Those forewarned were hardly persuaded at all; those not forewarned were persuaded.

Research by Charles Kiesler and Sara Kiesler (1964), and by Richard Petty and John Cacioppo (1977; 1979), has found that announcing a speaker's persuasive intent diminishes persuasion especially when the announcement comes a few minutes *before* the speech (thus allowing one to prepare counterarguments) and when the audience is involved enough with the topic to prepare a defense. In short, when people are involved and the message runs counter to what they believe, a sneak attack will provoke less counterarguing than an introduction that forewarns them of the speaker's intent. Ironically, however, when the issue is trivial, even blatant propaganda (as that for most aspirin and toothpaste) can be effective. Few bother to construct counterarguments. Similarly, when a premise is subtly slipped into a conversation—"Why was Sue hostile to Mark?"—people tend simply to accept it (in this instance, the premise that Sue was, in fact, hostile) (Swann, Giuliano, & Wegner, 1982).

Verbal persuasion can also be increased by distracting people with something that attracts their attention enough to inhibit their counterarguing, yet is not so powerful that the message gets ignored (Festinger & Maccoby, 1964; Osterhouse & Brock, 1970; Keating & Brock, 1974). Political ads often employ this technique. While the words promote the candidate, the visual images of the candidate in action restrain our analyzing what is being said. Distraction is especially effective when the message is simple or easily refuted; with difficult messages, distraction interferes with thoughtful reflection (Regan & Cheng, 1973; Harkins & Petty, 1981a).

This research on how persuasion increases as counterarguing decreases makes me wonder: Are fast talkers more persuasive partly because they leave us less time to counterargue? Are easy messages less persuasive when written because readers pace themselves and can therefore pause to counterargue? And does television shape important attitudes more through its subtle or hidden messages (for example, concerning sex roles) than through its explicit persuasive appeals? After all, if we do not consciously notice a message, we cannot counterargue it.

"People are usually more convinced by reasons they discover themselves than by those found by others."

Blaise Pascal

There is a practical moral to research on audience responses: Effective communicators will be concerned not only with their images and their messages, but also with how the recipients are likely to react. Are the recipients likely to think and to remember favorable thoughts? If so, the message will likely be persuasive. In fact, researchers have explored various ways to stimulate people's thinking—using rhetorical questions when people are relatively uninterested, presenting multiple speakers (for example, having three speakers each give one argument instead of one speaker give three), and making people feel responsible for evaluating the message. Each of these techniques for stimulating thinking tends to make strong messages even more persuasive and (because of counterarguing) weak messages less persuasive (Petty, Harkins, & Williams, 1980; Petty, Cacioppo, & Heesacker, 1981; Harkins & Petty, 1981a; 1981b).

Communicators can employ such techniques to trigger desired cognitive responses. For example, during the closing days of his 1980 presidential campaign, Ronald Reagan effectively used rhetorical questions to stimulate anti-Carter thoughts in the voters' minds. His summary statement in the presidential debate began with two rhetorical questions that were repeated often during the remaining week of the campaign: "Are you better off than you were four years ago? Is it easier for you to go and buy things in the stores than it was four years ago?"

Note that this new emphasis on the self-persuasive effects of one's own thinking is consistent with the emphasis in Chapter 2 on the self-persuasive

BEHIND THE SCENES

Richard E. Petty

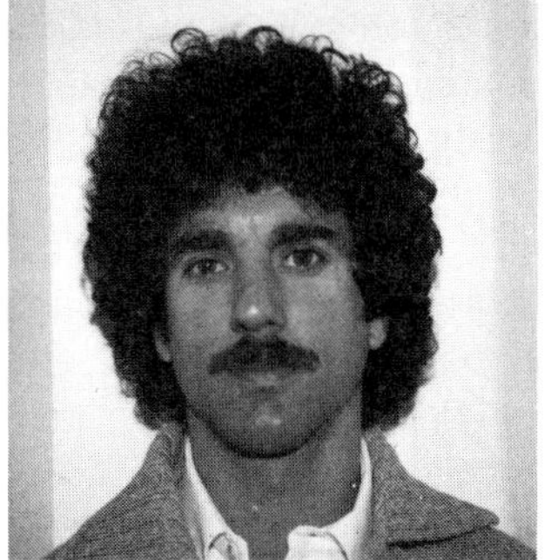

John T. Cacioppo

In the research on persuasion that we began as graduate students at Ohio State University, we have found two major benefits of measuring the particular cognitive responses (thoughts) that a persuasive message triggers. First, a cognitive-response analysis reveals the *nature and direction* of a person's thinking. In our earliest studies, we were astonished to find that what we thought were brilliant persuasive arguments sometimes provoked our subjects to express heated counterarguments. (In retrospect, this should not have surprised us, since we do this to each other all the time!) Other subjects, given arguments that we had assumed were rather ridiculous, sometimes produced favorable thoughts. Clearly, the personal significance of an argument is more important than its seemingly objective significance.

Second, an analysis of cognitive responses reveals the *amount* of thinking about a communication. We have found that the more issue-relevant thoughts people have, the more their persuasion endures; thoughtful attitude change tends to be long-lasting. After reading and scoring the thought listings of hundreds of people whom we have tried to persuade, we are convinced that the study of how people relate incoming information to their previous experiences and knowledge will unlock the secret of both persuasion and resistance to persuasion. *(Richard E. Petty, University of Missouri—Columbia, and John T. Cacioppo, University of Iowa)*

aftereffects of our actions. We do not sit idly by while manipulators inject new attitudes into us with their loaded syringes. What's crucial for attitude change is how *we* react, what *we* do and think in response to a persuasive appeal.

Age

As is well known, today's older people tend to have different social and political attitudes than younger people. There are at least two plausible explanations for this generation gap. One is a *life-cycle explanation*: Attitudes change (for example, become more conservative) as people grow older. The other is a *generational explanation*: The attitudes young people adopted in earlier generations have persisted largely unchanged; since these attitudes are

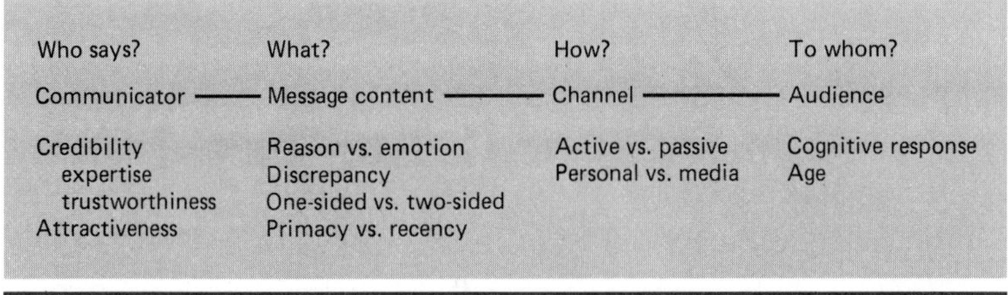

FIGURE 8-9 Summary of variables known to affect the impact of persuasive communications. In real life, these variables may interact; the effect of one variable may depend on the level of another.

different from those being adopted by today's young people, a generation gap has developed. Which explanation strikes you as more correct?

David Sears (1979) reports that the evidence supports the generational explanation. In surveying and resurveying groups of younger and older people over several years, and in studying the extent to which younger and older people change after moving into new situations, it is almost always found that the attitudes of older people change less than do those of young people. As Sears puts it, researchers have

> almost invariably found generational rather than life cycle effects. People do not become more racially prejudiced . . . as they age. Generational effects hold instead; being of recent vintage has bred less racial prejudice. Hence the attitudes with which each [age group] has entered adulthood have largely persisted.

We must be careful not to overstate the point; people now in their fifties and sixties do tend to have more liberal sexual and racial attitudes than they had in their thirties and forties (Glenn, 1980; 1981). Nevertheless, the teens and early twenties are important formative years. The attitudes formed then tend to be stable thereafter.

CASE STUDIES IN PERSUASION: CULT INDOCTRINATION

Cult: *A religious group typically characterized by (1) the distinctive ritual of its devotion to a god or a person, (2) isolation from the surrounding "evil" culture, and (3) a living charismatic leader.*

Have the persuasion principles described in this chapter been applied, whether consciously or not, in ways that indicate their power? Let us consider a recent phenomenon: Can the principles be used as spectacles through which we can see more clearly the social influences that have caused hundreds of thousands of Americans in recent years to join one of 3000 religious cults (Singer, 1979a)? Hare Krishna chanters, Moonies, Jonestown suicide victims—how are they persuaded to adopt beliefs radically different from those they had previously held? Do their experiences illustrate the dynamics of human persuasion?

Bear two things in mind: First, this is hindsight analysis. It uses persuasion principles as categories for explaining a fascinating social phenomenon. If the principles seem applicable, this analysis will illustrate them, but it will not prove them. With hindsight, almost any type of analysis can seem valid. Second, explaining *why* people have been convinced to believe what they believe says nothing about the truth of their beliefs. That is a logically separate issue. Explaining *why* someone believes that Columbus discovered America does not tell us whether Columbus did, in fact, discover America. Explaining a cultist's belief and a skeptic's disbelief would tell us nothing about the truth of their views. The point extends to your beliefs or your arguing against another's. It is a logical blunder for someone to say, "Your belief is not true. You just believe it because. . . ." Explaining a belief need not explain it away. Once, after Archbishop William Temple gave an address at Oxford, a questioner opened the discussion with a challenge: "Well, of course, Archbishop, the point is that you believe what you believe because of the way you were brought up." To which the Archbishop replied: "That is as it may be.

How are people persuaded to follow cult leaders such as the Rev. Sun Myung Moon? (Wide World Photos)

But the fact remains that you believe I believe what I believe because of the way I was brought up, because of the way you were brought up."

In the eyes of the public the two most troubling and mystifying cults have been Sun Myung Moon's Unification Church and Jim Jones's Peoples Temple. The Reverend Moon's curious mixture of Christianity, anticommunism, and glorification of Moon himself as a new messiah has attracted a worldwide following. In response to Moon's declaration, "What I wish must be your wish," many have committed themselves and their incomes to the Unification Church. How are they persuaded to do so?

In 1978, 911 followers of the Reverend Jones shocked the world when they complied with his order to drink cupfuls of strawberry drink laced with tranquilizers, painkillers, and a lethal dose of cyanide. How could such a thing happen? What persuaded these people to give Jones such total allegiance? Since this will be hindsight analysis, we can't be sure of our answers to these questions. But it looks as if the attitude-change principles have been at work.

Attitudes Follow Behavior

Compliance Breeds Acceptance

As Chapter 2 indicated over and again, a commitment that is voluntarily chosen, substantial, made public, and repeated, is likely to be internalized. Cult leaders seem to know this. Their new converts soon learn that membership is no peripheral matter. They are quickly made active members of the team, not mere spectators. Disciplined rituals within the cult community, and canvassing and fund raising for the cult in public, strengthen the initiates' identities as cult members. Just as the participants in social-psychological experiments come to believe in those things for which they have suffered and witnessed (Aronson & Mills, 1959; Gerard & Mathewson, 1966), so do the cult's initiates: The greater the personal commitment, the more the need to justify it.

The Foot-in-the-Door Phenomenon

How are we induced to make substantial commitments? Seldom by an abrupt, conscious decision. One does not just one day up and decide, "I'm through with mainstream religion. I'm gonna find a cult." Nor do cult recruiters approach people on the street with, "Hi. I'm a Moonie. Care to join us?"

In actuality, the recruitment strategy skillfully applies the foot-in-the-door principle. Unification Church recruiters may invite people to a dinner and then to a weekend of warm fellowship and discussions of life philosophy. At the weekend retreat, they encourage the attenders to join in songs, activities, and discussion. Once potential converts are identified, they are urged to sign up for longer training retreats. Eventually the activities become more arduous—soliciting contributions and attempting to convert others.

Jim Jones used this foot-in-the-door technique with his Peoples Temple members. At first, monetary offerings were voluntary. He next inaugurated a required 10 percent tithe, which soon increased to 25 percent. Finally, he ordered members to turn over to him everything they possessed. Work loads also became progressively more demanding. As exmember Grace Stoen recalls,

> Nothing was ever done drastically. That's how Jim Jones got away with so much. You slowly gave up things and slowly had to put up with more, but it was always done very gradually. It was amazing, because you would sit up sometimes and say, wow, I really have given up a lot. I really am putting up with a lot. But he did it so slowly that you figured, I've made it this far, what the hell is the difference? (Conway & Siegelman, 1979, p. 236)

Persuasion

The Communicator

Nearly all successful cults have a charismatic leader—someone who can attract and direct the support of the members. As in experiments on persuasion, a credible communicator is someone the audience perceives as an expert and worthy of their trust—for example, as "Father" Moon.

Jim Jones reportedly used devious "psychic readings" to establish his credibility. Newcomers were asked to identify themselves as they entered the church before Jones's services. Then one of his aides would call the person's home and say "Hi. We're doing a survey and we'd like to ask you some questions." Later, one exmember recalls, with this information in hand Jones would call out the person's name and say,

> Have you ever seen me before? Well, you live in such and such a place, your phone number is such and such, and in your living room you've got this, that, and the other, and on your sofa you've got such and such a pillow. . . . Now do you remember me ever being in your house? (Conway & Siegelman, 1979, p. 234)

Trust is another aspect of credibility. Cult researcher Margaret Singer (1979b) notes that middle-class Caucasian youths are more vulnerable because they are more trusting. They lack the "street smarts" of lower-class youths (who know how to resist a hustle) and the wariness of upper-class youths (who have been warned of kidnappers since childhood). Also, many cult members have been recruited by their own friends or relatives, people whom they have come to trust (Stark & Bainbridge, 1980).

The Message and the Channel

To people who are lonely and depressed, the vivid, emotional messages and the warmth and acceptance with which they are showered by the group can be strikingly appealing: Trust the master, join the family; we have the answer, the "one way." And the message comes through channels as varied as lectures, small-group discussions, and direct social pressure.

The Audience

Who is most receptive to the message? New recruits are disproportionately young—people under twenty-five, those still at that comparatively open age before attitudes and values become stable. Some, such as the followers of Jim

Cults: Do their methods illustrate principles of effective persuasion? (Douglas Nigel Marlette/*The Charlotte Observer*)

Jones, are less educated people, people who are attracted by the simplicity of the message and who find it difficult to counterargue. Potential converts tend also to be at a turning point in life or facing a personal crisis. They have needs and aspirations; the cult offers them an answer (Singer, 1979b; Lofland & Stark, 1965). Times of social and economic upheaval are therefore especially conducive to an Ayatollah or a "Father" who can make what appears to be simple sense out of the confusion (O'Dea, 1968; Sales, 1972).

Group Isolation

Cults seem also to illustrate a major topic of the next chapter: the power of a group to magnify its members' views. Members are usually separated from their previous social support systems and isolated with a group of fellow cultists. There may occur what Rodney Stark and William Bainbridge (1980) call a "social implosion": External ties weaken until the group socially collapses inward, each person engaging only with other group members. Cut off from families and former friends, they begin to lose their access to counterarguments. The group now defines reality. And since disagreements are frowned upon—or in the case of the Peoples Temple even punished—the apparent consensus helps eliminate lingering doubts.

These techniques—binding behavior commitments, persuasion, and group isolation—do not have unlimited power. As Jim Jones made his demands more extreme, he increasingly had to control his people with intimidation. He used threats of harm to any who fled the community, beatings for noncompliance, and drugs to neutralize disagreeable members. By the end, he was said to have become as much an arm twister as a mind bender.

Still, cult techniques of social influence are disconcerting because of their power and their similarity to techniques used by groups more familiar to us. Fraternity and sorority members, for example, have reported that the initial "love bombing" of potential cult recruits is not unlike their own "rush" period, during which prospective pledges are lavished with warm attention and made to feel special. During the subsequent "pledge" period, new members are somewhat isolated, cut off from old friends who did not pledge. They spend time studying the history and rules of their new group, they suffer and commit time on its behalf, and they are expected to comply with all demands. Not surprisingly, the end result is usually a new member genuinely committed to the organization.

I choose this familiar example not to disparage fraternities and sororities but to preface a concluding personal observation. That the Peoples Temple abused the power of persuasion does not mean that the power is itself intrinsically bad. Nuclear power can be used to light up homes or to blacken cities. Sexual power can be used to express and celebrate love or to use and abuse people for selfish gratification. Persuasive power can be used to enlighten or to deceive. That these powers can be exploited for evil purposes should warn us to guard against their immoral use. The powers themselves are neither inherently evil nor good. How we use them determines whether they are constructive or destructive.

RESISTING PERSUASION: ATTITUDE INOCULATION

I hope that recognizing how your attitudes can be manipulated has provoked you to consider how to *resist* unwanted persuasion. In Chapter 7 on conformity, we saw one way to build resistance: Before encountering others' judgments, make a public commitment to your position. Once people have stood up for their convictions, they are less susceptible (or should we say less "open"?) to what others have to say. How can people be stimulated to commit themselves in everyday situations?

From his experiments, Charles Kiesler (1971) offers one possible way: Mildly attack their position. Kiesler found that when people who were already committed to a position were attacked strongly enough to cause them to react, but not so strongly as to overwhelm them, they became even more committed. Kiesler explains it this way:

> When you attack a committed person and your attack is of inadequate strength, you drive him to even more extreme behaviors in defense of his previous commitment. His commitment escalates, in a sense, because the number of acts consistent with his belief increases. (p. 88)

Perhaps you can recall a time when this happened in an argument, as those involved escalated their rhetoric, committing themselves to increasingly extreme positions.

There is a second reason why a mild attack might build resistance. Since people can resist persuasion by counterarguing, a mild attack can elicit counterarguments that will then be available should a stronger attack come. William McGuire (1964) documented this in a series of experiments on *attitude inoculation*. McGuire wondered: Could we inoculate people against persuasion much as we inoculate them against a virus? Consider what happens when you receive polio vaccine. You subject yourself to a weak polio virus, thus stimulating your body's defenses in preparation for a strong polio virus. Might a similar technique be used to ward off undesired persuasion? Could we take people raised in a "germ-free ideological environment"—people who hold some unquestioned belief—and stimulate their mental defenses by subjecting them to a small "dose" of belief-threatening material?

Inoculation: *Exposing people to weak attacks upon their attitudes, so that when stronger attacks come they will have refutations available.*

Such is what McGuire did. First, he found some cultural truisms—statements people wholeheartedly agreed with, such as "It's a good idea to brush your teeth after every meal if at all possible." McGuire then found that people were vulnerable to a massive, credible assault upon these truisms (for example, prestigious authorities were said to have discovered that too much toothbrushing can damage one's gums). If, however, prior to having their belief attacked they were "immunized" by first receiving a small challenge to their belief, and if they read or wrote an essay in refutation of this mild attack, then they were better able to resist the subsequent powerful attack.

In a clear demonstration of how laboratory research findings can lead to practical application, a research team led by Alfred McAlister (1980) had high school students "inoculate" seventh graders against peer pressures to smoke. For example, the seventh graders were taught to respond to advertisements implying that liberated women smoke by saying, "She's not really liberated if she is hooked on tobacco." They also acted in role plays in which, for example, after being called "chicken" for not taking a cigarette, they answered with statements like "I'd be a real chicken if I smoked just to impress you." After several such sessions during the seventh and eighth grades, the inoculated students were half as likely to begin smoking as uninoculated students at a sister junior high school that had an identical parental smoking rate (see Figure 8-10). Comparable reductions were also achieved in alcohol and marijuana use. Moreover, research with Houston seventh graders by Richard Evans, Richard Rozelle and others (1981) confirms that education-inoculation procedures can indeed reduce the smoking rate.

Researchers are also now studying how to immunize young children so they can more effectively analyze and evaluate television commercials. This research is prompted partly by recent studies indicating that children, especially those under eight years, (1) have trouble distinguishing commercials from programs and fail to grasp their persuasive intent, (2) trust television advertising

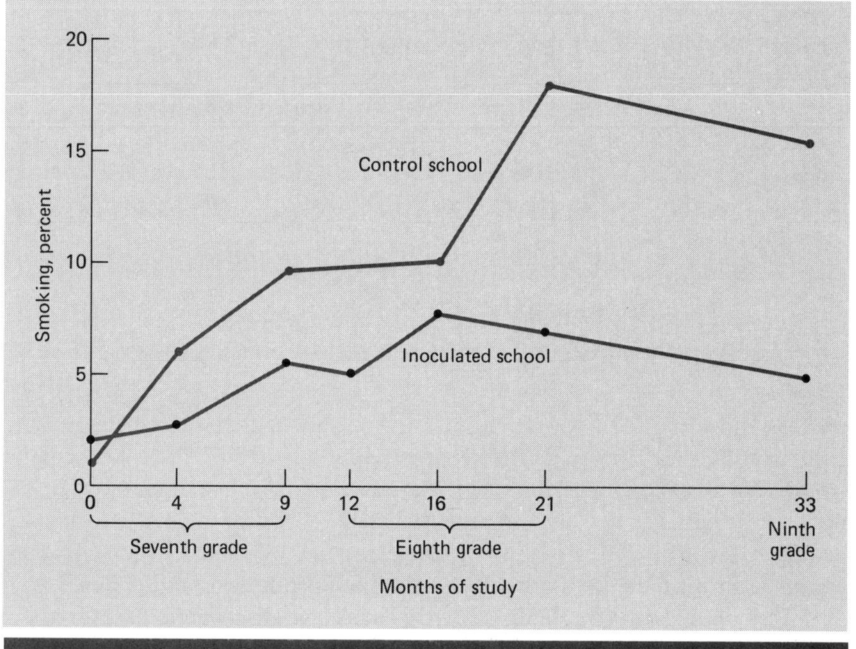

FIGURE 8-10 The percentage of cigarette smokers at an "inoculated" junior high school was much less than at a matched control school using a more typical smoking education program. (Data from McAlister et al., 1980; Telch et al., 1981.)

rather indiscriminately, and (3) desire and badger their parents for whatever products are advertised (Adler et al., 1980; S. Feshbach, 1980; Palmer & Dorr, 1980). Children, it seems, are an advertiser's dream: the gullible, vulnerable, easy sell. Moreover, approximately half of the 20,000 ads the typical child sees in a year are for low-nutritious, often sugary foods. Armed with such data, citizens groups have given the advertisers of such products a chewing out (Moody, 1980): "When a sophisticated advertiser spends millions to sell unsophisticated, trusting children an unhealthy product, this can only be called exploitation. No wonder the consumption of dairy products has declined since the advent of television, while soft-drink consumption has almost doubled." On the other side are the commercial interests, who claim that such ads allow parents to teach their children consumer skills and, more important, finance children's television programs. In the United States, the Federal Trade Commission has been in the middle, pondering both research findings and political pressures while deciding whether to place new constraints on TV ads aimed at young children.

A currently debated question: *What is the cumulative effect on children's materialism of witnessing some 350,000 commercials during their growing-up years?*

Meanwhile, researchers have wondered whether children might be taught how to resist deceptive ads. In one such effort, a team of investigators led by Norma Feshbach (1980; S. Cohen, 1980) gave small groups of elementary

Unlike Linus, many children, especially those under age eight, have difficulty distinguishing commercials from programs. (© United Features Syndicate, Inc.)

school children in the Los Angeles area three half-hour lessons that sought to stimulate their abilities to analyze commercials. The children were inoculated by viewing ads and discussing them. For example, after viewing a toy ad they were immediately given the toy and challenged to make it do what they had just seen on the television. Such experiences helped breed a more realistic understanding of the credibility of certain commercials.

This inoculation research also has some provocative implications. It suggests that the best way to build resistance to brainwashing may not be, as some senators thought after the Korean war, to introduce more courses on patriotism and Americanism. Teachers might be better advised, suggested McGuire, to inoculate—to challenge somewhat the concepts and principles of democracy, helping their students to develop defenses.

"The SLA . . . read me news items they clipped from the newspapers almost every day. Some of their stories were indisputable, sometimes I did not know what to believe. It was all very confusing. I realized that my life prior to my kidnapping had indeed been very sheltered; I had taken little or no interest in foreign affairs, politics, or economics."

Patricia Campbell Hearst, Every Secret Thing

For the same reason, religious educators should be wary of creating a "germ-free ideological environment" in their churches and schools. For example, Daniel Batson (1975) observed that teenage churchgoers who rejected a belief-threatening message actually *intensified* their belief commitment. An attack refuted is apparently more likely to solidify one's position than to undermine it, particularly if the threatening material can be examined with some like-minded others. Cults apply this principle by forewarning members of how their families and friends will dispute the cult's beliefs. When the expected attack comes, the member will be armed with counterarguments.

Another implication is that, for the persuader, an ineffective appeal can be worse than none at all. Why? Those who reject an appeal are thereby inoculated against further such appeals. This seemed evident in an experiment in which Susan Darley and Joel Cooper (1972) invited students to write essays advocating a strict dress code. Since this was against the students' own positions and the essays were to be published, all chose *not* to write the essay—even those offered $1.50 to do so. The interesting finding was that the students who turned down the $1.50 then became even more extremist and confident in their anti-dress code opinions. Having now made an overt decision against the dress code, they became even more resistant to it. Similarly, those who

BEHIND THE SCENES

William McGuire

One testimonial to the success of our immunization research is the extent to which it has been applied. Actually, I'm worried about this applicability, for two reasons. First, I confess to having felt like Mr. Clean when doing this immunization work because I was studying how to help people resist being manipulated. But now I appreciate more that people must be open to influence; it is not economical to learn everything by direct experience.

Second, I'm uneasy about how advertisers use our research. After the research was published, an advertising agency executive called and said, "Very interesting, Professor: I was delighted to read about it." Somewhat righteously, I replied, "Very nice of you to say that, Mr. Executive, but I'm really on the other side. You're trying to persuade people, and I'm trying to make them more resistant." "Oh, don't underrate yourself, Professor," he said. "We can use what you're doing to diminish the effect of our competitors' ads." And sure enough, it has become almost standard for advertisers to mention other brands and deflate their claims. *(William McGuire, Yale University)*

have rejected initial appeals to quit smoking may become immune to further appeals. So it seems that ineffective persuasion, by stimulating the listener's defenses, may be counterproductive—"hardening the heart" against subsequent appeals.

Perhaps inoculation research has a personal implication, too. Do you want to build up your resistance to persuasion without becoming closed to valid messages? Be an active listener. Force yourself to counterargue. After hearing a political speech, discuss it with others. In other words, don't just listen; react. If the message cannot withstand careful analysis, so much the worse for it. If it can, its effect on you will be the more enduring for having done so.

SUMMING UP

What makes for effective persuasion? Four factors have been extensively researched: the communicator, the message, the channel by which the message is communicated, and the audience.

The Communicator

Credible communicators are perceived as trustworthy experts. People who speak unhesitatingly, who talk fast, and who look listeners straight in the eye are more credible. So also are people who are overheard without their knowledge or who argue against their own self-interest. An attractive communicator—for example, someone similar to the audience—is also usually more effective. An exception is when an unattractive communicator succeeds in getting people to do something unpleasant; since doing so cannot be justified by the attractiveness of the communicator, people may improve their opinion of the act to explain their compliance.

The Message

Emotional factors can play a role. Associating a message with the good feelings one has while eating, drinking, or listening to music makes it more convincing. Messages that arouse fear can also be effective, perhaps because they are vivid and memorable.

How discrepant should a message be from the audience's existing opinions? That depends on the communicator's credibility. Highly credible people are able to elicit the greatest changes in opinion when they argue a relatively extreme position; less credible people are more successful when they advocate positions closer to those of the audience.

Is a message most persuasive when it presents only its position or when it introduces the opposing side as well? This depends on the listeners. When the audience already agrees with the message, is unaware of opposing arguments, and is unlikely later to be subjected to the opposition, then a one-sided appeal is most effective (although perhaps not most ethical). With more sophisticated audiences or with those not already agreeing, two-sided messages are most successful.

If two sides of an issue are to be presented, do the arguments presented first or second have the advantage? The most common finding is what is called a primacy effect: Information presented early is most potent, especially when it affects one's interpretation of the later information. However, if a time gap separates the two sides, the effect of the early information diminishes; if a decision is made right after hearing the second side, which is therefore still fresh in the mind, the result will likely be a recency effect.

The Channel

Another important consideration is *how* the message is communicated. Attitudes developed from actual experience are usually stronger than those shaped by appeals passively received. Nevertheless, although not as potent as face-to-face personal influence, the mass media can be effective when the issue is minor (such as which brand of aspirin to buy) or unfamiliar (such as deciding between two otherwise unknown political candidates). Some of the media's effect may, however, be transmitted in two steps: directly to opinion leaders and then on to others through their personal influence.

The Audience

Finally, it matters *who* receives the message. Traits such as intelligence bear no simple relation to persuasibility, apparently because a trait that contributes to one's receiving and comprehending a message will often work against yielding to it. More crucial is what the audience thinks while receiving a message. Do they think agreeing thoughts? Do they counterargue? Forewarning an audience that a disagreeable message is coming reduces persuasion by stimulating counterarguments. On the other hand, distracting people while they hear a disagreeable message can interfere with their counterarguing and thus increase persuasion.

The age of the audience also makes a difference. Researchers who have resurveyed people over time find that older people's attitudes are more stable. Apparently we form most of our basic attitudes and values when young and then carry them through adulthood. As succeeding generations form new attitudes, generation gaps result.

The recent successes of religious cults, such as the Unification Church and the Peoples Temple, provide an opportunity to see powerful persuasion processes at work. It appears that their success has resulted partly by their eliciting behavior commitments (as described in Chapter 2), by applying principles of effective persuasion (this chapter), and by isolating members in like-minded groups (to be discussed in Chapter 9).

How do people resist persuasion? A prior public commitment to one's own position, stimulated perhaps by a mild attack on the position, breeds resistance to later persuasion. A mild attack can also serve as an inoculation, stimulating one's attitudinal defenses to develop counterarguments that will then be available if and when a strong attack comes. This implies, paradoxically, that one way to strengthen existing attitudes is to challenge them, though not so strongly as to overwhelm them.

Chapter

Group Influence

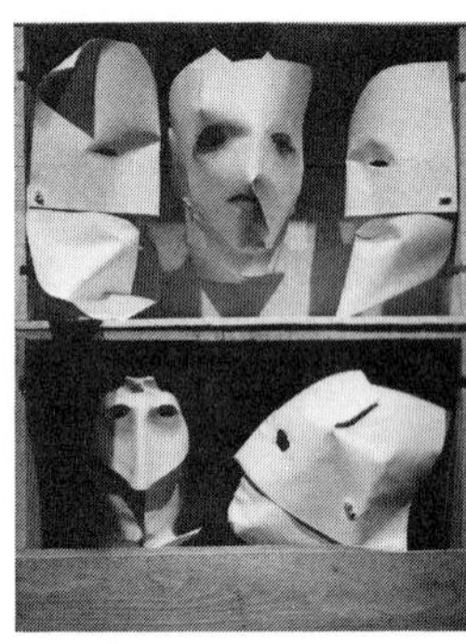

Our world contains not only 4.3 billion individuals, but also 200 nation-states, 4 million local communities, 20 million economic organizations, 200 million extended families, and hundreds of millions of other formal and informal groups—couples on dates, psychology departments, churches, dorm bull sessions. How do such groups influence their individual members? Consider six concrete examples of the sorts of group influences studied by social psychologists:

Wanda is wearily nearing the end of her daily jog. Her head prods her to keep pushing it; her body begs her to walk it in. She compromises and slogs home. The next day's conditions are identical, except that a friend runs with her. Wanda runs her route two minutes faster. She wonders: "Wow! Did I run better merely because Gail was with me?"

In a team tug-of-war, will eight people on a side exert as much force as the sum of their best efforts in individual tugs-of-war? More than a half century ago, a German psychologist found that the collective effort of such teams was but half the sum of the individual efforts. Were the participants coasting on the group's effort? If so, does such loafing also occur in work groups?

In preparation for battle, warriors in some tribal cultures are depersonalized with body and face paints or special masks. After the battle, some cultures kill, torture, or mutilate any remaining enemies; other cultures take prisoners alive. Robert

Watson (1973) scrutinized anthropological files and discovered that the cultures with depersonalized warriors are also the cultures that are brutal to the enemy. Are people in modern cultures ever depersonalized by their groups? If so, how, and with what results?

Educational researchers have been fascinated with a curious "accentuation phenomenon." Initial attitude differences among students in different colleges tend to become accentuated as they progress through college. Likewise, attitude differences between those who belong to a fraternity or a sorority and those who do not are modest at the freshman level, more pronounced in the senior year. Does this phenomenon occur because group interaction among like-minded people accentuates their initial leanings? If so, why?

The executives of a soft-drink company enthusiastically discuss plans for their new asparagus-flavored soda pop. The group invites no contrary opinions and, since group members who harbor doubts hesitate to puncture the group's enthusiasm, the group deludes itself that all endorse the product and overestimates its probable success. In real social situations, do group influences often work against optimal decisions? If so, what group forces are hampering the decision making and how can they be avoided?

The movie *12 Angry Men* opens at the conclusion of a murder trial as twelve weary jurors file into the juryroom. It is a hot day, they are tired, close to agreement, and eager for a quick verdict convicting a teen-age boy of killing his father with a knife. But one maverick, played by Henry Fonda, refuses to vote guilty. As the heated deliberation proceeds, all the jurors, one by one, change their verdicts until consensus is reached: "Not guilty." In real juries, a lone individual seldom sways the entire group. Yet, history is made by minorities that sway majorities. What helps make a minority persuasive?

These examples illustrate six intriguing phenomena of group influence: "social facilitation," "social loafing," "deindividuation," "group polarization," "groupthink," and "minority influence." We will examine them one at a time. But first things first: what is a group, and why do groups exist?

WHAT IS A GROUP?

The answer seems self-evident—until several people compare their definitions. Are Wanda and her jogging partner a group? Are the passengers on an airplane a group? Is a group a set of people who identify with one another, who sense they belong to one another? Is it people who share common goals and rely on one another? Does a group form when a number of individuals become organized? Such are among the characteristics that various social psychologists have used to define a group.

Group: *Two or more people who, for longer than a few moments, interact with and influence one another.*

Group dynamics expert Marvin Shaw (1981) argues that all groups have one thing in common: Their members interact. He therefore defines a *group* as two or more people who interact with and influence one another. So Wanda and her jogging companion might indeed be considered a group. And most certainly the fraternity and sorority members and corporate decision makers would be members of groups. Such groups may exist for several reasons—to meet one's need to belong, to provide information, to supply rewards, to accomplish goals.

By Shaw's definition, the passengers on a routine airplane flight would seem *not* to be a group. Although physically together, they are more a collection of individuals than a true, interacting group. But the distinction between simple collective behavior among unrelated individuals on a plane and the more influential group behavior among interacting individuals sometimes blurs. For example, people who are merely in one another's presence do sometimes significantly influence one another. In this chapter, we will first consider three examples of such collective influence: social facilitation, social loafing, and deindividuation. These phenomena transpire in situations that involve minimal interaction, and hence only border on group behavior. Then we will consider three examples of social influence in interacting groups: group polarization, groupthink, and minority influence. These phenomena indisputably involve group behavior.

SOCIAL FACILITATION

Co-actors: *A group of people working simultaneously and individually on a noncompetitive task.*

The most elementary question in social psychology could be: How are we affected by the mere presence of other people? "Mere presence" means people are not competing, do not reward or punish, and in fact do nothing except be present as a passive audience or as *co-actors*. Would the mere presence of other people affect your jogging, eating, typing, or exam performance? The search for the answer is a delightful scientific mystery story.

The Presence of Others Can Boost Performance

Almost ninety years ago, Norman Triplett (1898), a psychologist interested in bicycle racing, noticed that cyclists' times were faster when racing together than when racing alone against the clock. Before he peddled his hunch (that the presence of others boosts performance), Triplett conducted one of social psychology's early laboratory experiments. Children told to wind string on a fishing reel as rapidly as possible wound faster when they worked with co-actors than when working alone.

Subsequent experiments—in the early decades of this century—found that the presence of others also improves the speed with which people do

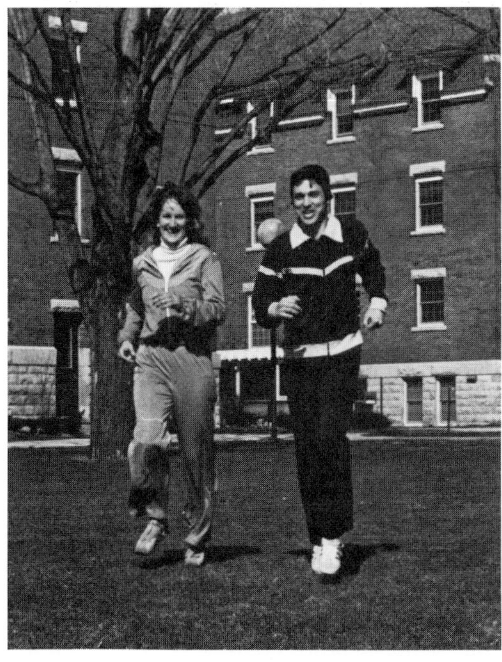

Co-action: the presence of others facilitates well-learned behavior. (Photo by Tom Renner)

simple multiplication problems and cross out designated letters, and improves the accuracy with which people perform simple motor tasks such as keeping a metal stick in contact with a dime-size disc on a moving turntable (F. W. Allport, 1920; Dashiell, 1930; Travis, 1925). This *social-facilitation* effect, as it came to be called, also occurs with animals. In the presence of others of their species, ants excavate more sand and chickens eat more grain (Bayer, 1929; Chen, 1937).

The Presence of Others Can Hurt Performance

On the other hand, some studies conducted about the same time revealed that the presence of others could also hinder performance on certain tasks. In the presence of others, cockroaches, parakeets, and greenfinches learn mazes more slowly than when alone (Allee & Masure, 1936; Gates & Allee, 1933; Klopfer, 1958). This disruptive effect also occurs with people. The presence of others diminishes people's efficiency at learning nonsense syllables, completing a maze, and performing complex multiplication problems (Dashiell, 1930; Pessin, 1933; Pessin & Husband, 1933).

Saying that the presence of others sometimes facilitates performance and sometimes hinders it is about as satisfying as a weather forecast predicting that it might be sunny, but then again it might rain. Consequently, by 1940, research activity in this area fizzled. For twenty-five years it lay dormant until awakened by the touch of a new idea.

The General Rule

Can these seemingly contradictory findings be reconciled by a general rule? Social psychologist Robert Zajonc (pronounced *Zy-ence*, rhymes with *science*), wondered. As often happens at creative moments in science, Zajonc (1965) used one field of research to illuminate another. In this case the illumination came from a well-established principle in experimental psychology: Arousal enhances whatever response tendency is dominant. That is, on easy tasks [for which the most likely ("dominant") response is the correct one], increased arousal enhances performance. For example, people solve easy anagrams, such as akec, fastest when they are anxious. On complex tasks (for which the correct answer is not the dominant response), increased arousal accentuates incorrect responding. Thus on harder anagrams people do worse when anxious.

Social facilitation: *(1) Original meaning—the tendency of people to perform simple or well-learned tasks better when others are present. (2) Current meaning (see text below)—the strengthening of dominant (prevalent, likely) responses due to the presence of others.*

Could this principle solve the mystery of social facilitation? It seemed reasonable to presume that people are more aroused or energized in the presence of others. (Most of us can recall feeling more tense or excited when before an audience.) If social arousal facilitates dominant responses, it should boost performance on easy tasks and hurt performance on difficult tasks. Looking back at the confusing results, everything seemed to fit. Winding fishing reels, doing simple multiplication problems, and eating were all easy tasks for which the observed reponses were well-learned or naturally dominant. And sure enough, having others around boosted performance. On the other hand, learning new material, doing a maze, or solving complex math problems were more difficult tasks for which the correct responses were initially less probable. And sure enough, the presence of others increased *incorrect* responding on these tasks. The same general rule—arousal facilitates dominant responses—seemed to work in both cases. Suddenly, what had been assumed to be contradictory results were now recognized as not contradictory at all.

"Discovery consists of seeing what everybody has seen and thinking what nobody has thought."

Albert Axent-Gyorgyi, The Scientist Speculates

Zajonc's solution, so simple and elegant, left other social psychologists thinking what Thomas H. Huxley thought after first reading Darwin's *Origin of Species*: "How extremely stupid not to have thought of that!" It seemed obvious—once Zajonc had pointed it out. Perhaps, however, the pieces appeared to merge so neatly only because they were being viewed through the spectacles of hindsight. But a question no hindsight can answer yet remained: Would the solution survive direct experimental tests?

Indeed it has survived. First, several experiments in which Zajonc and his associates manufactured an arbitrary dominant response confirmed that an audience enhanced this response. In one, Zajonc and Stephen Sales (1966) asked people to pronounce various nonsense words between one and sixteen times. The people were then told that the same words would be flashed on a screen, one at a time. Each time, they were to guess which had appeared. When the people were actually shown only random black lines for 1/100 second, people "saw" mostly the words they had pronounced most frequently.

These words had become the dominant responses. The same test was also given in the presence of two others. From what you have learned thus far, what do you think the effect was? As Figure 9-1 indicates, Zajonc and Sales found exactly what they had predicted: to an even greater extent, the people guessed the most frequently practiced words.

Subsequent experiments have confirmed this effect—the facilitation of dominant responses—in various ways. For example, Peter Hunt and Joseph Hillery (1973) found that in the presence of others, University of Akron students took less time to learn a simple maze and more time to learn one that was complex (just as the cockroaches did in the experiment previously cited). And James Michaels and his collaborators (1982) found that good pool players in the Virginia Polytechnic Institute student union (who had made 71 percent of their shots while being unobtrusively observed) did even better (80 percent) when four observers came up to watch them play. Poor shooters (who had previously averaged 36 percent) did even worse (25 percent) when closely observed.

We have seen that people do respond to the presence of others. But are people really aroused by the presence of observers? In times of stress, a comrade can be comforting. However, researchers have occasionally found that with others present, people perspire more, breathe faster, tense their muscles more, and have higher blood pressure and a faster heart rate (Geen, 1980; Moore & Baron, 1983).

Why Are We Aroused in the Presence of Others?

Deodorant producers certainly have capitalized on this effect. Nearly all their advertising depicts the phenomenon. What is it about other people that causes arousal? Is it their mere presence? The answers are still being debated. However, there is evidence to support three possible factors, each of which may play a role.

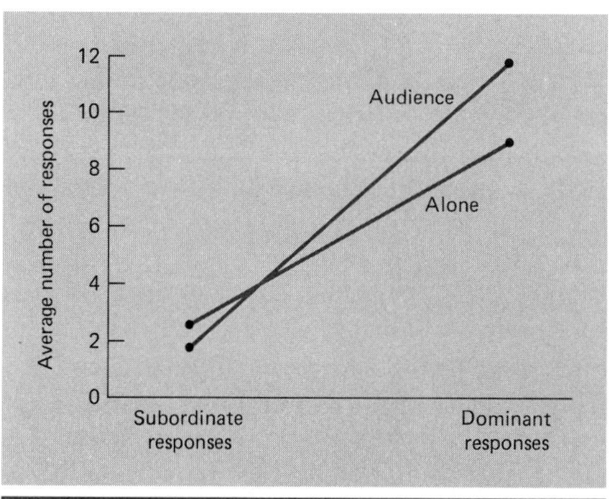

FIGURE 9-1 Social facilitation of dominant responses. People responded with dominant words (practiced sixteen times) more frequently, and subordinate words (practiced but once) less frequently, when observers were present. (Data from Zajonc & Sales, 1965.)

Evaluation apprehension: *Concern for how others are evaluating oneself.*

Nickolas Cottrell surmised that observers make us apprehensive because we know they may be evaluating us. To test whether this *evaluation apprehension* exists, Cottrell and his associates (1968) repeated Zajonc and Sales' nonsense-syllables study at Kent State University and added a third condition. In this "mere presence" condition the observers, supposedly in preparation for a perception experiment, were blindfolded in order to prevent them from evaluating the subjects' performance. In contrast to the effect of the watching audience, the mere presence of these blindfolded people did *not* boost well-practiced responses. Other experiments confirmed Cottrell's conclusion: The enhancement of dominant responses is strongest when people think they are being evaluated (e.g., Sasfy and Okun, 1974; Bray & Sugarman, 1980). Perhaps this is one reason why two-thirds of college basketball games are won by the home team (Hirt & Kimble, 1981), why in both laboratory and everyday situations the larger the audience, the more apprehensive people feel (Jackson & Latané, 1981), and why people perform best when their co-actor is slightly superior (Seta, 1982). What is more, those most affected by the presence of others tend to be socially anxious; they are people concerned with how others evaluate them (Geen, 1980; Gastorf, Suls, & Sanders, 1980).

Glenn Sanders, Robert S. Baron, and Danny Moore (1978; Baron, Moore, & Sanders, 1978; Sanders & Baron, 1975) carry evaluation apprehension a step further. They theorize that people who are concerned with how co-actors are doing on the task or how an audience is reacting get distracted from the task at hand. Their experiments suggest that this *conflict* between paying attention to others and paying attention to the task makes people even more aroused. Evidence that people are indeed "driven by distraction" comes from experiments in which social facilitation is produced not just by the presence of another person, but by even a nonhuman distraction, such as bursts of light (Sanders, 1981a; 1981b).

Zajonc, however, believes that the mere presence of others does produce some arousal even when there exists no evaluation apprehension or conflict. For example, people's color preferences are stronger when they make judgments with others present (Goldman, 1967). On such a task, there is no "good" or "right" answer for others to evaluate, hence no reason to be concerned with their reactions.

Similarly, Hazel Markus (1978) had University of Michigan men prepare for an experiment by putting on special socks, shoes, and a lab coat. She then "canceled" the experiment, so the students put their own clothes back on. This clothes changing was done either alone, in front of a supposed fellow subject who watched, or in the presence of someone else who, with back to the subject, acted as if he were repairing some equipment. When someone else was in the room the unfamiliar clothes took longer to put on, and the familiar clothes were put on more quickly, even when the other person's back was turned. So it seems that even when people are not being evaluated for "correct" answers, the "bodily presence of another," as Triplett surmised back in 1898, "serves to liberate latent energy not ordinarily available."

Perhaps, however, the mere presence of another is arousing because it distracts. Nevertheless, the fact that facilitation effects also occur with animals, which probably are not consciously worrying about how other animals are evaluating them, hints at some type of innate social arousal mechanism running through much of the zoological world. I think that Wanda, our jogger, would agree. Most joggers report that jogging with someone else, even one who neither competes nor evaluates, somehow energizes.

This may in turn be due to joggers' being slower to feel fatigue when a fellow jogger is diverting their attention (Pennebaker & Lightner, 1980).

This is a good time to remind ourselves of the purpose of a theory. As we noted in Chapter 1, a good theory is a scientific shorthand: It simplifies and summarizes a variety of observations. Social facilitation theory does this well. It is a simple summary of many research findings. A good theory also offers clear predictions that can be used (1) to confirm or modify the theory, (2) to generate new exploration, and (3) to suggest practical application. Social facilitation theory has definitely generated the first two types of prediction: (1) the basics of the theory (that the presence of others is arousing, and that this social arousal enhances dominant responses) have been confirmed, and (2) the theory has brought new life to a long dormant field of research. Does it also suggest (3) some practical applications?

Application is properly the last phase of research. In their study of social facilitation, researchers have yet to work much on this. That gives us the opportunity to speculate on what some applications might be. For example, as Figure 9-2 illustrates, many new office buildings are replacing private

FIGURE 9-2 In the "open office plan" people work in the presence of others. How might this affect worker efficiency? (Photograph courtesy of Herman Miller Inc.)

offices with large, open areas divided by low partitions. Might the resulting awareness of others' presence help energize the performance of well-learned tasks, but disrupt creative thinking on complex tasks? Can you think of other possible applications?

The "social energizing" effect we've been examining usually occurs in situations where people are working toward individual goals and where their efforts, whether winding fishing reels or solving math problems, can be individually evaluated. These situations parallel some everyday work situations, but not those situations that require cooperative effort, where people pool their efforts toward a *common* goal and where individuals are *not* accountable for their efforts. A team tug-of-war provides one such example. The effects of organizational fund raising might well be another. People on a work crew might be yet another. On such "additive tasks"—tasks where the group's achievement depends on the sum of the individual efforts—will team spirit boost productivity? Will bricklayers lay bricks faster when working as a team than when working alone?

"Mere social contact begets . . . a stimulation of the animal spirits that heightens the efficiency of each individual workman."

Karl Marx, Das Kapital

One way to attack a question such as this is with laboratory simulations. Like the aeronautical engineer's wind tunnel, a controlled miniature reality can enable researchers to isolate and study important variables.

Many Hands Make Light Work

Contrary to the common notion that "in unity there is strength," the tug-of-war experiment suggested that group members may actually be *less* motivated when performing additive tasks. However, Ivan Steiner (1972) noticed a problem with the tug-of-war experiment. Perhaps the group's poor performance stemmed from poor coordination—people pulling in slightly different directions at slightly different times. A group of Massachusetts researchers led by Alan Ingham (1974) cleverly eliminated this problem by making individuals think others were pulling with them, when in fact they were pulling alone. Blindfolded participants assigned the first position in the apparatus shown in Figure 9-3 and told to "pull as hard as you can" pulled 18 percent harder when they knew they were pulling alone than when they believed that behind them from two to five people were also pulling.

Social loafing: *The tendency for people to exert less effort when they pool their efforts toward a common goal than when they are individually accountable.*

At Ohio State University, researchers Bibb Latané, Kipling Williams, and Stephen Harkins (1979; Harkins, Latané, & Williams, 1980) kept their ears open for other ways to investigate *social loafing* as they dub this phenomenon. They observed that the noise produced by six people shouting or clapping "as loud as you can" was less than three times that produced by one person alone. However, like the tug-of-war task, noisemaking is vulnerable to group inefficiency. Latané and his associates needed to follow Ingham's

FIGURE 9-3 The rope-pulling apparatus. People in the first position pulled less hard when they thought people behind them were also pulling. (Data from Ingham, Levinger, Graves, & Peckham, 1974.) (Photo by Alan G. Ingham)

example by leading participants to believe others were shouting or clapping with them, when in fact they were doing so alone.

Their solution was to blindfold six people, seat them in a semicircle, and have them put on headphones, over which they were blasted with the sound of people shouting or clapping. People could not even hear their own shouting or clapping, much less that of others. On various trials they were instructed to shout or clap either alone or along with the group. Other people told about the experiment guessed they would shout louder when with others, because they would be less embarrassed (Harkins, 1981). The actual result? Once again, social loafing: When they believed five others were also either shouting or clapping, the participants produced one-third less noise than when they thought themselves alone. However, those who clapped both alone and in groups did not view themselves as loafing; they perceived themselves clapping equally in both situations.

John Sweeney (1973), a political scientist interested in the policy implications of social loafing, obtained similar results in an experiment at the University of Texas. He found that students pumped exercise bicycles more energetically (as measured by electrical output) when they knew they were being individually monitored than when they thought their output was being pooled with that of other riders. In the group condition, people were tempted to *free ride* on the group effort.

Free riders: *People who benefit from the group but give little in return.*

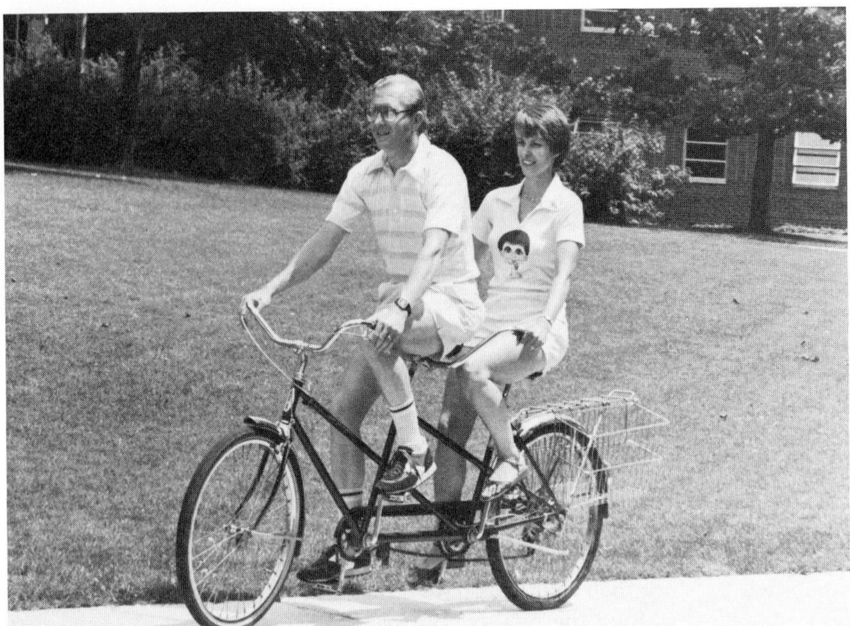

Social loafing. People who pool their efforts toward a common goal without being individually accountable tend to exert less effort than when performing the same task alone. (Tom Renner)

At work here is a twist on one of the psychological forces that contributes to the social facilitation effect: evaluation apprehension. In the experiments dealing with social loafing, individuals are open to evaluation only when acting alone. The group situation (rope pulling, shouting, and so forth) *decreases* evaluation apprehension; when individuals are not accountable, responsibility is diffused across all group members (Kerr & Bruun, 1981). By contrast, in the social facilitation experiments, the presence of the group *increased* the individual's vulnerability to evaluation.

However, it is possible to make group members' performances identifiable. Some football coaches do this by individually filming and evaluating each lineman. The Ohio State researchers did the same by having group members wear individual microphones while engaged in group shouting (Williams, Harkins, & Latané, 1981). They found that, whether they were in a group or not, people exerted more effort when their outputs were individually identifiable.

Social Loafing in Everyday Living

How widespread is social loafing? In the laboratory, the phenomenon has been observed not only among people who are pulling ropes, cycling, shouting, and clapping, but also among those who are pumping water or air, evaluating poems or editorials, producing ideas, typing, and detecting signals. But can the results of these experiments be generalized to worker productivity in everyday situations? We can, at this point, only speculate, noting situations that at least superficially parallel the laboratory phenomenon.

It is reported that on their collective farms, Russian peasants work one field one day, another field the next, with little direct responsibility for any given plot. For their own use, they are given small private plots. Interestingly, the private plots occupy but 1 percent of the agricultural land yet produce 27 percent of the Soviet farm output (H. Smith, 1976). In Hungary, private plots account for only 13 percent of the farmland, but produce one-third of the produce (Spivak, 1979).

In America, workers who do not pay dues or volunteer time to their union or professional association nevertheless are usually happy to accept its benefits. This hints at another possible explanation of social loafing. When rewards are divided equally, regardless of how much one contributes to the group, any individual gets more reward per unit of effort by free riding on the group. Hence, people may be motivated to slack off when their efforts are not individually monitored and rewarded. For example, in a pickle factory the key job is picking the right size dill-pickle halves off the conveyor belt and stuffing them in jars. Unfortunately, workers are tempted to stuff any size pickle in, since their output is not identifiable (the jars go into a common hopper before reaching the quality-control section). Williams, Harkins, and Latané (1981) note that research on social loafing suggests "making individual production identifiable, and raises the question: 'How many pickles could a pickle packer pack if pickle packers were only paid for properly packed pickles?'."

Sometimes a group goal may be so compelling that little social loafing occurs. The traditional Hope College freshman versus sophomore "pull" generates near-maximum effort. (Hope College Photo)

But surely, collective effort does not always lead group members to slack off. Sometimes the goal is so compelling, and maximum output from everyone is so essential, that team spirit can at least maintain effort if not intensify it. In an Olympic crew race, will the individual rowers in an eight-person crew pull their oars with less effort than those in a one- or two-person crew? My hunch is that they will not. Similarly, Latané notes that Israel's communal kibbutz farms have actually outproduced Israel's noncollective farms (Leon, 1969), and Williams (1981) reports that groups of friends loaf less than do groups of strangers. Perhaps, then, the cohesiveness of the kibbutz organization somehow intensifies effort. If so, then will social loafing not occur in less individualistic, more group-centered cultures? Shortly before this book went to press, Latané, Williams, and their associates returned from the Orient where they repeated their sound production experiments in Japan, Thailand, and Taiwan. Their findings? Social loafing was evident there, too.

Perhaps research will one day more precisely identify the group circumstances that intensify and those that diminish individual effort and productivity. For now, laboratory experiments suggest that when group members perform additive tasks without individual accountability, many hands can make light the work. While collective effort enables people to fulfill certain goals more easily, it also permits social loafing.

DEINDIVIDUATION

Experiments on social facilitation indicate that groups can arouse people; social loafing experiments indicate that groups can diffuse responsibility. When high levels of arousal are combined with diffused responsibility, one's normal inhibitions may diminish. The result may be acts ranging from a mild lessening of restraint (throwing food in the dining hall, snarling at a referee, screaming during a rock concert) to impulsive self-gratification (group vandalism, orgies, thefts) to destructive social explosions (riots, lynchings, torturings). In a 1967 incident, 200 University of Oklahoma students gathered to watch a disturbed fellow student threatening to jump from a tower. They began to chant "Jump. Jump. . . ." The student jumped to his death (UPI, 1967).

Deindividuation: *Loss of self-awareness and evaluation apprehension; occurs in group situations that foster anonymity and draw attention away from oneself.*

Doing Together What We Would Not Do Alone

One thing these unrestrained behaviors have in common is that they are somehow provoked by the power of a group. It is hard to imagine a single rock fan screaming deliriously at a private rock concert, or a single Oklahoma student trying to coax someone to suicide. For it is in group situations that people are most likely to abandon their normal restraints, to lose their sense of individuality, to become what Leon Festinger, Albert Pepitone, and

Theodore Newcomb (1952) labeled *deindividuated*. What circumstances elicit this psychological state?

A Group

A group not only has the power to arouse its members, but also to render them unidentifiable. The snarling crowd protects the snarling basketball fan from accountability. A lynch mob enables its members to believe that they will not be prosecuted; the action is perceived as the *group's*. Rioters, made faceless by the mob, are freed to loot. In an analysis of twenty-one instances in which crowds were present as someone threatened to jump from a building or bridge, Leon Mann (1981) found that when the crowd was small and exposed by daylight, people usually did not try to bait the person. But when a large crowd or the cover of night gave people anonymity, the crowd usually baited and jeered. In each of these examples, from the sports crowd to the jeering mob, evaluation apprehension plummets. And because "everyone is doing it," all can attribute their behavior to the situation rather than to their own choices.

Philip Zimbardo (1970) speculated that the mere immensity of crowded cities contributes to anonymity and thus to norms that permit vandalism. He once purchased two 10-year-old cars and left them with the hood up and license plates removed, one on a street near the Bronx campus of New York University and one near the Stanford University campus in Palo Alto, a much smaller city. In New York the first auto strippers arrived within ten minutes, taking the battery and radiator. After three days and twenty-three incidents of theft and vandalism by neatly dressed white people, the car was reduced to a battered, useless hulk of metal. By contrast, the only person observed to touch the Palo Alto car in over a week was a passerby who lowered the hood when it began to rain.

Physical Anonymity

How can we be sure that the crucial difference between the Bronx and Palo Alto is greater anonymity in the Bronx? We can't. But we can experiment with anonymity to see if it actually lessens inhibitions. In one such experiment, Zimbardo (1970) dressed New York University women in identical white coats and hoods, making them resemble members of the Ku Klux Klan (see Figure 9-4). Asked to deliver electric shocks to a woman, they pressed the shock button twice as long as did women who were visible and wearing large name tags.

A research team led by Edward Diener (1976) cleverly demonstrated the effect both of being in a group *and* of being physically anonymous. At Halloween, they observed 1352 Seattle children trick-or-treating. As the children, either alone or in groups, approached one of twenty-seven homes scattered throughout the city, an experimenter greeted them warmly, invited them to "take *one* of the candies," and then left the room. Hidden observers noted that children in groups were more than twice as likely to take extra candy as those alone. Also, children left anonymous were more than twice as

FIGURE 9-4
Anonymous women delivered more shock to helpless victims than did identifiable women. (Data from Zimbardo, 1969.) (Photo courtesy of Philip Zimbardo)

likely to transgress as those who had been asked their names and where they lived. The transgression rate thus varied dramatically with the situation, from 8 percent among children alone and identified up to 80 percent among anonymous children.

These experiments make me think about the effect of wearing uniforms. In Zimbardo's prison simulation the guards and prisoners were dressed in depersonalizing common outfits (see Chapter 6). Did this contribute to the depraved behavior that followed? Recall, too, the discovery by Robert Watson that warriors wearing depersonalizing masks or face paints treat their victims more brutally. Does becoming physically anonymous always unleash our worst impulses?

Fortunately, no. For one thing, the situations in which some of these experiments took place had clear antisocial cues. For example, Robert Johnson and Leslie Downing (1979) point out that the Klan-like outfits worn by Zimbardo's subjects may have been cues that encouraged hostility. So, in an experiment at the University of Georgia, they had women put on nurses' uniforms before deciding how much shock someone should receive. When those wearing the nurses' uniforms were made anonymous, they became *less* aggressive in administering shock than when their names and personal identities were stressed. Evidently being anonymous makes one less self-conscious and more responsive to cues present in the situation, whether negative (for example, Klan uniforms) or positive (for example, nurses' uniforms).

Moreover, even if anonymity unleashes our impulses we must remember that not all our impulses are sinister. Picture yourself in this heartwarming experiment conducted by Swarthmore College researchers Kenneth Gergen, Mary Gergen, and William Barton (1973). You are ushered through double doors into a totally darkened environmental chamber, where you will spend the next hour (unless you choose to leave) with seven strangers of both sexes. You are told that "There are no rules as to what you should do together. At the end of the time period you will be escorted from the room alone, and will subsequently depart from the experimental site alone. There will be no opportunity to [formally] meet the other participants."

Control participants, who spent the hour in a lighted room with more conventional expectations, chose simply to sit and converse the whole time. By contrast, the experience of being anonymous in the dark room with unclear expectations "unleashed" intimacy and affection. People in the dark talked less, but they talked more about "important" things. Ninety percent purposefully touched someone; 50 percent hugged another. Few disliked the anonymity; most deeply enjoyed it and volunteered to return without pay. Anonymity had "freed up" intimacy and playfulness.

Activities that Arouse and Distract

Aggressive outbursts by large groups are often preceded by minor actions that arouse and divert people's attention. Group shouting, chanting, clapping, or dancing serve both to hype people up and to reduce their self-consciousness. One Moonie observer recalls how the "choo-choo" chant helped deindividuate:

> All the brothers and sisters joined hands and chanted with increasing intensity, choo-choo-choo, Choo-choo-choo, CHOO-CHOO-CHOO! YEA! YEA! POWW!!! The act made us a group, as though in some strange way we had all experienced something important together. The power of the choo-choo frightened me, but it made me feel more comfortable and there was something very relaxing about building up the energy and releasing it. (Zimbardo, Ebbesen, & Maslach, 1977, p. 186)

In William Golding's (1962) *Lord of the Flies*, a group of marooned boys gradually descended into savagery. The boys sometimes preceded their savage acts by group activities, such as dancing in a circle and chanting "*Kill the beast! Cut his throat! Spill his blood!*" By doing so the group became "a single organism" (p. 182).

"A mob is a society of bodies voluntarily bereaving themselves of reason."

Ralph Waldo Emerson, "Compensation," Essays, First Series

Edward Diener's experiments (1976; 1979) at the University of Washington and the University of Illinois have shown that such activities as throwing rocks and group singing can set the stage for more disinhibited behavior. There is a self-reinforcing pleasure in doing an impulsive act while observing others doing it also. Moreover, impulsive group action arouses people and absorbs their attention. When we yell at the referee we are not thinking about our values; we are reacting to the immediate situation. Consequently, when we stop to think about what we have done or said, we sometimes feel chagrined. Sometimes. Not always. For at other times we intentionally seek deindividuating group experiences—dances, worship experiences, group encounters—where we can enjoy intense positive feelings and a sense of closeness with others.

"The use of self-control is like the use of brakes on a train. It is useful when you find yourself going in the wrong direction, but merely harmful when the direction is right."

Bertrand Russell, Marriage and Morals

Deindividuation as Diminished Self-Awareness

The research on deindividuation shows that a group experience that diminishes people's self-consciousness also tends to disconnect their behavior from their attitudes (Prentice-Dunn & Rogers, 1980; Diener et al., 1980). Deindividuated people are less restrained, more likely to act without thinking about their own values, more responsive to the immediate situation. These findings complement and reinforce the experiments on *self-awareness* we considered in Chapters 2 and 3. Self-awareness is the other side of the coin from deindividuation. Those made self-aware, say by acting in front of a mirror or TV camera, exhibit *increased* self-control, and their actions are more strongly rooted in their attitudes. For example, people made self-aware are less likely to cheat when given a convenient chance to do so (Diener & Wallbom, 1976; Beaman et al., 1979). They exhibit greater consistency between their words outside a situation and their deeds in it.

Therefore, we may expect that circumstances that increase self-awareness will also decrease deindividuation: mirrors and cameras, small towns, bright lights, large name tags, undistracted quiet, individual clothes and houses (Ickes, Layden, & Barnes, 1978). When a teenager leaves for a party a parent's parting advice could well be, "Have fun, and remember who you are"—in other words, enjoy the group, but be self-aware; don't become deindividuated.

One can also view the effects of self-awareness versus deindividuation from the perspective of impression-management theory. As formulated by James Tedeschi, Barry Schlenker, Jerald Jellison, Svenn Lindskold, and others, impression-management theory assumes that when we are identifiable and self-conscious our social behavior is guided by our concern for how others perceive and react to us. For example, when we groom ourselves in front of a mirror we are not so much trying to project our true selves as we are trying to create a favorable impression. Likewise, to create a favorable impression we normally behave properly. However, sometimes, as in the deindividuation experiments, we are *not* identifiable; we are just one of a group. Impression-management theory predicts that in such situations we will be less concerned with the impression we are making on others (Lindskold & Propst, 1981). Thus our behavior will reflect less concern for social propriety.

GROUP POLARIZATION

Which effects—good or bad—does group interaction more often have? On the one hand, mob violence demonstrates the destructive potential of groups. On the other, group therapists, management consultants, and educational theorists proclaim the benefits of certain group experiences, and leaders of social and religious movements urge their followers to strengthen their identities by group fellowship with like-minded others.

Recent research helps clarify our understanding of such effects. From studies of people in small groups, a principle has emerged that helps explain both apparently destructive and constructive outcomes: In general, group discussion strengthens group members' initial inclinations. The unfolding of this research literature illustrates beautifully the very process of inquiry—how an interesting discovery often leads researchers to hasty and erroneous conclusions, which are ultimately replaced with better conclusions and new ideas for research. This research on group polarization is the one scientific mystery I can discuss firsthand, having been one of the detectives. So let us take the story from the beginning.

The Story Begins

A research literature of more than 300 studies originated in a surprising finding by James Stoner (1961), then a MIT graduate student. For his master's thesis in industrial management, Stoner decided to compare risk-taking by individuals and groups. He wanted to test the commonly held belief that groups are more cautious than individuals. Stoner's procedure, which was followed in dozens of later experiments, posed some decision dilemmas to people by themselves. Each problem described a decision faced by a fictional character. The participant's task was to advise the character how much risk to take. Put yourself in the participant's shoes: What advice would you give the character in this item?

Henry is a writer who is said to have considerable creative talent but who so far has been earning a comfortable living by writing cheap westerns. Recently he has come up with an idea for a potentially significant novel. If it could be written and accepted it might have considerable literary impact and be a big boost to his career. On the other hand, if he is not able to work out his idea or if the novel is a flop, he will have expended considerable time and energy without remuneration.

Imagine that you are advising Henry. Please check the *lowest* probability that you would consider acceptable for Henry to attempt to write the novel.

Henry should attempt to write the novel if the chances that the novel will be a success are at least:

_______ 1 in 10
_______ 2 in 10
_______ 3 in 10
_______ 4 in 10
_______ 5 in 10
_______ 6 in 10
_______ 7 in 10
_______ 8 in 10
_______ 9 in 10
_______ 10 in 10 (Place a check here if you think Henry should attempt the novel only if it is certain that the novel will be a success.)

After making your decision, guess what the average reader of this book would advise.

After marking their advice on some items similar to this one, five or so individuals would then gather in a group to discuss and reach agreement on each item. How do you suppose the group decisions compared to the average of the decisions made prior to the discussions? Were the groups likely to take greater risks? Were they more cautious? About the same? Much to everyone's amazement, the decisions chosen by the group were by and large *riskier* than those selected before discussion. This finding was immediately dubbed the "risky shift" phenomenon, and it set off a wave of investigations into group risk-taking. These studies revealed that this effect occurs not only when a group makes a unanimous decision; after a brief period of discussion individuals also alter their decisions. What is more, Stoner's finding was successfully repeated in a dozen different nations with people of varying ages and occupations.

People's opinions did converge during discussion. However, it was curious that the point toward which they converged was usually a lower (riskier) number than their initial average. Here was a delightful puzzle, for the risky shift effect, while not huge, was nevertheless reliable, unexpected, and without any immediately obvious explanation. Why? What group influence produces such an effect? And how widespread is the effect? Do discussions in juries, business committees, and military organizations also tend to promote risk-taking?

After about five years of speculation and research on groups being more prone to take risks, indications surfaced that the risky shift was not as universal as first thought. One could write decision dilemmas that did *not* yield a reliable risky shift, or on which people even became more *cautious* after discussion. One such dealt with "Roger," a young married man with two school-age children and a secure but low-paying job. Roger can afford life's necessities, but few of its luxuries. He hears that the stock of a relatively unknown company may soon either triple in value, if its new product is favorably received, or decline considerably if it does not sell. Roger has no savings. So in order to invest in the company, he is considering selling his life insurance policy.

Is there a general principle that will predict both the tendency to give riskier advice after discussing Henry's situation, and more cautious advice after discussing Roger's? Yes. If you are like most, you would likely advise Henry to take greater risk than Roger, even before talking with others. It turns out that there is a strong tendency for discussion to accentuate these initial leanings.

Group polarization: *Group-produced enhancement of members' preexisting tendencies. Refers to a strengthening of the members' average tendency,* not *to a split within the group.*

Investigators therefore began to realize that this group phenomenon was *not*, as originally assumed, a consistent shift to risk, but perhaps rather a tendency for group discussion to *enhance* the initially dominant point of view. This idea led investigators to postulate a *group polarization* phenomenon:

Discussion generally strengthens the average inclination of group members before discussion.

Do Groups Intensify Opinions?

Experiments on Group Polarization

This new view of the changes induced by discussion prompted experimenters to have people discuss statements that most of them favored or most of them opposed. Will talking in groups enhance their initial inclinations as it did with the decision dilemmas? The group polarization hypothesis predicts that, yes, the initial average position will be strengthened (see Figure 9-5).

Group polarization has been confirmed in dozens of studies. For example, Serge Moscovici and Marisa Zavalloni (1969) observed that engaging in discussion enhanced French students' initially positive attitude toward their Premier and negative attitude toward Americans. Likewise, Willem Doise (1969) found that the negative attitudes that French architectural students had toward their school were magnified after they discussed them.

Another research strategy has been to pick issues on which opinions are divided and then isolate people who hold the same view. Once each person's opinion is assessed, he or she is assigned to a group of like-minded people. There they discuss the issue, while people on the other side of the issue also confer. The researchers' purpose is to see whether discussion with similarly minded people polarizes the two types of groups, whether it magnifies the gap between their attitudes.

For example, George Bishop and I (Myers & Bishop, 1970) set up groups of relatively prejudiced and unprejudiced high school students and asked them to respond—both before and after discussion—to issues involving racial attitudes, such as property rights versus open housing. We found that the discussions among like-minded students did indeed increase the initial gap between the two groups (see Figure 9-6).

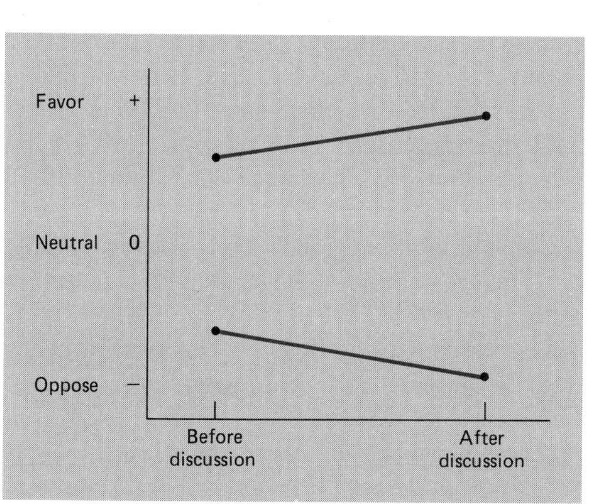

FIGURE 9-5 The group-polarization hypothesis predicts that an attitudinal leaning shared by group members will usually be strengthened by discussion. For example, if people initially tend to favor risk on a life dilemma question (such as that concerning Henry), they tend to favor it even more after discussion. If initially they tend to oppose risk (as in the case of Roger's decision about selling his life insurance), they tend to oppose it even more after discussion.

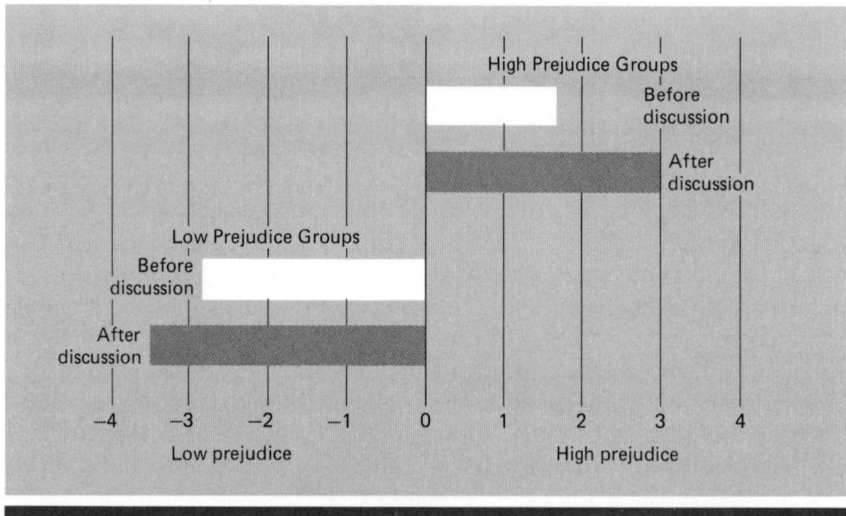

FIGURE 9-6 Discussion increased polarization between homogeneous groups of high- and low-prejudice high school students. (Data from Myers & Bishop, 1970.)

Naturally Occurring Group Polarization

There is plenty of evidence that in everyday life people associate mostly with others whose attitudes are similar to their own (see Chapter 13). Most of us need only look at our circle of friends to illustrate this point. Does group interaction in everyday situations also intensify shared attitudes? In naturally occurring events, it is difficult to disentangle cause and effect, but the laboratory phenomenon does seem to have real-life parallels.

One such parallel is what education researchers call the "accentuation phenomenon": Initial differences among college student groups are accentuated with time in college. For instance, if the students at college X are initially more intellectual than the students at college Y, that difference will likely expand as they progress through college. Researchers believe this effect results at least partly from the tendency of group members to reinforce their shared inclinations (Feldman & Newcomb, 1969; Chickering & McCormick, 1973; Wilson et al., 1975).

Observations of societal polarization also parallel the laboratory experiments. According to sociologist James Coleman (1957), during community conflicts like-minded people increasingly associate with one another, thus amplifying their shared tendencies. Similarly, investigators of gang delinquency have observed a process of mutual reinforcement within neighborhood gangs whose members have a common socioeconomic and ethnic background (Cartwright, 1975). In a laboratory analogy to such occurrences, Norris Johnson, James Stemler, and Deborah Hunter (1977) had University of Cincinnati students imagine how they would likely respond to a perceived

Box 9-1

Group Polarization

Shakespeare portrayed the polarizing power of the like-minded group in this dialogue of Julius Caesar's followers:

Antony: Kind souls, what weep you when you but behold
Our Caesar's vesture wounded? Look you here,
Here is himself, marr'd, as you see, with traitors.
First Citizen: O piteous spectacle!
Second Citizen: O noble Caesar!
Third Citizen: O woeful day!
Fourth Citizen: O traitors, villains!
First Citizen: O most bloody sight!
Second Citizen: We will be revenged!
All: Revenge! About! Seek! Burn! Fire! Kill! Slay! Let not a traitor live!

Note: From *Julius Caesar* by William Shakespeare, Act III, Scene III, ll. 199-209.

injustice (for example, a college administration that refused to negotiate with student organizations). Given seven options, ranging from "no action" up to a potentially violent march, most students, prior to holding a discussion on the options, favored some type of action. After discussing the options, they favored an even more radical action.

Explaining Group Polarization

Why polarization takes place at all became a tantalizing puzzle for a number of social psychologists: Why do groups of people seem to adopt stances more exaggerated than the average opinions of their individual members? Researchers hoped that solving the mystery of group polarization might provide new general insights into how people influence one another. Solving small problems sometimes solves larger ones.

A satisfactory theory of group polarization must neatly summarize past findings and predict new ones. Such predictions give us a basis for testing the truth of the theory and may also suggest some useful applications.

"The great tragedy of Science—the slaying of a beautiful hypothesis by an ugly fact."

Thomas Henry Huxley, Collected Essays

When we sought to explain group polarization, several possibilities soon emerged. For example, perhaps the arousal produced by being in the presence of others enhances group members' initial leanings. But this good idea failed its tests. For example, stating one's response in front of an observer does not polarize responses (Myers, 1967).

Among several other possible theoretical explanations, two have held up under scrutiny. One deals with the arguments presented during a discussion, the other with how members of a group view themselves vis-à-vis the other members. To use terminology introduced in Chapter 7, the first idea is an example of informational influence, the second of normative influence.

Informational Influence

According to the best supported explanation, group discussion elicits a pooling of ideas, most of which favor the dominant viewpoint. These ideas may include persuasive arguments that some group members had not previously considered. When discussing Henry the writer, for example, someone may cogently observe that "Henry has little to lose, since if his novel flops he can always go back to writing cheap westerns." But such statements combine information about the person's *arguments* regarding the issue with cues concerning the person's *position* on the issue. Disentangling these two factors, it has been found that when people hear relevant arguments without learning the specific stands that other people assume, they still shift their positions (Burnstein & Vinokur, 1977). Arguments, in and of themselves, are apparently a principal factor in polarizing attitudes.

Researchers have also found that active verbal participation in discussion elicits more changes in attitude than does passive listening. Both participants and observers hear the same ideas, but when participants put them into their own words the resulting verbal commitment seems to magnify the impact of the discussion. This finding parallels attitude research done by Anthony Greenwald (1968) showing that people who actively reformulate a persuasive message in their own words remember it best and are most influenced by it (see also Tesser, 1978). It also illustrates the point made in Chapter 8 that people's minds are not just blank tablets for persuaders to write on; what people think in response to a message is crucial. Indeed, just *expecting* to discuss an issue with an equally expert person of an opposing view can motivate people to marshal their arguments, and thus to adopt an even more extreme position (Fitzpatrick & Eagly, 1981).

Normative Influence

Social comparison: *Evaluating one's opinions and abilities by comparing oneself to others.*

In the second explanation of polarization, social comparison with others plays an important role. As Leon Festinger (1954) argued in his influential theory of social comparison, it is human nature to want to evaluate our opinions and abilities, something we can do by comparing our views with those held by other people like ourselves. Moreover, since people want to be perceived favorably, they may express stronger opinions if they discover that other people share their views more than they had supposed.

Perhaps you can recall a time when you and others were guarded and reserved in a group, until someone broke the ice and said, "Well, to be perfectly honest, I think . . . ," and soon you were all surprised to discover strong support for views you had each assumed were not widely shared. When people are asked (as you were earlier) to predict how others would respond to items such as the "Henry" dilemma, they typically guess others' opinions to be less supportive of the socially preferred tendency (in this case, writing the novel) than their own. An average respondent might advise writing the novel even if its chance of success is only 4 in 10, but estimate that most other people would require 5 or 6 in 10. Thus, when the discussion begins, many group members will soon discover that they are not outshining the others as they had supposed; in fact, some are already out ahead of them, having taken even a stronger position on behalf of writing the novel. No longer restrained by a misperceived group norm, they will now be liberated to give stronger expression to their preferences. What is more, research indicates that people tend to admire as most sincere and competent those persons who are on their side of an issue but who are more extreme (Eisenger & Mills, 1968). This, too, may contribute to polarization.

This finding is reminiscent of the self-serving bias (Chapter 3): People tend to view themselves as better-than-average embodiments of socially desirable traits and attitudes.

This normative influence theory prompted a series of experiments that exposed people to others' positions without exposing them to others' arguments. This is roughly the experience we have when reading the results of an opinion poll. When people learn others' positions—without opportunity for discussion—will they adjust their responses so as to maintain a favorable position relative to others? When people have not already made a prior commitment to a particular response, seeing others' responses does indeed stimulate a small polarization (Sanders & Baron, 1977; Goethals & Zanna, 1979). (See Figure 9-7 for an example.) The polarization is usually not as great as that produced by a lively discussion. Still, it surprised researchers that instead of simply conforming to the group average, people more often go it one better. Are people seeking to "one-up" the observed norm in order to differentiate themselves from the group? Is this another indication of what some researchers

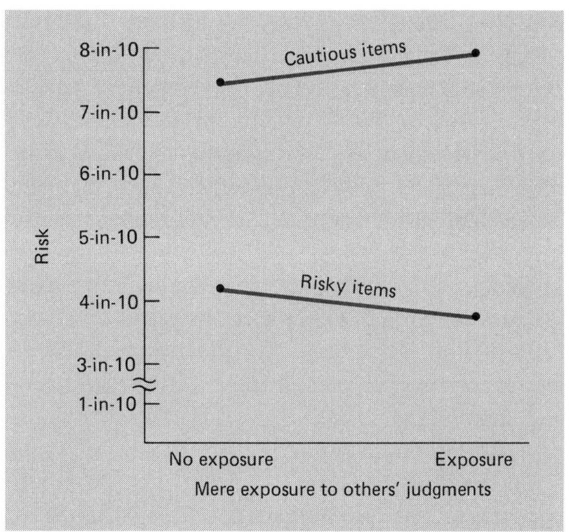

FIGURE 9-7 On "risky" dilemma items (such as the case of Henry), mere exposure to others' judgments enhanced individuals' risk-prone tendencies. On "cautious" dilemma items (such as the case of Roger), exposure to others' judgments enhanced their cautiousness. (Data from Myers, 1978.)

(see Chapter 7) believe is our need to feel unique? Roger Brown (1974) believes so: "To be virtuous, in any of an indefinite number of situations, is to be different from the [average]—in the right direction and to the right degree."

Conclusions

The accounts of group polarization based on persuasive arguments (a type of informational influence) and social comparison (a type of normative influence) help explain results from several discussion experiments which show that accentuation of the average response is *not* inevitable. When people are given a choice between contributing to charity or keeping their earnings from an experiment, group interaction can bring out selfish inclinations, even if individuals had seemed to favor generosity before the discussion (Wolosin, Sherman, & Mynatt, 1975; Yinon, Jaffe, & Feshbach, 1975). Most of these results are, however, consistent with the explanation of group polarization. For even if social inhibitions cause people to conceal their private leanings—to keep their earnings—discussion may lead them to reveal and accentuate such inclinations. This suggests, too, that social comparison and persuasive arguments work together. Discovering that others share one's feelings (social comparison) can unleash arguments (informational influence) supporting what everyone secretly wants to do.

Recently, the natural human inclination toward forming small groups to discuss issues and solve problems seems to have grown. Alcoholics, dieters, and educators are drawing on the presumed power of support groups, and group-oriented management methods are competing with traditional methods. Group polarization research suggests reasons for the potency of small groups. In them, people may be motivated to present themselves favorably, and to engage in active thinking and commitment.

The research on group polarization also illustrates several characteristics of social psychological inquiry. First, one area of research usually stands on the shoulders of another. Group polarization researchers drew upon and provided new tests of the concepts of social influence developed in earlier research.

A second characteristic is that much as we like our explanations to be simple, more often than not no one explanation of a phenomenon can by itself account for all the data. Because people are complex, more than one factor frequently influences a phenomenon.

Finally, pursuing small problems in depth sometimes pays unexpected dividends. Note how far the social-comparison experiments strayed from our original concern with risk-taking. This illustrates the unexpected ways in which a program of basic research often develops. An interesting discovery is followed by a plethora of generalizations and studies, in this case stimulated by our having misnamed the phenomenon as "risky shift." Subsequent research then casts doubt on the original conclusions. But ultimately there emerges both a better conception of the phenomenon and a spin-off of interesting new experiments. Such surprises are one reason science is so fascinating. Who knows? Maybe as this particular research continues our current ideas about "group polarization" and its explanations will themselves be supplanted.

GROUPTHINK

Are the social-psychological phenomena that we have been considering in these first nine chapters evident in highly sophisticated decision-making groups? In a corporate boardroom or a meeting of the President's Cabinet is there likely to be self-justification? Self-serving bias? A cohesive "we feeling" provoking conformity and rejection of nonconformers? Public commitment producing resistance to change? Group polarization? Irving Janis (1971; 1982a), a Yale social psychologist, wondered whether such phenomena might help explain good and bad group decisions made by recent American presidents and their advisers. Thus he analyzed the decision making procedures that led to several major fiascos, such as:

Pearl Harbor. In the weeks preceding the Pearl Harbor attack, military commanders in Hawaii were fed a steady stream of information about Japan's preparations for attack—somewhere. Then military intelligence lost radio contact with Japanese aircraft carriers, which had begun moving full-steam straight for Hawaii. Air reconnaissance could have spotted the carriers, or at least provided a few minutes warning of the impending attack. But the complacent commanders decided against such precautions. Thus, no alert was sounded until the Japanese were directly attacking the virtually defenseless ships and airfields.

The Bay of Pigs invasion. "How could we have been so stupid?" asked President John Kennedy after he and his advisers learned their attempt to overthrow Castro by sending into Cuba 1400 CIA-trained Cuban exiles proved a disaster. Nearly all the invaders were soon killed or captured, the United States was humiliated, and Cuba allied itself even closer to the U.S.S.R.

The Vietnam war. From 1964 to 1967 President Lyndon Johnson and his "Tuesday lunch group" of policy advisers escalated the Vietnam war on the assumption that U.S. aerial bombardment, defoliation, and search and destroy missions were likely to bring North Vietnam to the peace table while maintaining the appreciative support of the South Vietnamese populace. The escalation decisions were made despite warnings from government intelligence experts as well as from leaders of nearly all of the U.S. allies. The resulting disaster cost 56,500 American and more than one million Vietnamese lives, drove the President from office, and created huge budget deficits that helped fuel inflation in the 1970s.

Groupthink: "*The mode of thinking that persons engage in when* concurrence-seeking *becomes so dominant in a cohesive ingroup that it tends to override realistic appraisal of alternative courses of action.*"

Irving Janis (1971)

Janis argues that these blunders were bred by the tendency of these decision-making groups to suppress dissent in the interests of group harmony,

A meeting in late 1967 of President Johnson's "Tuesday Lunch Group." (Photo by Okamoto/Lyndon B. Johnson Library, University of Texas, Austin.)

Note that the conditions thought to breed groupthink—cohesiveness, isolation, directive leader—appear similar to those found in some religious cults. Are the symptoms of groupthink similarly embodied in such cults?

a phenomenon he calls *groupthink*. The soil from which groupthink seems to sprout includes an amiable, cohesive group, relative isolation of the group from contrary viewpoints, and a directive leader who signals what decision he or she favors. For example, when planning the ill-fated Bay of Pigs invasion, the newly elected President Kennedy and his advisers enjoyed a strong esprit de corps; arguments critical of the plan were suppressed or excluded; and the President himself soon indicated his endorsement of the invasion.

Symptoms of Groupthink

From historical records and the memoirs of participants and observers, Janis identified eight symptoms of groupthink that ran through these bad decisions.

1 An Illusion of Invulnerability

The groups Janis studied all developed an excessive optimism that blinded them to warnings of danger. When told that radio contact with the Japanese carriers had been lost, Admiral Kimmel, the chief naval officer at Pearl Harbor, joked about their possibly being about to round Honolulu's Diamond Head. Kimmel's laughing at the idea was a way of dismissing the very possibility of its being true.

2 Rationalization

The groups discounted challenges to their past decisions by collectively justifying them. For example, President Johnson's Tuesday lunch group spent far more time rationalizing than reflecting upon and rethinking their prior decisions to escalate. Each of their initiatives became an action to be defended and justified.

3 Unquestioned Belief in the Group's Morality

Since the members assumed the inherent morality of their group, ethical and moral issues were ignored. For example, although the group knew that Kennedy adviser Arthur Schlesinger, Jr., and Senator J. William Fulbright had moral reservations about invading a small, neighboring country, these moral qualms never were discussed.

4 Stereotyped View of Opponent

Participants in these groupthink tanks appeared to consider their enemies too evil to negotiate with, or so weak and unintelligent that they could not possibly defend themselves against the planned initiative. For instance, the Kennedy group convinced itself that Castro's military was so weak and his popular support so shallow that a mere brigade could easily overwhelm his regime.

5 Conformity Pressure

Dissent was not appreciated. Group members who raised doubts about the group's assumptions and plans were readily refuted, at times not by argument but by personal sarcasm. Once, when President Johnson's assistant Bill Moyers arrived at a meeting, the President derided him with "Well, here comes Mr. Stop-the-Bombing."

"All those in favor say 'Aye.'"
"Aye." "Aye." "Aye." "Aye." "Aye."

Self-censorship can contribute to an illusion of unanimity. (Drawing by H. Martin; © 1979 *The New Yorker* Magazine, Inc.)

6 Self-Censorship

Since disagreements were often discomforting and the groups seemed in consensus, the members tended to withhold, even discount, their own misgivings. In the months following the Bay of Pigs invasion, Arthur Schlesinger (1965) reproached himself

> for having kept so silent during those crucial discussions in the Cabinet Room, though my feelings of guilt were tempered by the knowledge that a course of objection would have accomplished little save to gain me a name as a nuisance. I can only explain my failure to do more than raise a few timid questions by reporting that one's impulse to blow the whistle on this nonsense was simply undone by the circumstances of the discussion. (p. 255)

7 Illusion of Unanimity

Self-censorship and pressure against puncturing the group's apparent consensus led to an illusion of unanimity. What is more, this "consensus" of "all these brilliant people" appeared to the public to further validate the group's decision. This appearance of consensus was evident in the three fiascos, and in other fiascos before and since. Albert Speer (1971), an adviser of Adolf Hitler, describes the atmosphere around Hitler as one where conformity pressure suppressed all deviation. The absence of dissent created an illusion of unanimity that seemed to justify the most heinous acts.

> In normal circumstances people who turn their backs on reality are soon set straight by the mockery and criticism of those around them, which makes them aware they have lost credibility. In the Third Reich there were no such correctives, especially for those who belonged to the upper stratum. On the contrary, every self-deception was multiplied as in a hall of distorting mirrors, becoming a repeatedly confirmed picture of a fantastical dream world which no longer bore any relationship to the grim outside world. In those mirrors I could see nothing but my own face reproduced many times over. No external factors disturbed the uniformity of hundreds of unchanging faces, all mine. (p. 379)

8 Mindguards

Some members protected their groups from information that would have disputed the effectiveness or the morality of its decisions. Prior to the Bay of Pigs, Robert Kennedy took Schlesinger aside and told him "Don't push it any further," and Secretary of State Dean Rusk withheld diplomatic and intelligence experts' warnings against the invasion.

Janis believes that these groupthink symptoms cause several defects in making decisions. As summarized in Figure 9-8, these involve a failure to seek and discuss contrary information and alternative possibilities.

Preventing Groupthink

Does this bleak analysis imply that group decision making is inherently defective? To pose the question with contradictory proverbs, do "too many cooks always spoil the broth" or can "two or more heads sometimes be better than one?"

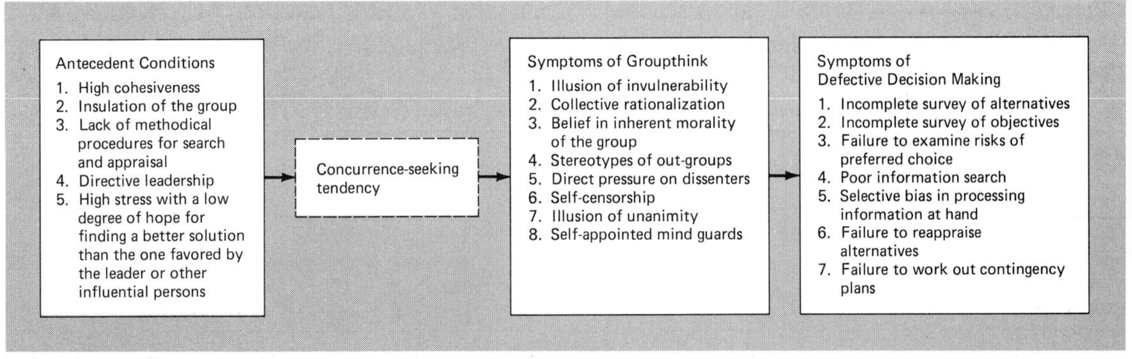

FIGURE 9-8 Theoretical analysis of groupthink. (Data from Janis & Mann, 1977, p. 132.)

Group insights are often better. In laboratory experiments, most individuals err on the horse-trader problem (Chapter 4), but when deciding collectively they arrive at the right decision (Hill,1982). Patrick Laughlin (1980; Laughlin & Adamopoulos, 1980) finds this also true with other types of cognitive tasks. For instance, consider this analogy: *Assertion* is to *disproved* as *action* is to (*hindered*, *opposed*, *illegal*, *precipitate*, or *thwarted*). Most college students miss this question when answering alone, but answer correctly after discussion. (See the marginal note on page 324 for the answer.) Moreover, Laughlin finds that if but two members of a six-person group are initially correct, two-thirds of the time they convince all the others; however, if but one person is correct, this "minority of one" almost three-fourths of the time fails to convince the wayward group. Dell Warnick and Glenn Sanders (1980) confirmed that several heads can be better than one when they studied the accuracy of eyewitnesses' reports of videotaped crime. Groups of eyewitnesses gave accounts that were far more accurate than those provided by the average isolated individual.

"Like the child who first remarked on the Emperor's lack of clothes, minorities may be effective mainly when majorities have blinded themselves to naked reality. If the Emperor were in fact dressed, the child would, of course, be ignored."

Bibb Latané and Sharon Wolf (1981)

Janis also analyzed two highly successful group decisions: the Truman administration's formulation of the Marshall Plan for getting Europe back on its feet after World War II, and the Kennedy administration's handling of Russia's attempts to install missile bases in Cuba. Janis's recommendations for preventing groupthink (see Box 9-2) incorporate many of the good group procedures used by both the Marshall Plan and the missile-crisis groups. These suggestions attempt to remedy the defects that characterize groupthink by ensuring that the group seeks information from all sides and improves its evaluation of possible alternatives. Management researchers A. H. Van de Ven and A. L. Delbecq (1971) propose a "nominal-group" technique for accomplishing this goal of more complete processing of information:

The answer to the question on p. 323 is thwarted.

Imagine a meeting room in which seven to ten individuals are sitting around a table in full view of each other. However, they are not speaking to each other. Instead, each individual is writing on a pad of paper in front of him. At the end of 10 to 20 minutes, a very structured sharing of ideas takes place. Each individual, in round-robin fashion, provides from his private list one idea which is written on a flip-chart by a recorder in full view of other members. There is still no discussion, only the recording of privately generated ideas. This round-robin listing continues until each member indicates that he has no further ideas to share. . . . Generally, a spontaneous discussion then follows for a period (in the same fashion as an interactive group meeting) before. . . voting.

Box 9-2

Ten Prescriptions for Preventing Groupthink

1. Tell group members about groupthink, its causes and consequences.
2. The leader should be impartial, should not endorse any position.
3. The leader should instruct everyone to critically evaluate, should encourage objections and doubts.
4. One or more members should be assigned the role of "devil's advocate."
5. From time to time subdivide the group. Have the subgroups meet separately and then come together to air differences.
6. When the issue concerns relations with a rival group, take time to survey all warning signals and identify various possible actions by the rival.
7. After reaching a preliminary decision, a "second-chance" meeting should be called at which each member is asked to express remaining doubts.
8. Outside experts should attend meetings on a staggered basis and be asked to challenge the group's views.
9. Each group member should air the group's deliberations with trusted associates and report their reactions.
10. Several independent groups should work simultaneously on the same question.

Note: Adapted from "Counteracting the Adverse Effects of Concurrence-Seeking in Policy-Planning Groups: Theory and Research Perspectives" by I. L. Janis. In H. Brandstätter, J. H. Davis, & G. Stocker-Kreichgauer (Eds.), *Group Decision Making*. New York: Academic Press, 1982, pp. 477-501.

BEHIND THE SCENES

Irving Janis

The main theme of my book, *Groupthink*, occurred to me while reading Arthur Schlesinger's chapters on the Bay of Pigs in *A Thousand Days*. At first, I was puzzled: How could bright, shrewd men like John F. Kennedy and his advisers be taken in by the CIA's stupid, patchwork plan? I began to wonder whether some kind of psychological contagion, similar to social conformity phenomena observed in studies of small groups, had interfered with their mental alertness. I kept thinking about the implications of this notion until one day I found myself talking about it in a seminar.

When I reread Schlesinger's account, I recalled concurrence-seeking behavior that had impressed me time and again in my research on face-to-face groups, particularly when a "we-feeling" of solidarity is running high. Additional accounts of the Bay of Pigs—some turned up by my daughter Charlotte Janis while working on a high school term paper—yielded more such observations, leading me to conclude that group processes had been subtly at work, preventing the members of Kennedy's team from debating the real issues posed by the CIA's plan and from carefully appraising its serious risks.

By this time, I was sufficiently fascinated by what I began to call the groupthink hypothesis to start looking into a fairly large number of historical parallels. I selected for intensive analysis three additional United States foreign-policy decisions and again found consistent indications of the same kind of detrimental group processes. In a revised edition of *Groupthink* published in 1982, I have added a new case study of the Watergate cover-up, based largely on unedited transcripts of Richard M. Nixon's tapes. What I tried to do in all the cases was to show how the evidence at hand could be viewed as forming a consistent psychological pattern, in the light of what is known about group dynamics. *(Irving Janis, Yale University)*

Evaluating Groupthink Concepts

Janis's diagnoses and remedies for inferior group decision making integrate his social psychological perspective with careful analysis of historically significant group decisions. However, we must recognize that these groupthink concepts are not facts. They are defensible hypotheses that need further testing. We can evaluate the concepts by (1) asking how they harmonize with other research findings and (2) putting them directly to the test.

Do Groupthink Concepts Harmonize with Research on Group Influence?

In general terms, the "symptoms of groupthink" seem to fit and illustrate the findings pertaining to self-justification, self-serving bias, and conformity that we discussed previously. Ivan Steiner (1982) believes the hypothesized groupthink processes coincide also with previous research on group influence. For example, researchers have noted that problem solving groups have a strong tendency to converge on a single solution. This convergence phenomenon (which Janis calls concurrence seeking) is also evident in the group polarization experiments: A group's average position may polarize, but its members also converge.

Similarly, experiments on group problem solving document self-censorship and biased discussion. Once a margin of support for one alternative develops, better ideas have little chance of being accepted. Likewise, reports Steiner, descriptions of mob lynchings indicate that once a lynching was suggested, misgivings, if not immediately expressed, were drowned out. Drawing on biased information is evident in group polarization experiments. The arguments that surface in group discussion tend to be more one-sided than those volunteered by individuals privately. For example, when asked to write whatever arguments relevant to "Henry the writer" come to mind, individuals typically volunteer fewer than twice as many reasons for attempting the novel as opposing it. In discussion, this tendency is magnified; the expressed arguments average about 3 to 1 in favor of attempting the novel.

Based on previous research, Steiner does, however, suggest that it is probably not cohesiveness per se that breeds groupthink. Highly cohesive groups (for example, a secure married couple) may provide their members with freedom to disagree. Steiner argues that the prime determinant of groupthink is instead *desire for cohesion*. Group members are likely to suppress disagreeable thoughts when they are striving to build or maintain good group feeling, or looking to the group for acceptance and approval.

Putting Groupthink Remedies to the Test

Janis looks forward to having his prescriptive hypotheses tested with a full range of research studies. First, he anticipates collecting a much larger set of case studies. Do the group processes leading to good and bad decisions differ in the ways his groupthink analysis predicts? For example, one of Janis's students, William Wong-McCarthy, analyzed Watergate tapes and found that when events seemed most threatening and hopeless, President Nixon and his advisers made more of the self-justifying statements symptomatic of groupthink (cited by Janis, 1982b; see also Raven, 1974).

The prescriptions also can be tested in laboratory experiments. Matie Flowers (1977) had students from Indiana University and Syracuse University imagine they were school officials discussing what to do about a teacher who had become incompetent. Those groups that operated with a leader who was noncommittal and encouraged all viewpoints aired more facts and considered more possible solutions before reaching their decision than did groups operating with a closed, directive leader.

Janis hopes to further test his prescriptions in workshops where significant issues are deliberated by experts who are either trained or not trained in how to avoid groupthink. If the antigroupthink program proves successful, he envisions eventually testing it with actual groups of policy-making executives.

MINORITY INFLUENCE

Each of the four chapters in this unit on social influence has concluded with a reminder of our power as individuals. We have seen that while cultural situations mold us, we also help create and choose these very situations; that while pressures to conform sometimes overwhelm our better judgments, blatant pressure nevertheless can motivate us to assert our individuality and freedom; and that while persuasive forces are indeed powerful, we can still resist persuasion by making public commitments to our positions and by anticipating persuasive appeals. This particular chapter has emphasized group influences upon the individual. It is therefore fitting that we conclude with a look at how individuals can influence their groups.

As the beginnings of most social movements illustrate, a small minority will sometimes sway, and then even become, the majority. "All history," wrote Ralph Waldo Emerson, "is a record of the power of minorities, and of minorities of one." Think of Copernicus and Galileo, of Martin Luther, of the suffragettes.

What makes a minority persuasive? What might Arthur Schlesinger have done to get the group deciding on the fate of the Bay of Pigs to consider seriously his misgivings? Experiments on minority influence by Serge Moscovici in Paris and Charlan Nemeth at the University of California, Berkeley, have identified several determinants of minority influence.

Consistency

More influential than a minority that wavers is a minority that unswervingly sticks to its position. For instance, Moscovici and his associates (1969) have found that if a minority consistently judges blue slides as green, members of the majority will occasionally agree; but if the minority wavers, saying blue to one-third of the blue slides and green to the rest, virtually no one in the majority will ever concur with the "green" judgments. Still being debated is the nature of this influence. Moscovici believes that a minority's going along with the majority usually indicates public submissiveness (compliance). But a majority's being influenced by a minority more likely demonstrates genuine acceptance—for example, really perceiving the blue slide as green (Moscovici & Personnaz, 1980; but see also Doms & Van Avermaet, 1980; Sorrentino, King, & Leo, 1980).

"If the single man plant himself indomitably on his instincts, and there abide, the huge world will come round to him."

Ralph Waldo Emerson, Nature, Address, and Lectures: The American Scholar

Experiments show—and experience confirms—that nonconformity, especially persistent nonconformity, is often painful. If you set out to be

Emerson's minority of one, be prepared for ridicule. When Nemeth (1979) planted a minority of two within a simulated jury and had them oppose the majority's opinions, the duo was inevitably disliked. However, the majority did nevertheless acknowledge that the persistence of the two did more than anything else to make them rethink their positions. One need not win friends to influence people.

A persistent minority is influential, even if not popular, partly because it soon becomes the focus of debate (Schachter, 1951). Being the center of conversation allows one to contribute a disproportionate number of arguments. And Nemeth reports that in experiments on minority influence, as in the studies dealing with group polarization, the position supported by the most arguments usually wins. Similarly, in a group problem-solving experiment, Edwin Thomas and Clinton Fink (1961) found that when only one person in a group initially solved a problem correctly the group eventually converted to this minority answer *if* (and only if) the one correct person talked more than anyone else. Based on many experiments we can indeed therefore generalize: Influential group members tend to be talkative (Stein & Heller, 1979).

Self-Confidence

Consistency and persistence in one's positions convey an image of self-confidence. Furthermore, Nemeth and Joel Wachtler (1974) report that any behavior by a minority that conveys self-confidence—for example, taking the head seat at the table—will tend to raise self-doubts among the majority. By being reasonably firm and forceful, the minority's apparent self-assurance may prompt the majority to reconsider its position and consider other alternatives.

Self-confidence tends also to be a trait of leaders, such as the Reverend Jim Jones, who have had the "charisma" to kindle the allegiance of their followers. Although what makes for good leadership usually depends on the situation—the best person to lead the sales force may not be the best person to captain the bowling team—charismatic leaders tend to have an unshakable faith in their cause, utter confidence in their ability to succeed, and an ability to communicate this faith and confidence in clear and simple language (Fiedler, 1981; House, 1977).

Defections from the Majority

A persistent minority will at the very least puncture any illusion of unanimity the group might otherwise have had. When a minority consistently doubts the majority wisdom, members of the majority who might otherwise have self-censored their own doubts will feel freer to express them, and may even switch to the minority position. In research with University of Kansas students, Charles Kiesler and Michael Pallak (1975) found that those in the majority disliked defectors, but had their own self-doubts accentuated by the defection. John Levine and his colleagues (1980) obtained similar results with University of Pittsburgh students; in fact, they found that a minority person who defected from the majority was even more persuasive than one who consistently voiced

To influence the group, an individual should appear self-confident. (Drawing by Zeigler; © 1980 *The New Yorker* Magazine, Inc.)

the minority position. And in her jury-simulation experiments, Nemeth found that once defections begin, others often soon follow, thus initiating a "snowball" effect. As President Carter slipped in the polls in the months preceding the 1980 election, some of his former supporters began to yearn for another alternative and called for an "open" Democratic National Convention. Speculating from the experiments, we might surmise that observing these defections aroused strong self-doubts among the President's remaining supporters.

Are these factors that strengthen minority influence unique to minorities? Probably not. Bibb Latané and Sharon Wolf (1981) argue that the same social forces work for both majorities and minorities. If consistency, self-confidence, and defections from the other side contribute to the strength of a minority, such variables likely contribute to the strength of a majority also. The impact of any position—whether held by a majority or a minority—depends on the strength, immediacy, and number of those who support it.

I find a delightful irony in this new emphasis on how individuals can influence the group. Until recently, the idea that the minority could sway the majority was itself a minority view in social psychology. Nevertheless, by arguing consistently, persistently, and forcefully, Moscovici, Nemeth, and others have convinced the majority of group-influence researchers that minority influence is indeed a phenomenon worthy of study.

SUMMING UP

We spend much of our lives in groups—with family members, friends, fellow students, coworkers, etc. What influences do such groups have upon their individual members? This chapter examined six recently researched phenomena of group influence.

Social Facilitation

Perhaps the most elementary issue in social psychology concerns how we are affected by the mere presence of others. Some early experiments on this question found that one's performance improved when either observers or co-actors were present (social facilitation). Other experiments found that the presence of others can hurt one's performance. Robert Zajonc reconciled these seemingly contradictory findings by applying a well-known principle from experimental psychology: Arousal facilitates dominant responses. If we assume that the presence of others is arousing (an assumption confirmed by later research), it follows that the presence of observers or co-actors should boost performance on easy tasks (for which the correct response is dominant) and hinder performance on difficult tasks (for which incorrect responses are dominant). Such is precisely what has consistently been found, both in the earlier experiments that Zajonc sought to reconcile and in newer ones.

But why are we aroused by others' presence? Experiments suggest that the arousal stems partly from "evaluation apprehension" and partly from a conflict between paying attention to others and concentrating on the task. Other experiments, including some with animals, suggest that the presence of others can be arousing even when the actor is not being evaluated or distracted.

Social Loafing

Social-facilitation researchers study people's performance on tasks where they can be individually evaluated. However, in many work situations people pool their efforts and work toward a common goal without individual accountability. What does research reveal about our behavior under these conditions? Experiments indicate that group members work less hard when performing such "additive tasks." This finding seems to parallel everyday situations in which responsibility is diffused, tempting individual group members to free ride on the group's effort.

Deindividuation

When high levels of social arousal are combined with diffused responsibility, people may both abandon their normal restraints and lose their sense of individuality. Such "deindividuation" is especially likely when, after being aroused and distracted, people can assume anonymity by being in a large group or wearing indistinct garb. The net result? Diminished self-awareness and self-restraint and, therefore, increased responsiveness to the immediate situation, be it negative or positive. On the other hand, circumstances that *increase* self-awareness reduce one's being controlled by the situation by increasing one's self-control.

Group Polarization

The potentially positive and negative results of group interaction can also be explained by findings from research on the effects of group discussion. While trying to understand the curious finding that group discussion enhanced risk taking, investigators discovered that discussion actually tends to strengthen whatever is the initially dominant point of view, whether risky or cautious, whether it be for or against a position on some attitudinal issue. Observations of naturally occurring social polarization suggest that in everyday situations, too, group interaction tends to intensify opinions.

The group polarization phenomenon provided a window through which researchers could observe the influence of a group. Experiments have confirmed the presence of two social influences: informational and normative. The information gleaned from a discussion mostly favors the initially preferred alternative, thus reinforcing people's support for it. Moreover, people may go further out on the limb when, after they have compared their positions, they discover surprising support for their initial inclinations.

Groupthink

Analysis of the decisions that led to several international fiascos indicates that a group's desire for harmony can override its realistic appraisal of contrary views. This is especially true when group members strongly desire unity, when they are isolated from opposing ideas, and when the leader signals what he or she wants from the group. Symptomatic of this overriding concern for harmony, labeled "groupthink," are (1) an illusion of invulnerability, (2) rationalization, (3) unquestioned belief in the group's morality, (4) stereotyped views of the opposition, (5) pressure to conform, (6) self-censorship of misgivings, (7) an illusion of unanimity, and (8) "mind guards" who protect the group from unpleasant information.

However, both in experiments and in actual history, groups do sometimes make intelligent decisions. The circumstances under which such have been made suggest remedies for groupthink. By taking steps to ensure that the group seeks information from all sides and improves its evaluation of possible alternatives, the group can benefit from the combined insights of its members.

Minority Influence

It is important also to examine how individuals can influence their groups. After all, if minority viewpoints were always impotent, history would be more static than it is. Experiments indicate that a minority is most influential when it is consistent and persistent in its views, when its actions convey self-confidence, and when it begins to elicit some defections from the majority. And, even if such factors do not persuade the majority to adopt the minority's views, they will likely increase the majority's self-doubts and prompt it to consider other alternatives more seriously.

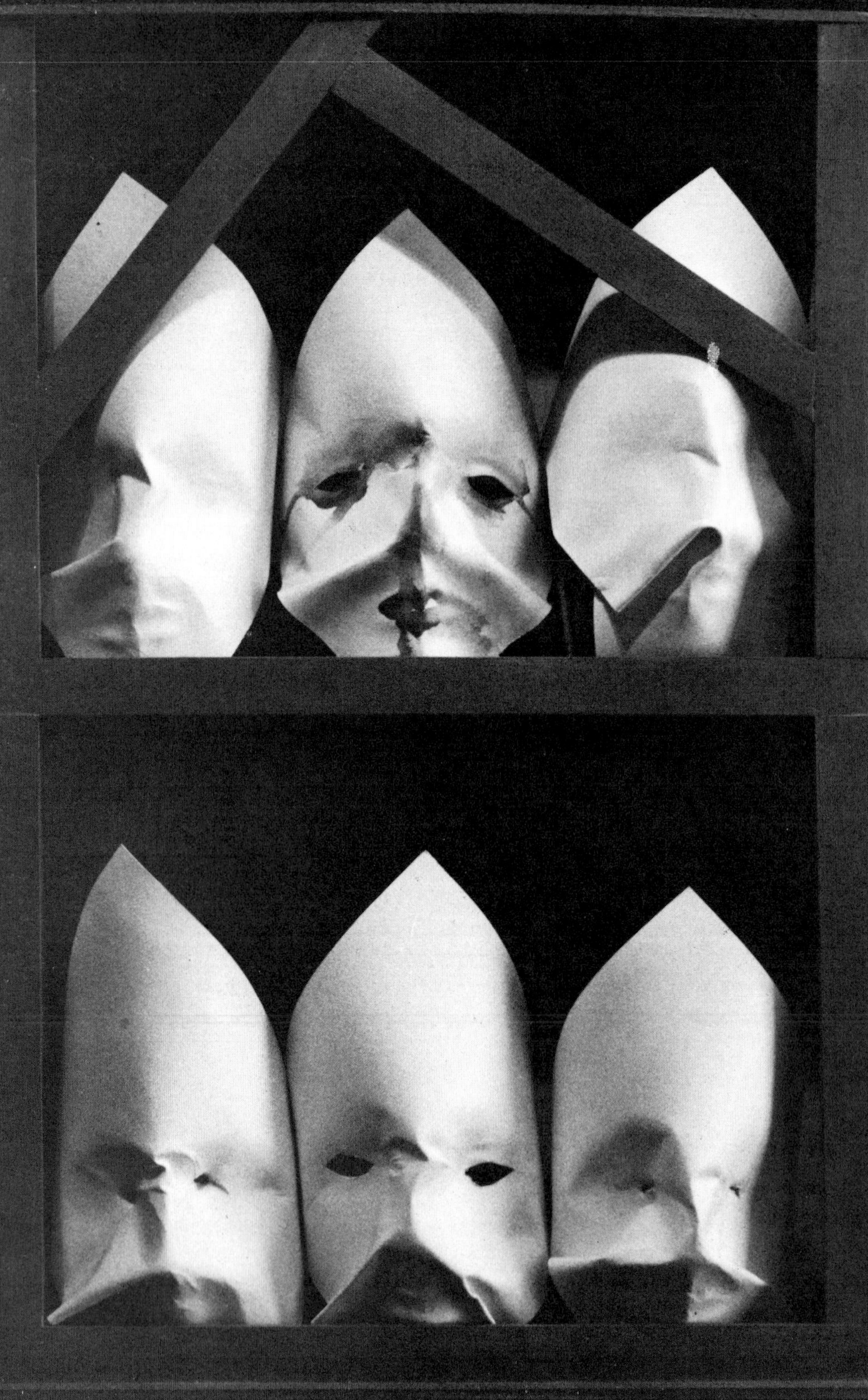

SOCIAL RELATIONS

Part 1 defined social psychology as the scientific study of how people think about, influence, and relate to one another. Part 2 on social thinking and Part 3 on social influence explored the first two aspects of this definition. We shall now, in Part 4 on social relations, examine how we actually treat and feel about one another.

Some 300 years ago, La Rochefoucauld remarked, "Men's natures are like most houses—many sided; some aspects are pleasant and some not." In order to keep our perspective balanced, we will scrutinize both the pleasant and unpleasant aspects. In Chapter 10, we will look at *aggression*: Why and when do we hurt one another? Then in Chapter 11 we will analyze *altruism*: Why and when do we help one another? After studying the Chapter 12 analysis of *prejudice*—why we dislike, even despise one another—we shall in Chapter 13 consider *attraction*—why we like and love one another. Finally, in Chapter 14 on *conflict and peacemaking*, we shall consider how social conflicts develop and how they can sometimes be justly and amicably resolved.

Chapter

Aggression: Hurting Others

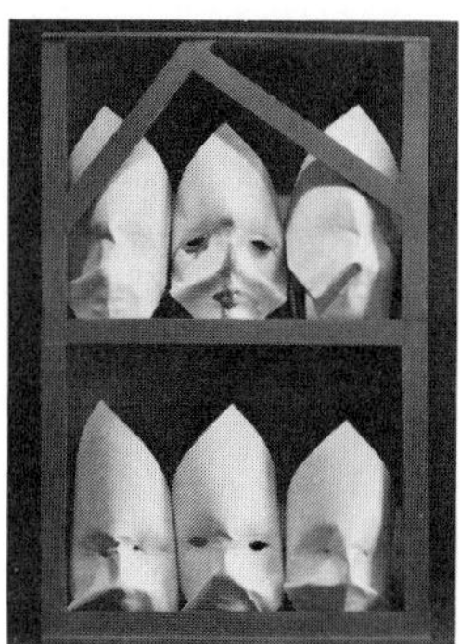

Humanity's potential for inhumanity threatens us all as never before. Spending for arms and armies now approaches $2 billion per *day*, or more than $100 per year for every person on earth—millions of whom have never in their lives received $100 in one year. An ever-enlarging stockpile of nuclear warheads has the capability to destroy the world's population more than two dozen times over. As never before, human civilization is threatened by atomic devastation. And along with this awesome global threat, many live in fear of personal violence. Since 1930 in the United States, the rate of violent crime has staggered upward. Even since 1970, the FBI's base year for evaluating recent trends, reports of violent crime have continued to increase drastically.

Humanity has more lethal potential than ever before. But is barbarism unique to the latter part of this twentieth century? The *Guinness Book of World Records* suggests not. Consider the following:

Bloodiest war: World War II, which cost 55 million battle and civilian deaths.

Bloodiest battle: The First Battle of the Somme in World War I, which took more than one million lives.

Bloodiest civil war: The T'ai-p'ing rebellion in China about the time of the American Civil War, in which 20 to 30 million lives were lost.

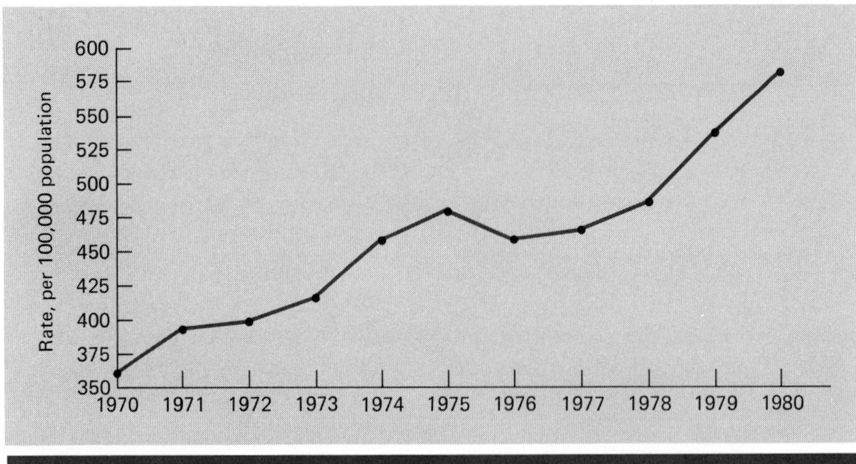

FIGURE 10-1 Violent crime in the United States increased 62 percent between 1970 and 1980. (Rate per 100,000 of murder, forcible rape, robbery and aggravated assault.) (Data from FBI Uniform Crime Reports, 1971-1980.)

"Our behavior toward each other is the strangest, most unpredictable, and most unaccountable of all the phenomena with which we are obliged to live. In all of nature, there is nothing so threatening to humanity as humanity itself."

Lewis Thomas (1981)

Greatest mass killings: 26 million Chinese are reported to have been liquidated in the first sixteen years of Mao Tse-tung's regime. Eight to 10 million Russians are estimated to have been killed during Stalin's purge of 1936 to 1938.

Cultural sophistication does not exempt one from inhumanity. Camp commanders at Auschwitz—where up to 6000 people a day were exterminated—would spend their evenings relaxing to the music of Beethoven and Schubert. The potential for inhumanity seems present among all peoples, whether "cultured" or not, whether red or yellow, black or white. War, murder, and lesser cruelties have been ever with us.

Why this propensity to aggress? Is it because we, like the mythical Minotaur, are half human, half beast? What circumstances prompt aggressive outbursts? Can aggression be controlled? If so, how? In this chapter, these are our questions. However, let us first clarify this nebulous term, "aggression."

WHAT IS AGGRESSION?

The term is nebulous. We use it in many ways, for many reasons. Clearly, the "Thugs," members of a former murdering fraternity in northern India, were aggressing when between 1550 and 1850 they strangled more than 2 million people. But when "aggressive" is used to describe a dynamic salesperson or a straight-talking woman, it takes on a different meaning. Social psychol-

Box 10-1

The Slaughter of Native Americans

"So tractable, so peaceable, are these people," Columbus wrote to the King and Queen of Spain,

> that I swear to your Majesties there is not in the world a better nation. They love their neighbors as themselves, and their discourse is ever sweet and gentle, and accompanied with a smile; and though it is true that they are naked, yet their manners are decorous and praiseworthy (Brown, 1976, p. 1).

In time the friendly Taino Indians who welcomed Columbus ashore had been completely obliterated, save for those who were sold as slaves in Europe.

When the English landed in Plymouth in 1620 they met friendly natives who saved them from starvation by sharing their food and by teaching the newcomers how to grow corn and catch fish. By the end of the century, their kindness was repaid by the invasion of their lands, and when this was resisted, by almost complete extermination.

On Manhattan Island, which the Dutch purchased for fishhooks and glass beads, the invaders massacred two entire villages by bayoneting men, women, and children during the middle of the night, hacking their bodies to pieces, and then burning what remained.

The white people's insatiable drive for more land led to the breaking of treaty after treaty. When Indians fought the taking of their land, they were slaughtered by the superior firepower of the invaders or displaced to more barren land. In the process, the Indian population was reduced to about 25 percent of what it was before the Europeans arrived.

Note: Based on *Bury My Heart at Wounded Knee* by Dee Brown, New York: Holt, Rinehart, & Winston, 1971, and *The World Book Encyclopedia*.

ogists debate how to define aggression. But on this much they agree: We should sharpen our vocabulary by distinguishing between self-assured, energetic, go-getting behavior and behavior that hurts, harms, or destroys. The former can be called assertion. The latter clearly and surely is aggression.

Chapter 6 defined aggression as physical or verbal behavior that is intended to hurt someone. This excludes accidental hurts, such as a baseball pitcher's unintentionally hitting the batter. But it does include a wide variety of actions aimed at hurting someone, whether such acts succeed or not. Thus gossipy "digs" about a person are usually considered aggressive. Researchers have struggled to find appropriate ways to study aggression in laboratory experiments. As we shall see, they typically measure aggression by having people decide how much to hurt someone, such as by having them choose how much electric shock to impose.

Hostile aggression: *Aggression driven by emotions such as anger and performed as an end in itself.*

Instrumental aggression: *Aggression that is a means to some other end.*

Our definition encompasses two distinct types of aggression. *Hostile aggression* springs from anger. Its goal is to injure. *Instrumental aggression* also aims to hurt, but only as a means to some other end (Feshbach, 1970; Buss, 1971). Many wars, for example, have been undertaken not out of cruel desire to harm the enemy, but because the nation has seen the war as instrumental (useful) in gaining new territory or resources. Hostile aggression is "hot"; instrumental aggression is "cool." Distinguishing between hostile and instrumental aggression is sometimes difficult (Bandura, 1979). What begins as a cool, calculating act can ignite hostility. Still, social psychologists find the distinction useful. Most murders are hostile. They are impulsive, emotional outbursts. On the other hand, Chicago's more than 1000 murders since 1919 by mobster "hit men" have most likely been calculated to attain specific goals.

The distinction between people's hostile and instrumental aggression is paralleled by the distinction between animals' "social aggression," characterized by displays of rage, and "silent aggression," as when a predator stalks its prey. Peter Marler (1974) reports that these two distinct types of animal aggression even involve separate brain regions.

THE NATURE OF AGGRESSION

Social psychologists have analyzed three primary ideas about aggression's root cause: (1) there is an inborn aggressive drive, (2) aggression is a natural response to frustrating experiences, and (3) aggressive behavior, like other social behaviors, is learned. Because different kinds of aggression (for example, hostile and instrumental) may well have different causes, a combination of these major ideas about the nature of aggression could well be valid.

Is Aggression an Instinct?

Philosophers have long debated whether our human nature is fundamentally that of a benign, contented "noble savage" or that of a potentially explosive brute. The first view, popularly associated with the eighteenth-century philosopher Jean-Jacques Rousseau, blames society, not human nature, for the evils of human existence. The second, associated often with the philosopher Thomas Hobbes, sees society's restrictions as necessary to restrain and control the human brute. In this century, the "brutish" view—that aggressive drive is inborn and thus inevitable—has been most prominently argued by Sigmund Freud and by Konrad Lorenz.

Instinctive behavior: *An innate, unlearned behavior pattern exhibited by all members of a species.*

Psychoanalytic Theory

After witnessing the savagery of World War I, Sigmund Freud surmised that our human nature has within it a death instinct, a drive toward self-destruction. However, a counterforce, the life instinct, usually compels us to turn and release this destructive energy outward. In short, Freud proposed that human aggression springs from our redirecting the energy of the death instinct toward others.

Although a few psychoanalytic thinkers have accepted Freud's idea of a death instinct [psychiatrist Karl Menninger (1969) has referred to our "innate suicidal propensities"], most have not. However, psychoanalysts do tend to agree that there is an innate aggressive energy that, if not discharged, builds up and explodes. This is commonly described as the "hydraulic model": Like steam pressure building up in a boiler, aggression must be allowed to drain off. Psychoanalyst Bruno Bettelheim (1966) concluded:

> We shall not be able to deal intelligently with violence unless we are first ready to see it as a part of human nature, and then we shall come to realize [that] the chances of discharging violent tendencies are now so severely curtailed that their regular and safe draining-off is not possible anymore.

Ethology

Ethology: The study of naturally occurring animal behavior, especially its fixed patterns.

Generalizing from his observations of animal behavior, Konrad Lorenz, Nobel Prize–winning ethologist, has proposed a theory of instinctive aggression. Lorenz, differing from Freud, views aggression as adaptive rather than self-destructive, and gives greater prominence to environmental stimuli that trigger aggression. He too, however, concurs with the basic hydraulic model. Aggressive energy accumulates until "released" by an appropriate stimulus, much as a mouse releases the pent-up energy of a mousetrap. Lorenz (1967) believes

> Knowledge of the fact that the aggression drive is a true, primarily species-preserving instinct enables us to recognize its full danger: it is the spontaneity of the instinct that makes it so dangerous. If it were merely a reaction to certain external factors, as many sociologists and psychologists maintain, the state of mankind would not be as perilous as it really is, for, in that case, the reaction-eliciting factors could be eliminated with some hope of success. (p. 47)

"To fight is a radical instinct; if men have nothing else to fight over they will fight over words, fancies, or women, or they will fight because they dislike each other's looks, or because they have met walking in opposite directions. To knock a thing down, especially if it is cocked at an arrogant angle, is a deep delight to the blood."

George Santayana, Soliloquies in England: On War

From the perspective of evolution, aggression has survival value. For example, in many species, the males that are most aggressive become socially dominant. The number 1 aggressor thus becomes the number 1 copulator. While other males look on, one dominant male elephant seal can go about contributing his genes to several dozen females. Such selective breeding maximizes aggressiveness.

On the other hand, it would hardly be adaptive for members of the same species to destroy one another. In fact, among animals deadly combat is rare.

"Man, biologically considered, . . . is the most formidable of all the beasts of prey, and indeed, the only one that preys systematically on its own species."

William James,
Memories and Studies

Lorenz contends that killing another of one's species is rare among animals because gestures of submission instinctively *inhibit* the attacker. "Inhibitory mechanisms" are especially strong with species naturally equipped for hunting and killing. For example, at the height of a struggle between two timber wolves, the one losing will turn its head upward, exposing its jugular vein. This automatically triggers the inhibition of the victor's aggression. Waving the white flag or making oneself defenseless by raising one's hands will usually cause the same response in a human aggressor. Lorenz therefore argued that humans, lacking the natural weapons of such creatures as wolves and lions, had less need to develop automatic inhibitory mechanisms. Instead, we came to rely more on those social inhibitions that stem from personal bonds of friendship and love.

"Some say the world will end in fire,
Some say in ice.
From what I've tasted of desire
I hold with those who favour fire."

Robert Frost,
"Fire and Ice" *in* The Poetry of Robert Frost, *New York: Holt, Rinehart and Winston, 1969*

If animals and humans are, as Lorenz believed, endowed with both a "fighting instinct" and the means to inhibit it, why then did he so gloomily predict a perilous future? He feared that with the development of modern weaponry, our capacity for destruction has far outstripped our capacity for inhibition. We have armed our "fighting instinct" without comparably arming our inhibitions. Consequently, nature's balance has fallen into a human imbalance, and our survival is threatened.

"Of course, we'll never actually use it against a potential enemy, but it will allow us to negotiate from a position of strength."

Humanity has armed its capacity for destruction without comparably arming its capacity for the inhibition of aggression. (John Ruge/*Saturday Review,* 1980)

Evaluating the Instinct Theory

The idea common to both Freud and Lorenz—that aggressive energy instinctively wells up from within, quite apart from one's encounters with the environment—has been sharply criticized by social psychologists. For one thing, the use of "instincts" to explain social behavior fell into disrepute after sociologist Luther Bernard scanned books by 500 social scientists and in 1924 compiled a list of 5759 supposed human instincts (Barash, 1979, p. 4). What the social scientists had tried to do was *explain* social behavior by *naming* it. It is terribly tempting to play this explaining-by-naming game: "Why do sheep stay together?" "It's because of their herding instinct." "How do you know they have a herding instinct?" "Just look at them: They're always together!" Such circular explanation is, of course, no explanation at all.

It is also very tempting to assume that what is true of lower animals is true of humans. Spiders instinctively weave nets to catch their prey. People who fish for a living also weave nets to catch their prey. Can it therefore be said that the fishers are simply doing what comes instinctively? Obviously not.

With higher animals, aggressive tendencies are modifiable by circumstance. A kitten reared with a rat will, when grown, usually refuse to attack rats (Kuo, 1930). Among humans, aggressiveness varies widely from culture to culture, from the gentle Philippine Tasaday tribe, which has no word for war, to the warring Yanomamo Indians of South America (Nance, 1975; Eibl-Eibesfeldt, 1979). Even within a culture, aggressiveness may change with circumstance. As their native forests were cut down by white invaders, the Iroquois Indians changed from peaceful hunters to aggressive warriors (Hornstein, 1976).

If the aggressive drive, like the hunger drive, spontaneously builds with the mere passage of time, then there must be physiological events that create the drive. With the hunger drive, such physiological events have been identified. But not with the presumed aggressive drive. As researcher J. P. Scott (1958) put it, "There is no physiological evidence of any spontaneous stimulation for fighting arising within the body" (p. 62).

Biological Influences upon Aggression

Although the human propensity to aggress may not qualify as an instinct, aggression *is* biologically influenced. Because aggression is a complex behavior, we cannot expect it to be controlled by any single, precise spot in the brain (Valenstein, 1973). But in both animals and humans, researchers have found complex neural systems that facilitate aggression. When these areas in the brain's inner core are activated, hostility increases; when activity in them is blocked, hostility decreases. Docile animals can thus be provoked into rage, and raging animals into submission. Similar effects have been observed with human patients. For example, after receiving electrical stimulation in her amygdala (a part of the brain core), one woman smashed her guitar against the wall, barely missing her psychiatrist's head (Moyer, 1976).

The individual members of any species vary in the sensitivity of their neural systems controlling aggression. One source of differing sensitivity is heredity. Animals of many species have been bred for aggressiveness. At times, this is done for practical purposes (for example, fighting cocks are bred). Sometimes, breeding is done for purposes of research. For example, Kirsti Lagerspetz (1979), a Finnish psychologist, took normal albino mice and bred the most aggressive ones with one another and the least aggressive ones with one another. After repeating this for twenty-six generations she had one set of fierce mice and one set that was placid. We, too, vary in aggressiveness (Olweus, 1979). Moreover, the characteristic reactiveness of our temperaments—for example, how easygoing and nonreactive we are—is partly something we bring with us into the world. A person's temperament, observed in infancy, tends to endure (Thomas, Chess, & Birch, 1970).

Blood chemistry is another influence upon the neural system's sensitivity to aggressive stimulation. Both laboratory experiments and police data indicate that when people are provoked, alcohol can enhance aggressive responses (Boyatzis, 1977; 1980; Frieze & Knoble, 1980; Pagano & Taylor, 1981; Schmutte & Taylor, 1980). It may do so by reducing self-awareness, producing a more deindividuated state (Hull, 1981; Hull et al., 1982). Low blood sugar also can boost aggressiveness. And in males, aggressiveness can be influenced by the injection of male hormones (Moyer, 1976; Reinisch, 1981). Interestingly,

"Go right ahead. I realize you're bred to be violent, just as I'm bred to be passive."

Animals can be bred for aggressiveness. (Sidney Harris)

though perhaps coincidentally, after age twenty-five androgens and rates of violent crime both decrease.

Urges to commit violent crime can also rise from brain injuries and diseases. Charles Whitman, who in 1966 killed his wife and mother and then went to the top of the University of Texas Tower and shot to death fourteen people, left a letter in which he recalled his "overwhelming violent impulses" and "tremendous headaches." Whitman's autopsy revealed a malignant brain tumor the size of a walnut (R. N. Johnson, 1972).

Is Aggression a Response to Frustration?

It is a warm evening. Tired and thirsty after two hours of studying, you borrow some change from a friend and head for the nearest pop machine. As the machine devours the change, you can almost taste the cold, refreshing cola. But when you push the button, nothing happens. You push it again. Then you flip the coin return button. Not even your investment is returned. Your throat is now feeling parched. Again, you hit the buttons. You slam them. And finally you shake and whack the machine. You stomp back to your studies, empty-handed and shortchanged. Should your roommate beware? Are you now more likely to say or do something hurtful?

One of the first psychological theories of aggression, the popular frustration-aggression theory, answers yes, yes indeed. In fact, John Dollard and several of his Yale colleagues (1939) went so far as to propose that "aggression is always a consequence of frustration" and "frustration always leads to some form of aggression" (p. 1). One cannot arise without the other.

Frustration: *The blocking of goal-directed behavior.*

Frustration, said Dollard and his colleagues, is anything (such as the malfunctioning vending machine) that blocks one's attaining a goal. Frustration is especially pronounced when one's motivation to achieve a goal is very strong and the blocking is complete. If this experience is repeated, the aggressive

FIGURE 10-2 Summary of the classic frustration-aggression theory. Frustration creates a motive to aggress. Fear of punishment or disapproval for aggressing against the source of one's frustration may cause the aggressive drive to be displaced against some other target, or even redirected against oneself. (Based on Dollard et al., 1939, and Miller, 1941.)

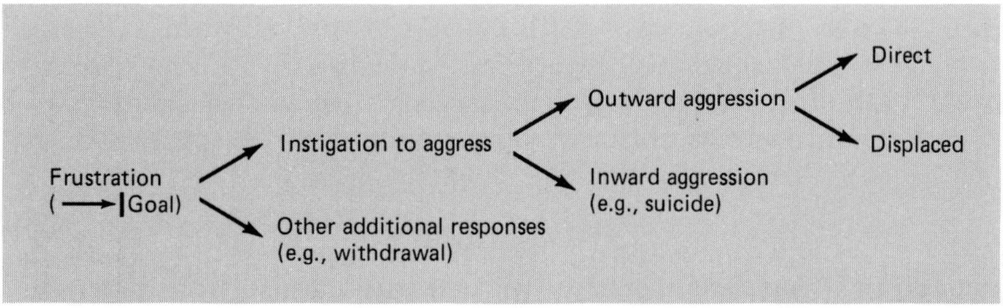

drive builds, until released. (Note that this theory also assumes the hydraulic model, except now the aggressive energy originates not from within but rather from frustrating experiences.)

Displacement: *Redirecting aggression to a target other than the source of the frustration. Generally, the new target is a safer target, one that is less likely to retaliate or against whom aggression is more socially accepted.*

As Figure 10-2 suggests, the aggressive energy need not be released directly against its source. We have often been taught to inhibit direct retaliation, especially when others might disapprove or punish; we learn instead to displace our hostilities to safer targets. *Displacement* is illustrated in an anecdote about a man who, having been humiliated by his boss, berates his wife, who yells at their son, who kicks the dog, which bites the mail carrier.

Frustration-Aggression Theory Revised

Laboratory tests of the frustration-aggression theory have produced mixed results: Sometimes frustration increases aggressiveness; however, surprisingly it often does not (R. A. Baron, 1977; Zillmann, 1979). For example, if the frustration is understandable—if, as in one experiment by Eugene Burnstein and Philip Worchel (1962), a confederate disrupts a group's problem solving because his hearing aid malfunctions (rather than just because he failed to pay attention)—then aggression does not increase.

Note that frustration-aggression theory is designed to explain hostile aggression, not instrumental aggression.

Since it is clear that the original theory overstated the frustration-aggression connection, Leonard Berkowitz (1978), has revised the theory. Berkowitz theorizes that frustration produces anger, an emotional readiness to aggress. Anger is especially likely when someone who frustrates us could have chosen to act otherwise (Weiner, 1981). And a frustrated person is presumed especially likely to lash out when there are also aggressive cues that, so to speak, pull the cork, thus releasing the bottled-up anger. Sometimes the cork will blow without such cues; but when stimuli associated with aggression are present they tend to amplify aggression.

For instance, Berkowitz (1968; 1981b) and other researchers have found that the mere sight of a weapon—an obvious aggressive cue—can heighten aggression. In one experiment, children who had just played with toy guns became more willing to knock down another child's blocks. In another experiment, angered University of Wisconsin men gave more electric shocks to their tormentor when a rifle and a revolver were nearby (supposedly having been left from a previous experiment), than when badminton racquets had been left behind (Berkowitz & LePage, 1967). Some experiments have failed to replicate this "weapons effect" (Page & Scheidt, 1971; Epstein, O'Neal, & Jones, 1980). But enough have replicated it so that Berkowitz is not surprised that over half of all murders in the U.S. are committed with handguns: "Guns not only permit violence, they can stimulate it as well. The finger pulls the trigger, but the trigger may also be pulling the finger."

The Distinction between Frustration and Deprivation

Picture someone feeling extremely frustrated—economically, or sexually, or politically. My hunch is that most will imagine someone economically, or sexually, or politically *deprived*. Ironically, however, frustration often is unrelated to deprivation. The most sexually frustrated people are probably

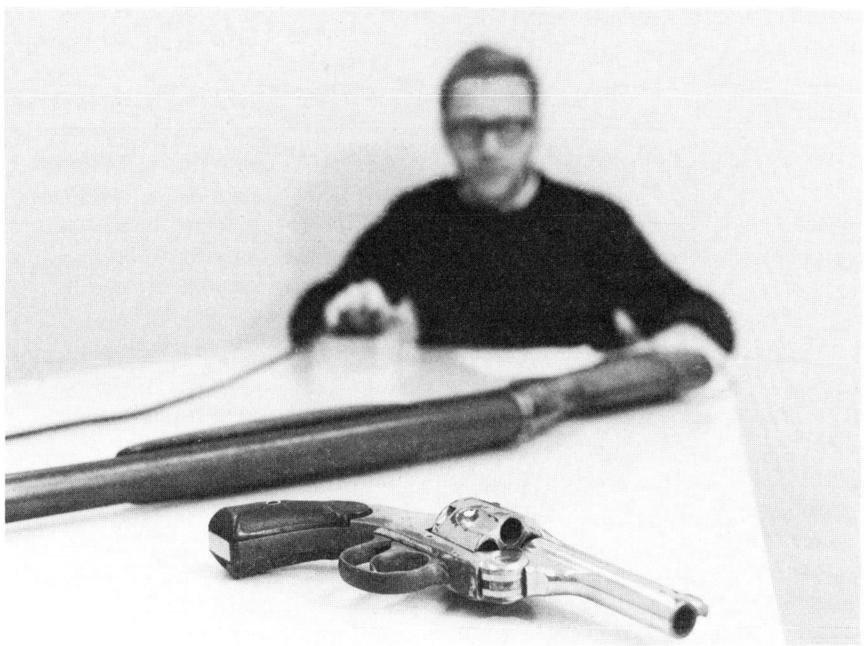

Since guns are obvious aggressive cues, their presence may "uncork" aggressive impulses. One experiment by Leonard Berkowitz and Anthony LePage (1967) found that the mere presence of guns increased the number of shocks that angry men gave their tormentors. (Photo courtesy of Leonard Berkowitz)

not those who are celibate. The most economically frustrated people are probably not the impoverished residents of Jamaican shantytowns. In fact, the 1969 National Commission on the Causes and Prevention of Violence concluded that economic advancements may even exacerbate frustration and escalate violence. Let's pause to examine this paradoxical conclusion.

Prior to Detroit's 1967 riot, in which 43 people were killed and 683 structures damaged or destroyed by fire, I watched Michigan's Governor, George Romney, boast on television's *Meet the Press* about his state's leadership in civil rights legislation and about the $367 million in federal aid pumped into Detroit during the five preceding years. No sooner were his words ringing across television land, than a large black neighborhood in Detroit exploded into this century's worst U.S. civil disorder. People were stunned. Why Detroit? Although things were still bad there, relative to the general affluence of the white populace, the injustices were even greater in certain other American cities. The National Advisory Commission on Civil Disorders, established to answer the question, concluded that an immediate psychological cause was the frustration of expectations that had been fueled by the legislative and judicial civil rights victories of the 1960s. When there occurs a "revolution

"I would say a person is deprived *if he lacks a goal object people generally regard as attractive or desirable, but is* frustrated *only when he had been anticipating the pleasure to be gotten from this object and then cannot fulfill this expectation."*

Leonard Berkowitz (1972)

BEHIND THE SCENES

Leonard Berkowitz

In 1955, my first year of teaching at the University of Wisconsin, I was assigned a "special-topics" course that allowed me to cover any research area. I chose the topic aggression. As I studied the research for my lectures, I became fascinated by questions and ambiguities in these early investigations. The more I thought and talked about these problems, the more interested I became. My lecture notes became the basis of an article on the frustration-aggression hypothesis. But of course, the questions didn't go away, so I began a series of experiments.

It has always been very helpful for me to write things down. In preparing journal articles, I see problems and relationships that hadn't occurred to me before. So writing up one study has often been the spur to another. For example, many questions popped into my head during the time I was writing my 1962 book on aggression, especially questions regarding how TV and movie violence affects members of the audience. This was a relatively unexplored area of research. So I undertook experiments on the impact of observing aggression. Soon I found that my findings and thinking were readily translated into a coherent theory. Because I reported initial findings during the 1960s, a time when our society was very concerned with the violence in our midst, my research attracted considerable attention. Who could want better reinforcements? The research results were theoretically interesting, bringing me intrinsic satisfactions, and the attention this research drew was extrinsically gratifying. *(Leonard Berkowitz, University of Wisconsin)*

of rising expectations," as happened in Detroit and elsewhere, frustrations may escalate, even while conditions improve.

"Evils which are patiently endured when they seem inevitable become intolerable when once the idea of escape from them is suggested."

Alexis de Tocqueville, 1856

The principle works internationally. The political scientist–social psychologist team of Ivo and Rosaline Feierabend (1968; 1972) applied the frustration-aggression theory in a study of political instability within eighty-four nations. They found that when people in rapidly modernizing nations become urbanized and when their literacy improves, they then become more aware of material improvements. However, since the growing affluence of a nation usually diffuses slowly, the increasing gap between aspirations and achievements tends to intensify frustration. Expectation outstrips reality. Even

WORLD'S HIGHEST STANDARD OF LIVING
There's no way like the American Way

Deprivation without hope produces apathy. It has been true in American cities and in impoverished countries. Similarly, when the Indians of the American plains gave up hope of resisting white power they ceased aggression and became passively resigned to their fate. (Margaret Bourke-White, *Life* Magazine, © 1937 Time, Inc.)

as people's deprivation diminishes, their frustration and political aggression may therefore nevertheless escalate.

The point is not that actual deprivation and social injustice are irrelevant to social unrest. (Injustice can be a root cause, even if not the immediate psychological cause.) The point is simply this: Frustration is created by the *gap* between our expectations and our attainments. Thus liberation movements can, by raising their adherents' aspirations, simultaneously stimulate achievement and discontentment. A woman's becoming a feminist likely will *not* alleviate her frustrations. In the short run, her frustration may in fact increase.

Box 10-2

Is Deprivation Frustration?

Historian Carl Gustavson has identified several common errors in people's beliefs about revolutions. Error 1 is that "A revolution is caused by the misery of the people." Not so, says Gustavson.

This error is more than simply another instance of oversimplified causation, for the statement itself seems to have little verity. Eyewitness accounts of the French Revolution do give an impression that the people were suffering from great want. . . .

[But] the general direction of the economy of France had been upward throughout the eighteenth century; if misery caused revolution, why did it not occur earlier, instead of taking place at the end of the century of relative progress? The French peasants, who were so vocal and restless in 1789 and who, it is true, had seen a worsening of their condition in the last decades, were nevertheless probably as well off as in any other country in Europe. Less than a million of the twenty million farmers were even nominally serfs, a sharp contrast to the countries farther east. If exasperation with poor circumstances were the principle cause for a revolution, the French would have been among the last to revolt.

Extreme suffering or poverty seems to induce apathy rather than rebellion, for people in these circumstances are too busy simply surviving to give much thought to government. . . . The revolution was born, not out of misery, but out of strength and hope.

Note: from *A Preface to History* by C. Gustavson, New York: McGraw-Hill, 1955, pp. 99–101.

Does Money Buy Happiness?

The principle "frustration equals expectations minus attainments" also can help us understand why our own feelings of satisfaction and frustration fluctuate. Consider the following rather bewildering set of facts: Fact 1: Americans at every income level, except the very top, insist that just 10 or 20 percent more income would make them happier (Strumpel, 1976). More money would relieve their financial woes and buy more happiness, they believe. Fact 2: As the 1980s began, the average American was enjoying a disposable income (corrected for inflation and taxes) about double that of the 1950s. Even during the inflationary 1970s, when U.S. prices rose 93 percent, per-person incomes rose 143 percent (*U.S. Department of Commerce News*, 1981). Since most Americans believe money increases happiness and since

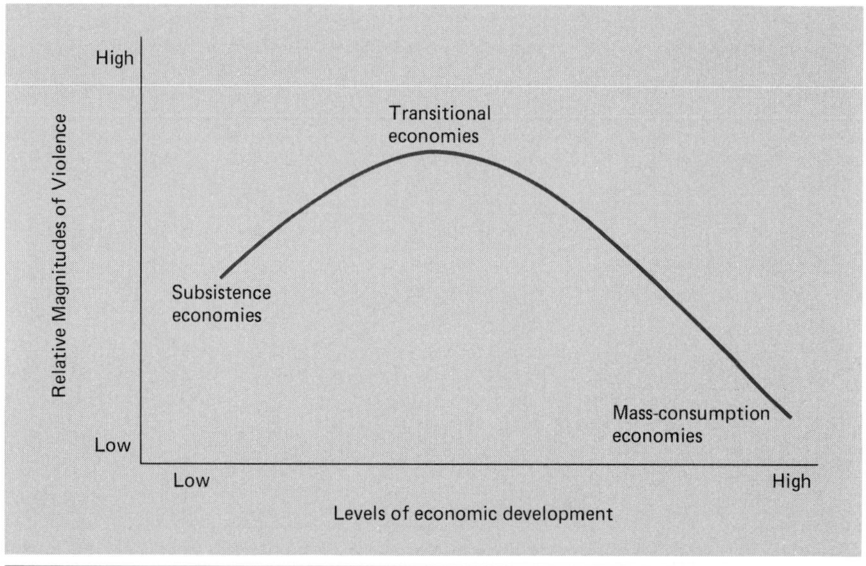

FIGURE 10-3 The relationship between social violence and economic development. Since 1950, violent conflict has been greatest in developing nations. (Data from Gurr, 1972.)

Americans do, in fact, have more money today than in decades past, they must be happier, right?

Wrong. Americans in recent years have been no more likely than those of the 1950s to report feeling happy and satisfied with their lives. In 1957, for example, 35 percent reported themselves "very happy." By 1980, after two decades of growing affluence, 33 percent declared themselves "very happy" (see Figure 10-4).

Why are we not happier with our economic circumstances? Why all the commiserating about inflation and other financial woes among people whose affluence has doubled? And why do yesterday's luxuries—color television sets, electric can openers, stereo sound systems—become today's necessities, leading people always to feel their needs are greater than their incomes can provide?

Parkinson's second law: *Expenditures rise to meet income.*

Two principles developed by research psychologists help explain our rising expectations. The *adaptation-level phenomenon* implies that our feelings of success and failure, satisfaction and dissatisfaction, are relative to our prior achievements. Therefore, if our current achievements fall below what we previously accomplished, we feel dissatisfied, frustrated; if they rise above, we feel successful, satisfied.

Adaptation-level phenomenon: *The tendency to adapt to a given level of stimulation and thus to notice and react to* changes *from that level.*

If we continue to achieve, however, we soon adapt to the success, and what we formerly felt positive about then registers as neutral, and that which formerly left us neutral is now perceived as negative. This helps explain why,

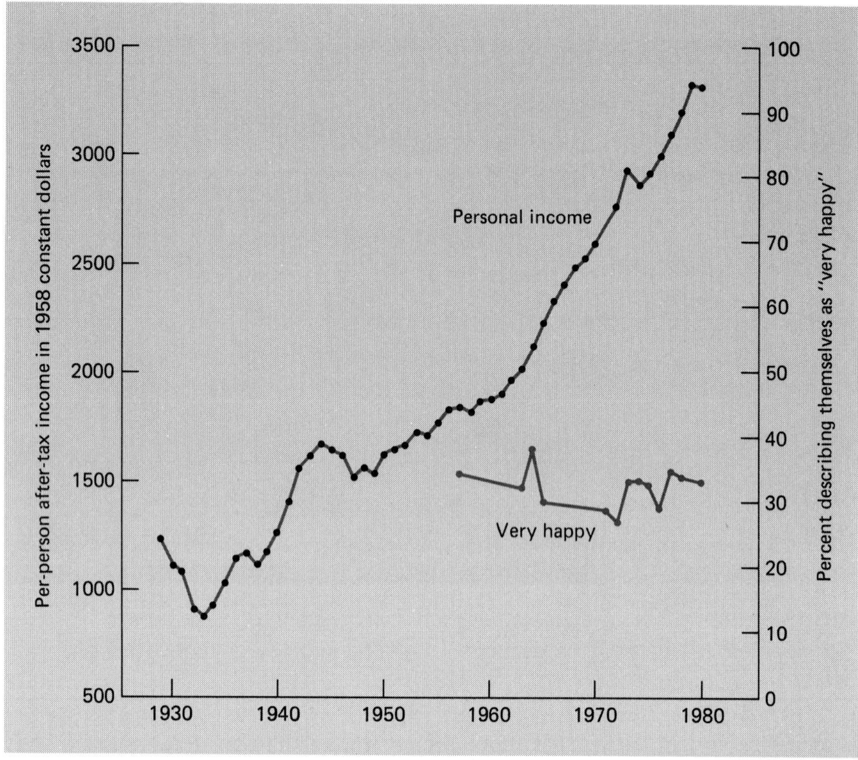

FIGURE 10-4 Money. Does it buy happiness? It can surely enable us to evade or overcome certain types of pain. Yet, while buying power has doubled since the 1950s, self-reported happiness has not increased. [Income data from *Historical Statistics of the U.S.* (data for 1929-1970), *Statistical Abstract of the United States, 1980* (data for 1971-1978), and *Survey of Current Business*, February 1981 (data for 1979-1980). Happiness data cited by Smith (1979) and personal communication.]

despite the rapid increase in real income during the past several decades, the average American is no happier. Donald Campbell (1975b) thus concludes that we humans will never create a social paradise on earth. If we would achieve such, we would soon redefine "utopia" and would once again feel sometimes pleased, sometimes deprived, sometimes neutral.

Most of us have experienced the adaptation-level phenomenon. Increased material goods, or academic achievement, or social prestige provide an initial surge of pleasure. Yet, all too soon the feeling wanes. Now, we need an even higher level to give us another surge of pleasure. "Even as we contemplate our satisfaction with a given accomplishment, the satisfaction fades," noted Philip Brickman and Donald Campbell (1971), "to be replaced finally by a new indifference and a new level of striving."

The adaptation-level principle is well illustrated by a recent study of state lottery winners. Brickman and his colleagues, Dan Coates and Ronnie Janoff-Bulman (1978), found that at first the winners typically felt elated: "Winning the lottery was one of the best things that ever happened to me." Yet their self-reported overall happiness did not increase. In fact, the ordinary activities they had previously enjoyed, activities such as reading or eating a good breakfast, actually became less pleasurable. Winning the lottery was apparently such an emotional high that, by comparison, their ordinary pleasures paled.

The dissatisfactions bred by adapting to new attainments often become compounded when we compare ourselves with others. Ephraim Yuchtman (1976) observed that feelings of well-being, especially among white-collar workers, are closely connected with whether their compensation is equitable to others in their line of work. For instance, a salary raise for a city's police officers, while temporarily lifting their morale, may deflate that of the firefighters.

"A house may be large or small; as long as the surrounding houses are equally small, it satisfies all social demands for a dwelling. But let a palace arise beside the little house, and it shrinks from a little house into a hut."

Karl Marx

In everyday life, when people increase in affluence, or status, or achievement, they similarly raise the standards by which they evaluate their own attainments. When climbing the ladder of success, people look up, not down (Gruder, 1977; Martin, 1980; Suls & Tesch, 1978). They attend to where they are going, usually neglecting where they have come from. Such upward comparison is conducive to feelings of *relative deprivation* (Bernstein & Crosby, 1980; Crosby, 1976; Williams, 1975).

This term, "relative deprivation," was coined by researchers studying the satisfaction felt by American soldiers in World War II (Merton & Kitt, 1950; Stouffer et al., 1949). Ironically, those in the Air Corps, where promotions were rapid and widespread, were *more* frustrated about their own rate of promotion than were those in the Military Police, for whom promotions were slow and unpredictable. In retrospect, we can see that since the Air Corps' promotion rate was rapid, and since most Air Corps personnel probably perceived themselves as better than the average Air Corps member (the self-serving bias), it is quite likely that their aspirations soared higher than their achievements. The result? Frustration.

Relative deprivation: *The perception that one is less well off than others to whom one compares.*

Lucy fails to appreciate the adaptation-level phenomenon. (© 1962 United Feature Syndicate, Inc.)

One possible source of such frustration is the affluence depicted on television. Karen Hennigan and her coworkers (1982) analyzed crime rates in American cities around the time that television was introduced. In thirty-four cities where television ownership became widespread in 1951, the 1951 larceny theft rate (for crimes such as shoplifting and stealing a bicycle) took an observable jump. In thirty-four other cities, where a government freeze had delayed the introduction of television until 1955, a similar jump in the theft rate occurred—in 1955. Why? Hennigan and her colleagues believe that

> television caused younger and poorer persons (the major perpetrators of theft) to compare their life-styles and possessions with (a) those of wealthy television characters and (b) those portrayed in advertisements. Many of these viewers may have felt resentment and frustration over lacking the goods they could not afford, and some may have turned to crime as a way of obtaining the coveted goods and reducing any "relative deprivation."

The principles of adaptation-level and relative deprivation have several thought-provoking implications (Austin, McGinn, & Susmilch, 1980). Ironically, seeking satisfaction through material achievement requires continually expanding one's level of affluence merely to maintain the same level of satisfaction. "Poverty," said Plato, "consists not in the decrease of one's possessions but in the increase of one's greed."

"All our wants, beyond those which a very moderate income will supply, are purely imaginary."

Henry St. John, Letter to Swift, *1719*

Fortunately, the adaptation-level phenomenon also can enable us to adjust downward, should we choose or be forced to adopt a simplified way of life. If our buying power shrinks, as it did in 1980, we initially will feel some pain. But eventually most of us will adapt to the new reality. In the aftermath of the 1970s gas price hikes, Americans have already managed to substantially reduce their "need" for large gas-slurping cars. Even paraplegics, the blind, and other severely handicapped people generally adapt to their tragic situation and eventually find a normal or near-normal level of life satisfaction (Brickman et al., 1978; Cameron, 1977). Victims of traumatic incidents surely must envy those who are not paralyzed, as many of us envy those who have won a state lottery. Yet, after a period of adjustment, none of these three groups differs appreciably from the others in moment-to-moment happiness. Human beings have an enormous capacity to adapt.

"However great the discrepancies between men's lots, there is always a certain balance of joy and sorrow which equalizes all."

La Rochefoucauld, Maxims

Finally, experiences that lower our expectations or standards of comparison can renew our appreciation for present blessings (Wills, 1981). As Abraham Maslow (1972) noted,

> All you have to do is to go to a hospital and hear all the simple blessings that people never before realized *were* blessings—being able to urinate, to sleep on your side, to be able to swallow, to scratch an itch, etc. Could *exercises* in deprivation educate us faster about all our blessings? (p. 108)

A research team led by Marshall Dermer (1979) put a number of University of Wisconsin—Milwaukee women through some imaginative exercises in deprivation. After viewing vivid depictions of how grim life was in Milwaukee in 1900, or after imagining and then writing about various personal tragedies, such as being burned and disfigured, the women expressed a greater sense of satisfaction with the quality of their own lives. So it seems that pausing to recall the deprivations of our more distant past, and comparing ourselves with those who have less rather than those who have more, can increase our contentment.

Is Aggression Learned Social Behavior?

The theories of aggression based on instinct and frustration assume that the aggressive urge erupts from inner emotions, and that under certain conditions it is both natural and unlearned. In contrast to this assumption that aggression is "pushed" from within, social psychologists have increasingly contended that, through learning, aggression is also "pulled" out of us.

How Is Aggression Learned?

By experience and by observing others we learn that *aggression often pays*. Animal-training experiments reveal that animals can be transformed from docile creatures into ferocious fighters through a series of successful bouts. Severe defeats, on the other hand, create submissiveness (Ginsburg & Allee, 1942; Kahn, 1951; Scott & Marston, 1953).

Children, too, can be thus affected. A child whose aggressive acts successfully intimidate other children will likely become increasingly aggressive (Patterson, Littman, & Bricker, 1967). Similarly, aggressive hockey players—the ones sent most often to the penalty box for rough play—score more goals than nonaggressive players (McCarthy & Kelly, 1978a; 1978b). In both these cases, aggression seems to be instrumental in achieving certain rewards.

Collective violence also sometimes pays. After the 1980 riot in Miami's Liberty City neighborhood, President Carter came to the neighborhood to assure residents personally both of his concern and of forthcoming federal aid. After the 1967 Detroit riot, Ford Motor Company accelerated its efforts to hire minority workers, prompting comedian Dick Gregory to joke, "Last summer the fire got too close to the Ford plant. Don't scorch the Mustangs, baby." I don't mean to suggest that these riots were consciously planned for their instrumental value or that their benefits exceeded their costs. Still, sometimes the unintended lesson is that aggression has its payoffs. If nothing more, it gets attention.

Albert Bandura, the leading proponent of the "social learning" theory of aggression, believes that we learn aggression not only by experiencing its payoffs, but also by *observing others*. Like many social behaviors, aggression can be acquired by watching others act and noting the resultant consequences.

Picture this scene from one of Bandura's experiments (Bandura, Ross, & Ross, 1961). A Stanford Nursery School child is put to work on an interesting art activity. An adult is in another part of the room, where there are Tinker Toys, a mallet, and a big, inflated Bobo doll. After a minute of working with the Tinker Toys, the adult gets up and for almost ten minutes attacks the Bobo doll—pounding it with the mallet, kicking it, and throwing it, all the while yelling such remarks as "Sock him in the nose. . . . Hit him down. . . . Kick him."

After observing this outburst, the child is then taken to a different building and placed in a room that has many very attractive toys. But after two minutes the experimenter interrupts, stating that these are her best toys and she has decided to "save them for the other children." The frustrated child now goes into an adjacent room containing a variety of toys for aggressive and nonaggressive play, two of which are a Bobo doll and a mallet.

Seldom did children not exposed to the aggressive adult model display any aggressive play or talk. Frustrated though they may have been over being deprived of the attractive toys, they nevertheless played calmly. However, those who previously had observed the aggressive adult were many times more likely to pick up the mallet and lash out at the doll. Watching the adult's aggressive behavior apparently lowered their inhibitions. But the children's observations did more than disinhibit them, for not just any aggressive behavior arose. Rather, the children often reproduced the very acts and said the very words they had previously observed. In short, observing aggressive behavior can both lower inhibitions and teach ways to be aggressive.

Bandura (1979) believes that in everyday life aggressive models are found most often in (1) one's family, (2) one's subculture, and (3) the mass media. Children of parents who discipline with physical aggression tend to use similar tactics when relating to others. For example, the parents of violent teenage boys and of abused children have often had parents who disciplined them with lots of physical punishment (Bandura & Walters, 1959; Silver, Dublin, & Lourie, 1969; Strauss & Gelles, 1980). Within families, violence breeds violence.

Outside the home, one's social environment can be a source of aggressive models. In communities where "macho" images not only abound but are admired, aggression is readily transmitted to new generations (Cartwright, 1975; Short, 1969; Wolfgang & Ferracuti, 1967). The violent subculture of teenage gangs, for instance, provides its junior members with numerous aggressive models.

Although one's family or subculture may at times demonstrate brutal aggression, additional opportunities to observe a wide range of violent actions are now provided by television. As we shall note later in this chapter, research indicates that viewing televised violence tends to (1) increase aggressiveness, (2) desensitize viewers to violence, and (3) shape their assumptions about social reality.

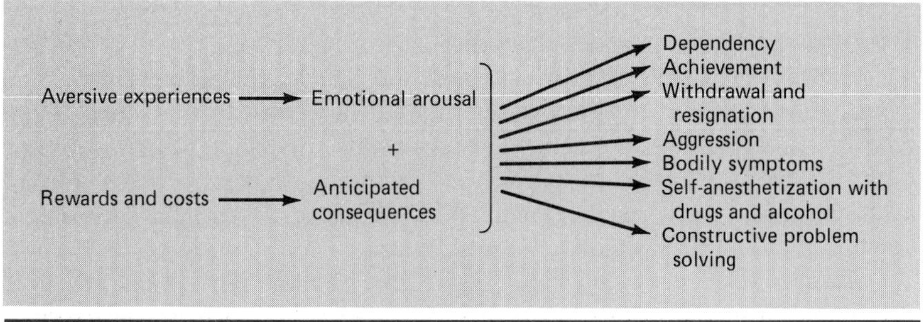

FIGURE 10-5 The social-learning view of aggression. Aggression is motivated by the emotional arousal stemming from an aversive experience. Whether aggression or some other response actually occurs depends on what consequences we have learned to expect. (Based on Bandura, 1979.)

When Is Aggression Provoked?

To say that aggressive responses are learned both by experience and by observing aggressive models does not help us predict when such responses will actually occur. Bandura (1979) contends (see Figure 10-5) that aggressive acts are motivated by a variety of aversive experiences—frustration, pain, insults. Such experiences arouse us emotionally. But whether we act aggressively or instead react in some other way depends upon what consequences we anticipate. Aggression is most likely when we are aroused *and* it seems safe and rewarding to aggress.

The social-learning theory of how aggressive behavior is acquired and provoked offers a perspective from which we can view some specific influences upon aggression. In more depth, let us look now at a few of these influences.

INFLUENCES UPON AGGRESSION

To a greater or lesser extent, all of us have learned aggressive responses. We are each a potential aggressor. So, what conditions tend to provoke our acts of aggression?

Aversive Incidents

Pain

Researcher Nathan Azrin wanted to know if switching off foot shocks could be used to reinforce two rats' positive interactions with each other. Azrin planned to turn on the shock and then, once the rats began to approach each other, cut off the pain. To his great surprise, the experiment proved impossible. No sooner did the rats feel pain than they attacked each other, even before the experimenter could switch off the shock. Azrin then dropped his initial research plans, and with colleagues Roger Ulrich, Ronald Hutchinson, and Don Hake undertook a series of studies on this pain-attack reaction.

First, they found that the greater the shock, the more violent the aggression. They also noted that the rats did not adapt to the shock. Even when given up to several thousand shocks a day, the effect did not wear off. What is more, rats reared in isolation reacted much the same way, suggesting an innate pain-attack reaction much like the natural frustration-aggression reaction that had been theorized decades earlier.

Do rats alone react this way? The researchers wanted to know. So next they found that with a wide variety of species, the cruelty the animals imposed upon each other matched zap for zap the cruelty imposed upon them. As Azrin (1967) explained, the pain-attack response occurred

"I like pussy, her coat is so warm; and if I don't hurt her she'll do me no harm."

Jane Taylor,
I Like Little Pussy

> in many different strains of rats. Then we found that shock produced attack when pairs of the following species were caged together: some kinds of mice, hamsters, opossums, raccoons, marmosets, foxes, nutria, cats, snapping turtles, squirrel monkeys, ferrets, red squirrels, bantam roosters, alligators, crayfish, amphiuma (an amphibian), and several species of snakes including the boa constrictor, rattlesnake, brown rat-snake, cottonmouth, copperhead, and black snake. The shock-attack reaction was clearly present in many very different kinds of creatures. In all the species in which shock produced attack it was fast and consistent, in the same "push-button" manner as with the rats.

And, in addition to these findings, it was noted that the animals were not choosy about their targets. Not only would they attack target animals of their own species but also those of a different species, or stuffed dolls, or even a tennis ball. Lastly, the researchers varied the source of pain. It was found that not only shocks induce attack, but also intense heat and "psychological pain"—for example, suddenly not rewarding hungry pigeons that have been trained to expect a grain reward after pecking at a disk. Such "psychological pain" is, of course, what we call frustration.

Consistent with the formulation of social learning shown in Figure 10-5, these experiments demonstrated that in many (though not all) animal species, aversive stimulation can fuel aggression. Further consistent with Figure 10-5, aversive stimulation also increases the likelihood of other behaviors, especially escape. Given a choice, many animals prefer to flee rather than fight. Azrin and his colleagues prevented such alternative responses by restricting the animals to a small enclosure. Escape was impossible. So, the animals did the next best thing—attack. In retrospect we can see how pain-provoked fight and flight could both have survival value. Both fight and flight can terminate aversive stimulation.

Pain heightens aggressiveness in humans, also. Many of us can recall such a reaction after stubbing a toe or suffering a headache. Leonard Berkowitz and his associates demonstrated this by having University of Wisconsin

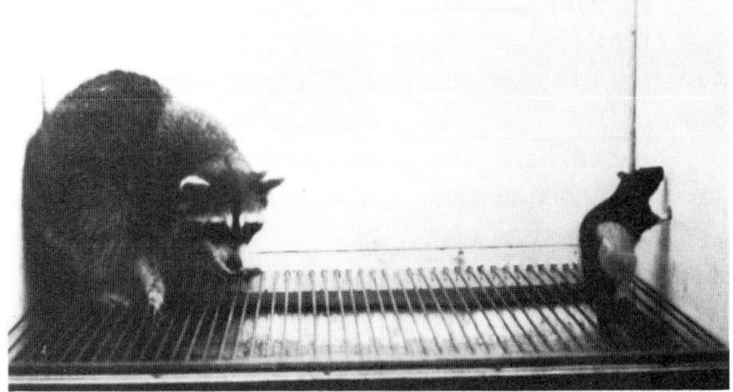

The pain-attack reaction. (Data from Nathan Azrin, 1967.) (Photo by Dr. Nathan Azrin, courtesy of Dr. Ronald Hutchinson)

students supervise someone else while holding one hand in either lukewarm water or painfully cold water (Berkowitz & Frodi, 1977; Berkowitz, Cochran, & Embree, 1980). Those whose hands were submerged in the cold water reported feeling more irritable and more annoyed, and they were more willing to blast the person with unpleasant noise. In view of such results, Berkowitz (1978; 1981a) now believes that pain rather than frustration is the more basic stimulus for hostile aggression. Frustration is certainly one important type of pain. But, says Berkowitz, any decidedly aversive event, whether a dashed expectation, a personal insult, or a physical pain, can incite an emotional outburst.

Heat

People have theorized for centuries about the effect of climate on human action. Hippocrates, comparing the civilized Greece of his day to the savagery (for example, human sacrifice) in what we now know as Germany and Switzerland, believed the cause to be Europe's harsher climate. Later, the British based their superior culture on *England's* ideal climate. French thinkers proclaimed the same for France. Since climate remains steady while cultural traits change, the climate theory of culture obviously has limited validity.

However, temporary climate variations can affect one's behavior. For example, William Griffitt (1970; Griffitt & Veitch, 1971) found that, compared to Kansas State University students who answered questionnaires in a room with a normal temperature, those who worked in an uncomfortably hot room (over 90°F) reported feeling more tired and aggressive and expressed more hostility toward a stranger they were asked to rate. Similarly, Paul Bell (1980) observed that after being angered by an experimenter while in a hot room, Colorado State University men retaliated with more negative recommendations concerning reemployment of the experimenter than did those who suffered the same provocation in a comfortable room. Yet, other experiments by Bell and Robert Baron indicated that being in a very hot room can sometimes reduce aggression—if the participants think that not making trouble will quickly end the experiment (Baron, 1977). As we noted above, pain motivates aggression and pain motivates escape. Sometimes the urge to escape is stronger.

So, in laboratory experiments, discomfiting heat sometimes, but not always, increases aggression. Does such happen in real life as well? Two Stanford University investigators, J. Merrill Carlsmith and Craig A. Anderson (1979), analyzed major riots occurring in seventy-nine United States cities between 1967 and 1971. They wanted to find out whether such outbreaks were more likely on hot rather than on cool days. As Figure 10-6 indicates, they were indeed. Moreover, Carlsmith and Anderson noted that within any given city, a riot was more likely to occur on its hottest days. And John Cotton (1981) reports that on summer days in Des Moines, Iowa, individual acts of violence (for example, assault or murder) also are somewhat more likely on hot days.

Does this indicate that the discomfort of hot days fuels aggressiveness? While this conclusion appears plausible, we had best not hastily assume it. Figure 10-6 presents simply a *correlation* between temperature and riots. People certainly could be more irritable when suffering through hot sticky weather. However, there may be other contributing factors. Maybe hot summer evenings lead people into the streets. There, other group influence factors may well take over. Judging from laboratory experiments on aversive stimulation and from those on collective aggression (see the discussion below), my hunch is that such behavior is stimulated by both the heat and the group.

Attacks

Being attacked by another is especially conducive to aggression. Experiments at Kent State University by Stuart Taylor (Taylor & Pisano, 1971) and at Washington State University by Harold Dengerink (Dengerink & Myers, 1977) reveal that attacks breed retaliatory attacks. In these experiments one person competes with another in a reaction-time contest. After each test trial, the winner gets to choose how much shock to give the loser. Actually, each subject is playing a programmed opponent, one who steadily escalates the amount of shock. Do the real subjects respond charitably, "turning the other cheek"? Hardly. Extracting "an eye for an eye" is the more likely response. When attacked, subjects usually retaliate in kind.

"Military violence must be answered with violence."

Jeane Kirkpatrick (1981), U.S. Ambassador to the United Nations

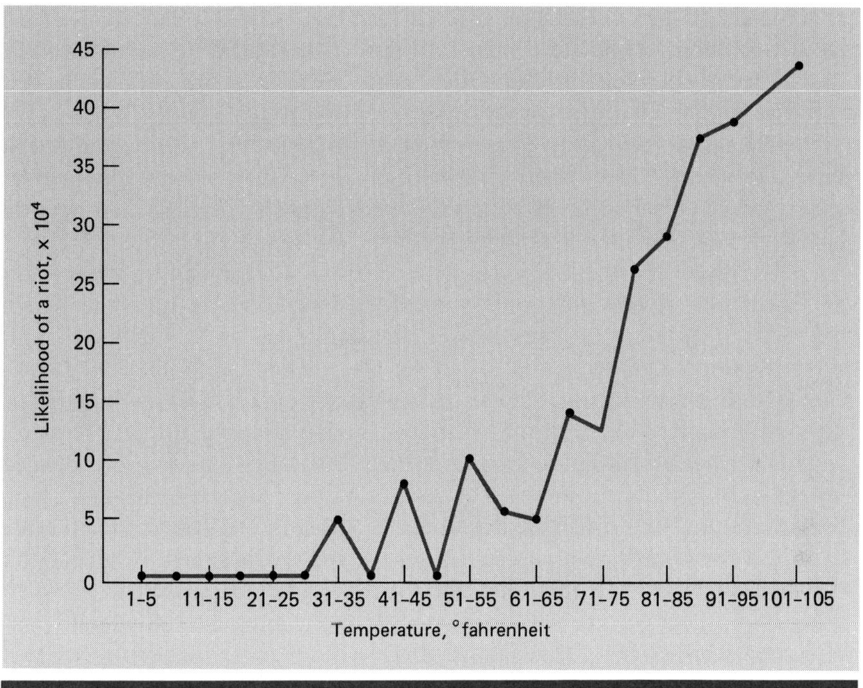

FIGURE 10-6 Between 1967 and 1971 the likelihood of a riot increased with temperature. This does not mean that most riots occurred at temperatures above 90°F. Rather, on any given day above 90°F a riot was more likely than on any given day of lower temperature. (Data from Carlsmith & Anderson, 1979.)

Arousal

So far we have seen that various aversive stimulations can arouse people's anger. Do other types of arousal, such as those that accompany exercise or sexual excitement, have a similar effect?

General Arousal

Imagine that Wanda, having just finished a stimulating short run, comes home to discover that her date for the evening called and left word that he had made other plans. Will Wanda more likely explode in fury after her run than if she discovered the same message just after awakening from a nap? Or, having just exercised, will her aggressive tendencies have been exorcised? To look for an answer, let's examine some intriguing research on how we interpret and label our bodily states.

In a now famous experiment, Stanley Schachter and Jerome Singer (1962) found that an aroused bodily state can be experienced in different ways. A group of men from the University of Minnesota were aroused by an injection of adrenalin, producing feelings of body flushing, heart palpitation, and more rapid breathing. When they were forewarned that the drug would produce these effects, they felt little emotion, even when with either a hostile or a euphoric person. Of course—they could readily attribute their bodily sensations to the drug. Another group of men were led to believe the drug produced no such side effects. Then they, too, were placed in the company of a person either hostile or euphoric. How did they feel and act? Angrily when with the hostile person. Joyfully when with the person who was euphoric.

The principle that arousal facilitates dominant responses (see Chapter 9) could also explain this. If the situation makes one angry, being aroused can amplify one's anger.

This discovery—that a given state of bodily arousal can be steered into an experience of one emotion or another, depending on how the person interprets and labels the arousal—was later confirmed by Russell Geen, John Rakosky, and Roger Pigg (1972; but see also Leventhal, 1980). They had a confederate subject administer electric shocks to some University of Missouri men while they were reading a sexually stimulating story. Either experience would have been sufficient to arouse the men. But, while wired to physiological instruments, some were shown dials indicating they were experiencing strong "shock arousal" but little "sexual arousal." Others were shown dials that led them to believe their arousal came from the story. Those led to believe that the shocks had aroused them had their emotion steered into anger. So when it was their turn to shock, they reciprocated by shocking the confederate more often and more strongly (see Figure 10-7).

In similar experiments, Dolf Zillmann, Jennings Bryant, and their collaborators (see Zillmann & Bryant, 1974; Bryant & Zillmann, 1979; Zillmann, Katcher, & Milavsky, 1972) found that when aroused people—people who have just pumped an exercise bike or watched a film of a Beatles rock concert—are provoked, they often find it easy to misattribute their arousal to the provocation. They then retaliate with heightened aggression.

FIGURE 10-7 What emotion we experience depends upon how we interpret and label our bodily states. For example, if we attribute arousal to aggressive stimuli, we will likely experience anger.

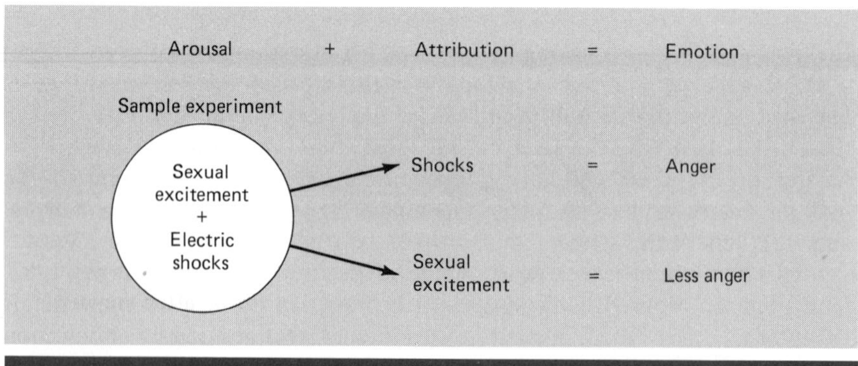

While common sense might assume that Wanda's run would have drained her aggressive tensions, enabling her to accept the insulting news calmly, these studies suggest that being aroused can actually feed emotions.

Having followed this theoretical reasoning, you should be able to predict the outcome of the following experiment. Jonathan Younger and Anthony Doob (1978) gave University of Toronto women a fake pill, telling half of them that the pill would produce arousal, the other half that it would produce a "general feeling of calm and relaxation." After a confederate subject had insulted and annoyed the women, they were invited to shock the confederate as part of a study of "the effects of punishment on creative responding." Question: Which group of women delivered the most shocks—those who had expected to be aroused by the pill or those who expected to feel relaxed?

Younger and Doob predicted that those who had expected the pill to be arousing would attribute their arousal to the pill; hence they would be neither very angry nor aggressive. Indeed, these women were no more aggressive than those who had been provoked not at all. On the other hand, the women who had expected to feel relaxed, but now felt aroused, could only attribute their arousal to the irritating confederate. It was they who more strongly retaliated.

Sexual Arousal

The arousal study summarized in Figure 10-7 is suggestive. It hints that sexual arousal might in an angered person actually amplify aggression. If true, our knowledge of such could prove beneficial. In the United States, the tolerance of sexually explicit stimuli has increased ever since the 1970 U.S. Commission on Obscenity and Pornography concluded that, as far as it could determine, viewing such stimuli has no adverse effects. Even on commercial television, "seductive behaviors and sexual innuendos" have "substantially increased in frequency since 1975" (Silverman, Sprafkin, & Rubinstein, 1978; 1979).

"Research . . . has found no evidence to date that exposure to explicit sexual materials plays a significant role in the causation of delinquent or criminal behavior among youth or adults."

U. S. Commission on Obscenity and Pornography (1970, p. 27)

Generalizing from laboratory research, we can speculate that television's comparatively mild sexual stimuli likely do not increase aggression. Robert Baron (1977) and others have found in their experiments that mild erotic stimuli (for example, pictures of seminude women shown to young men) can actually *decrease* aggressive behavior. Apparently, after being angered, viewing such stimuli is as likely to distract attention from the provocation as to amplify the anger.

However, highly erotic stimuli—say, X-rated magazine pictures or a passionate excerpt from an X-rated film—seem, at least upon normal college males, to have a different effect. For example, assume that, like the Iowa State University men in an experiment by Edward Donnerstein, Marcia Donnerstein, and Ronald Evans (1975), you were shown either nonsexual pictures or those mildly or highly erotic. Either before or after viewing the pictures, a supposed fellow participant in the experiment insults and curses you. Then, later, as feedback for this fellow's incorrect answers on a learning

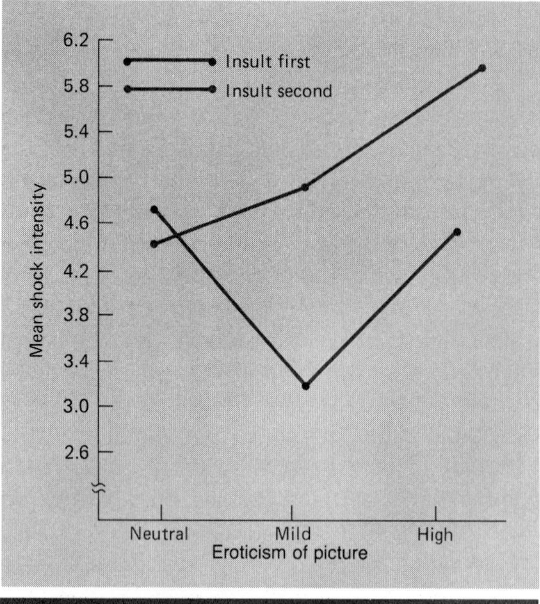

FIGURE 10-8 After viewing highly erotic pictures, participants delivered more intense shock than after viewing mildly arousing pictures. Aggression was especially high when the participants were insulted *after* rather than *before* being sexually aroused, thus enabling them to attribute their arousal to their anger. (Data from Donnerstein, Donnerstein, & Evans, 1975.)

task, you must choose how much to shock him. As indicated in Figure 10-8, those who had viewed the highly arousing pictures applied stronger shocks than those who viewed the mildly erotic pictures. What is more, those who were insulted *after* being aroused were especially aggressive. Following the simple theory in Figure 10-7, can you reason why?

The most recent experiments have been especially concerned with one type of increasingly popular pornography: that depicting aggression against women (Malamuth & Spinner, 1980). A typical episode of sexual violence might depict a rapist forcing himself upon a female victim. She at first resists, tries to fight off her attacker. But gradually she becomes sexually aroused and as she does, her resistance melts. By the end she is in ecstacy, pleading for more. We have all viewed or read nonpornographic versions of this sequence: Dashing man grabs and forcibly kisses protesting woman. Within moments, the arms that were pushing him away are clutching him tight, her resistance overwhelmed by her unleashed passion.

Such portrayals, though out of touch with reality, are common, and they affect people. In what ways do you suppose? Experiments suggest three effects (Donnerstein & Malamuth, 1982). First, not only are convicted rapists sexually aroused by rape depictions, but (assuming the woman is portrayed as enjoying the rape) college men and women as well (Able et al., 1977; Malamuth, 1981; Malamuth, Heim, & Feshbach, 1980; Schmidt, 1975). (If that is disturbing, remember that the viewer or reader is given a vivid sexual depiction, not just the idea of a rape, as you just were.)

Second, viewing scenes of a man overpowering and arousing a woman can distort one's sense of how women actually respond to sexual violence. For example, Neil Malamuth and James Check (1981) compared University of Manitoba men who were shown either two nonsexual movies or two movies nonpornographically depicting a man sexually overpowering a woman. A week later, when surveyed by a different experimenter, those who had seen the films with mild sexual violence more readily accepted the myth that many women enjoy rape. Note that the film's sexual message was subtle: It was unlikely to elicit counterarguing. (Recall from Chapter 8 that persuasion is greatest when a message is slipped in without provoking people to counterargue.) If viewing just two such movies can have a discernible effect upon beliefs about women, what cumulative learning occurs from viewing many such films? Perhaps we should not be surprised that while Malamuth, Scott Haber, and Seymour Feshbach (1980) found that a sample of UCLA women all believed that they would personally derive absolutely no pleasure from being victimized, many believed there are *other* women who would: "Some women might be turned on by an overpowering man. But me? Not on your life." Believing that women enjoy rape is especially common among rapists, many of whom slur their victims with such slanderings as "You know you want it! You *all* want it!" (Gager & Schurr, 1976).

Third, recent experiments indicate that viewing sexual violence can increase aggression, particularly that of men against women. Edward Donnerstein (1980) showed 120 University of Wisconsin men either a neutral, an erotic, or an aggressive-erotic (rape) film. Then, the men, supposedly as part of another experiment, "taught" a male or female confederate some nonsense syllables by choosing how much shock to administer for incorrect answers. The men who had watched the rape film administered markedly stronger shocks—but only toward female victims (see Figure 10-9). In subsequent experiments, Donnerstein and Leonard Berkowitz (1981) found the same result, and it did not matter whether the rape film depicted the woman as suffering or enjoying herself. Evidently, just as children's inhibitions against aggression are lowered after observing an aggressive model, so too are men's, especially when the men are angered and when their potential victim is like (for example, in gender) the filmed victim.

If you are troubled by the ethics of conducting experiments such as these, rest assured that these researchers appreciate the controversial and powerful experience they are giving their participants. Thus the participants are forewarned about what they may be shown. Only after giving their knowing consent do they participate. Moreover, after the experiment any rape myths that the film may have communicated are discredited. One hopes that such debriefing sufficiently offsets the vivid image of a supposedly ecstatic rape victim (C. W. Sherif, 1980). Judging from a study with University of Minnesota students by Check and Malamath (1983), it does. Those who viewed an aggressive-erotic film and were then debriefed became less accepting of the

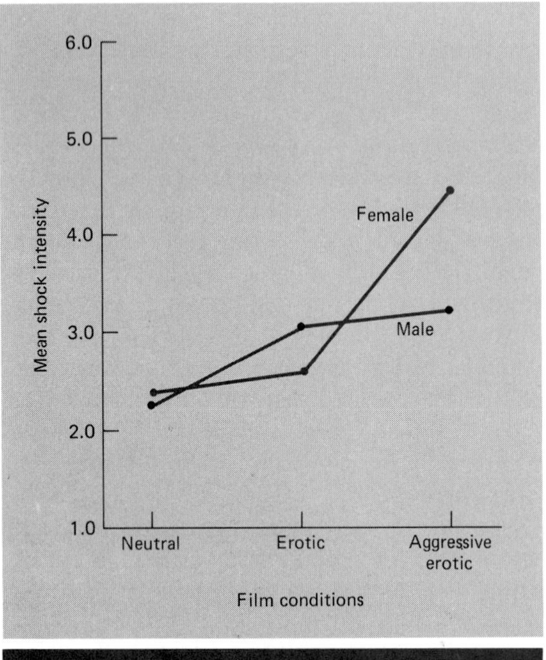

FIGURE 10-9 After viewing an aggressive-erotic film, college men delivered stronger shocks than before, especially to a woman. (Data from Donnerstein, 1980.)

"women-enjoy-rape" myth than were students who had not seen the film. Similarly, Donnerstein and Berkowitz (1981) found that Wisconsin students who viewed pornography and were then thoroughly debriefed were later *less* likely than other students to agree that "Being roughed up is sexually stimulating to many women."

Justification for this experimentation is not only scientific, but also humanitarian. In 1980, some 82,000 American females—one every six minutes—were known to have suffered the horror of forcible rape, more than twice the number reported during the mid-1960s (FBI, 1971 to 1980). How many more unreported and unconfirmed cases occur is anybody's guess. When "normal" college males are asked whether there is any likelihood that they would rape a woman "if you could be assured that no one would know and that you could in no way be punished," a disturbing proportion—about 35 percent—admit to at least a possibility of their doing so. Is this result believable? Researcher Malamuth (1981) concludes that it is. Compared to men who indicate no possibility of their raping, those who do are more like convicted rapists in their beliefs in rape myths and in their being sexually aroused even by rape depictions that portray a resistant, unaroused victim. Moreover, those who indicate most likelihood of raping behave more aggressively toward women in laboratory settings.

Malamuth and Donnerstein are among those alarmed by the increasing vulnerability of women to rape. Without oversimplifying the complex causes

BEHIND THE SCENES

Ed Donnerstein and Neil Malamuth

Rape and other forms of violence against women continue to be a major social problem. As social psychologists we are fortunate to have skills that allow us to investigate some of the causes of this violence. We began by examining pornography as one possible cause, and soon recognized that various media depictions of women could lead to negative attitudes and behaviors toward women. This type of research is a good example of how social issues can be translated into empirical research. There are many questions still unanswered, but the work is exciting from both theoretical and applied viewpoints.

It has been quite interesting to see how TV and newspapers have treated our work. There seems to be a strong tendency for the press to "read into" many of our published reports. While one individual will state that pornography leads to aggression, another will write that it does not. It is not surprising that research on highly sensitive social issues, like pornography, should be of considerable interest to the press. Learning how to deal with the public media has been a valuable experience for us both. *(Ed Donnerstein, University of Wisconsin, and Neil Malamuth, University of Manitoba)*

of rape, they conclude that viewing sexual violence can have antisocial effects. Commenting on these results, Susan Brownmiller (1980), author of *Against Our Will: Women and Rape*, argues against our tolerance of aggressive pornography. Liberal thinkers, she states, would not tolerate pornographic depictions of Jewish victims being abused by Gentiles, or of blacks being abused by whites, but have condoned such when women are the victims of men. Brownmiller calls for an end to this double standard.

Television

In this chapter we have seen that children's observations of an aggressive model can unleash their aggressive urges and teach them new ways to aggress. And we have seen that, after viewing sexual violence against a woman, college men tend to act more violently toward a woman who has angered them. Such findings prompt many people to be concerned about television's effect on the behavior and thinking of its viewers.

Consider these few facts about watching television. In 1945, the Gallup poll asked Americans, "Do you know what television is?" (Gallup, 1972, p. 551). Today, 98 percent of American households have a TV set, more than have bathtubs or telephones. In the average home, the set is on some $6\frac{3}{4}$ hours per day; the typical member of the household watches it 3 to 5 of these hours (Nielsen, 1981; Comstock et al., 1978). Women watch more than men, nonwhites more than whites, the very old and young more than the middle-aged, and the less educated more than the highly educated. For the most part, these facts about Americans' viewing habits also characterize those of Europeans, Australians, and Japanese (Murray & Kippax, 1979).

During all those hours, what social behaviors are being modeled? Since 1967, George Gerbner, Larry Gross, and their fellow TV watchers (1980) at the University of Pennsylvania have been sampling prime-time and Saturday morning entertainment network programs in the United States. Their findings? Eight of ten programs contained violence. Prime-time programs have averaged five violent acts per hour; Saturday morning children's programs almost eighteen per hour. During the late 1960s and the 1970s the yearly rates of televised cruelty varied by no more than 10 percent from the average for the whole period. [By comparison the frequency of sexual innuendos on prime-time programs increased tenfold during the last half of the 1970s (Sprafkin & Silverman, 1981).]

Televised violence: *"The overt expression of physical compelling action against one's will on pain of being hurt or killed, or actually hurting or killing."*

George Gerbner et al. (1980)

Analyses of television's content during the 1970s revealed that violence levels changed little and that sexual content increased. (Drawing by Barsotti; © 1978 *The New Yorker* Magazine, Inc.)

So, given these two facts—(1) an enormous amount of television watching—more than 1000 hours a year per person, and (2) a heavy dose of aggression in the typical television diet—it is difficult to resist being concerned about the cumulative effects of such viewing. Does prime-time crime stimulate the behavior it depicts? Or, as viewers vicariously participate in aggressive acts, do the shows drain off aggressive energy?

The latter idea, a variation on the *catharsis* hypothesis, postulates that experiencing an emotion is a way to release it. Generalized to viewing aggression, the catharsis hypothesis would maintain that violent drama enables people to release their pent-up hostilities. Defenders of the media cite this theory frequently, and remind us that violence predates television. In an imaginary debate with one of television's critics, the medium's defender might argue, "The genocides of Jews and American Indians were certainly not provoked by television. Television mostly just reflects and caters to our tastes." "Agreed," responds the critic, "but it's also true that during America's TV age violent crime has increased several times faster than the population rate." The defender objects: "That national trend is the result of many complex factors. At the time television was introduced, *violent* crime did not jump. In fact, TV may even reduce aggression by keeping people off the streets and by offering them a harmless opportunity to vent their aggression."

Catharsis: *Emotional release. The catharsis view of aggression is that aggressive drive is reduced when one "releases" aggressive energy, either by acting aggressively or by fantasizing aggression.*

And so the debate goes on. However, the approximately 3000 studies of television and human behavior (Murray, 1980) do shed some light on this controversy. Two issues are addressed by this research: (1) how television affects viewers' *behavior* (for example, are people more or less aggressive after viewing aggressive behavior?), and (2) how television affects viewers' *thinking* (for example, do heavy doses of violence desensitize people to violence?).

"One of television's great contributions is that it brought murder back into the home where it belongs. Seeing a murder on television can be good therapy. It can help work off one's antagonisms."

Alfred Hitchcock

Effects on Behavior

Do viewers tend to imitate the behavior of violent models? Examples abound of people reenacting crimes portrayed on television: Recall the six teenagers who, after watching a movie about youth who set derelicts on fire for kicks, then went out and did the same to a Boston woman. In one informal survey of 208 prison convicts, 9 out of 10 admitted that by watching crime programs they learn new criminal tricks. And 4 out of 10 said they had attempted specific crimes they had seen on television (*TV Guide*, 1977).

Correlation of TV Viewing and Behavior

But such is not scientific evidence. Nor does it tell us how television affects the aggressiveness of those who have never committed violent crimes. Researchers therefore have used both correlational and experimental studies to examine the effects of viewing violence. One technique, commonly used with schoolchildren, is simply to see whether individuals' TV watching predicts their aggressiveness. Results indicate that the more violent the content of the child's TV viewing, the more aggressive the child (Eron, 1982;

Huesmann, 1982). The relationship is modest, but consistently found, in the United States, Europe, and Australia.

So, may we conclude that a violent TV diet contributes to aggression? Perhaps you are already thinking that this is correlational research, so the cause-effect relation could also work in the opposite direction. Maybe aggressive children prefer aggressive programs. Or maybe some underlying third factor, such as lower intelligence, predisposes some children both to prefer aggressive programs and to act out their own aggression.

Researchers have developed two ways to test these alternative explanations. The "hidden-third-factor" explanation can be tested by statistically pulling out the influence of some of these possible factors. For example, British researcher William Belson (1978; Muson, 1978) studied 1565 London boys and found that, compared to those who watched little violence, those who watched a great deal (especially realistic rather than cartoon violence) admitted to 50 percent more violent acts during the preceding six months (for example, "I busted the telephone in a telephone box"). Belson also examined twenty-two likely "third factors," such as family size. The heavy and light viewers still differed after equating them on the potential third factors, so Belson surmised that the heavy viewers were indeed more violent *because* of their TV exposure.

Similarly, Leonard Eron and Rowell Huesmann (1980) also found that viewing violence correlates with aggressiveness even after statistically pulling out several obvious possible third factors. Moreover, they restudied 211 boys ten years after studying them as eight-year-olds, and discovered that viewing violence at age eight somewhat predicted their aggressiveness at age nineteen, but that aggressiveness at age eight did *not* predict their viewing of violence at age nineteen. Aggression followed viewing violence. But the reverse did not occur (findings that have been confirmed in a new study of 700 Chicago-area youngsters). Thus, Eron and Huesmann surmise that viewing violence does indeed enhance aggressiveness.

Is televised violence senseless? One network vice-president explained that in his network's shows, violence "is in context, is germane to the plot, advances character development, and is never [senseless]." (Swafford, 1980.) (© 1980 King Features Syndicate)

Notice that these studies illustrate how researchers are now using correlational findings to *suggest* cause and effect. Yet, an infinite number of possible "third factors" could be creating a merely coincidental relation between viewing violence and aggression. To identify and extract all these is impossible. Fortunately, however, the experimental method can control all these extraneous factors. If some children are randomly assigned to watch a violent film, and others a nonviolent film, any subsequent aggression difference between the two groups must be due to the only factor that distinguishes them: what they watched.

Experiments on TV Viewing

The pioneering experiments were conducted by Albert Bandura and Richard Walters (1963), who sometimes had young children view the adult pounding the Bobo doll on film instead of observing it live, and by Leonard Berkowitz and Russell Geen (1966), who found that angered college students who viewed a violent film acted more aggressively than did similarly angered students who viewed nonaggressive films. These laboratory experiments, coupled with the American public's growing concern, were sufficient to prompt the U.S. Surgeon General to commission fifty new research studies during the early 1970s. By and large, these studies confirmed that viewing violence amplifies aggression.

In a later series of experiments, a team of researchers led by Ross Parke (1977) in the United States and Jacques Leyens (1975) in Belgium showed institutionalized American and Belgian delinquent boys a series of either aggressive or nonaggressive commercial films. Their consistent finding: "Exposure to movie violence . . . led to an increase in viewer aggression." For example, compared to the week preceding the film series, physical attacks increased sharply in cottages where boys were viewing violent films.

"Then shall we simply allow our children to listen to any story anyone happens to make up, and so receive into their minds ideas often the very opposite of those we shall think they ought to have when they are grown up?"

Plato,
The Republic

Television research has involved a variety of methods and participants. One ambitious researcher, Susan Hearold (1979), recently assembled results from 230 correlational and experimental studies involving more than 100,000 people. Her conclusion: Viewing antisocial portrayals is indeed associated with antisocial behavior. Its effect is not overwhelming and is, in fact, at times not evident. Moreover, the aggression provoked by these studies is not assault and battery; it is more on the scale of a shove in the lunch line, a cruel comment, a threatening gesture.

Nevertheless, the convergence of evidence from this variety of studies is striking. Experimental studies point most clearly to cause and effect, but they are sometimes remote from real life (for example, pushing a hurt button). Moreover, the experiments can but hint at the cumulative effects of witnessing 13,000 murders, as does the average American child during the elementary and junior high school years. On the other hand, while the correlational studies are complicated by the inclusion of an unidentifiable number of other influences, they do tap the cumulative effects.

"The consensus among most of the research community is that violence on television does lead to aggressive behavior by children and teen-agers who watch the programs."

National Institute of Mental Health (1982)

The conclusion drawn both by the Surgeon General and by these researchers is *not* that television is a primary cause of social violence, any more than cyclamates are a primary cause of cancer. However, it is a cause. And even if it is just one among many contributors, it is one that, like cyclamates, is potentially controllable. Given this convergence of correlational and experimental evidence, researchers have turned some of their attention to exploring *why* viewing violence has this effect. Perhaps from earlier sections of this chapter you can anticipate their explanations.

Three possibilities have been suggested. One is that it's not the violent content per se that causes social violence, but the *arousal* produced by the exciting action (Tannenbaum & Zillmann, 1975). Being aroused can energize behavior.

Other research indicates that viewing violence also can produce *disinhibition*. In Bandura's experiment, the adult's punching the Bobo doll seemed to legitimate such outbursts; thus the children's own inhibitions were lowered. Similarly, Berkowitz (1964) found that after college men view someone getting a well-deserved beating, they are less inhibited about shocking someone who is similar to (for example, even merely having the same name as) the film's victim.

That media portrayals also evoke *imitation* was made apparent when the children in Bandura's experiments reenacted the specific behaviors they had witnessed. The $10 billion-a-year American television industry is hard-pressed to dispute that television prompts viewers to imitate what has been seen. Its advertising income is supported by this conclusion. Thus, advertisers employ models, the observation of which presumably affects viewers' behavior. Television's critics agree—and are troubled that on TV programs assaults outnumber affectionate acts 4 to 1, and that most allusions to sexual intercourse occur between unmarried couples or involve a prostitute (Fernandez-Collado & Greenberg, 1978; Lowry, Love, & Kirby, 1981).

Prosocial behavior: *Positive, constructive, helpful social behavior; the opposite of antisocial behavior.*

If the ways of relating and problem solving modeled on television do tend to produce imitation, especially among young viewers, then modeling *prosocial* behavior should be socially beneficial. Chapter 11 contains good news: Television's subtle influence can indeed teach children positive lessons in behavior.

Effects on Thinking

Other researchers are examining the cognitive effects of viewing violence: Does prolonged viewing desensitize us to cruelty? Does it distort our perceptions of reality?

Take some emotion-arousing stimulus, say an obscene word, and repeat it over and over. What happens? If you have studied introductory psychology, you may recall that the emotional response is likely to "extinguish." After witnessing thousands of cruelties, there is good reason to expect a similar emotional numbing. Perhaps the most common response might well become "Doesn't bother me at all." Such a response is precisely what Victor Cline, Roger Croft, and Steven Courrier (1973) observed when they measured the physiological arousal of 121 Utah boys viewing a brutal boxing match.

Compared to boys who watched little television, those who watched a great deal were minimally aroused; their responses to the beating resembled more a shrug than a concern.

"All television is educational. The question is, what is it teaching?"

Nicholas Johnson, Former Commissioner, Federal Communications Commission (1978)

Of course these boys might differ in ways other than their television viewing. Yet, in a series of experiments, Ronald Drabman and Margaret Thomas (1974; 1975; 1976; Thomas & Drabman, 1975; Thomas, Horton, Lippincott, & Drabman, 1977; Geen, 1981) confirmed that viewing violence breeds indifference—a more blasé reaction when later viewing the film of a brawl or when actually observing two children fighting.

Does viewing television's fictional world also mold our conceptions of the real world? George Gerbner and his University of Pennsylvania associates (1979) suspect this is television's most potent effect. Their surveys of both adolescents and adults show that heavy viewers (four hours a day or more) are more likely than light viewers (two hours or less) to exaggerate the frequency of violence in the world around them and to fear being personally assaulted. Similarly, a recent national survey of American seven- to eleven-year-old children gave evidence that heavy viewers were more likely than light viewers to admit to fears "that somebody bad might get into your house," or that "when you go outside, somebody might hurt you" (Peterson & Zill, 1981).

Researchers are also investigating other positive and negative effects of television. My own hunch is that television's most influential effect occurs indirectly, as it each year replaces in people's lives a thousand or more hours of other activities they could be engaged in.

What Does Television Preempt?

Most American children spend more time watching television than in school, in fact more time than in *any* other activity save one: sleep. If there were no television, would they spend those thousands of hours in more worthwhile pursuits or not?

It is interesting to discover what people spend less time doing once television is introduced into their homes. According to a multination UNESCO study, television owners sleep less, read less, and talk less. They also spend less time in religious activities, leisure travel, and socializing with friends (Robinson, 1972). Other researchers have found that the introduction of television into a culture greatly shrinks activities that are most similar to television watching—namely, entertainments such as movie attendance, radio listening, and comic book reading (Murray & Kippax, 1979).

Developmental psychologists such as Jerome Bruner (1975) and Jean Piaget have stressed the contribution of active play to children's intellectual development. As one National Institute of Mental Health report put it, "The child lives and grows through action" (Lichtenbert & Norton, 1970). If this is so, then the passivity that accompanies television watching may slow intellectual growth. Dorothy Singer and Jerome Singer (1979), codirectors of Yale University's television research center, note that even quiet reading is

"I'll tell you what we did with our evenings before television. We gave dinner parties. We went to dinner parties. We read. We worked jigsaw puzzles. We went to plays. We went to concerts. We went to movies. We popped corn. We played cards. We went dancing. We took walks. We bowled. We attended meetings. We took classes. We went . . ."

(Reprinted from *Better Homes and Gardens* Magazine. (© Copyright Merideth Corporation 1977. All rights reserved.)

more conducive to cognitive activity. When reading, unlike when viewing most television programs, they further write,

> You are in control of the pace. You can reread a sentence, turn back to an earlier page and take the time to piece together combinations of images and words. As you read you are also more likely on occasion to drift away into more extended private images and thoughts about the material.
>
> In effect, you are engaging in a more creative act of imagination and perhaps also in the forming of new combinations of words and images. Reading seems, therefore, harder work than watching television but ultimately more rewarding because it enhances your own imaginative capacities.

Group Aggression

In this chapter we have considered the circumstances that induce *individuals* to aggress. Because social psychologists study the social thinking and actions of individuals, it is appropriate for them to study individual aggression. But much aggression, such as gang fights, riots, and wars, is collective. Sociologists' analyses of "subcultures of violence" and of the stages through which a riot usually unfolds have deepened our understanding of aggression by groups. Social psychology likewise can enhance our understanding of group aggression.

First, the same circumstances that provoke individuals to aggress can provoke groups to do likewise. If frustrations, insults, and aggressive models heighten the aggressive tendencies of isolated people, then such factors will likely prompt the same reaction in those gathered together. For example, at a riot's beginning, acts of aggression often spread rapidly after being "triggered" by the aggressive example of one antagonistic person. Normally law-abiding bystanders, after observing looters freely helping themselves to TV sets or steaks, often drop their ethical inhibitions and imitate.

Laboratory experiments reveal two ways in which a group situation can actually amplify aggressive reactions of individuals. Consider decisions made in wartime. Decisions to attack typically are made by strategists remote from the front lines. The strategists have a buffer between themselves and the actual violence: They give orders. Others carry them out. Does such distancing make it easier to recommend aggression?

Jacquelin Gaebelein and Anthony Mander (1978) created a laboratory version of this situation. They asked their University of North Carolina at Greensboro students either to shock someone or to advise another person how much shock to administer. When the subjects who were asked to do the shocking were provoked by the recipient, they and the advisers independently favored approximately the same amount of shock. But when the recipient was relatively innocent of any provocation, as are most victims of mass aggression, the front-line person was inclined to give lower shock levels than those recommended by the advisers. Apparently the advisers' inhibitions against aggression were diminished by their not being directly responsible for the hurting.

As the wartime examples suggest, aggressive decisions often are made not by an individual strategist, but by a group of strategists. Does group interaction magnify the aggressive tendencies of individuals, much as it polarizes other individual tendencies? (See Chapter 9.) Experiments by two Israeli social psychologists, Yoram Jaffe and Yoel Yinon (1979) indicate that it does. In one, university men who were angered by a supposed fellow subject retaliated with decisions to give much stronger shocks when in groups than when alone. In another experiment (Jaffe, Shapir, & Yinon, 1981), unskilled workers decided, either alone or in groups, how much punishing shock to give someone for incorrect answers on an ESP task. As Figure 10-10 indicates, individuals administered progressively more of the assumed shock as the experiment proceeded, and group decision making magnified this individual

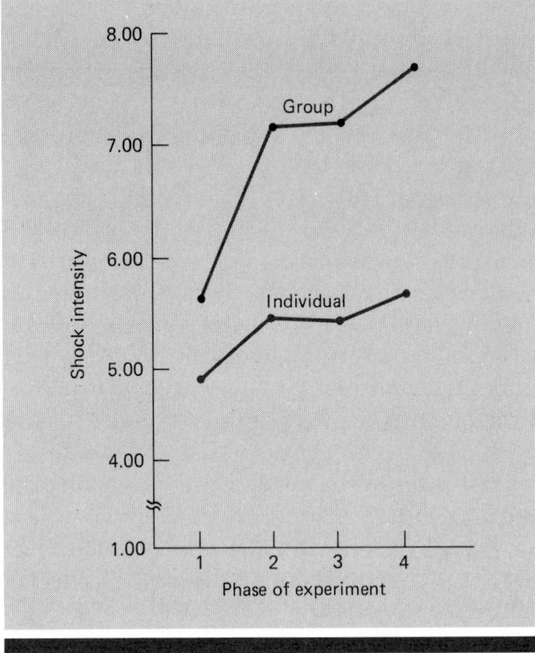

FIGURE 10-10 When individuals chose how much shock to administer as punishment for wrong answers, they escalated the shock level as the experiment proceeded. Group decision making further polarized this tendency. (Data from Jaffe, Shapir, & Yanon, 1981.)

tendency. These experiments suggest that when circumstances provoke an individual's aggressive reaction, the addition of group interaction will often amplify it. Thus, children's imitation of televised aggressive acts tends to increase when they view and then play in pairs, rather than alone (Drabman & Thomas, 1977).

REDUCING AGGRESSION

We have examined three prominent theories about the causes of aggression (instinct, frustration-aggression, and social learning), and we have scrutinized several influences upon aggression. Obviously, the forces producing aggression cannot be eliminated. How, then, might aggression be minimized? Do theory and research suggest ways to control aggression?

Catharsis

"Youngsters should be taught to vent their anger." So advises Ann Landers (1969). If a person "bottles up his rage, we have to find an outlet. We have to give him an opportunity of letting off steam." So asserted the prominent psychiatrist, Fritz Perls (1973). Both statements assume what earlier we called the hydraulic model—that one's accumulated aggressive energy, be it from the buildup of instinctual impulses or from frustrations, needs a release.

The catharsis hypothesis straightforwardly implies the hydraulic model. Catharsis usually is credited to Aristotle. Although Aristotle actually said nothing about aggression, he did argue that one can purge emotions by experiencing them, and that viewing the classic tragedies therefore enabled a catharsis ("purgation") of pity and fear. To have an emotion excited, he believed, is subsequently to have that emotion released (Butcher, 1951). The catharsis hypothesis has been extended to include the emotional release supposedly obtained not only by the observations of drama, but also through the recall and reliving of past events, through the expression of emotions, and through various actions. In such ways, one can supposedly "blow off a little steam."

Assuming that aggressive action or fantasy drains pent-up aggression, thus reducing the aggressive urge, some therapists and group leaders have encouraged people to ventilate their suppressed aggression by acting it out—by whopping one another with foam bats, or beating a bed with a tennis racket while screaming. Parents have been similarly advised to encourage their children's release of emotional tension in various kinds of aggressive play. Is the catharsis approach valid? Does it work?

The catharsis hypothesis predicts that aggressive drive will be reduced after one releases aggressive energy. (Paolo Koch/Rapho/Photo Researchers, Inc.)

The idea indeed does have a long and distinguished history. Yet, a distinguished history does not validate a truth. Contrary to the suppositions of Freud, Lorenz, and their followers, the near consensus among social psychologists today is that the catharsis view of aggression has not been confirmed (Geen & Quanty, 1977). For example, Robert Arms and his associates report that Canadian and American spectators of football, wrestling, and hockey exhibit *more* hostility after viewing the event than before (Arms, Russell, & Sandilands, 1979; Goldstein & Arms, 1971). Not even a war seems to purge a people's aggressive feelings. In fact, after a war, a nation's murder rate tends to jump (Archer & Gartner, 1976).

In more direct laboratory tests of the catharsis hypothesis, Jack Hokanson and his colleagues (1961; 1962a; 1962b; 1963; 1966) found that when Florida State University students were allowed to counterattack someone who had provoked them, their arousal (as measured by their blood pressures) more quickly returned to normal. This calming effect of retaliation seems to occur only in very specific circumstances—when the target is one's actual tormentor, not a substitute, and when the retaliation is justifiable and the target nonintimidating, so that one does not afterward feel guilty or anxious.

However, a key question is: Does such aggressing reduce subsequent aggression? We need here to distinguish between consequences in the short run and the long run. Experiments dealing with aggression's short-run consequences give mixed results. Sometimes people who have aggressed do become less aggressive. But this result could have occurred because the procedures in these experiments produced *inhibition* rather than catharsis. The aggressor may have been inhibited by thinking, "If I overdo it, I could get into trouble" or "The poor guy has suffered enough."

"He who gives way to violent gestures will increase his rage."

Charles Darwin
The Expression of Emotion in Man and Animals

In other experiments, aggressing has actually led to heightened aggression. Ebbe Ebbesen, Birt Duncan, and Vladimir Konecni (1975) interviewed 100 engineers and technicians shortly after they were angered by layoff notices. Some were asked questions that gave them the opportunity to express their hostility against their employer or supervisor—for example, "What instances can you think of where the company has not been fair with you?" Afterwards, a secretary administered a questionnaire assessing their attitudes toward the company and the supervisor. Did the previous opportunity to "vent" or "drain off" their hostility reduce it? To the contrary, their hostility substantially increased. Expressing hostility bred more hostility.

Sound familiar? Recall from the Chapter 2 discussion of actions and attitudes that cruel acts beget cruel attitudes. Or, as we noted in analyzing Stanley Milgram's obedience experiments, little aggressive acts can breed their own justification, thus facilitating further aggressive acts. Even if retaliation may sometimes (in the short run) reduce tension, in the long run it may also reduce one's inhibitions. We can speculate that this will be true especially when, as often happens, the force of one's aggressive outburst is an overreaction to the provocation. Moreover, when people discover that retaliation is tension-reducing, this reinforcement may increase the likelihood of future retaliation. So, in the long run, aggression more likely breeds aggression than reduces it.

Should we therefore bottle up our anger and aggressive urges? Fortunately, there are other, nonaggressive ways to express our feelings and to inform others how their behavior affects us. Perhaps stating "I'm angry" or "When you talk like that I feel irritated" might communicate one's feelings in a way that leads the other to make amends rather than further escalate the aggression.

A Social Learning Approach

If aggressive behavior is learned rather than instinctive, then there is more hope for its control. However, such control will not be achieved by any simple formula. Unlike the simplicity of our instinctive kneejerk, aggression is very complex; it is influenced by a host of factors. Let us briefly review some and speculate how to counteract them.

We have seen that aversive experiences such as frustrated expectations and personal attacks arouse people, creating in them a readiness to aggress. Thus, it is likely wise to refrain from planting false, unreachable expectations in people's minds, as some believe President Lyndon Johnson did with his vision of the "Great Society"—a vision ironically followed by the 1960s riots. And in order not to provoke retaliation, we might teach people nonattacking ways to communicate their feelings.

"It was in the middle of rising expectations and the increased, though inadequate, social spending of the Great Society that the U.S. riots of 1967 and 1968 took place."

Jesse Jackson (1981)

We have seen that instrumental aggression is controlled by anticipated rewards and costs. This suggests that we should devote increased attention to how we might reward cooperative, nonaggressive behavior. For example, experiments have found that children become less aggressive when their aggressive behavior is ignored instead of being rewarded with attention, and when their nonaggressive behavior is reinforced (Hamblin et al., 1969). Punishing the aggressor is less consistently effective. Under ideal conditions—when the punishment is strong, prompt, and sure, when it is combined with reward for the desired behavior, and when the potential aggressor is not angry—the threat of punishment can deter aggression (R. A. Baron, 1977). Such was evident in 1969 when the Montreal police force went on a sixteen-hour strike. Widespread looting and destruction erupted—until the police returned. But the side effects of punishment, particularly physical punishment, can make it backfire. Punishment is aversive stimulation. It often models the very behavior it seeks to prevent. And it is coercive (recall that actions which are coerced with strong external justifications are not likely to be internalized). Perhaps these are some reasons why violent teenagers and child-abusing parents tend to come from homes where discipline took the form of harsh physical punishment (Bandura & Walters, 1959; Lefkowitz et al., 1976; Strauss & Gelles, 1980).

We have seen that observing aggressive models can lower one's inhibitions against aggression and elicit imitation. This suggests new steps to reduce brutal, dehumanizing portrayals on television, steps comparable to those already taken to reduce racist and sexist portrayals. Even more so, it suggests the desirability of providing nonaggressive models, people who exemplify effective nonviolence. Laboratory studies consistently find that restraint is as contagious as belligerence (Donnerstein & Donnerstein, 1977; R. A. Baron, 1977). Recall, too, the liberating power of a (disobedient) nonaggressive model in Milgram's obedience research. In this century, leaders such as Ghandi and Martin Luther King have been powerful exemplars of nonviolence.

We have seen that aggression is also learned by direct experience and is elicited by aggressive stimuli. This suggests reducing the availability of weapons, such as handguns. Jamaica in 1974 implemented a sweeping anticrime program that included strict gun control and censorship of guns scenes from television and movies (Diener & Crandall, 1979). In the following year, robberies dropped 25 percent, nonfatal shootings 37 percent. In Sweden, the toy industry has discontinued the sale of war toys. According to the Swedish Information Service (1980), Sweden decided that "Playing at war means learning to settle disputes by violent means."

Since arousal can be "steered" into hostility or other emotions, depending on the context, one can try to redirect a person's anger. This often works with children, whose anger can sometimes be converted to intense laughter. Once laughter occurs it is likely to breed a happier emotion. Similarly, mild sexual arousal and empathy are incompatible with anger.

All such incompatible responses tend to diminish aggression. Robert A. Baron (1976) illustrated this at an intersection near Purdue University. He instructed a driver to hesitate fifteen seconds in front of another car after the light changed to green. In response to this mild frustration, 90 percent of the drivers did what we might expect: They honked, a mildly aggressive act. If, while the light was red, a female pedestrian crossed between the two cars, disappearing by the time the light changed to green, the honking rate was still close to 90 percent. However, when this procedure was repeated with the pedestrian on crutches (evoking empathy), or dressed in a revealing outfit (evoking mild sexual arousal), or wearing an outlandish clown mask (evoking humor), the honking rate dropped to about 50 percent.

Experiments by Norma Feshbach and Seymour Feshbach (1981) confirm that empathy is indeed incompatible with aggression. They put some Los Angeles elementary school children through a ten week program that trained them to recognize others' feelings, to assume the perspective of other people, and to share their emotions. Compared to other children in control groups, those who received this empathy training became significantly less aggressive in their school behavior.

Suggestions such as these can help us minimize aggression (for more suggestions, see Goldstein et al., 1981). But given the complexity of aggression's causes, and the difficulty of controlling them, who can feel the optimism expressed by Andrew Carnegie when, in 1900, he forecast that in the twentieth century, "To kill a man will be considered as disgusting as we in this day consider it disgusting to eat one." Since Carnegie uttered those cheery words, some 200 million human beings have been killed. It is a sad irony that although we, today, understand human aggression better than ever before, we still express horror at the extent of humanity's inhumanity.

SUMMING UP

Aggression manifests itself in two forms: *hostile aggression* springing from emotions such as anger and intending to injure, and *instrumental aggression*, which while also aiming to hurt, is a means to some other end.

There are three broad theories of aggression. The *instinct* view is most commonly associated with Sigmund Freud and Konrad Lorenz. It contends that, if not discharged, aggressive energy will accumulate from within, like water accumulating behind a dam. Although the available evidence tends not to support the instinct view, aggression is biologically influenced by heredity, blood chemistry, and brain diseases.

According to the second view, *frustration* creates anger, and when aggressive cues are present this anger may be released as aggression. Frustration stems not from deprivation per se, but from the gap between one's expectations and one's achievements. Since expectations are driven higher by past achievements and by comparing oneself with others, affluent people often feel as frustrated as those who have less.

The third view, that of *social learning*, presents aggression as a learned behavior. By experience and by observing others' success we learn that aggression sometimes pays. Thus when we are aroused by an aversive experience and when it seems both safe and rewarding to aggress, we will likely do so. Aversive experiences include not only frustration, but also discomfort, pain, and personal attacks, both physical and verbal. In fact, arousal from almost any source, even physical exercise or sexual stimulation, can be steered by the environment into anger.

American television portrays considerable violence. Laboratory studies have found that viewing violent models increases aggressive behavior. So it is no wonder that researchers are now studying the impact of television. Correlational and experimental studies converge on the conclusion that viewing violence breeds a modest increase in aggressive behavior. It seems also both to desensitize viewers to aggression and to alter their perceptions of reality. However, television's greatest effect may be indirect as it preempts other activities.

Much aggression is committed by groups. Circumstances that provoke individuals may also provoke groups. In fact, the group situation seems to amplify aggressive reactions.

Can aggression be minimized? Contrary to the catharsis hypothesis, aggression seems more often to breed than to reduce further aggression. The social learning approach suggests controlling aggression by counteracting the factors that provoke it—for example, by teaching people how to minimize aversive stimulation, by rewarding and modeling nonaggression, and by eliciting reactions incompatible with aggression.

Chapter

Altruism: Helping Others

Discovered on October 26, 1965, in Indianapolis, Indiana, was the half-starved, brutalized body of sixteen-year-old Sylvia Likens. Since July, she had boarded with Gertrude Braniszewski, who, aided by her three teenage children and two neighborhood boys, had beaten, burned, and branded her. Sylvia had not accepted her degradation passively. She had fought back. Many neighbors had heard Sylvia's screams. Her biographer, Kate Millet (1979), records:

> They heard it for weeks on end. Judy Duke observed Sylvia's beatings and even described them to her mother once in the kitchen over the dinner dishes; the verdict was that the child deserved punishment. Mrs. Vermillion, living next door, her house a mere fourteen feet from Sylvia's basement window, must have heard the child's sufferings almost to madness week after week, before another sound, the sound of a coal shovel scraping the floor, made her trouble herself with the notion of calling the police. And stopped short of doing it. Just as Sylvia stopped short, the shovel no longer moving, signaling, crying out finally for help. . . .
>
> And so Mrs. Vermillion put down the phone, grumbled one more time to her husband . . . and slumped back into moral lassitude again. (pp. 22-23)

Why had Sylvia's neighbors not come to her aid? Were they callous, indifferent, apathetic? Were they, as Millet surmises, "vegetable minds"? If so, there are many such minds. Consider the following:

Kitty Genovese is set upon by a knife-wielding stalker as she returns to her apartment house at 3:00 a.m. Thirty-eight of her neighbors are aroused by her screams of terror and pleas for help: "Oh my God, he stabbed me! Please help me! Please help me!" Many of them come to their windows and watch while, for 35 minutes, she struggles to escape her attacker. Not until her attacker departs does anyone so much as call the police. Soon after, she dies.

Andrew Mormille is knifed in the stomach as he rides the subway home. After his attackers leave the car, eleven other riders watch the young man bleed to death.

An 18-year-old switchboard operator, working alone, is sexually assaulted. She momentarily escapes and runs naked and bleeding to the street, screaming for help. Forty pedestrians passively watch as the rapist tries to drag her back inside. Fortunately, two police officers happen by and arrest the assailant.

Eleanor Bradley trips and breaks her leg while shopping. Dazed and in pain, she pleads for help. For 40 minutes the stream of shoppers and executives simply parts and flows around her. Finally, a cab driver helps her to a doctor (Darley & Latané, 1968).

What is shocking is not that in these cases some people failed to help, but that virtually none did. In each of these groups (groups of thirty-eight, eleven, forty, and hundreds) almost 100 percent of those involved failed to respond. Why? Placed in the same or similar situations, would you, would I, react as they?

Of course, there are also anecdotes of great heroism:

Hearing the rumble of an approaching subway train, Everett Sanderson leapt down onto the tracks and raced the approaching headlights to rescue Michelle De Jesus, a four-year-old who had fallen from the platform. Three seconds before the train would have run her over, Sanderson flung Michelle into the crowd above. As the train roared in, he himself failed in his first effort to jump back to the platform. Then at the last instant, bystanders pulled him to safety (Young, 1977).

On a hillside in Jerusalem, 800 trees form a simple line, The Avenue of the Righteous. Beneath each tree is a plaque with the name of a European Christian who, during the Nazi holocaust, gave refuge to a Jew or Jews. These Christians knew that if the refugees were discovered, Nazi policy dictated that both host and refugee would suffer a common fate. Many did (Hellman, 1980).

Lesser acts of comforting, caring, and helping abound: People offer directions, donate money, give blood, without asking anything in return. Why and when will people perform such acts? And what can be done to lessen indifference and increase altruism? These are this chapter's primary questions.

Altruism is distinct from self-centeredness. An altruistic person is concerned and helpful even when no benefits are offered or expected in return. The classic illustration of altruism is Jesus' parable of the Good Samaritan:

Altruism: *Concern and help for others that asks nothing in return; devotion to others without conscious regard for one's self-interests.*

> There was once a man who was going down from Jerusalem to Jericho when robbers attacked him, stripped him, and beat him up, leaving him half dead. It so happened that a priest was going down that road; but when he saw the man, he walked on by on the other side. In the same way a Levite also came there, went over and looked at the man, and then walked on by on the other side. But a Samaritan who was traveling that way came upon the man, and when he saw him, his heart was filled with pity. He went over to him, poured oil and wine on his wounds and bandaged them; then he put the man on his own animal and took him to an inn, where he took care of him. The next day he took out two silver coins and gave them to the innkeeper. "Take care of him," he told the innkeeper, "and when I come back this way I will pay you whatever else you spend on him." (Luke 10:30–35)

The Samaritan illustrates altruism in a pure form. Filled with compassion, he voluntarily gives time, energy, and money to a total stranger, expecting neither repayment nor appreciation.

To study altruistic acts, social psychologists have examined the conditions under which people will perform such deeds. Before looking at what these experiments reveal, let us first set a foundation by considering three theories of altruism.

WHY DO WE HELP ONE ANOTHER?

Social Exchange: The Benefits and Costs of Helping

One explanation for altruism comes from what is called the *social-exchange theory:* Human interactions are guided by a "social economics." We exchange not only material goods and money, but also *social* goods—love, services, information, status (Foa & Foa, 1975). In doing so, we are said to use a "minimax" strategy—minimize costs, maximize rewards. Social-exchange theory does not contend that we consciously keep track of costs and rewards, but only that such considerations can be used to predict our behavior. Thus if we walk by an empty car with its lights on, we may briefly pause to try the driver's door, but if it is locked, we are unlikely to make the more costly effort of searching for the owner. We are more likely to give telephone change to a classmate (someone who can later reciprocate our help or whose esteem we covet) than to a stranger.

Social-exchange theory: *The theory that human interactions are transactions that aim to maximize one's rewards and minimize one's costs.*

How might this cost-benefit theory explain a person's decision whether to donate blood? Suppose that your campus is having a blood drive and

Minimax: *Minimize costs, maximize rewards.*

someone solicits your participation. Might you not weigh the *costs* of donating (pain, time, fatigue) versus not donating (guilt, disapproval) as well as the *benefits* of donating (feeling good about helping someone, free refreshments) versus not donating (saving the time, discomfort, and anxiety)? According to social exchange theory—and to studies of Wisconsin blood donors by Jane Allyn Piliavin, Dorcas Evans, and Peter Callero (1982) such are the subtle calculations that precede decisions to help or not.

"Men do not value a good deed unless it brings a reward."

Ovid, Epistulae ex Ponto

Rewards that motivate altruism may be either external or internal. When businesses donate money to improve their corporate image, or when someone offers a ride to another hoping to receive appreciation or friendship, the

BEHIND THE SCENES

Jane Allyn Piliavin

I gave blood twice as a teenager in New Jersey. On the second occasion—a hot summer day—a nurse had to do the venipuncture seemingly a dozen times before she found the vein. By the time the needle was in, I was drenched with sweat. It was perhaps fifteen years before I gave again, and only in response to a personal request to give for a little girl who was to have open-heart surgery. Five years later, I was asked to give again—this time for my husband's department chairman, who was having a bypass operation. This time, though, I kept going . . . and one morning I woke up realizing I had given a gallon of blood! "Why am I doing this?" I asked myself. Then, because I'm a social psychologist interested in altruism and helping, I asked, "Why would anybody do this?" That is how I began my research on commitment to regular blood donation.

I am much more interested in basic, theoretically oriented research than I am in research directed toward the solution of specific problems. However, my youthful ambition was to be a social worker, and my immediate family—father, mother, and sister—were blood donors. So, in this research, I am able to combine my basic theoretical interests in the determinants of altruism and helping behavior with the possibility of being able to contribute to the solution of a real human problem: the need for ever-increasing amounts of blood. I am therefore more excited about this research than I have been with any of my past work—because it's me. *(Jane Allyn Piliavin, University of Wisconsin)* desired reward is external. We give to get. Not surprisingly, we therefore seem most eager to help someone attractive to us, someone whose approval we desire (Krebs, 1970; Unger, 1979b).

The benefits of altruism also include internal self-rewards, such as calming one's own anxiety. When near someone in distress, people typically respond with empathy. A woman's scream outside your window will arouse and distress you. If you cannot reduce your arousal by interpreting the scream as a playful shriek, then you may take steps to help the person, thereby reducing your distress (Piliavin & Piliavin, 1973). Indeed, Dennis Krebs (1975) found that Harvard University men whose physiological responses and self-reports revealed the most empathy in response to another's distress also gave the most help to the person. As Everett Sanderson remarked after saving the child who fell from the subway platform, "If I hadn't tried to save that little girl, if I had just stood there like the others, I would have died inside. I would have been no good to myself from then on." Altruistic acts also increase our sense of self-worth. For example, nearly all the blood donors in Jane Piliavin's research agreed that giving blood "makes you feel good about yourself" and "gives you a feeling of self-satisfaction."

Some readers may object that the cost-benefit business is demeaning, because it takes the altruism out of altruism. Perhaps. In defense of the theory, however, is it not a credit to humanity that we can derive pleasure from helping others, that much of our behavior is not antisocial but "prosocial," that we can even find fulfillment in the giving of love? How much worse if we gained pleasure only by serving ourselves.

"True," the reader may reply, "Still, doesn't social-exchange theory imply that a helpful act is never truly altruistic, that we merely *call* it altruistic when its rewards are inconspicuous? If we help the screaming woman so that we might gain social approval, relieve our distress, or boost our self-image, is it really altruistic?" This is reminiscent of B. F. Skinner's (1971) analysis of altruism. We give credit to people for their good deeds, says Skinner, only when we don't know why they do them. (In the language of attribution theory, we attribute their behavior to their inner dispositions when we lack external explanations.) When the causes are conspicuous, we credit the causes, not the person.

Daniel Batson and his associates (1981) reasoned that an act is truly altruistic if, after observing another's distress, people seek to help even when they will no longer be troubled by observing the suffering person (for example, after passing a stranded motorist). On the other hand, if people are eager to help only when doing nothing means they must continue to be troubled by the other's suffering, then the act would be self-serving: Reducing the other's distress serves only to relieve one's own distress while observing. To simulate such conditions, Batson's research team had University of Kansas women observe a young woman suffering while she supposedly received electric shocks. During a pause in the experiment, the obviously upset victim explained to the experimenter that a childhood fall against an electric fence left her acutely sensitive to shocks. In sympathy, the experimenter suggested that perhaps the observer (the actual subject in this experiment) might be willing to trade places with her and so take the remaining shocks for her. Previously, half of these actual subjects had been led to feel a kinship with the suffering person (thus arousing their empathy). Half also believed that their part in the experiment was completed, so that in any case they were done observing the woman's suffering. Nevertheless, their empathy aroused, virtually all these student observers willingly offered to substitute for the victim, taking on her suffering. This suggests that helping behavior is sometimes motivated by a genuine altruistic concern for others. Relieving another's suffering can be inherently rewarding (Hoffman, 1981).

There is, however, a weakness in social-exchange theory. It easily degenerates into explaining-by-naming. If someone volunteers for the Big Sister tutor program, it is tempting to "explain" her compassionate action in terms of the satisfaction it brings her. But such after-the-fact naming of rewards creates a circular explanation: "Why did she volunteer?" "Because of the inner rewards." "How do you know there are inner rewards?" "Why else would she have volunteered?" It is precisely because of such circularity that the philosophical doctrine of "psychological egoism"—the idea that all behavior is motivated by self-interest—has fallen into disrepute. It is called a tautology: a statement that cannot be falsified. Egoism can be stretched to include all possible motivations. When a theory excludes nothing, it says nothing.

To escape the circularity, we must define the rewards and costs independently of the behavior that is being explained. Thus, if social approval is presumed to motivate helping, then in experiments we should find that when approval is tied to helping, helping increases. And it does (see Staub, 1978). Moreover, the cost-benefit analysis says something else. It suggests that the passive bystanders who observed the switchboard operator being dragged by the rapist may not have been apathetic. They might actually have been greatly distressed, yet paralyzed by their awareness of the potential costs of intervening.

Social Norms

Often we help others not because we have consciously calculated that such behavior is in our self-interest, but simply because something tells us we *ought* to. We ought to help a new neighbor move in. We ought to turn off a vacant car's lights. We ought to return the wallet we found. Norms (as you may recall from Chapter 6) are social expectations. They *prescribe* proper behavior, the *oughts* of our lives. Researchers studying helping behavior have identified two social norms that seem to motivate altruism.

The Reciprocity Norm

Sociologist Alvin Gouldner (1960) contends that a universal component of moral codes is a *norm of reciprocity*: We should return help, not harm, to those

"Are you all right, Mister? Is there anything I can do?"

B TOBEY
"Young man, you're the only one who bothered to stop! I'm a millionaire and I'm going to give you five thousand dollars!"

Helping sometimes yields benefits. (Drawing by B. Tobey; © 1972 *The New Yorker* Magazine, Inc.)

who have helped us. Gouldner believes that this norm is as universal as the incest taboo. We "invest" in others and expect dividends. Politicians know that the one who gives a favor can later expect a favor in return. The reciprocity norm even applies within marriage; sometimes one may give more than one receives. But in the long run, one expects the exchange to balance out. In all such interactions, to receive without giving in return violates the reciprocity norm. Those who do so can expect rejection.

Reciprocity norm: *An expectation that people will help, not hurt, those who have helped them.*

The norm may well be universal; yet the extent of one's obligation to reciprocate varies according to circumstance. We feel deeply indebted when someone freely makes a big sacrifice on our behalf, but less so when the sacrifice is small and expected (Tesser, Gatewood, & Driver, 1968; Wilke & Lanzetta, 1970). Consider, for example, the white South African high school students who took part in an experiment by Stanley Morse and his colleagues (1977). Each student won a hit record, aided by hints from a quizmaster. Later, when the quizmaster asked for help on a project, those who had not expected any hints volunteered nearly twice as much of their time as those who had been led to expect help. So the norm seems to be: Return favors, especially big, unexpected favors.

"There is no duty more indispensable than that of returning a kindness."

Cicero

The reciprocity norm applies to many interactions, but not to our dealings with children, with the severely impoverished and handicapped, with any perceived as unable to return as much as they receive. Fortunately, another widespread social norm urges us to help those who cannot reciprocate.

The Social-Responsibility Norm

The reciprocity norm governs social exchange; it reminds us to balance giving and receiving in our social relations. However, if only a reciprocity norm existed, the Samaritan would not have been the Good Samaritan. In the parable, Jesus obviously had something more humanitarian in mind, something explicit in his other teachings: "If you love those who love you [the reciprocity norm] what right have you to claim any credit? . . . I say to you, Love your enemies" (Matthew 5:46, 44).

Social-responsibility norm: *An expectation that people will help those dependent upon them.*

The belief that people should help those who need help, without regard for future exchanges, has been labeled the *norm of social responsibility* (Berkowitz, 1972b; Schwartz, 1975). The norm ranges from one's retrieving a dropped book for a person on crutches to parents caring for their children (R. D. Clark, 1975).

Experiments show that people are frequently willing to help needy people—even when they remain anonymous and have no expectation of receiving any social reward (Berkowitz, 1972b). In practice, however, people usually apply the social-responsibility norm selectively—to those whose need seems not due to their own negligence. The norm seems to be: Give people what they deserve. If they are victims of circumstance, say of natural disaster, then by all means be generous. If, however, they seem to have created their own problem, by laziness or lack of foresight, then they should get what they deserve. People's responses are closely tied to their *attributions*. If we attribute the need to an uncontrollable predicament, we help. If we attribute another's need to the person's choices, fairness does not require us to help; after all, it's the person's own fault (Weiner, 1980).

Attribution: *See Chapter 3, pages 72–84.*

To make this point concrete, imagine yourself as one of the University of Wisconsin students in a study by Richard Barnes, William Ickes, and Robert Kidd (1979). You receive a call from a "Tony Freeman" who explains that he is in your introductory psychology class. He says he needs help for the upcoming exam, and that he has gotten your name from the class roster. "I don't know. I just don't seem to take good notes in there," Tony explains. "I know I can, but sometimes I just don't feel like it, so most of the notes I have aren't very good to study with." How sympathetic would you feel toward Tony? How much of a sacrifice would you make to loan him your notes? If you are like the students in this experiment, you would probably be much less inclined to help than if Tony had just explained that his troubles were beyond his control. Other experiments have produced similar results: When people need our help, we are often willing to help them—if we do not blame them for their problem (Gruder, Romer, & Korth, 1978; Meyer & Mulherin, 1980).

Our attributions (to controllable or uncontrollable factors) also affect our political responses. To what shall we attribute young blacks experiencing more unemployment than young whites? To such controllable factors as a presumed lack of self-discipline and initiative? Or to uncontrollable factors, such as discrimination, lack of jobs, or poor schools? One's political responses depend on which type of attribution one makes.

Sociobiology

The third explanation of altruism is rooted in evolutionary theory. Chapter 6 briefly explained how sociobiologists study and speculate about the evolution of social behavior. Sociobiology contends that the essence of life is gene survival. Our genes drive us in ways that maximize their chance of survival. When we die, they usually live on.

As each new person (each new set of genes) competes with others, those genes that survive are being selected over those that die out. Thus, any behavior that contributes to the perpetuation of one's genes will flourish. This doesn't mean we are rigidly programmed by our genes. In fact, part of what distinguishes us from lower forms of life is the extent to which our genes predispose our openness to learning from and adapting to our environment.

"Genes hold culture on a leash. The leash is very long, but inevitably values will be constrained in accordance with their effects on the human gene pool."

Edward O. Wilson, On Human Nature (1978, p. 167)

Still, it is a humbling human image. *The Selfish Gene* is the title of one prominent sociobiology book (Dawkins, 1976). Psychologist Donald Campbell (1975a; 1975b) has called it a biological reaffirmation of "original sin"—that is, a deep, self-serving tendency. Sociobiologist David Barash (1979) puts it bluntly: "Real, honest-to-God altruism simply doesn't occur in nature" (p. 135). Genes that would incline people to selflessly promote others' welfare would not survive in the evolutionary competition. Self-sacrifice has no biological survival value. However, genetic selfishness actually could prompt several types of altruistic behavior.

Kin Selection: Genes Care for Relatives in Whom They Reside

One form of self-sacrifice that *would* contribute to the survival of our genes is devotion to our children. Parents who put their children's welfare ahead of their own will be more likely to have their genes passed on to posterity than parents who ignore their children's welfare. One could say then that evolution *has* selected altruism, at least toward one's children. (Children have less at stake in the survival of their parents' genes. This may explain why parents are generally more devoted to their children than their children are to them.)

Other relatives share genes in proportion to their biological closeness. You share one-half your genes with your brothers and sisters, one-eighth with your cousins. That "genes help themselves by being nice to themselves, even if they are enclosed in different bodies" (Barash, 1979, p. 153), led the evolutionary biologist J. B. S. Haldane once to jest that while he would not give up his life for his brother, he would sacrifice himself for *three* brothers, or for nine cousins. The point is not that we calculate genetic relatedness before helping, but that the social world operates in such a way that close kin are usually favored. The Carnegie Medal for bravery is never awarded for saving the life of a relative. That is expected. What is unexpected (and therefore honored) are those who, like our subway hero Everett Sanderson, risk themselves to save a nonrelative.

We also share common genes with many others. Genes for blue eyes are shared with other blue-eyed people. But how do we detect the people in which copies of our genes will be found most abundantly? As the blue-eyes example suggests, one clue lies in physical similarities. Also, in evolutionary history, one's genes were more likely found in neighbors than in foreigners. Are we to conclude therefore that we are biologically biased to act more altruistically toward those similar to us and those who live near us? In the aftermath of natural disasters, the order of who gets helped would not surprise a sociobiologist: family members first, friends and neighbors second, strangers last (Form & Nosow, 1958).

Kin selection: *The idea that evolution has selected altruism toward one's close relatives to enhance the survival of mutually shared genes.*

Although biased altruism may no longer be conducive to human survival, some sociobiologists believe our evolutionary past has endowed us with such tendencies. If so, sociobiologist E. O. Wilson (1978) concludes that kin selection is a mixed blessing, for "altruism based on kin selection is the enemy of civilization. If human beings are to a large extent guided . . . to favor their own relatives and tribe, only a limited amount of global harmony is possible" (p. 167).

Striking instances of "selfish genes" predisposing altruism toward others carrying the same genes is provided by the social insects. Soldier and worker ants, bees, and termites have no offspring: within a colony there is no genetic competition. Instead, their genetic stake is entirely in perpetuating the colony's genes. Consequently, self-sacrificial behavior—true altruism—is commonplace. To support the colony, these insects divide the labor cooperatively. If necessary, bees will even engage in kamikaze suicide to defend the colony. Sociobiologists would say that such altruism occurs because natural selection favors colonies possessing genes that promote the colony's survival. The altruistic insects do not reproduce. Thus, they waste no genes while serving and protecting the colony's genes.

Reciprocity

The theory that genetic self-interest underlies altruism toward others who carry one's genes also predicts reciprocity. An organism helps another, biologist Robert Trivers argues, because it expects help in return (the giver expects later to be the getter) and because failing to reciprocate is punished and thus not favored by natural selection (Binham, 1980). The cheat, the turncoat, the traitor are universally despised.

Reciprocity works best in small, isolated groups, groups in which one will again interact with the people for whom one does favors. Thus reciprocity is stronger in the remote Cook Islands of the South Pacific than in New York City (Barash, 1979, p. 160). And small towns, small schools, small churches, small work teams, small dorms, are all conducive to a community spirit in

"The story takes place in a small, sleepy, typically American New England town, and the gimmick is that all the inhabitants are fine, decent, normal, upright, God-fearing people who—while respecting their neighbors' privacy—manage to be helpful to one another."

Reciprocal altruism works best in small communities. (John Ruge/*Saturday Review*)

which people are more likely to care for each other and enjoy being cared for in return. Perhaps this is why researchers have observed that, compared to people in nonurban environments, those in big cities are less willing to relay a phone message, less likely to mail "lost" letters, less cooperative with survey interviewers, less helpful to a lost child, and less willing to do small favors (Korte, 1980).

Individual Selection versus Group Selection

Perhaps you resist: Reciprocity is pseudo altruism. It denies true altruism, which is selfless. Apart from altruism toward one's kin, is there no biological basis for true altruism? Is there not deep in our nature some altruistic impulse that drives an Everett Sanderson to risk life and limb to save Michelle, that causes a soldier to throw himself on a live grenade to save his buddies, that causes a Mother Theresa to live a life of poverty and exhausting hard work while caring for the desperate of Calcutta?

We could answer affirmatively if natural selection has favored not only behaviors conducive to individual survival, but also behaviors conducive to group survival. Early humans apparently lived in groups of about twenty-five (Buys & Larson, 1979). Perhaps groups composed of truly altruistic members survived better than did those whose members were solely selfish. Perhaps the more cooperative, the more loyal the members of our ancestral groups were, the more likely those groups were to survive. It sounds reasonable. And some evolutionary biologists believe such "group selection" does indeed occur. If so, it would provide the biological basis for true altruism.

"We must all hang together, or assuredly we shall all hang separately."

Benjamin Franklin

Increasingly, though, most sociobiologists have concluded that individual selection prevails over that of the group. If, within a group, some individuals have genes predisposed to altruism and some to selfishness, inevitably the selfish genes win the genetic competition. E. O. Wilson (1978) puts it simply: "Fallen heroes do not have children. If self-sacrifice results in fewer descendants, the genes that allow heroes to be created can be expected to disappear gradually from the population" (pp. 152-153).

However, if individual self-interest inevitably wins in genetic competition, then why does altruism toward strangers occur? What causes an Everett Sanderson to act as he does? A Mother Theresa to act as she does?

Donald Campbell's (1975a; 1975b) answer is that human societies have evolved ethical and religious rules that serve as brakes on the biological bias toward self-interest. Commandments such as "Love your neighbor" admonish us to balance self-concern with concern for the group, and so contribute to the survival of the group. Sociobiologist Richard Dawkins (1976) reaches a similar conclusion: "Let us try to *teach* generosity and altruism, because we are born selfish. Let us understand what our own selfish genes are up to, because we may then at least have the chance to upset their designs, something which no other species has ever aspired to" (p. 3).

Comparing and Evaluating Theories of Altruism

By now you have perhaps noticed similarities between the social exchange, social norm, and sociobiological views of altruism. The parallels are indeed striking. As Table 11-1 indicates, each proposes two types of prosocial behavior: a tit-for-tat reciprocal exchange, and a more authentic, unconditional altruism. In fact, we might think of these theories as three complementary levels of explanation, mirroring one another. For example, if the sociobiological view of altruism is correct, then our genetic predispositions should manifest themselves in psychological and sociological phenomena.

Each theory appeals to logic. Yet each is vulnerable to charges of being speculative and after-the-fact. When one starts with a known effect (for example, the give and take of everyday life) and explains it simply by

TABLE 11-1 Comparing Theories of Altruism

		How is Altruism Explained?	
Theory	**Level of Explanation**	**Mutual "Altruism"**	**Inner-Directed Altruism**
Social norms	Sociological	Reciprocity norm	Social responsibility norm
Social exchange	Psychological	External rewards for helping	Empathy → inner rewards for helping
Sociobiology	Biological	Reciprocity	Kin selection Group selection?

conjecturing a social exchange process, a "reciprocity norm," or an evolutionary origin, one might be merely explaining-by-naming. For example, the argument that a behavior occurs because of its survival function is hard to disprove. With hindsight, it's easy to think that it had to be that way for survival. As we have noted before, each theory's task is to generate predictions that enable us to test it. If any conceivable behavior can be explained as the result of a social exchange, a norm, or natural selection, then the theories cannot be falsified.

An effective theory provides not only specific predictions, but also a coherent scheme for summarizing diverse observations. On this criterion, the three theories of altruism get higher marks. Although most studies of helping have not directly tested these theories, the theories do give us a broad perspective from which we can understand human altruism.

Research on altruism has involved several different types of helping: compliance with requests for help, spontaneous spur-of-the-moment helping, and (less often) a more enduring commitment of one's time. Perhaps future research will reveal that the explanation of each of these types of helping is somewhat different from that of the others. Nevertheless, the recent experiments on helping do address a common question: Precisely when do people help?

WHEN WILL WE HELP?

Social psychologists were curious and concerned about bystanders' lack of involvement during such events as the Kitty Genovese murder. So they undertook experiments to identify when people will help in an emergency. More recently, the question has been broadened to also ask: When will people help in nonemergencies—by doing such deeds as giving money, donating blood, or contributing time? Let's examine these experiments, looking first at the *circumstances* that enhance helpfulness and then at the characteristics of *people* who help.

When it comes to giving, some people stop at nothing.

Situational Influences: When are We Likely to be Good Samaritans?

Number of Bystanders

The passivity of bystanders during such emergencies as the Genovese murder has prompted social commentators to lament our culture's alienation, apathy, indifference, and unconscious sadistic impulses. Note that all these explanations attribute the nonintervention to the bystanders' dispositions. This leaves room for us to reassure ourselves that we are not the type of people who would not help. If we feel appalled merely upon reading about these incidents, we can tell ourselves we are not similarly indifferent or sadistic. Why then were those bystanders such dehumanized characters?

Two social psychologists, Bibb Latané and John Darley (1970) were not convinced that the bystanders were dehumanized. So Latané and Darley

BEHIND THE SCENES

John M. Darley

Shocked by the Kitty Genovese murder, Bibb Latané and I met over dinner and began to analyze the bystanders' reactions. Because we were social psychologists, we thought not about how people are different nor about the personality flaws of the "apathetic" individuals who failed to act that night, but rather about how people are the same and how anyone in that situation might react as did these people. By the time we finished our dinner, we had formulated several factors that together could lead to the surprising result: no one helping. Then we set about conducting experiments that isolated each factor and demonstrated its importance in an emergency situation. *(John M. Darley, Princeton University)*

staged a number of ingenious emergencies and found that a single situational factor—the presence of other bystanders—could result in nonintervention, even among nice, normal people. By 1980 some four dozen comparisons had been accumulated of help given by bystanders who perceived themselves to be either alone or with others. In about 90 percent of these comparisons, involving nearly 6000 people, lone bystanders were more likely to help (Latané & Nida, 1981). Sometimes, the victim was actually less likely to get help if many people could help. Why? Latané and Darley surmised that as the number of bystanders increases, any given bystander is less likely to *notice* the incident, less likely to *interpret* the incident as an emergency, and less likely to *assume responsibility* for taking action. Taking these one at a time, let us examine why.

Noticing

Twenty minutes after Eleanor Bradley fell and broke her leg on a crowded city sidewalk, you come by. Your eyes are focused on the backs of the pedestrians in front of you (it is bad manners to stare at those you pass) and your private thoughts are focused on the events of your day. Would you therefore be less likely to notice the fallen woman than if the sidewalk were virtually deserted?

To check this conjecture, Latané and Darley (1968) had Columbia University men fill out a questionnaire in a room, either by themselves or with two strangers. While working (and being observed through a one-way mirror) there was a staged emergency: Smoke poured into the room through a wall vent. *Solitary* students, who often glanced idly about the room while working, noticed the smoke almost immediately—usually in less than five seconds. Those in *groups* kept their eyes on their work. It typically took them about twenty seconds to notice the smoke.

Interpreting

Once an ambiguous event is noticed, it calls for an interpretation. Put yourself in the smoke-filling room. Though a bit worried, you don't want to embarrass yourself by getting flustered. You glance at the others. They look calm, indifferent. Assuming everything must be okay, you shrug it off and go back to work. Then one of the others notices the smoke and, noting your apparent concern, reacts similarly. This is what we called in Chapter 7 "informational influence"—each person using the behavior of others as clues to reality.

This is similar to what happened in the actual experiment. When those working alone noticed the smoke, they usually hesitated a moment, then got up, walked over to the vent, felt, sniffed, and waved at the smoke, hesitated again, and then went to report it. In dramatic contrast, those in groups of three did not move. Among the twenty-four men in eight groups, only one person reported the smoke within the first four minutes. By the end of the six-minute experiment, the smoke was so thick that the men's vision was becoming obscured and they were rubbing their eyes and coughing. Still, in only three of the eight groups did even a single person leave to report the problem.

Equally interesting, subsequent interviews revealed that the group's passivity had affected members' interpretations. What caused the smoke? "A leak in the air conditioning," "Chemistry labs in the building," "Steam pipes," "Truth gas." They offered many explanations. Not one said "fire."

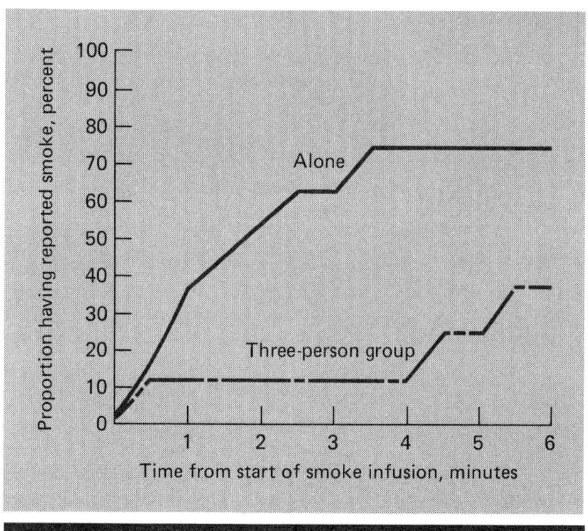

FIGURE 11-1 The smoke-filled room experiment. Smoke pouring into the testing room was much more likely to be reported by individuals working alone than by three-person groups. (Data from Latané & Darley, 1968.)

The group members, in serving as nonresponsive models, had influenced each other's interpretation of the situation as not being an emergency.

This experimental dilemma parallels dilemmas each of us have faced. Are the shrieks outside merely playful antics, or the desperate screams of someone being assaulted? Is the boys' scuffling a friendly tussle, or a vicious fight? Is the woman slumped in the doorway sleeping, or is she seriously ill, perhaps in a diabetic coma?

Bystander effect: *The finding that a person is less likely to provide help when there are other bystanders.*

Unlike the smoke-filled-room experiment, however, each of these everyday situations involves danger to another person rather than to oneself. To see if the same "bystander effect" could occur in such situations, Latané and Judith Rodin (1969) staged an experiment around a "lady in distress." In this experiment, a female researcher set Columbia University men to work on a questionnaire and then left through a curtained doorway to work in her adjacent office. Four minutes later she could be heard (from a high-fidelity tape recorder) climbing up on a chair to reach some papers. This was followed by a scream and a loud crash as the chair collapsed and she fell to the floor. "Oh, my God, my foot . . . I . . . I . . . can't move it," she sobbed. "Oh . . . my ankle. . . . I . . . can't get this . . . thing . . . off me." Only after two minutes of moaning did she manage to make it out her office door.

Seventy percent of those who were alone when the "accident" was overheard came into the room or called out to offer help. But in only 40 percent of the pairs of strangers confronting the emergency did either person offer help. This again demonstrates that the more people known to be aware of an emergency the *less* likely it is that any given person will act. For the victim there was no safety in numbers. Those who did not intervene apparently interpreted the situation as a nonemergency. "A mild sprain," said some. "I didn't want to embarrass her," explained others.

Assuming Responsibility

But what about those times when it is obvious that an emergency is occurring? Those who watched Kitty Genovese being attacked and heard her pleas for help correctly interpreted what was happening. But the lights and silhouetted figures in neighboring windows told them that others were also watching. This diffused the responsibility for action.

Few of us have observed a murder. But all of us have at times been slower to react to a need when others are present. To explore further why bystanders can inhibit our acting, Darley and Latané, (1968) simulated the Genovese drama. They placed people in separate rooms from which the subjects would hear a victim crying for help. To create this situation, Darley and Latané, asked some New York University students to discuss over a laboratory intercom their problems with university life. The students were told that to guarantee their anonymity they would not see each other, nor would the experimenter eavesdrop. During the ensuing discussion, the participants heard one person, when the experimenter turned his microphone on, lapse into an epileptic seizure in which, with increasing intensity and speech difficulty, he pled for someone to help.

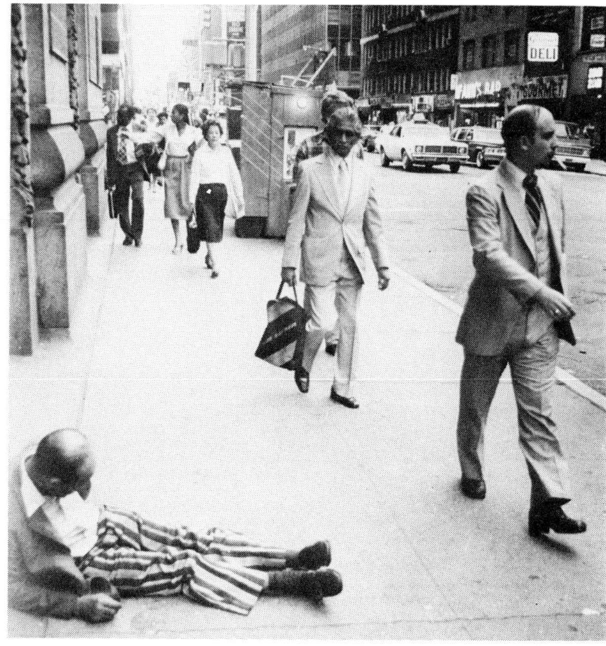

In everyday life, situations are often ambiguous. Is this an emergency? Or is the man drunk or asleep? Other people's reactions in such a situation can influence our interpretation. (© 1980 Jan Halaska/ Photo Researchers, Inc.)

Box 11-1

Diffusion of Responsibility

"But, I Thought You Called"

ALBUQUERQUE. N.M. (UPI) — Everyone thought someone else had taken care of it, but after more than an hour and a half of watching a fire at a small apartment complex, the 30 onlookers realized that no one had called the fire department.

A neighbor finally made the call, and a fire truck arrived three minutes later, but it was too late to save the building.

"It was just a case of everybody thinking someone else had called us," said Lt. Phil Silva, an investigator for the Albuquerque Fire Department.

Note: From United Press International, June 24, 1978.

Of those led to believe they were the only listener, 85 percent sought help. Of those who believed four others also overheard the victim, only 31 percent went for help. Were those who did not respond apathetic and indifferent? When the experimenter entered the room to terminate the experiment, she did not find them so. In fact, most of these subjects immediately expressed concern; many had trembling hands and sweating palms. They believed an emergency had occurred, but were undecided about whether they should act.

After the smoke-filled-room, the lady-in-distress, and the seizure experiments, Latané and Darley asked the participants whether the others' presence had influenced them. Obviously, the other bystanders had actually had a dramatic effect. Yet, the participants almost invariably denied that they had been influenced. The typical reply? "I was aware of the others, but I would have reacted just the same if they weren't there." This response once again demonstrates a point stressed in Chapter 4: We often do not know why we do what we do. And that, of course, is why experiments such as these are revealing. A survey of uninvolved bystanders following a real emergency likely would have left the bystander effect hidden.

Further experiments, however, have revealed some situations in which the presence of others sometimes does *not* inhibit people from offering help. Irving Piliavin, Judith Rodin, and Jane Piliavin (1969) staged an emergency in a laboratory on wheels, the unwitting subjects being 4450 riders of New York's subways. On each of 103 occasions, a confederate entered a subway

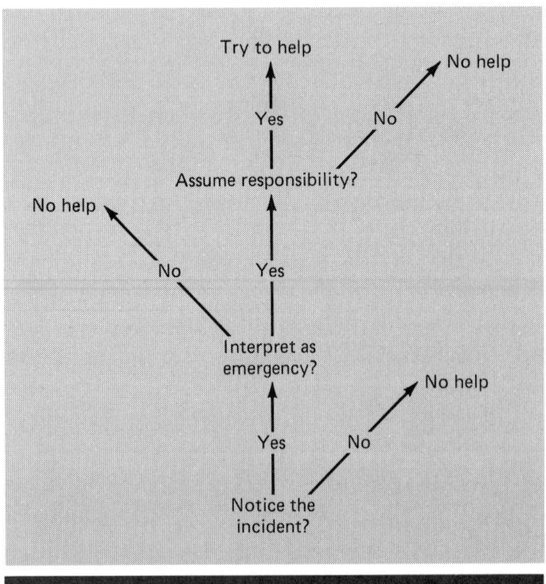

FIGURE 11-2 Latané and Darley's decision tree. Only one path up the tree leads to helping. At each fork of the path, the presence of other bystanders may divert a person down a branch of not helping. (Adapted from Darley & Latané, 1968.)

car and stood in the center next to a pole. After the train pulled out of the station, he staggered, then collapsed. When the victim carried a cane, one or more bystanders almost always promptly offered help, regardless of whether or not the seats were all taken. Even when the victim carried a bottle and smelled of liquor, he was often promptly offered aid—aid that was especially prompt when several male bystanders were close by. Why? Did the presence of other passengers provide a sense of security to those who helped? Was it because the situation was unambiguous? (The passengers couldn't help but notice and realize what was happening.)

To test this latter possibility, Linda Solomon, Henry Solomon, and Ronald Stone (1978) conducted a series of experiments in which New Yorkers either saw and heard someone's distress, as in the subway experiment, or only heard it, as in the lady-in-distress experiment (leaving the situation more open to interpretation). When the emergencies were unambiguous, those in groups were only slightly less likely to be helpful than were those alone. However, when the emergencies were somewhat ambiguous, the subjects who were in groups were far less likely to help than were solitary bystanders.

In the subway experiment, a significant factor may have been that the passengers sat face to face, allowing them to see the alarm on one another's faces. To explore this idea, Darley, Allan Teger, and Lawrence Lewis (1973) created a situation in which people were working either face to face or back to back when they heard a crash in the adjacent room as several metal screens fell on a workman. Unlike those who were working alone, who almost always offered help, pairs working back to back seldom offered help. However, a person working face to face with a partner was able to notice that the other was startled and knew that the other had observed likewise. Apparently this led both to interpret the situation as an emergency and to feel some responsibility to act, for these pairs were virtually as likely to give aid as were those working alone. To summarize: The presence of other bystanders seems to inhibit one's helping, especially when either the emergency is ambiguous or the bystanders cannot read one another's reactions.

Finally, this seems an appropriate time to raise again the issue of research ethics. Is it right to force hundreds of subway riders to witness someone's apparent collapse? Were the researchers in the seizure experiment ethical when they forced people to decide whether to abort the discussion to report the problem? Would you object to being in such a study? Note that it would have been impossible to obtain your "informed consent"; doing so would have destroyed the cover for the experiment.

Two things can be said in defense of the researchers. First, they were always careful to debrief their laboratory participants, explaining both the experiment and its purposes. After explaining the seizure experiment, probably the most stressful, the experimenter gave the participants a questionnaire. One hundred percent said the deception was justified and that they would be willing to take part in similar experiments in the future. None of the participants said they were angry at the experimenter. Other researchers similarly report that the overwhelming majority of subjects in such experiments say afterwards that their participation was both instructive and ethically justified (Schwartz & Gottlieb, 1981). In the field experiments, an accomplice assisted the victim if no one else did, thus eventually reassuring bystanders that the problem was dealt with.

Second, remember that the social psychologist has a twofold ethical obligation: to protect the participants and to enhance human welfare by discovering influences upon human behavior. The ethical principle seems to be this: if the welfare of participants is protected, as it apparently was in this research, social psychologists fulfill their responsibility to society by doing such research.

Models: Helping when Someone Else Does

If observing a model of aggression can heighten aggression (Chapter 10), and if models who are unresponsive can inhibit responding, then might not models of helpfulness promote helping? Imagine hearing a crash followed by sobs and moans. If another bystander's reaction implied, "Uh oh. This is an emergency! I've got to do something," would this not also help stimulate others to help?

The evidence is clear: Prosocial models do indeed enhance the altruism of others. James Bryan and Mary Ann Test (1967) found that Los Angeles drivers were more likely to offer help to a female driver with a flat tire if a quarter mile earlier they had seen someone helping another woman change a tire. In another experiment, Bryan and Test observed that New Jersey Christmas shoppers were more likely to drop money in a Salvation Army kettle if they had just observed someone else do the same. And in a study with British adults, Philippe Rushton and Anne Campbell (1977) found people usually unwilling to donate blood, unless they were approached after observing a confederate consent to donating.

Sometimes models contradict in practice what they preach. Parents sometimes advise their children to "Do as I say, not as I do." Experiments indicate that children learn moral judgments from both what they hear preached and what they see practiced (Rice & Grusec, 1975; Rushton, 1975). Thus, when exposed to hypocrites, they tend to model the model: They do what the model does and say what the model says.

"We are, in truth, more than half what we are by imitation. The great point is, to choose good models and to study them with care."

Lord Chesterfield, Letters, *January 18, 1750*

However, models are not always emulated. The example set by a disliked model can boomerang. Imagine being one of the several hundred Madison, Wisconsin, residents who found an addressed envelope with several personal documents showing. Wrapped around the documents was a note from someone who had found the envelope but dropped it. In the note, this first finder identified himself as a South African who was "very disappointed with how self-centered and childish Americans are," adding, "You have much to learn from the honest way we keep our Negroes down," and "I must say, it has been annoying to have to get involved with the whole problem of returning

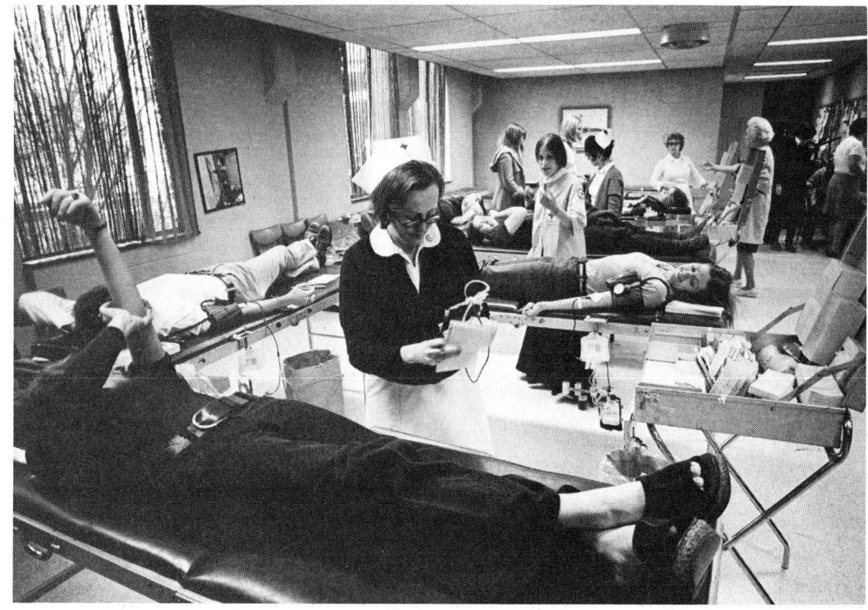

Modeling: Observing other's altruism can enhance one's own. (Christopher Morrow/ Stock, Boston)

these things" (Schwartz & Ames, 1977). Under these conditions—having a repulsive model who disliked helping—fully three-fourths of the second finders mailed the envelopes. It seemed that the typical subject felt, "If he's against helping, I'm for it." When the model was disliked, yet expressed *enjoyment* of helping, only about half the second finders mailed the envelope. "I'm not sure I want to go along with what a jerk like that does."

People in a Hurry

Darley and his fellow researcher, Daniel Batson (1973), discerned another determinant of helping in the Good Samaritan parable. The priest and the Levite were both busy, important people, probably hurrying to their duties. The lowly Samaritan surely was less pressed for time. To see whether people in a hurry would behave as the priest and Levite did, Darley and Batson cleverly staged the situation described in the parable.

After being asked to collect their thoughts prior to recording a brief extemporaneous talk (which, for half the participants, was on the Good Samaritan parable), Princeton Theological Seminary students were directed to a recording studio in an adjacent building. En route, they passed a man sitting slumped in a doorway, head down, coughing and groaning. Some of the students had been sent off nonchalantly: "It will be a few minutes before they're ready for you, but you might as well head on over." Of these, almost two-thirds stopped to offer help. Others were told, "Oh, you're late. They were expecting you a few minutes ago . . . so you'd better hurry." Of these, only 10 percent offered help.

Reflecting on these findings, Darley and Batson remarked that

> A person not in a hurry may stop and offer help to a person in distress. A person in a hurry is likely to keep going. Ironically, he is likely to keep going even if he is hurrying to speak on the parable of the Good Samaritan, thus inadvertently confirming the point of the parable. (Indeed, on several occasions, a seminary student going to give his talk on the parable of the Good Samaritan literally stepped over the victim as he hurried on his way!)

That is one of the most ironically humorous scenes ever noted in a social psychology experiment: a contemporary "priest" passing by a slumped, groaning victim while pondering the parable of the Good Samaritan.

Yet, perhaps we are being unfair to the seminary students, who were, after all, hurrying to *help* the experimenter. Perhaps they keenly felt the social responsibility norm, but found it pulling them two ways—toward the experiment and toward the victim. In another enactment of the Good Samaritan situation, Batson and his associates (1978) directed forty University of Kansas students to an experiment in another building. Half were told they were late; half knew they had plenty of time. Half thought their participation was vitally important to the experimenter; half thought it was unessential. The results: Those who, like the White Rabbit in *Alice's Adventures in Wonderland*, were late for a very important date, seldom stopped to help. They had a pressing social obligation elsewhere. Those on their way to an unimportant appointment usually stopped to help.

Can we conclude that those who were rushed were callous? For example, did the seminarians notice the victim's distress and then consciously choose to ignore it? No. In their hurry, they never fully grasped the situation. Harried, preoccupied, rushing to meet a deadline, they simply did not take time to tune into the person in need.

Whom Do We Help?

When we discussed the social-responsibility norm, we noted the tendency to help those most in need, those most deserving. In the subway experiment, the "victim" was helped far more promptly when carrying a cane than when carrying a liquor bottle. Grocery store shoppers have been found to be more willing to give change to a woman who, they are led to believe, wants to buy milk than to one who wants to buy cookie dough (Bickman & Kamzan, 1973).

If, indeed, one's perception of another's need strongly determines one's willingness to help, will women, if perceived as less competent and more dependent, receive more help than men? In the United States, such indeed is the case (Deaux, 1976). Several experiments have found that women with disabled cars (for example, with a flat tire) get many more offers of help than do men (Penner, Dertke, & Achenbach, 1973; Pomazal & Clore, 1973; West, Whitney, & Schnedler, 1975). Similarly, solo female hitchhikers receive far more offers of help than do solo males or couples (Pomazal & Clore, 1973;

M. Snyder, Grether, & Keller, 1974). Of course, men's chivalry toward solo women may be motivated by something other than altruism. The cost of helping a woman can be minimal (at least in terms of risk to one's safety), but the potential benefits maximal. So it won't come as a great surprise to learn that men more frequently help attractive women than those they see as unattractive (Mims, Hartnett, & Nay, 1975; Stroufe et al., 1977; West & Brown, 1975).

Perhaps because similarity is conducive to liking (see Chapter 13) and liking is conducive to helping, we are also biased toward those *similar* to us. The similarity bias applies to both dress and beliefs. Tim Emswiller, Kay Deaux, and Jerry Willits (1971) had confederates, dressed either conservatively or in counterculture garb, approach "straight" and "hippie" Purdue University students seeking a dime for a phone call. Fewer than half the students did the favor for those dressed differently from themselves, but two-thirds did so for those dressed similarly. Similarly, on election day, 1972, Stuart Karabenick, Richard Lerner, and Michael Beecher (1973) had Nixon and McGovern workers "accidentally" drop campaign leaflets near voting polls. The workers were helped by fewer than half the passersby who preferred the other candidate, but by more than two-thirds of those whose preference was the same.

In an era when a leading social issue continues to be racial prejudice, one wonders whether the similarity bias extends to those of one's own race. During the 1970s, numerous experiments explored this question. The results are confusing. Some studies found a same-race bias (Benson, Karabenick, & Lerner, 1976; R. D. Clark, 1974; Franklin, 1974; Gaertner, 1973; Gaertner & Bickman, 1971; Sissons, 1981). Others found no bias (Gaertner, 1975; R. M. Lerner & Frank, 1974; D. W. Wilson & Donnerstein, 1979; Wispe & Freshley, 1971). And still others—especially those involving face-to-face situations—found a bias toward helping those of a different race (Dutton, 1971; 1973; Dutton & Lake, 1973; I. Katz, Cohen, & Glass, 1975). Is there a general rule that can resolve these seemingly contradictory findings?

One possibility is that people tend to favor their own race, but keep this bias secret in order to preserve a positive image. Few want to appear prejudiced. If this explanation is correct, the same-race bias should appear when, and only when, one's failure to help someone of another race can be attributed to factors other than race. For example, Samuel Gaertner and John Dovidio (1977) found white University of Delaware women less willing to help a black than a white "lady in distress" when their responsibility could be diffused among the bystanders ("I didn't help the black woman because there were others who could") but equally helpful when there were no other bystanders.

Similarly, John Brigham and Curtis Richardson (1979) found white store clerks in Tallahassee, Florida, less willing to help a man short of money on a small purchase when he was black than when he was white. In this situation, the clerks could easily attribute their neglect to store policy: "I'm sorry, but I'm not allowed to sell it to you unless you can pay for it."

So, does prejudice still lurk beneath the surface, sometimes emerging when it can be disguised by other excuses? We shall turn to this question in the next chapter.

Personal Influences: Who Are the Good Samaritans?

We have considered several influences upon one's decision to help—number of bystanders, modeling, hurrying, and characteristics of the person in need. We also need to consider internal factors, factors having to do with the state or the characteristics of the helper.

Guilt

Throughout recorded history, guilt has been a painful emotion, so painful, in fact, that cultures have institutionalized a variety of ways to relieve it: sacrifices both animal and human, offerings of grain and money, penitent behavior, confession, denial. In ancient Israel, periodically the sins of the people were laid on a "scapegoat" animal that was then led into the wilderness, thus carrying away the people's guilt (de Vaux, 1965).

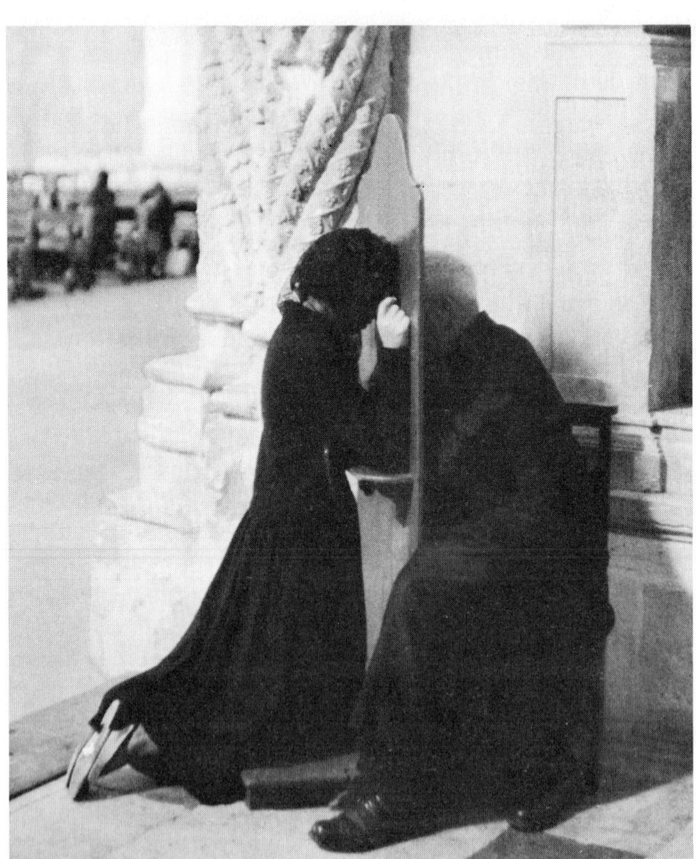

Guilt is alleviated in various ways, such as by confession or doing good deeds. (Henri Cartier-Bresson/ Magnum Photos)

To examine the consequences of guilt, social psychologists have induced people to either accidentally or intentionally transgress: to lie, to deliver shock, to knock over a table loaded with alphabetized cards, to break a machine, to cheat. Afterward, the guilt-laden participants have been subtly offered a convenient way to relieve their guilt, such as by confessing, by disparaging the one harmed, or by doing a benevolent deed to offset the malevolent one. The results are remarkably consistent: People will do whatever can be done to expunge the guilt and restore their self-image.

Picture yourself as a participant in one such experiment conducted by David McMillen and James Austin (1971) with Mississippi State University students. You and another student, each seeking to earn credit toward a course requirement, arrive for the experiment. Soon after, an accomplice of the experimenter enters, portraying himself as a previous subject looking for a book he had lost. He strikes up a conversation in which he mentions that the experiment involves taking a multiple-choice test, for which most of the correct answers are "B." After the accomplice departs, the experimenter arrives, explains the experiment, then asks, "Has either of you been in this experiment before or heard anything about it?" Would you lie?

The behavior of those who have gone before you in this experiment—100 percent of whom told the little lie—suggests that you would. After you have taken the test (without receiving any feedback on it), the experimenter mentions, "You are free to leave. However, if you have some spare time, I could use your help in scoring some questionnaires." Assuming you have told the lie, do you think you would now be more willing to volunteer some time? Judging from the results, the answer again is yes. On the average, those who had not been induced to lie volunteered only two minutes of time. But those who had lied were apparently eager to redeem their self-image; on the average they offered a whopping sixty-three minutes. One moral of this experiment was well expressed by a seven-year-old girl, who, in one of our own experiments, wrote, "Don't Lie or youl Live with gilt." And if you suffer guilt, you will feel a need to relieve it.

Our eagerness to do good after doing bad seems to reflect both our need to reduce *private* guilt and restore our shaken self-image, and our desire to reclaim a positive *public* image (Darlington & Macker, 1966; Konecni, 1972; J. W. Regan, 1971). In an upstate New York shopping center, Dennis Regan, Margo Williams, and Sondra Sparling (1972) had a confederate ask women shoppers to take his picture. When the camera wouldn't work, he either implied that the subject had broken it (inducing guilt) or explained that the camera "acts up a lot." A few moments later a second confederate, carrying a shopping bag with candy spilling out, crossed paths with the subject. Of women not feeling guilty, only 15 percent bothered to inform the confederate about the spilled candy. Of those made to feel guilty, 55 percent did so. Since the guilt-laden subjects had no need to redeem themselves in the eyes of the second confederate, their behavior seems most readily explained as an expiation of private guilt. Another indication that guilt motivates one to help comes from experiments in which people who have transgressed are given opportunity to confess. Confession apparently reduces guilt, for it also reduces subsequent helping (Carlsmith, Ellsworth, & Whiteside, 1968).

Closely connected with our private feelings of guilt is our concern for our public image. We are therefore even more likely to redeem ourselves with altruistic behavior when other people know about our misdeeds (Carlsmith & Gross, 1968).

"Open confession is good for the soul."

Old Scottish proverb

Mood

If guilt increases helping, do other negative feelings, such as sadness, likewise increase helping? If, just after being depressed by a bad grade, you saw someone in front of you spill papers on the sidewalk, would you be more likely than usual to help? Or less likely?

At first glance, the results are confusing. Putting people in a negative mood (for example, by having them read or think about something sad) sometimes increases altruism, sometimes decreases it. Such an apparent contradiction excites the scientist's detective spirit. Looking more closely, we indeed can find clues to an order in what appears to be confusion. First, the studies in which negative mood decreases helping generally have involved children (Isen, Horn, & Rosenhan, 1973; Kenrick, Baumann, & Cialdini, 1979; Moore, Underwood, & Rosenhan, 1973); those that find increased helping usually have studied adults (Aderman & Berkowitz, 1970; Apsler, 1975; Cialdini, Darby, & Vincent, 1973; Cialdini & Kenrick, 1976). Why, do you suppose, are children and adults affected differently?

Robert Cialdini, Douglas Kenrick, and Donald Baumann (1981; Baumann, Cialdini, & Kenrick, 1981) surmise that for adults, altruism is self-gratifying. As we noted earlier, it can carry its own inner rewards. Blood donors feel better about themselves for having donated. Thus, when an adult is in a negative mood, be it guilt or sadness, a helpful deed (or any other mood-improving experience) can help neutralize the bad feelings. Also, this implies (and experiments confirm) that if someone in a negative mood is first given some other mood boost (for example, finding money, listening to a humorous tape) and then given an opportunity to be helpful, helping will be unaffected by the original negative mood (Cialdini, Darby, & Vincent, 1973; M. R. Cunningham, Steinberg, & Grev, 1980; R. F. Kidd & Berkowitz, 1976). To repeat: When being helpful is a means to improve one's mood, a sad adult is helpful.

But why does this not work with children? Cialdini, Kenrick, and Baumann argue that altruism is not similarly rewarding for young children. Although young children are not without empathy, they do not take much pleasure in being helpful; such behavior is a product of socialization, or so Cialdini and his colleagues believe. To test their belief, they had children in early elementary school, late elementary school, and high school reminisce about sad or neutral experiences prior to being given a chance to donate prize coupons privately to other children (Cialdini & Kenrick, 1976). When sad, the youngest children donated slightly less, the middle groups donated slightly more, and the teenage group donated significantly more. Only the teenagers seemed to find generosity a self-gratifying technique for cheering themselves up. As the researchers note, these results are consistent with Donald Campbell's sociobiological view: We are born selfish; thus, altruism must be socially indoctrinated. Such results are, however, also consistent with the view that, like height, altruism naturally grows with age as the child develops the capacity to see things from another person's point of view (Bar-Tal, in press; Rushton, 1976; Underwood & Moore, 1982). Do you suppose some combination of these ideas ("altruism as socialized," "altruism as natural") is even closer to the truth?

Can we conclude that among well-socialized adults the "Feel-bad, do-good" phenomenon is always to be expected? No. In the previous chapter, we saw that one negative mood, anger, produces anything but compassion. Another likely exception to the phenomenon is profound grief. People who have suffered the loss of a spouse or a child, whether through death or separation, often undergo a period of intense self-focus during which it is difficult to be self-giving to others.

In a powerfully involving laboratory simulation of self-focused grief, William Thompson, Claudia Cowan, and David Rosenhan (1980) had Stanford University students privately listen to a taped description of a person (who they were to imagine was their best friend of the other sex) dying of cancer. For some, the experiment focused their attention on their own worry and grief:

> He (she) could die and you would lose him, never be able to talk to him again. Or worse, he could die slowly. You would know every minute could be your last time together. For months you would have to be cheerful for him while you were sad. You would have to watch him die in pieces, until the last piece finally went, and you would be alone.

For others, it focused their attention on the friend:

> He spends his time lying in bed, waiting those interminable hours, just waiting and hoping for something to happen. Anything. He tells you that it's not knowing that is the hardest.

The researchers report that, regardless of which tape was heard, the participants were profoundly moved and sobered by the experience, yet not the least regretful of having participated (although some of the participants in a control condition who listened to a boring tape were regretful). Did their mood affect their helpfulness? When immediately thereafter they were given a chance to anonymously help a graduate student with her research, 25 percent of those whose attention had been self-focused did so, while of those whose attention was other-focused, 83 percent helped. The two groups were equally touched. But only the other-focused participants found helping someone especially rewarding. In short, the "Feel-bad, do-good" effect seems to occur with people whose attention is focused on others, people for whom altruism is therefore rewarding (Barnett et al., 1980; McMillen, Sanders, & Solomon, 1977). Unless self-preoccupied, sad people are often sensitive, helpful people.

So, are happy people unhelpful? Quite the contrary. There are few more consistent findings in the entire literature of psychology: Happy people are helpful people. As Table 11-2 indicates, this effect occurs with both children and adults, regardless of whether the good mood is produced by an ego-boosting success, by pondering happy thoughts, or by any of several other positive experiences. One woman recalled her experience after falling in love:

> At the office, I could hardly keep from shouting out how deliriously happy I felt. The work was easy; things that had annoyed me on previous occasions were taken in stride. And I had strong impulses to help others; I wanted to share my joy. When Mary's typewriter broke down, I virtually sprang to my feet to assist. Mary! My former "enemy"! (Tennov, 1979, p. 22)

TABLE 11-2 Doing Well and Doing Good: In Experiment after Experiment, People Put in a Good Mood Are More Helpful

Researchers	Participants	Happiness Is	Helpfulness Is
Berkowitz & Connor (1966)	University of Wisconsin students	Success at a jigsaw puzzle	Working hard to help a peer
Isen (1970)	Pennsylvania teachers	Success at perceptual judgments	Contributions; picking up a dropped book
	Stanford students	Success at perceptual judgments	Picking up a dropped book
Isen & Levin (1972)	Philadelphia area students	Receiving cookies	Helping an experimenter
	San Francisco and Philadelphia shoppers	Finding 10¢ in a phone booth	Picking up dropped papers
Aderman (1972)	University of Wisconsin students	Reading happy statements	Helping experimenters
Isen, Horn & Rosenhan (1973)	Fourth graders	Success at a game	Contributions for "poor children"
Moore, Underwood, & Rosenhan (1973)	Second and third graders	Thinking happy thoughts	Contributions for "other kids"

TABLE 11-2 (Cont.) Doing Well and Doing Good: In Experiment after Experiment, People Put in a Good Mood Are More Helpful

Researchers	Participants	Happiness Is	Helpfulness Is
Rosenhan, Underwood, & Moore (1974)	Second and third graders	Thinking happy thoughts	Contributions for "other kids"
Isen, Clark, & Schwartz (1976)	Pennsylvania and Maryland residents	Receiving a free sample	Relaying a wrong-number call
Sherrod et al. (1977)	College students	Writing positive thoughts; viewing attractive slides	Helping another experimenter
Veitch, DeWood, & Bosko (1977)	Bowling Green University students	Hearing a radio broadcast of good news	Helping look for a contact lens
Weyant (1978)	Florida State University students	Success in solving anagrams	Contributions
Cunningham (1979)	Minneapolis residents	Sunshine	Assisting an interviewer
	Chicagoans	Sunshine	Big restaurant tips
Fried & Berkowitz (1979)	University of Wisconsin students	Soothing music	Helping an experimenter
Cunningham, Steinberg & Grev (1980)	Minneapolis residents	Finding 10¢ in a phone booth	Picking up dropped papers; contributions
Yinon & Bizman (1980)	Israeli college students	Success on aptitude test	Tutoring a foreign student
Rosenhan, Salovey, & Hargis (1981)	Stanford students	Imagining a Hawaiian vacation	Helping another experimenter
Wilson (1981)	Texas A&M students	Listening to a Steve Martin comedy	Loaning money

In experiments the one helped usually is someone encountered "after" the experiment—someone seeking a donation, an experimenter seeking help with paperwork, a woman who drops papers. For example, Alice Isen, Margaret Clark, and Mark Schwartz (1976) had a confederate who had supposedly spent her last dime on a wrong number, call people who, from zero to twenty minutes earlier, had been given a free sample of stationery. As Figure 11-3 indicates, their willingness to relay the phone message rose slightly during the first four or five minutes afterward, perhaps as the gift "sank in" or as they became less distracted. But as the good mood wore off, helpfulness dropped.

If sad people are, at least under some conditions, extra helpful, how can it be that happy people are also helpful? One team of researchers, led by Alice Isen (1978), believes that whereas a negative mood can often be alleviated by

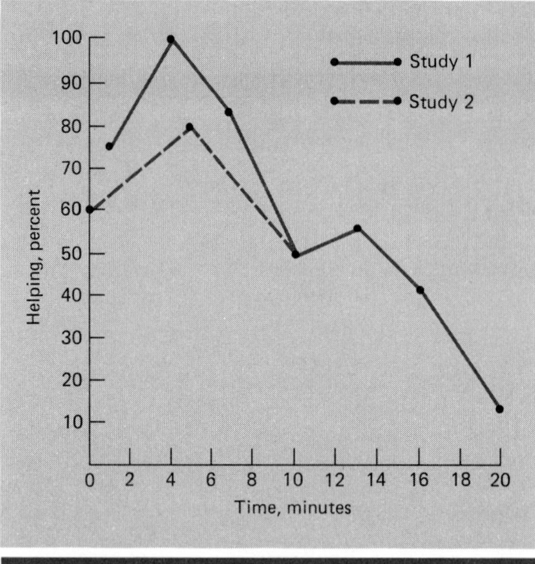

FIGURE 11-3
Percentage of those willing to relay a phone message 0 to 20 minutes after receiving a free sample. Of control subjects who did not receive a gift, only 10 percent helped. (Data from Isen, Clark, & Schwartz, 1976.)

positive behavior, a positive mood is conducive to positive thoughts, which are conducive to positive behavior. They report that people given a gift, or feeling the warm glow of success, are more likely to have positive thoughts on other topics. Furthermore, they surmise, positive thinkers are positive actors.

Personality Traits

We have thus far seen that the mood and guilt of a person dramatically affect altruism. Are there similar dramatic effects of a person's enduring personality traits? Surely there must be some traits which distinguish the other-focused Albert Schweitzers and Mother Theresas from those blinded by their own self-centeredness.

Surely. But as yet social psychologists have been unable to discover a single personality trait that predicts altruistic behavior with anything close to the predictive power of the situational, guilt, and mood factors. Modest relationships between helping and some personality variables, such as need for social approval and empathy, have occasionally been observed (Staub, 1978). But by and large, personality tests have been unable to identify altruists (Gergen, Gergen, & Meter, 1972; Huston et al., 1981; Latané & Darley, 1970).

In short, the situation can powerfully affect one's willingness to help; the influence of personality seems modest. If that has a familiar ring, it could well be because we examined a similar conclusion in our study of the research on conformity (Chapter 7): Conformity too is influenced greatly by the situation, but is essentially unpredictable by personality tests. My hunch, however, both then, and now, is that who we are nevertheless does affect what we do, and that just as attitude researchers have discovered methods that enable them to predict behavior, so future research may demonstrate that one's personality does indeed affect one's social behavior. Recall that attitudes seldom precisely predict a *specific* act (which is what most experiments on altruism measure, in contrast to the lifelong altruism of an Albert Schweitzer). But expressed attitudes better predict a person's general behavior (across many situations). So, too, personality scores—or a cluster of personality scores—may better predict altruistic behavior in general (Rushton, 1980, pp. 81–85).

People's long-term altruism may also be influenced by their personal values. For example, Peter Benson and his colleagues (1980) found that during the preceding year religiously committed Earlham College students recalled volunteering more hours as tutors, relief workers, campaigners for social justice, and so forth than did those who were less religiously committed (see also, Batson & Gray, 1981; Batson & Ventis, 1982). No doubt we will also learn more about how personality *interacts* with the situation to determine altruism—for example, about how a given situation affects some personality types one way and other types another.

HOW CAN ALTRUISM BE INCREASED?

As social scientists, our goal is to understand human behavior, thus also suggesting ways to improve it. Social psychologists therefore wonder how the insights emerging from research on altruism can be used to increase altruism.

Undoing the Restraints on Helping

One way to promote altruism is to reverse those factors that inhibit altruism. Since it appears that hurried, preoccupied people are less likely to help, can we think of ways to encourage them to slow down and turn their attention outward? If the presence of others diminishes each bystander's sense of responsibility, how can we enhance a bystander's sense of responsibility?

Reduce Ambiguity, Increase Responsibility

If Latané and Darley's decision tree (Figure 11-2) describes accurately the dilemmas bystanders face, then assisting people to correctly interpret an incident and to assume responsibility should increase their involvement. That is the presumption Leonard Bickman and his colleagues (1975; 1979; Bickman & Green, 1977; Bickman & Rosenbaum, 1977) tested in a series of experiments on crime reporting. In each experiment, supermarket or bookstore shoppers witnessed a shoplifting. Some witnesses had seen signs that attempted both to sensitize them to shoplifting and to inform them how to report it. But the signs had little effect. Other witnesses heard a bystander interpret the incident:

"Say, look at her. She's shoplifting. She put that into her purse." (The bystander then left to look for a lost child.) Still others heard this person add, "We saw it. We should report it. It's our responsibility." Both of these face-to-face comments substantially boosted reporting of the crime.

The potency of direct personal influence has been apparent in other research as well. Robert Foss (1978) surveyed several hundred blood donors and found that neophyte donors, unlike veterans, were usually there because someone had personally asked them. Nonverbal appeals also can be effective, when personalized. Mark Snyder, John Grether, and Kristine Keller (1974) found that hitchhikers doubled the number of rides they were offered by looking drivers straight in the eye. Being personally approached seems to make one feel less anonymous, more responsible.

A similar effect of reduced anonymity was observed in experiments by Henry Solomon and Linda Solomon (1978; Solomon et al., 1981). They found that bystanders who had identified themselves to one another by name, age, and so forth were more likely to offer aid to a sick person than were those who remained anonymous. Similarly, when a female experimenter caught the eye of a fellow shopper and gave her a warm smile prior to stepping on an elevator, that shopper was far more likely than other shoppers to offer help when the experimenter later said, "Damn. I've left my glasses. Can anyone tell me what floor the umbrellas are on?" Even a trivial momentary conversation—"Excuse me, aren't you Suzie Spear's sister?" "No, I'm not."—dramatically increased the subsequent helpfulness of the person addressed.

Altruism also increases when one expects later to meet and talk with a victim and other witnesses. Using a laboratory intercom system, Jody Gottlieb and Charles Carver (1980) led University of Miami students to believe they were discussing problems of college living with other students. (Actually, the other discussants were tape-recorded.) When one of the supposed fellow discussants had a choking fit and cried out for help, she was helped most quickly by subjects who believed they would soon be meeting their fellow discussants face to face. In short, anything that personalizes bystanders—a personal request, eye contact, stating one's name, anticipation of interaction—seems also to increase their willingness to act.

Bystanders' feeling that they are being treated personally probably makes them more self-aware and therefore more attuned to their own altruistic ideals. Recall (from Chapters 2 and 9) that people made self-aware (for example, by acting in front of a mirror or TV camera) usually exhibit increased consistency between their attitudes and their actions. By contrast, people who are "deindividuated" tend to be less responsible. This implies that circumstances that increase self-awareness—name tags, being watched and evaluated, undistracted quiet—will also increase altruism. Shelley Duval, Virginia Duval, and Robert Neely (1979) confirmed this supposition by showing University of Southern California women their own image on a TV screen, or having them complete a biographical questionnaire, just before giving them a chance to contribute time and money to people in need. Those made self-aware contributed more. Note that while these mild boosts to self-awareness strengthened the connection between the participants' ideals and their deeds, the self-awareness was apparently not so strong as to leave the participants preoccupied with themselves.

Guilt and Concern for Self-Image

Earlier we noted that people who have transgressed are eager to reduce their private feelings of guilt and to reestablish their self-worth. Can heightening people's awareness of their transgressions therefore increase their desire to help? A Reed College research team led by Richard Katzev (1978) wondered. So when visitors to the Portland Art Museum disobeyed a "Please do not touch" sign, they reprimanded some of them: "Please don't touch the objects. If everyone touches them, they will deteriorate." Likewise, when visitors to the Portland zoo fed unauthorized food to the bears, some of them were admonished with, "Hey, don't feed unauthorized food to the animals. Don't you know it could hurt them?" In both cases, 58 percent of the now guilt-laden subjects shortly thereafter offered help to another experimenter who had "accidentally" dropped something. Of those not so reprimanded, only about one-third helped.

People are also concerned about their public images. This, too, can be used as a means to get them to help others. When Robert Cialdini and his colleagues (1975) asked some of their Arizona State University students to chaperon delinquent children on a zoo trip, only 32 percent agreed to do so. With other students the questioner first made a very large request—that the students commit two years as volunteer counselors to delinquent children. After getting the "door-in-the-face" in response to this request (all refused), the questioner then counteroffered with the chaperoning request, saying, in effect, "Ok, if you won't do that, would you do just this much?" With this technique, nearly twice as many—56 percent—agreed to help. Other research indicates that people who refuse a large but reasonable request fear that the person refused may consider them as not helpful or concerned (Pendleton & Batson, 1979). Such heightened worry about one's image apparently predisposes the person to be more willing to help with a lesser request.

Door-in-the-face technique: *A strategy for gaining a concession in which, after someone is first given opportunity to turn down a large request (the door-in-the-face), the same requester counteroffers with a more reasonable request.*

When, in another experiment, Cialdini and David Schroeder (1976) had a solicitor approach suburbanites and say, "I'm collecting money for the American Cancer Society," 29 percent contributed, averaging $1.44 each. When the solicitor added "Even a penny will help," 50 percent contributed, averaging $1.54 each. Apparently, it's hard to turn down a request for a paltry contribution and still maintain one's altruistic self-image.

Socializing Altruism

If altruism is indeed not inborn, but learned, then how can it be taught? Here are three possibilities.

Reprimanding people can shrink their self-images. (Drawing by Joseph Farris; © 1980 *The New Yorker* Magazine, Inc.)

Modeling Altruism

Earlier we learned that when we see our fellow bystanders not respond, we are not likely to help; whereas, if we see someone being helpful, we are more likely to offer assistance. A similar modeling effect has been observed within families. Studies of European Christians who risked their lives to rescue Jews, and of the civil rights activists of the late 1950s, revealed that in both cases these exceptional altruists had close relationships with at least one parent who was, similarly, a strong "moralist" or committed to humanitarian causes (London, 1970; Rosenhan, 1970).

Do the effects of positive models extend to television, much as aggressive portrayals promote aggression? To date, the research indicates that television's prosocial models have actually had even greater effects than its antisocial models. Susan Hearold (1979; also Rushton, 1979) statistically combined 108 comparisons of prosocial versus either neutral programs or no program and found that, on the average, "If the viewer watched prosocial programs instead of neutral programs, he would [at least temporarily] be elevated from the 50th to the 74th percentile in prosocial behavior—typically altruism."

In one such study, researchers Lynette Friedrich and Aletha Stein (1973; Stein & Friedrich, 1972) showed preschool children *Mister Rogers' Neighborhood* episodes each day for four weeks as part of their nursery school program. (*Mister Rogers* is an educational program designed to enhance young children's social and emotional development.) During this viewing period, children from less educated homes became more cooperative, helpful, and likely to state their feelings. In a subsequent study, kindergarteners who viewed four *Mister Rogers* programs were able to state its prosocial content, both on a test and in puppet play (Friedrich & Stein, 1975; also Coates, Pusser, & Goodman, 1976).

"Children can learn to be altruistic, friendly and self-controlled by looking at television programs depicting such behavior patterns."

Television and Behavior
National Institute of Mental Health, 1982

Attributing One's Helpful Behavior to Altruistic Motives

Another clue to socializing altruism comes from research on what is called the "overjustification effect": When the justification for an act is overly sufficient, the person may attribute the act to the extrinsic justification rather than to an inner motive. Thus, rewarding people for doing what they would do anyway can undermine their intrinsic motivation. This principle can be stated positively: By providing people with just enough justification to prompt a good deed (weaning them from bribes and threats when possible), we may help maximize their pleasure in doing such deeds on their own.

Overjustification effect: *See Chapter 2, pages 64–66.*

The overjustification phenomenon has been illustrated by Daniel Batson and his associates (1978; 1979) in research with University of Kansas students. In several experiments they found that students felt most altruistic after they had agreed to help someone without payment or implied social pressure. When pay had been offered or social pressures were present, people felt less altruistic after helping. In another experiment, students who were drawn into helping someone were led to attribute their doing so either to compliance ("I guess we really don't have a choice") or to compassion ("The guy really needs help . . ."). Subsequently, when the students were asked to volunteer their time to a local service agency, 25 percent of those who had been led to perceive their previous helpfulness as mere compliance now volunteered; of those led to see themselves as compassionate, 60 percent volunteered. The moral? Simple: When people wonder, "Why am I helping?" it's best if the circumstances enable them to answer, "Because I am a caring, giving, helpful person."

It is important to remember that rewards don't always undermine intrinsic motivation. As you may recall from Chapter 2, what matters is whether the reward functions as a bribe, leading people to see their behavior as controlled rather than inner directed, or as an unanticipated compliment, leading people to feel competent and worthy. When Joe is coerced with "If you'll quit being chicken and give blood, we'll win the fraternity prize for most donations," he'll likely not attribute his donation to altruism. When Jocelyn is rewarded with "That's terrific that you'd choose to take an hour out of such a busy week to give blood," she's more likely to walk away with an altruistic self-image—and thus to contribute again (J. A. Piliavin, Evans, & Callero, 1982; G. C. Thomas & Batson, 1981; Thomas, Batson, & Coke, 1981).

The importance of one's self-image is also apparent in research on the effect of labeling people. After they had made a charitable contribution, Robert Kraut (1973) told some New Haven, Connecticut, women, "You are

"I can think of at least a half-dozen good deeds we could do if we got paid for them."

The overjustification effect: Extrinsic rewards can undermine intrinsic motivation. (Al Ross/*Saturday Review* 10/18/75)

a generous person." Two weeks later, these women were more willing than those not labeled to contribute to a different charity. Likewise, Angelo Strenta and William DeJong (1981) told some students that their personality test revealed that "You are a kind, thoughtful person." These students were later more likely than other students to be kindly and thoughtful toward a confederate who dropped a stack of computer cards.

Learning about Altruism

Researchers have found one other way to boost altruism, one that provides a happy insight to conclude our chapter. Some social psychologists have been concerned that as people become more aware of social psychology's findings, their behavior may change, thus invalidating the findings (Gergen, 1973). Will having learned about the factors that inhibit altruism make people less influenced by these factors? Sometimes, such "enlightenment" is not our problem but one of our goals, a goal that leads to more compassionate behavior.

Experiments with University of Montana students by Arthur Beaman and his colleagues (1978) indicate that once people understand why the presence of bystanders inhibits helping, they become more likely to help in group situations. The researchers used a lecture to inform some students how bystanders' refusal to help can affect both one's interpretation of an emergency and one's feelings of responsibility. Other students heard either a different lecture, or no lecture at all. Two weeks later, as part of a different experiment in a different location, the participants found themselves walking (with an unresponsive confederate) past someone slumped over, or past a person sprawled beneath a bicycle. Of those who had not heard the helping lecture, about a fourth paused to offer help; of the "enlightened," twice as many did so.

Coincidentally, shortly before I wrote the last paragraph, a former student, now living in Washington, D.C., stopped by. She mentioned that she recently found herself part of a stream of pedestrians striding past a man lying unconscious on the sidewalk. "It took my mind back to our social psych class and the accounts of why people fail to help in such situations. Then I thought, well, if I just walk by, too, who's going to help him?" So she made a call to an emergency help number and waited with the victim—and other bystanders who now joined her—until help arrived.

SUMMING UP

Why Do People Help?

Three prominent theories attempt to explain altruistic behavior. The *social-exchange theory* assumes that helping, like other social behaviors, is motivated by people's desire to minimize their costs and maximize their rewards—rewards either external (for example, social approval) or internal (for example, reducing distress, increasing self-satisfaction).

It is also theorized that one's willingness to help is motivated by *social norms*. The *reciprocity norm* stimulates us to return help, not harm, to those who have helped us. The *social-responsibility norm* leads us to feel we should help needy, deserving people, even if they cannot reciprocate.

Sociobiology assumes two types of altruism: that favored by natural selection, such as devotion to one's kin, and that of reciprocity. Some biologists also believe that groups whose members are altruistic will survive better than groups whose members are selfish. However, most sociobiologists believe that the genes of selfish individuals are more likely to survive than the genes of self-sacrificing individuals, and that society must therefore teach altruism.

These three theories complement one another. Each uses psychological, sociological, or biological concepts to account for two types of altruism: (1) an "altruism" of reciprocal exchange—when you scratch my back, I'm more likely to scratch yours—and (2) an unconditional altruism. Yet each theory is vulnerable to charges both of being speculative and of inventing explanations, explanations that more clearly describe than predict altruism.

When Will People Help?

Several situational influences work either to inhibit or encourage altruism. As the number of bystanders at an emergency increases, any given bystander is (1) less likely to notice the incident, (2) less likely to interpret it as an emergency, and (3) less likely to assume responsibility. This is especially true when the situation is ambiguous, or when the bystanders cannot easily detect one another's alarm.

When are people most likely to help? (1) After observing someone else helping and (2) when not hurried. And who are those most likely to elicit our help? (1) Those who both need and deserve it and (2) those similar to us.

Helping is further affected by such personal influences as people's moods. After transgressing, one often becomes more willing to offer help, apparently hoping to expunge guilt or to restore one's self-image. People who are sad also tend to be altruistic, especially when being helpful is a way to eliminate the mood. However, this "Feel-bad, do-good" effect is generally not found in young children, suggesting that the inner rewards gained from altruism are a product of later socialization. Finally, it has consistently been found that happy people are helpful people.

In contrast to altruism's potent situational and mood determinants, personality test scores have served only modestly as predictors of helping.

Increasing Altruism

Research suggests that altruism can be particularly enhanced in two ways. First, reverse those factors that inhibit altruism. We can take steps to reduce the ambiguity of an emergency situation, or to increase people's feelings of responsibility (for example, by reducing feelings of anonymity or increasing self-awareness). And we can even use reprimands or the door-in-the-face technique to evoke guilt feelings or a concern for people's self-images.

Second, we can teach altruism. For example, research into television's portrayals of prosocial models clearly indicates the medium's power to teach positive behavior. Children who view helpful behavior tend to act similarly. However, if we attempt to coax altruistic behavior from people, we had best also remember the "overjustification effect": When either excessive rewards or threats are used to coerce good deeds, people's intrinsic love of the activity often diminishes. If people are provided with enough justification for them to decide to do good, but not much more, they are likely to attribute their behavior to their own altruistic motivation and henceforth be more willing to help.

Chapter

Prejudice: Disliking Others

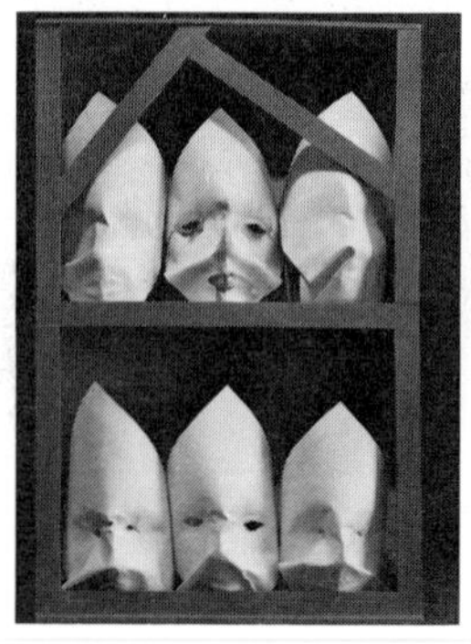

Prejudice and discrimination come in many forms. Consider a few actual occurrences:

Several years ago, a group of homosexual students at the University of Illinois announced that the motto for one spring day would be: "If you are gay, wear blue jeans today." When the day dawned, many who usually wore jeans woke up with an urge to dress up in skirt or slacks. The homosexual group had made its point—that attitudes toward homosexuals are such that many would rather give up their usual clothes lest anyone suspect. . . . (*RCAgenda*, 1979)

Yoshio, one of a group of Japanese university students visiting an American college, matter-of-factly reveals to his Japanese peers that he is a "Burakumin," one of Japan's "ghetto-people" whose ancestors had a polluting occupation. Their response: hands come to the mouth and brows furrow, revealing their shock and astonishment. For though physically indistinguishable from other Japanese, the Burakumin have for generations been segregated in Japan's slums, considered eligible only for the most menial occupations and unfit for intermarriage with other Japanese. So, how could it be that this obviously bright, attractive, ambitious student was a Burakumin?

Shortly after World War II a Canadian social scientist simultaneously mailed 100 Ontario resorts two letters asking for room reservations for the same dates. In response to one letter, signed by "Mr. Lockwood," 93 percent of the resorts offered accommodations. In response to the other, signed by "Mr. Greenberg" (a frequently Jewish name), 36 percent offered accommodations. (Wax, 1948)

WHAT IS PREJUDICE?

Prejudice, stereotyping, discrimination, racism, sexism. The terms often overlap. So, before seeking to understand prejudice, let's first sharpen our vocabulary by clarifying the terms. Each of the situations described above involved people harboring or acting upon bad feelings toward a particular group. And that is the essence of *prejudice*: an unjustifiable negative attitude toward a group and its individual members. Prejudice involves prejudgment; it biases us against a person based solely on the person's membership in a particular group.

Prejudice: *An unjustifiable negative attitude toward a group and its individual members.*

Prejudice is an attitude. As we saw in Chapter 2, an attitude is a distinct combination of feelings, inclinations to act, and beliefs. This combination we called the ABC of attitudes: *a*ffect (feelings), *b*ehavior tendency (inclination to act), and *c*ognition (beliefs). A prejudiced person might therefore *dislike* the Burakumin and be inclined to *behave* in a discriminatory manner, *believing* them ignorant and dangerous.

The beliefs out of which prejudicial feelings grow are called *stereotypes*. To stereotype is to generalize. In attempts to simplify the world, people often generalize: Blacks are better basketball players than whites. Professors are absentminded. Members of fraternity X are animals. Such shorthand summaries of the world can sometimes be helpful. The problem with stereotypes arises when they are inaccurate, or *over*generalized, or resistant to change. Thus, if you told me I was about to meet Mike, an avid organic gardener, I might form an image of someone in bib overalls sporting a neatly trimmed beard and driving a VW Microbus displaying a "Ban Handguns" bumper sticker. Certainly I would not expect someone to pull up in a Cadillac and emerge wearing a vested blue suit with a "We Need Nukes" lapel button. My stereotype of organic gardeners may contain a kernel of truth. Yet it is likely an overgeneralization. There may well be some conservatively dressed, Cadillac-driving organic gardeners. Were I to meet one I might just shrug it off by telling myself, "The exception proves the rule."

Stereotype: *A generalization about a group of people that distinguishes those people from others. Stereotypes can be overgeneralized, inaccurate, and resistant to new information.*

Prejudice is a negative *attitude; discrimination* is negative *behavior*. And discriminatory behavior, though it often erupts from prejudicial attitudes, does not always do so. As Chapter 2 emphasized, attitudes and behavior are often loosely linked, partly because our behavior is influenced not only by our inner convictions but also by the requirements of particular situations. Prejudiced attitudes need not breed hostile acts, nor does all oppression spring from prejudice. *Racism* and *sexism*, for example, refer not only to individuals' prejudicial attitudes, but also to institutional practices that discriminate, even when there is no prejudicial intent.

Discrimination: *Unjustifiable negative behavior toward a group and its members.*

Racism: *(1) Individuals' prejudicial attitudes and discriminatory behavior toward people of a given race, or (2) institutional practices (even if not motivated by prejudice) that subordinate people of a given race.*

Sexism: *(1) Individuals' prejudicial attitudes and discriminatory behavior toward people of a given sex, or (2) institutional practices (even if not motivated by prejudice) that subordinate people of a given sex.*

Imagine a state police force that set a height requirement of 5 feet 10 inches for all its officers. If this institutional requirement were irrelevant to on-the-job effectiveness but tended to exclude Hispanics, Orientals, and women, the requirement might then well be labeled racist and sexist. Note also that one could make this allegation even if such discrimination were not intended. Similarly, if, by word of mouth, the hiring practices in an all-white business had the effect of excluding employees different from those presently employed, the practice could be called racist, even if the employer were open-minded and intended no discrimination. In this chapter we will explore the sources and consequences of prejudiced attitudes; we will not deal with racism and sexism in their institutional forms.

HOW PERVASIVE IS PREJUDICE?

Is prejudice inevitable? Can it be eradicated? As a case example, let's look at prejudice in the United States, examining trends in both racial and gender prejudice.

Racial Prejudice

To judge from what Americans tell survey takers, racial prejudice has plummeted since the early 1940s. In 1942, a majority of Americans agreed that "there should be separate sections for Negroes on streetcars and buses" (Hyman & Sheatsley, 1956); today, the question would seem bizarre to most people. In 1942, fewer than a third of all whites (only 1 in 50 in the south) supported school integration; in 1980, support for such was nearing 90 percent (National Opinion Research Center). A near consensus of white adults believe, "Blacks should have as good a chance as whites to get any kind of job"; they would be willing to send their children to an integrated school; and as we saw in Chapter 11, they are, at least in most face-to-face situations, unlikely to let race interfere with their aiding a person in need. Recently, in questioning a sample of Pennsylvanians ranging from high school students to church choir members, Clark McCauley and Christopher Stitt (1978) found that when white people estimated the relative frequency of blacks' and whites' being on welfare, having "a female head of family," or having four or more children at home, if they erred at all, they erred by tending to *under*estimate the real black-white differences. In earlier decades, stereotypes concerning such differences were strong (Karlins, Coffman, & Walters, 1969).

This decrease in expressing prejudice occurred primarily before 1972; since then, racial attitudes have stabilized (see Figure 12-1). Still, considering what a thin slice of history is covered by the years since 1942, or even since the time when human enslavement was an accepted American practice, the changes are dramatic.

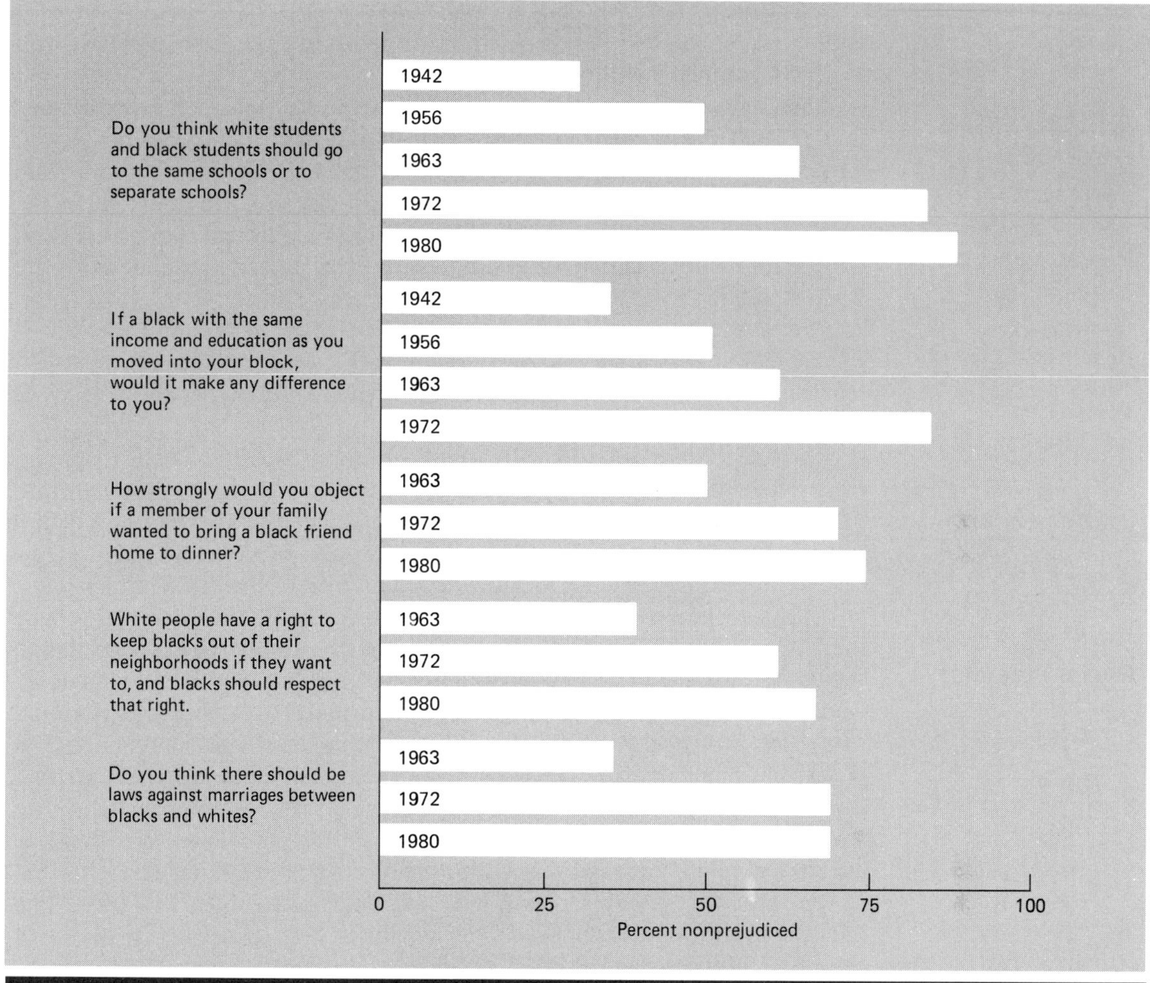

FIGURE 12-1 Expressed racial attitudes of white Americans from 1942 to 1980. (Data from Condran, 1979; Hyman & Sheatsley, 1956; 1964; National Opinion Research Center, 1980.)

Black Americans' attitudes also have changed. A significant influence upon the Supreme Court's 1954 decision declaring segregated schools unconstitutional was research by Kenneth Clark and Mamie Clark (1947) demonstrating that black Americans held antiblack prejudices. Given a choice between black dolls and white dolls, black children tended to choose the white. In recent studies, black children have tended to prefer black dolls, and black adults have viewed blacks and whites as essentially equal in such traits as intelligence, laziness, and dependability (Banks, 1976; Brand, Ruiz, & Padilla, 1974; Y. M. Epstein, Krupat, & Obudho, 1976; Jackman & Senter, 1978; Smedley & Bayton, 1978).

So, shall we conclude that racial prejudice is extinct in America? Americans may at least congratulate themselves that today, far more than in decades past, racial prejudice is unfashionable. If a judge asks prospective jurors, "Do any of you have racial prejudice that would bias your consideration of the defendant?" even bigots will likely keep their hands in their laps. Yet, there are several indications that racial prejudice still exists underground, surfacing when it is safe.

First, prejudice is evident in the residue of white Americans who, as Figure 12-1 indicates, unabashedly dislike blacks. Their attitudes are mirrored by a smaller percentage of black Americans who, similarly, dislike and avoid whites (Farley et al., 1978).

"I will buy with you, sell with you, talk with you, walk with you, and so following; but I will not eat with you, drink with you, nor pray with you."

Shylock in William Shakespeare's The Merchant of Venice

Second, while variations on the question, "Should America oppress blacks?" no longer detect prejudice, questions concerning more intimate interracial contacts do. "I would probably feel uncomfortable dancing with a black person in a public place," is a more sensitive detector of racial feelings than "I would probably feel uncomfortable riding a bus with a black person."

Third, when racial attitudes are measured using techniques that reduce the likelihood of people's simply stating what they think is socially desirable, prejudice reappears. In an earlier chapter, we saw that when white university students indicate their racial attitudes while hooked to an elaborate machine that supposedly acts as a lie detector, they often admit to more prejudice than do students responding under normal conditions. Other researchers have invited people to evaluate someone's behavior, that someone being either white or black. For example, Birt Duncan (1976; also Sagar & Schofield, 1980c) had white University of California, Irvine, students observe on a TV screen what they thought was a live confrontation between two men. The men's conversation developed into an argument that culminated with one of the two lightly shoving the other. When a white shoved a black man, only 13 percent of the observers rated the act as "violent behavior." They more often interpreted the action as "playing around" or "dramatizing." Not so when a black shoved a white man: Then, 73 percent of the observers said the act was "violent."

Fourth, many experiments have subtly assessed people's actual behavior toward blacks and whites. As noted in Chapter 11, research during the 1970s found that white Americans were as likely to aid a needy black person (for example, one who dropped groceries) as a white—except when the person in need was remote (for example, a wrong number caller who needed a phone message relayed). In studies by Edward Donnerstein and Marcia Donnerstein and others, white people were asked to use electric shocks to "teach" a task to either a white or a black person. As in the helping studies, people were not consistently affected by the recipient's race—except when the aggression was safe (when the recipient could not retaliate or when the aggressor was anonymous) (Crosby, Bromley, & Saxe, 1980). And, in an experiment at the University of Alabama, Ronald Rogers and Steven Prentice-Dunn (1981) found that nonangered whites administered less shock to a black victim than a white victim, but that *angered* whites behaved quite differently. When the victim had insulted them, they responded with *more* shocks when he was black than when he was white (see Figure 12-2).

Fifth and finally, recent surveys have detected that people's friends, neighbors, and classmates still tend to be of the same race. For example, Janet Schofield, Andrew Sagar, and their colleagues have observed thousands of students in desegregated middle school classrooms (Sagar & Schofield, 1980b; Francis & Schofield, 1982). Girls, especially, spent most of their time with those of their own race.

As Figure 12-1 indicated, the overwhelming majority of white Americans now claim that it would make no difference to them if a black of similar income and education were to move onto their block. And nearly all oppose housing discrimination: In recent surveys by CBS News (1978) and ABC News (1981), 93 percent agreed that "Blacks have a right to live wherever they can afford to, just like whites" (although 55 percent still favored a law saying that "a homeowner can decide for himself who to sell his house to even if he prefers not to sell to blacks"). But when Reynolds Farley, Howard Schuman, and their colleagues (1978) posed yet another question in surveying

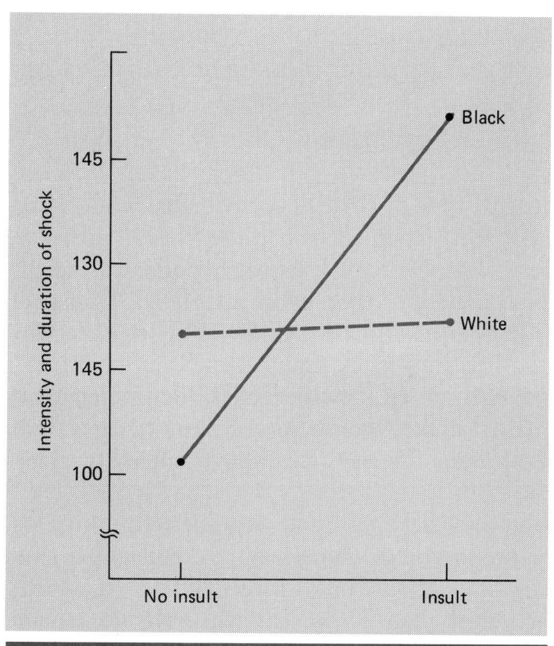

FIGURE 12-2 Does anger trigger latent prejudice? When white students administered electric shock, supposedly as part of a "behavior-modification experiment," they behaved less aggressively toward an agreeable black victim than toward a white victim. But when the victim objected to the shocks and insulted the subjects, they responded with more aggression toward the black victim. (Data from Rogers & Prentice-Dunn, 1981.)

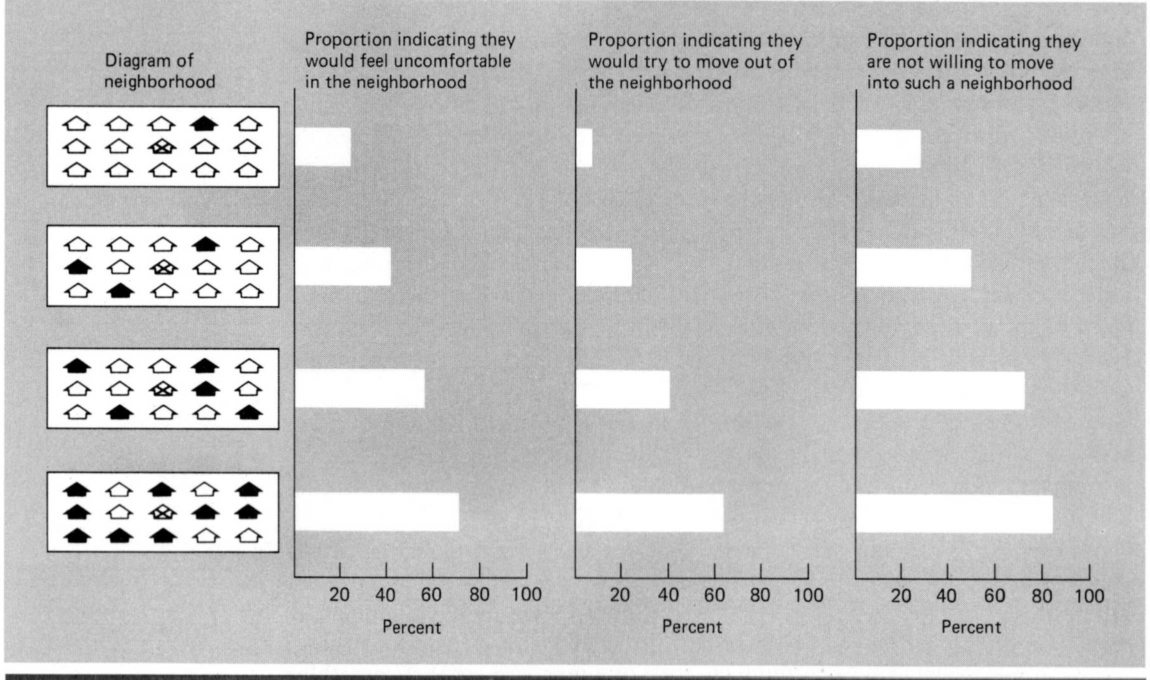

FIGURE 12-3 Neighborhood preferences of white Detroit area residents. People were shown diagrams representing neighborhoods of different racial mixes (combinations of black houses and white houses). The house in the center was designated "your house." (Data from Reynolds Farley et al., 1978.)

the heavily segregated Detroit area, they discovered considerable white racial bias. Contrary to the notion that segregation exists because "blacks prefer to be with their own kind," most *black* Detroiters shown hypothetical neighborhood patterns said they would prefer one thoroughly integrated. Similarly, in a nationwide 1981 Gallup Poll, black Americans, by an 8 to 1 margin, preferred a neighborhood "that has both black families and white families" over an all-black neighborhood. Whites, on the other hand, found integrated neighborhoods unappealing; half said they would be unwilling to move into a neighborhood where only three of the fifteen homes were occupied by black families (see Figure 12-3).

If all whites in the Detroit area held the same attitudes, the "tipping point"—the point at which the proportion of whites leaving the neighborhood would begin to exceed those entering—should be 70 percent white, 30 percent black. Neighborhoods that are more than 70 percent white should remain stably integrated. But they seldom do. Why? Farley, Schuman, and their colleagues reason it's because white attitudes vary. Few whites would be troubled by a black family's moving into their neighborhood. But as Figure 12-3 shows, 7 percent said they would be bothered enough to move out. If any of these vacancies were filled by blacks—an increasingly likely possibility once the racial barrier was broken (since blacks overwhelmingly prefer integrated areas)—then the proportion of blacks would rise to the threshold where a few more whites might leave. And so forth, until the neighborhood would ultimately become all-black. It's unfortunate, especially because most whites are open to and most blacks prefer some degree of racial integration. On the other hand, if white residents are similarly open to at least minimal integration, or if whites continue to develop more liberal attitudes, as they have since 1940, or if the number of whites migrating back into the cities equals the number migrating outward, stable integration may eventually occur. As yet, however, researchers Farley and Schuman conclude that the reality in many urban areas is aptly summarized by the words of a pop tune: "chocolate city, vanilla suburbs."

Survey researchers, too, have found that prejudice, though no longer blatant, still exists in subtle forms (McConahay, Hardee, & Batts, 1981). One such form can be opposition to school busing to achieve better racial balance. If busing is serenely accepted when it transfers students of certain grades between two white schools but vehemently resisted when it includes a school with a substantial minority enrollment, then one may suspect that something more is involved than a commitment to neighborhood schools. [In 1980, school busing for racial purposes was in fact opposed by 82 percent of white Americans, though only by 33 percent of blacks (Gallup).] John McConahay (1982) in surveying residents of the Louisville, Kentucky, area, found that people who strongly opposed busing for desegregation also exhibited other signs of subtle prejudice—for example, agreeing that "Over the past few years the government and news media have shown more respect to blacks than they deserve." And Donald Kinder and David Sears (1981) report that whites in the Los Angeles area who exhibited subtle prejudice (for example, strong opposition to busing) were unlikely to vote for black mayoral candidate Thomas Bradley.

To summarize: The good news—during the past four decades blatant prejudice against black Americans has plunged. White racial attitudes are far more egalitarian than a generation ago, and as of 1980 the upward trend was continuing, although more slowly. The bad news—racial fears, resentments, and partiality still lurk, though now camouflaged by a more pleasant exterior.

Prejudice against Women

How pervasive is prejudice against women? In Chapter 6, we examined sex-role norms. Are these norms undergirded by gender stereotypes? There is, as you might imagine, considerable overlap between people's conceptions of how women and men *should* differ (norms) and how they *do* differ (stereotypes)

Recall that sex-role norms *are* prescriptions *for how males and females* ought *to behave; gender* stereotypes *are* descriptive *beliefs about how they* actually *differ.*

"All the pursuits of men are the pursuits of women also, and in all of them a woman is only a lesser man."

Plato, Republic

"I love men, not because they are men, but because they are not women."

Queen Christina of Sweden

(Stoppard & Kalin, 1978). But stereotypes needn't imply sex-role norms. If an employer believes that women employees have higher turnover rates than do men hired for the same work [generally a false stereotype (Frieze et al., 1978, p. 249)], this need not mean that the employer believes women ought to quit sooner. Nevertheless, such a stereotype could undergird prejudice and discrimination against female applicants.

From research on stereotypes, two conclusions are indisputable: Strong gender stereotypes exist, and, as often happens, members of the stereotyped group accept the stereotypes. Men and women agree that you *can* judge the book by its sexual cover. Analyzing responses from a 1975 University of Michigan survey of adult Americans, Mary Jackman and Mary Senter (1981) found that gender stereotypes were much stronger than racial stereotypes. For example, only 22 percent of men thought the two sexes equally "emotional." Of the remaining 78 percent, those who believed females were more emotional outnumbered those who thought males were by 15 to 1. And what did the women believe? To within 1 percentage point, their responses were identical.

Those who saw some differences between the sexes were also asked *why* men and women differ:

Which of the statements on this card comes closest to what you think? Just tell me the letter of your answer.

X. Most differences are there because they're born different.

Y. Most differences come from the way they're brought up at home.

Z. Most differences come from the different opportunities they have in America.

How would you answer this question? Although more men (28 percent) than women (21 percent) favored the "born different" explanation, a plurality of both men and women favored the second explanation (socialization). Similarly, a 1979 Roper survey found that Americans by a better than 2 to 1 margin believe that men's "masculine ways" and women's "feminine ways" result more from the way people are raised and taught than from inherent physical differences. So, while Americans have clear stereotypes of how the sexes differ, most do not see these differences as biologically immutable.

When Inge Broverman, Paul Rosenkrantz, and their colleagues (Rosenkrantz et al., 1968; Broverman et al., 1972) surveyed New England college students and adults, they too found men and women in striking agreement: males were seen as generally more competent (aggressive, independent, dominant, decisive, ambitious) and females as warmer and more expressive (aware of others' feelings, tactful, gentle, exhibiting tender feelings). At the University of Delaware, Natalie Porter and Florence Geis (1981) found that women were not likely to be seen as leaders. They showed students pictures

FIGURE 12-4 Which one of these people would you guess is the strongest contributor to the group? Shown this picture, college students usually guessed one of the two men, despite the fact that in same-sex groups the person at the head of the table is the most commonly guessed. (Photograph courtesy of Porter and Geis, 1981.)

of "a group of graduate students working as a team on a research project" (see Figure 12-4). Then they gave them a test of "first impressions," asking them to guess which member contributed most to the group. When the group was either all-male or all-female, the students overwhelmingly chose the person at the head of the table. When the group was mixed-sex, a man occupying the head position was again overwhelmingly chosen. But a woman occupying that position was ignored. Each of the men in Figure 12-4 received more of the leadership choices than all three women combined. This stereotype of men as leaders seemed to operate unconsciously, for it was true not only of women as well as men, but also of feminists as well as nonfeminists. How pervasive are gender stereotypes? Quite pervasive.

It is important to remember that stereotypes are simply generalizations about a group of people, and as such may be true, false, or overgeneralized based on a kernel of truth. How males and females *actually* differ was a topic of Chapter 6. There, we noted that men and women do tend to differ in aggressiveness, social power, spatial ability, and empathy. So, might we conclude that gender stereotypes are accurate?

At best, they are probably overgeneralizations. The stereotypes are strong; the actual behavioral differences are small. Moreover, some gender stereotypes exist even where behavioral differences do not. You can likely recall struggling to decide whether to call someone's new baby a "he" or a "she." Differences in the size, appearance, and behavior of newborn boys and girls are too trivial to allow one to discriminate between the sexes. Nevertheless, parents, especially fathers, have been found to rate their day-old daughters as softer, smaller, and more beautiful, and their sons as firmer, stronger, and better coordinated (J. Z. Rubin, Provenzano, & Luria, 1974).

It is also important to remember that stereotypes (beliefs) are not prejudices (attitudes). Stereotypes may support prejudice (as does the false notion about the turnover rate of female employees). But then again one might believe without prejudice that men and women are "different yet equal." Let us therefore see how researchers have probed for gender prejudice both in its overt and in its subtle forms. Is there such prejudice?

Judging from what Americans tell survey researchers, attitudes toward women have changed as rapidly as racial attitudes. In 1937, one-third of Americans said they would vote for a qualified woman whom their party nominated for President; in 1978, more than 4 in 5, male and female alike, said they would. In 1938, 1 in 5 approved "of a married woman earning money in business or industry if she has a husband capable of supporting her"; in 1978, 3 out of 4 approved. In 1970, Americans were split 50-50 on whether they favored or opposed "efforts to strengthen women's status." By 1979 this fundamental tenet of the women's movement was favored by better than 2 to 1. (See Figure 12-5.) And should there be "equal pay for women and men when they are doing the same job?" (NBC, 1977b) Yes, say both men and women—by a 16 to 1 margin, as close to absolute consensus as Americans ever get. From the days in which they were legally relegated to second-class citizenship and denied the right to vote, women have indeed "come a long way."

And there is more good news for those who are upset by gender bias. Two heavily publicized findings of prejudice against women seem either no longer to hold true or not to have the implications initially feared. In one study, Philip Goldberg (1968) gave women students at Connecticut College several short articles, asking them to judge the value of each. Sometimes a given article was attributed to a male author (for example, John T. McKay), other times to a female author (for example, Joan T. McKay). In general, the articles received lower ratings when attributed to a female. The historic mark of oppression—self-deprecation—surfaces again. Women were prejudiced against women.

Eager to demonstrate the subtle reality of gender prejudice, I obtained Goldberg's materials and repeated the experiment for the benefit of my own students. They showed no such tendency to deprecate women's work. So Janet Swim and I searched the literature and corresponded with investigators

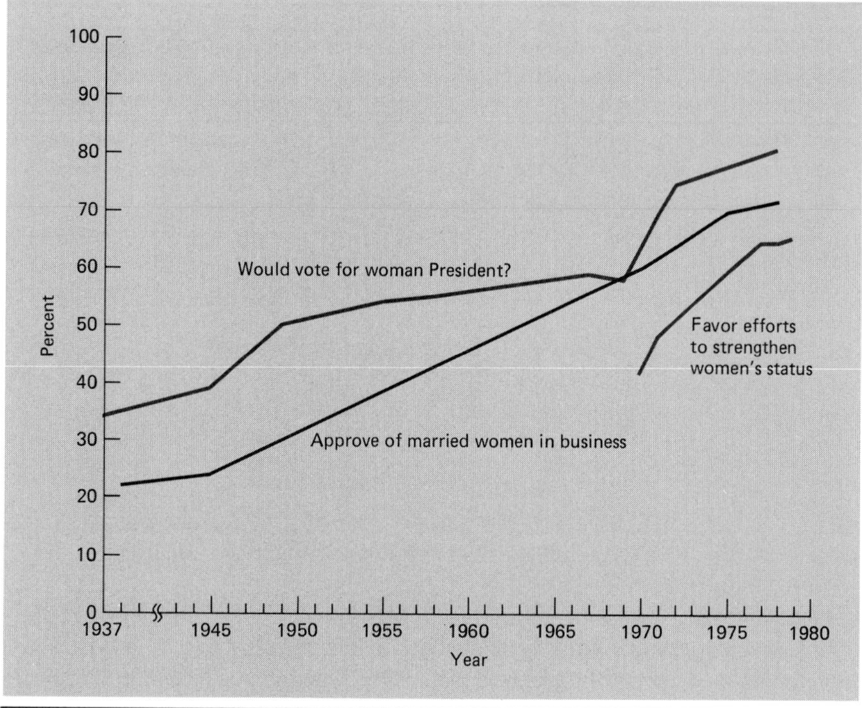

FIGURE 12-5 Prejudice against women: an idea whose time has passed? The percentage of Americans who say they (1) favor efforts to strengthen women's status, (2) would vote for a qualified woman candidate for president, and (3) approve of married women earning money in business and industry has steadily increased since the mid-1930s. (Data from Gallup, Roper, Harris, and National Opinion Research Center polls summarized in *Public Opinion*, September–October 1978, p.36; January-February 1979, p.36; and December-January 1980, pp. 33-34. Copyright American Enterprise Institute.)

to learn all that we could about studies of gender bias in the evaluation of men's and women's work. Table 12-1 indicates that in experiments during the 1970s, bias occasionally surfaced, though as often against men as against women. But the most common result was no difference: On two-thirds of the comparisons, people's judgments of someone's work were not significantly affected by whether the work was attributed to a female or a male.

The second widely publicized finding, by Inge Broverman and her associates (1970), suggested that mental health workers (psychologists, psychiatrists, social workers) view the "healthy person" as virtually synonymous with the "healthy male," but view the "healthy female" as one who adjusts

TABLE 12-1 Evaluations of Work Attributed to Women and to Men

Researchers	Participants	Stimuli	Who Was Favored
P. Goldberg (1968)	Connecticut College Women	Articles on masculine, feminine, and neuter topics	Males
Pheterson (1969)	Middle-aged women	Articles	No difference
Pheterson, Kiesler, & Goldberg (1971)	Connecticut College women	Painting entries Painting winners	Males No difference
Baruch (1972)	Swarthmore College women	Articles on masculine, feminine, and neuter topics	No difference
Gold (1972)	Columbia Univ. men	Articles	No difference
	Columbia Univ. women	Articles	Females
	Univ. of Massachusetts students	Articles	No difference
Robison (1972)	Western Illinois Univ. students	Persuasive essays	No difference
S. Higgins (1973)	Western Illinois Univ. women	Articles	No difference
	Middle-aged women	Articles	No difference
Wallies (1973)	Western Illinois Univ. women	Articles on masculine, feminine, and neuter topics	No difference
Chobot et al. (1974)	Univ. of Connecticut students	Articles	No difference
Etaugh & Sanders (1974)	Bradley Univ. students	Paintings	No difference
H. N. Mischel (1974)	High school & Stanford Univ. students	Masculine articles Feminine articles	Males Females
	Israeli youths and adults	Articles on masculine and feminine topics	No difference
Etaugh & Rose (1975)	Seventh, ninth, & eleventh graders	Articles on masculine, feminine, and neuter topics	No difference
Levenson et al. (1975)	Texas university students	Articles on masculine, feminine, and neuter topics	No difference
	Men students	A political science test essay	No difference
	Women students	A political science test essay	Females

TABLE 12-1 (Cont.) Evaluations of Work Attributed to Women and to Men

Researchers	Participants	Stimuli	Who Was Favored
Cline, Holmes, & Werner (1977)	Kansas collegians and residents	Sketches	No difference
	Men only	Quotations	Males
	Women only	Quotations	Females
Panek et al. (1976)	Connecticut collegians	Goldberg's articles	No difference
Peck (1978)	Univ. of Wisconsin, Parkside, students	Articles	No difference
Friend, Kalin, & Giles (1979)	British university men	Articles on masculine & feminine topics	Males
Linsenmeier & Wortman (1979)	Northwestern Univ. students	Minicourses with expert leaders	No difference
	Men only	Minicourses with inexpert leaders	No difference
	Women only	Minicourses with inexpert leaders	Males
C. Ward (1979)	British art and university students	Painting No. 1	Females
		Painting No. 2	No difference
C. Ward (1981)	British undergraduates	Article	No difference
	British art and university students	Painting	No difference

to feminine norms of submissiveness, emotionality, and dependence. Thus, mental health workers seemed to share their culture's sex-role norms. If they also imposed them on their clients, then they would be agents for the status quo, as when a therapist would tell a battered wife that she caused her husband's outbursts by her "hostile" failure to keep the house spotless.

Do counselors and psychotherapists in fact endorse and help perpetuate male domination? That is, do they share the prevailing sex-role norms? And do they apply these norms in making mental health judgments and in giving advice? In separate analyses of several dozen recent experiments examining the charge that mental health workers are sexist, Bernard Whitley (1979) and Mary Lee Smith (1980) concur on a verdict: not guilty. Although mental health workers agree with some of the common sex-role norms, they have nevertheless been observed to evaluate and treat men and women similarly.

The attention given the highly publicized studies of prejudice against women's work and of gender bias in psychotherapy illustrates once more a point emphasized in Chapter 1: Social scientists' values often penetrate their conclusions. This comment is not directed at the researchers who conducted the publicized studies; they did as they should in reporting their findings.

However, as often happens, my colleagues and I more readily accepted, generalized, and proclaimed the findings supporting our preconceived biases than those opposing them.

So, can Americans congratulate themselves that gender bias too is fast becoming extinct? Has the women's movement nearly completed its work? No. Despite the above findings, other research indicates that while blatant gender prejudice is dying, subtle bias still lives. While 3 out of 4 Americans may approve of a married woman's being employed, only one-third disagree with the seemingly contradictory proposition that "women's place is in the home" (Yankelovich, 1978, p. 34). (Perhaps it's considered okay for a woman to work outside the home, but better that she be home.) An even clearer indication is the repeated finding that people not only stereotype men and women differently, but they also tend to judge the perceived characteristics of women as less desirable (Broverman et al., 1972). Men are "logical" and "independent," women "emotional" and "submissive." In these and many other ways, it is considered better to be like a man than like a woman.

Furthermore, just as those who study racial prejudice have developed new, more sensitive techniques for detecting bias, so have those who study gender prejudice. For example, the bogus pipeline method has been used to elicit admissions of bias. As we noted in Chapter 2, men led to believe the experimenter could read their true attitudes with a sensitive lie detector expressed less than usual sympathy toward women's rights.

Bias can also be subtly measured by having people evaluate the behavior of someone who just happens to be either male or female. From an experiment with Houston area students and residents by Kenneth Burstin, Eugene Doughtie, and Avi Raphaeli (1980) here is one such item (the alternate version is indicated by parentheses):

Tulsa, Okla.—"While the cat's away, the mice will play," says the old saying. However, for an Oklahoma woman (man), the mouse got caught at the game.

It seems that last month, Karl (Kathy) Michaels was away visiting relatives for a few days, leaving the two Michaels youngsters in the care of their mother (father), Kathy (Karl). Mrs. (Mr.) Michaels, however, took the opportunity to rendezvous with her (his) secret lover, leaving the two children, Mark, 5, and Tommy, 3, as she (he) had apparently done on several such occasions. This time, however, fear and hunger after many hours of neglect drove the Michaels children to the streets in search of their wayward parent.

A pair of city residents found the children wandering in the street almost 3 miles from the Michaels home. The police were called in, and in the process of reuniting the children and their mother (father), the whole story came out.

"I don't see that what I did was too terrible," Kathy (Karl) told an obviously upset spouse.

WOULD YOU AGREE THAT MRS. (MR.) MICHAELS IS A POOR PARENT? (CIRCLE ONE)

1	2	3	4	5	6	7
STRONGLY DISAGREE						STRONGLY AGREE

Men given the "Kathy Michaels" version were more harshly judgmental than were men given the "Karl Michaels" version. And women exhibited a similar same-sex bias; they judged Kathy *less* harshly than they did Karl. Yet, afterward, when asked whether they would more harshly judge a father or a mother who "abandons two small children for several hours in order to meet secretly with a lover," 97 percent claimed they would judge them "equally poor parents." The typical person seemed to be thinking, "Would I use a double standard in judging such behavior by a father and a mother? Of course not." However, many had.

In a series of experiments at Purdue University, Kay Deaux and her colleagues had people likewise evaluate only a male or a female, thus hiding the experiment's purpose. In one, students observed a fellow student succeeding on a perceptual task and were asked to explain it (Deaux & Emswiller, 1974). When the task involved recognizing masculine objects (for example, a tire jack), a male's success was generally attributed to his ability; equivalent success by a female was attributed less to her ability, more to luck. However, with feminine objects, the student observers showed no such tendency to explain female success differently from male success. Apparently, the students believed that anyone could perform the feminine tasks, but it took a man's skill (or else good luck) to perform the masculine tasks. In other experiments, females said to have succeeded in traditionally masculine activities—becoming a successful physician, heroically helping police apprehend a gunman—were seen as less competent than a similarly successful male, but more highly motivated or deserving of a reward. However, men who succeeded in feminine tasks were not similarly considered as highly deserving (Feldman-Summers & Kiesler, 1974; Taynor & Deaux, 1973; 1975). In short, women who succeed in a "man's world" are often viewed as either uncommonly lucky or highly motivated, thus offsetting their presumed lesser abilities.

Gender bias is also plainly evident in the hopes of prospective parents. When asked what sex they would prefer their first (or only) child) to be, the overwhelming majority of both men and women say "A boy" (Tavris & Offir, 1977, p. 21; Frieze et al., 1978, p. 283). Moreover, women whose first children are girls conceive a second child sooner and are happier about the new pregnancy than women who have had sons. And when survey researchers have asked people whether they wish they had been born the other sex, the number of women who do, though decreasing (from 25 percent in 1946 to 16

Question: *"Misogyny" is the hatred of women. What is the corresponding word for the hatred of men?*
Answer: *In most dictionaries, no such word exists.*

"And just why do we always call my *income the second income?"*

Gender prejudice is usually expressed subtly. (Drawing by Vietor; © 1981 *The New Yorker* Magazine, Inc.)

percent in 1970 to 10 percent in 1976), has always far exceeded the 4 percent or less of men who would rather be women (Erskine, 1971; Gallup, 1978b).

To conclude: Overt prejudice against racial minorities and women is far less prevalent today than it was just four decades ago. Although sex stereotypes remain, blatant racial and gender prejudices have largely disappeared. Nevertheless, techniques that are sensitive to subtle prejudice still detect widespread bias.

By cxamining thc traditional social and cmotional cxplanations of racial prejudice we will see how these also help explain gender prejudice. We will also consider some intriguing new findings that reveal how prejudice can be created and sustained by illusory thinking.

SOCIAL SOURCES OF PREJUDICE

Prejudice springs from numerous interrelated factors. One cluster of factors helps to explain how prejudice is produced and maintained by the social environment.

Social Inequalities

Prejudice Rationalizes Inequalities

Principle number one: Unequal status breeds prejudice. Slaves are likely to be viewed by their masters as lazy, irresponsible, lacking ambition—as having just those traits that justify the existing social structure: slavery. What the historical forces were that created the unequal status is a question for historians. But once inequalities exist, prejudice can be used to justify the economic and social superiority of those who have wealth and power. Thus, although prejudice and discrimination are but modestly associated—one often occurs without the other—they do support each other: Discrimination breeds prejudice, and prejudice legitimizes discrimination (Pettigrew, 1980).

Examples abound of prejudice rationalizing unequal status. Until recently, prejudice was greatest in regions of the U.S. where slavery had been practiced. Nineteenth-century European politicians and writers justified their imperial expansion by describing the exploited, colonized people as "inferior," "requiring protection," and a "burden" to be borne altruistically (G. W. Allport, 1958, pp. 204–205). Three decades ago, sociologist Helen Mayer Hacker (1951) noted how stereotypes of blacks and women helped rationalize the inferior status of each: Both groups were viewed as being inferior in intelligence, as being emotional and primitive, and as "contented" with their subordinate role. Blacks were "inferior," women were "weaker." Blacks were all right in their place; women's place was in the home.

That attitudes easily adjust themselves to existing social relations is also evident in times of conflict. One often views one's enemies as subhuman and depersonalizes them with a label. Thus during World War II the Japanese people became the "sly Japs," and then after the war was over they became the "intelligent" Japanese whom Americans today admire. Attitudes are amazingly adaptable.

In Chapter 2, we noted laboratory experiments revealing that oppressive acts do indeed breed negative attitudes. Harming an innocent victim typically leads aggressors to disparage their victims, thus helping to justify the hurtful behavior. And in a recent experiment at the University of Virginia, Stephen Worchel and Virginia Andreoli (1978) found that, compared to students whose task was to reward someone for right answers on a learning task, those who instead gave shocks for wrong answers dehumanized their victim. They were less able to recall his unique characteristics (for example, name and physical characteristics) and better able to recall attributes such as race and religion that served to depersonalize the victim by identifying him with his groups. Thus, cruelty begets cruel attitudes and corrodes the aggressor's personal sensitivities.

"It is human nature to hate those whom we have injured."

Tacitus, Agricola

Those who benefit from social inequalities, yet avow that "all are created equal," may especially need to construct self-serving justifications for the way things are. And what more powerful justification than to believe that God has ordained the existing social order? For all sorts of cruel deeds, noted William James, "piety is the mask," (1902, p. 264)—the mask that sometimes portrays lovely expressions while hiding ugly motives.

In almost every country, religion is invoked on significant national occasions to sanctify the present order. In a remarkable turnabout, Father George Zabelka (1980), chaplain to the aircrews that bombed Hiroshima, Nagasaki, and other civilian targets in Japan, years later came to regret that he had provided religion's blessing upon these missions of devastation. "The whole structure of the secular, religious, and military society told me clearly that it was all right to 'let the Japs have it.' God was on the side of my country."

That religion can easily be used to justify injustice is one possible explanation of a remarkably consistent pair of findings: (1) American church members are more racially prejudiced than nonmembers, and (2) those professing traditional Christian beliefs are more prejudiced than those with less traditional beliefs (Gorsuch & Aleshire, 1974). These findings have been repeatedly observed no matter where and when the study was conducted or what type of racial prejudice was studied.

Although these findings are well-established, it is not clear what they mean. Knowing the relationship between two variables—religion and prejudice—tells us nothing about their causal connection. There might be no causal connection at all; perhaps, for example, people with less education are more fundamentalist in their beliefs and also, for reasons having nothing to do with religion, more prejudiced in their attitudes. Or perhaps prejudice causes religion, by leading people to seek out religions that support their prejudices. Or perhaps religion causes prejudice, by leading people to believe that since all persons possess free will, impoverished minorities have no one but themselves to blame for any perceived lack of virtue or achievement.

If indeed religion causes prejudice, then the more religious one is, the more prejudiced one would be. But three other findings consistently indicate this plainly is not so. First, among church members, faithful church attenders are, in twenty-four out of twenty-six comparisons, less prejudiced than irregular attenders (Batson & Ventis, 1982). Second, Gordon Allport and Michael Ross (1967) found that those for whom religion is an end in itself (those who agree, for example, with the statement "My religious beliefs are what really lie behind my whole approach to life") express less prejudice than those for whom religion is more a means to other ends (for example, those who agree with the statement "A primary reason for my interest in religion is that my church is a congenial social activity"). Third, Protestant ministers and Roman Catholic priests have generally been far more supportive of civil rights efforts than have lay people (Hadden, 1969; Fichter, 1968).

So, what is the relationship between religiosity and prejudice? As we have seen now several times in this chapter, the answer one gets depends on *how* one asks the question. If religiousness is defined in terms of church membership (not attendance), or willingness to agree at least superficially with traditional beliefs, then the more religious are the more racially prejudiced—hence the Ku Klux Klan, who rationalize bigotry with the aid of religion.

However, if intensity of religious commitment is assessed in any of several other ways, then the very devout seem, on the average, less prejudiced than the nominally religious—hence the religious roots of the modern civil rights movement, among whose leaders were many ministers and priests. As Gordon Allport concluded, "The role of religion is paradoxical. It makes prejudice and it unmakes prejudice" (1958, p. 413).

"We have just enough religion to make us hate, but not enough to make us love one another."

Jonathan Swift, Thoughts on Various Subjects

Blaming the Victim: The Self-Fulfilling Prophecy Lurks Again

Attitudes may coincide with the social order not only as a rationalization for it, but also because discrimination hurts its victims. "One's reputation," wrote Gordon Allport, "cannot be hammered, hammered, hammered into one's head without doing something to one's character" (1958, p. 139). In his classic book, *The Nature of Prejudice*, Allport catalogued 15 possible effects of victimization. Allport believed these reactions were reducible to two basic types—those that involve blaming oneself (for example, withdrawal, self-hate, aggression against one's own group), and those that involve blaming external causes (for example, fighting back, suspiciousness, increased group pride). If the net results are negative—for example, higher rates of illegitimacy, broken families, and delinquency—they can be used to justify continuing the prejudice and discrimination that help maintain them: "If we let those people in our nice neighborhood, property values will plummet."

But does discrimination affect its victims as this analysis supposes? Social psychology has helped answer this question with its repeated findings (see Chapters 4, 5, and 6) that people's beliefs about others tend to be self-confirming. We have seen how, in laboratory experiments, people's sex stereotypes can lead them to treat others in ways that create the reality fantasized (Skrypnek & Snyder, 1982).

"If we foresee evil in our fellow man, we tend to provoke it; if good, we elicit it."

Gordon Allport, The Nature of Prejudice

That even subtle discrimination can affect its victims was evident in a clever pair of experiments by Carl Word, Mark Zanna, and Joel Cooper (1974). In the first experiment, white Princeton University men interviewed white and black job applicants. When the applicant was black, the interviewers sat further away, terminated the interview 25 percent sooner, and made 50 percent more speech errors than when the applicant was white. Imagine yourself being interviewed by someone who sat at a distance, stammered, and ended the interview rather quickly. Would it affect your performance or your feelings about the interviewer? To find out, the researchers conducted a second experiment in which trained interviewers treated students as the interviewers in the first experiment had treated either the white or black applicants. When videotapes of the students being interviewed were later rated, those who had been treated as were the blacks in the first experiment were judged to have been more nervous and to have performed less effectively. Moreover, those being interviewed could themselves sense a difference; those treated as were the blacks judged their interviewers as less adequate and less friendly. The experimenters concluded "that the 'problem' of black performance resides not entirely within the blacks, but rather within the interaction setting itself."

"I know you said you had no vacancies, but on the phone you sounded as though you thought I might be coloured."

In one experiment, white people who were treated as if they were black sensed a lack of acceptance. (From *Cartoons from Punch* edited by W. Hewison, St. Martin's Press, Inc. Copyright © 1979 Punch Publications Ltd.)

Social inequalities are surely not the only cause of prejudice. Behind the anti-Semitism of Hitler and the anti-Mormon hostility in nineteenth century America lay something more. Nevertheless, prejudice often rationalizes a group's social and economic superiority and acts powerfully as a self-fulfilling prophecy.

Ingroup and Outgroup

Ingroup: *A group of people who share a sense of belonging, a feeling of common identity.*
Outgroup: *A group that is perceived as distinctively different from or apart from the ingroup.*

The social definition of who you are—your race, religion, sex, academic major—can also imply a definition of who you are not. The circle that includes "us" excludes "them." Thus, the mere experience of people's being formed into groups, quite apart from any relationship between the groups, may promote *ingroup bias*. Ask children, "Which are better, the children in this town or the children in Jonesville [a neighboring town whose children they've never met]?" Most will say their own town has better children.

In a series of experiments, two British social psychologists, Henri Tajfel and Michael Billig (1974; Tajfel, 1970; 1981; 1982), have found that even when the us-them distinction is inconsequential, people still immediately favor their own group. In one study, British teenagers evaluated modern abstract paintings and then were told they and some others had favored the art of Paul Klee over that by Wassily Kandinsky. Then, without ever meeting the other members of their group, they were asked to divide some monetary awards among members of both groups. In experiment after experiment, when groups were defined even in this way, favoritism toward one's own group resulted. Researcher David Wilder (1981) summarizes the typical result: "When given the opportunity to divide 15 points [worth money], subjects generally award 9 or 10 points to their own group and 5 or 6 points to the other group." This bias, he reports, has been observed with both sexes and among many different age groups and nationalities.

Ingroup bias: *The tendency to favor one's own group.*

Other researchers report that members of one's artificial group are also more positively rated (Brewer, 1979). In fact, some researchers report that even forming conspicuous groups on *no* logical basis—say, merely by composing groups X and Y with a lottery—is sufficient to produce ingroup bias (Brewer & Silver, 1978; Billig & Tajfel, 1973; Locksley, Ortiz, & Hepburn, 1980). In Kurt Vonnegut's novel *Slapstick*, computers gave everyone a new middle name; all "Daffodil-11's" then felt unity with one another and distance from "Raspberry-13's." The self-serving bias (Chapter 3) again surfaces: "We" are better than "they," even when "we" and "they" are the same.

Ingroup bias is the favoring of one's own group. Such relative favoritism could reflect (1) liking for the ingroup, or (2) dislike for the outgroup, or some combination of the two. If both, the implication would be that loyalty to one's group is generally accompanied by a devaluing of other groups. Is that true? Is ethnic pride conducive to ethnocentrism? Does women's solidarity with other women stimulate them to dislike men? Does enthusiastic loyalty to a particular fraternity or sorority lead its members to deprecate independents and members of other fraternities and sororities?

Ethnocentrism: *Belief in the superiority of one's ethnic or cultural group.*

Results from experiments reveal support for both explanations, especially for the first: Apparently ingroup bias results primarily from perceiving that one's own group is good, and to a lesser extent from a sense that other groups are bad (Brewer, 1979). Although, as always, we must be cautious about generalizing from laboratory experiments, it seems that positive feelings for our own groups need not be mirrored by equally strong negative feelings for outgroups. Granted, there appears to be some tendency for devotion to one's own race, religion, and social groups to be accompanied by a devaluation of other races, religions, and social groups, but the combination is not a given.

In everyday life, ingroup bias gets magnified by the tendency for people to interact primarily with the members of their own groups. A group's members interacting mostly with each other usually intensifies both their loyalty to the group and their sense of mutual dependence. For example, segregation was devised to confine feelings of sympathy and equality to those in the group (G. W. Allport, 1958, p. 205). Also, when interaction occurs mostly within group lines it frequently leads to exaggerated stereotyping of outgroups; to vested interests in maintaining the group's separation; and to thinking, feeling, and acting in ways unique to each group. Thus, ingroup bias is often amplified by patterns of interaction that further widen the gap between the groups.

Conformity

Once established, prejudice is maintained largely by its own social inertia. If prejudice is a social norm—if it is expected—then many people will follow the path of least social resistance: They will conform to the social fashion. They will act not so much out of a need to hate as from a need to be liked and accepted (Pettigrew, 1980).

Studies by Thomas Pettigrew (1958) of whites in South Africa and the American south revealed that during the 1950s those who conformed most to other social norms were also most prejudiced; those who in general were less conforming mirrored less of the surrounding prejudice. That nonconformity can exact a price was painfully evident to the ministers of Little Rock, Arkansas, where the Supreme Court's 1954 school desegregation decision was first implemented. Most ministers favored integration, but usually only privately; they knew that if they were to advocate it vigorously they would risk losing members and contributions (Campbell & Pettigrew, 1959). Or consider the Indiana steelworkers and West Virginia coal miners of the same era. In the mills and the mines, integration was accepted. However, in the

BEHIND THE SCENES

Thomas Pettigrew

One's best ideas in social psychology often evolve from direct experience. As a white southerner, I was fascinated when I read *The Authoritarian Personality* as an undergraduate at the University of Virginia in the early 1950s. Yet the book did not explain most of what I thought I knew about antiblack prejudice in the south. In particular, I knew many family members and white friends who evinced the region's traditional racial views but few of the characteristics of authoritarians. To explain the discrepancy, I needed only to recall the times I had been expelled from the public schools of Richmond, Virginia, for opposing the traditional racial norms. These ideas led directly to my research and emphasis on the importance of societal pressures to conform in shaping individual attitudes and behavior. *(Thomas Pettigrew, University of California, Santa Cruz)* neighborhoods, the norm was rigid segregation (Reitzes, 1953; Minard, 1952). Prejudice was clearly *not* a manifestation of "sick" personalities, but more simply of the norms that operated in one situation but not another.

Conformity also maintains other prejudices. "If we have come to think that the nursery and the kitchen are the natural sphere of a woman," wrote George Bernard Shaw in an 1891 essay, "we have done so exactly as English children come to think that a cage is the natural sphere of a parrot—because they have never seen one anywhere else." Children who *have* seen women elsewhere—children of employed women, for example—tend to have less stereotyped views of men and women (Broverman et al., 1972; Hoffman, 1977). In short, it appears that people's attitudes are formed partly as mirrored images of surrounding attitudes, be those attitudes of "white pride," "black pride," "male superiority," or "feminist consciousness."

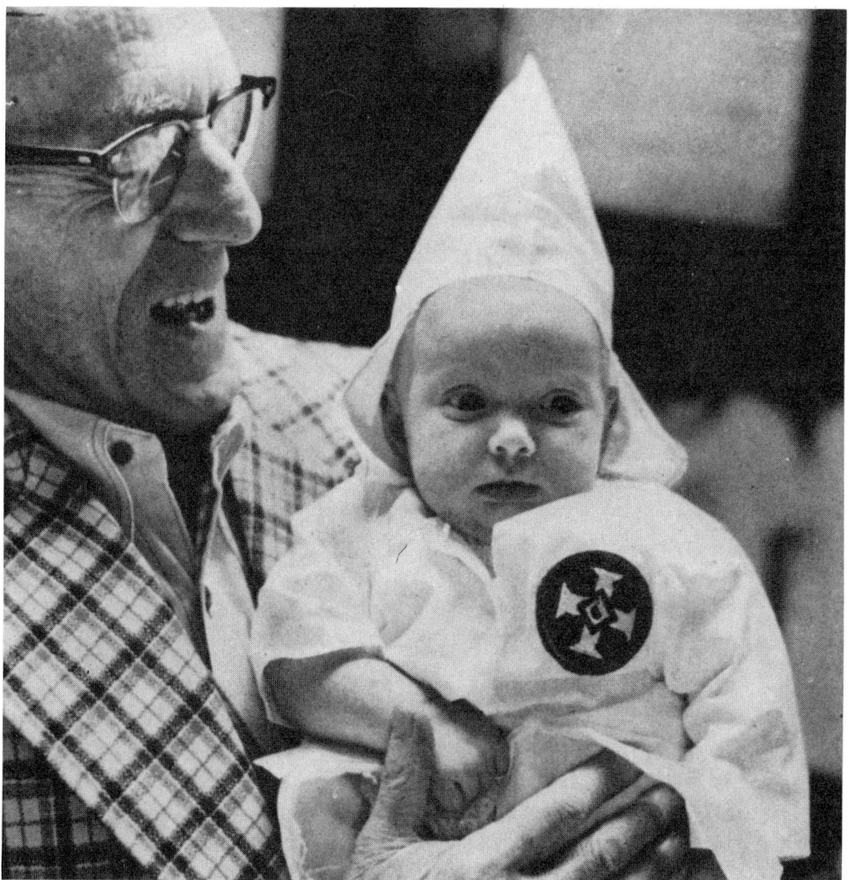

Much prejudice results not from "sick" personalities but simply from conformity to the surrounding norms of prejudice. (Jack Edwards)

In all this, there is a message of hope. If much prejudice is not deeply ingrained in one's personality, then as fashions change and new norms evolve, prejudice can diminish. And so it has.

Institutional Supports

Segregation is but one way that social institutions bolster widespread prejudice. Prejudice also may be supported by political leaders, leaders who tend not only to reflect the prevailing attitudes but also to legitimize and reinforce them. When Arkansas' Governor Faubus barred the doors of Central High School in Little Rock, he was doing more than representing the majority of his constituents; he was helping to perpetuate their views.

Schools too reinforce dominant cultural attitudes. One analysis of stories in 134 children's readers written prior to 1970 found that stories focusing on boys outnumbered those on girls by better than 2 to 1 and men characters outnumbered women 3 to 1 (Women on Words and Images, 1972). Who was portrayed as showing initiative, bravery, and competence? In an old children's reader, the answer was vividly illustrated. Jane, sprawled out on the sidewalk, her roller skates beside her, listened as Mark explained to his mother:

"She cannot skate," said Mark.
"I can help her.
I want to help her.
Look at her, mother.
Just look at her.
She's just like a girl.
She gives up."

Not until the 1970s, not until our changing ideas about males and females fostered new perceptions of such portrayals, was this blatant stereotyping widely noticed. The institutional supports for prejudice are often unnoticed. Usually, they are not deliberately hateful attempts to oppress a group; more often they simply reflect how a culture at that time assumes things to be.

Many films and television programs also embody and reinforce prevailing cultural attitudes. The stupid, wide-eyed black butlers and maids in the old Shirley Temple movies helped perpetuate the stereotypes they reflected. On radio and in the early years of television, the popular *Amos 'n' Andy* show provoked Americans to laugh at a portrayal of irresponsible, fun-loving blacks. In 1978, three Amherst College researchers, Russell Weigel, James Loomis, and Matthew Soja (1980), analyzed the racial content of American prime-time television and found it still modeling a segregated world: Fewer than 2 percent of the interactions were cross-racial. The prime-time world is also overwhelmingly male: Men outnumber women by at least 3 to 1. Moreover, most women portrayed on television do not work outside the home and are younger than the men they deal with (Gerbner, 1981).

Widespread prejudice is usually supported by such social institutions as the mass media. The popular 1950s radio program *Amos 'n' Andy* personified and reinforced the stereotyped image of blacks as lazy, irresponsible, and unintelligent. Ironically, the two men who played Amos and Andy were white. (Culver Pictures)

Since the media's stereotypes support prejudice, might satirizing bigotry undermine prejudice? One of television's most popular programs of the 1970s, *All in the Family*, portrayed a crude, outspoken white bigot, Archie Bunker. How did this program affect its 50 million weekly viewers? Did the devastating satire, as actor Carroll O'Connor and producer Norman Lear intended, help eliminate prejudice? [O'Connor: "I think we are doing something that needs to be done and that is to show a racist what he is doing" (C. Sanders, 1972).] Or did it, as some critics maintained, reinforce prejudice by institutionalizing a "lovable bigot"? Three separate studies each found that the program's message lay in the eyes and ears of the beholders (Brigham & Biesbrecht, 1976; Surlin, 1974; Vidmar & Rokeach, 1974). Relatively nonprejudiced whites saw the satire, laughed at Archie Bunker, and believing he usually lost his arguments, responded, "Isn't it obvious what a buffoon he is?" However, to prejudiced people this point was not obvious. They were far more likely to perceive Archie's view of the world as accurate, to like him and those he liked, to dislike those he disliked, to laugh with him when he laughed, to laugh at those he laughed at. The satire that was so obvious to more liberal viewers had failed to penetrate the minds of prejudiced viewers. So once again we see illustrated a familiar principle: Our preconceptions control our interpretations. To protect our preexisting biases, information is readily bent, folded, or mutilated.

EMOTIONAL SOURCES OF PREJUDICE

That prejudice is not easily penetrated by satirical or logical appeals suggests that it has emotional roots. Prejudice springs not only from intellectual justifications but also from passionate emotions.

Frustration and Aggression: The Scapegoat Theory

Chapter 10 emphasized that pain and frustration can evoke hostility. When the cause of our frustration is too intimidating or too vague, we often redirect our hostility. This phenomenon of "displaced aggression" may have contributed to the lynchings of black people in the U.S. south. Between 1882 and 1930, there was a tendency for more lynchings to occur in years when the cotton price was low and economic frustration was therefore presumably high (Hovland & Sears, 1940; Mintz, 1946).

Our targets for displaced aggression vary. Following their defeat in World War I and their country's subsequent economic chaos, many Germans treated Jews as villains. Long before Hitler came to power, one German leader explained, "The Jew is just convenient. . . . If there were no Jews, the anti-Semites would have to invent them" (quoted by G. W. Allport, 1958, p. 325). In earlier centuries hostilities were vented on witches. More recently, people who have watched inflation devour their wage increases can hardly direct their anger at the whole complex economic system. Some simplistic target more often bears the wrath, be it "lazy welfare bums" or "greedy oil companies."

Evidence for this "scapegoat theory" of prejudice comes from both surveys and experiments. In separate surveys, those whose job satisfaction is low, or who claim while in the Army to have had a "bad break," have been more racially intolerant than less frustrated people who are satisfied with their jobs or feel that the Army gave them a "good break" (Bettelheim & Janowitz, 1950; A. A. Campbell, 1947). A famous experiment by Neal Miller and Richard Bugelski (1948) conducted with college-age men working at a summer camp also confirms the scapegoat theory. The men were asked to state their attitudes toward Japanese and Mexicans, both before and after being forced to stay in camp to take tests rather than attend a long-awaited free evening at a local theatre. Compared to a control group that did not undergo this frustration, the deprived group displayed increased prejudice following the frustration. Additional research suggests that frustration does not, however, breed prejudice against all outgroups; rather, it seems to intensify hostilities against those already disliked (Weatherley, 1961).

Compelling as these results are, the scapegoat theory of prejudice is incomplete: It does not explain why certain groups are treated as scapegoats while others are not. Moreover, aggression is not always displaced; when possible, people prefer to retaliate against the perceived source of their frustration.

One source of frustration is competition. When two groups compete for jobs, housing, or social prestige, one group's goal fulfillment can become the other group's goal frustration. An ecological principle, Gause's law, states that maximum competition will exist between those species with identical needs (E. O. Wilson, 1978, p. 175). Similarly, researchers have consistently detected the strongest antiblack prejudice among whites who are closest to blacks on the socioeconomic ladder (Greeley & Sheatsley, 1971; Tumin, 1958; Pettigrew, 1978; Vanneman & Pettigrew, 1972). (See Box 12-1.) When interests clash, prejudice pays, for some people. Certainly prejudice paid the white men who, for most of this century, managed to protect their own interests by excluding women and minorities from their trade unions.

But as an explanation of prejudice, competition, too, is inadequate. Surveys of residents in both suburban Los Angeles and Louisville reveal that opposition to busing for desegregation is nearly as strong among those unaffected by busing as it is among those whose children are involved (Kinder & Sears, 1981; McConahay, 1982; Sears, Hensler, & Speer, 1979). Thus, we can see that racial attitudes are not merely responses to a threat to one's immediate self-interest; rather they appear to be socialized over one's lifetime.

Box 12-1

Competition Can Breed Frustration and Prejudice

Whites in [Boston's] ethnic neighborhoods complain that the blacks are being hired preferentially by the telephone company and by the police and fire departments, which have been strongholds of the Irish. But blacks see a white-run city with a police department that is only three percent black after several years of concerted effort at special recruitment. Blacks, complaining of father-son union discrimination, are demanding jobs on construction sites in black neighborhoods. After a clash at one site, about 2,000 white workers gathered at City Hall to complain that Federal monies were being spent to put them out of work.

Note: New York Times, May 23, 1976, p. 2E.

Clearer evidence that competition can, however, breed prejudice comes from experiments that eliminate such variables as educational level, variables that often intertwine with competition. As Chapter 14 will show, competition by itself—competition even between two very similar groups—provokes prejudice. But for now, it is sufficient to note that frustration often spawns hostility, and this hostility is at times displaced to acceptable scapegoats and at other times aimed directly at one's competitors.

Personality Dynamics

Two people, with equal reason to feel frustrated or threatened, will often not be equally prejudiced. The search for why this is so led social psychologists to apply an idea of Sigmund Freud's: People sometimes hold to beliefs and attitudes that satisfy their unconscious needs.

Needs for Status and Group Identification

Status is relative: To perceive ourselves as having status, we need people below us. Thus one psychological benefit of prejudice, or of any status system, is the feeling of superiority it offers. Most of us can recall a time when we took secret satisfaction in another's failure—perhaps when seeing a sibling reprimanded, or upon hearing of a classmate's difficulty on a test. From such comparisons our own esteem derives a boost. Is this why those low or slipping on the socioeconomic ladder tend to be more prejudiced (Bettelheim & Janowitz, 1950)? Perhaps people whose status is high or rising have less need for a group to feel superior to.

"By exciting emulation and comparisons of superiority, you lay the foundation of lasting mischief; you make brothers and sisters hate each other."

Samuel Johnson, quoted in James Boswell's Life of Samuel Johnson

But there is some ambiguity in these findings because other factors associated with low or falling status could also account for the prejudice. An experiment would help determine whether a threat to status can by itself cause prejudice. Imagine yourself as one of the Arizona State University students who took part in such an experiment by Robert Cialdini and Kenneth Richardson (1980). You are walking alone across campus. Someone approaches you and solicits your participation in a five-minute survey. You agree. After the researcher gives you a brief "creativity test," he deflates you with the news that "you have scored relatively low on the test." The researcher then completes the survey by asking you some evaluative questions about either your school or its traditional rival, the University of Arizona. Would your feelings of failure affect your ratings of either school? Cialdini and Richardson found that, compared with those in a control group whose self-esteem was not threatened, the students who experienced failure gave higher ratings to their own school, lower ratings to their rival. Apparently, boasting of one's own group and denigrating outgroups can boost one's ego. Likewise, Teresa Amabile and Ann Glazebrook (1982) found that when Dartmouth College men were made to feel insecure, they judged others' work more harshly. This suggests, for example, that a man who doubts his own strength and independence might, by proclaiming women to be pitifully weak and dependent, boost his masculine image. Indeed, when Joel Grube, Randall Kleinhesselink, and Kathleen Kearney (1982) had Washington State University men view young women's videotaped job interviews, men with low self-acceptance disliked strong, nontraditional women. But men with high self-acceptance tended to be more attracted to *non*traditional than traditional women.

A despised outgroup serves yet another need: the need to belong to an ingroup. As we shall see in Chapter 14, the perception of a common enemy can serve as powerful cement for any group. School spirit is seldom so strong as when the game is with the arch-rival. The sense of comradeship among workers is often highest when they all feel a common antagonism toward management. To solidify the Nazi hold over Germany, Hitler used the "Jewish menace." Despised outgroups can strengthen the ingroup.

The Authoritarian Personality

The emotional needs that contribute to prejudice are said to predominate in the "authoritarian personality." In the 1940s, a group of University of California, Berkeley, researchers, two of whom had fled from Nazi Germany, devised a test for authoritarianism that sought to assess tendencies toward rigid thinking, punitiveness, intolerance of weakness, and submission to authorities (Adorno et al., 1950). Their major finding was that people who agreed with such items as "Obedience and respect for authority are the most important virtues children should learn," tended to be prejudiced against all ethnic minorities.

The Berkeley researchers also found that frequently authoritarians had been harshly disciplined as children. This apparently led them to repress their own hostilities and impulses and to "project" such onto outgroups. Also, the insecurity of the authoritarian child was believed to predispose an excessive concern with power and status and an inflexible right-wrong way of thinking that made ambiguity difficult to tolerate; therefore, such people tended to be submissive to those with power over them and aggressive toward those beneath them.

The research on authoritarian personality has been criticized on several counts. For example: (1) Perhaps mere lack of education accounted for the simplistic prejudices of authoritarian individuals. (2) The Berkeley researchers, by focusing on right-wing authoritarianism, seemed to overlook a dogmatic authoritarianism of the left. (3) The democratic values of these researchers were hardly disguised: The contemptibly "rigid" authoritarian character which they described was strikingly similar to the "stable" character identified by psychologists in pre-Nazi Germany. Personal values thus determined whether such personalities were to be condemned for their "ethnocentrism" (American psychologists' label) or praised for their strong "ingroup loyalty" (German psychologists' label) (Brown, 1965).

Still, the main conclusion of this ambitious research has survived: There *do* appear to be individuals whose hostilities surface as prejudice; and prejudices against different minorities do often coexist (M. Snyder & Ickes, in press). The authoritarian attitude is only one among many sources of prejudice. But it can breed intolerance of those different from oneself, or even a political attitude of minimal concern for the people of other nations (Tetlock, 1981c).

COGNITIVE SOURCES OF PREJUDICE

Much of the foregoing explanation of prejudice could have been written in the 1960s. Not so what follows. This new look at prejudice supplements the established ideas by applying what has been learned from the explosion of research on social thinking. The basic point is this: Stereotyped beliefs and prejudiced attitudes exist not only because of social conditioning; not only because they serve an emotional function, enabling people to displace and project their hostilities; but also as by-products of our normal thinking processes. One should not assume that stereotypes always spring from malice. Rather, stereotypes are often a price we pay for simplifying our complex world. Stereotypes, by this view, are roughly analogous to perceptual illusions, a price we often pay for the benefits we derive from our perceptual knack for simplifying.

Categorization

One way we simplify our worlds is to "catcgorizc"—to organize the world by clustering objects into groups. A biologist organizes the world by classifying plants and animals. Once we have organized people into categories, we can more easily think and remember information about them. To the extent that persons in a group are similar, knowing their group enables us to predict better their individual behavior. Customs inspectors and airplane antihijack personnel are therefore taught "profiles" of individuals to suspect (Kraut & Poe, 1980). Such are categorization's benefits. However, the benefits exact a cost.

We have already considered one social cost: the ingroup bias. Merely dividing people into groups can trigger discrimination. There are other costs as well. Ethnicity and sex are, in our current world, powerful ways of categorizing people (S. E. Taylor et al., 1978). Imagine Tom, a forty-year old, black real estate agent in New Orleans. I suspect that your image of "black male" predominates over the categories "middle-aged," "business person," and "southerner." By itself such categorization is not prejudice. But, as we shall see, categorization does provide a foundation for prejudice.

Perceived Similarities within Groups, Differences Between Groups

Picture the following objects: apples, chairs, pencils. There is a strong tendency to see objects within a group as being more uniform than they really are. Were your apples all medium size and red, your chairs all straight-backed, your pencils all yellow? Similarly, once people are assigned to groups—athletes, theatre majors, math professors—we are prone to exaggerate the similarities within groups and the differences between them (S. E. Taylor, 1981; Wilder, 1978). Consequently, mere division into groups can create a sense that members of another group are "all alike" but different from oneself and one's own group (Allen & Wilder, 1979). It is well established that we tend to like people we think are similar to us and dislike those we perceive to be different. So this could provide a basis for the ingroup bias (Byrne & Wong, 1962; Rokeach & Mezei, 1966; Stein, Hardyck, & Smith, 1965).

This tendency to see people in another group as more similar to one another than they really are is less true of perceptions of one's own group. Many non-Europeans see the Swiss as a fairly homogeneous people. But to the people of Switzerland, the Swiss are a diverse group, encompassing French-, German-, and Italian-speaking people. White Americans readily identify "black leaders" who supposedly can speak for black Americans. Whites apparently presume that whites are considerably more diverse, for they do not assume that there are "white leaders" who can speak for white America (Watson, 1981). Similarly, to members of Princeton "Eating Clubs," the members of any given other club are perceived as less diverse than the members of one's own club (E. E. Jones, Wood, & Quattrone, 1981).

"You want to know what we need around here? I'll tell you what we need around here. We need name tags around here."

Compared to those in one's own group, people in other groups often seem, and even look, more alike. To the human cartoonist, all penguins look alike. (Bill Maul/*Saturday Review*)

The perception that "they are alike, we are diverse" extends even to our perception of physical characteristics. Many of us can recall being embarrassed by having confused two people of another racial group, prompting the person we've misnamed to surmise, "You think we all look alike." A number of recent experiments, by John Brigham, Roy Malpass, Jane Chance, and others, reveal that people of other races do in fact appear to look more alike than do people of one's own race (Brigham & Williamson, 1979; Malpass & Kravitz, 1969; Chance & Goldstein, 1981). For example, when white students are shown faces of a few white and a few black individuals and then asked to pick these individuals out of a photographic lineup, they more accurately recognize the white faces than the black.

"Women are more like each other than men [are]."

Lord (not *Lady*) *Chesterfield*

I am white. When I first read this research, I thought, of course: White people *are* more physically diverse than blacks. But my reaction was apparently just an illustration of the phenomenon. For if my reaction were correct, black people, too, would better recognize a white face among a lineup of whites than a black face in a lineup of blacks. But in fact the opposite appears true: In most studies, blacks more easily recognize a fellow black than they do a white. This intriguing "own-race bias" appears to be a cognitive phenomenon that is automatic, for it is usually unrelated to both the racial attitudes and the interracial experience of the perceiver (Brigham & Barkowitz, 1978).

This phenomenon is quite well established; its explanation is not. What do you suppose accounts for it?

The Persuasive Power of Distinctive Stimuli

Other ways we perceive our worlds also breed stereotypes.

Distinctive People Draw Attention

In Chapter 4 we noted that a group's most distinctive member draws attention. A black in an otherwise white group, a man in an otherwise female group, or a woman in an otherwise male group is perceived as more prominent and influential, and is evaluated more extremely than the same individual when not a minority of one (S. E. Taylor et al., 1979).

In an experiment at Harvard, Ellen Langer and Lois Imber (1980) found that students watching a videotape of a man reading paid closer attention when they were led to think he was out of the ordinary—a cancer patient, a homosexual, or a millionaire. They detected characteristics of the man that were ignored by other viewers, and their evaluation of him was more extreme. For example, those who thought the man a cancer patient noticed his distinctive facial characteristics and bodily movements, and thus perceived him as much more "different from most people" than did the other viewers. So the extra attention paid to distinctive people can create an illusion that such people differ more from others than they really do. If people thought you were an ex-mental patient, they would likely notice things about you that otherwise would pass unnoticed.

However, it is possible for people to perceive others reacting to their distinctiveness when actually they aren't. At Dartmouth College, researchers

Robert Kleck and Angelo Strenta (1980) discovered this when they led college women to feel disfigured. The women thought the purpose of the experiment was to assess how another woman student would react to a huge facial scar that was created with theatrical makeup on the right cheek, running from the ear to the mouth. Actually, the purpose was to see how the women themselves, when made to feel deviant, would perceive another's behavior toward them. After applying the makeup, the experimenter gave the subject a small hand mirror so she could see the authentic-looking scar. When she put the mirror down, he then applied some "moisturizer" to "keep the makeup from cracking." What the "moisturizer" really did was remove the scar.

The scene that followed was poignant. A young woman, feeling terribly self-conscious about her supposedly disfigured face, is talking with another woman who sees no such disfigurement and knows nothing of what has gone before. If you have ever felt similarly self-conscious—perhaps about a physical handicap, adolescent acne, even just "awful-looking hair"—then perhaps you can sympathize with the self-conscious woman. Compared to women in a control condition, who were led to believe their conversational partner merely thought they had an allergy, the "disfigured" women became acutely sensitive to how their partners were looking at them; they rated their partners as more tense, distant, and patronizing. But in fact, observers who later analyzed videotapes of how the "disfigured" persons were treated could find no such differences in treatment. Speculating from these results, it would seem that if we are self-conscious about being different, we may misinterpret mannerisms and comments that we would otherwise not notice.

Vivid, Distinctive Cases Get Remembered

Our minds also use distinctive cases as a shortcut to judging groups. Are blacks good athletes? "Well, there was Jesse Owens and Muhammed Ali and O. J. Simpson. And look at the professional basketball teams. Yeah, I'd say so." Note the thought process at work here: One recalls instances of a particular category and, based on those recalled, forms a generalization, which may or may not be correct. Hence the tourist who concluded, "All Indians walk single file. At least the one I saw did." The problem, as noted in Chapter 4, is that vivid instances, though persuasive because of their greater impact on memory, are seldom representative of the larger group. Exceptional athletes, though distinctive and memorable, are not the best basis for judging the distribution of athletic talent among an entire race.

Two recent experiments demonstrate how distinctive cases fuel stereotypes. In one, Myron Rothbart and his colleagues (1978) had University of Oregon students view fifty slides, each of which stated the height of a man. For one group of students, ten of the men were said to be slightly over 6 feet (up to 6 feet 4 inches). For other students, these ten men were well over 6 feet (up to 6 feet 11 inches). When asked later how many of the men were over 6 feet, those given the moderately tall instances recalled 5 percent too many, while those given the extreme instances recalled 50 percent too many.

Similarly, when other students were told the actions of fifty men, ten of whom had performed either nonviolent crimes (for example, forgery), or violent crimes (for example, rape), those shown the list with the violent crimes most overestimated the number of criminal acts. Because distinctive cases are most easily remembered, they tend to dominate our images of various groups. Ask some people to picture the type of person who opposed the Vietnam war and you are more likely to call up images of televised bearded protestors occupying buildings than of the many ordinary people who were less noticeable but who also opposed the war.

That we are prone to overgeneralize from vivid cases is indisputable. The question has become, when are we most likely to do so? George Quattrone and Edward Jones (1980) report that the tendency to form stereotypes from the behavior of a single person is especially strong when one's prior expectations are weak and when the person is a member of an unfamiliar group. Princeton and Rutgers students were shown a videotape of a student who was said to attend either Princeton or Rutgers, and who decided, in one version of the tape, to wait alone for an experiment or, in another version of the tape, to wait with others. When the students were asked to guess what most other students would decide, they guessed that most students would choose as did the one they saw on the tape. But viewing a single student deciding whether to listen to rock or classical music—an area in which students have stronger expectations about other students' preferences—had less effect on their guesses of what most students would choose. Moreover, the tendency to generalize from the single case was much greater when the student was said to be from the other university, not one's own. Rutgers students who saw a supposed Princeton student choosing to wait alone thus ended up with an impression of Princeton students as rather solitary; those who saw the Princeton student choosing to be with others formed a more sociable impression of Princeton students. In other words, the less knowledge we have about a group and its behavior, the more likely we are to be influenced by a vivid case or two. To see is to believe.

Distinctive Events Produce Illusory Correlations

Stereotypes assume a correlation between people's group membership and their characteristics ("Italians are emotional," "Jews are shrewd," "Accountants are perfectionists"). Even under the best of conditions, our attentiveness to unusual occurrences can create illusory correlations. Because we are sensitive to distinctive events, the co-occurrence of two such events is especially noticeable—more noticeable than each of the times the unusual events do not occur together.

Illusory correlation: *A false impression that two variables, say gender and intelligence, are associated.* *See Chapter 4, pages 129–130.*

David Hamilton and Robert Gifford (1976) demonstrated this in a clever experiment with students at Southern Connecticut State College. The students were shown slides on which various people, members of "Group A" or "Group B," were said to have done something desirable or undesirable. For example, "John, a member of Group A, visited a sick friend in the hospital." Twice as many statements described members of Group A as Group B, but both groups were associated with nine desirable behaviors for every four undesirable behaviors. Since both Group B and the undesirable acts were less frequent, their co-occurrence—for example, "Allen, a member of Group B, dented the fender of a parked car and didn't leave his name"—was an infrequent combination that caught people's attention. The students therefore overestimated the frequency with which the "minority" group (B) acted undesirably; consequently, they judged Group B more harshly.

Remember, Group B members actually committed undesirable acts in the same proportion as Group A members. Moreover, the students had no preexisting biases for or against Group B, and they received the information more systematically than daily experience ever offers it. Evidently, the joint occurrence of two distinctive events grabs attention. This illusory correlation phenomenon provides yet another source for the formation of racial stereotypes.

The mass media reflect and feed this phenomenon. For instance, when an avowed homosexual murders someone, the homosexuality often gets mentioned. When a heterosexual person murders someone, this is a less distinctive event; thus the person's sexual orientation is seldom mentioned. Likewise, when an ex-mental patient shoots someone (such as John Lennon or President Reagan), the person's mental history commands attention. Assassins and mental hospitalization are both relatively infrequent, making their combination especially newsworthy. Such reporting can add to the illusion of a large correlation between (1) homosexuality or mental hospitalization and (2) violent tendencies.

Unlike those who judged Groups A and B, we often have preexisting biases. Further research by David Hamilton and Terrence Rose (1980) reveals that our preexisting stereotypes can lead us to "see" correlations that aren't there. They had University of California, Santa Barbara, students read sentences in which the members of different occupational groups were described by various adjectives (for example, "Doug, an accountant, is timid and thoughtful"). In actuality, each occupation was described equally often by each adjective; accountants, doctors, and salespeople were equally often reported to be timid, wealthy, and talkative. However, the students *thought* they had more often read descriptions of timid accountants, wealthy doctors, and talkative salespeople. Their stereotyping led them to perceive correlations that weren't there, thus helping to perpetuate the stereotypes (McArthur & Friedman, 1980). To believe is to see.

Attribution: Is it a Just World?

Fundamental attribution error: *See Chapter 3, pages 75–84*.

In explaining others' actions, we frequently commit the fundamental attribution error. We attribute their behavior so much to their inner dispositions that we discount important situational forces. The error occurs partly because our attention is focused on the persons themselves, not on the constraints of their situations. For example, the race or sex of a person is vivid and attention-getting; the role requirements or situational forces working upon the person are more invisible. In the last century, even slavery was generally overlooked as an explanation for certain behaviors of slaves. Rather, their behavior was attributed to their own nature. Until recently, the same was true of how we explained the perceived differences between women and men. Since sex-role constraints were hard to see, we were more likely to attribute men's and women's behavior to their innate dispositions.

The Ultimate Attribution Error

Thomas Pettigrew (1979; 1980) argues that this fundamental attribution error becomes "the ultimate attribution error" when people explain the actions of people in groups. Members of one's own group are granted the benefit of the doubt: "She donated because she has a good heart; he refused because he had to under the circumstances." Members of other groups are less often given the benefit of the doubt; more often the worst is assumed: "He donated to gain their favor; she refused because she's selfish." Hence, as we noted earlier in this chapter, the shove that is perceived by whites as mere "horsing around" when done by a fellow white man becomes a "violent gesture" when done by a black. However, positive behavior by outgroup members is more likely to be dismissed, in one of several ways: as a "special case" ("He is certainly bright and hardworking—not at all like other Hispanics"), as due to luck or some special advantage ("She probably got admitted just because her med school had to fill its quota for women applicants"), as demanded by the situation ("Under the circumstances, what could the cheap Scot do but pay the whole check?"), or by attributing it to extra effort ("Jewish students get better grades because they're so compulsive").

The ultimate attribution error: *Granting the benefit of the doubt to members of one's own group, but not to members of other groups. Thus negative behavior by outgroup members is attributed to their dispositions, positive behavior explained away.*

Earlier we noted that laying blame on the victim can be a way to justify one's own superior status. Now we see that blaming the victim needn't have only self-serving motives; it can also stem from a cognitive bias toward attributing people's outcomes to their own dispositions. If women, blacks, or Jews have been abused, they must somehow have brought it on themselves. When the British marched a group of German civilians around the Belsen concentration camp at the close of World War II, one German responded, "What terrible criminals these prisoners must have been to receive such treatment."

The Just-World Phenomenon

Notice in the previous example that the person blaming the victim had done the victim no harm. In a series of experiments conducted at the University of Waterloo and the University of Kentucky, Melvin Lerner and his colleagues (Lerner & Miller, 1978; Lerner, 1980) learned that merely *observing* another person being innocently victimized is enough to make the victim seem less worthy. Imagine that you along with some others are participating in a study on the perception of emotional cues (Lerner & Simmons, 1966). One of the participants, a confederate, is selected by lottery to perform a memory task. This person receives painful shocks whenever she gives a wrong answer. You and the others note her emotional responses. After watching the victim receive a number of these apparently painful shocks, you are asked to evaluate her. How would you respond? With compassionate sympathy? We might legitimately expect such. As Ralph Waldo Emerson wrote, "The martyr cannot be dishonored." But on the contrary, the experiments reveal that when observers were powerless to alter the victim's fate, they, by and large, rejected and devalued the victim. Juvenal, the Roman satirist, anticipated these results: "The Roman mob follows after Fortune . . . and hates those who have been condemned."

Lerner (1980) suggests that such disparaging of hapless victims results from our need to believe "I am a just person living in a just world, a world where people get what they deserve." From early childhood, he argues, we are taught that good is rewarded and evil punished. Hard work and virtue pay dividends; laziness and immorality do not. From this it is but a short leap to assuming, furthermore, that those who are rewarded must be good and those who suffer must likewise deserve their fate. The classic illustration of such thinking is found in the Old Testament story of Job. Job's friends surmise that, this being a just world, Job must have done something wicked to elicit such terrible suffering.

Just-world phenomenon: *The tendency of people to believe the world is just, and that therefore people get what they deserve, and deserve what they get.*

All this suggests that one reason why people may seem indifferent to social injustice is not because they are unconcerned for justice, but because they *see* no injustice. What is more, believing in a just world—that rape victims must have behaved seductively, that battered spouses have provoked their beatings, that welfare people don't deserve better—enables successful people to reassure themselves that they, too, have gotten what they deserve.

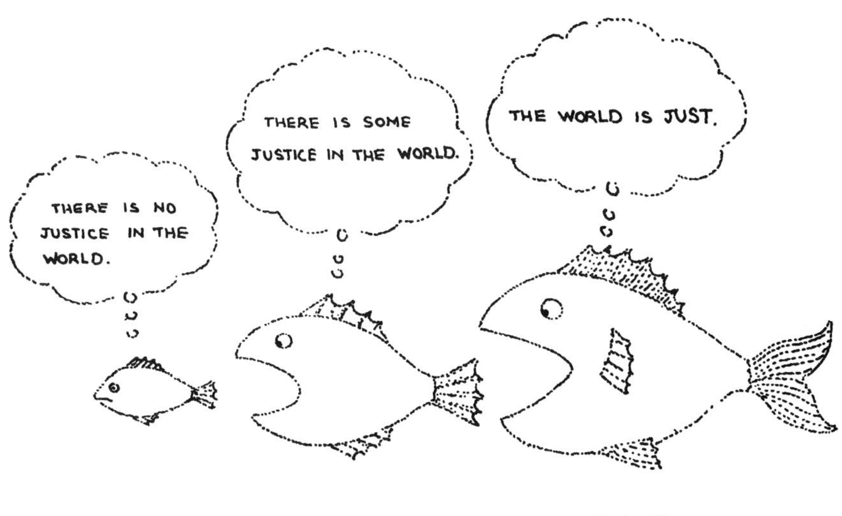

The just-world phenomenon. (Drawing by Mankoff; © 1981 *The New Yorker* Magazine, Inc.)

If, on the other hand, the poor could not be blamed for their poverty, then it would become more difficult to credit the wealthy for their success. Linking poverty with moral failure thus allows the affluent to link wealth with virtue and to relieve their guilt about the poor.

Although it is true that people tend to loathe a loser, even when the loser's suffering results merely from bad luck, we should not forget that self-initiative and feelings of self-efficacy are indeed conducive to achievement. Nevertheless, the problem with the "It's-a-just-world" type of thinking is that it discounts the situational constraints that leash one's best efforts.

Self-efficacy: *See Chapter 3, pages 95–100.*

On a more hopeful note, our yearning to see and to have a just, equitable world lies waiting to be tapped. The same motive that leads us to disparage life's losers when we can do little to help, can, when we finally recognize injustice, lead us to act (D. T. Miller, 1977). Once we perceive injustice, we are not indifferent to it.

Cognitive Consequences of Stereotypes

Stereotypes Are Self-Perpetuating

Prejudice is prejudgment. Prejudgments are inevitable. None of us is a dispassionate bookkeeper of social happenings, tallying evidence for and against our biases. Rather, our prejudgments direct our *interpretations* and our *memories* (Rose & Hamilton, 1979). Let's take these one at a time.

First, stereotyping directs our interpretations. Whenever a member of a group behaves as expected, the fact is duly noted; the prior belief is confirmed. When a member of the group behaves inconsistently with the observer's expectation, the behavior may be explained away as due to special circumstances (Crocker, Hannah, & Weber, 1982); or it may be misinterpreted, leaving the prior belief intact.

For example, have you ever felt that, try as you might, you could not overcome someone's opinion of you? That no matter what you did, you were misinterpreted? William Ickes and his colleagues (1982) demonstrated one reason this happens in an experiment with pairs of college-age men. Upon arrival, one member of each pair was falsely forewarned by the experimenters that the other subject was "one of the unfriendliest people I've talked to lately." The two were then introduced and left alone together for five minutes. As did students in another condition, who were led to think the other subject was exceptionally friendly, those who expected him to be *un*friendly went out of their way to be friendly to him, and their smiles and other friendly behaviors elicited a warm response from him. But unlike the positively biased students, those expecting an unfriendly person apparently attributed this reciprocal friendliness to their own "kid-gloves" treatment of him. Hence they afterward expressed more mistrust and dislike for the person and rated his behavior as less friendly. It seemed that, despite their partner's actual friendliness, the negative bias had induced these students to "see" hostilities lurking beneath his "forced smiles."

It would be an overstatement to say that we are absolutely blind to disconfirming facts. When David Hamilton and George Bishop (1976) interviewed suburban Connecticut homeowners several times during the year following the arrival of a first black neighbor, they found initial opposition melting. Fears that the new black neighbors would not take care of their property or that property values would decline apparently proved groundless, thus partially disconfirming the negative stereotypes. Still, it is fair to say that disconfirming facts have less effect on stereotypes than we might logically expect. Genuine friendliness is easily misinterpreted as mere superficial smoothness. Or the basic stereotype can be retained by splitting off a new category. Homeowners who have desirable black neighbors can form a new stereotype of "professional, middle-class" blacks. This subgroup stereotype can help them still maintain the larger stereotype that *most* blacks make irresponsible neighbors. Likewise, one who believes that women are basically passive and dependent can split off a new stereotype category of "aggressive feminist" to handle women who don't fit the basic female stereotype (S. E. Taylor, 1981). Similarly, people's images of the elderly seem to be split into stereotypes of the "grandmotherly" type, the "elder-statesman" type, and the inactive "senior-citizen" type (Brewer, Dull, & Lui, 1981).

Stereotypes perpetuate themselves not only by directing our interpretations but also by creating a selective memory for confirming events (Hamilton, 1981). In one experiment, Myron Rothbart, Mark Evans, and Solomon Fulero (1979) had some University of Oregon students read statements describing fifty members of a group (for example, "Jim invited friends to a potluck dinner at his house"). These statements equally often portrayed the group members as intelligent and as friendly. Nevertheless, those who had been led to believe the group was intellectually inclined recalled more of the "intelligent" statements, and those led to believe the group was friendly recalled more "friendly" statements.

In a follow-up experiment with Rothbart, John Howard (1980) placed students into an ingroup and an outgroup, based merely on a trivial criterion: whether they had over- or underestimated the number of dots on three cards. Then they were shown favorable and unfavorable statements said to have been made by others whose dot judgments were similar to or different from their own (for example, "I spread rumors that my roommate was dishonest"). When later given a memory test for these statements, the students better remembered the negative behaviors of the outgroup than those of their ingroup. The researchers' conclusion: the bias we hold for our ingroup is powerful enough to distort our memories. The net result: " 'Evidence' for group differences may be generated even when such differences have no bases in reality."

Do Stereotypes Bias Our Judgments of Individuals?

There is an upbeat note on which we can conclude our chapter. Anne Locksley, Eugene Borgida, and Nancy Brekke found that, once one knows a person, "stereotypes may have minimal, if any, impact on judgments about that person" (Locksley et al., 1980; 1982; Borgida, Locksley, & Brekke, 1981).

They discovered this by giving some University of Minnesota students anecdotal information about recent incidents in the life of "Nancy." In a supposed transcript of a telephone conversation, Nancy told a friend how she responded to three different situations (for example, being harassed by a seedy character while shopping). Some of the students read transcripts portraying Nancy responding assertively (telling the seedy character to leave); others read a report of passive responses (simply ignoring the character until he finally drifted away). Still other students received the identical information, except that the person was named "Paul" instead of Nancy. A day later the students predicted how Nancy (or Paul) would respond to other situations. Did knowing the person's sex have any effect on these predictions? None at all. Their expectations of how assertive the person would be were affected solely by what they had learned about that individual the day before. Even their judgments of the person's masculinity and femininity were unaffected by knowing the person's sex. Sex stereotypes had been left on the shelf; Nancy and Paul were evaluated as individuals.

The explanation for this finding is implied by an important principle discussed in Chapter 4. Given (1) general information about a group from which someone comes and (2) rather trivial, though vivid, anecdotal information about a particular person in that group, the vivid information usually overwhelms the general information when making judgments about that person. For example, after being told how most people in an experiment actually behaved and then viewing a brief interview with one of the supposed subjects, the typical viewer, when judging how this person behaved, makes little use of the "base-rate" information concerning how most people actually behaved.

Stereotypes are general beliefs about the distribution of traits in groups of people. For example, "Assertiveness is found more often in men, passiveness in women." Such stereotypes are often believed, yet, like other general knowledge, are at times ignored when in competition with vivid, anecdotal information. Thus many people seem to believe that "politicians are crooks" but "our Senator Jones has integrity." Similarly, the bigot may hold extreme stereotypes and yet claim, "One of my best friends is. . . ." Borgida, Locksley, and Brekke explain: "People may sustain general prejudices while simultaneously treating individuals with whom they frequently interact in a nonprejudicial manner."

This may well resolve a puzzling set of findings considered early in this chapter. Recall the evidence indicating that sex stereotypes (1) are strong, yet (2) seem to have very little effect on people's judgments of particular pieces of writing attributed to a man or a woman, or of individual male or female mental health clients. Now we see why. Mental health workers may have strong sex-role stereotypes, yet ignore them when confronted with a particular individual.

That stereotypes may not be as pervasive as feared should not allay our concern. Sometimes stereotypes are so strong that they do color our judgments of individuals, just as under some circumstances we do pay attention to base-rate information. Also, sometimes we make judgments about someone, or begin interacting with someone, with little to go on but our stereotype. In such cases, stereotypes can bias our interpretations and memories of people. Such bias was evident in a recent experiment by John Darley and Paget Gross (1982). Princeton University students viewed a videotape of a fourth-grade girl, Hannah, showing her either in a depressed urban neighborhood, supposedly the child of lower class parents, or in an affluent suburban setting, the child of professional parents. Asked to guess Hannah's ability level in various subjects, both groups of viewers refused to use Hannah's class background to prejudge her ability level; each group reluctantly rated her ability level at her grade level. Other students were also shown a second videotape in which Hannah took an oral achievement test, getting some questions right, some wrong. Now, those who had previously been introduced to "high class" Hannah judged her answers as indicating high ability, and later recalled her getting most questions right; those who had met "lower class" Hannah judged her ability as below grade level, and recalled her missing almost half the questions. But remember: this second videotape was *identical* for both groups. So we see that when stereotypes are strong, and the information about someone is ambiguous (unlike the cases of Nancy and Paul), stereotypes can *subtly* bias our judgments of individuals.

Stereotypes more surely bias our judgments of groups. Sometimes, such as when we vote, we make judgments about groups as a whole. On such occasions, that "One of my best friends is . . ." becomes trivial; what matters, what shapes public policy toward a large group of people, is our impression of the group as a whole. So, even if, once we come to know a particular person, we are often able to set aside our stereotypes and our prejudices, both still remain potent social forces.

SUMMING UP

Stereotypical beliefs, prejudicial attitudes, and discriminatory behavior have long poisoned our social existence. Judging by what Americans have told survey researchers during the last four decades, prejudice against blacks and women has plunged. Nevertheless, subtle survey questions, and indirect methods for assessing people's attitudes and behavior, still reveal strong sex stereotypes and a fair amount of disguised racial and gender bias. Prejudice, though less obvious, yet lurks.

Prejudice arises from an intricate interplay of social, emotional, and cognitive sources.

The social situation breeds and maintains prejudice in several ways. A group that enjoys social and economic superiority will often justify its standing with prejudicial beliefs. Moreover, prejudice can lead people to treat others in ways that trigger expected behavior, thus seeming to confirm the view one holds. Many recent experiments also reveal that prejudice, or more specifically an ingroup bias, may arise from the mere fact of people's being divided into groups. Once established, prejudice is maintained partly through the inertia of conformity, and partly through institutional supports, such as the mass media.

It has long been thought that prejudice has emotional roots, too. Frustration breeds hostility, which is sometimes vented on scapegoats, and sometimes expressed more directly against competing groups that are perceived as responsible for one's frustration. Prejudice, by providing a feeling of social superiority, may also help cover one's feelings of inferiority. Research has revealed that different types of prejudice are often found together in those who, apparently because of repressed hostilities, have an "authoritarian" attitude.

During the last decade, a new look at prejudice has emerged. This new research shows how the stereotyping that underlies prejudice can be a by-product of the normal ways by which we simplify the world. First, clustering people into categories tends to make those within a group seem more uniform than they really are and to exaggerate the seeming differences between groups. Once in a group, there is also a tendency when viewing another group to perceive that "they act and look alike, we don't." Second, there is a compelling quality to anyone who is distinctive, such as a solo member of a minority. Distinctive people draw our attention, making us aware of differences that we would otherwise not notice. We also better remember distinctive, extreme occurrences. Thus, knowing little about another group, one may even form a stereotype based on but a vivid case or two. The co-occurrence of two distinctive events—say a minority person committing an unusual crime—can also help create the illusion of a correlation between such people and such behavior. Finally, the tendency to attribute others' behavior to their dispositions can lead to the ultimate attribution error: attributing the undesirable behavior of outgroup members to their natural character, while explaining away their positive behaviors. Such blaming of the victim also results from the common presumption that this is a just world in which people get what they deserve.

Stereotypes have cognitive consequences as well as cognitive sources. By directing our interpretations and our memories, they lead us to "find" supportive evidence, even when none exists. Stereotypes are therefore resistant to disconfirmation. Yet, when people get to know a particular individual, they seem quite able to set aside their stereotypes of the individual's group and to judge the person individually. Stereotypes are more potent when judging unknown individuals and when judging and making decisions about whole groups.

Social psychologists have more successfully explained than alleviated prejudice. Since prejudice results from many interrelated factors, it has no simple remedy. Nevertheless, we can now anticipate some techniques for reducing prejudice (to be discussed further in Chapters 13 and 14): If unequal status breeds prejudice, then seek to create cooperative, equal-status relationships; if prejudice often rationalizes discriminatory behavior, then mandate nondiscrimination; if social institutions support prejudice, then pull out those supports (for example, have the media model interracial harmony); if outgroups seem more unlike one's own group than they really are, then make efforts to personalize their members. Such are among the prescribed antidotes for the poison of prejudice.

Since World War II, some of these antidotes have begun to be applied, and racial and gender prejudice have indeed diminished. It now remains to be seen whether, during the remaining years of this century, this progress will continue, or whether, as could easily happen in an age of diminishing resources, antagonisms will again erupt.

Chapter

13 Attraction: Liking and Loving Others

What predisposes one person to like, or to love, another? Few questions about human nature arouse greater interest. The ways that people's affections flourish and fade form the stuff and fluff of soap operas, popular music, novels, and much of our everyday conversation. Long before I knew there was such a field as social psychology, I had memorized Dale Carnegie's recipe for *How to Win Friends and Influence People*. In fact, so much has been written about liking and loving that almost every conceivable explanation—and its opposite—has been already proposed. Does absence make the heart grow fonder? Or is someone who is out of sight also out of mind? Is it likes that attract? Or opposites?

While scientific observation gave us an almost exact estimate of the earth's circumference more than 2000 years ago, it was not until our lifetime that liking and loving became the objects of vigorous scientific scrutiny. And then when they did, the very idea of scientifically analyzing such "subjective" phenomena was greeted with some scorn. When the National Science Foundation awarded an $84,000 grant for research on love, Wisconsin Senator William Proxmire was irate:

> I object to this not only because no one—not even the National Science Foundation—can argue that falling in love is a science; not only because I'm sure that even if they spend $84 million or $84 billion they wouldn't get an answer that anyone would believe. I'm also against it because I don't want the answer.

I believe that 200 million other Americans want to leave some things in life a mystery, and right at the top of things we don't want to know is why a man falls in love with a woman and vice versa. . . .

So National Science Foundation—get out of the love racket. Leave that to Elizabeth Barrett Browning and Irving Berlin! (T. G. Harris, 1978)

The press loved it. They had a field day with Proxmire's comments. Some columnists echoed his derision, others rebutted it. In the *New York Times*, James Reston (1975) acknowledged that love has unfathomable depths of mystery, yet argued, "If the sociologists and psychologists can get even a suggestion of the answer to our pattern of romantic love, marriage, disillusion, divorce—and the children left behind—it could be the best investment of federal money since Jefferson made the Louisiana Purchase."

Fortunately, social-psychological analyses of friendship and intimate love are not meant to compete with Elizabeth Barrett Browning and Irving Berlin. The social psychologist and the poet deal with love at quite different "levels." The social psychologist examines who attracts whom. The poet describes love as a sometimes sublime experience. Though social psychologists and poets might glean insights from one another, the study of who attracts whom does not preempt poetic description of the experience of love, nor does poetry decisively answer the questions posed in psychological research.

Levels of explanation: *See Chapter 1, pages 7–8.*

A SIMPLE THEORY OF ATTRACTION

Asked why they like one person and not another, or why they were attracted to their fiance or spouse, most people can readily answer. "I like Carol because she's warm, witty, and well-read." What such explanations leave out—and what social psychologists believe most important—is ourselves (Berscheid & Walster, 1978). Attraction involves the one who is attracted as well as the attractor. Thus a more psychologically accurate answer might be, "I like Carol because of how I feel when I'm with her." We are attracted to those whom *we* find it satisfying and gratifying to be with.

The point can be expressed as a simple psychological principle: Those who reward us, or who are associated with rewards, we like. This principle is elaborated in two allied theories. First, from our discussion in Chapter 11 of social-exchange theory, you may recall the "minimax" motive: Minimize costs, maximize rewards. This implies that if a relationship rewards more than it costs us, we will like it and will therefore wish to continue. Such will be especially true if the relationship is more profitable than alternative relationships (Burgess & Huston, 1979; Kelley, 1979; Rusbutt, 1980). Minimax: Minimize boredom, conflicts, expenses; maximize self-esteem, pleasure, security. Some 300 years ago La Rochefoucauld (1665) similarly conjectured:

Reward theory of attraction: *The theory that we like those whose behavior is rewarding to us, or who have been associated with rewarding events.*

"Friendship is a scheme for the mutual exchange of personal advantages and favors whereby self-esteem may profit."

If in a relationship, both partners pursue their personal desires willy-nilly, the relationship is not likely to survive long. Therefore, our society teaches us to exchange rewards by a rule that Elaine Hatfield, William Walster, and Ellen Berscheid (1978) call *equity*: What you and your partner get out of a relationship should be proportional to what you each put into it. If two people receive equal outcomes, then their contributions should be equal; otherwise the relationship is likely to be perceived as unfair. If both feel that the outcomes correspond to the assets and efforts each contributes to their relationship, then both will perceive equity.

Equity: *A condition in which what people receive from a relationship is proportional to what they contribute to it.* Note: *Equitable outcomes needn't always be equal outcomes.*

Casual acquaintances maintain equity by directly exchanging benefits: You loan me your class notes, later I'll loan you mine; I invite you to my party, you invite me to yours. Those in love feel not so bound to trade benefits "in kind": notes for notes, parties for parties. They feel freer to maintain equity by exchanging a variety of benefits ("When you drop by to loan me your notes, why don't you stay for dinner?"), or even to stop keeping track of who owes whom.

That friendship and love are rooted in an equitable exchange of rewards may seem crass. Do we not sometimes give in response to a loved one's need, without expecting a reciprocal benefit? Indeed, those involved in an equitable *long-term* relationship are usually less concerned with *short-term* equity. Margaret Clark and Judson Mills (1979; Clark, 1981; Mills & Clark, 1982) argue that people even take pains to *avoid* calculating any exchange of benefits. When we help a good friend, we do so not wanting instant repayment. We would far rather the friend simply offer us help when we are in need. Likewise, if someone entertains us at dinner, we wait before reciprocating, lest the return invitation be attributed merely to paying off a social obligation. Not being calculating is a mark of true friendship. In experiments with University of Maryland students, Clark and Mills found that tit-for-tat exchanges boosted people's liking for one another when their relationship was relatively formal, but *diminished* liking when the two sought true friendship. They surmise from this that marriage contracts (those in which each partner specifies what is expected from the other) are more likely to undermine than enhance the couple's love. When the other's positive behavior is voluntary, it is more likely to be attributed to love.

Although communal relationships are not based on explicit exchange, they are mutually beneficial. The participants do not (and should not) keep a conscious ledger of their exchanges. Nevertheless, when either party feels that the costs of the relationship exceed its rewards, or when the relationship becomes inequitable rather than being mutually beneficial, the relationship itself is threatened. While a scorekeeping, tit-for-tat exchange nurtures neither deep friendship nor love, such feelings *can* be nourished by the subtle exchange of rewards—the meeting of one another's needs—that occurs whenever two people become interdependent.

We not only like people who are rewarding to be with, we also, according to the second version of the reward principle, like those we *associate* with good feelings. According to theorists Donn Byrne and Gerald Clore (1970), and to Albert Lott and Bernice Lott (1974), social conditioning creates positive feelings toward those who have been linked to rewarding events. When, after a strenuous week, we relax in front of a fire, enjoying good food, drink, and music, we will likely feel a special warmth toward those around us, even if in their own right they are not especially rewarding.

Experiments by William Griffitt (1970) and others confirm this phenomenon of liking—and disliking—by association. In one, college students who evaluated strangers in a pleasant room liked them better than did those in an uncomfortably hot room. Another experiment asked people to evaluate photographs of other people, while in either an elegant, sumptuously furnished, softly lit room or a shabby, dirty, stark room (Maslow & Mintz, 1956). Again, the warm feelings evoked by the elegant surroundings were transferred to the people being rated. It has even been found that a stranger who merely happens on the scene is liked better by someone who has just heard a radio broadcast of good rather than bad news (Veitch & Griffitt, 1976). Elaine Hatfield and William Walster (1978) find a practical tip in these research studies: "Romantic dinners, trips to the theatre, evenings at home together, and vacations never stop being important. . . . If your relationship is to survive, it's important that you *both* continue to associate your relationship with good things."

This simple theory of attraction—we like those who reward us and those associated with rewards—is helpful, but as with most sweeping generalizations it leaves many questions unanswered. What, precisely, *is* rewarding? Of course, the answer will vary from person to person and situation to situation. But, in general, is it more rewarding to be with someone who differs from us or one who is similar to us? To be lavishly flattered or constructively criticized? A theory is no better than the precision of its predictions.

Our liking and disliking of people is influenced by the events with which they are associated. (*Miss Peach* by Mell Lazarus Courtesy of Mell Lazarus and Field Newspaper Syndicate.)

With so many possibilities, we had better examine specifics that contribute to attraction. For most people most of the time, what factors are conducive to liking and loving? We will start with those factors that help initiate a friendship and then consider those that help sustain and deepen a relationship. First, however, you might pause to identify the factors that, in your experience, seem to have been conducive to your close friendships. Having done so, you can compare your list with the factors that social psychologists have found conducive to liking and loving.

LIKING: WHO LIKES WHOM?

Initially we are powerfully attracted to other people by what seem to be, yet are not, trivial factors: mere geographical proximity, or superficial physical attributes—factors to which few of us likely attribute our friendships.

Proximity

Proximity: *Geographical nearness. Proximity (or, more precisely, "functional distance") is a powerful predictor of liking.*

One of the most powerful predictors of whether any two people are friends is their sheer proximity to one another. Proximity can also breed hostility; most assaults, most murders, involve people living in close proximity, often within the same walls. But fortunately far more often, proximity kindles liking. Though it may seem trivial to those pondering the mysterious origins of romantic love, sociologists have found that most people marry someone who lives in the same neighborhood, or works at the same job, or sits in the same class (Bossard, 1932; Burr, 1973; Clarke, 1952; Katz & Hill, 1958). Look around. If you choose to marry, it will likely be to someone who has lived or worked or studied within walking distance.

FIGURE 13-1 Diagram of a married-student apartment building at MIT. Had you desired to make friends after moving into one of these buildings, which of the apartments should you have preferred? Leon Festinger, Stanley Schachter, and Kurt Back (1950) found that residents of apartments 1 and 5, who were functionally close to several of the upper apartments as well as to the lower apartments, had the best opportunities to form friendships.

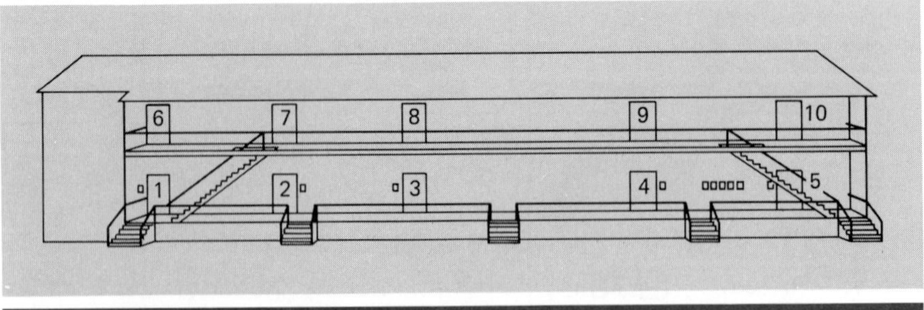

Leon Festinger, Stanley Schachter, and Kurt Back (1950), discovered this proximity → liking when they observed the formation of friendships in the married student apartments at the Massachusetts Institute of Technology. Since people were assigned apartments essentially at random, without any prior friendships, the researchers could assess the importance of proximity—and important was what it turned out to be. When wives were asked to name their three closest friends within the entire complex of buildings, some two-thirds of those named lived in the same building, while two-thirds of these lived on the same floor. The person most frequently chosen? One who lived next door.

Interaction

Actually, geographical distance per se is not what is critical, but rather the "functional distance"—how often people's paths cross. People frequently become friends with those who use the same entrances, parking lots, and recreation areas. A recent study of workers at a California naval training center found that they most enjoyed talking to those coworkers whom they most often ran into (Monge & Kirste, 1980). At the college where I teach, the men and women students once lived on opposite sides on the campus. They understandably bemoaned the dearth of cross-sex friendships. They now occupy different areas of the same dormitories, sharing common sidewalks, lounges, and laundry facilities, and cross-sex friendships are far more frequent. So, if you're new in town and want to make friends, try to get an apartment near the complex's mailboxes, an office desk near the coffee pot, a parking spot near the main buildings. Such is the architecture of friendship.

Further evidence that what's crucial in forming friendships is not just geographical distance, but the opportunity for interaction, comes from a clever study with University of North Carolina students by Chester Insko and Midge Wilson (1977). They sat three students in a triangle facing one another and then had persons A and B converse about themselves while C observed, and B and C converse while A observed. Thus, for example, B and C were equally near A and therefore observed the same behavior from A. But who most liked A? Usually person B, with whom person A had talked. Interacting with another generally stimulates one's liking for that person. In this case it did so partly because it enabled the two conversants to explore their similarities and to sense one another's liking. Likewise, randomly assigned college roommates, who of course can hardly avoid frequent interaction, are far more likely to become good friends than enemies (Newcomb, 1961).

But why does proximity breed liking? For one thing, partly just the availability of people nearby; obviously, there are fewer opportunities to get to know someone who attends a different school or lives in another town. But there is more to it than that, else why do people tend to like their roommates, or those one door away, better than those two doors away? After all, those just a few doors away, or even a floor below, hardly live at an inconvenient distance. Moreover, those close by are potential enemies as well as friends. So why *does* proximity encourage affection more often than animosity?

"When I'm not near the one I love, I love the one I'm near."

E. Y. Harburg
Finian's Rainbow, *London: Chappell Music, 1947*

Anticipation of Interaction

Already we have noted one answer: Proximity, especially functional proximity, enables people through interaction to discover commonalities and exchange rewards. What is more, one's merely anticipating interaction can boost liking. John Darley and Ellen Berscheid (1967) demonstrated this when they gave some women students at the University of Minnesota ambiguous information about two other women, one of whom the students expected to have a rather intimate conversation with. Asked how much they liked each, the women were more attracted to the person they expected to meet.

Does this occur because the anticipation of interacting with someone creates a feeling that the two of you are a group? (Recall from Chapter 12 the "ingroup bias.") Or is it because we are stimulated to perceive the other person as pleasant, thus maximizing the chance of a rewarding relationship (Knight & Vallacher, 1981; Tyler & Sears, 1977)? Likely, it is both, because people tend to feel a kinship with those in their group. Regardless, this much seems clear: The phenomenon is adaptive. Our lives are filled with relationships with people whom we may not have chosen but with whom we anticipate continuing interactions—dormmates, grandparents, teachers, classmates, co-workers. Liking such people is surely conducive to better relationships with them.

Mere Exposure

Mere-exposure effect: *The tendency for novel stimuli to be liked more or rated more positively after one has been repeatedly exposed to them.*

There is yet another reason why proximity leads to liking. A host of recent studies by Robert Zajonc and others have found, quite contrary to the old proverb about familiarity breeding contempt, that familiarity breeds fondness. Mere repeated exposure to all sorts of novel stimuli—nonsense syllables, Chinese characters, musical selections, faces—boosts people's ratings of such stimuli. Do the Turkish words *nansoma*, *saricik*, and *afworbu* mean something better or something worse than the words *iktitaf*, *biwojni*, and *kadirga*? University of Michigan students tested by Zajonc (1968; 1970) preferred whichever of these words they had seen most frequently. The more times they had seen a meaningless word or Chinese ideograph, the more likely they were to say it meant something good.

In 1969, residents of Grand Rapids, Michigan, were presented with their new downtown landmark, a huge metal sculpture created by the artist Alexander Calder. Their reaction? "An abomination," "an embarrassment," "a waste of money," scorned some letter writers and commentators. Other people were neutral; few citizens seemed enthusiastic. But within a decade, the sculpture became an object of civic pride, its critics silent, its picture adorning bank checks, city posters, and tourist literature. Similarly, when completed in 1889, the Eiffel Tower in Paris was mocked as grotesque. Today this giant is the friendly, beloved symbol of Paris (Harrison, 1977). Such changes make one wonder about some people's initial reactions to art (Brown, 1965). Do visitors to the Louvre in Paris really adore the *Mona Lisa*, or are they simply delighted to find a familiar face? Perhaps both: To know her is to like her.

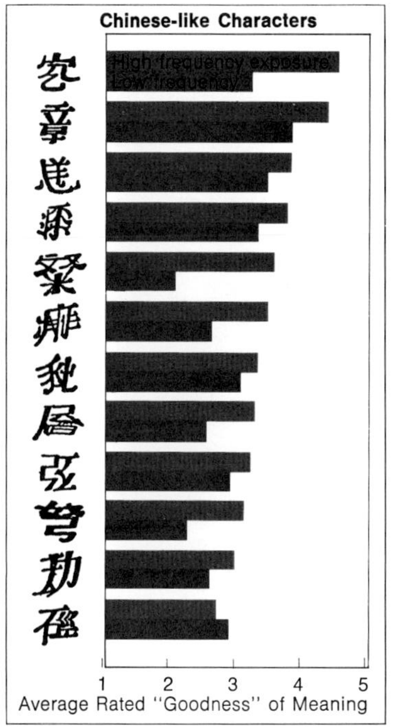

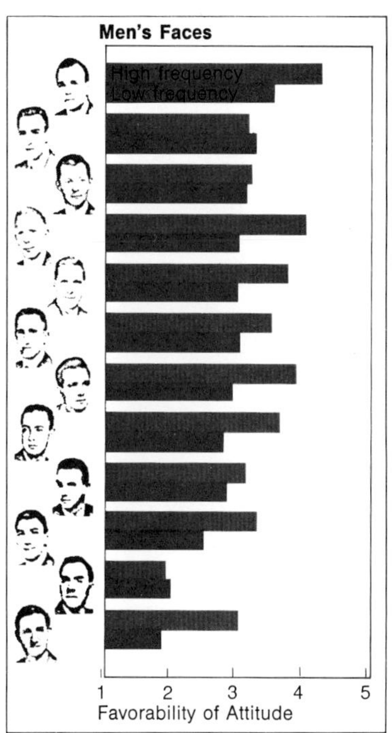

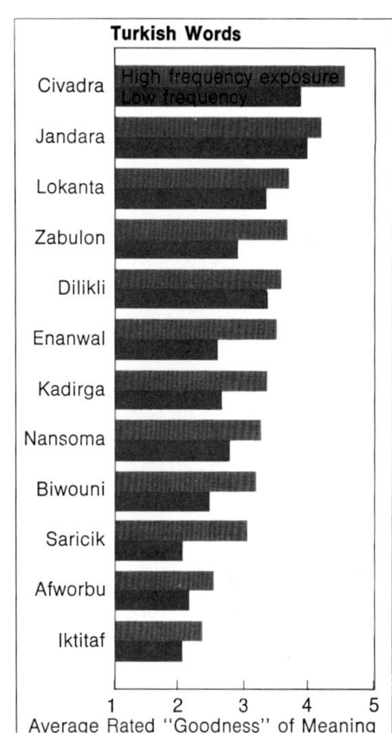

FIGURE 13-2 The mere-exposure effect. Stimuli are rated more positively after being shown repeatedly. (Data from Zajonc, 1968.) (Reprinted from *Psychology Today* Magazine. Copyright © 1970 Ziff-Davis Publishing Company.)

Perhaps you are objecting, feeling that one really has to know some people in order to *dis*like them, or that some stimuli lose appeal when *over*exposed. A new musical piece that grows on you can, after the hundredth hearing, become wearisome. To be sure, the "Exposure-breeds-liking" principle must be qualified. Continuing repetitions not only have a diminishing positive effect but can, sometimes, eventually have a negative effect (Suedfeld, Rank, & Borrie, 1975). This negative effect seems especially likely when people's initial reactions to the stimulus are already negative, rather than neutral or positive (Brickman et al., 1972; Grush, 1976). Second, positive responses are lessened when repetitions are incessant rather than distributed among other experiences (Harrison, 1977). Third, the exposure effect, like many other influences upon us, is modest; being but one of many influences, it won't by itself overcome strong feelings from other sources.

Still, as a generalization, the principle now seems indisputable. Moreover, Zajonc and his co-workers, William Kunst-Wilson and Richard Moreland, have found that exposure can lead to liking even when people are unaware of

Familiarity often boosts liking of artistic and musical stimuli, as happened with this Alexander Calder sculpture in Grand Rapids, Michigan. (Photograph by William Mayer.)

what they have been exposed to (Wilson, 1979; Kunst-Wilson & Zajonc, 1980; Moreland & Zajonc, 1980). In one experiment, women students listened in one ear over headphones to a prose passage, repeated the words out loud, and compared them to a written version, checking for errors. Meanwhile, brief and novel melodies were played into their other ear. This procedure focused their attention upon the verbal material and away from the tunes. Later, when they heard these same tunes interspersed among similar ones not previously played, they did not recognize them. Nevertheless, the tunes they *liked best* were the ones they had previously heard. In another experiment, people were shown a series of geometric figures, one at a time, each for a millisecond—just long enough to perceive but a flash of light. Although later they were unable to recognize the figures they had been shown, they nevertheless liked them best.

"'Tis strange—but true; for truth is always strange— Stranger than fiction."

Lord Byron, Don Juan

Note that in both experiments people's conscious judgments about the stimuli were a far less reliable clue to what they had heard or seen than were their instant feelings. Though not consciously reasoned out, their preferences were nevertheless real. Perhaps you, too, can recall immediately liking or disliking something or someone without consciously knowing why. Only later were you able to verbalize why you felt that way. Zajonc (1980) argues that our emotions are often more instantaneous, more primitive than our thinking. For example, fearful or prejudicial feelings aren't always bred by stereotyped beliefs; sometimes the beliefs arise later as justifications for one's intuitive feelings.

What causes the familiarity-liking relationship? Although the phenomenon is indeed well-established, its explanation remains uncertain (Grush, 1979). Some believe it stems from a natural "neophobia," an adaptive tendency to be wary of unfamiliar things until one accumulates evidence that they are not dangerous. Animals, too, tend to prefer familiar over unfamiliar stimuli (Hill, 1978).

Whatever the explanation, the phenomenon colors our evaluations of people. Other things being equal, the more times people see a given stranger during an experiment, the more the stranger is liked (Saegert, Swap, & Zajonc, 1973; Swap, 1977). Similarly, Canadian preschoolers who had watched two brief *Sesame Street* excerpts featuring North American Indians and Japanese-Canadians were much more likely than children not exposed to express a desire to play with such children (Goldberg & Gorn, 1979). We even like ourselves better when we are the way we're used to seeing ourselves. In a delightful experiment, Theodore Mita, Marshall Dermer, and Jeffrey Knight (1977) photographed women students at the University of Wisconsin—Milwaukee and later showed each one her actual picture along with a mirror image of it. Asked which picture they liked better, most preferred their mirror image, which is of course the image they were used to seeing. (No wonder our photographs never look quite right.) However, when close friends of the

"All you lack for my vote, sir, is a little more media exposure."

Mere exposure boosts votes. (Drawing by Dana Fradon; © 1979 *The New Yorker* Magazine, Inc.)

subjects were shown the same two pictures, they preferred the true picture, the image to which *they* were accustomed.

Advertisers and politicians have learned that "mere exposure" works to their advantage. It is hard to separate out the many factors that lead to purchases and to winning elections. But when people don't have strong feelings about a product or a candidate, mere repetition seems to boost sales or votes (McCullough & Ostrom, 1974; Winter, 1973). If the candidates are relatively unknown, as often happens in congressional and presidential primaries and in local elections, those who gain the most media exposure usually win (Patterson, 1980; Schaffner, Wandersman, & Stang, 1981). Joseph Grush, Kevin McGeough, and Robert Ahlering (1978) exhaustively analyzed 1972 U.S. congressional primaries and found that, overwhelmingly, the winners were either incumbents or big spenders. Even in presidential debates, it seems that, other things being equal, the lesser-known challenger has more to gain than does the already familiar incumbent. As one political campaign handbook put it, "Repetition breeds familiarity and familiarity breeds trust" (Meyer, 1966).

Physical Attractiveness

"We should look to the mind, and not to the outward appearance."

Aesop, Fables

"Personal beauty is a greater recommendation than any letter of introduction."

Aristotle, Diogenes Laertius

What do you look for in a potential date? Sincerity? Good looks? Character? Conversational ability? Asked to rank such attributes, most collegians put physical attractiveness near the bottom of the list (Tesser & Brodie, 1971; Vreeland, 1972). Of course. Sophisticated, intelligent people are not greatly concerned with such superficial qualities as good looks; they know that "beauty is only skin deep." At least they know that's how they *ought* to feel. As Cicero counseled, "The final good and the supreme duty of the wise man is to resist appearance."

This intuition that looks matter little may be another instance of our denying real influences upon us (Chapter 4), for there is now a file drawer full of research studies indicating that appearance is a powerful determinant of initial attraction. The consistency and pervasiveness of this effect is startling, perhaps even disconcerting. Good looks are a great asset.

Dating

Like it or not, the fact is that a young woman's physical attractiveness is a moderately good predictor of how frequently she dates: a young man's attractiveness, slightly less a predictor of how frequently he dates (Berscheid et al., 1971; Krebs & Adinolfi, 1975; Reis, Nezlek, & Wheeler, 1980; Walster et al., 1966). Does this imply, as many have surmised, that women are better at following Cicero's advice to "resist appearance"? Or does it merely reflect the fact that men more often do the inviting? If women were to indicate their preferences among various men, would looks be as important to them as to men?

Some researchers have addressed this question by providing men and women students with various pieces of information about someone of the other sex, including a picture of the person, or by briefly introducing a

Do men care more about women's attractiveness than women do about men's? Perhaps. But research indicates that "a pretty face" is a definite asset for men, too. (© 1959 United Feature Syndicate, Inc.)

man and a woman, and later asking them how interested they would be in dating one another. In these experiments, women were virtually as much influenced by a man's looks as men were by a woman's (S. M. Andersen & S. L. Bem, 1981; Crouse & Mehrabian, 1977; Nida & Williams, 1977; Stretch & Figley, 1980). Other researchers have matched students on blind computer dates to see what qualities and combinations led to liking. One such study sent some University of Texas men and women on thirty-minute coke dates (Byrne, Ervin, & Lamberth, 1970). Immediately afterwards, and again three months later, the students evaluated their dates and speculated about *why* they felt as they did. Men more than women suspected their date's physical attractiveness was important, thus seeming to confirm Bertrand Russell's observation, "On the whole, women tend to love men for their character, while men tend to love women for their appearance." But, to the contrary, the date's physical attractiveness *actually* predicted the women's attraction to their dates more than the men's.

In an even more ambitious study, Elaine Hatfield and her co-workers (1966) matched 752 University of Minnesota freshmen for a "Welcome Week" computer dance. For each person, the researchers secured a variety of personality and aptitude test scores, but then actually matched the couples randomly. On the night of the dance, the couples danced and talked for two and one-half hours and then took a brief intermission to evaluate their dates. How well did the personality and aptitude tests predict attraction? Not well at all. So far as the researchers could discern, only one thing mattered: how physically attractive the person was. The more attractive a woman, as rated by the experimenters and, especially, as rated by her date, the more he liked her and wanted to date her again. Similarly, the more attractive the man, the more she liked and wanted to date him again. Pretty pleases.

The Matching Phenomenon

After a brief date, physically attractive people are liked best. But not everyone can end up paired with someone stunningly attractive. So how do people pair off?

Judging from research by Bernard Murstein (1972; 1976) and others, they pair off with people who are about as attractive as they are. For example, several studies have found a strong correspondence between the attractiveness of husbands and wives (Cavior & Boblett, 1972; Murstein & Christy, 1976; Price & Vandenberg, 1979; G. L. White, 1980). People tend to marry those who are a "good match" not only to their level of intelligence, but also to their level of attractiveness. So, while people might prefer someone maximally attractive, they tend actually to choose and marry someone not "out of their league." This "matching phenomenon" has also been verified in experiments. When choosing whom to approach, knowing the other is free to say yes or no, people tend to seek equity by approaching someone whose attractiveness roughly matches their own (Berscheid et al., 1971; Huston, 1973; Stroebe et al., 1971).

Matching phenomenon: *The tendency for men and women to choose as partners those who are a "good match" in attractiveness and other traits.*

Good physical matches may also be conducive to good relationships. When Gregory White (1980) studied some UCLA dating couples, he found that those who were most similar in physical attractiveness were most likely, nine months later, to have fallen more deeply in love. Based on this finding, whom might we expect to be most closely matched for attractiveness—married couples or couples casually dating? White found, as have other researchers (Cavior & Boblett, 1972), the answer to be married couples.

Perhaps this research has prompted you to think of happy couples dissimilar in attractiveness. In such cases, the less attractive person often has compensating qualities, as when a beautiful young woman marries an aged but prestigious and wealthy statesman. Each one brings assets to the social marketplace, and the value of their respective assets caused them to be viewed as an equitable match. In the 1930s, researchers observed Oakland, California, preadolescent girls, noting which were strikingly attractive and which were not. Years later, sociologist Glen Elder (1969) tracked them down and found that the beautiful ones had managed to marry men whose social status exceeded their own. Knowing that attractiveness is correlated with upward social mobility does not prove that attractiveness per se is the cause. But such data are easily explained by the principle of equity in matching. Similarly, Ellen Berscheid, Elaine Hatfield, and George Bohrnstedt (1973) found that men and women who were unequal with their partner on one dimension—say physical attractiveness—were often compensatingly unequal on some other dimension. If one person was more attractive, the other tended to be richer or more self-sacrificing.

"A proposal of marriage in our society tends to be a way in which a man sums up his social attributes and suggests to a woman that hers are not so much better as to preclude a merger or partnership in these matters."

Erving Goffman (1952)

The Physical-Attractiveness Stereotype

Do the benefits of being good-looking spring entirely from one's being sexually attractive? Clearly not. Young children are favorably biased toward attractive children much as adults are biased toward attractive adults (Dion, 1973; Dion & Berscheid, 1974; Langlois & Stephan, 1981). When adults judge children they are similarly biased. Margaret Clifford and Elaine Hatfield (Clifford & Walster, 1973) showed Missouri fifth-grade teachers identical information

Exceptionally attractive people often marry someone of higher social status. (Wide World Photos)

about a boy or girl, but with the photograph of an attractive or unattractive child attached. The teachers who judged an attractive child saw the child as more intelligent and more likely to do well in school. Or think of yourself as a playground supervisor having to discipline an unruly child. Might you, like the University of Minnesota women studied by Karen Dion (1972; also Berkowitz & Frodi, 1982), be tempted to give more benefit of the doubt if the child is attractive?

What is more, beautiful people, even if of the same sex, are assumed also to possess certain desirable traits. Other things being equal, they are guessed to be happier, more intelligent, more sociable, more successful, and more competent (Dion, Berscheid, & Walster, 1972; Cash et al., 1975; Landy & Sigall, 1974; Maruyama & Miller, 1980). When in need, they receive more help (Benson, Karabenick, & Lerner, 1976; Stroufe et al., 1977). When good things happen (for example, a promotion) attractive people are perceived as more responsible for the outcome than are unattractive people; when bad things happen, attractive people are seen as less responsible (Seligman, Paschall, & Takata, 1974). To top it off, attractive people, more than unattractive people, are guessed to have personalities like one's own (Marks, Miller, &

Physical-attractiveness stereotype: *The presumption that physically attractive people possess other socially desirable traits as well: What is beautiful is good.*

Maruyama, 1981). Added together, the findings point to a *physical-attractiveness stereotype*: What is beautiful is good. Children are taught the stereotype quite early. Snow White and Cinderella are beautiful—and kind; the witch and the stepsisters are ugly—and wicked. As one kindergarten girl put it when asked what it means to be pretty, "It's like to be a princess. Everybody loves you" (Dion, 1979).

If physical attractiveness is this important, then permanently changing people's attractiveness should change the way others react to them. But would it be ethical to alter someone's looks? In the United States, such manipulation is performed more than a million times a year—by plastic surgeons and orthodontists (Berscheid, 1981). To examine the effect of such alterations, Michael Kalick (1977) had Harvard students indicate their impressions of eight women, judging from profile photographs taken either before or after cosmetic surgery. Not only were the women judged as more physically attractive after the surgery, but also as kinder, more sensitive, more sexually warm and responsive, more likable, and so on. Likewise, Karen Korabik (1981) found that University of Guelph (Ontario) students rated girls as more intelligent, better-adjusted, and so forth after they had completed orthodontic treatment. Amazingly, ratings were based on before and after pictures taken with mouths closed and teeth not showing. Orthodontic treatment affects facial structure as well as teeth, and the raters were apparently responding to these subtle facial changes. Ellen Berscheid (1981) notes that while such cosmetic improvements tend to boost one's self-image, they can also be temporarily disturbing:

Most of us—at least those of us who have *not* experienced swift alterations of our physical appearance—can continue to believe that our physical attractiveness level plays a minor role in how we are treated by others. It is harder, however, for those who have actually experienced swift changes in appearance to continue to deny and to minimize the influence of physical attractiveness in their own lives—and the fact of it may be disturbing, even when the changes are for the better.

However, we should not overstate the potency of the attractiveness stereotype. To say that attractiveness is important, other things being equal, is not to say that physical appearance is always more important than other qualities. Attractiveness probably most affects first impressions; one's appearance is vivid, it draws immediate attention. As a relationship develops, appearance *may* diminish in importance. [One study disputed this by finding attractiveness *increased* in importance with subsequent dates (Mathes, 1975).] Nevertheless, first impressions are important, not only for one's prospects for dating, but also for job interviews. If first impressions are bad, there may never be a chance for second impressions. Indications are that attractiveness does figure strongly in hiring decisions (Cash, Gillen, & Burns, 1977; Marvelle & Green, 1980). Moreover, as society has seemingly become more mobile and urbanized—our contacts with doctors, colleagues, and neighbors more fleeting—first impressions have probably become more important than ever before (Berscheid, 1981).

Is the physical-attractiveness stereotype accurate? Or was Leo Tolstoy correct when he wrote that it's "a strange illusion . . . to suppose that beauty is goodness"? There well might be a trace of truth to the stereotype. Children and young adults who are attractive tend to have higher self-esteem (B. P. Allen, 1978, p. 116; Maruyama & Miller, 1981). They are more assertive, although they are also believed to be more egotistical (Jackson & Huston, 1975). They are neither more nor less academically capable (contrary to the negative stereotype that "beauty times brains equals a constant") (Sparacino & Hansell, 1979). However, they are somewhat more socially polished. William Goldman and Philip Lewis (1977) demonstrated this by having sixty University of Georgia men call and talk for five minutes with each of three women students. When, afterward, the men and women rated their unseen telephone partners, those partners who happened to be most attractive were rated as somewhat more socially skillful and likable.

Surely these small average differences between attractive and unattractive people are the result of self-fulfilling prophecies. Attractive people are valued and favored, and so may develop more social self-confidence. (You may recall from Chapter 4 an experiment in which unseen women who were *thought* to be attractive were treated in a way that led them to respond more warmly.) By this analysis, what's crucial to your social skill is not how you look but how you are treated and how you feel about yourself—whether you accept yourself, like yourself, feel comfortable with yourself. Sara Kiesler and Roberta Baral (1970) led several dozen Yale men to feel either good about themselves—

BEHIND THE SCENES

Ellen Berscheid

I vividly remember the afternoon I began to appreciate the far-reaching implications of physical attractiveness for social behavior. Karen Dion (now a professor at the University of Toronto) was a graduate student in our University of Minnesota lab at that time, and had learned that researchers in our university's Institute of Child Development had collected some popularity ratings from nursery school children and, as part of the procedure, had also taken a photo of each child. She suggested that we try to obtain the photos to examine the relationship between the child's physical attractiveness and his or her popularity rating.

On an informal basis, we had previously talked to elementary school teachers and other caretakers of young children, but they had persuaded us that "all children are beautiful" and that no reliable discrimination along the physical-attractiveness dimension could be made. Thus, at that time we shared the views of many that the impact of physical attractiveness was probably limited to adolescents and young adults and probably even limited further to heterosexual dating relationships.

Nevertheless, because the photos were readily available, we went ahead and obtained ratings of each child's physical attractiveness. To do so, we simply instructed graduate students to make those ratings. (We gave them no choice in the matter, because we also had found that most people refused to try to make such ratings.) When we looked at the correspondence between these physical attractiveness ratings (made by adults who were totally unacquainted with the children) and the children's popularity with their nursery school playmates, as well as their ratings of each other's behavior along a number of other dimensions, we realized that the long shot had hit home: Attractive children were popular children. This effect of attractiveness was far more potent than we and others had assumed, with a host of implications that investigators in many of the behavioral sciences are still tracing. *(Ellen Berscheid, University of Minnesota)*

by leading them to think they were scoring high on a test of intelligence and creativity—or bad about themselves. During a break in the testing the experimenter and subject went for coffee and sat down next to a female acquaintance of the experimenter's from another college. The woman, actually a confederate, was groomed either as her very attractive self or very sloppily and with her hair tied back severely and grotesque eye glasses. When the experimenter excused himself to make a phone call, the confederate observed how warm and romantic the man was. Did he talk to her? Compliment her? Buy her coffee? Ask her out? Men who were feeling good about themselves behaved most romantically toward the attractive confederate. Those whose self-esteem had been lowered exhibited more interest in the plain woman.

Thus far, I have described attractiveness as if it were an objective quality like height, something some people have more of, some less. Actually, attractiveness is whatever the people of any given place and time find attractive. This, of course, varies (Cross & Cross, 1971; Marshall & Suggs, 1971). And even in a given place and time, there is (fortunately) some disagreement about who's attractive and who's not (Morse & Gruzen, 1976). Generally, though, "attractive" facial and bodily features do not deviate too drastically from the average (Symons, 1981; Beck, Ward-Hull, & McLear, 1976; Graziano, Brothen, & Berscheid, 1978). Noses, legs, or statures that are not unusually large or small tend to be perceived as relatively attractive.

What's attractive to you also depends on what you have adapted to. Douglas Kenrick and Sara Gutierres (1980) had male confederates interrupt Montana State University men in their dormitory rooms, explaining, "We have a friend coming to town this week and we want to fix him up with a date, but we can't decide whether to fix him up with her or not, so we decided to conduct a survey. . . . We want you to give us your vote on how attractive you think she is . . . on a scale of 1 to 7." When shown a picture of an average young woman, those who had just been watching three beautiful women on *Charlie's Angels* rated her less attractive than those who hadn't. Laboratory experiments confirmed this "contrast effect" (Gutierres & Kenrick, 1979). Students shown slides of highly attractive people found average people less attractive than did those who were first shown unattractive people. It makes one wonder: Does viewing beautiful people on television and in ads, or ogling the bodies in *Playboy* or *Playgirl*, diminish the perceived attractiveness of one's mate?

We can conclude our discussion of attractiveness on a heartwarming note. Not only do we perceive attractive people as likable, but we also perceive likable people as physically attractive. Perhaps you can recall individuals who, as you grew to like them, became more attractive, their physical imperfections no longer so noticeable. For example, Alan Gross and Christine Crofton (1977) had University of Missouri—St. Louis students view someone's photograph after reading a favorable or unfavorable description of the person's personality. Those perceived as good appeared more attractive (see also Owens & Ford, 1978; Felson & Bohrnstedt, 1979). Other researchers have found that the more in love a woman is with a man, the more physically attractive she finds him (Price et al., 1974). Apparently Plato was right: "The good is the beautiful."

Similarity versus Complementarity

From our discussion so far, one might surmise that Leo Tolstoy was entirely correct: "Love depends . . . on frequent meetings, and on the style in which the hair is done up, and on the color and cut of the dress." Proximity and physical attractiveness do indeed help initiate a relationship. However, as people get to know one another other influences enter to help each decide whether their acquaintance is to develop into a friendship.

Do Birds of a Feather Flock Together?

Of this much we may be sure: Birds who flock together are of a feather. Friends, engaged couples, and spouses are far more likely than people randomly paired to share common attitudes, beliefs, and values. Furthermore, among married couples, the greater the similarity between husband and wife, the more likely they are to be happily married and the less likely they are to divorce (Byrne, 1971). Such findings are intriguing. But, being correlational, their cause and effect remain an enigma. Does similarity lead to liking? Does liking lead to similarity? Or do attitude similarity and liking both spring from some third factor, such as a common cultural background?

To discern cause and effect we experiment. Imagine that at a campus party Laurie gets involved in a long discussion of politics, religion, and personal likes and dislikes with Les and Larry. She and Les discover they agree on most everything, she and Larry on few things. Afterwards, she reflects, "Les is really intelligent, and he's so likable. I hope we meet again." In numerous controlled experiments, Donn Byrne (1971) and his colleagues captured the essence of Laurie's experience. Over and again they found that if you are simply told about someone's attitudes on various issues, the more similar the attitudes are to your own, the more likable you will find the person. This "Likeness-leads-to-liking" relationship holds true not only for college students, but for children and the elderly, for people of various occupations, and those in various nations. What matters is not only the number of similar attitudes expressed by the other person (Kaplan & Anderson, 1973) but the proportion: One who shares your opinions on four out of six topics is liked better than one who agrees on eight out of sixteen (Byrne & Nelson, 1965).

The extent to which people of another race are perceived as similar also helps determine our racial attitudes. In fact, except for intimate relationships, such as dating, the perception of like minds seems more important for attraction than like skins. Most whites express more liking for, and willingness to work with, a similarly minded black than a dissimilarly minded white (Rokeach, 1968; M. Goldstein & E. E. Davis, 1972; B. I. Silverman, 1974).

This "agreement" effect has also been tested in real-life situations by observing over time who comes to like whom. At the University of Michigan, Theodore Newcomb (1961) studied two groups of seventeen unacquainted male transfer students. After thirteen weeks of living together in a boarding-house, those whose agreement was initially highest were most likely to have formed close friendships. One group of friends was composed of five liberal arts students, each a political liberal with strong intellectual interests. Another was made up of three conservative veterans who were all enrolled in the engineering college.

Because the men living in the boardinghouse spent much of their time out of the house, it took a while for likes to attract. William Griffitt and Russell Veitch (1974) compressed the getting-to-know-you process by confining thirteen unacquainted men in a fallout shelter. (The men were paid volunteers.) The researchers found that, given information about the men's opinions on various issues, they could predict with better-than-chance accuracy whom each man would most like and most dislike during the stay underground. As in the boardinghouse, the men liked best those most similar to themselves. Such is true not only of men. In the coke-date experiment described earlier, the couples were matched so that half shared the same opinions, half did not. When they returned, the well-matched couples stood closer to one another in front of the experimenter's desk and later expressed the most liking one for another.

"And they are friends who have come to regard the same things as good and the same things as evil, they who are friends of the same people, and they who are the enemies of the same people. . . . We like those who resemble us, and are engaged in the same pursuits."

Aristotle, Rhetoric

Like all generalizations, the similarity-attraction principle needs to be qualified. First, if we are made to feel like a faceless member of a homogeneous crowd, we will be more open to associating with people who enable us to feel a bit distinctive and unique (Snyder & Fromkin, 1980). Second, similarity sometimes divides people—when they are competing for scarce payoffs, such as A grades in a curve-graded class. Third, similarity matters more on important issues than on trivial ones. Finally, similarity is relative: Being merely from the same country is enough to breed mutual warmth when one is a foreign student or tourist. Americans who have "nothing in common" in the United States may greet one another like old friends in a Bangkok restaurant.

Nevertheless, the generalization is a powerful one. Studies with a variety of methods and people consistently verify that similar attitudes are a potent source of attraction. Birds of a feather do indeed flock together.

Do Opposites Attract?

But are we not also attracted to people who are in some ways *different* from ourselves, different in ways that complement our own characteristics? Researchers have explored this question by comparing friends and spouses not only in attitudes and beliefs, but also in age, religion, race, smoking behavior, economic level, education, height, intelligence and as we saw earlier, appearance. In all these ways and more, similarity still prevails (Berscheid & Walster, 1978; Kandel, 1978). Smart birds flock together. So do rich birds, Protestant birds, tall birds, pretty birds.

Still we resist: Are we not attracted to people whose needs and personalities complement our own? Wouldn't a wonderful relationship develop from the acquaintance of a sadist and a masochist? Or, to pose the question as sociologist Robert Winch (1958) has done, wouldn't the needs of someone who is outgoing and domineering complement those of someone who is shy and submissive? It sounds reasonable, even compelling. And most of us can think of couples whose differences do indeed seem complementary. Perhaps you have heard

There is at least one dimension on which complementary needs often produce attraction. (Copyright © 1943 James Thurber. Copyright © 1971 Helen W. Thurber and Rosemary T. Sauers. From *Men, Women and Dogs*, published by Harcourt, Brace Janovich.)

"I love the idea of there being two sexes, don't you?"

someone explain: "My husband and I are perfect for each other. I'm Aquarius—a decisive person. He's Libra—can't make decisions; but he's always happy to go along with arrangements I make."

Complementarity: *The tendency, in a relationship between two people, for each to supply what is missing in the other. The complementarity hypothesis proposes that people are attracted to those whose needs are different, in ways that complement their own.*

Given how persuasive the idea is, the inability of researchers to confirm it is astonishing. Although some "complementarity" may evolve as a relationship progresses (even a relationship between two identical twins), people seem, if anything, slightly more prone to marry those whose needs and personalities are similar (Berscheid & Walster, 1978; Nias, 1979; D. Fishbein & Thelen, 1981a; 1981b). Perhaps we shall yet discover some ways (other than heterosexuality) in which differences breed liking. But of this much we are now sure: the "Opposites-attract" rule, if it's ever true, is of miniscule importance compared to the powerful tendency of likes to attract.

Liking Those Who Like Us

With hindsight, we can use the reward principle to explain the conclusions noted so far. *Proximity* is rewarding because when someone lives or works close by it costs less time and effort to receive the friendship's benefits. We like *attractive* people because they touch our aesthetic taste, because we perceive that they offer other desirable traits, and because we benefit by associating with them. If others have *similar* opinions we feel rewarded because they validate our own beliefs. Hence, we especially like them if we have successfully converted them to our way of thinking (Lombardo, Weiss, & Buchanan, 1972; Riordan, 1980; Sigall, 1970).

If, indeed, we especially like those whose behavior is rewarding, then surely we ought to adore those who like and admire us. Do we in fact like those who like us? Let's examine the evidence. It is true that we tend strongly to believe that those we like also like us (Curry & Emerson, 1970). Yet maybe they don't; maybe we only assume that those we adore feel the same way about us. In the University of Minnesota Welcome Week dating experiment, how much a man said he liked his date actually was unrelated to how much she reported liking him.

With such a disconcerting finding—Do we wrongly imagine that our friends like us?—David Kenny and William Nasby (1980) wondered whether there needed to be a refining of the research method. Would doing so reveal that liking does after all tend to be reciprocated? To answer this question, they analyzed various dyads to see how person A felt about person B, *relative* to how other people felt about B and *relative* to how A felt about other people. Sure enough, one person's relative liking for another predicted the other's relative liking in return. Liking was mutual.

But does one person's liking another *cause* the other to return the appreciation? Experiments thus far indicate the answer, "Yes, indeed." Those told that certain others liked them or evaluated them highly felt immediately a reciprocal affection (Berscheid & Walster, 1978). Ellen Berscheid, William Walster, and Elaine Hatfield (1969) even found that University of Minnesota students liked better a fellow student who said eight positive things about them than one who said seven positive things and one negative thing. Evidently we are very sensitive to the slightest hint of criticism in other's appraisals.

This general principle—that we like those who like us—was recognized long before it was confirmed by social psychologists. Observers from the ancient philosopher Hecato ("If you wish to be loved, love") to Ralph Waldo Emerson ("The only way to have a friend is to be one") to Dale Carnegie ("Dole out praise lavishly") anticipated the findings. However, what they seem not to have anticipated are the more precise conditions under which the principle is most often true.

Attribution

As we've seen, flattery *will* get you somewhere. But not everywhere. If someone's praise clearly violates what we know is true—if someone says "Your hair looks great" when we haven't washed it in days and it feels like a greasy mop—we may lose respect for the flatterer or wonder whether the compliment springs from ulterior motives (Shrauger, 1975). Laboratory experiments reveal something we've noted in previous chapters: Our reactions depend on our attributions. Do we attribute the other's flattery to some "ingratiating" selfish motive? Is the person trying to con us—to get us to buy something, to sexually acquiesce, to do a favor? If so, both the flatterer and the comments lose appeal (E. E. Jones, 1964; Lowe & Goldstein, 1970). But if there is no apparent ulterior motive, then both flattery and flatterer are warmly received.

Ingratiation: *Strategies, such as flattery, by which people seek to gain another's favor.*

What we attribute our own actions to is similarly important. Clive Seligman, Russell Fazio, and Mark Zanna (1980) paid undergraduate dating couples to indicate "why you go out with your girl friend/boy friend." Some were asked to rank seven intrinsic reasons, such as "I go with ______ because we always have a good time together" and "because we share the same interests and concerns." Others ranked possible extrinsic reasons: "because my friends think more highly of me since I began seeing her/him," "because she/he knows a lot of important people." Asked later to respond to a "love scale," those whose attention had been drawn to possible extrinsic reasons for their relationship expressed less love for their partner and even saw marriage as a less likely possibility than did those made aware of possible intrinsic reasons. (Sensitive to ethical concerns, the researchers debriefed all the participants afterward and later confirmed that the experiment had no long-term effects on the participants' relationships.)

Self-Esteem and Attraction

The reward principle also indicates that another's approval should be especially rewarding after one has been deprived of approval, much as eating is most powerfully rewarding when we are extremely hungry. To test this idea, Hatfield (Walster, 1965) gave some Stanford University women either very favorable or very unfavorable analyses of their personalities, thus offering an affirming boost to some while temporarily wounding the self-esteem of others. Then they were asked to evaluate several people, including an attractive male confederate who just before the experiment had struck up a warm conversation with each subject and had asked each for a date. (Not one turned him down.) After the affirmation or criticism, which women most liked the man? Those whose self-esteem had been temporarily shattered, and who were presumably hungry for social approval. This finding supports psychoanalyst Theodor Reik's (1944) contention that people are most likely to fall in love on the rebound, when their egos are bruised.

After this experiment Dr. Hatfield spent almost an hour explaining the experiment and talking with each woman. She reports that in the end, none remained disturbed by the temporary ego blow or the broken date.

Gaining Another's Esteem

If approval after disapproval is powerfully rewarding, then would we most like (1) someone who liked us after initially disliking us or (2) someone who liked us from the start? Dick is in a small discussion class with his roommate's cousin, Jan. After the first week of classes, Dick learns via his "pipeline" that Jan thinks him rather dull, shallow, and socially awkward. However, as the semester progresses, he learns that Jan's opinion of him is steadily rising; gradually she comes to view him as bright, thoughtful, and charming. Will Dick now like Jan as much as he would had she thought well of him from the beginning? If Dick is simply counting the number of approving comments he receives, then the answer will be no; he would like Jan better had she consistently offered affirmative comments. But if after her initial disapproval, Jan's rewards become more potent, Dick then might like her just as much as if she had been consistently affirming.

To see which is most often true, Elliot Aronson and Darwyn Linder

(1965) captured the essence of Dick's experience in a controlled experiment. Eighty University of Minnesota women were allowed to overhear a sequence of evaluations of themselves by another woman. Some women heard consistently positive things about themselves, some consistently negative. Still others heard evaluations that changed either from negative to positive (like Jan's evaluations of Dick), or from positive to negative. The results of this experiment, and several others since, are somewhat varied. Generally, however, the target person is liked as much or even more when the subject experiences a *gain* in the other's esteem, especially when the gain is both gradual and reverses the earlier criticism (Aronson & Mettee, 1974; Clore, Wiggins, & Itkin, 1975). Perhaps Jan's nice words have more credibility coming after her not-so-nice words. Or perhaps after being withheld they are especially potent.

Aronson even speculates that constantly approving a loved one can lose value. When Mr. Doting says for the 500th time, "Gee, honey, you look great," the words carry far less impact than were he now to say, "Gee, honey, you don't look good in that dress." A loved one you've doted upon is hard to powerfully reward, but easy to powerfully hurt. This suggests that an open, honest relationship—one where people enjoy one another's esteem and acceptance, yet are candid about their negative feelings—is more likely to offer continuing rewards than one dulled by the suppression of unpleasant emotions, one in which people try only, as Dale Carnegie advised, to "lavish praise." Aronson (1980) put it this way:

> As a relationship ripens toward greater intimacy, what becomes increasingly important is authenticity: the ability of individuals to communicate a wide range of feelings to each other under appropriate circumstances and in ways that reflect their caring. Thus, to return again to the Dotings, if two people are genuinely fond of each other, they will have a more satisfying and exciting relationship over a longer period of time if they are able to express both positive and negative feelings than if they are completely "nice" to each other at all times. (p. 270)

LOVING

Social psychologists have effectively studied both first impressions and the initial stages of friendship. What is more, that which initially influences one's liking another—proximity, attractiveness, similarity, being liked—also influences the development of loving relationships. For example, if romances in the United States flourished *randomly*, without regard to proximity and similarity, then most Catholics (being a minority) would marry Protestants, most blacks would marry whites, and college graduates would be as apt to marry high school dropouts as fellow graduates.

BEHIND THE SCENES

Elaine Hatfield

I have always been intensely curious—especially about things people are not *supposed* to ask about. All those fascinating topics that are forbidden because they appeal to "prurient interest," "morbid curiosity," and so forth are just what I want to know about. In addition, I am interested in the truth—even if it means saying the unsayable. Thus, I've found it most exciting to spend my time investigating critically important, but difficult, perplexing, sometimes overlooked topics, topics that scientists once dismissed as impossibly difficult, taboo, or "trivial"—but which common sense said were critically important: physical attractiveness, love, sex, and emotion. *(Elaine Hatfield, University of Hawaii at Manoa)*

Nevertheless, loving is not merely intense liking (Z. Rubin, 1973). Loving is more complex, and thus more difficult to measure, more perplexing to study. People yearn for it, live for it, die for it. Yet only in the last few years has loving—despite Senator Proxmire's scorn—become a serious topic in social psychology. Let's take a look at what so far has been concluded.

What is this thing called love? The first step in scientifically studying love, as in studying any variable, is to decide how to define and measure it. We have ways to measure aggression, altruism, prejudice, and liking, but how do we measure love? Elizabeth Barrett Browning asked a similar question: "How do I love thee? Let me count the ways." Social psychologist Zick Rubin (1970; 1973) counted three ways. To tap each, he wrote questionnaire items:

1 *Attachment* (for example, "If I were lonely, my first thought would be to seek ______ out.")

2 *Caring* (for example, "If ______ were feeling bad, my first duty would be to cheer him [her] up.")

3 *Intimacy* (for example, "I feel that I can confide in ______ about virtually everything.")

Rubin administered his Love Scale to hundreds of dating couples at the University of Michigan. He later invited to the laboratory some of the couples whose scores suggested their relationship was either strong and loving or weak. While each couple awaited the session, observers behind a one-way mirror clocked the time they maintained eye contact. The "weak-love" couples looked at one another less than the "strong-love" couples, who gave themselves away by gazing into one another's eyes.

Just as it is helpful to distinguish between loving and liking, so it is also useful to distinguish among the varieties of loving. Elaine Hatfield and William Walster (1978) discerned two distinct types: passionately romantic love, and a more enduring "companionate" love.

Romantic Love

Romantic love is passionate, emotional, intense. Hatfield and Walster (1978) define it as a state of "absorption in the other." It is, they say, characterized by "a confusion of feelings: tenderness and sexuality, elation and pain, anxiety and relief, altruism and jealousy."

Romantic love: *An aroused state of intense absorption in another. Lovers long for their partners and feel ecstatic at having attained their partner's love.*

Infatuation: What people call romantic love when it's over: "I was infatuated with Julia. But now I'm in love with Wanda."

As this definition implies, people can feel passionate love toward someone who evokes pain, anxiety, and jealousy. Why? Romantic love sometimes seems not to follow the sensible principle that we like those who reward us and dislike those who cause us pain. Douglas Kenrick and Robert Cialdini argue one possible answer: While the loved one may cause pain and anxiety, the loved one also alleviates those emotions. The lover triggers jealousy when with someone else, yet also offers ecstatic relief upon returning. Loving those associated with the termination of negative feelings actually illustrates the reward principle (Kenrick & Cialdini, 1977). Perhaps you can recall a "lover's quarrel" that was almost justified by the intense pleasure of making up.

Hatfield and Walster have a quite different explanation of passionate love, one that applies a theory of emotion we considered in Chapter 10. There, we saw that a given state of arousal can be steered into any of several emotions, depending upon how one attributes the arousal. An emotion involves both body and mind, both arousal and how we interpret and label the arousal. Imagine yourself with pounding heart, trembling hands: Are you experiencing fear, anxiety, joy? Physiologically, one emotion is quite similar to another. You thus likely experience the arousal as joy if you are in a euphoric situation, anger if your environment is hostile and (Hatfield and Walster contend) passionate love if the situation is romantic.

If indeed passion is a revved-up state that's labeled love, then one's experience of "love" should be intensified by whatever revs one up. In several experiments, college men aroused sexually by reading or viewing erotic materials had a heightened response to a woman (for example, by scoring much higher on Rubin's Love Scale when describing their girl friend) (Carducci, Cosby, & Ward, 1978; Dermer & Pysczynski, 1978; Stephan, Berscheid, & Walster, 1971). Proponents of the "two-factor theory of emotion" argue that when revved-up men respond to a woman, they easily misattribute some of their arousal to her.

Two-factor theory of emotion: *Arousal × label = emotion.*

According to this theory, one's being aroused by *any* source should

Proponents of the two-factor theory of emotion theorize that passionate love is an aroused state that is attributed to the romantic partner. (© 1981 Andy Levin/Black Star)

intensify one's passionate feelings—providing one's mind is free to attribute some of the arousal to a romantic stimulus. Donald Dutton and Arthur Aron (1974) invited University of British Columbia men to participate in a learning experiment. After meeting their attractive female partner, some were frightened with the news that they would be suffering some "quite painful" electric shocks. Before the experiment was to begin, the researcher gave a brief questionnaire, "to get some information on your present feelings and reactions, since these often influence performance on the learning task." Asked how much they would like to date and kiss their female partner, the aroused (frightened) men expressed more intense attraction toward the woman than did men who had not been aroused. Likewise, Gregory White, Sanford Fishbein, and Jeffrey Rutsein (1981) found that when college men were aroused—whether by running in place, by listening to a Steve Martin comedy, or by hearing a grisly tape of human mutilation—they then responded more intensely to a confederate female; they expressed greater liking for an attractive woman and disliking for an unattractive woman.

Does this phenomenon occur also outside the laboratory? Dutton and Aron (1974) had an attractive young woman individually approach young men as they crossed a narrow, wobbly 450-foot-long suspension walkway hanging 230 feet above British Columbia's rocky Capilano River. She asked each man to help her fill out a class questionnaire. When he had finished, she scribbled out her name and phone number and invited him to call if he wanted to hear more about the project. Of those who had helped, most accepted the phone number, and half who did so called. By contrast, men approached on a low, solid bridge, and men approached on the high bridge by a *male* interviewer, rarely called. So, once again, physical arousal seemed to accentuate the men's romantic responses. Adrenaline made the heart grow fonder.

But does it usually? Social psychologists are debating this (Kenrick, Cialdini, & Linder, 1979; Furst, Burnam, & Kocel, 1980). The two-factor theory of romantic love predicts that arousal will most intensify love when its source is ambiguous, leaving us free to misattribute the arousal as passion. My hunch is that sometimes the source of our arousal is *un*ambiguous; we know all too well why we're feeling anxious, irritated, or frightened. Ruminating on the problem can leave us *less* open to experiencing romantic love. Other times, as when we are elated or stirred by a happening that doesn't gnaw at our minds, our arousal is more open to being steered into passion.

Companionate Love

Though passionate love burns hot, it inevitably burns out. The romantic high may be sustained for a few months, even a year or two. Then, if the love is to endure, it settles to a steady, warm afterglow that Hatfield and her associates call *companionate love*. Unlike the wild emotions of passionate love, companionate love is lower-key; it's a deep, affectionate attachment. And it is just as real.

Companionate love: *The affection we feel for those with whom our lives are deeply intertwined.*

Companionate love thrives where a relationship is intimate and mutually rewarding. But what is "intimacy"? And what is "mutually rewarding"?

Self-Disclosure

Deep, companionate relationships are intimate. They enable us to be known as we truly are and feel accepted. This delicious experience we enjoy in a good marriage or a very close friendship—a relationship where we are free to be open without fear of losing the other's affection. Such relationships are characterized by what the late Sidney Jourard called *self-disclosure*, or what Dalmas Taylor (1979) and Irwin Altman (Altman & Taylor, 1973) have called "social penetration." As such a relationship grows, those involved reveal more and more of themselves to one another; their knowledge of one another penetrates to deeper and deeper levels, until it reaches an appropriate level. Lacking such opportunities for intimacy, one may experience the pain of loneliness.

Self-disclosure: *Revealing intimate aspects of oneself to others.*

Experiments have probed both the causes and the effects of self-disclosure. Researchers have wondered: When are people most willing to disclose intimate information concerning "what you like and don't like about yourself" or "what you're most ashamed and most proud of"? And what effects do such revelations have upon those who reveal and receive them?

The most reliable finding is the "reciprocity" effect: Disclosure begets disclosure (Cosby, 1973; R. B. Taylor, De Soto, & Loeb, 1979). We reveal ourselves more to those who have been open with us. But intimacy is seldom instant. Far more often it progresses as a dance: I reveal a little, you reveal a little—but not too much; you then reveal more, as do I.

What are the effects of such self-disclosure? Jourard (1964) argued that dropping our masks, letting ourselves be known as we are, nurtures love. He presumed that it is gratifying to open up to another, and then to receive the trust another implies by being open with us.

"What is a Friend? I will tell you. It is a person with whom you dare to be yourself."

Frank Crane, A Definition of Friendship

While it is surely true that intimacy can be rewarding, the results of many experiments caution us not to presume that self-disclosure will automatically kindle love. It's just not that simple. While it seems true that we like best those to whom we've disclosed ourselves (Skotko, 1980; R. L. Archer, Berg, & Burleson, 1980), it has not been consistently found that we

BEHIND THE SCENES

Dalmas Taylor

My interest in self-disclosure grew as I observed pairs of sailors getting acquainted during periods of social isolation. In the early 1960s the new Polaris submarine assignments to Antarctica, where men wintered in for long periods, brought about behavior problems that the Navy wanted to understand and alleviate. In our laboratories at the Naval Hospital in Bethesda, Maryland, we simulated such confinement by having pairs of men live and work in soundproofed rooms for up to twenty-one days. During this isolation the men turned to each other for enrichment and stimulation. Established rules for developing relationships were abandoned; self-disclosure seemed to occur rapidly. So we developed ways to quantify both the amount and intimacy of self-disclosure. Then we initiated a program of research on self-disclosure in which we investigated reward/cost factors, and personality and situational variables in an attempt to understand better how human relationships develop. Out of this research came the concept that Irwin Altman and I termed "social penetration." *(Dalmas A. Taylor, University of Maryland)* are also most fond of those who most intimately reveal themselves to us (Archer & Burleson, 1980; Archer, Berg, & Runge, 1980; Dalto, Ajzen, & Kaplan, 1979). Researchers have indeed found that sometimes people like an open, self-disclosing person better than one who holds back. This is especially true when the self-disclosing individual is perceived as normally more reserved, but indicates that "something" about the partner "made me feel like opening up" (D. A. Taylor, Gould, & Brounstein, 1981). Apparently, it is gratifying to be singled out for disclosure. On the other hand, someone who early in an acquaintanceship rushes to tell us intimate details may come across as indiscreet, immature, even unstable (Dion & Dion, 1978; Miell, Duck, & La Galpa, 1979).

Even if it does not automatically trigger attraction, intimate self-disclosure does seem to be one of the delights of companionate love. Those dating and married couples who most reveal themselves to one another tend to express most satisfaction with their relationship, and are more likely to endure in it (Adams & Shea, 1981; Hendrick, 1981; Z. Rubin et al., 1980). Researchers have also found that women are often more willing to disclose their fears and weaknesses than are men (J. D. Cunningham, 1981). As Kate Millett (1975) put it, "Women express, men repress." Nevertheless, men today, particularly men with egalitarian sex-role attitudes, seem increasingly willing to reveal their intimate feelings, and to enjoy the satisfactions that accompany a relationship of mutual trust and self-disclosure.

Equity

Earlier, we noted an equity rule at work in the matching phenomenon: People usually bring equal assets to their romantic relationships. Often, they are matched for attractiveness, status, and so forth. And if mismatched in one area (for example, in attractiveness), they tend to be compensatingly mismatched in some other area (for example, status); thus in total assets they are an equitable match. No one says, and likely few even think, "I'll trade you my good looks for your big income." But especially in relationships that last, it often works out that way.

In the long run, those in a relationship that is equitable are more content (Hatfield, Walster, & Traupmann, 1979). Those who perceive their relationship as inequitable frequently feel discomfort; the one who has the better deal may feel guilty, and the one who senses a raw deal may feel strong irritation. (Given the self-serving bias, the person who is "overbenefited" may be less sensitive to the inequity.) Robert Schafer and Patricia Keith (1980) surveyed several hundred married couples of all ages, noting those who felt their marriage was somewhat unfair because one spouse contributed too little to the cooking, housekeeping, and tasks of providing, or to the roles of companion and parent. Inequity took its toll: those who perceived some inequity also tended to feel more distressed and depressed.

What do people do when they perceive a relationship as inequitable?

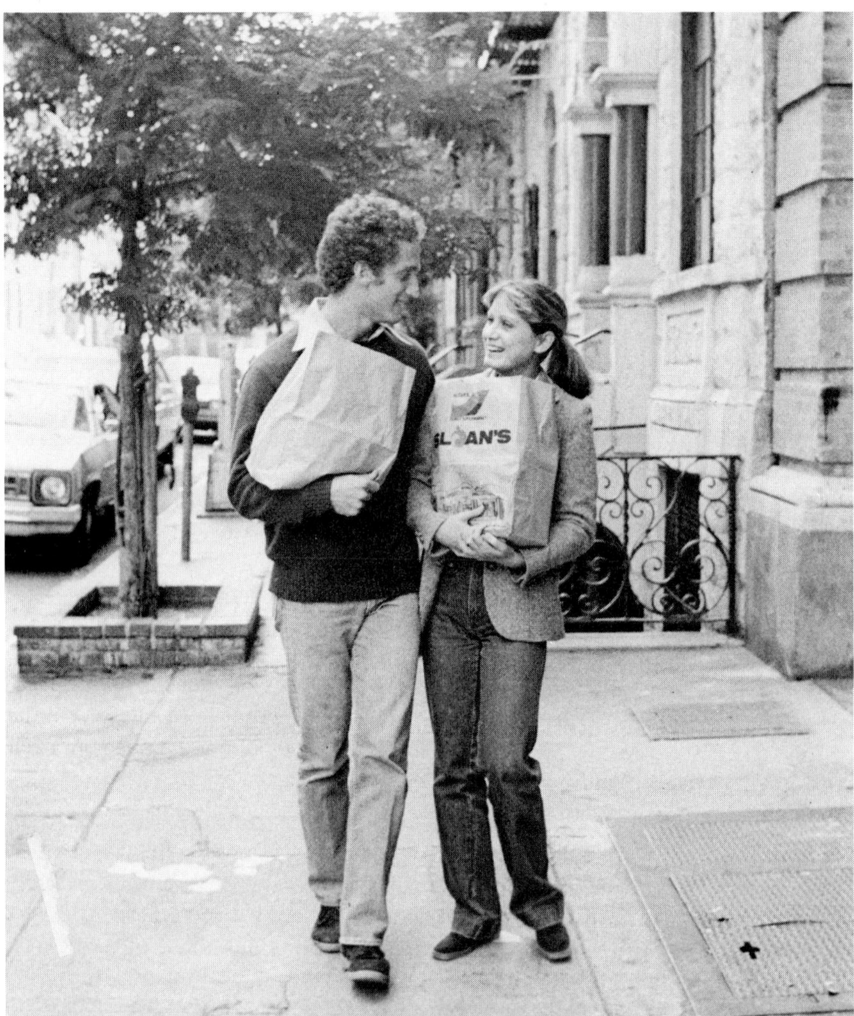

People are usually more contented in a relationship that they feel is equitable. (Erika Stone/Peter Arnold, Inc.)

There are two possible initiatives. The first: Strive to restore equity by setting things right. If John feels he is getting less than he has coming, he can demand better treatment. If wife Marsha acknowledges inequity, she may reluctantly agree to the changes. Perhaps you can recall doing many favors for a friend and then feeling it was time the friend gave you the same consideration. And perhaps you can recall receiving many favors from another friend and then feeling relieved at a chance to reciprocate. Whether "underbenefited" or "overbenefited," most feel better when a more equitable relationship is restored.

If efforts to restore equity fail, the other initiative is to terminate the relationship. When the relationship is marriage, this alternative has its own costs: shocked parents and friends, restricted parental rights, guilt over broken vows. Still, annually millions of couples are willing to pay such costs in order to extricate themselves from what they perceive as the greater costs of continuing a painful, unrewarding relationship. Others, unable to bear the emotional and financial costs of separation, continue to endure their broken relationship, some of them hoping that it may yet again become mutually rewarding.

"Hot love soon cold."

John Heywood Proverbs

We can all hope that this new social psychological study of love will explore further the dynamics of companionate love. What causes companionate love to shrivel? What enables it to endure and deepen? Difficult questions they are, but few questions are more important for human well-being.

Box 13-1

Endless Love? Emotions Were Bottled Up

SEATTLE, WASH.—UPI—Ten years ago a man wrote a love poem to his wife, slipped it into a bottle with an envelope and dropped it into the Pacific Ocean halfway between Seattle and Hawaii.

Chris Wille, an employe of the National Wildlife Federation, found the bottle recently while jogging on a beach in Guam. After replacing the envelope—the 10-cent stamp was a bit behind the times—he dutifully mailed the letter to Seattle.

When it was returned with "no longer at this address," Wille sent it to the Seattle Times.

The printed note was unabashed, old-fashioned romanticism.

"If, by the time this letter reaches you, I am old and gray, I know that our love will be as fresh as it is today.

"It may take a week or it may take years for this note to find you. Whatever the case may be, it shall have traveled by a strange and unpredictable messenger—the sea.

"If this should never reach you, it will still be written in my heart that I will go to extreme means to prove my love for you. Your husband, Bob."

The woman to whom the letter was addressed was reached by phone and the note was read to her. She burst out laughing—and the more she heard the harder she laughed.

"We're divorced," she said, slamming down the phone.

Note: Milwaukee Journal, August 27, 1981, p. 1.

SUMMING UP

Who likes whom, and why? Few of social psychology's questions have been of more perennial interest. Several influences upon our attraction to one another can be explained with the aid of a simple principle: We like people whose behavior is rewarding to us, or who have been associated with rewarding events.

This chapter examined four powerful influences upon liking. The best predictor of whether any two people are friends is their sheer *proximity* to one another. Proximity is conducive to interaction, which enables people to discover their similarities and to feel one another's liking. Liking also receives a boost from the mere anticipation of interacting with someone. Finally, proximity exposes one to others, and mere repeated exposure tends to trigger liking.

A second determinant of one's initial attraction to another is the person's *physical attractiveness.* Both in laboratory studies and in field experiments involving blind dates, college students tend to like best someone who's attractive. In everyday life, however, people tend actually to choose and marry someone whose attractiveness roughly matches their own (or someone who, if less attractive, has other compensating qualities). Positive attributions about attractive people are so wide-ranging that many researchers believe there exists a strong physical-attractiveness stereotype—an assumption that what is beautiful is good. But then again, attractiveness is relative—not only relative to our culture's definition of attractiveness, but also relative to whom we're comparing a person to, and relative to how much we like the person.

As an acquaintance progresses, two other factors further help determine whether the acquaintance becomes a friendship. One's liking for another is greatly aided by *similarity* of attitudes, beliefs, and values. A wide variety of laboratory and field experiments have consistently found that likeness leads to liking. Researchers so far have been unable to discover needs and traits for which people seek out those different from themselves. Apparently, opposites rarely attract.

We are also likely to develop friendships with people who *like us.* The tendency to be fond of those who like and admire us is especially strong when (1) we do not attribute the other's flattery to ingratiating motives, (2) we have recently been deprived of approval, and (3) the other's praise reverses earlier criticism.

Occasionally, an acquaintance develops not just into friendship, but into passionate, *romantic love.* Such love is often a bewildering confusion of ecstasy and anxiety, elation and pain. Advocates of the reward principle argue that we can love someone who causes us pain because the loved one also alleviates the pain. Advocates of the two-factor theory of emotion argue that when one is in a romantic context, arousal from any source, even painful experiences, can be steered into passion.

In the best of relationships, the initial romantic high settles to a steadier, more affectionate relationship called *companionate love*. One delight of companionate love is intimate self-disclosure, a state achieved gradually as each partner reveals more and more. Companionate love is most likely to endure when both partners feel it to be equitable, in that both receive from the relationship in proportion to what they contribute to it.

Chapter

Conflict and Peacemaking

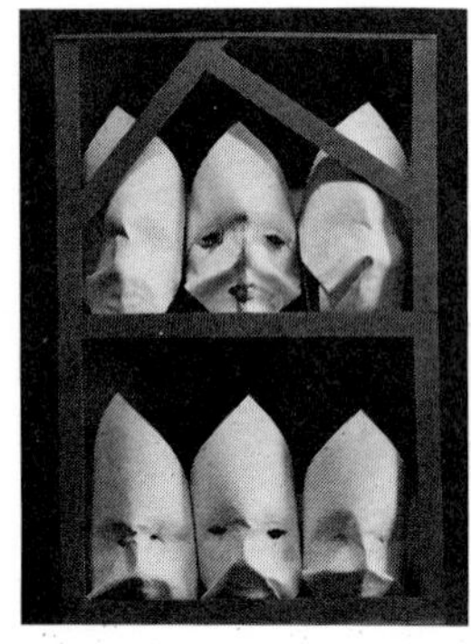

Sometimes a destructive drain on human potential; sometimes a constructive stimulus for growth: Such is conflict—conflict between individuals, between groups, between nations. Consider the following instances of each.

Between individuals: Warren Peace and his roommate are hardly speaking to one another. Apart from a few snide allusions to "the lousy socks on the floor," and "that loud, distracting music," they have each settled into a quiet smolder. The longer silence prevails, the more Warren assumes his roommate feels hostile, and the more hostile Warren feels in return. Where will it lead? Will they split? Or will they somehow reach a new understanding that restores the friendship they once enjoyed?

Between groups: Workers at the Acme Manufacturing Company are out on strike. Disgruntled over low pay and minimal benefits, they insist they'll not return without a significant boost in their compensation. The company's reply: "Given your high absenteeism and low productivity, we simply can't afford to meet your demands." Where will it end? Will the strike force the company into bankruptcy and the workers out of their jobs? Or might it be possible to recast the current employer-employee relationship, making possible both higher productivity and profits for the company and higher wages for the workers?

Between nations: There is a speech that has been spoken in many languages, by the leaders of many countries. It goes like this: "The intentions of our country are entirely peaceful. Yet, we are also aware of the world's unrest, and of the threat that other nations, with their new weapons, pose to us. Thus we would be remiss not to take adequate steps to increase our ability to defend against attack. By so doing, we shall help protect our way of life and preserve the peace" (L. F. Richardson, 1969). Every nation claims concern only for peace but, mistrusting other nations, arms itself in self-defense. The end result: a world in which there is 1 soldier for every 250 people, 1 doctor for every 3700; a world in which every nine hours humanity spends as much on arms as it does annually on the United Nations (*Context*, 1980).

As suggested in these examples, conflict varies. It is at times minimal, at times immense; at times hidden, at times open; at times destructive, at times constructive. Despite such variation, this much can be said for sure: Any time people, or groups, are so bound together that their actions affect one another, conflict is natural and inevitable. Granted, it may be suppressed. But unless the two parties have identical needs and desires, their wishes will sometimes clash. A relationship or an organization without conflict is likely an apathetic one. So conflict is not inherently evil. Rather, it signifies people's involvement, commitment, and caring; if understood, if recognized, it can stimulate renewed and improved human relations. Without conflict, problems seldom are faced and resolved.

"We . . . are not the creators of tension. We merely bring to the surface the hidden tension that is already alive. We bring it out in the open, where it can be seen and dealt with.

Martin Luther King, Jr.

Let's clarify our terms. We shall define *conflict* as a perceived incompatibility of actions or goals. Whether their perceptions are accurate or inaccurate, people in conflict sense that one side's gain is the other's loss. "I'd like the music off." "I'd like it on." "We want more pay." "We can't give it to you." "We want peace and security." "So do we, but you threaten us."

Peace, in its most positive sense, is more than the suppression of open conflict, more than a tense, fragile, surface calmness. Peace is the outcome of a creatively managed conflict, one in which the parties reconcile their perceived differences and reach genuine accord. "We got our increased pay. You got your increased profit. Now we're helping each other achieve our aspirations."

But what kindles conflicts? And what steps can be taken to help transform closed fists into open arms? The more than 1000 social-psychological studies of conflict have identified several ingredients of conflict (Deutsch, 1980). What's striking (and what simplifies our task considerably) is that these social-psychological ingredients are common to all levels of social conflict, whether interpersonal conflicts or more complex intergroup or international conflicts.

Conflict: *A perceived incompatibility of actions or goals.*

CONFLICT

First, we will examine several of the ingredients of conflict. As we do so, bear in mind that social psychology provides but one perspective on significant social conflicts. For example, international conflicts also spring from differing histories, ideologies, and economies—all of which are carefully studied by political scientists. Having identified some important elements of conflict, we can then ponder ways to promote peace.

Social Dilemmas: Individual Rationality, Group Irrationality

"Right now we can destroy the Soviet Union about 16 times and they can destroy us about nine times. Do we really need to increase it to 17 and 10?"

U.S. Congressman Paul Simon (1980)

Several of the problems that most threaten our human future—the nuclear arms race, pollution, overpopulation, and depletion of natural resources—arise as various parties rationally pursue or protect their self-interest, but do so, ironically, to their collective detriment. Anyone can reason: "It would cost me lots of money to buy expensive pollution controls. And, besides, by itself my pollution is trivial." Many others reason similarly, resulting in befouled air and water. Likewise, in some societies individuals benefit by having lots of children who, it is assumed, can assist with the family tasks and provide security for their parents' old age. But when nearly everyone has lots of children, the end result can be the collective devastation of overpopulation. Therefore, we have an urgent dilemma: How can the well-being of individual parties—their rights to freely pursue their personal interests—be reconciled with the well-being of the community?

Laboratory Dilemmas

Social psychologists have used laboratory games to isolate this dilemma. Although they were initially designed for experiments on conflict behavior, these games also expose the heart of many real social conflicts. By showing us how well-meaning people easily become trapped in mutually destructive behavior, they illuminate some fascinating, yet troubling, paradoxes of human existence. Consider the following three examples.

The Prisoner's Dilemma The first and the most widely researched game was derived from an anecdote concerning two suspects who are questioned separately by the district attorney (Rapoport, 1960). They are indeed guilty; however, the DA presently has only enough evidence to convict them of a lesser offense. So the DA offers each a chance to confess privately. The DA explains that if one confesses and the other doesn't, the confessor will be granted immunity and the confession will be used to convict the other of a maximum offense. If both confess, each will receive a moderate sentence for the lesser offense. The dilemma faced by each prisoner can be summarized in the form of a matrix (see Figure 14-1). Faced with such a dilemma, would you confess?

Many would, despite the fact that mutual confession would elicit more severe sentences than would mutual nonconfession. Note from the matrix that no matter what the other prisoner decides, one is better off confessing. Even if the other confesses, one then gets a moderate sentence instead of a severe one. If the other does not confess, one goes free. Of course, each prisoner reasons the same. Hence, the social trap.

In hundreds of experiments, university students have been faced with

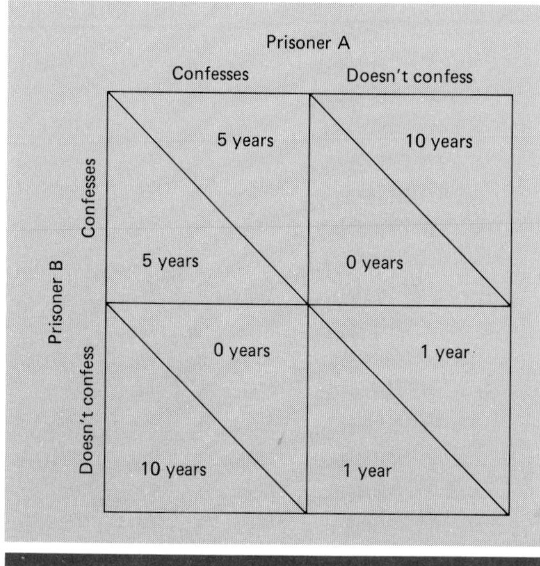

FIGURE 14-1 The Prisoner's Dilemma. In each box, the number above the diagonal is prisoner A's outcome. Thus, if both prisoners confess, both get five years. If neither confesses, each gets a year. If one confesses, that prisoner is set free in exchange for evidence used to convict the other of a crime bringing a ten-year sentence. If you were one of the prisoners, would you confess?

variations on the Prisoner's Dilemma with the outcomes being not prison terms, but chips, money, or course points. As Figure 14-2 illustrates, on any given decision a person is better off not cooperating (because such behavior either exploits the other's cooperation or protects against exploitation by the other). However—and here's the rub—by mutually not cooperating both parties end up far worse off than if they would trust each other and cooperate. This dilemma often traps each in a maddening predicament, a predicament in which both realize they *could* mutually profit but, mistrusting one another, become "locked in" to not cooperating.

In such dilemmas, the unbridled pursuit of self-interest can be detrimental to all. So is it between the United States and the Soviet Union. A disinterested observer from another planet would likely note that the military policy of "Mutually Assured Destruction," is, as its acronym implies, MAD. As Dwight D. Eisenhower lamented,

> Every gun that is made, every warship launched, every rocket fired signifies, in the final sense, a theft from those who hunger and are not fed, those who are cold and are not clothed. This world in arms is not spending money alone. It is spending the sweat of its laborers, the genius of its scientist, the hopes of its children. . . . This is not a way of life, at all, in any true sense. Under the cloud of threatening war, it is humanity hanging from a cross of iron.

It may be true that maintaining a "balance of terror" helps prevent wars that might occur if one nation believed it could exploit another's weakness. But surely the peoples of both nations would be more secure, less tense, if there

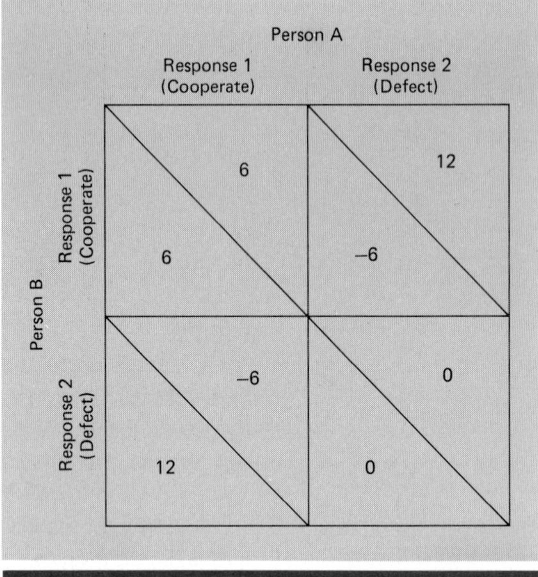

FIGURE 14-2
Laboratory version of the Prisoner's Dilemma. The numbers represent some reward, such as money. In each box, the number above the diagonal line is the outcome for person A.

were no weapons threat, and if their billion-dollar-per-day military spending were made available for productive rather than destructive purposes.

Granted, such a solution is easily said. The dilemma faced by national leaders—and by college students faced with laboratory simulations of the arms-race dilemma—is that disarmament makes one vulnerable to exploitation. [Indeed, in the laboratory, pacifists often are exploited (Oskamp, 1971; Reychler, 1979; Shure, Meeker, & Hansfield, 1965).] So, alas, the arms race continues.

Unlike the United States–Soviet Union arms race, many of our other pressing social dilemmas involve numerous participants. For example, those who pollute and exploit limited natural resources are generally anonymous, and the harm they do is diffused over many people. Therefore, researchers have developed new laboratory dilemmas that simultaneously involve several people.

The Commons Dilemma A powerful metaphor for the insidious nature of social dilemmas is what ecologist Garret Hardin (1968) has called the "tragedy of the commons." He derived the name from the pasture often centrally located in old New England towns. However, the "commons" can be air, water, whales, cookies, or any jointly used finite resource. If all use the resource in moderation, it may replenish itself as rapidly as it's harvested. The grass will grow, the whales will reproduce, the cookie jar will get restocked.

But imagine 100 farmers surrounding a commons capable of sustaining 100 cows. When each grazes one cow, the common feeding ground is fully used, without being overtaxed. But then one may reason: "If I put a second cow in the pasture, I'll double my output, minus the mere one percent increase in the overcrowding of the meadow." So this farmer adds a second cow. Then so does each of the other farmers. The inevitable result? The tragedy of the commons.

Many real-life predicaments parallel this story. Environmental pollution is the sum of many minor pollutions, each of which benefits the individual polluters much more than they could benefit themselves (and the environment) if they stopped only their small "contribution" to pollution. We litter public places—dorm lounges, parks, zoos—but keep our personal spaces clean. And we deplete our natural resources, because the immediate personal benefits of consumption outweigh the costs; the costs appear inconsequential for they are diffused among all.

The elements essential to the Commons Dilemma have been isolated in such laboratory games as the following. Put yourself in the place of Arizona State University students playing Julian Edney's (1979a; 1979b) Nuts Game. You and several others are sitting around a shallow bowl that initially contains ten metal nuts. The experimenter explains that your goal is to accumulate as many nuts as possible, that each of you at any time may take as many as you want, and that every ten seconds the number of nuts remaining in the bowl will be doubled. Would you leave the nuts in the bowl to regenerate, thus producing a greater harvest for all?

Likely not. Unless they were given time to devise and agree upon a strategy for conservation, 65 percent of Edney's groups never reached the first ten-second replenishment. In fact, often the people knocked the bowl on the floor grabbing for their share.

Edney's nut bowl reminds me of the cookie jar in our home. What we *should* do is conserve cookies during the interval between weekly restockings, so that each day we can each enjoy two or three. But, lacking regulation and believing that the resource will soon be depleted, what we actually do is "maximize our individual cookie consumption" by downing one after the other. The result: Within twenty-four hours the cookie glut ends, the jar sits empty, and we are forced to await its replenishment.

The Dollar Auction Another provocative example of individual rationality that leads to group irrationality is the Dollar Auction game (Shubik, 1971). The auction is simple, yet easily traps people in a spiraling conflict that can escalate furiously. (*Warning*: While this game will liven up a party, it can damage friendships.) One merely offers to sell a dollar to the highest bidder, with one simple rule: The two highest bidders must *both* pay their bids, although only the highest bidder gets the dollar.

The bidding starts at a nickel. Hoping for an easy buck, people quickly join in. Soon, however, it becomes apparent that the bidders, not the auctioneer, are the easy mark. The first moment of truth dawns as the bidding passes 50 cents. If one bidder reaches 50 cents and the other 45 cents, the one at 45 cents now reasons, "If I raise to 55 cents, this jerk with the dollar will get $1.05. But if I don't, I lose 45 cents instead of potentially making 45 cents." So the bidding escalates.

The trap now apparent, the bidding narrows to two people. Their next moment of truth comes as the bidding passes $1. At 95 cents the lower bidder realizes that "The other has bid a buck. If I raise to $1.05, even if I win, I'll lose a nickel. But if I don't raise, I'll lose even more." Now the auctioneer leans back and smugly watches. Allan Teger (1980) has played the Dollar Auction game with forty groups. He reports that the bidding always went over a dollar. Once, it even went as high as $20.

When Teger afterward asked the bidders why they bid beyond $1, many replied that they were forced to by the bids of their opponent (a situational explanation). But why did the opponent continue to bid? Most expressed bewilderment, some even implying that the other person must be crazy (a dispositional explanation). Remarkably, most bidders never realized that their fellow bidders faced identical pressures. This again illustrates the fundamental attribution error (Chapter 3). And "more than anything else," reports Teger, this error explains why the bidders felt unable to escape the conflict.

During the bidding, the participants' motives usually change. They are at first lured by the desire to make some easy money. But then at moments of realization, their motives shift: They now struggle to minimize their losses, and then shift to motives less economic—to save face and to defeat the other person. These shifting motives are strikingly similar to President Johnson's apparently shifting motives during the buildup of the Vietnam war. At first, his speeches included many positive references to America's concern for democracy, freedom, and justice. As the conflict escalated, his expressed concern became increasingly to protect America's honor and to avoid the national humiliation of losing a war.

The Prisoner's Dilemma, the Commons Dilemma, and the Dollar Auction games have several similar features. Like many real-life conflicts, they are *non-zero-sum games*: The two sides' profits and losses need not add up to zero; both can win, both can lose. Each game pits the immediate interests of individuals against the well-being of the group. Each is a diabolical social trap that shows how, even when individuals behave "rationally," harm can result. No malicious person planned for Los Angeles to be smothered in smog, nor for the horrendous destruction of the Vietnam war.

Non-zero-sum-games: *Games in which one side's winning need not be balanced by the other's losing; that is, outcomes need not sum to zero. With cooperation, both can win; with competition, both can lose.*

However, we must take care not to overstate the point. Certainly, not all self-serving behavior leads to collective doom. In a plentiful commons—as in the world of the eighteenth century capitalist economist Adam Smith—individuals who seek to maximize their own profit may also give the community what it needs: "It is not from the benevolence of the butcher, the brewer, or the baker, that we expect our dinner, but from their regard to their own interest" (Smith, 1776, p. 18).

But in those situations that are indeed social traps, how can we induce people to cooperate for their mutual betterment?

Resolving Social Dilemmas

Research with the laboratory dilemmas has revealed several methods for promoting cooperation.

Regulation Reflecting on the Commons Dilemma, Garrett Hardin (1968) observed, "Ruin is the destination to which all men rush, each pursuing his own best interest in a society that believes in the freedom of the commons. Freedom in a commons brings ruin to all." For example, if taxes were entirely voluntary, how many would pay full taxes?

Likely many would not. Thus, people evolve laws and regulations for their common good. An International Whaling Commission is established to set agreed-upon "harvest" rates that will enable whales to regenerate. The United States and the Soviet Union mutually commit themselves to the Atmospheric Test Ban Treaty that reduces radiation in our common air. When enforced, environmental regulations similarly equalize the burden for all; no steel company need fear that other companies will gain a competitive advantage by disregarding their environmental responsibilities.

Similarly, participants in laboratory games often seek ways to regulate their behavior for what they know to be their common good. For example, players of the Nuts Game may agree to take but one or two nuts every ten seconds, leaving the rest to regenerate. Bidders in the Dollar Auction game may, on the side, agree to stop bidding and split the dollar.

We can see then that regulating behavior is one solution to social dilemmas. But in everyday life, regulation may itself have costs—costs of administering and enforcing the regulations, costs of diminished personal freedom. A volatile political question can thus arise: At what point does the cost of a regulation exceed its benefits?

Small Is Beautiful Given the costs of regulation, other ways of resolving social dilemmas are also needed. One suggestion: Keep the group small. In laboratory dilemma games, people who interact with but a few others cooperate more than do those in larger groups (Dawes, 1980). The smaller the commons, the more responsibility each person feels for it.

On the Puget Sound island where I grew up, our small neighborhood shared a communal water supply. On hot summer days when the reservoir ran low, a light came on, signaling our fifteen families to conserve. Recognizing our responsibility to one another, each of us conserved. Never did the reservoir run dry. In a much larger commons—say a large city—such voluntary conservation is generally far less successful. The harm one does is diffused across many others. Thus one can rationalize away personal accountability.

"For that which is common to the greatest number has the least care bestowed upon it."

Aristotle

Some political theorists and social psychologists have therefore argued that, where feasible, the commons should be divided into smaller territories (Edney, 1980). Perhaps, for example, neighborhood governments could take over more responsibility for sanitation, beautification, policing, and so forth (M. O. Hatfield, 1972; 1975).

Communication To escape a social trap, people must communicate with one another. In the laboratory, groups able to communicate sometimes degenerate into threats and name calling (Deutsch & Krauss, 1960). But often, communication enables groups to cooperate more (Dawes, 1980; Jorgenson & Papciak, 1981)—much more. Being able to discuss the dilemma and to make a commitment to cooperate sometimes even doubles the extent of the actual cooperation.

Open, clear, forthright communication can reduce people's mistrust of one another. Without communication, those who expect others not to cooperate usually refuse to cooperate themselves (Messe & Sivacek, 1979; Pruitt & Kimmel, 1977). One who mistrusts almost has to be uncooperative (to protect against exploitation), and noncooperation is rationalized by further mistrust ("What else could I do? It's a dog-eat-dog world"). In experiments, communication seems to reduce mistrust greatly, enabling people to reach agreements that lead to their common betterment. In times of serious social conflict, how can we structure communication in order to produce similar results? To this question, we shall later return.

"My own belief is that Russian and Chinese behavior is as much influenced by suspicion of our intentions as ours is by suspicion of theirs. This would mean that we have great influence on their behavior—that, by treating them as hostile, we assure their hostility."

U.S. Senator J. William Fulbright (1971)

Changing the Payoffs Experimenters have repeatedly found that cooperation rises when the payoff matrix is changed to make cooperation more rewarding, exploitation less rewarding (Pruitt & Kimmel, 1977).

Changing payoffs might likewise help resolve actual dilemmas. In some major cities, drivers are given an incentive to conserve gas and alleviate traffic congestion. Those who drive to work in carpools are allowed on fast freeway lanes while single-occupant cars bide their time in the crowded lanes. Added incentive for conservation has come from the skyrocketing cost of gasoline. As U.S. gas prices streaked past $1 per gallon, gas consumption began to diminish.

Appeals to Altruistic Norms In Chapter 11, we noted a social responsibility norm, and saw how increasing people's feelings of responsibility for others can boost altruism. In light of this finding, can we assume that appeals to altruistic motives will therefore prompt people to leash their selfish desires and to act instead for the common good?

The evidence is mixed. On the one hand, it seems that just *knowing* about the dire consequences of noncooperation has little effect. In laboratory dilemma games, people realize that their self-serving choices are mutually destructive, yet they continue to make such choices (Cass & Edney, 1978;

Edney & Harper, 1978). Outside the laboratory, warnings of doom and appeals to conserve have triggered little response. Knowing the good does not necessarily lead to doing the good.

Still, most people do have feelings of social responsibility. The problem is how to tap such feelings. When participants in laboratory games are permitted to communicate, frequently they appeal emphatically to the social-responsibility norm: "If you defect on the rest of us, you're going to have to live with it for the rest of your life" (Dawes, McTavish, & Shaklee, 1977). Noting this, researcher Robyn Dawes (1980) and his associates gave people a short sermon about group benefits, exploitation, and ethics. Then the people played a dilemma game. The appeal worked. People were convinced to forgo immediate personal gain for the common good.

Could such appeals ever work in large-scale dilemmas? My prediction is yes. If great are the benefits of cooperation and the costs of noncooperation, then one can, with reasonable assurance of success, appeal to the social-responsibility norm. Basketball players will pass up a good shot to offer a teammate a better shot. Struggling for civil rights, many marchers willingly agreed, for the sake of their larger group, to suffer harassment, beatings, and jailings. In wartime, people can be persuaded to make great personal sacrifices for the good of their group.

Competition

In Chapter 12 we noted that racial hostilities arise most often when groups must compete for jobs and housing. When interests clash, conflict erupts. This was powerfully evident in the Shantung Compound, a World War II internment camp into which the Japanese military herded foreigners residing in China. According to one of those interned, theologian Langdon Gilkey (1966), the need to distribute the barely adequate food and floor space provoked frequent conflicts involving people of various types—doctors, missionaries, lawyers, professors, business people, junkies, prostitutes. The potential effects of such competition for space, jobs, and political power has also been tragically evident in Northern Ireland, where since 1969, hostilities between the ruling Protestant majority and the Catholic minority have claimed more than 2000 lives (Hodgson, 1981).

However, we must question whether it is competition itself that provokes such hostile conflicts. Real life situations are so complex that it is hard to be sure. If competition is indeed responsible, then it should be possible to provoke conflict in an experiment. We would want to randomly divide people into two groups, then have the groups compete for a scarce resource, and note what happens. Such is precisely what Muzafer Sherif (1966) and his colleagues did in a dramatic series of experiments with typical eleven- and twelve-year-old boys. After ascertaining what seemed the conditions necessary to provoke hostility between the groups, Sherif introduced these apparent essentials into several three-week summer camping experiences.

In one such experiment, twenty-two unacquainted Oklahoma City boys were divided into two groups, taken to a Boy Scout camp in separate buses, settled in bunkhouses about a half mile apart, and for most of the first week kept unaware of the other group's existence. By cooperating in various activities—preparing meals, camping out, fixing up a swimming hole, building a rope bridge—each group soon became close-knit. They even gave themselves names: "Rattlers" and "Eagles." Typifying the good feeling, a sign was put up in one cabin: "Home Sweet Home."

Group identity thus established, the stage was set for the conflict. Toward the end of the first week, the Rattlers "discovered the Eagles on 'our' baseball field." Antagonisms soon surfaced. So when the camp staff proposed a tournament of competitive activities between the two groups (baseball games, tugs-of-war, cabin inspections, treasure hunts, and so forth), both groups responded enthusiastically. This was win-lose competition. The spoils (medals, knives) would all go to the tournament victor.

The result? Within several days the camp degenerated into open warfare. It was like a scene from William Golding's novel *Lord of the Flies* which depicted the social disintegration of some boys of similar age marooned on an island. In Sherif's experiment, the conflict began with each side calling the other derogatory names during the competitive activities, and soon escalated to "garbage wars" in the dining hall, flag burnings, cabin ransackings, and even fistfights that had to be broken up by the camp staff. Asked to describe the other group, the boys invariably said "they" were "sneaky," "smart alecks," "stinkers," while referring to their own group as "brave," "tough," "friendly."

Competition kindles conflict. Here one group of boys raids the bunkhouse of another. (Muzafer Sherif)

This win-lose competition had produced intense conflict, negative images of the outgroup, and strong in-group cohesiveness and pride. Note that all this occurred without any cultural, physical, or economic differences between the two groups, and with boys who were the "cream of the crop" of their communities. Sherif commented that had you or I visited the camp at this point we likely would have concluded that these "were wicked, disturbed, and vicious bunches of youngsters" (1966, p. 85). But, in fact, their evil behavior was triggered by an evil situation.

Fortunately, Sherif not only made strangers into enemies; he then made the enemies into friends. How? The secret of his peacemaking will be explained shortly.

Perceived Injustice

"That's unfair!" "What a ripoff!" "We deserve better!" Such comments typify conflicts bred by perceived injustice. But what is "justice"? According to a number of social-psychological theorists, people perceive justice as equity—the distribution of rewards in proportion to individuals' contributions (Deutsch, 1977; E. Walster (Hatfield), G. W. Walster, & E. Berscheid, 1978). If you and I have a relationship (for example, employer-employee, teacher-student, colleague-colleague), it is equitable if:

$$\frac{\text{My outcomes}}{\text{My inputs}} = \frac{\text{Your outcomes}}{\text{Your inputs}}$$

But if you contribute more and benefit less than I do, you likely will feel exploited and irritated; I may feel exploitative and guilty. Chances are, though, you more than I will be sensitive to the inequity and eager to remedy it (Messick & Sentis, 1979).

"Do unto others 20% better than you would expect them to do unto you, to correct for subjective error."

Linus Pauling (1962)

While we may agree with the equity principle's definition of justice, we may, however, strongly disagree on whether our relationship is equitable. For example, if we are colleagues, what shall we consider a relevant input? If I include my having a Ph.D., being forty years old, white, and male, you may object, and propose a more relevant set of criteria. If I am older, I may favor basing pay on seniority, you on current productivity.

"Awards should be 'according to merit'; for all men agree that what is just in distribution must be according to merit in some sense, though they do not all specify the same sort of merit."

Aristotle

Given such a disagreement, whose definition is likely to prevail? More often than not, researchers have found that those with the most social power more successfully convince themselves and others that they deserve what they're getting. Karl Marx anticipated this finding: "The ideas of the *ruling* class are in every epoch the ruling ideas: i.e., the class, which is the ruling material force of society, is at the same time its ruling intellectual force" (E. H. Walster et al., 1978, p. 220). This has been called a "golden" rule: Whoever has the gold makes the rules.

As this suggests, the exploiter can relieve guilt not only by actual compensation but also by valuing or devaluing inputs so as to justify the existing outcomes. Some men may perceive the lower pay of women as equitable, given women's "less important" inputs. As we noted in Chapter 12, those who inflict harm may even blame the victim, and thus maintain their belief in a just world.

And those exploited? How do they react? Elaine Hatfield, William Walster, and Ellen Berscheid (1978) detect three possibilities. They can accept and justify their inferior position ("We're poor; it's what we deserve, but we're happy"). They can demand compensation, perhaps by harassing, embarrassing, even cheating their exploiter. Or, if all else fails, they may attempt to restore equity by retaliating, perhaps vindictively.

"When the rich gather to take action about the poor, it is called philanthropy. When the poor gather to take action about the rich, it is called revolution."

Sam Levenson, You Don't Have to Be in Who's Who to Know What's What

An interesting implication of equity theory—an implication that has been confirmed experimentally—is that the more competent and worthy people feel (the more they value their inputs), the more likely they are to feel that a given outcome is insufficient and thus to retaliate (M. Ross, Thibaut, & Evenbeck, 1971). Intense social protests generally come from those who believe themselves worthy of more than they are receiving.

Critics argue that equity is not the only conceivable definition of justice. For example, Edward Sampson (1975) says that equity theorists wrongly assume that the economic principles that guide western, capitalist nations are universal. Some noncapitalist cultures define justice not as equity (deservingness) but as equality, or even fulfillment of need: "From each according to his abilities, to each according to his needs." And conflict theorist Morton Deutsch (1977) adds that, even within capitalist nations, criteria other than equity sometimes define justice. In a family or an altruistic helping institution, the criterion may be need. In a friendship, it may be equality. In a competitive relationship, the winner may take all the reward.

Indeed, people's criteria for justice do vary. When the appropriate criteria are unclear, men tend to favor making rewards proportional to input, whereas women lean more toward equality (Kahn et al., 1980; Kahn, Nelson, & Gaeddert, 1980; Reis & Jackson, 1981). When social harmony is stressed, an equality norm often prevails; for example, roommates tend to overlook merit and distribute rewards equally (Austin, 1980). When productivity is stressed, or when people's attention is drawn to their responsibility for the outcomes, equity is favored (Greenberg, 1979; 1980).

How universal, then, is the tendency to define justice as equity? And on what basis should rewards be distributed? Need? Equality? Merit? Some combination of these? Is equality a special case of equity—one in which humanity is considered the relevant input? Such questions are being debated still. However, one thing is clear: One source of human conflict is the perception of injustice.

Misperception

Recall that conflict is a *perceived* incompatibility of actions or goals. It is important to realize that conflicts often contain but a small core of truly incompatible goals. The bigger problem is their being surrounded by many

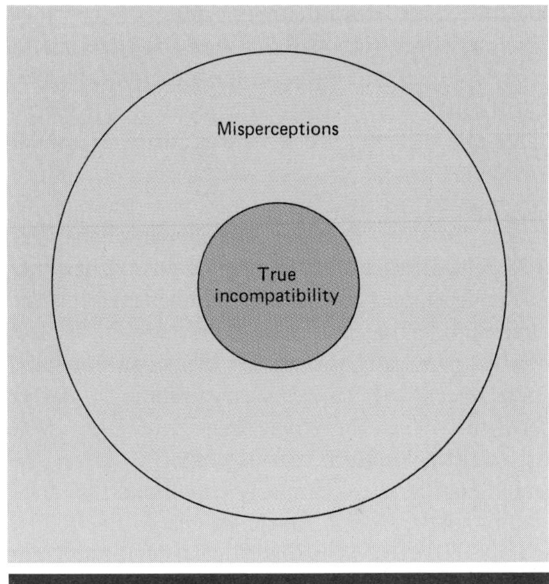

FIGURE 14-3 Most conflicts contain a core of truly incompatible goals surrounded by a larger exterior of misperceptions.

misperceptions of the other's motives and goals. The Eagles and the Rattlers did indeed have some genuinely incompatible aims. But their hateful perceptions of each other soon subjectively magnified their differences.

In earlier chapters we considered several seeds of such misperception. The *self-serving bias* leads individuals and groups to accept credit for their good deeds and shuck responsibility for bad deeds, without according others the same benefit of the doubt. A tendency to *self-justify* further inclines people to deny the wrong of evil acts that cannot be shucked off. One filters the information and interprets it to fit one's *preconceptions*. Groups frequently *polarize* these self-serving, self-justifying, biasing tendencies. One symptom of *groupthink* is the tendency to perceive one's own group as moral and strong, the opposition as evil and weak; the daring attempt to rescue the American hostages in Iran was to President Carter "a humanitarian mission" and to Iranian leaders "an act of war" (*Time*, 1980c). Indeed, the mere fact of being in a group can trigger an *ingroup bias*. And negative *stereotypes* once formed, are often resilient to contradictory evidence.

Given these seeds of social misperception, it should not surprise us, though it should sober us, to discover that people in conflict frequently form distorted, diabolical images of one another. Yet the types of misperception are intriguingly predictable.

Mirror-Image Perceptions

To a striking degree, the misperceptions of those in conflict are mutual. They tend to attribute the same virtues to themselves and vices to the other. When American psychologist Urie Bronfenbrenner (1961) visited Russia in 1960 and conversed with many ordinary citizens in his Russian tongue, he was astonished

"The present tensions with their threat of national annihilation are kept alive by two great illusions. The one, a complete belief on the part of the Soviet world that the capitalist countries are preparing to attack it; that sooner or later we intend to strike. And the other, a complete belief on the part of the capitalist countries that the Soviets are preparing to attack us; that, sooner or later, they intend to strike."

General Douglas MacArthur (1966)

to hear most Russians saying the same things about America that most Americans were saying about Russia. The Soviets said that the U.S. government was militarily aggressive; that it exploited and deluded the American people; that in diplomacy it was not to be trusted. "Slowly and painfully, it forced itself upon one that the Russian's distorted picture of us was curiously similar to our view of them—a mirror image."

Quantitative analysis of the content of American and Soviet mass media has identified similar perceptions. "We are peaceful and altruistic; they are unpredictable warmongers" (Angell, Dunham, & Singer, 1964). When two sides see things so differently, at least one of the two is misperceiving the other. And when such misperceptions exist, noted Bronfenbrenner, "It is a psychological phenomenon without parallel in the gravity of its consequences . . . for *it is characteristic of such images that they are self-confirming*." As we have seen before, if A expects B to be hostile, A may treat B in such a way that B fulfills A's expectations, thus beginning a vicious circle.

Observers of the Arab-Israeli conflict have similarly concluded that such negative mirror-image perceptions are a chief obstacle to peace. Both sides insist that "we" are motivated by our need to protect our security and our territory, while "they" want to obliterate us and gobble up our land (R. K. White, 1977; Heradstveit, 1979). Neither side recognizes and appreciates how its own actions sustain the other's fear and anger. Given such intense mistrust, negotiation is next to impossible.

Mirror-image perception: *Reciprocal views of one another often held by parties in conflict; for example, each may view itself as moral and peace-loving and the other as evil and aggressive.*

Destructive mirror-image perceptions also operate in conflicts between small groups and even between individuals. As we saw in the dilemma games, both parties may say, "We want to cooperate. But their refusal to cooperate forces us to react defensively." In a study of executives, Kenneth Thomas and Louis Pondy (1977) uncovered similar self-serving attributions. Asked to describe their behavior during a significant recent conflict, 74 percent perceived themselves as cooperative, only 21 percent as competitive. Only 12 percent felt the other party was similarly cooperative; 73 percent judged the other party as competitive. The executives explained that they had "suggested," "informed," and "recommended," while their antagonist had "demanded," "disagreed with everything I said," and "refused."

The Blacktop Illusion

Blacktop illusion: *The belief that the real enemy is the other group's leaders, who intimidate and mislead their innocent people.*

International conflicts are also fueled and prolonged by what Ralph White (1969) has called the *blacktop illusion*: The enemy's top leaders are evil and coercive; their people, though controlled and manipulated, are much more pro-us. Such beliefs have characterized Americans' and Russians' views of each other. Likewise, the United States entered the Vietnam war believing that in areas dominated by the communist Vietcong "terrorists," many of the people were our allies-in-waiting. As suppressed information later revealed, these beliefs were mere wishful thinking. White wondered:

> Suppose our policy-makers had known that most of the emotionally involved [Vietnamese] people were against us, and had known it clearly, at the time they

were making those fateful commitments and staking American prestige on the outcome. . . . Would we now have all the tragedy of the Vietnam War? . . . I doubt it. (p. 37)

Similarly, the recent Iranian-American conflict was characterized by Americans' belief that Iran's Ayatullah Khomeini and student radicals were manipulating and leading astray a people who had been our friends. Iranians, at least during the early stages of the conflict, were buoyed by a false belief that the American people were unsupportive of President Carter's unsympathetic response to Iranian demands (*Time*, 1980a). The belief that evil resides primarily in the leaders of the opposing group is also illustrated by the frequent contention that one's employees, or one's minority citizens, are really contented and loyal, and that if they voice or show disapproval they are being misled by outside agitators.

The blacktop illusion serves several psychological functions. It reinforces one's own "good intentions." It provides a convenient devil—the leaders—on whom to focus hostility. And it provides hope that the other group's people, if no longer intimidated, would gladly overthrow those who are controlling them and rally to the correct side, one's own.

Shifting Perceptions

If perceptions accompany conflict, then they should appear and disappear as conflicts wax and wane. And so they do, with startling ease. The same processes that create the enemy's image can reverse that image when the enemy becomes an ally. Thus the "bloodthirsty, cruel, treacherous, buck-toothed little Japs" of World War II became soon after—in American minds (Gallup, 1972) and in the American media (Hesselink, 1973)—our "intelligent, hardworking, self-disciplined, resourceful allies." Our World War II allies, the Russians, now became the "warlike, treacherous" ones. The Germans, whom Americans after two world wars hated, then admired, and then again hated, were once again admired—apparently no longer plagued by cruelty in their national character. And within the memory of many of us, the despicable Chinese "Reds" whom we fought in North Korea have become the more gracious, industrious people of the enchanting Republic of China. Clearly, our images of those with whom we are in conflict not only justify our actions, but also are adjusted with amazing ease.

The extent of misperceptions during conflict provides a chilling reminder that people need not be insane or abnormally evil to form distorted, diabolical images of their antagonists. When in conflict with another nation, another group, or simply a roommate or parent, we readily develop a host of misperceptions that allow us to perceive our own motives and actions as wholly good, the other's as evil. And our antagonists most likely form a mirror-image perception of us. So the conflict continues until something enables us both to peel away our perceptions and work at reconciling our actual differences.

PEACEMAKING

We have seen how conflicts are ignited: by social traps, perceived injustices, competition, and social misperceptions. The picture indeed appears grim. But the reality is not hopeless. Sometimes hostilities are transformed into friendships, conflicts into harmony. Social psychologists have focused their research upon four possible strategies for helping enemies become comrades. These might be called the four C's of peacemaking: contact, cooperation, communication, conciliation.

Contact

Might putting two conflicting groups into close contact enable them better to know and like each other? We have previously noted some reasons why it might. In Chapter 13, we saw that proximity—and the accompanying interaction, anticipation of interaction, and mere exposure—boosts liking. In Chapter 2, we noted that the recent downturn in blatant racial prejudice in the U.S. followed closely on the heels of desegregation, seemingly illustrating the principle that "attitudes follow behavior." [If this social-psychological principle now seems obvious, remember, that's how things usually seem—once you know them. To the U.S. Supreme Court in 1896 (Plessy v. Ferguson) the idea that desegregated behavior might influence racial attitudes was anything but obvious. What seemed obvious at the time was that "Legislation is powerless to eradicate racial instincts."]

During the last thirty years in the United States, segregation and prejudice have diminished together. But was the *cause* of these improved attitudes interracial contact? Were those who actually experienced desegregation affected by it?

Does Desegregation Improve Racial Attitudes?

The evidence is mixed. On the one hand, many studies conducted during and shortly after the desegregation following World War II found whites' attitudes toward blacks improving markedly. Whether the people were department store clerks and customers, merchant marines, government workers, police officers, neighbors, or students, racial contact led to diminished prejudice (Amir, 1969; T. F. Pettigrew, 1969). For example, near the end of World War II, the Army partially desegregated some of its rifle companies (Stouffer et al., 1949). When asked their opinions of such desegregation, 11 percent of the white soldiers in segregated companies, and 60 percent of those in desegregated companies, approved.

When Morton Deutsch and Mary Collins (1951) took advantage of a made-to-order natural experiment, they observed similar results. In accordance with state law, two New York City public housing units were desegregated; families were assigned apartments at random, without regard to race. In a similar development in nearby Newark, blacks and whites were assigned to separate buildings. When a survey was conducted with white women in the two developments, those in the desegregated development were far more likely to favor interracial housing and to say that their attitudes toward blacks had improved. Exaggerated stereotypes had wilted in the face of reality. As one woman put it, "I've really come to like it. I see they're just as human as we are."

Less encouraging, on the other hand, are the results of school desegregation studies (Stephan, 1978; McConahay, 1978; 1981). Stuart Cook (1975; 1979), a social psychologist who coauthored an influential social science brief prior to the 1954 U.S. Supreme Court desegregation ruling, summed up twenty-five years of subsequent research: "As for such race relations indicators as racial interaction, cross-race friendships, respect and liking for schoolmates of the other race, and generalized racial attitudes, neither positive nor negative changes have prevailed."

Some readers may be bewildered by such conflicting evidence; sometimes desegregation improves racial attitudes, sometimes it doesn't. But these findings are precisely the kind that excite the scientist's detective spirit. When one set of research findings points to one conclusion and another to a differing one, an important factor is probably at work. So far, we've been lumping all desegregation together. Actual desegregation occurs in many ways, and under vastly different conditions. So it is surely an oversimplification to say that desegregation, per se, has either this effect or that.

When Does Desegregation Improve Racial Attitudes?

To discern the crucial differences between our two sets of studies we can compare the two in detail. But there is a simpler method. Drawing upon theories developed from laboratory research, we can speculate what factors might make a difference, and then see whether these factors are indeed present in one set of studies but not the other.

Let us go back to where we began: Is the amount of interracial *contact* a factor? Indeed it seems to be. Researchers have gone into dozens of desegregated schools and observed with whom children of a given race eat, loiter, and talk. Though less decisive than sex, race is nevertheless a potent factor. Whites disproportionately associate with whites, blacks with blacks (Schofield, 1981). And academic tracking programs often amplify such resegregation by separating academically advantaged white students into predominantly white classes (Schofield & Sagar, 1977). Researchers Andrew Sagar and Janet Ward Schofield (1980a) conclude that "simply throwing alienated groups together in the same school offers little hope of . . . dispelling the misunderstandings, biases, and fears which continue to divide the American people."

In contrast, the more encouraging older studies of store clerks, soldiers, and housing project neighbors involved considerable interracial contact. Recent studies involving prolonged, personal contact—between black and white prison inmates, and between black and white girls in an interracial summer camp—have shown similar benefits of contact (Clore et al., 1978; Foley, 1976).

It is also important to note that the social psychologists who advocated

Equal-status contact: *Just as a relationship between people of unequal status breeds attitudes consistent with their relationship, so do relationships between those of equal status. Thus, to reduce prejudice, interracial contact should be between persons equal in status.*

desegregation never claimed that contact of *any* sort would improve attitudes. Prior to 1954, many prejudiced whites had ample contact with blacks—with the latter in subordinate roles, as slaves, shoe-shine boys, and domestic workers. But as we saw in Chapter 12, contacts on such an unequal basis breed attitudes that merely justify the continuation of such relations. So it's important that people in contact have *equal status*. Such were the contacts between the store clerks, the soldiers, the neighbors, the prisoners, the summer campers. This kind of contact has been lacking in desegregated schools: Researchers report that white students are generally more active, more influential, more successful (E. G. Cohen, 1980a; Riordan & Ruggiero, 1980). When an eighth grade black girl from an academically inferior school is dropped suddenly into a predominantly white middle-class junior high school with white middle-class teachers who expect less of her, chances are she will be perceived both by her classmates and herself as having lower academic status.

Cooperation

Though equal-status contact can help, it is sometimes not enough. It didn't help when Sherif terminated the Eagles versus Rattlers competition and brought the groups together for noncompetitive activities such as watching movies, shooting off fireworks, and eating. By this time, their hostility was so strong that mere contact provided the opportunity for taunts and attacks. When an Eagle was bumped by a Rattler his fellow Eagles urged him to "brush off the dirt." Obviously, desegregating the two groups had hardly promoted their social integration.

Given such preexisting hostilities, it may seem that bringing about peace is hopeless. What can a peacemaker do? Think back to some of the successful and unsuccessful desegregation efforts. The Army's racial mixing of rifle companies not only brought blacks and whites into equal-status contact, but also made them interdependent. Together, they were fighting against a common enemy, striving toward a shared goal.

Contrast this interdependence with the competitive situation found in the typical school classroom, desegregated or not. There, students compete for good grades, teacher approval, and various honors and privileges. Is the following scene familiar (Aronson, 1980)? The teacher asks a question. Several students' hands shoot up; other students sit, eyes downcast, trying to look invisible. When the teacher calls on one of the eager faces, the others hope for a wrong answer, giving them a chance to display their knowledge. Those who fail to answer correctly, and those with the downcast looks who already feel like losers in this academic sport, often resent those who succeed. The situation abounds with both competition and painfully obvious status inequalities; it could hardly be better designed to create divisions among the children.

Does this suggest a second factor that predicts whether the effect of desegregation will be favorable? Does competitive contact divide and cooperative contact unite? Let's examine what happens to people who together face a common predicament or work together toward a shared goal.

Common External Threats

Together with others, have you ever been victimized by the weather; harassed as part of your initiation into a group; punished by a teacher; or persecuted and ridiculed because of your social, racial, or religious identity? If so, you may recall sharing feelings of closeness with those who faced the predicament with you. Perhaps previous normal social barriers were dropped as you helped one another dig out of the snow or struggled to cope with your common enemy.

Such friendliness is what research on experiencing a shared threat leads us to expect. John Lanzetta (1955) observed such a phenomenon thirty years ago when he put four-man groups of Naval ROTC cadets to work on several problem-solving tasks, and then began informing them over a loudspeaker that their answers were wrong, their productivity inexcusably low, their thinking stupid. Other groups did not receive this harassment. Lanzetta observed that the group members under duress became friendlier to one another, more cooperative, less argumentative, less competitive. They were in it together. And the result was a cohesive spirit.

The unifying effect of having a common enemy was also evident within the groups of competing boys in Sherif's camping experiments, and in many subsequent experiments (K. L. Dion, 1979). America's conflicts with Germany and Japan during World War II, and with Iran during 1980, aroused Americans' feelings of patriotism and heightened their sense of unity. Conflict between groups promotes unity within groups. Times of interracial strife are frequently therefore times of heightened racial pride. When keenly conscious of who "they" are, we also know who "we" are.

Leaders have even been known to create a threatening external enemy as a technique for building group cohesiveness. George Orwell's novel *Nineteen Eighty-Four* illustrates the tactic: The leader of the protagonist nation uses border conflicts with the other two major powers to lessen internal strife. From time to time the enemy shifts, but there is always an enemy. Indeed, the nation seems to *need* an enemy. We can fantasize that in response to some extraterrestrial threat, perhaps a feared invasion of our planet, the earth's nations would draw together. For the world, for a nation, for a group, having a common enemy is powerfully unifying. Our enemy's enemy readily becomes our friend (Aronson & Cope, 1968).

Superordinate Goals

Superordinate goal: *A shared goal that necessitates cooperative effort; a goal that overrides people's differences from one another.*

Closely related to the unifying power of an external threat is the unifying power of *superordinate goals*, goals compelling for all in a group and requiring cooperative effort. Sherif introduced such goals in an effort to create harmony among his warring campers. For example, he created a problem with the camp water supply. Since this predicament affected them all, they cooperated in a successful effort to restore the water. Later, when given an opportunity to rent a movie, one expensive enough to require the joint resources of both

Superordinate goals. Rattlers and Eagles work to reestablish their shared water supply. (Muzafer Sherif)

groups, they again cooperated. When a truck "broke down" on a camping trip, a staff member casually left the tug-of-war rope nearby, prompting one boy to suggest that they all pull the truck to get it started. When it did, a backslapping celebration ensued over their victorious "tug-of-war against the truck."

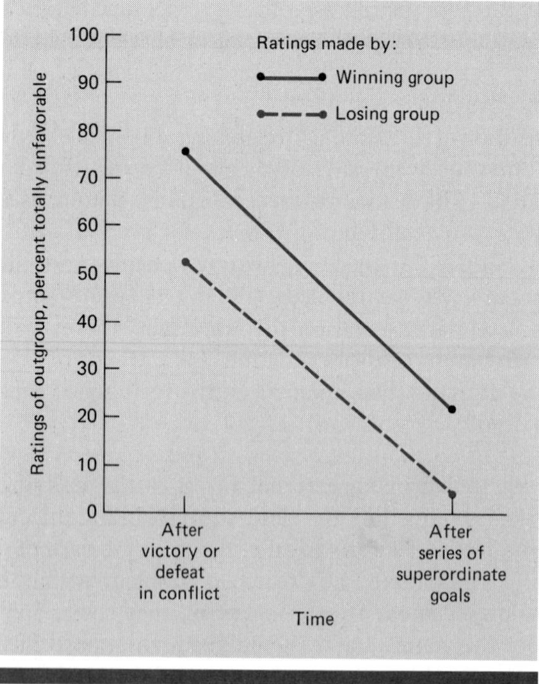

FIGURE 14-4 After competition, the Eagles and Rattlers rated each other unfavorably. After working cooperatively to achieve superordinate goals, hostility dropped sharply. (Data from Sherif, 1966, p. 84.)

BEHIND THE SCENES

Muzafer Sherif

My rejection of research theory by analogy with the physical sciences and my commitment to appropriate levels and units of analysis led me to assume unlikely roles in our various research projects. In the 1949 intergroup field experiment I was Mr. Musee, the camp "caretaker." I assumed this role so as not to be an unaccounted factor by disrupting the homogeneity of the researchers and campers with my foreign accent. In the 1954 Robbers Cave experiment I was just a "visitor" of the "camp director." In both situations the researchers assumed normal camp roles—as counselors, custodians, etc.—and gathered data as part of the natural flow of events. By creating a seemingly natural camp experience we removed "demand characteristics" that might have distorted their behavior had the boys been consciously acting as "subjects." This basic approach—adapting the method of inquiry so as to capture important aspects of everyday life—was also used in our later studies of attitude change and in our studies using the "autokinetic situation" to study the creation of social norms (see Chapter 7). *(Muzafer Sherif)*

After working together to achieve such superordinate goals, the boys began eating together and enjoyed themselves around a campfire. Friendships sprouted across group lines. Hostilities plummeted (see Figure 14-4). And, on the last day, the boys agreed they wanted to travel home together on one bus. During the trip they sat no longer by groups. As the bus approached Oklahoma City and home, they as one spontaneously sang "Oklahoma" and then bade their friends farewell. With isolation and competition, Sherif had made strangers into bitter enemies. With superordinate goals, he had made enemies into friends.

Are Sherif's experiments mere child's play? Or can pulling together to achieve superordinate goals be similarly beneficial with conflicting groups of adults? Robert Blake and Jane Mouton (1979) wondered. So in a series of two-week experiments involving more than 1000 executives in 150 different groups, they recreated the essential features of the situation experienced by the Rattlers and Eagles. Each group first engaged in activities by itself, then competed with another group, and then cooperated with the other group in working toward superordinate goals decided upon by both. Their results were indeed similar to Sherif's, providing, in the words of the researchers, "unequivocal evidence that adult reactions parallel those of Sherif's younger subjects."

Now, however, recall that all the cooperative efforts by Rattlers and Eagles ended in success. Would the same harmony have emerged if the water had remained off, the movie unaffordable, the truck still stalled? Likely not. In experiments with University of Virginia students, Stephen Worchel and his associates (1977; 1978; 1980) confirmed that *successful* cooperation between two groups boosts their attraction for one another. However, if previously conflicting groups *fail* in a cooperative effort, *and* if conditions allow them to attribute their failure to each other, their conflict may actually be worsened. For example, since Sherif's groups were already feeling hostile to one another, we can speculate that a failure to raise sufficient funds for the movie might have been attributed to the "stinginess" and "selfishness" of the other group, and thus might have exacerbated rather than alleviated their conflict.

Cooperative Learning

So far we have noted the apparently meager social benefits of typical school desegregation, and the apparently dramatic social benefits of successful, cooperative contacts between members of rival groups. Could putting these two findings together suggest a constructive alternative to traditional desegregation practices? Several independent research teams speculated "yes." Each wondered whether, without hurting academic achievement, one might promote interracial friendships by replacing competitive learning situations with cooperative ones. Given the diversity of their methods, their consistently positive results are striking and very heartening.

Are students who participate in already existing cooperative activities, such as interracial athletic teams and class projects, less prejudiced? Robert Slavin and Nancy Madden (1979) analyzed survey data from 2400 students in seventy-one American high schools and found encouraging results. Those of different races who play and work together are more likely to report having friends of another race and to express positive racial attitudes.

From this correlational finding can we conclude that cooperative interracial activity at school improves racial attitudes? One way to find out is to experiment. Randomly designate some students to work together in racially mixed groups. For example, David DeVries and Slavin (1978) divided dozens of classes into interracial "teams," each composed of four or five students from all achievement levels. The team members sit together, study a variety of subjects together, and at the end of each week compete with the other teams in a class tournament. All team members can contribute to their team's score by doing well, sometimes by competing with other students whose recent achievements are similar to their own, sometimes by competing with their own previous scores. Therefore everyone stands a chance to succeed, and the team's members are motivated to help one another prepare for the weekly tournament—perhaps by drilling each other on fractions, or spelling, or historical events—

whatever is the next event. Competition is thus used not to isolate students from one another but to bring them into closer contact and to draw out their mutual support.

Other research teams, led by Elliot Aronson (1978; 1979), elicited similar group cooperation with a "jigsaw" technique. In experiments in elementary schools both in Texas and California, children were assigned to racially and academically diverse six-member groups. The material to be learned was then divided into six parts, with each student becoming the expert on his or her part. For example, in a unit on Chile, one student might be the expert on Chile's history, another on its geography, another on its culture, and so on. First, the various "historians," "geographers," and so forth got together to master their material. Then they each returned to their home group to teach it to their classmates. Each group member held, so to speak, a piece of the jigsaw. Note that the self-confident students had therefore to draw out and listen to the normally more reticent students, who in turn could soon realize that they had something important to offer their peers.

Other research teams—led by David Johnson and Roger Johnson (1975) at the University of Minnesota, Elizabeth Cohen (1980b) at Stanford University, Shlomo Sharan and Yael Sharan (1976) at Tel Aviv University, and Stuart Cook (1978) at the University of Colorado—have devised additional methods for cooperative learning. From all this research, what can we conclude? The investigators speak for themselves. Slavin (1980), for example, observes that cooperative learning is an "effective means of increasing positive race relations and achievement in desegregated schools." Aronson reports that "children in the interdependent, jigsaw classrooms grow to like each other better, develop a greater liking for school, and develop greater self-esteem than children in traditional classrooms" (1980, p. 232). Researchers also note that cross-racial friendships begin to blossom, that the exam scores of minority students improve (perhaps because academic achievement is now peer-supported), and that many teachers continue using cooperative learning after the experiments are over (D. W. Johnson et al., 1981). "It is clear," writes race-relations expert John McConahay (1981), that cooperative learning "is the most effective practice for improving race relations in desegregated schools that we know of to date."

We should be cautious not to overstate the results. There is no one solution to conflict and prejudice, and some unresolved issues about cooperative learning yet remain (S. W. Cook, 1980). But after the discouraging results of traditional means of implementing desegregation, the consistency and strength of these findings are most certainly encouraging.

Should we have "known it all along"? At the time of the 1954 Supreme Court decision, Gordon Allport spoke for many social psychologists in predicting that "Prejudice . . . may be reduced by equal status contact between majority and minority groups in the pursuit of common goals" (1958, p. 281). Unfortunately, school desegregation did not usually meet these conditions.

Rather, it was carried out under conditions already known to minimize its effectiveness, and did little if anything to improve student achievement, self-esteem, and race relations (S. W. Cook, 1979). On the other hand, the experiments that designed and then tested the results of a more constructive method of desegregation have confirmed Allport's insight. Indeed, Allport's 1954 prediction is echoed strikingly by John McConahay's 1981 synopsis of recent research: "The data point clearly to this conclusion: racial prejudice can be reduced in desegregated schools by bringing students together under conditions of equal status that emphasize common goals."

So, because cooperative, equal-status contacts exert a positive influence upon boy campers, industrial executives, college students, and schoolchildren, can we assume that the principle extends to all levels of human relations? Are families unified by pulling together to farm the land, restore an old house, or sail a sloop? Are communal identities forged by barn raisings, group singing, or cheering on the football team? Is international understanding bred by

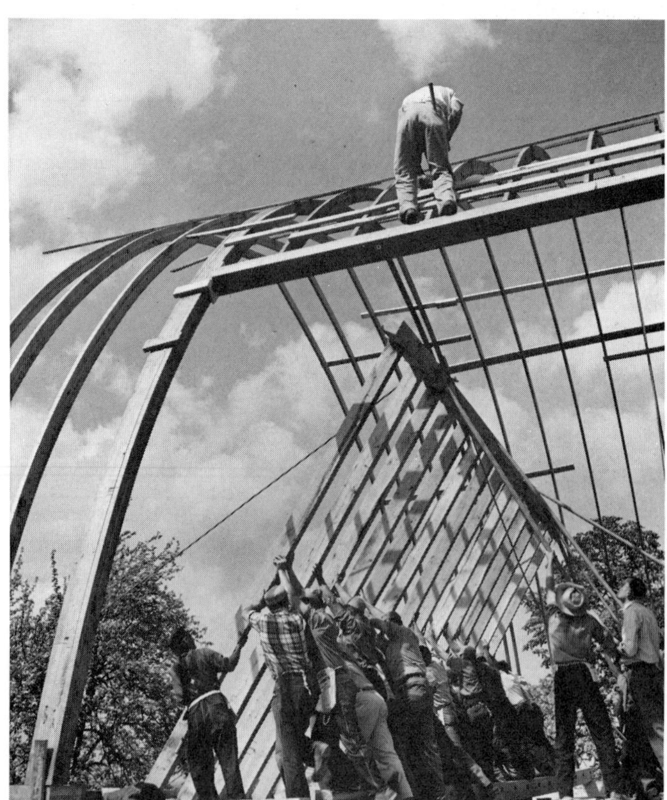

Successful cooperation builds cohesiveness. (H. Armstrong Roberts)

international collaboration in science and space, by joint efforts to feed the world and conserve resources, by friendly personal contacts between people of different nations? Indications are that the answer to all these questions is yes (Kelman, 1965; M. Sherif, 1966). Thus an important challenge facing our divided world is to identify and agree on our superordinate goals, and to structure cooperative efforts to achieve them.

Communication

Conflicting parties have several other means by which they can try to resolve their differences. When husband and wife, or labor and management, or nation X and nation Y disagree, they can *bargain* with one another directly; they can ask a third party to *mediate* by making suggestions and facilitating their negotiations; or they can *arbitrate* by submitting their disagreement to someone who will study the issues and impose a settlement (Houlden et al., 1978). We shall consider the first two options, both of which have been studied by social psychologists.

Bargaining

Bargaining: *Seeking an agreement through direct negotiation between parties to a conflict.*

Mediation: *Attempts by a neutral third party to help resolve a conflict by facilitating communication and offering suggestions.*

Arbitration: *Resolution of a conflict by a neutral third party who studies both sides and imposes a settlement.*

When conflicts are neither intense nor at an impasse, people usually prefer to bargain on their own (J. Z. Rubin, 1980). If you or I want to buy or sell a new car or house, are we better off adopting a tough bargaining stance—opening with an extreme offer so that splitting the difference will yield a favorable result? Or are we better off beginning with a sincere "good-faith" offer?

Experiments suggest no simple answer. On the one hand, those who demand more do in fact often get more (Deutsch, 1980). This finding, obtained in many laboratory studies, was confirmed by Robert Cialdini, Leonard Bickman, and John Cacioppo (1979) in an actual car sale. In a control condition, they approached various Chevrolet dealers and asked the price of a new Monte Carlo sports coupe with designated options. In an experimental condition, they approached other dealers and first struck a tougher bargaining stance, asking for and rejecting a price on a *different* car ("I need a lower price than that. . . . That's a lot"). When they then asked the price of the Monte Carlo, exactly as in the control condition, they received offers that averaged some $200 lower.

Tough bargaining may lower the other party's expectations, making the other side willing to settle for less (Yukl, 1974). But being tough can sometimes backfire. Many a conflict is not over a pie of fixed size, but over a pie that may shrink if the conflict continues. When a strike is prolonged, both labor and management are the losers. Being tough can also diminish the chances of actually reaching an agreement. If the other party responds with an equally extreme position, both may be locked into positions from which neither can back down without losing face.

Mediation

In such situations, a third-party mediator may be able to offer suggestions that enable the conflicting parties to make concessions and still save face (Pruitt, 1981b). If my concession can be attributed to a mediator, who is

"Gentlemen, instead of trying to mediate this thing, why don't you just slug it out?"

In an intense conflict, third-party mediators may aid in its resolution. (Henry Martin/*Personnel*)

gaining an equal concession from my antagonist, then neither of us will be viewed as caving in to the other's demands.

Mediators can also help resolve conflicts by facilitating constructive communication. Their first task is to help the parties rethink the conflict. By prodding them to identify the costs of continuing the conflict and the benefits of resolving it, the mediator aims to replace a competitive "win-lose" orientation with a cooperative "win-win" orientation that leads both parties to seek a mutually beneficial resolution. In experiments with students at the State University of New York at Buffalo, Dean Pruitt and his colleagues have found that getting bargainers to adopt such an orientation often leads them to communicate more openly and to offer more proposals to each other (Pruitt & Lewis, 1975; 1977; Kimmel et al., 1980). The end result is usually a better deal for both.

Communication often helps by peeling away the self-fulfilling misperceptions. Perhaps you can recall experiences similar to that of the following college student:

> Often, after a prolonged period of little communication, I perceive Martha's silence as an indication of her dislike for me. She, in turn, thinks that my quietness is a result of my being mad at her. My silence induces her silence, which makes me even more silent . . . until this snowballing effect is broken by some occurrence that makes it necessary for us to interact. And the communication then unravels all the misinterpretations we had made about one another.

The outcome of such conflicts often depends on *how* people communicate their feelings to one another. Roger Knudson, Alison Sommers, and Stephen Golding (1980) invited married couples to come to the University of Illinois psychology laboratory and relive, through role playing, one of their past conflicts. Before, during, and after their conversation (which often generated as much emotion as their actual previous conflict) the couples were closely observed and questioned. These observations revealed that those who evaded the issue—by failing to make their positions clear or failing to acknowledge their spouse's position—tended to be left with the illusion that they were more in harmony and agreement than they really were. Often, they afterward believed they now agreed more when actually they agreed less. In contrast, those who engaged the issue—by making their positions clear and by taking one another's views into account—achieved more actual agreement and gained more accurate information about one another's perceptions.

Those who have done research concerning conflict believe that a key factor is *trust.* If you believe the other is well-intentioned, not out to exploit you, you will then more likely divulge your needs and concerns. If, however, you lack such trust, you probably will be cautious, fearing that being open will give the other party information that might be used against you.

When the two parties mistrust each other and communicate unproductively, a third party mediator—be it a marriage counselor, a labor mediator, a diplomat—can sometimes help. After coaxing the conflicting parties to rethink their perceived win-lose conflict, the mediator often then has each party identify and rank its goals. If the actual incompatibility of their goals is not great, the ranking procedure may make it easier for each to concede on less important goals so that both may be able to achieve their chief goals (Erickson et al., 1974; Schulz & Pruitt, 1978). For example, once labor and management both believe that management's goal of higher productivity and profit is not necessarily incompatible with labor's goal of better wages and working conditions, they can begin to work for a win-win solution.

When the parties are then convened to communicate directly, they are usually *not* set loose in the hope that, because they are meeting eyeball to eyeball, the conflict will resolve itself. In the midst of a threatening, stressful conflict, people's emotions often disrupt their ability to understand the other party's point of view. Thus communication may become most difficult just when it is most needed (Tetlock, 1981a). So the mediator will often structure the encounter in hopes of assuring that each party will both feel understood by and understand the other.

For example, in order to build mutual understanding the conflicting parties may be encouraged to restrict their own arguments to statements of fact, including statements of how they feel and how they respond when the other acts in a given way: "I enjoy having music on. But when it's loud, I find it difficult to concentrate. That makes me crabby." Also, they may be asked to reverse roles and argue one another's position or to restate one another's positions before replying with their own: "My turning up the stereo seems to bug you." Such communication may cut away many of the accumulated misperceptions, for when the parties are flooded with information that contradicts their misperceptions, the misperceptions may change. This differs from everyday life, in which we receive contradictory information bit by bit, making it easier to rationalize or dismiss each contradictory bit (Jervis, 1973).

These peacemaking principles, based partly on laboratory experiments, partly on practical experience, have been successful in mediating both international and industrial conflicts (Blake & Mouton, 1962; 1979; Burton, 1969; Wehr, 1979). For example, a small team of Arab and Jewish Americans, led by social psychologists Herbert Kelman and Stephen Cohen (1979), have conducted several workshops bringing together influential Arabs and Israelis. By using methods such as those we've cited, Kelman and Cohen have sought to eliminate misperceptions and to have the participants creatively seek solutions for their common good. Isolated, the participants are free to speak directly to their adversaries without fearing their constituents' reactions to what they are saying. The result? Participants from both sides typically come to understand better the other country's perspective and how its people respond to their own country's actions.

When direct communication is impossible, a third party can meet with one party, then the other. Henry Kissinger's "shuttle diplomacy" in the two years after the Arab-Israeli war of 1973 produced three disengagement agreements between Israel and its Arab neighbors. Kissinger's mediating strategy gave him considerable control over the communications and enabled both sides to concede to him without appearing to capitulate to one another (Pruitt, 1981a).

The complex process of international negotiation can sometimes receive

Structured communication can help unravel misperceptions, enabling antagonists to understand each other better. (Malik/National Peace Academy Campaign)

an added boost from smaller mediating efforts. In 1976, Kelman drove an Egyptian social scientist, Boutros Ghali, to the Boston airport. En route, they formulated plans for an Egyptian conference on misperceptions in Arab-Israeli relations. The conference later took place, and Kelman conveyed its promising results to influential Israelis. A year later, Ghali became Egypt's acting foreign minister, and Egyptian President Anwar Sadat made an historic trip to Israel, beginning a road to peace. Afterward, Ghali said happily to Kelman, "You see the process that we started at the Boston airport last year" (Armstrong, 1981). A year later, mediator Jimmy Carter secluded Sadat and Israel Prime Minister Begin at Camp David. Thirteen days later, the trio emerged with "A Framework for Peace in the Middle East" in hand. Six months later, after visits to both countries by Carter in order to mediate further, a treaty was signed, ending the state of war that had existed since 1948.

Conciliation

So, direct communication often helps. But sometimes the tension and suspicion run so high that genuine communication becomes all but impossible. In such times, each party may threaten, coerce, or retaliate against the other. Unfortunately, such acts tend to be reciprocated, thus escalating the conflict (Tedeschi, Schlenker, & Bonoma, 1973; Kimble, Fitz, & Onorad, 1977). So, would an opposite strategy—appeasing the other party by being unconditionally cooperative—likely produce a satisfying result? Often not. In laboratory games, those who are 100 percent cooperative are frequently exploited. Politically, a one-sided pacifism is generally out of the question; neither the Soviets nor the Americans are about to disarm without the assurance that the other is doing likewise.

Is there a third alternative—one conciliatory rather than retaliatory, yet strong enough to discourage exploitation? Charles Osgood (1962; 1980), a University of Illinois social psychologist, has for twenty years advocated one such alternative. Osgood calls it *G*raduated and *R*eciprocated *I*nitiatives in *T*ension-reduction, nicknamed GRIT, a name that delightfully and insightfully suggests the kind of determination it requires. GRIT aims to reverse the arms race, by triggering reciprocal deescalating acts. To do so, it draws upon social psychological concepts, such as the norm of reciprocity and research on attribution of motives.

GRIT: *Graduated and Reciprocated Initiatives in Tension-reduction—a strategy designed to de-escalate international tensions.*

GRIT requires one side to initiate a few small deescalatory actions, undertaken in ways that encourage the adversary's reciprocation. The first steps in the strategy *announce* one's conciliatory intent. The initiator states its desire to reduce tension, declares each conciliatory act prior to making it, and invites the adversary to reciprocate. Such announcements create a framework that helps the adversary interpret correctly what otherwise might be seen as weak or tricky actions, and they elicit public pressure on the adversary to adhere to the reciprocity norm.

Next, the initiator establishes credibility and genuineness by carrying out, exactly as announced, several verifiable *conciliatory acts*. This intensifies

When tension runs high, retaliation may displace communication. (Drawing by Dana Fradon; © 1980 *The New Yorker* Magazine, Inc.)

"And I say one bomb is worth a thousand words."

pressure to reciprocate. Making the conciliatory acts diverse—perhaps offering medical information, closing a military base, and lifting a trade ban—keeps the initiator from making a significant sacrifice in any one area and leaves the adversary freer to choose its own means of reciprocation. If the adversary reciprocates voluntarily, its own conciliatory action may also soften its hostile attitudes.

GRIT *is* conciliatory. But it is not "surrender on the installment plan." The remaining aspects of the plan protect one's self-interest by *maintaining retaliatory capability*. The initial conciliatory steps entail some small risk, but do not jeopardize one's security; rather they simply are calculated to begin edging both sides down the tension ladder. If one side takes an aggressive action, it is reciprocated in kind, making it clear that no exploitation will be tolerated. Yet, this reciprocal act is not to be an overresponse which would likely reescalate the conflict. If the adversary offers its own conciliatory acts, these too are matched, or even slightly exceeded.

Does it really work? In a series of experiments at Ohio University, Svenn Lindskold and his associates (1976 to 1981) have tested various aspects of the GRIT plan. Lindskold concludes (1978) that his own and others' studies provide "strong support for the various steps in the GRIT proposal." In laboratory games, announcing one's cooperative intent does boost cooperation. Repeated conciliatory acts do breed greater trust (although self-serving biases often make one's own acts seem more conciliatory and less hostile than those of one's adversary). Maintaining an equality of power does protect one against being exploited.

Lindskold is not contending that the world of the laboratory experiment mirrors the more complex world of everyday life. Rather, as we noted way back in Chapter 1, experiments enable us to formulate and to verify powerful theoretical principles such as the reciprocity norm, the self-serving bias, and the principles that predict whether one will attribute cooperative or deceitful motives to another. And, notes Lindskold (1981), "It is the theories, not the individual experiments that are used to interpret the world."

"I am not suggesting that principles of individual behavior can be applied to the behavior of nations in any direct, simple-minded fashion. What I am trying to suggest is that such principles may provide us with hunches about internation behavior that can be tested against experience in the larger arena."

Charles E. Osgood (1966)

GRIT-like strategies have occasionally been tried outside the laboratory, and with promising results. During the Berlin Crisis of the early 1960s, U.S. and Soviet tanks faced one another barrel-to-barrel. The crisis was defused when the Americans pulled back their tanks step-by-step. The Russians reciprocated each step. More recently, small concessions by Israel and Egypt (for example, Israel allowing Egypt to open up the Suez Canal, Egypt allowing ships bound for Israel to pass through) helped reduce tension to a point where the negotiations between the two nations became possible (J. Z. Rubin, 1981).

To many, the most significant attempt at GRIT was the so-called "Kennedy experiment" (Etzioni, 1967). On June 10, 1963, President Kennedy gave a major speech, "A Strategy for Peace." In it he noted that "our problems are man-made . . . and can be solved by man," and then announced his first conciliatory act: The U.S. was stopping all atmospheric nuclear tests and would not resume them unless another country did. In the Soviet Union, Kennedy's speech was published in full. Five days later Premier Khrushchev reciprocated, announcing he had halted production of strategic bombers. There soon followed further reciprocal gestures: the U.S. agreed to sell wheat to Russia, the Soviets agreed to a "hot line" between the two countries, and the two countries soon achieved a test-ban treaty. These conciliatory initiatives did, for a time, warm relations between the two countries.

The GRIT strategy was formulated as a plan for reversing the arms race and reducing international tensions. Might such conciliatory efforts also help reduce tension between groups, or between individuals? The theoretical principles that underlie the strategy are derived from research with individuals and small groups, so its applicability to the tensions of our daily existence seems promising. When a relationship is strained and communication non-existent, it sometimes takes only a conciliatory gesture—a soft answer, a warm smile, a gentle touch—for both parties to begin easing down the tension ladder, to a rung where communication can be reestablished and the conflict creatively resolved.

SUMMING UP

Conflict

Whenever two people, two groups, or two nations interact, their perceived needs and goals may conflict. In this chapter, we identified some common ingredients of conflicts, and we considered ways to resolve them constructively and peacefully.

Social Dilemmas

Many social problems arise as people pursue their individual self-interests, to their common detriment. Three laboratory games, the Prisoner's Dilemma, the Commons Dilemma, and the Dollar Auction, capture this clash of individual versus communal well-being. In each game, the participants choose whether to pursue their immediate interests or to cooperate for their common betterment. Ironically and tragically, each game often traps well-meaning participants into decisions that shrink their common pie. In real life, as in laboratory experiments, such traps can be avoided by establishing rules that regulate self-serving behavior; by keeping social groups small so that people feel responsibility for one another; by enabling people to communicate, thus reducing mistrust; by changing payoffs to make exploitation less and cooperation more rewarding; and by invoking altruistic norms.

Competition

When people compete for scarce resources, human relations can sink into prejudice and hostility. In a famous series of experiments, Muzafer Sherif found that win-lose competition quickly made strangers into enemies, triggering outright warfare even among normally upstanding boys.

Perceived Injustice

Conflicts are also kindled when people feel unjustly treated. According to equity theory, people define justice as equity—the distribution of rewards in proportion to people's contributions. Conflicts occur when people disagree on the extent of their contributions and thus on the equity of their outcomes. Other theorists argue that people sometimes define justice not as equity, but as equality, or even in terms of people's needs.

Misperception

Conflicts frequently contain a small core of truly incompatible goals, surrounded by a thick layer of misperceptions of the adversary's motives and goals. Often, conflicting parties have *mirror-image perceptions*—each attributing the same virtues to themselves and vices to each other. When both sides believe "We are peaceloving, they are hostile," each may treat the other in ways that provoke confirmation of their expectations. International conflicts are also fed by a *blacktop illusion*: One's enemy's leaders are perceived as evil and coercive, its people as more innocent or even as sympathetic to one's own point of view. Such perceptions of our antagonists easily adjust themselves as conflicts wax and wane.

Peacemaking

Conflicts are readily kindled and fueled by these ingredients, but fortunately some equally powerful forces can transform hostility into harmony.

Contact

Might putting people into close contact reduce their hostilities? There are good reasons to think so. Yet, despite some encouraging early studies of desegregation, more recent studies in the U.S. show that mere desegregation of schools has little effect upon racial attitudes. However, in most schools, interracial contact is seldom prolonged or intimate. When it is, and when it is structured to convey *equal status,* hostilities often lessen.

Cooperation

Contacts are especially beneficial when people work together to overcome a common threat or to achieve a superordinate goal. In his boys' camp experiments, Sherif used the unifying effect of a common enemy to create cohesive groups. Then he used the unifying power of cooperative effort to reconcile the warring groups. Taking their cue from experiments on cooperative contact, several research teams have replaced competitive classroom learning situations with opportunities for cooperative learning. Their heartening results suggest how desegregation might be more constructively implemented, and strengthen our confidence that cooperative activities can benefit human relations at all levels.

Communication

Conflicting parties can also seek to resolve their differences by bargaining either directly with one another or through a third-party mediator. When a pie of fixed size is to be divided, adopting a tough negotiating stance tends to gain one a larger piece (for example, a better price). When the pie can vary in size, as in the dilemma situations, toughness more often backfires. Third-party mediators can help by prodding the antagonists to replace their competitive win-lose view of their conflict with a more cooperative win-win orientation. Mediators can also structure communications that will peel away misperceptions and increase mutual understanding and trust.

Conciliation

Sometimes tensions run so high that genuine communication is impossible. In such times, small conciliatory gestures by one party may elicit reciprocal conciliatory acts by the other party. Thus tension may be reduced to a level where communication can occur. One such conciliatory strategy, Graduated and Reciprocated Initiatives in Tension-reduction, aims to alleviate tense international situations.

Those who mediate tense labor-management and international conflicts sometimes use one other peacemaking strategy. They instruct the participants, as this chapter instructed you, in the dynamics of conflict and peacemaking. The hope is that understanding—understanding how conflicts are fed by social traps, perceived injustice, competition, and misperceptions, and understanding how conflicts can be resolved through equal-status contact, cooperation, communication, and conciliation—can help us as we seek to establish and enjoy peaceful, rewarding relationships.

APPLIED SOCIAL PSYCHOLOGY

Thus far we have identified principles that describe and explain how we think about, influence, and relate to one another. We have also studied the methods by which these principles have been discerned, and we have pondered their significance for our everyday living.

To review some of these principles, we will briefly consider two areas in which they are being applied. In Chapter 15 we will look at our relation to the physical environment. How, for example, are we affected by crowding and by the architectural design of our environments? How can we be stimulated to conserve our natural environment? Then in Chapter 16 we will see how both the concepts and methodology of social psychology can help us understand what happens in the world of law. For example, in courtrooms, how do people form impressions of defendants, and how do juries reach decisions?

Chapter

Social Psychology and the Physical Environment

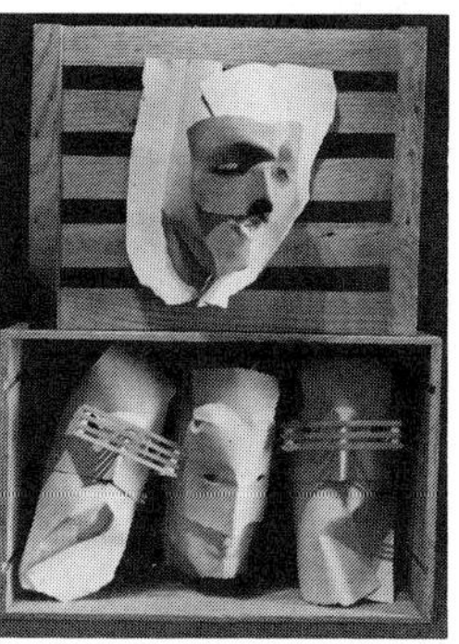

As we have become more environmentally conscious, there has emerged a new breed of psychologist. Their purpose? To study the relations between human behavior and the physical environment. These "environmental psychologists" apply concepts and methods from the more established areas of psychology in their study of how we perceive and adapt to our physical environment; how we are affected by its temperature, its noise, its structure; how we can design less stressful, more humane environments.

In this chapter we will examine three environmental issues that are among those of particular interest to social psychologists: crowding, architectural design, and energy conservation.

CROWDING

What Is Crowding?

First we must recognize that *crowding* is subjective. Jammed with others in a small room, most of us would feel crowded. Snuggled in bed on a cold night, my wife and I feel anything but crowded. The first situation is less *dense* (fewer people per square feet), yet more crowded. So crowding and density, though related, are distinguishable (Stokols, 1972; 1978). Add to a given room more light, mirrors, windows, and a sweeping view, and though the

Density: *An objective* measure *of the amount of space per person.*
Crowding: *A subjective* feeling *of not enough space per person.*

density would be unchanged, the people in it would likely feel less crowded (Schiffenbauer et al., 1977; Sundstrom, 1978).

Feeling crowded is an unpleasant emotion. As you may recall from Chapters 10 and 13, the two-factor theory of emotion proposes that "emotion = arousal × label," which means that a given state of arousal can be steered into an experience of one emotion or another, depending on how one labels the arousal. If aroused in a hostile environment, a person may feel angry; in a romantic environment, one aroused similarly may feel passionate; in a room too densely packed, the person may feel crowded.

Several research teams, led by Stephen Worchel, Miles Patterson, and John Keating, have successfully applied this two-factor theory of emotion to crowding. Worchel and Steven Yohai (1979) had University of Virginia students in groups of five discuss several questions while seated either comfortably in a circle or, supposedly for tape recording purposes, in a circle so tight that the front legs of each chair touched. Afterward, those in the tightly packed group reported feeling quite confined—unless they had been told beforehand that "subliminal noise" would be played during the experiment. "You won't be able to hear it with your naked ear," the experimenter explained, "but it may make you feel somewhat stressed and uncomfortable." Actually, no such noise was played. Yet thinking such was occurring, the participants attributed to it the arousal caused by their density; hence, though ill at ease, they did not label and experience their arousal as crowding.

But why is human density arousing? Researchers have identified several reasons (Evans, 1978).

Space Invasions

Personal space: *The buffer zone we like to maintain around our bodies. Its size depends upon our familiarity with whoever is near us.*

Around our bodies, each of us has a *personal space*, a sort of portable bubble or buffer zone that we like to maintain between ourselves and others. As the situation changes, the bubble varies in size. With strangers we maintain a fairly large personal space, keeping a distance of 4 feet or more between us. On uncrowded buses, or in restrooms or libraries, we protect our space and respect others' space. We let friends come closer, often within 2 or 3 feet. Some prefer more personal space than others: Adults maintain more distance than children; men keep more distance from one another than do women; Americans, the British, and Scandinavians prefer more distance than do Arabs, the French, and Latin Americans (H. W. Smith, 1981; Sommer, 1969; Stockdale, 1978).

Does one's encroaching on another's personal space produce arousal? You can answer the question the way researchers have, by playing space invader. Stand or sit but a foot or so from someone and strike up a conversation. Does the person fidget, look away, back off, show other signs of discomfort? Such are among the signs of arousal noted by researchers (Altman & Vinsel, 1978). One controversial experiment even observed that men require more time to begin urination and less time to complete the act (known symptoms of mild emotional arousal) when another man is standing at an adjacent urinal (Middlemist, Knowles, & Matter, 1976; 1977).

Constrained Behavior

Imagine yourself crammed in the back of a bus, or trapped in slow-moving traffic on a densely packed freeway. Such situations are stressful and can be frustrating: they constrain us; they restrict our accustomed freedom of action. As we noted in Chapter 7, what threatens our sense of freedom frequently produces "reactance"—an aroused state that prompts us to restore our freedom. So, when the available space is insufficient for a given activity, we feel constrained, and thus aroused and crowded. Two couples playing a doubles match on a racquetball court may feel crowded; on a dinner date afterward, the same two couples will not feel crowded sitting in a much smaller area.

If, indeed, people are aroused in situations where they feel constrained, then increasing their freedom and control should alleviate their distress. For example, New York high school students, in an experiment by Drury Sherrod (1974), were set to work in a small, packed room, and half of them were told, "Although we prefer that you take the test in this special room, you are free to leave this booth at any time and work out here in the main room." Interestingly, those given this freedom never used it. But they did later show fewer signs of stress.

In a field experiment that tested the same idea, solo individuals entered an elevator in Yale University's library with four confederates. As they did

In which position would you feel least crowded? In an experiment conducted in the elevator at the Yale library, researchers found that individuals felt least crowded when jockeyed by four confederates into the position in front of the control panel. (Kenneth Karp.)

so, two of the confederates went straight to the back. The other two maneuvered the unsuspecting individual to a place either in front of the floor selection buttons or to the opposite front corner. After the individual left the elevator, one of the confederates asked him or her to complete a class survey on elevator design. Who rated the elevator as more crowded? The researchers, Judith Rodin, Susan Solomon, and John Metcalf (1978), report it was those who had stood away from the elevator's controls. Feeling less in control of the elevator, they apparently felt more constrained, and thus more aroused and crowded.

Stimulus Overload

To be stimulated is to be aroused. Hence, too much stimulation—for example, too many people—may produce stress. As research on social facilitation (Chapter 9) indicated, the mere presence of another can be arousing. For some, at times, the presence of many others becomes too much to contend with, too arousing.

How much is "too much"? As we have already noted, the answer depends on the situation. And it also depends on the individual. Some prefer the low-stimulation level of near utter privacy. Others prefer high stimulation—stereo blaring, loud parties, studying in the student coffee shop (Altman, 1975).

"I would rather sit on a pumpkin and have it all to myself than be crowded on a velvet cushion."

Henry David Thoreau, Walden

A common thread runs through space invasions, constrained behavior, and stimulus overload. Each involves a perceived *loss of personal control* (Schmidt & Keating, 1979). When we lose control over the space around our bodies, when our behavior cannot control our environment, when we are unable to control the level of social stimulation, then we show signs of arousal. And when this arousal is attributed to the density of people around us, we feel crowded.

FIGURE 15-1 Model of crowding. Dense situations diminish one's sense of personal control, causing arousal. If arousal is correctly attributed to the density, one feels crowded; if the arousal is misattributed to something else, one feels less crowded. (After Schmidt and Keating, 1979.)

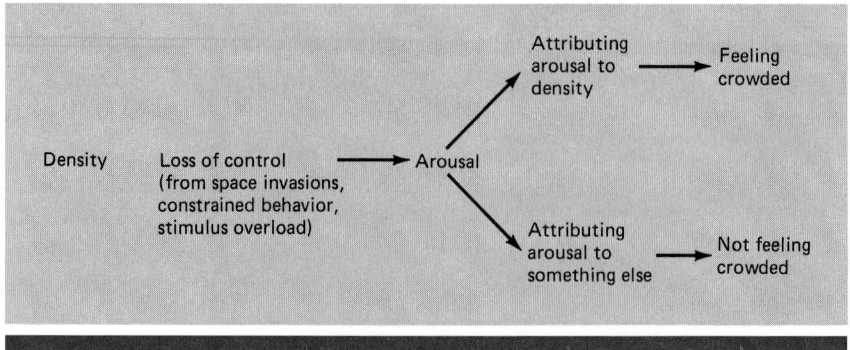

The Effects of Human Density

Given this understanding of density and crowding, we now can ask: How does human density affect us? To this question, two quite different answers are currently being debated. The first: Density merely intensifies tendencies already present, good or bad. The second: Density's effects are mostly negative.

Density-Intensity

The first view, offered by social psychologist Jonathan Freedman (1975), theorizes that density amplifies people's typical reactions to a situation. If their reactions are positive, increasing density will magnify their positive response; if negative, density will intensify their negative response. Recently I took my fifteen-year-old son and several of his buddies to a rock concert. Clearly, the density of the crowd magnified their pleasure, my displeasure.

Density-intensity: *The theory that high density intensifies people's positive or negative reactions.*

Several experiments confirm the density-intensity principle. For example, when they sit very close, friendly people are liked even more, *un*friendly people are *dis*liked even more (Schiffenbauer & Schiavo, 1976; Storms & Thomas, 1977). In experiments both with students at Columbia University and with visitors to the Ontario Science Center, Freedman and his co-workers (1979; 1980) had an accomplice listen to a humorous tape or watch a movie with other subjects. The accomplice could more readily induce the subjects to laugh and clap when all sat close together. As theatre directors know, a "good house" is a full house. Perhaps you've noticed that a class of thirty-five students tends to be more warm and lively in a room that seats just thirty-five than when spread around a room that seats 100.

Why this effect? Freedman has a simple answer: in dense situations other people are more prominent stimuli; we are more aware of and responsive to their reactions. Thus one person's laughter or clapping is more readily noticed and imitated.

Research on social facilitation suggests a second possible reason. As you may recall from Chapter 9, the arousal produced by the mere presence of others tends to magnify dominant responses (for example, correct answers on easy tasks, incorrect answers on hard tasks). So, if density is arousing, the arousal may intensify people's responses. Gary Evans (1979) found support for this idea. He tested ten-person groups of University of Massachusetts students, either in a room 20 by 30 feet or in one 8 by 12 feet. Compared to those in the large room, those in the one densely packed had higher pulse rates and blood pressure (indicating arousal), and though their performance on simple tasks did not suffer, on difficult tasks they made more errors.

Density as Stressful

The second view is that not only is density arousing, it's stressful. Space invasions, constrained behavior, and stimulus overload are inherently negative experiences that usually produce negative consequences (Epstein, Woolfolk, & Lehrer, 1981). Losing personal control causes frustration, tension, and other harmful consequences.

Do facts support this view? Some researchers have found that animals allowed to overpopulate a confined environment do experience severe stress (Calhoun, 1962; Christian, Flyger, & Davis, 1960). As a result, they may exhibit abnormal sexual behavior, heightened aggressiveness, and even an inflated death rate. But of course, it is a rather large leap from rats in an enclosure or deer on an island to human beings in a city (R. M. Baron & Needel, 1980; Freedman, 1979). Nevertheless, it's true that dense urban areas do suffer higher rates of crime and emotional distress (Kirmeyer, 1978). Moreover, children growing up in "dense" home situations are less likely to assert personal control [for example, by wanting to choose their own candy reward rather than have an experimenter choose for them (Rodin, 1976)]. Compared to people in rural areas, urbanites are also less likely to accept a handshake from a stranger, less prone to make eye contact with passersby, and less helpful to someone in need (Milgram, 1977; Newman & McCauley, 1977). And within a given prison, death, psychiatric commitment, and suicide rates tend to rise and fall as the prison's population rises and falls (McCain, Cox, & Paulus, 1982).

Lest we hold population density responsible for all our social ills, it is important to note that such correlations between urban density and social problems need not imply that density is *causing* the problems. Urbanites not only experience higher density than small-town people, but they may also differ in income, education, cultural history, and a host of other ways. These factors, too, are often associated with particular social behaviors. So, which is more crucial? The density of city life? Certain of these other factors? Both?

Actually, studies show that the effect of population density upon crime and mental disorder is smaller than often supposed. After adjusting for differences in income and education, the population density of one's home or neighborhood is not all that closely related to such social problems (Freedman, Heshka, & Levy, 1975; Verbrugge & Taylor, 1980). Density has more effect on other behaviors, such as willingness to make eye contact with passersby. An office worker in midtown Manhattan is surrounded by nearly a quarter million people (Milgram, 1970). One adapts to such an unmanageable stimulus overload by ignoring most of it. Small-town tourists trying to take in all of Manhattan may be wide-eyed for a day or two. But if they stay long enough, they too will begin to filter the input and respond more selectively.

The behavior of people in cities may also differ because of other environmental factors that accompany high population density. One such factor is noise. Researchers have found that people who are exposed to prolonged loud noise in factories, in homes near airports, and in apartments adjacent to highways and trains tend to suffer higher-than-usual rates of stress-related medical and psychological impairments (for example, S. Cohen et al., 1980). But again, the research is correlational: Perhaps people who choose to work and live in noisy environments are somehow different.

To eliminate this ambiguity, investigators have conducted laboratory experiments. For example, David Glass and Jerome Singer (1972) simulated

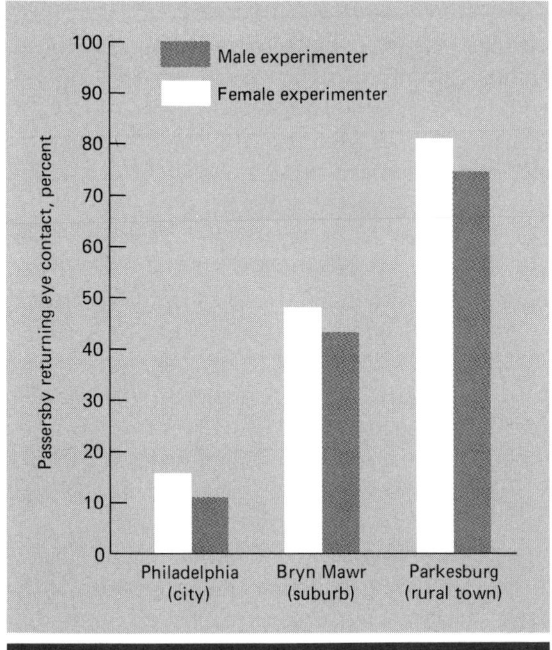

FIGURE 15-2 An effect of human density? In an urban post office or grocery store, people were unlikely to reciprocate eye contact from a stranger; in a rural town, they usually did so. (Data from Joseph Newman and Clark McCauley, 1977.)

the din of city life by a tape-recorded mixing of the clattering of office machines and of people speaking in foreign languages. While people worked on various tasks this noise was played, either loudly or softly, at either predictable or unpredictable intervals. People soon adapted to the noise and, unless the tasks were very trying, performed about equally well in all conditions. More noticeable were the *aftereffects* of having coped with the noise. People who had been exposed to *unpredictable* loud noise later made more errors on a proofreading task and had lower tolerance for frustration on a difficult problem-solving task. From these and other results, we can speculate that noise will be most stressful when it is unpredictable and uncontrollable. Jackhammers, motorcycles, and yells in the dorm hallway will be considerably more disruptive than constant sound from your own stereo, car engine, or fan. Moreover, such stressful noises can make people more aggressive and less helpful (Bell, Fisher, & Loomis, 1978).

Even if one removes the noise factor, the associations that occur naturally between density and negative behavior are still ambiguous. So researchers have conducted experiments in which they have found, for example, that being in a packed laboratory room can indeed be frustrating, annoying, and stressful (Nicosia et al., 1979). Still, such effects are temporary and result from a brief experience. What are the effects of densely packed permanent living conditions? What dense living situation could researchers study? You perhaps have lived in one.

Most college dormitories meet the Census Bureau's criteria for "crowded" living accommodations—more than one person per room (Loo, 1980). And occasionally, large enrollments have prompted colleges and universities temporarily to squeeze three people into quarters designed for two. Since, to attempt some degree of fairness, such assignments are made at random, colleges have in actuality staged experiments in human density. Not surprisingly, several research teams have capitalized upon these.

At the University of Connecticut, Reuben Baron and his colleagues (1976) found that tripled students not only felt more crowded, but also perceived less personal control over room activities—effects independently confirmed by Steven McNeel (1980) at Bethel College in St. Paul, Minnesota. Other research teams led by Robert Karlin (1978; 1979) at Rutgers University and Joel Glassman (1978) at Auburn University, report that tripled students also earn slightly lower grades. And just as laboratory density seems to be more stressful for men than for women, so is dormitory tripling (Walden, Nelson, & Smith, 1981; Nicosia et al., 1979). Apparently, men require more personal space than do women.

The stress of tripling may, however, be due to more than lack of space. Three-person groups tend to be less stable than two-person groups. Often two of the three hit it off better, leaving the third person feeling somewhat isolated and left out of room activities (Chertkoff, 1975; Aiello, Baum, & Gormley, 1981). At Trinity College in Connecticut, Andrew Baum and his co-workers (1979) found that it was not all three roommates, but rather these isolates who most keenly felt the stresses of the tripled room.

Which of the two views—the density-intensity idea or the density-as-stress idea—is correct? Perhaps further research will show that both are correct. Maybe the effect of density is like the effect of music: If soft music evokes positive feelings, steadily increasing the volume may intensify those positive feelings, until one reaches a point at which the music—or the density—becomes stressful.

ARCHITECTURE AND SOCIAL BEHAVIOR

One of environmental psychology's most fascinating questions is: How are we affected by the design of our living and working spaces? How does the physical structure of an apartment building, a college dormitory, a classroom, an office, influence our morale and our behavior?

Building Design

High-Rise = High Crime?

In 1954 an architectural wonder arose on fifty-seven inner-city acres in St. Louis. When the massive Pruitt-Igoe public housing project opened its doors, nearly 12,000 people moved into the more than 2700 new apartments within its forty-three buildings. Imagine our taking a walk through the project only a few years later. Our walk reveals the extent to which the high hopes of these new residents had been dashed. Broken windows, urine-stained elevators and stairwells, and littered hallways and playgrounds hint at the social chaos within. We come upon a resident of one of the still-occupied buildings. She describes a nightmare of vandalism, rape, and robbery. Because such crimes occur most commonly in the elevators and stairwells, many of the upper floors have been abandoned (Yancey, 1971). Returning again after a few more years, we discover the nightmare ended, the entire project gone, demolished.

Is the Pruitt-Igoe nightmare illustrative of a general tendency for high-rise housing to have crime? Crime rates do often rise with the height of public housing projects (O. Newman, 1972; 1973). However, people are not assigned randomly to housing. Therefore, residents of average and of high-rise buildings may differ in many ways. So researchers are still debating whether high-rise housing per se is bad for us (D. P. McCarthy & Saegert, 1979).

The answer may depend on a building's architectural design. The Pruitt-Igoe complex was designed with two types of space—the private space of one's apartment, and the public stairwells, elevators, and outside areas shared by all. Lacking were small, semi-public commons areas around which social networks develop. For example, people who live around culs-de-sac interact more than do those living side by side on straight streets (Lansing, Marans, & Zehner, 1970). Had each few families in Pruitt-Igoe shared a given well-defined territory—a *small* commons—the chances are better that they would

The demolition of Pruitt-Igoe begins, 1972. (United Press International)

have come to know one another, to recognize and keep an eye on intruders, and to preclude yet another tragedy of the commons (see Chapter 14).

Leonard Bickman and his co-workers (1973) found evidence for the impersonality of high-rise living when they surveyed women students in massive high-rise dormitories at the University of Massachusetts and the University of Pennsylvania, and compared their findings to those gathered from students living in small units at the University of Pennsylvania and at Smith College. Asked whether they would ignore a male stranger in the dorm, 44 percent of those in the high-rise dorms and 8 percent of those in the very small dorms said they would. Bickman and his team also "accidentally dropped" in these buildings dozens of letters—stamped, addressed, and sealed, but without any return address. In the large dorms these "lost letters" were picked up and mailed less than two-thirds of the time; in the small dorms almost 100 percent were mailed.

"We shape buildings; thereafter they shape us."

Winston Churchill

Another architectural feature that seems to encourage crime in many high rises is the seclusion of public spaces. When children leave an upper-floor apartment, their parents immediately lose sight of them. The elevators and stairwells are shielded from surveillance. Some urban designers, therefore, now advise that public spaces in and around high rises have maximum exposure, such as elevators with see-through doors (O. Newman, 1972; 1973). Bank robbers report that they avoid banks with (1) large windows that expose them to passersby or (2) layouts that interfere with their viewing everyone in the bank. High visual exposure to the outside and low visual access to the bank's inside reduce a thief's sense of personal control (Archea, 1980).

Dormitory Design

Has dorm life ever felt hectic? Crowded? Unfriendly? Out of control? Social psychologists Andrew Baum, Stuart Valins, and their colleagues discovered that students' answers to such questions depend partly on the design of their dormitories. In a series of studies, these researchers have compared life in dorms that have long corridors with life in dorms designed either with short corridors or with suites of three rooms clustered around a small lounge and bathroom. In each design, the *spatial density* (amount of space per person) is the same. However, the *social density* (number of people who occupy a given space) is not. When those living in the traditional long-corridor design depicted in Figure 15-3 leave their rooms, they may run into any of thirty-three others with whom they share the same bathroom and lounge. Those in the suite experience less social density, for they may encounter any one of five others.

Spatial density: *Space per person.*
Social density: *Number of persons who occupy a given space.*

Which dorm would you prefer? In study after study, Baum and his associates (Baum & Valins, 1977) report that those living in long-corridor dorms are less likely to evolve informal social groups, and they feel more crowded and forced into unwanted interactions with others. Remarkably, the effects of such dormitory stress appear even in laboratory situations remote from the dorm. Those who have lived for several weeks or more in a long-corridor dorm tend to be more socially withdrawn, to sit farther away from

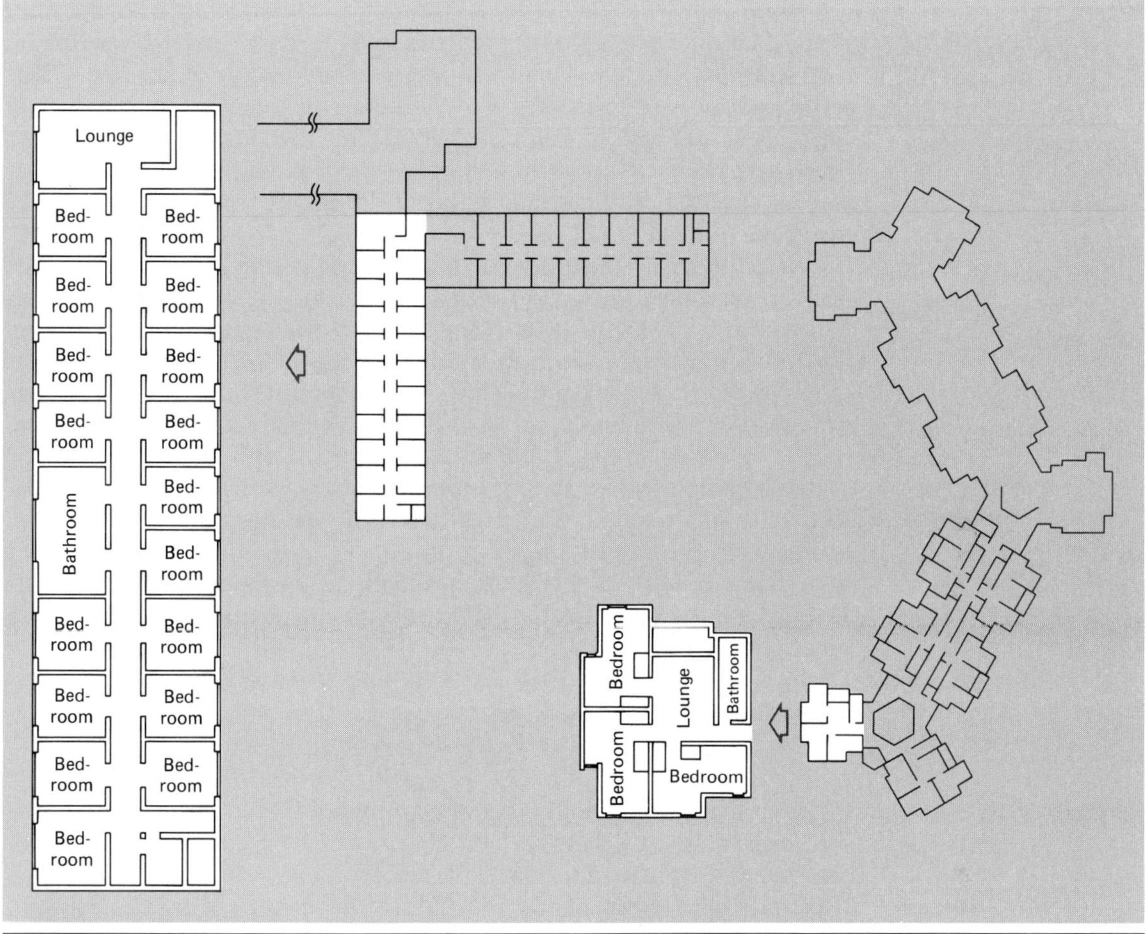

FIGURE 15-3 Floor plans of long-corridor dormitories and suite-design dormitories at the State University of New York at Stony Brook. (From Baum & Valins, 1977.) Which of these dorms would you prefer to live in?

a stranger and make less eye contact (Baum et al., 1975; 1978; 1981). Suite residents, by contrast, seem to welcome social stimulation outside the dorm (Reichner, 1979).

The consistency of these findings is striking. Moreover, that the differences only appear after a few weeks of living in the dorms suggests that the stress and withdrawal are caused by dorm design, not inherent differences in the people assigned to long-corridor dorms. Still, it would be helpful if we could experimentally manipulate the design of a given dorm and observe whether stress and withdrawal change.

Baum and Glenn Davis (1980) did precisely this. They divided one floor of a long-corridor women's dorm into two short-corridor sections by, as Figure 15-4 illustrates, installing unlocked doors in the middle of the floor. This psychologically transformed a forty-three-student group into two groups of twenty. For comparison, the floor just above was left undivided. The two floors were otherwise indistinguishable—same building, same view, similar people—and thus, any resulting behavior differences could be traced to the architectural modification.

And differences there were. After ten weeks, those living in the divided corridor were more likely than their long-corridor counterparts on the floor above to leave their doors open, signaling their willingness to interact. They also reported making more friends and were less likely to view dorm life as hectic, crowded, and uncontrollable. When observed in the laboratory, they exhibited a less withdrawn posture, sat closer to a stranger, and looked at her more.

"An ideal prison . . . would be relatively small (certainly less than 1,000 and preferably 500) and consist of single rooms or cubicles."

Paul Paulus, Garvin McCain, and Verne Cox (1981)

Paul Paulus, Garvin McCain, and Verne Cox (1981) discovered a similar effect of social density in their analysis of 1400 inmates of six U. S. prisons. As Figure 15-5 indicates, inmates who slept in large open dorms had many more illness complaints than those who slept in single cubicles. This effect was not due to spatial density, since the amount of space allotted to each inmate was essentially constant.

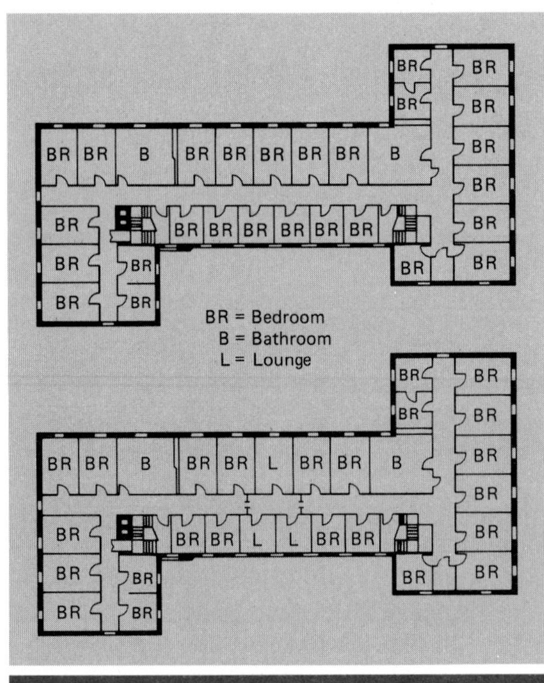

FIGURE 15-4 Floor plans of a long-corridor dormitory floor (*above*) and a similar floor divided with doors in the middle. After several weeks, residents of the divided corridor were more likely to have made friends and less likely to view dorm life as hectic and uncontrollable. (From Baum & Davis, 1980.)

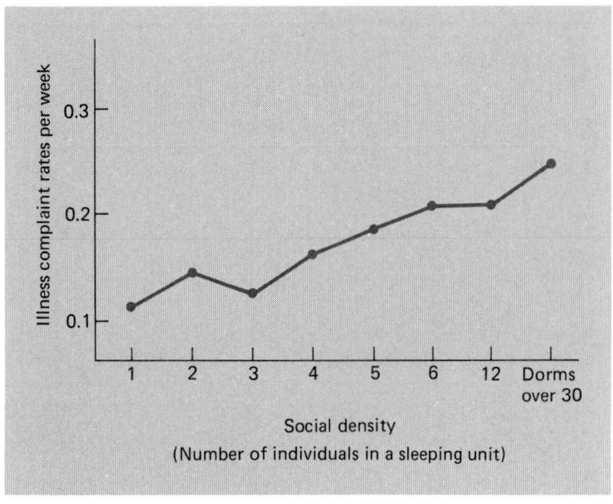

FIGURE 15-5
Frequency of illness complaints among 1400 inmates in six U.S. prisons. Those who slept in large dorms had double the illness complaints of those who slept in individual cubicles. (Data from Paulus, McCain, & Cox, 1981.)

The "Small-is-beautiful" impression one gets from reading this research is reinforced by comparisons of institutions with high or low social density. Roger Barker (1978), Allan Wicker (1979), and others (Morgan & Alwin, 1980) have extensively studied people in schools and churches, both small and large. Their consistent finding: Those in the small institutions are more involved. Large schools and churches can offer more activities, but in the smaller institutions nearly everyone feels needed. One religious group, the Jehovah's Witnesses, maximizes member participation by splitting a congregation whenever numbers exceed about 250. Similarly, Stephen Harkins and Bibb Latané (1980) report that the smaller a Massachusetts town, the more likely its citizens are to attend town meetings and vote in local elections. Does this apparent diffusion of responsibility in large groups also typify colleges and universities? For example, as the size of a school increases, does the percentage of students voting in campus elections decrease? Such effects are presumed to be due not directly to the physical size of the institution or community, but rather to its social size; when a church or school or town has few people, they tend to be more involved.

Classroom Environment

How would you describe your social psychology classroom? Cold or warm? Impersonal or intimate?

One way to make an environment more friendly is to seat people facing one another. Robert Sommer and Hugo Ross (1958) noted that patients in a newly remodeled Saskatchewan geriatrics ward seemed depressed—as they sat in chairs lined up along the walls, side by side. The researchers rearranged the chairs in circles around tables. Within a few weeks, conversation almost doubled. More formal laboratory experiments yield similar results (Argyle &

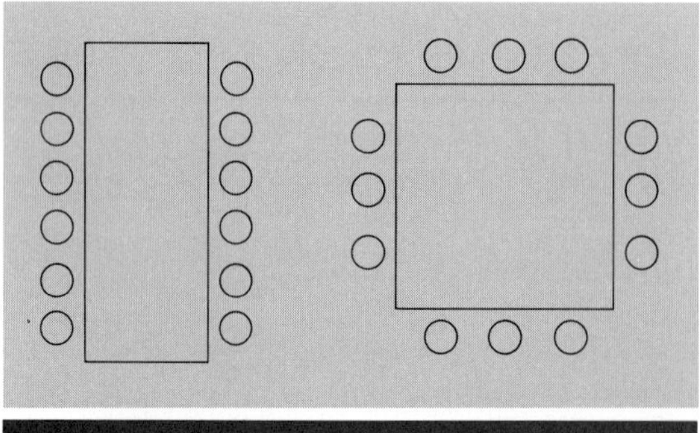

FIGURE 15-6 In the rectangular seating arrangement each person has easy eye contact with the six group members seated across the table. In the square seating arrangement, each has easy eye contact with virtually everyone in the group. Since eye contact facilitates communication, the second seating arrangement is preferable for group discussion.

Dean, 1965; Mehrabian & Diamond, 1971): People tend to talk to those with whom they have eye contact, such as those who, at a table, sit across from rather than alongside them.

Most classrooms seat students in straight rows, giving them easy eye contact only with the teacher. So it's not surprising that students' public comments are directed to the instructor, and seldom, if ever, to other students. For that matter, students don't discuss much with the instructor either—two or three minutes worth during the average lecture class at one university, and only five or six minutes during the average seminar (F. D. Becker et al., 1973). Robert Sommer and Helge Olsen (1980) observed that in introductory psychology discussion groups held in straight-row classrooms at the University of California, Davis, only 48 percent of the students participated, averaging 1.4 statements per student during a class hour. After one of these classrooms was converted to a "soft" room with circular seating, 79 percent of its students contributed, averaging 5 comments per student per hour, one-fourth of which were directed to other students.

If people talk with those whom they face, then instructors in traditional classrooms should interact most with those who sit front and center, least with those in the rear corners. And so they do (Sommer, 1967). But perhaps those front and center participate most not because of seating position per se, but rather because those who select these seats are more eager to begin with. To examine this possibility, researchers have randomly assigned students to seats. Still, those closest to the instructor participate most (Caproni et al., 1977; Levine et al., 1980; Schwebel & Cherlin, 1972). In addition there seems to be a slight tendency for those seated front and center to obtain higher

Traditional straight-rowed classroom *(above)* remodeled as "soft" classroom (*below*). Which do you prefer? At the University of California, Davis, 7 percent rated their straight-rowed room as "excellent." In the several semesters after the remodeling, nearly 80 percent rated the same room as excellent. (From Sommer & Olsen, 1980.) (Photos courtesy of Robert Sommer.)

grades and enjoy the course more than those in the back and on the sides (F. D. Becker et al., 1973; Stires, 1980; but not Levine et al., 1980).

In short, architects and professors can design and arrange classrooms that serve varied purposes. And students can choose seats that serve their purposes.

Office Design

In Chapter 13 we noted that people often come to know and like those who are in functional proximity. This suggests some practical advice for office planners who want to encourage cohesive work groups: Arrange clusters of offices that share the same lounge, walkways, and restrooms. When paths cross, friendships tend to form.

Office arrangements vary from private offices to huge rooms with undivided rows of desks. In recent years the "open office plan" has become a popular third alternative (Sundstrom & Sundstrom, 1983). By 1980, furniture designed for the open office plan had captured 50 percent of all office-furniture

When U.S. Senator Mark Hatfield's office was partitioned under the open-office plan, staff productivity increased. (Photographs from Propst, Adams, & Propst, 1977, courtesy of Herman Miller Research, Inc.)

Dormitory sleeping lofts increase usable floor space and create semiprivate study spaces underneath. (Photograph courtesy of Hope College.)

sales (Root, 1980; Ruff, 1980). Movable partitions give each worker a semiprivate work space at considerably less expense than an individual office. Although partitioned rooms are less quiet and private than individual offices, several experiments reveal that partitioning an undivided room alleviates stress and feelings of crowding, and may also increase workers' satisfaction and productivity (Desor, 1972; Gaskie, 1980; Nicosia et al., 1979). Partitions help by defining each person's territory and by restricting people's visual access to one another.

On some campuses, students have invented a way to partition semiprivate study spaces while adding floor space to their dormitory rooms. When they construct lofts for their beds, the area underneath the beds becomes a small but well-defined territory for study. This area is usually highly organized and personalized, and sometimes even curtained for added privacy. Furthermore, the loft arrangement opens the middle of the room into a minilounge area for relaxing (Wichman & Healy, 1979).

We have considered ways to create environments that are both pleasant and productive. Now let's ponder one example of how we might preserve and protect the natural environment that we have.

ENERGY CONSERVATION

Announcing his energy program, President Carter in 1977 called upon Americans to fight "the moral equivalent of war." Surveyed after this plea, a slight majority of Americans agreed that the energy crisis was indeed real (Olsen, 1981). Yet the troops did not rush to the battlefront. Rather, the calls for energy conservation seemed to produce nothing more than an agreeable nod. People proceeded to consume more energy than ever.

"I know many of you are bitter at our generation for using all of the oil reserves. But I would like to remind you of one thing. It was our oil and our gas, and we could do anything we wanted with it. Your generation has to find its own oil and gas reserves."

Art Buchwald at Georgetown University

Since 1977, the benefits of conservation have become more apparent. As energy costs inflate, conservation saves more and more money for the individual. And for a society that needs time to develop alternative energy sources, conservation's benefits are immediate and without the risks that some believe accompany coal burning and nuclear fusion. It is also apparent that some people consume far more energy than others. People living in identical houses use widely varying amounts of energy, and when the occupants of a house change, energy consumption may go sharply up or down (Darley, Seligman, & Becker, 1979). So though conservation is desirable, some people are conserving far less than others.

Policymakers would like to motivate us all to conserve, but so far their persuasive efforts have not been notably successful. Would attention to the psychological dynamics underlying energy use help? Recently, research teams at Princeton University, the University of Colorado, and elsewhere have drawn from social psychology's stockpile of principles in devising some strategies that seem to work. Let us sample a few of their many findings.

Energy Attitudes and Behavior

During the 1970s most appeals to conserve sought to persuade people that because the energy crisis was real, we should all voluntarily conserve. The assumption was that such appeals would change people's attitudes about energy consumption, and that such change would trigger them to change their behavior. Certainly this was President Carter's hope when he summoned us to the "war on energy."

To confirm this assumption's accuracy, many researchers have studied the linkage between people's general attitudes toward energy (for example, their belief that there is a serious energy crisis) and their energy-conserving behavior. To the astonishment of many, no such attitude-behavior linkage appeared (Olsen, 1981). People's broad attitudes concerning the energy crisis and the desirability of conservation were unrelated to their own energy consumption.

Does this finding astonish you? Perhaps you recall from Chapter 2 that general attitudes are seldom good predictors of behavior. So it should not have surprised us that appeals to conserve energy had little effect.

However, perhaps you recall also that one's attitude toward a specific behavior usually better predicts that behavior. And sure enough, Clive Seligman and his co-workers (1979; Becker et al., 1981) found that people who felt that a warm house in winter or a cool house in summer was essential for their personal comfort and health did indeed use more energy than their neighbors.

Perhaps, then, persuasive appeals might be more successful if they attacked the specific attitudes that underlie energy consumption. Inform people that hot houses in winter and cool houses in summer are *not* better for their health. Persuade them that sweaters in winter and fans in summer can provide much the same comfort at less cost. Encourage fashion designers to offer white-collar males more efficient alternatives to the year-round formula of shirt, tie, long trousers, and jacket (Rholes, 1981). (Perhaps men could learn from women's freer dress norms, which allow sweaters in winter and sleeveless blouses and sandals in summer.) Door-to-door personal appeals and home energy checks could respond to people's individual apprehensions about energy conservation. In neighborhoods where Seattle City Light undertook one such program, electricity consumption dropped 9 percent (Olsen, 1981).

In Chapter 2 we also noted that general attitudes can trigger action *if* people's attention is drawn to them. Lacking such reminders, good intentions often lie dormant. Lawrence Becker and Clive Seligman (1978) devised and tested one reminder with willing New Jersey residents. When the outside air temperature dropped below 68°F while the air conditioner was running, a blue light began blinking in the kitchen. Those given this very specific appeal—in essence, "Conserve *now*, by turning off the air conditioner"—consumed 16 percent less electricity than comparable households without the device.

Finally, we noted previously how attitudes are strengthened by making a public commitment. Michael Pallak, David Cook, and John Sullivan (1980) found that public commitment can provide a similar boost to conservation. Iowa City residents who agreed to have their names publicized as attempting to conserve used less energy in the year following than did those who also agreed to conserve but were told their names would not be mentioned.

Feedback

Another way to help laudable attitudes become laudable behavior is to give people feedback on their behavior. Tell them how they are doing relative to their previous consumption, relative to other people's consumption, or relative to some goal. Becker, Seligman, and John Darley (1979) note that such feedback is to an energy diet what the bathroom scale is to a food diet. Someone unconcerned about losing weight will be unaffected by stepping on the scale. But for someone who wants to reduce, the scale is essential; it provides encouragement either to continue or to intensify one's efforts.

For the energy dieter, how can feedback best be provided? One's monthly gasoline-credit-card bill provides feedback, though feedback that is remote from the day's joyride or extra trip to the store. The social dilemma that seduces us into depleting scarce resources arises partly because we find the lure of immediate personal benefits more compelling than our knowledge of ultimate costs. So, maybe we should make the costs immediate, too. Would people be more conscious of the cost of gas consumption if cars came not only with trip odometers, indicating mileage, but also with cost meters, indicating the estimated gasoline cost of each trip?

Many recent experiments confirm that if people are motivated to conserve, then prompt, effective feedback can enable them to achieve energy savings of 10 to 15 percent. For example, in addition to their usual oil bill, Burleigh Seaver and Arthur Patterson (1976) gave some Pennsylvania residents monthly information comparing their rate of consumption to that during the same period of the previous year. When they were also informed of the dollars saved or lost by virtue of their decreased or increased consumption and were given praise for conserving, their savings were significant.

In his research with New Jersey residents, Lawrence Becker (1978) made feedback more immediate. In one experiment, he asked some residents to commit themselves to a goal: Cut back by 20 percent. Then three times a week the experimenters taped a chart to the residents' patio doors, showing them how they were doing (see Figure 15-7). Those given both the goal and the feedback used 13 percent less electricity than a control group given neither.

Becker's experiment confirms the principle that those desiring to go on an energy diet need feedback that gauges their success. But to implement it nationwide would require an army of feedback givers. Could we automate the feedback? Perhaps one way would be to install a device inside the home that would continuously display electricity usage—not in kilowatt-hours but, like our imaginary automobile cost meter, in dollars and cents. One such device has been tested in several experiments. It displays in red digital numbers the cost per hour of one's current level of electricity use.

Would this device make a difference if it were used in your home? In experiments, the evidence is mixed. Becker and his co-workers found that, despite glowing testimonies from some users, the cost meter had no effect on actual energy use (Becker et al., 1979). But when the device was installed in some all-electric homes in North Carolina, Lou McClelland and Stuart Cook (1979–1980) observed an eleven-month electricity savings of 12 percent.

Note that the device provides immediate feedback but does not allow residents to compare their present and past consumption. To continue our dieting analogy, it is like a device that would tell dieters how many calories they were consuming at any instant without letting them know whether their total body weight was going up or down. We can speculate that perhaps such a dietary device would be more useful in combination with a bathroom scale. And that perhaps the cost meter would be more useful if combined with a computerized monthly bill that, based on the weather and one's past consumption, compared predicted usage with actual usage.

One further suggestion of the importance of feedback comes from a very large residential group that receives no feedback about their usage—those who live in master-metered apartment buildings with energy costs paid by

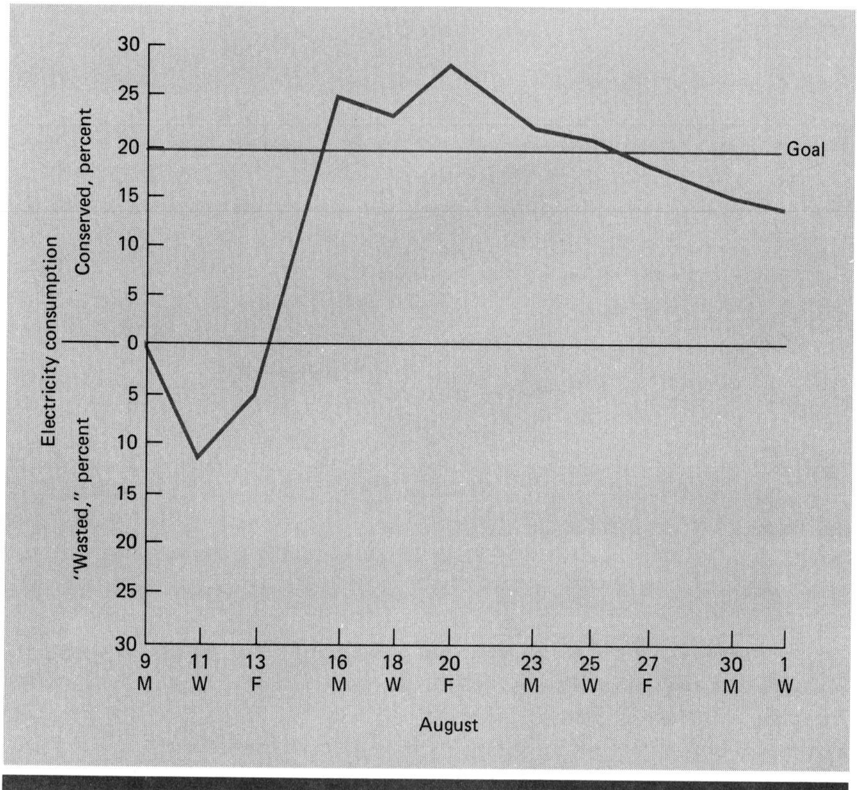

FIGURE 15-7 Example of chart used to give residents feedback on their electricity consumption during the air conditioning season. Taking into account the outdoor temperature and their own past usage, the chart indicated whether the household increased or decreased its energy use. (From Becker, Seligman, & Darley, 1979.)

the landlord. This is another instance of the commons dilemma. For even if the landlord divides the energy costs among all the building's tenants, any given tenant can still free-ride on the rest of the group, reasoning that he or she will pay virtually nothing for an extra few hours of air conditioning. Not surprisingly, master-metered apartment buildings use about 25 percent more energy than comparable individually metered buildings (McClelland & Cook, 1980; Darley et al., 1979).

All in all it seems clear that, given a motive to conserve, users are helped when given feedback that informs them how they are doing relative to their own past consumption.

Might comparison with other consumers also boost conservation? In the Chapter 3 discussion of the self-serving bias we noted that few people perceive themselves as energy gluttons; most believe they already are using less electricity than their average neighbor. Then in the Chapter 9 discussion of group polarization we noted what can happen when people favor a given course of action, but each thinks he or she favors it more than most others: Comparing their positions with one another often accentuates their leanings. So, since most people favor conservation, and think they practice it more than most others, would learning others' energy use accentuate conservation? Michael Pallak and his associates (1980) provided such social comparison information and found that it did, by more than 15 percent.

SUMMING UP

Environmental psychologists apply psychology's concepts and methods in their study of the interrelations between human behavior and the physical environment. This chapter examined three environmental concerns to which social psychology has been applied.

Crowding

Human *density* is a physical measure—the amount of space per person. *Crowding* is the stressful feeling that there's not enough space for the number of people. For several reasons, dense conditions are often arousing or even stressful. When strangers invade the *personal space* immediately around our bodies, we feel uncomfortable. Being crammed in dense traffic or a dense room *constrains* our behavior. Attempting to attend simultaneously to many other people may cause *stimulus overload*. In short, it is arousing to sense a *loss of control*.

There are two views of how density affects us. Advocates of the *density-intensity* principle state that density will intensify people's typical reactions to a situation, positive or negative. Others believe that high density is far more often a negative, *stressful* experience. They point not only to laboratory experiments, but also to the social disorganization that often accompanies population density in cities, prisons, and tripled dormitory rooms.

Architecture and Social Behavior

The way we shape our living and working spaces shapes us in return. High-rise apartments and dormitories often create an impersonal environment that encourages crime and discourages altruism. But the actual design of the structure makes a big difference. For example, students living in long-corridor dormitories tend to feel more crowded, experience more stress, and become more socially withdrawn than those living in short-corridor dorms or in dorms with small suites of rooms.

Classroom seating designs also influence the social atmosphere. In general, eye contact promotes interaction. So students in rooms with straight-row seating tend to discuss less than those with seating arrangements that maximize student-to-student eye contact. Within a given room, those seated with best eye contact with the instructor (for example, front and center) tend to participate most.

Office designers can create office layouts that draw together groups of workers, and that use partitions to create privacy and alleviate crowding.

Energy Conservation

How can people be motivated to conserve their environment? Studies of energy use have yielded many intriguing findings. For example, although people's general attitudes about the energy crisis are unrelated to their own consumption, their more specific attitudes concerning how energy use affects their personal comfort and health do predict their consumption. This explains why general appeals to believe in the crisis and conserve energy have not been notably successful. Among the more promising techniques for promoting conservation is giving people *feedback* on their energy use. Savings of 10 to 15 percent have been achieved when those who desire to conserve are informed about how they are doing relative to their own past consumption or to others' consumption.

Chapter

Social Psychology in Court

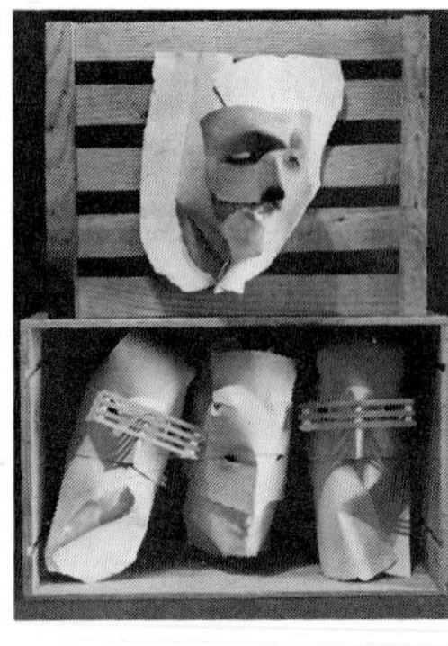

Some days the crowd lined up for courtroom seats before dawn. They were drawn by a real-life soap opera starring Jean Harris, former headmistress of an elite Virginia girls' school and mistress of Herman Tarnower, wealthy author and physician, whom she stood accused of murdering in a jealous rage over his affections for a younger rival. Testifying before the eight women and four men of the jury, Harris maintained that she had gone to Tarnower's home intending to take her own life, and that the fatal shot was fired accidentally as she and Tarnower struggled over the gun (*Newsweek*, 1981).

Would the jury nevertheless attribute the fatal shot to Jean Harris' intent? (They did.) Were they biased, positively or negatively, by her attractiveness and social status? Did they heed the judge's instructions to ignore testimony that had been ruled inadmissible? Did the jurors' preexisting attitudes and personal characteristics prejudice their judgments? After deliberations began, how did the jurors influence one another? Such questions are of great interest to lawyers, judges, and defendants. And they are questions to which social psychology can suggest answers.

Therefore, social psychologists are now studying jurors' judgments, believing that the courtroom offers a context for studying how people form judgments of others, and that social psychology can in turn shed new light on legal questions such as those above. In this chapter, we will see some of what these investigators of social psychology and law have so far concluded.

And we will note how their findings reconfirm many familiar principles of social thinking, social influence, and social relations.

There exists a long list of topics applicable to social psychology and law. For example, in criminal cases, psychological factors may influence decisions involving arrest, interrogation, prosecution, and plea bargaining. Of criminal cases disposed of in U.S. District Courts during 1979, 83 percent never came to trial (U.S. Department of Justice, 1980). Thus, much of the trial lawyer's work "is not persuasion in the courtroom but bargaining in the conference room" (Saks & Hastie, 1978, pp. 119-120). But even in the conference room, decisions are made based on speculations about what a jury or judge might do. Thus in most legal cases, the courtroom plays an important role. Let us therefore focus our attention upon two sets of factors that have been heavily researched: (1) features of the courtroom drama that can influence jurors' judgments of a defendant and (2) the characteristics of both the jurors and their deliberations.

JUDGING THE DEFENDANT

As the courtroom drama unfolds, jurors hear testimony, form impressions of the defendant, listen to instructions from the judge, and render a verdict. Let's take these steps one at a time to see how social psychology can help us understand the jurors' behaviors.

Such research seeks answers to two fundamental questions: First, to what extent do extraneous biases erode the judicial goal of fairness? Second, what reforms could minimize such biases? An aim of the judicial system is to guarantee impartial judgments. Oaths, opposing attorneys, and cross-examinations exist partly to provide fairness. But people, jurors included, are not dispassionate computing machines, so they can be influenced by irrelevant psychological factors.

Eyewitness Testimony

How Persuasive is Eyewitness Testimony?

In Chapter 4 we noted that anecdotes and personal testimonies, being vivid and concrete, can be powerfully persuasive, often more so than information that is logically compelling but abstract. Especially when spoken in the unhesitating straightforward style of "men's speech" (Chapter 6), vivid accounts are hard to resist. There's no better way to end an argument than to say "I saw it with my own eyes!" Seeing is believing.

At the University of Washington, Elizabeth Loftus (1974; 1979a) found that those who had "seen" were indeed believed, even when their testimony was known to be essentially useless. When students were presented with a hypothetical robbery-murder case with circumstantial evidence but no eyewitness testimony, only 18 percent voted for conviction. Others received the same information but with the addition of a single eyewitness testimony; now 72 percent, knowing that someone had declared "That's the one!", voted for conviction. A third group received the same information as this second group, except that the testimony was discredited by the defense attorney (the witness had but 20/400 vision and was not wearing glasses at the moment of the crime). To what extent did this discrediting reduce the effect of the testimony? Hardly at all—68 percent still voted for conviction. Attempts to replicate this disturbing finding have met with uneven success, suggesting that sometimes eyewitnesses can be effectively discredited (Cavoukian, 1980; Hatvany & Strack, 1980; Saunders & Vidmar, 1981; Weinberg & Baron, 1980; 1981). Still, a vivid eyewitness description of what transpired often seems difficult to erase once pictured in the jurors' minds.

Experiments at the University of Alberta reinforced this conclusion. Gary Wells, R. C. L. Lindsay, and their colleagues staged the theft of a calculator hundreds of times before individual eyewitnesses. Afterward, each eyewitness was asked to identify the culprit from a photo lineup. Other people, acting as jurors, then observed the eyewitnesses being questioned and evaluated their testimony. Are eyewitnesses who make incorrect identifications believed less often than those who are accurate? To the contrary, Wells, Lindsay, and Tamara Ferguson (1979) found that both correct and incorrect eyewitnesses were believed 80 percent of the time. This led them to speculate categorically "that human observers have absolutely no ability to discern eyewitnesses who have mistakenly identified an innocent person" (Wells, Lindsay, & Tousignant, 1980).

In a follow-up experiment Lindsay, Wells, and Carolyn Rumpel (1981) staged the theft under conditions that sometimes allowed witnesses a good, long look at the thief and sometimes not. The jurors believed the questioned witnesses more when witnessing conditions were good. But even when witnessing conditions were so poor that two-thirds of the witnesses had actually misidentified an innocent person, 62 percent of the jurors still usually believed the witnesses.

In yet another experiment, Wells and Michael Leippe (1981) found that jurors were more skeptical of eyewitnesses whose memory for trivial details had been tested in cross-examination. However, the cross-examination did most to discredit the *accurate* witnesses, whose memories of trivial details actually were poorer than the memories of those who had misidentified the culprit. Jurors seemed to think that a witness who could remember that there were three pictures hanging in the room must have "really been paying attention." Actually, those who paid attention to such details were *less* likely to have paid attention to the culprit's face.

Though the lesson of this research is predictable from our earlier consideration of the persuasive power of vivid information, it is nonetheless sobering that jurors find eyewitnesses quite persuasive, even those whose testimony is inaccurate.

BEHIND THE SCENES

Gary L. Wells

When I first thought of testing how well people could detect the inaccuracy of false eyewitness testimony, I barely considered the possibility that people would be functionally incapable of discriminating between accurate and false eyewitness identifications. I did expect that people would rely too heavily on the eyewitnesses' confidence, which my colleagues and I had earlier shown to be a useless predictor of eyewitness accuracy. However, as the experiments progressed, the excitement grew. It is now clear that a centuries-old assumption of the criminal justice system does not hold up to empirical scrutiny.

I consider this research to be part of a larger interest in social psychology, an interest in helping criminal-justice officials clarify and refine their assumptions about human behavior and cognition. Indeed, students of social psychology would do well to note that the criminal-justice system operates on a large number of assumptions about human behavior and cognition that are yet to be tested. That is the excitement of social psychology in court. *(Gary L. Wells, University of Alberta)*

How Accurate Are Eyewitnesses?

Are eyewitness testimonies, in fact, often inaccurate? Stories abound of innocent people who have wasted years in prison because of the erroneous testimony of eyewitnesses—witnesses who were sincere, but sincerely wrong (Brandon & Davies, 1973). (See Box 16-1.) Still, given the thousands of criminal trials each year, even several dozen such cases wouldn't establish that eyewitness accounts are not to be trusted. Whether assessing the accuracy of eyewitnesses' recollections or psychics' predictions, one needs to ascertain their overall "hit" and "miss" rates. One way to gather such information is to stage crimes comparable to those in everyday life and later solicit eyewitness reports.

This has now been done many times, with disconcerting results. For example, at the California State University, Hayward, 141 students witnessed an assault on a professor. Seven weeks later, when Robert Buckhout (1974) asked them to identify the assailant from a group of six photographs, 60 percent chose an innocent person. So it's not surprising that eyewitnesses to actual crimes frequently disagree about what they witnessed.

Of course, some witnesses are more confident than others. And Wells and his colleagues report that it's the confident witnesses whom jurors find

Box 16-1

Mistaken Identity

Fifty years ago, Yale law professor Edwin Borchard (1932) documented sixty-five convictions of people whose innocence was ultimately established beyond a doubt. Most resulted from mistaken identifications of the culprit by eyewitnesses. Borchard observed that

> In several of the cases the convicted prisoner, later proved innocent, was saved from hanging or electrocution by a hairbreadth. Only by rare good fortune were some of the sentences of hanging and electrocution commuted to life imprisonment or indictments for first-degree murder modified by verdicts of second-degree murder, so that the error could still be corrected. How many wrongfully convicted persons have actually been executed, it is impossible to say. (pp. xviii-xix)

most believable. Thus it is disconcerting that unless witnessing conditions are very favorable, eyewitnesses' "certainty" is unrelated to their accuracy (Deffenbacher, 1980; Leippe, 1980; Brigham et al., 1982). Incorrect witnesses express considerable confidence in their judgments, virtually as much as correct witnesses. The overconfidence phenomenon rides again.

Overconfidence phenomenon: *See Chapter 4, pages 117–120.*

Sources of Error Errors sneak into our perceptions and our memories because our minds are not videotape machines. Rather, we construct our memories, based partly on what we perceived at the time and partly on our expectations, beliefs, and current knowledge. (See Figures 16-1 and 16-2.)

Elizabeth Loftus, David Miller, and Helen Burns (1978) provide a dramatic demonstration of memory construction. University of Washington students were shown thirty slides depicting successive stages of an automobile-pedestrian accident. One critical slide showed a red Datsun, stopped either at a stop or at a yield sign. (See Figure 16-3.) Afterward, the students were asked questions, among which was, for half of them, "Did another car pass the red Datsun while it was stopped at the stop sign?" The other half were asked the same question but with the words "stop sign" replaced by "yield sign." Later, when shown both slides in Figure 16-3 and asked which one they had previously seen, those previously asked the question consistent with what they had seen were 75 percent correct. But those previously asked the misleading question were only 41 percent correct; more often than not, they denied seeing what they had actually seen and instead "remembered" a picture they had never seen! In other experiments, Loftus (1979a) has found that after suggestive questioning, witnesses may believe that a red light was actually green or that a robber had a mustache when he didn't. When interrogating

FIGURE 16-1 Cultural expectations affect perceiving, remembering, and reporting. In a 1947 experiment on rumor transmission, Gordon Allport and Leo Postman showed people this picture of a white man holding a razor blade and then had them tell a second person about it, who then told a third person, and so on. After six tellings, the razor blade in the white man's hand usually shifted to the black man's. (From "Eyewitness Testimony" by Robert Buckhout. Copyright © 1974 by Scientific American, Inc. All rights reserved.)

FIGURE 16-2 Expectations affect perception. Is the drawing on the right a face or figure? (From Fisher, 1968, adapted by Loftus, 1979.) (Drawing by Anne Canevari Green.)

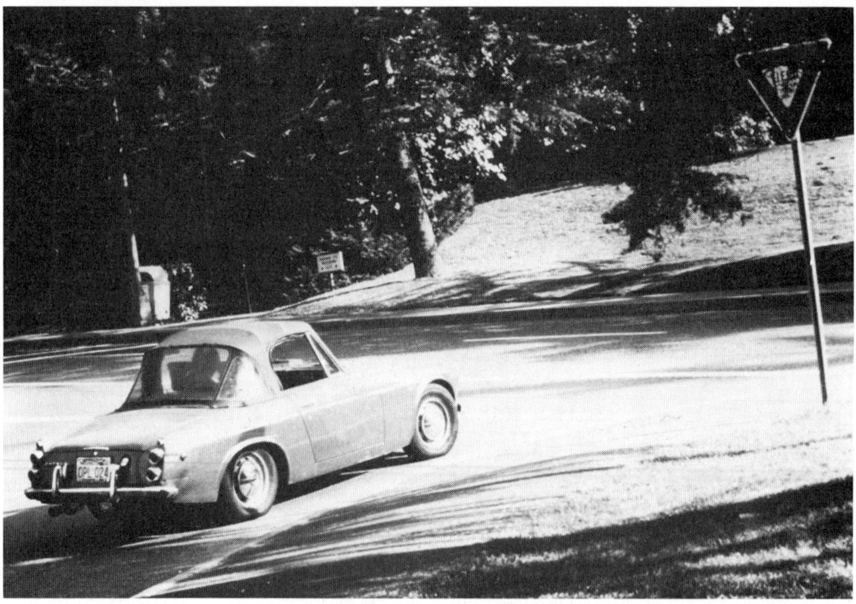

FIGURE 16-3 When shown one of these two pictures and then asked a question suggesting the sign not seen, most people later "remembered" seeing the nonexistent object. (From Loftus, Miller, & Burns, 1978.) (Photos courtesy of Elizabeth Loftus.)

eyewitnesses, police and attorneys commonly ask questions that are framed by their own understanding of what transpired. So it is troubling to discover how easily witnesses incorporate misleading information into their memories.

Retelling the events commits people to their own version of the story, and can further harden their construction of it. Perhaps you can recall a time when the more you retold a story the more you convinced yourself of what turned out to be a falsehood. Wells, Ferguson, and Lindsay (1981) demonstrated this by having some eyewitnesses to a staged theft rehearse their answers to questions before taking the witness stand. Doing so increased the confidence of those who were inaccurate, and thus made jurors who heard their false testimony more likely to vote the innocent person guilty.

Chapter 2 noted that people tend to adjust what they say to please their listeners and, having done so, often come to believe their altered message. Keeping this in mind, imagine that you witnessed an argument that erupted into a fight in which one person injured the other. Afterward, the injured party sues the other, and prior to the trial a smooth lawyer for one of the two parties interviews you. Might you slightly adjust your testimony, giving a version of the fight that tends to support this lawyer's client? If you did so, might your later recollections in court be similarly slanted? Blair Sheppard and Neil Vidmar (1980) report that the answers to these questions are "yes." At the University of Western Ontario, they had some students serve as witnesses to a fight and others as lawyers and judges. When interviewed by lawyers for the defendant rather than the plaintiff, the witnesses later gave the judge testimony that was more favorable to the defendant.

"A leading question is simply one that, either by its form or content, suggests to the witness what answer is desired or leads him to the desired answer. . . . While the rules of evidence and other safeguards provide protection in the courtroom, they are absent in the backroom of the precinct station."

Ernest Hilgard & Elizabeth Loftus (1979)

Reducing Error Given these error-prone tendencies, what constructive steps can be taken to increase the accuracy of eyewitnesses and jurors? Eyewitness experts such as Wells and Loftus have several ideas. For example, when police first interview eyewitnesses they should let them tell the story in their own words. Unprompted recollections are most accurate (Lipton, 1977). Then they should ask specific questions, but treat the answers skeptically. Moreover, they should keep such questions free of hidden assumptions. For example, Loftus and Guido Zanni (1975) report that questions such as "Did you see the broken headlight?" trigger twice as many "memories" of nonexistent events as questions without the hidden assumption: "Did you see a broken headlight?"

Researchers have also found that accuracy improves when witnesses are interviewed soon after the event, when their memories are not distorted by scanning mug shots or assisting with composite drawing before trying to identify the culprit in a lineup, and when the lineup is not biased against an innocent suspect who happens to fit the culprit's general description.

The case of Ron Shatford illustrates how the composition of a lineup can promote misidentification (Doob & Kirshenbaum, 1973). After a suburban Toronto department store robbery, the cashier involved could only recall that

FIGURE 16-4 An innocent suspect who fits the culprit's general description is more likely to be misidentified when placed in a lineup with others not fitting the same general description. (Drawing by Anne Canevari Green.)

the culprit was not wearing a tie and was "very neatly dressed and rather good looking." Nevertheless, when the good-looking Shatford was placed in a lineup with eleven unattractive men, all of whom wore ties, the cashier readily identified him as the culprit. Only after Shatford served fifteen months of a long sentence did another person confess, allowing Shatford to be retried and found not guilty.

Finally, experts on this research occasionally give testimony about eyewitness testimony (Fishman & Loftus, 1978). They offer jurors the sort of information that you have just been reading, thus helping them critically evaluate the testimony of both prosecution and defense witnesses. They explain that eyewitnesses often perceive events selectively, that subsequent discussions about the events can alter or add to their memories, that research using staged crimes has shown that witnesses often choose a wrong person from a lineup, that eyewitnesses are especially prone to error when trying to identify someone of another race (see Chapter 12), and that jurors should disregard the confidence with which an eyewitness offers testimony. Experiments (Hosch, Beck, & McIntyre, 1980; Loftus, 1980; Wells, Lindsay, & Tousignant, 1980) show that such testimony can prompt jurors to analyze eyewitness testimonies more skeptically and discuss them more fully.

The Defendant's Characteristics

"Jurymen seldom convict a person they like, or acquit one they dislike. The main work of the trial lawyer is to make a jury like his client, or at least to feel sympathy for him." So said the famed trial lawyer, Clarence Darrow (1933). Was he right? Is jurors' liking or disliking the defendant crucial? And is it true, as Darrow also said, that "facts regarding the crime are relatively unimportant"?

Darrow overstated the matter. One study of over 3500 criminal cases and some 4000 civil cases found that 4 times in 5 the judge concurred with the jury's decision (Kalven & Zeisel, 1966). Sometimes this may only indicate that judges and jurors share common biases. Still, usually the evidence is clear enough that jurors can set aside their differing personal sympathies and readily agree on a verdict (Saks & Hastie, 1978). So we needn't be as cynical as Darrow. Facts matter.

But jurors often must make difficult social judgments: Did the defendant commit the offense? If so, was the offense intended? When making difficult judgments, the facts are not all that matter. Inevitably, jurors bring into the courtroom certain stereotypes that influence their instant impressions of the defendant. Can they then lay these preconceived judgments aside and decide the case based on the facts alone? To some extent they surely can and surely do. As you may recall from Chapter 12, once people get to know an individual in a stereotyped group they often lay aside their stereotypes and respond to

"I ask you, Your Honor, does my client look like a crook?"

Other things being equal, socially or physically attractive defendants may be judged more leniently. (Drawing by Modell; © 1980 *The New Yorker* Magazine, Inc.)

the person as an individual. But analyses of actual cases suggest that some bias often persists. For example, defendants with high socioeconomic status sometimes get lenient treatment (McGillis, 1979).

Actual cases can vary in so many ways (for example, status, age, race, type of crime) that it's hard to be sure which factor is responsible. So experimenters have controlled such factors by giving people the same basic facts of a case while varying just one of the defendant's characteristics, such as physical attractiveness or similarity to the jurors. Taking the experiments using attractiveness and similarity, let us see what these revealed.

Physical Attractiveness

Chapter 13 described the physical attractiveness stereotype: Beautiful people are good people. Michael Efran (1974) wondered whether this stereotype might bias students' judgments of another student who was accused of cheating. He asked some of his University of Toronto students whether attractiveness should affect one's presumption of guilt. Their answer: "No, it shouldn't." But did it? Yes. When Efran gave other students a description of the case with a photograph of either an attractive or an unattractive defendant, the accused who were most attractive were judged least guilty and recommended for least punishment.

Other experimenters have confirmed that justice is not blind to a defendant's physical attractiveness (Cash, 1981). Nor is it blind to the defendant's social attractiveness; in experiments, defendants believed to be warm and selfless, for example, are less often judged guilty and are sentenced more leniently than those who come across as cold and self-centered (for example, Weiten, 1980). There are, however, limits to the effect of the attractiveness. Harold Sigall and Nancy Ostrove (1975) showed University of Maryland students either an attractive or unattractive woman who was said either to have committed a burglary or to have charmed a middle-aged bachelor into giving her $2200 to invest in a nonexistent corporation. Asked to sentence the woman, those given the burglary case sentenced the attractive woman much more leniently; those given the swindle case were, if anything, more lenient with the unattractive woman. In the swindle case, attractiveness could facilitate the crime. So it seems that if attractiveness is perceived to be helpful in committing a crime, then it does not benefit the defendant to be attractive.

Note: *Generally, juries determine guilt, not punishment. As a further indication of attitudes toward the accused, experimenters nevertheless sometimes ask their jurors also to recommend a sentence.*

We have so far seen that when experimenters present people with a fixed but meagre amount of evidence, defendants' looks do indeed affect the judgments they receive. But this is a far cry from real defendants facing real judges and jurors in real trials. So John Stewart (1980) had observers go into Pennsylvania criminal courtrooms and rate the defendants' physical attractiveness. When sentences were handed down, the physically attractive defendants were no more likely to be judged innocent, but when found guilty, they did receive slightly shorter sentences. Of course, as with all such correlational findings, some other factor perhaps associated with attractiveness (for example, a steady job) could also have triggered the shorter sentences.

Ideally, justice is blind. (Drawing by Anne Canevari Green.)

Similarity to the Jurors

If Clarence Darrow was even partially right in his declaration that one's liking for a defendant colors one's judgments, then other factors that influence one's liking for a person should also have an impact in the courtroom. Among such influences is the principle of similarity-attraction: Likeness leads to liking. So it probably will not surprise you that when people pretend they are jurors, they are more sympathetic to a defendant who shares their attitudes, religion, race, or (in cases of sexual assault) gender (for example, Griffitt & Jackson, 1973; Ugwuegbu, 1979; Selby, Calhoun, & Brock, 1977). More generally, someone who causes a severe accident is judged less responsible if made to appear similar to the one who judges (Burger, 1981).

To see one reason why this might be, recall from Chapter 3 the fundamental attribution error—a tendency when explaining *others'* behavior to attribute it so much to their inner dispositions that important situational factors get discounted. When judging our own behavior, we are more sensitive to situational pressures; hence, we are usually not so quick to blame ourselves for mistakes and negative behavior. Perhaps, then, people who can identify with a defendant tend to blame the defendant less or believe the defendant less likely to repeat the crime. This is similar to what Kelly Shaver (1970) has called "defensive attribution"; we sometimes defend ourselves against feeling vulnerable to catastrophes by attributing less blame to people who are similar to ourselves.

Blinding the Jurors

"Jurors will introduce into their verdict a certain amount—a very large amount, so far as I have observed— of popular prejudice, and thus keep the administration of the law in accord with the wishes and feelings of the community."

Oliver Wendell Holmes (1889)

Some have argued that it's okay for jurors to be biased, for such bias reflects the conscience of their community (Brooks & Doob, 1975). For example, community values are important in determining what is pornography, and in determining when prosecutors are being fair in their enforcement of an unpopular law. But apart from representing community values and presuming "innocent until proven guilty," we hold that jurors should be objective. Ideally, they should leave their other biases outside the courtroom door and begin a trial with blank minds. So implies the Sixth Amendment to the U.S. Constitution: "the accused shall enjoy the right to a speedy and public trial by impartial jury."

How, then, might we minimize the effects of jurors' biases? In experiments at Northern Illinois University, researchers Martin Kaplan and Cynthia Schersching (1980) have found that when the facts of a case are undisputed, the jurors' own biases have much less effect than when the evidence is ambiguous. Moreover, anything that focuses jurors' attention on the evidence seems to lessen the effects of their biases. Discussing the case does this. Kaplan and Schersching speculate that allowing jurors to take notes or view videotapes of testimony might further minimize the effects of their personal biases.

To forewarn new jurors of potential biases, Daniel McGillis (1979) suggests having their orientation sessions draw upon social-psychological research. However, could there be an even simpler remedy? Judges do commonly instruct jurors when to ignore biasing information. Could it be

"The jury will disregard the witness's last remarks."

It's not easy for jurors to erase inadmissible testimony from memory. (Drawing by Lorenz; © 1977 *The New Yorker* Magazine, Inc.)

sufficient for the judge to remind the jurors that "the issue is not whether you like or dislike the defendant, but whether the defendant committed the offense"?

How Effective Are the Judge's Instructions?

Likely all of us can recall courtroom dramas in which an attorney exclaimed, "Your honor, I object!" whereupon the judge sustained the objection and ordered the jury to ignore the other attorney's suggestive question or the witness's remark. For example, nearly all states in the U.S. now have "rape shield" statutes that prohibit or limit testimony concerning the victim's prior sexual activity. [Such testimony, though deemed irrelevant to the case at hand, tends to make jurors more sympathetic to the accused rapist's claim that the woman consented to sexual relations (Borgida, 1981; Cann, Calhoun, & Selby, 1979).] If such unreliable, illegal, or prejudicial testimony is nevertheless slipped in by the defense or blurted out by a witness, will jurors follow a judge's instruction to ignore it?

Very possibly not. Several experimenters report that it is hard for jurors to ignore damaging pretrial publicity or inadmissible evidence such as the defendant's previous convictions. In one study, Stanley Sue, Ronald Smith, and Cathy Caldwell (1973) gave University of Washington students a description of a grocery store robbery-murder and a summary of the prosecution's case and the defense's case. When the prosecution's case was weak, no one judged the defendant guilty. When a tape recording of an incriminating phone call made by the defendant was added to the weak case, about one-third judged him guilty. The judge's instructing jurors that the tape was not legal evidence and should be ignored did nothing to erase this effect of the damaging testimony.

Indeed, in an experiment at Duke University, Sharon Wolf and David Montgomery (1977) found that a judge's order to ignore testimony—"It must play no role in your consideration of the case. You have no choice but to disregard it"—can even boomerang, adding to the testimony's impact. Perhaps such statements create reactance in the jurors. Or perhaps they sensitize jurors to the inadmissible testimony, much as happens when I warn you *not* to look at your nose while you read the next sentence.

Reactance: *The desire to assert one's sense of freedom (see Chapter 7, pages 253–254).*

What is more, inadmissible testimony may influence jurors without their being aware of it. William Thompson, Geoffrey Fong, and David Rosenhan (1981) had people watch videotaped, simulated trials in which testimony obtained from a telephone wiretap was sometimes introduced and ruled inadmissible. Those who heard inadmissible evidence suggesting guilt thought they were influenced by it, but were not. (Apparently they sensed that the testimony was compelling, so they resisted it.) Those who heard inadmissible evidence suggesting innocence thought they had *not* been influenced, but they were. This illustrates one of the lessons of Chapter 4: People sometimes do not know why they act and feel as they do—which, of course, is why social

The courtroom of the future? (Illustration by Marvin Mattelson. Reprinted from *Psychology Today* Magazine. Copyright © 1972 Ziff-Davis Publishing Company.)

psychologists do experiments rather than merely relying upon people's introspections.

As this last experiment and several others suggest, a judge's instructions are not always ignored (R. L. Archer et al., 1979; Kerr et al., 1976). After all, on legal issues the judge is perceived as credible, of high status, impartial. Moreover, in actual trials the nature of the case and the way the judge admonishes the jury vary widely, so we had best be cautious in generalizing from the few available experiments. However, this much we can say: In light of the available research and all else we know about how people form and sustain their impressions of others, it is surely easier to strike inadmissible testimony from the court record than from the jurors' minds. As trial lawyers sometimes say, "You can't unring a bell."

What then can judges do to minimize the impact of inadmissible evidence?

Since forewarning people about an impending persuasive appeal tends to diminish its impact (see Chapter 8), judges might warn jurors about the credibility and admissibility of various types of evidence (Cavoukian & Doob, 1980). Initial impressions, once formed, can be difficult to erase and may color one's interpretation of later information. Thus when Saul Kassin and Lawrence Wrightsman (1979) showed University of Kansas students a one-hour videotaped trial with the judge afterward strongly reminding them of "innocence until proven guilty," 59 percent judged the accused thief guilty—hardly different from the 63 percent who found him guilty when the judge gave no such admonition. When the judge gave the same admonition *before* the trial, only 37 percent voted for conviction. Similarly, Eugene Borgida and Phyllis White (1980) found Minnesota jurors more likely to judge an accused rapist guilty if before as well as after the trial they were reminded that the victim's prior sexual history is irrelevant.

A more complete solution is simply to eliminate inadmissible testimony before the jurors hear it—by videotaping witnesses' testimony and removing objectionable material. If future research confirms the findings of recent experiments—that live and videotaped testimony have much the same impact—then perhaps we can anticipate courtrooms replete with life-size television monitors (G. R. Miller & Fontes, 1979b).

"We find the videotaped trial format not guilty *of any charges of detrimental effects on juror responses."*

Gerald Miller et al. (1974)

In Erie County, Ohio, monitors have been used already. In one-third of the civil cases tried from 1975 to 1979, witnesses were prerecorded (Miller & Fontes, 1979a). Courts in other states are doing the same. Critics object that the procedure prevents jurors from observing how the defendant and others react to the witness. Proponents argue that videotaping not only enables the judge to edit out inadmissible testimony but also speeds up the trial and allows witnesses to talk about crucial events before their memories fade further.

Thus far we have considered three courtroom factors—eyewitness testimony, the defendant's characteristics, and the judge's instructions. Researchers are also studying the influence of many other factors. For example, at Michigan State University, Norbert Kerr (1978a; 1978b; 1981) is researching such issues as: Might a severe potential punishment (for example, a death penalty) make jurors less willing to convict? Do experienced jurors' actions or judgments differ from those of novice jurors? Are defendants judged more harshly when the *victim* is attractive or has suffered greatly? Kerr's research suggests that the answer to all three questions is yes.

THE JURY

These courtroom influences upon "the average juror" are worth pondering. But most jurors are not "the average juror." They carry into the courthouse their individual attitudes and personalities, and when deliberating they influence one another. A key question is, how are their verdicts influenced by their individual dispositions and by their working together as a group?

The Jurors as Individuals

A close case can be decided by *who* gets selected for the jury. For example, in criminal cases people who do not oppose the death penalty—and who therefore are eligible to serve in cases where a death sentence is possible—are more prone to favor the prosecution (for example, see Cowan, Thompson, & Ellsworth, 1982). Thus if the court excuses potential jurors who are strongly opposed to the death penalty, it may also be composing a jury that leans toward conviction. Conviction-prone jurors tend also to be more authoritarian—more rigid, punitive, and contemptuous of those with lower status (Gerbasi, Zuckerman, & Reis, 1977; Kaplan & Schersching, 1980; Moran & Comfort, 1982).

"The kind of juror who would be unperturbed by the prospect of sending a man to his death . . . is the kind of juror who would too readily ignore the presumption of the defendant's innocence, accept the prosecution's version of the facts, and return a verdict of guilty."

Witherspoon v. Illinois, *1968*

Judges, too, vary widely in their attitudes, and in their sentencing practices. It is rather embarrassing to the ideal of impartiality that, given similar cases, two judges can pronounce drastically different penalties. But since each case *is* unique, maybe sentencing differences justly reflect the differing circumstances of different cases. To test this possibility, researchers have posed the *same* cases to different judges. Still the sentences vary in ways that could only be deemed unfair to those unfortunate enough to be assigned a harsh judge. For example, when fifty federal judges were asked to sentence someone for theft and possession of stolen goods, their sentences ranged from probation to $7\frac{1}{2}$ years in prison (Partridge & Eldridge, 1974). One way to reduce such variability might be to have judges fill in sentencing forms that indicate the average sentence for the crime committed and ask them to decide how much they wish to deviate from this norm. Defining an appropriate sentence norm does, however, require more consensus than now exists on the *purpose* of sentencing. Is it to protect the public? Or also to consider the well being of the convicted?

Given the variations among individual jurors, could trial lawyers use the jury selection processes to stack a jury in their favor? Often attorneys are severely limited in what questions they can ask prospective jurors. Nevertheless, legal folklore suggests they can sometimes "stack the jury." A recent president of the Association of Trial Lawyers of America boldly proclaimed, "Trial attorneys are acutely attuned to the nuances of human behavior, which enables them to detect the minutest traces of bias or inability to reach an appropriate decision" (Bigam, 1977).

Mindful of how error-prone people's subjective assessments of others tend to be (see Chapter 5), social psychologists are skeptical of the claim that attorneys come equipped with fine-tuned social Geiger counters. In several celebrated trials, survey researchers therefore assisted attorneys by using "scientific jury selection" to weed out potential jurors likely to be unsympathetic. For example, in a famous trial involving two of President Nixon's former cabinet members, John Mitchell and Maurice Stans, a survey revealed that from the defense's point of view the worst possible juror was "a liberal, Jewish, Democrat who reads the *New York Times* or the *Post*, listens to Walter Cronkite, is interested in political affairs, and is well-informed about Watergate" (Zeisel & Diamond, 1976). In nine trials where the defense is known to have relied on such methods, it has won seven (Wrightsman, 1978; Hans & Vidmar, 1982).

Despite the excitement—and ethical concern—about scientific jury selection, systematic experiments by Steven Penrod (1981) reveal that jurors' general attitudes and personal characteristics are actually poor predictors of their verdicts. Researchers Michael Saks and Reid Hastie (1978) similarly conclude that the composition of the jury is actually a minor determinant of most verdicts, one that at best may tip the scales only in an otherwise close case: "The studies are unanimous in showing that evidence is a substantially more potent determinant of jurors' verdicts than the individual characteristics of jurors" (p. 68). In courtrooms, jurors' public pledge of fairness and the judge's instruction to "be fair" strongly commit most jurors to the norm of fairness. In experiments, it's only when the evidence is made ambiguous that researchers find jurors' personalities and general attitudes having much effect. Variations in the situation, especially in the evidence, generally have far more effect. That echoes a conclusion reached in several previous chapters. As Saks and Hastie explain,

> What this implies about human behavior, on juries or off, is that while we are unique individuals, our differences are vastly overshadowed by our similarities. Moreover, the range of situations we are likely to encounter is far more varied than the range of human beings who will encounter them. (p. 69)

The Jury as a Group

Imagine a jury that, having finished hearing a trial, has entered the jury room to begin its deliberations. Jury researchers Harry Kalven and Hans Zeisel (1966) report that chances are about 2 in 3 that the jurors will initially *not* agree on a verdict. Yet, after discussion, the odds reach almost 95 percent that they will emerge with a consensus. Obviously, group influence has transpired.

Juries are decision-making groups. Are they therefore subject to the social influences that mold other decision groups—to patterns of majority and minority influence, to group polarization, to groupthink? Let's start with a simple question: If we knew the jurors' initial leanings, could we predict their verdict?

Predicting Jury Decisions

The law prohibits observation of actual juries. Therefore, to create their own "mock juries," researchers simulate the jury process by presenting a case to groups of people and having them deliberate as would a real jury. In a series of such studies at the University of Illinois, James Davis, Robert Holt, Norbert Kerr, and Garold Stasser tested various mathematical schemes for predicting group decisions, including decisions by mock juries (J. H. Davis et al., 1975; 1977; Kerr et al., 1976). Will some mathematical combination of people's initial decisions predict their eventual group decision? Davis and his colleagues found that the scheme which predicts best varies according to the nature of the case. But in several experiments, a "two-thirds majority" scheme fared best: The group verdict was usually the alternative favored by at least two-thirds of the jurors at the outset. The lack of such a majority was likely to result in a hung jury.

The experimental findings of Davis and his collaborators fit well the survey findings of Kalven and Zeisel, who report that 9 out of 10 juries reach the verdict favored by the majority on the first ballot. Although you or I might fantasize someday being the courageous lone juror who sways the majority, the fact is it seldom happens.

Minority Influence

Minority influence: *See Chapter 9, pages 327–329.*

Seldom, yet sometimes, the initial minority does prevail. For example, in the Mitchell-Stans trial the four jurors who favored acquittal persisted and eventually prevailed. From the research on minority influence we can speculate that jurors in the minority will be most persuasive when they are consistent, persistent, and self-confident, especially if they can begin to trigger some defections from the majority.

Ironically, the most influential minority juror in the Mitchell-Stans trial, Andrew Choa, was a well-educated *New York Times* reader—someone who did not fit the survey profile of someone likely to be sympathetic to the defense. But Choa was also a dedicated supporter of Richard Nixon and a bank vice-president who ingratiated himself with the other jurors through various favors, such as taking them to movies in his bank's private auditorium. True to the reciprocity norm, the jurors seemed to have given Choa's arguments special attention (Zeisel & Diamond, 1976). Choa also illustrates a finding from jury experiments—that jurors who are male and of high social status tend to be most influential (Gerbasi et al., 1977).

Group Polarization

Jury deliberation seems to shift people's opinions in some other intriguing ways as well. In six different experiments, jurors' initial sentiments have been magnified by their deliberation. For example, Robert Bray and Audrey Noble (1978) had University of Kentucky students listen to a thirty-minute tape of a murder trial and then, assuming the defendant was found guilty, recommend a prison sentence. Groups of high authoritarians initially recommended strong punishments (fifty-six years) and after deliberation were even more punitive (sixty-eight years). The low authoritarian groups were initially more lenient (thirty-eight years) and after deliberation became more so (twenty-nine years). Such findings hint that group polarization can occur in juries.

Group polarization: *See Chapter 9, pages 310–319.*

Juries are groups. Thus they are subject to many of the same influences found in other types of groups. (Wide World Photos)

Leniency

In many experiments, one other curious effect of deliberation has surfaced: Especially when the evidence is not highly incriminating, jurors after deliberating tend to become more lenient (for example, J. H. Davis et al., 1981; Hans, 1981). This qualifies the "two-thirds-majority-rules" finding, for if even a bare majority initially favor acquittal, it usually will prevail (Stasser, Kerr, & Bray, 1981). Moreover, a minority that favors acquittal stands a better chance than one that favors conviction. And once again, a survey of actual juries confirms the laboratory results: Kalven and Zeisel (1966) report that in those cases where the majority does not prevail it usually shifts to acquittal (as in the Mitchell-Stans trial), and that when a judge disagrees with the jury's decision, it is usually because the jury acquits someone whom the judge would have convicted. Might "informational influence" (stemming from others' persuasive arguments) account for the increased leniency? The "innocent-unless-proved-guilty" and "proof-beyond-a-reasonable-doubt" rules put the burden of proof on those who favor conviction, perhaps making evidence of the defendant's innocence more persuasive than that for conviction. Or perhaps "normative influence" creates the leniency effect, as jurors who view themselves as fair-minded confront other jurors who are even more concerned with protecting a possibly innocent defendant.

"It is better that ten guilty persons escape than one innocent suffer."

William Blackstone (1769)

Are Twelve Heads Better Than One?

In Chapter 9 we saw that on thought problems where there is an objective right answer, group rather than individual judgments are more often right. Does such hold true in juries? When deliberating, jurors not only exert normative pressure, trying to budge others' judgments by the sheer weight of their own, they also share information, thus enlarging one another's knowledge of the case. To the extent that informational influence moves jurors, we can hope that a jury's collective judgment will indeed be superior to that of its average member.

The evidence, though meagre, is encouraging. Some of the biases that contaminate the judgments of individual jurors have much less effect after the jurors have deliberated (Kaplan & Schersching, 1980). Deliberation seems not only to cancel out certain biases, but also to draw jurors' attention away from their own prejudgments, and to the evidence.

A court-related example of superior group performance comes from a recent experiment by Dell Warnick and Glenn Sanders (1980). Students at the State University of New York at Albany witnessed a brief, videotaped crime. Later, when they were asked to complete eyewitness questionnaires, those given an opportunity to discuss their observations with others, though no more confident of their reports, were far more accurate. Indeed, several heads were better than one.

Are Six Heads as Good as Twelve?

In keeping with their British heritage, juries in the United States and Canada have traditionally been composed of twelve people whose task is to reach consensus. However, in several cases appealed during the early 1970s, the U.S. Supreme Court declared that in civil cases and state criminal cases not potentially involving a death penalty, courts could use six-person juries. Moreover, the court affirmed a state's right to allow less than unanimous verdicts, even upholding one Louisiana conviction based on a 9 to 3 vote (Tanke & Tanke, 1979). There is no reason to suppose, argued the court, that smaller juries, or juries not required to reach consensus, will deliberate or ultimately decide differently from the traditional jury.

The court's assumptions triggered an avalanche of criticism from both legal scholars and social psychologists (Saks, 1974). Some criticisms were matters of simple statistics. For example, if 10 percent of a community's total jury pool is black, then 72 percent of twelve-member juries, but only 47 percent of six-member juries, may be expected to have at least one black representative. So smaller juries are less likely to embody a community's diversity. And if, in a given case, one-sixth of the jurors initially favor acquittal, that would be a single individual in a six-member jury and two people in a twelve-member jury. The court assumed that, psychologically, the two situations would be identical. But as you may recall from our discussion of conformity, resisting group pressure is generally far more difficult for a minority of one than for a minority of two.

Other criticisms were based on recent experiments by Michael Saks (1977), Charlan Nemeth (1977), and James Davis and others (1975)—experiments that put the court's assumptions to the test. In these mock jury experiments, the overall distribution of verdicts from small or nonunanimous juries did not differ much from the verdicts pronounced by unanimous twelve-member juries, although in their verdicts the smaller juries did, in a given case, seem slightly more inconsistent and unpredictable. There are, however, greater effects on the jury's deliberation. For example, a smaller jury has the advantage of greater and more evenly balanced participation per juror, but the disadvantage of eliciting less total deliberation. Moreover, once they realize that the necessary majority has been achieved, juries not required to reach consensus seem to discuss minority views rather superficially (Davis et al., 1975; Foss, 1981; Kerr et al., 1976; Nemeth, 1977).

In 1978, after these studies were reported, the Supreme Court rejected the state of Georgia's five-member juries (although it still retains the six-member jury). Announcing the Court's decision, Justice Harry Blackmun drew upon both the logical and the experimental data to argue that five-person juries would be less representative, less reliable, less accurate (Grofman, 1980). Ironically, many of these data actually involved comparisons of *six-* versus twelve-member juries, and thus also argued against the six-member jury. But, having made and defended a public commitment to the six-member jury, the Court has so far not been convinced that the same arguments apply (Tanke & Tanke, 1979).

"We have considered [the social science studies] carefully because they provide the only basis besides judicial hunch, for a decision about whether smaller and smaller juries will be able to fulfill the purposes and functions of the Sixth Amendment."

Justice Harry Blackmun (Ballew v. Georgia, *1978)*

Simulated Juries and Real Juries

Perhaps while reading this chapter you have wondered what some critics (Vidmar, 1979; Tapp, 1980) have wondered: Is there not an enormous gulf between college students discussing a simplified hypothetical case and real jurors deliberating a real person's fate? Indeed there is. It is one thing to ponder a pretend decision given minimal information, and quite another to agonize over the complexities and profound consequences of an actual case. So Reid Hastie, Martin Kaplan, James Davis, Eugene Borgida, and others are increasingly asking their participants, who sometimes are drawn from actual juror pools, to view enactments of actual trials. In some cases, participants have even been known to forget that a trial they are watching on television was not real, but staged (Thompson et al., 1981).

Yet some researchers also defend the laboratory simulations, noting that the laboratory offers a practical, inexpensive method for studying important issues under controlled conditions (Bray & Kerr, 1979; Dillehay & Nietzel, 1980). What is more, say the defenders, as researchers have begun testing them in more realistic situations, findings from the laboratory jury studies have often held up quite well. And besides, no one contends that the simplified world of the jury experiment mirrors the complex world of the courtroom. Rather, the experiments help us formulate theories, theories that can be used to interpret the complex world.

Come to think of it, are these jury simulations any different from social psychology's other experiments, all of which create simplified versions of complex realities? By varying just one or two factors at a time in this simulated reality, the experimenter can pinpoint how changes in these one or two aspects can affect us. And that takes us back to where we began this book.

SUMMING UP

In hundreds of recent experiments, courtroom procedures have been on trial. Social psychologists have conducted these experiments believing that the courtroom offers a natural context for studying how people form judgments, and that social psychology's principles and methods can shed new light on important judicial issues.

Judging the Defendant

During a trial, jurors hear testimony, form impressions of the defendant, and listen to the judge's instructions. At each of these stages, subtle factors may influence their judgments:

Eyewitness Testimony

Experiments reveal that both witnesses and jurors readily succumb to an illusion that a given witness's mental recording equipment functions free of significant error. But in fact, as witnesses construct and rehearse memories of what they have observed, errors creep in easily. Research suggests ways to alleviate such error, both in eyewitness reports and in jurors' use of such reports.

The Defendant's Characteristics

The facts of a case are usually compelling enough that jurors can lay aside their biases and render a fair judgment. But when the evidence is ambiguous, jurors are more likely to interpret it with the aid of their preconceived biases and to feel sympathetic to a defendant who is attractive or similar to themselves.

The Effectiveness of the Judge's Instructions

When jurors are exposed to damaging pretrial publicity or to inadmissible evidence, will they follow a judge's instruction to ignore it? In simulated trials, the judge's orders were sometimes followed, but often, especially when the judge's admonition came *after* the impression was made, they were not.

The Jury

What matters is what happens not only in the courtroom, but also within and among the jurors themselves.

The Jurors as Individuals

In a close case, the jurors' own characteristics can influence their verdicts. For example, jurors who favor capital punishment or who are highly authoritarian appear more likely to convict certain types of defendants. Thus lawyers, sometimes with the aid of survey researchers, seek to identify and eliminate potential jurors likely to be unsympathetic to their side. Nevertheless, in a trial as in other situations, what matters most is not the jurors' personalities and general attitudes, but rather the situation that they must react to.

The Jury as a Group

Juries are groups, groups that are swayed by the same influences that bear upon other types of groups—patterns of majority and minority influence, group polarization, information exchange. Researchers have also examined and questioned the assumptions underlying several recent Supreme Court decisions permitting smaller juries and nonunanimous juries.

Simulated juries are not real juries, so we must be cautious in generalizing these findings to actual courtrooms. Yet, like all experiments in social psychology, laboratory jury experiments can help us formulate theories and principles that we can use to interpret the more complex world of everyday life.

Bibliography

Abbey, A. Sex differences for friendly behavior: Do males misperceive females' friendliness? *Journal of Personality and Social Psychology*, 1982, **42**, 830–838.

ABC News/*Washington Post* survey. February 26–March 6, 1981. Reported in *Public Opinion*, April–May 1981.

Abelson, R. Are attitudes necessary? In B. T. King & E. McGinnies (Eds.), *Attitudes, conflict and social change*. New York: Academic Press, 1972.

Able, G. G., Barlow, D. H., Blanchard, E. B., & Guild, D. The components of rapists' sexual arousal. *Archives of General Psychiatry*, 1977, **34**, 895–903.

Abramson, L. Y., Alloy, L. B., & Rosoff, R. Depression and the generation of complex hypotheses in the judgment of contingency. *Behavior Research and Theory*, 1981, **19**, 34–45.

Adams, G. R., & Shea, J. A. Talking and loving: A cross-lagged panel investigation. *Basic and Applied Social Psychology*, 1981, **2**, 81–88.

Aderman, D. Elation, depression, and helping behavior. *Journal of Personality and Social Psychology*, 1972, **24**, 91–101.

Aderman, D., & Berkowitz, L. Observational set, empathy, and helping. *Journal of Personality and Social Psychology*, 1970, **14**, 141–148.

Aderman, D., & Brehm, S. S. On the recall of initial attitudes following counterattitudinal advocacy: An experimental reexamination. *Personality and Social Psychology Bulletin*, 1976, **2**, 59–62.

Adler, R. P., Lesser, G. S., Meringoff, L. K., Robertson, T. S., & Ward, S. *The effects of television advertising on children*. Lexington, Mass.: Lexington Books, 1980.

Adorno, T., Frenkel-Brunswik, E., Levinson, D., & Sanford, R. N. *The authoritarian personality*. New York: Harper, 1950.

Aiello, J. R., Baum, A., & Gormley, F. P. Social determinants of residential crowding stress. *Personality and Social Psychology Bulletin*, 1981, **7**, 643–649.

Ajzen, I., Dalto, C. A., & Blyth, D. P. Consistency and bias in the attribution of attitudes. *Journal of Personality and Social Psychology*, 1979, **37**, 1871– 1876.

Ajzen, I., & Fishbein, M. Attitude-behavior relations: A theoretical analysis and review of empirical research. *Psychological Bulletin*, 1977, **84**, 888–918.

Albee, G. Politics, power, prevention, and social change. Keynote address to Vermont Conference on Primary Prevention of Psychopathology, June 19, 1979.

Allee, W. C., & Masure, R. M. A comparison of maze behavior in paired and isolated shell-parakeets

(*Melopsittacus undulatus Shaw*) in a two-alley problem box. *Journal of Comparative Psychology*, 1936, **22**, 131–155.

Allen, B. P. *Social behavior: Fact and falsehood.* Chicago: Nelson Hall, 1978.

Allen, S. American Institute of Architects. Personal communication, 1980.

Allen, V. L. (Ed.). *Children as teachers.* New York: Academic Press, 1976.

Allen, V. L., & Levine, J. M. Consensus and conformity. *Journal of Experimental Social Psychology*, 1969, 5, 389–399.

Allen, V. L., & Wilder, D. A. Group categorization and attribution of belief similarity. *Small Group Behavior*, 1979, **10**, 73–80.

Allen, V. L., & Wilder, D. A. Impact of group consensus and social support on stimulus meaning: Mediation of conformity by cognitive restructuring. *Journal of Personality and Social Psychology*, 1980, **39**, 1116–1124.

Allgeier, A. R., Byrne, D., Brooks, B., & Revnes, D. The waffle phenomenon: Negative evaluations of those who shift attitudinally. *Journal of Applied Social Psychology*, 1979, **9**, 170–182.

Alloy, L. B., & Abramson, L. Y. Judgment of contingency in depressed and nondepressed students: Sadder but wiser? *Journal of Experimental Psychology: General*, 1979, **108**, 441–485.

Alloy, L. B., & Abramson, L. Y. The cognitive component of human helplessness and depression: A critical analysis. In J. Garber & M. E. P. Seligman (Eds.), *Human helplessness: Theory and applications.* New York: Academic Press, 1980.

Alloy, L. B., & Abramson, L. Y. Learned helplessness, depression, and the illusion of control. *Journal of Personality and Social Psychology*, 1982, **42**, 1114–1126.

Alloy, L. B., Abramson, L. Y., & Viscusi, Z. Induced mood and the illusion of control. *Journal of Personality and Social Psychology*, 1981, **41**, 1129–1140.

Allport, F. M. The influence of the group upon association and thought. *Journal of Experimental Psychology*, 1920, **3**, 159–182.

Allport, G. *The nature of prejudice.* New York: Doubleday Anchor Books, 1958.

Allport, G. W., & Postman, L. *The psychology of rumor.* New York: Henry Holt and Co., 1975. (Originally published, 1947.) Also In E. E. Maccoby, T. M. Newcomb, & E. L. Hartley (Eds.), *Readings in social psychology.* New York: Holt, Rinehart and Winston, 1958.

Allport, G. W., & Ross, J. M. Personal religious orientation and prejudice. *Journal of Personality and Social Psychology*, 1967, 5, 432–443.

Altman, I. *The environment and social behavior: Privacy, personal space, territory, crowding.* Monterey, Calif: Brooks/Cole, 1975.

Altman, I., & Taylor, D. *Social penetration: The development of interpersonal relations.* New York: Holt, Rinehart and Winston, 1973.

Altman, I., & Vinsel, A. M. Personal space: An analysis of E. T. Hall's proxemics framework. In I. Altman & J. Wohlwill (Eds.), *Human behavior and the environment.* New York: Plenum Press, 1978.

Amabile, T. M., & Glazebrook, A. H. A negativity bias in interpersonal evaluation. *Journal of Experimental Social Psychology*, 1982, **18**, 1–22.

American Council on Education. More college women pursue traditionally male careers. *Higher Education and National Affairs*, February 13, 1981, p. 4.

American Psychological Association. Ethical principles of psychologists. *American Psychologist*, 1981, **36**, 633–638.

Amir, Y. Contact hypothesis in ethnic relations. *Psychological Bulletin*, 1969, **71**, 319–342.

Anderson, C. A., Horowitz, L. M., & French, R. D. Attributional style of the lonely and the depressed. *Journal of Personality and Social Psychology*, 1982, in press.

Anderson, C. A., Lepper, M. R., & Ross, L. Perseverance of social theories: The role of explanation in the persistence of discredited information. *Journal of Personality and Social Psychology*, 1980, **39**, 1037–1049.

Andersen, N. H. A simple model of information integration. In R. B. Abelson, E. Aronson, W. J. McGuire, T. M. Newcomb, M. J. Rosenberg, & P. H. Tannenbaum (Eds.), *Theories of cognitive consistency: A sourcebook.* Chicago: Rand McNally, 1968.

Anderson, N. H. Cognitive algebra: Integration theory applied to social attribution. In L. Berkowitz (Ed.), *Advances in Experimental Social Psychology*, Vol. 7. New York: Academic Press, 1974.

Anderson, S. M., & Bem, S. L. Sex typing and androgyny in dyadic interaction: Individual differences in responsiveness to physical attractiveness. *Journal of Personality and Social Psychology*, 1981, **41**, 74–86.

Andrews, K. H., & Kandel, D. B. Attitude and behavior: A specification of the contingent consistency hypothesis. *American Sociological Review*, 1979, **44**, 298–310.

Angell, R. C., Dunham, V. S., & Singer, J. D. Social values and foreign policy attitudes of Soviet and American elites. *Journal of Conflict Resolution*, 1964, **8**, 329–491.

Apsler, R. Effects of embarrassment on behavior toward others. *Journal of Personality and Social Psychology*, 1975, **32**, 145–153.

Archea, J. The architectural basis for analyzing certain aspects of spatial behavior. Paper presented at the American Psychological Association convention, 1980.

Archer, D., & Gartner, R. Violent acts and violent times: A comparative approach to postwar homicide rates. *American Sociological Review*, 1976, **41**, 937–963.

Archer, R. L., Berg, J. M., & Burleson, J. A. Self-disclosure and attraction: A self-perception analysis. Unpublished manuscript, University of Texas at Austin. 1980.

Archer, R. L., Berg, J. M., & Runge, T. E. Active and passive observers' attraction to a self-disclosing other. *Journal of Experimental Social Psychology*, 1980, **16**, 130–145.

Archer, R. L., & Burleson, J. A. The effects of timing of self-disclosure on attraction and reciprocity. *Journal of Personality and Social Psychology*, 1980, **38**, 120–130.

Archer, R. L., Foushees, H. C., Davis, M. H., & Aderman D. Emotional empathy in a courtroom simulation: A person-situation interaction. *Journal of Applied Social Psychology*, 1979, **9**, 275–291.

Arendt, H. *Eichmann in Jerusalem: A report on the banality of evil.* New York: Viking Press, 1963.

Arendt, H. Organized guilt and universal responsibility. In R. W. Smith (Ed.), *Guilt: Man and society.* Garden City, N.Y.: Doubleday Anchor Books, 1971. Reprinted from *Jewish Frontier*, 1945, **12**.

Argyle, M., & Dean, J. Eye-contact, distance and affiliation. *Sociometry*, 1965, **28**, 289–304.

Argyle, M., Shimoda, K., & Little, B. Variance due to persons and situations in England and Japan. *British Journal of Social and Clinical Psychology*, 1978, **17**, 335–337.

Aristotle, *Poetics*, Book Six.

Arkin, R. M., Appelman, A., & Burger, J. M. Social anxiety, self-presentation, and the self-serving bias in causal attribution. *Journal of Personality and Social Psychology*, 1980, **38**, 23–35.

Arkin, R. M., Cooper, H., & Kolditz, T. A statistical review of the literature concerning the self-serving attribution bias in interpersonal influence situations. *Journal of Personality*, 1980, **48**, 435– 448.

Arkin, R. M., & Maruyama, G. M. Attribution, affect, and college exam performance. *Journal of Educational Psychology*, 1979, **71**, 85–93.

Arms, R. L., Russell, G. W., & Sandilands, M. L. Effects on the hostility of spectators of viewing aggressive sports. *Social Psychology Quarterly*, 1979, **42**, 275–279.

Armstrong, B. An interview with Herbert Kelman. *APA Monitor*, January 1981, pp. 4–5, 55.

Arnold, A. P. Sexual differences in the brain. *American Scientist*, 1980, **68**, 165–174.

Aronson, E. *The social animal.* San Francisco: Freeman, 1980.

Aronson, E., Blaney, N., Stephan, C., Sikes, J., & Snapp, M. *The jigsaw classroom.* Beverly Hills, Calif.: Sage Publications, 1978.

Aronson, E., & Bridgeman, D. Jigsaw groups and the desegregated classroom: In pursuit of common goals. *Personality and Social Psychology Bulletin*, 1979, 5, 438–446.

Aronson, E., & Carlsmith, J. M. Experimentation in social psychology. In G. Lindzey & E. Aronson (Eds.), *Handbook of Social Psychology* (2d ed.), Vol. 2. Reading, Mass: Addison-Wesley, 1969.

Aronson, E., & Cope, V. My enemy's enemy is my friend. *Journal of Personality and Social Psychology*, 1968, **8**, 8–12.

Aronson, E., & Linder, D. Gain and loss of esteem as determinants of interpersonal attractiveness. *Journal of Experimental Social Psychology*, 1965, **1**, 156–171.

Aronson, E., & Mettee, D. R. Affective reactions to appraisal from others. *Foundations of Interpersonal Attraction.* New York: Academic Press, 1974.

Aronson, E., & Mills, J. The effect of severity of initiation on liking for a group. *Journal of Abnormal and Social Psychology*, 1959, **59**, 177–181.

Aronson, E., Turner, J. A., & Carlsmith, J. M. Communicator credibility and communicator discrepancy as determinants of opinion change. *Journal of Abnormal and Social Psychology*, 1963, **67**, 31–36.

Asch, S. E. Forming impressions of personality.

Journal of Abnormal and Social Psychology, 1946, **41**, 258–290.

Asch, S. E. Opinions and social pressure. *Scientific American*, November 1955, pp. 31–35.

Asch, S. E. Studies of independence and conformity: A minority of one against a unanimous majority. *Psychological Monographs*, 1956, **70** (9, Whole No. 416).

Astin, A. W. *Four critical years*. San Francisco: Jossey-Bass, 1972.

Austin, W. Friendship and fairness: Effects of type of relationship and task performance on choice of distribution rules. *Personality and Social Psychology Bulletin*, 1980, **6**, 402–408.

Austin, W., McGinn, N. C., & Susmilch, C. Internal standards revisited: Effects of social comparisons and expectancies on judgments of fairness and satisfaction. *Journal of Experimental Social Psychology*, 1980, **16**, 426–441.

Ayeroff, F., & Abelson, R. P. ESP and ESB: Belief in personal success at mental telepathy. *Journal of Personality and Social Psychology*, 1976, **34**, 240–247.

Azrin, N. H. Pain and aggression. *Psychology Today*, May 1967, pp. 27–33.

Azrin, N. H., Hutchinson, R. R., & Hake, D. F. Extinction-induced aggression. *Journal of the Experimental Analysis of Behavior*, 1966, **9**, 191–204.

Babad, E. Y. Some observations on Sadat's visit. *APA Monitor*, February 1978, pp. 3, 19.

Bachman, J. G., & O'Malley, P. M. Self-esteem in young men: A longitudinal analysis of the impact of educational and occupational attainment. *Journal of Personality and Social Psychology*, 1977, **35**, 365–380.

Baer, R., Hinkle, S., Smith, K., & Fenton, M. Reactance as a function of actual versus projected autonomy. *Journal of Personality and Social Psychology*, 1980, **38**, 416–422.

Bales, R. F. Task roles and social roles in problem-solving groups. In E. E. Maccoby, T. M. Newcomb, & E. L. Hartley (Eds.), *Readings in Social Psychology*, (3d ed.). New York: Holt, Rinehart and Winston, 1958.

Bandura, A. Self-efficacy: Toward a unifying theory of behavioral change. *Psychological Review*, 1977, **84**, 191–215.

Bandura, A. The self system in reciprocal determinism. *American Psychologist*, 1978, **33**, 344–358.

Bandura, A. The social learning perspective: Mechanisms of aggression. In H. Toch (Ed.), *Psychology of crime and criminal justice*. New York: Holt, Rinehart & Winston, 1979.

Bandura, A. Self-efficacy: Mechanism in human agency. *American Psychologist*, 1982, **37**, 122–147.

Bandura, A., Ross, D., & Ross, S. A. Transmission of aggression through imitation of aggressive models. *Journal of Abnormal and Social Psychology*, 1961, **63**, 575–582.

Bandura, A., & Walters, R. H. *Adolescent aggression*. New York: Ronald Press, 1959.

Bandura, A., & Walters, R. H. *Social learning and personality development*. New York: Holt, Rinehart and Winston, 1963.

Banks, C. White preference in blacks: A paradigm in search of a phenomenon. *Psychological Bulletin*, 1976, **83**, 1179–1186.

Barash, D. *The whisperings within*. New York: Harper & Row, 1979.

Bar-Hillel, M. The base-rate fallacy in probability judgments. *Acta Psychologica*, 1980, **44**, 211–233.

Bar-Hillel, M., & Fischhoff, B. When do base rates affect predictions? *Journal of Personality and Social Psychology*, 1981, **41**, 671–680.

Barker, R. G. and associates. *Habitats, environments, and human behavior*. San Francisco: Jossey-Bass, 1978.

Barnes, R. D., Ickes, W., & Kidd, R. F. Effects of the perceived intentionality and stability of another's dependency on helping behavior. *Personality and Social Psychology Bulletin*, 1979, **5**, 367–372.

Barnett, M. A., King, L. M., Howard, J. A., & Melton, E. M. Experiencing negative affect about self or other: Effects on helping behavior in children and adults. Paper presented at the Midwestern Psychological Association convention, 1980.

Baron, R. A. The reduction of human aggression: A field study of the influence of incompatible reactions. *Journal of Applied Social Psychology*, 1976, **6**, 260– 274.

Baron, R. A. *Human aggression*. New York: Plenum Press, 1977.

Baron, R. M., Mandel, D. R., Adams, C. A., & Griffen, L. M. Effects of social density in university residential environments. *Journal of Personality and Social Psychology*, 1976, **34**, 434–446.

Baron, R. M., & Needel, S. P. Toward an understanding of the differences in the responses of humans and other animals to density. *Psychological Review*, 1980, **87**, 320–326.

Baron, R. S., Moore, D., & Sanders, G. S. Distraction as a source of drive in social facilitation research. *Journal of Personality and Social Psychology*, 1978, **36**, 816–824.

Bar-Tal, D. Sequential development of helping behavior: A cognitive-learning approach. *Developmental Review*, in press.

Bar-Tal, D., & Bar-Zohar, Y. The relationship between perception of locus of control and academic achievement. *Contemporary Educational Psychology*, 1977, **2**, 181–199.

Baruch, G. K. Maternal influences upon college women's attitudes toward women and work. *Developmental Psychology*, 1972, **6**, 32–37.

Barzun, J. *Simple and direct.* New York: Harper & Row, 1975, pp 173–174.

Batson, C. D. Rational processing or rationalization? The effect of disconfirming information on a stated religious belief. *Journal of Personality and Social Psychology*, 1975, **32**, 176–184.

Batson, C. D., Cochran, P. J., Biederman, M. F., Blosser, J. L., Ryan, M. J., & Vogt, B. Failure to help when in a hurry: Callousness or conflict? *Personality and Social Psychology Bulletin*, 1978, **4**, 97–101.

Batson, C. D., Coke, J. S., Jasnoski, M. L., & Hanson, M. Buying kindness: Effect of an extrinsic incentive for helping on perceived altruism. *Personality and Social Psychology Bulletin*, 1978, **4**, 86–91.

Batson, C. D., Duncan, B. D., Ackerman, P., Buckley, T., & Birch, K. Is empathic emotion a source of altruistic motivation? *Journal of Personality and Social Behavior*, 1981, **40**, 290–302.

Batson, C. D., & Gray, R. A. Religious orientation and helping behavior: Responding to one's own or to the victim's needs? *Journal of Personality and Social Psychology*, 1981, **40**, 511–520.

Batson, C. D., Harris, A. C., McCaul, K. D., Davis, M., & Schmidt, T. Compassion or compliance: Alternative dispositional attributions for one's helping behavior. *Social Psychology Quarterly*, 1979, **42**, 405–409.

Batson, C. D., & Ventis, W. L. *The religious experience: A social psychological perspective.* New York: Oxford University Press, 1982.

Baum, A., Aiello, J. R., & Calesnick, L. E. Crowding and personal control: Social density and the development of learned helplessness. *Journal of Personality and Social Psychology*, 1978, **36**, 1000–1011.

Baum, A., & Davis, G. E. Reducing the stress of high-density living: An architectural intervention. *Journal of Personality and Social Psychology*, 1980, **38**, 471–481.

Baum, A., & Gatchel, R. J. Cognitive determinants of reaction to uncontrollable events: Development of reactance and learned helplessness. *Journal of Personality and Social Psychology*, 1981, **40**, 1078–1089.

Baum, A., Harpin, R. E., & Valins, S. The role of group phenomena in the experience of crowding. *Environment and Behavior*, 1975, **7**, 185–198.

Baum, A., Shapior, A., Murray, D., & Wideman, M. V. Interpersonal mediation of perceived crowding and control in residential dyads and triads. *Journal of Applied Social Psychology*, 1979, **9**, 491–507.

Baum, A., & Valins, S. *Architecture and social behavior.* Hillsdale, N.J.: Lawrence Erlbaum, 1977.

Baumann, D. J., Cialdini, R. B., & Kenrick, D. T. Altruism as hedonism: Helping and self-gratification as equivalent responses. *Journal of Personality and Social Psychology*, 1981, **40**, 1039–1046.

Baumeister, R. F. A self-presentational view of social phenomena. *Psychological Bulletin*, 1982, **91**, 3–26.

Baumhart, R. *An honest profit.* New York: Holt, Rinehart & Winston, 1968.

Bayer, E. Beiträge zur zeikomponenten theorie des hungers. *Zeitschrift für Psychologie*, 1929, **112**, 1–54.

Beaman, A. L., Barnes, P. J., Klentz, B., & McQuirk, B. Increasing helping rates through information dissemination: Teaching pays. *Personality and Social Psychology Bulletin*, 1978, **4**, 406–411.

Beaman, A. L., Klentz, B., Diener, E., & Svanum, S. Self-awareness and transgression in children: Two field studies. *Journal of Personality and Social Psychology*, 1979, **37**, 1835–1846.

Beck, S. B., Ward-Hull, C. I., & McLear, P. M. Variables related to women's somatic preferences of the male and female body. *Journal of Personality and Social Psychology*, 1976, **34**, 1200–1210.

Becker, F. D., Sommer, R., Bee, J., & Oxley, B. College classroom ecology. *Sociometry*, 1973, **36**, 514– 525.

Becker, L. J. Joint effect of feedback and goal setting on performance: A field study of residential energy conservation. *Journal of Applied Psychology*, 1978, **63**, 428–433.

Becker, L. J., & Seligman, C. Reducing air conditioning waste by signalling it is cool outside. *Personality and Social Psychology Bulletin*, 1978, **4**, 412–415.

Becker, L. J., Seligman, C., & Darley, J. M. Psychological strategies to reduce energy consumption: Project summary report. Princeton, N.J.: Center for Energy and Environmental Studies, Princeton University, 1979.

Becker, L. J., Seligman, C., Fazio, R. H., & Darley, J. M. Relating attitudes to residential energy use. *Environment and Behavior*, 1981, **13**, 590–609.

Behavior Today. March 31, 1980, p. 8.

Bell, P. A. Effects of heat, noise, and provocation on retaliatory evaluative behavior. *Journal of Social Psychology*, 1980, **110**, 97–100.

Bell, P. A., Fisher, J. D., & Loomis, R. J. *Environmental psychology*. Philadelphia: Saunders, 1978.

Bell, R. Q., & Harper, L. V. *Child effects on adults*. Hillsdale, N.J.: Lawrence Erlbaum, 1977.

Beloff, J. Why parapsychology is still on trial. *Human Nature*, December 1978, pp. 68–74.

Belson, W. A. *Television violence and the adolescent boy*. Westmead, England: Saxon House, Teakfield Ltd., 1978.

Bem, D. J. Self-perception theory. In L. Berkowitz (Ed.), *Advances in experimental social psychology*. Vol. 6. New York: Academic Press, 1972.

Bem, D. J., & McConnell, H. K. Testing the self-perception explanation of dissonance phenomena: On the salience of premanipulation attitudes. *Journal of Personality and Social Psychology*, 1970, **14**, 23–31.

Bem, S. L. Gender schema theory: A cognitive account of sex typing. *Psychological Review*, 1981, **88**, 354–364.

Bem, S. L., & Bem, D. Case study of a non-conscious ideology: Training the woman to know her place. In D. Bem, *Beliefs, attitudes, and human affairs*. Belmont, Calif.: Brooks/Cole, 1970, pp. 89–99.

Benassi, V. A., Sweeney, P. D., & Drevno, G. E. Mind over matter: Perceived success at psychokinesis. *Journal of Personality and Social Psychology*, 1979, **37**, 1377–1386.

Benbow, C. P., & Stanley, J. C. Sex differences in mathematical ability: Fact or artifact? *Science*, 1980, **210**, 1262–1264.

Benson, P. L., Dehority, J., Garman, L., Hanson, E., Hochschwender, M., Lebold, C., Rohr, R., & Sullivan, J. Intrapersonal correlates of nonspontaneous helping behavior. *Journal of Social Psychology*, 1980, **110**, 87–95.

Benson, P. L, Karabenick, S. A., & Lerner, R. M. Pretty pleases: The effects of physical attractiveness, race, and sex on receiving help. *Journal of Experimental Social Psychology*, 1976, **12**, 409–415.

Bentler, P. M., & Speckart, G. Attitudes "cause" behaviors: A structural equation analysis. *Journal of Personality and Social Psychology*, 1981, **40**, 226–238.

Benware, C., & Deci, E. Attitude change as a function of the inducement for exposing a proattitudinal communication. *Journal of Experimental Social Psychology*, 1975, **11**, 271–278.

Berger, P. *Invitation to sociology: A humanistic perspective*. Garden City, N.Y.: Doubleday Anchor Books, 1963.

Bergin, A. E. The effect of dissonance persuasive communications on changes in a self-referring attitude. *Journal of Personality*, 1962, **30**, 423–438.

Berglas, S., & Jones, E. E. Drug choice as a self-handicapping strategy in response to noncontingent success. *Journal of Personality and Social Psychology*, 1978, **36**, 405–417.

Berkowitz, L. Group standards, cohesiveness, and productivity. *Human Relations*, 1954, **7**, 509–519.

Berkowitz, L. The effects of observing violence. *Scientific American*, February 1964, pp. 35–41.

Berkowitz, L. Impulse, aggression and the gun. *Psychology Today*, September 1968, pp. 18–22.

Berkowitz, L. Frustrations, comparisons, and other sources of emotional arousal as contributors to social unrest. *Journal of Social Issues*, 1972, **28**(1), 77–91. (a)

Berkowitz, L. Social norms, feelings, and other factors affecting helping and altruism. In L. Berkowitz (Ed.), *Advances in experimental social psychology* (Vol. 6). New York: Academic Press, 1972. (b)

Berkowitz, L. Whatever happened to the frustration-aggression hypothesis? *American Behavioral Scientist*, 1978, **21**, 691–708.

Berkowitz, L. Aversive conditions as stimuli to aggression. Paper presented at the Midwestern Psychological Association convention, 1981. (a)

Berkowitz, L. How guns control us. *Psychology Today*, June 1981, pp. 11–12. (b)

Berkowitz, L., Cochran, S. T., & Embree, M. C. Physical pain and the goal of aversively stimulated aggression. *Journal of Personality and Social Psychology*, 1980, **40**, 687–700.

Berkowitz, L., & Connor, W. H. Success, failure,

and social responsibility. *Journal of Personality and Social Psychology*, 1966, **4**, 664–669.

Berkowitz, L., & Frodi, A. Stimulus characteristics that can enhance or decrease aggression. *Aggressive Behavior*, 1977, **3**, 1–15.

Berkowitz, L., & Frodi, A. Reactions to a child's mistakes as affected by her/his looks and speech. *Social Psychology Quarterly*, 1982, in press.

Berkowitz, L., & Geen, R. G. Film violence and the cue properties of available targets. *Journal of Personality and Social Psychology*, 1966, **3**, 525–530.

Berkowitz, L., & LePage, A. Weapons as aggression-eliciting stimuli. *Journal of Personality and Social Psychology*, 1967, **7**, 202–207.

Berman, P. W. Are women more responsive than men to the young? A review of developmental and situational variables. *Psychological Bulletin*, 1980, **88**, 688–695.

Bernard, J. The good provider role: Its rise and fall. *American Psychologist*, 1981, **36**, 1–12.

Bernstein, M., & Crosby, F. An empirical examination of relative deprivation theory. *Journal of Experimental Social Psychology*, 1980, **16**, 442–456.

Bernstein, W. M. The private-public attribution distinction: Theoretical implications for egotism. Paper presented at the American Psychological Association convention, 1979.

Bernstein, W. M., Stephan, W. G., & Davis, M. H. Explaining attributions for achievement: A path analytic approach. *Journal of Personality and Social Psychology*, 1979, **37**, 1810–1821.

Berscheid, E. An overview of the psychological effects of physical attractiveness and some comments upon the psychological effects of knowledge of the effects of physical attractiveness. In W. Lucker, K. Ribbens, & J. A. McNamera (Eds.), *Logical aspects of facial form (craniofacial growth series)*. Ann Arbor: University of Michigan Press, 1981.

Berscheid, E., Boye, D., & Walster (Hatfield), E. Retaliation as a means of restoring equity. *Journal of Personality and Social Psychology*, 1968, **10**, 370–376.

Berscheid, E., Dion, K., Walster (Hatfield), E., & Walster, G. W. Physical attractiveness and dating choice: A test of the matching hypothesis. *Journal of Experimental Social Psychology*, 1971, **7**, 173–189.

Berscheid, E., & Walster (Hatfield), E. *Interpersonal attraction*. Reading, Mass.: Addison-Wesley, 1978.

Berscheid, E., Walster (Hatfield), E., & Bohrnstedt, G. The body image report. *Psychology Today*, November 1973, pp. 119–131.

Berscheid, E., Walster, G. W., & Walster (Hatfield), E. Effects of accuracy and positivity of evaluation on liking for the evaluator. Unpublished manuscript, 1969. Summarized by E. Berscheid and E. Walster (Hatfield) in *Interpersonal attraction*. Reading, Mass.: Addison-Wesley, 1978.

Bettelheim, B. Violence: A neglected mode of behavior. *Annals of American Academy of Political Social Science*, 1966, **364**, 50–59. Cited by K. Menninger, in *The crime of punishment*. New York: Viking, 1968, p. 173.

Bettelheim, B., & Janowitz, M. *Dynamics of prejudice: A psychological and sociological study of veterans*. New York: Harper, 1950.

Bickman, L. Bystander intervention in a crime: The effect of a mass-media campaign. *Journal of Applied Social Psychology*, 1975, **5**, 296–302.

Bickman, L. Interpersonal influence and the reporting of a crime. *Personality and Social Psychology Bulletin*, 1979, **5**, 32–35.

Bickman, L., & Green, S. K. Situational cues and crime reporting: Do signs make a difference? *Journal of Applied Social Psychology*, 1977, **7**, 1–18.

Bickman, L., & Kamzan, M. The effect of race and need on helping behavior. *Journal of Social Psychology*, 1973, **89**, 73–77.

Bickman, L., & Rosenbaum, D. P. Crime reporting as a function of bystander encouragement, surveillance, and credibility. *Journal of Personality and Social Psychology*, 1977, **35**, 577–586.

Bickman, L., Teger, A., Gabriele, T., McLaughlin, C., Berger, M., & Sunaday, E. Dormitory density and helping behavior. *Environment and Behavior*, 1973, **5**, 465–490.

Bierbrauer, G. Why did he do it? Attribution of obedience and the phenomenon of dispositional bias. *European Journal of Social Psychology*, 1979, **9**, 67–84.

Bigam, R. G. Voir dire: The attorney's job. *Trial 13*, March 1977, p. 3. Cited by G. Bermant & J. Shepard in The voir dire examination, juror challenges, and adversary advocacy. In B. D. Sales (Ed.), *Perspectives in law and psychology* (Vol. II): *The trial process*. New York: Plenum Press, 1981.

Billig, M., & Tajfel, H. Social categorization and similarity in intergroup behaviour. *European Journal of Social Psychology*, 1973, **3**, 27–52.

Binham, R. Trivers in Jamaica. *Science 80*, March–April 1980, pp. 57–67.

Blackstone, W. *Commentaries on the laws of England of public wrongs*. Boston: Beacon Press, 1972. (Originally published 1769.) Cited by M. F. Kaplan and C. Schersching in Reducing juror bias: An experimental approach. In P. D. Lipsitt & B. D. Sales (Eds.), *New directions in psycholegal research*. New York: Van Nostrand Reinhold, 1980.

Blake, R. R., & Mouton, J. S. The intergroup dynamics of win-lose conflict and problem-solving collaboration in union-management relations. In M. Sherif (Ed.), *Intergroup relations and leadership*. New York: Wiley, 1962.

Blake, R. R., & Mouton, J. S. Intergroup problem solving in organizations: From theory to practice. In W. G. Austin and S. Worchel (Eds.), *The social psychology of intergroup relations*. Monterey, Calif.: Brooks/Cole, 1979.

Blanchard, F. A., & Cook, S. W. Effects of helping a less competent member of a cooperating interracial group on the development of interpersonal attraction. *Journal of Personality and Social Psychology*, 1976, **34**, 1245–1255.

Blanck, P. D., Rosenthal, R., Snodgrass, S. E., DePaulo, B. M., & Zuckerman, M. Sex differences in eavesdropping on nonverbal cues: Developmental changes. *Journal of Personality and Social Psychology*, 1981, **41**, 391–396.

Block, J. H. Socialization influences on personality development in males and females. Washington, D. C.: American Psychological Association, 1979. Master Lecture Cassette Tape 15/11.

Boggiano, A. K., & Ruble, D. N. Self-perception vs. cued expectancy: Analyses of the effects of reward on task interest. Paper presented at the American Psychological Association convention, 1981.

Bond, M. H. Winning either way: The effect of anticipating a competitive interaction on person perception. *Personality and Social Psychology Bulletin*, 1979, **5**, 316–319.

Borchard, E. M. *Convicting the innocent: Errors of criminal justice*. New Haven: Yale University Press, 1932. Cited by E. R. Hilgard & E. F. Loftus, Effective interrogation of the eyewitness. *International Journal of Clinical and Experimental Hypnosis*, 1979, **27**, 342–359.

Borgida, E. Legal reform of rape laws. In L. Bickman (Ed.), *Applied Social Psychology Annual*. Vol. 2. Beverly Hills, Calif.: Sage Publications, 1981, pp. 211–241.

Borgida, E., & Brekke, N. The base rate fallacy in attribution and prediction. In J. H. Harvey, W. J. Ickes, & R. F. Kidd (Eds.), *New directions in attribution research*. Vol. 3. Hillsdale, N.J.: Lawrence Erlbaum, 1981.

Borgida, E., & Campbell, B. Belief relevance and attitude-behavior consistency: The moderating role of personal experience. *Journal of Personality and Social Psychology*, 1982, **42**, 239–247.

Borgida, E., Locksley, A., & Brekke, N. Social stereotypes and social judgment. In N. Cantor & J. Kihlstrom (Eds.), *Cognition, social interaction, and personality*. Hillsdale, N. J.: Lawrence Erlbaum, 1981.

Borgida, E., & Nisbett, R. E. The differential impact of abstract vs. concrete information on decisions. *Journal of Applied Social Psychology*, 1977, **7**, 258–271.

Borgida, E., & White, P. Judgmental bias and legal reform. Unpublished manuscript, University of Minnesota, 1980.

Bossard, J. H. S. Residential propinquity as a factor in marriage selection. *American Journal of Sociology*, 1932, **38**, 219–224.

Bourne, E. Can we describe an individual's personality? *Journal of Personality and Social Psychology*, 1977, **35**, 863–872.

Bower, G. H., & Masling, M. Causal explanations as mediators for remembering correlations. Unpublished manuscript, Stanford University, 1979.

Boyatzis, R. E. Alcohol and interpersonal aggression. In M. M. Gross (Ed.), *Alcohol Intoxication and Withdrawal*, Vol. 3B. (New York: Plenum Publishing, 1977, pp. 345–375.

Boyatzis, R. E. Alcohol and interpersonal aggression: An interdisciplinary perspective. Paper presented at the American Psychological Association convention, 1980.

Bradley, G. W. Self-serving biases in the attribution process: A reexamination of the fact or fiction question. *Journal of Personality and Social Psychology*, 1978, **36**, 56–71.

Brand, E. S., Ruiz, R. A., & Padilla, A. M. Ethnic identification and preference: A review. *Psychological Bulletin*, 1974, **81**, 860–890.

Brandon, R., & Davies, C. *Wrongful imprisonment: Mistaken convictions and their consequences*. Hamden, Conn.: Archon Books, 1973.

Bray, R. M., & Kerr, N. L. Use of the simulation method in the study of jury behavior: Some methodological considerations. *Law and Human Behavior*, 1979, **3**, 107-119.

Bray, R. M., & Noble, A. M. Authoritarianism and decisions of mock juries: Evidence of jury bias and group polarization. *Journal of Personality and Social Psychology*, 1978, **36**, 1424–1430.

Bray, R. M., & Sugarman, R. Social facilitation among interacting groups: Evidence for the evaluation apprehension hypothesis. *Personality and Social Psychology Bulletin*, 1980, **6**, 137–142.

Brehm, J. W. Post-decision changes in desirability of alternatives. *Journal of Abnormal Social Psychology*, 1956, **52**, 384–389.

Brehm, S., & Brehm, J. W. *Psychological reactance: A theory of freedom and control*. New York: Academic Press, 1981.

Brenner, S. N., & Molander, E. A. Is the ethics of business changing? *Harvard Business Review*, January–February 1977, pp. 57–71.

Brewer, M. B. In-group bias in the minimal intergroup situation: A cognitive-motivational analysis. *Psychological Bulletin*, 1979, **86**, 307–324.

Brewer, M. B., Dull, V., & Lui, L. Perceptions of the elderly: Stereotypes as prototypes. *Journal of Personality and Social Psychology*, 1981, **41**, 656–670.

Brewer, M. B., & Silver, M. In-group bias as a function of task characteristics. *European Journal of Social Psychology*, 1978, **8**, 393–400.

Brickman, P. Is it real? In J. Harvey, W. Ickes, & R. Kidd (Eds.), *New directions in attribution research*. Vol. 2. Hillsdale, N.J.: Lawrence Erlbaum, 1978.

Brickman, P., & Campbell, D. T. Hedonic relativism and planning the good society. In M. H. Appley (Ed.), *Adaptation-level theory*. New York: Academic Press, 1971.

Brickman, P., Coates, D., & Janoff-Bulman, R. J. Lottery winners and accident victims: Is happiness relative? *Journal of Personality and Social Psychology*, 1978, **36**, 917–927.

Brickman, P., Rabinowitz, V. C., Karuza, J., Jr., Coates, D., Cohn, E., & Kidder, L. Models of helping and coping. *American Psychologist*, 1982, **37**, 368–384.

Brickman, P., Redfield, J., Harrison, A. A., & Crandall, R. Drive and predisposition as factors in the attitudinal effects of mere exposure. *Journal of Personality and Social Psychology*, 1972, **8**, 31–44.

Brigham, J. C., & Barkowitz, P. Do they all look alike? The effect of race, sex, experience, and attitudes on the ability to recognize faces. *Journal of Applied Social Psychology*, 1978, **8**, 306–318.

Brigham, J. C., & Biesbrecht, L. W. All in the family: Racial attitudes. *Journal of Communication*, 1976, **26**(4), 69–74.

Brigham, J. C., & Richardson, C. B. Race, sex, and helping in the marketplace. *Journal of Applied Social Psychology*, 1979, **9**, 314–322.

Brigham, J. C., Maas, A., Snyder, L. D., & Spaulding, K. The accuracy of eyewitness identifications in a field setting. *Journal of Personality and Social Psychology*, 1982, **42**, 673–681.

Brigham, J. C., & Williamson, N. L. Cross-racial recognition and age: When you're over 60, do they still all look alike? *Personality and Social Psychology Bulletin*, 1979, **5**, 218–222.

Broad, W. J. Paranormal powers are so much hocus-pocus. *Science*, 1980, **207**, 389.

Brock, T. C. Communicator-recipient similarity and decision change. *Journal of Personality and Social Psychology*, 1965, **1**, 650–654.

Brockner, J., & Hulton, A. J. B. How to reverse the vicious cycle of low self-esteem: The importance of attentional focus. *Journal of Experimental Social Psychology*, 1978, **6**, 564–578.

Bronfenbrenner, U. The mirror image in Soviet-American relations. *Journal of Social Issues*, 1961, **17**(3), 45–56.

Brook, P. Filming a masterpiece. *Observer Weekend Review*, July 26, 1964. Cited by L. Tiger in *Men in groups*. New York: Random House, 1969, p. 163.

Brooks, W. N., & Doob, A. N. Justice and the jury. *Journal of Social Issues*, 1975, **31**, 171–182.

Broverman, I. K., Broverman, D. M., Clarkson, F. E., Rosenkrantz, P. S., & Vogel, S. R. Sex-role stereotypes and clinical judgments of mental health. *Journal of Consulting and Clinical Psychology*, 1970, **34**, 1–7.

Broverman, I. K., Vogel, S. R., Broverman, D. M., Clarkson, F. E., & Rosenkrantz, P. S. Sex-role stereotypes: A current appraisal. *Journal of Social Issues*, 1972, **28**(2), 59–78.

Brown, R. *Social psychology*. New York: Free Press, 1965.

Brown, R. Further comment on the risky shift. *American Psychologist*, 1974, **29**, 468–470.

Brownmiller, S. Comments on the "pornography and aggression" symposium at the American Psychological Association convention, 1980.

Bruck, C. Zimbardo: Solving the maze. *Human Behavior*. April 1976, pp. 25–31.

Bruner, J. S. Play is serious business. *Psychology Today*, January 1975, pp. 81–83.

Bryan, J. H., & Test, M. A. Models and helping: Naturalistic studies in aiding behavior. *Journal of Personality and Social Psychology*, 1967, **6**, 400–407.

Bryant, J., & Zillmann, D. Effect of intensification of annoyance through unrelated residual excitation on substantially delayed hostile behavior. *Journal of Experimental Social Psychology*, 1979, **15**, 470–480.

Buckhout, R. Eyewitness testimony. *Scientific American*, December 1974, pp. 23–31.

Burger, J. M. Motivational biases in the attribution of responsibility for an accident: A meta-analysis of the defensive-attribution hypothesis. *Psychological Bulletin*, 1981, **90**, 496–512.

Burger, J. M., & Petty, R. E. The low-ball compliance technique: Task or person commitment? *Journal of Personality and Social Psychology*, 1981, **40**, 492–500.

Burgess, R. L., & Huston, T. L. (Eds.). *Social exchange in developing relationships*. New York: Academic Press, 1979.

Burnstein, E., & Vinokur, A. Persuasive argumentation and social comparison as determinants of attitude polarization. *Journal of Experimental Social Psychology*, 1977, **13**, 315–332.

Burnstein, E., & Worchel, P. Arbitrariness of frustration and its consequences for aggression in a social situation. *Journal of Personality*, 1962, **30**, 528–540.

Burr, W. R. *Theory construction and the sociology of the family*. New York: Wiley, 1973.

Burstin, K., Doughtie, E. B., & Raphaeli, A. Contrastive vignette technique: An indirect methodology designed to address reactive social attitude measurement. *Journal of Applied Social Psychology*, 1980, **10**, 147–165.

Burton, J. W. *Conflict and communication*. New York: Free Press, 1969.

Buss, A. H. Aggression pays. In J. L. Singer (Ed.), *The control of aggression and violence: Cognitive and physiological factors*. New York: Academic Press, 1971.

Butcher, S. H. *Aristotle's theory of poetry and fine art*. New York: Dover Publications, 1951.

Buys, C. J., & Larson, K. L. Human sympathy groups. *Psychological Reports*, 1979, **45**, 547–553.

Byrne, D. *The attraction paradigm*. New York: Academic Press, 1971.

Byrne, D., & Clore, G. L. A reinforcement model of evaluative responses. *Personality: An International Journal*, 1970, **1**, 103–128.

Byrne, D., Ervin, C. R., & Lamberth, J. Continuity between the experimental study of attraction and real-life computer dating. *Journal of Personality and Social Psychology*, 1970, **16**, 157–165.

Byrne, D., & Nelson, D. Attraction as a linear function of proportion of positive reinforcements. *Journal of Personality and Social Psychology*, 1965, **1**, 659–663.

Byrne, D., & Wong, T. J. Racial prejudice, interpersonal attraction, and assumed dissimilarity of attitudes. *Journal of Abnormal and Social Psychology*, 1962, **65**, 246–253.

Bytwerk, R. L. Julius Streicker and the impact of *Der Stürmer*. *Wiener Library Bulletin*, 1976, **29**, 41–46.

Bytwerk, R. L., & Brooks, R. D. Julius Streicher and the rhetorical foundations of the holocaust. Paper presented to the Central States Speech Association convention, 1980.

Calhoun, J. B. Population density and social pathology. *Scientific American*, February 1962, pp. 139–148.

Cameron, P. *The life cycle: Perspectives and commentary*. Oceanside, N.Y.: Dabor, 1977.

Campbell, A. A. Factors associated with attitudes toward Jews. In T. M. Newcomb & E. L. Hartley (Eds.), *Readings in social psychology*. New York: Holt, 1947.

Campbell, D. T. The conflict between social and biological evolution and the concept of original sin. *Zygon*, 1975, **10**, 234–249. (a)

Campbell, D. T. On the conflicts between biological and social evolution and between psychology and moral tradition. *American Psychologist*, 1975, **30**, 1103–1126. (b)

Campbell, E. Q., & Pettigrew, T. F. Racial and

moral crisis: The role of Little Rock ministers. *American Journal of Sociology*, 1959, **64**, 509–516.

Cann, A., Calhoun, L. G., & Selby, J. W. Attributing responsibility to the victim of rape: Influence of information regarding past sexual experience. *Human Relations*, 1979, **32**, 57–67.

Cansler, D. C., & Stiles, W. B. Relative status and interpersonal presumptuousness. *Journal of Experimental Social Psychology*, 1981, **17**, 459–471.

Caplan, N. The new ghetto man: A review of recent empirical studies. *Journal of Social Issues*, 1970, **26**(1), 59–73.

Caproni, V., Levine, D., O'Neal, E., McDonald, P., & Garwood, G. Seating position, instructor's eye contact availability, and student participation in a small seminar. *Journal of Social Psychology*, 1977, **103**, 315–316.

Carducci, B. J., Cosby, P. C., & Ward, C. D. Sexual arousal and interpersonal evaluations. *Journal of Experimental Social Psychology*, 1978, **14**, 449–457.

Carlsmith, J. M., & Anderson, C. A. Ambient temperature and the occurrence of collective violence: A new analysis. *Journal of Personality and Social Psychology*, 1979, **37**, 337–344.

Carlsmith, J. M., Ellsworth, P., & Whiteside, J. Guilt, confession and compliance. Unpublished manuscript, Stanford University, 1968. Cited by J. L. Freeman, D. O. Sears, & J. M. Carlsmith in *Social psychology*. Englewood Cliffs, N.J.: Prentice-Hall, 1978, pp. 275–276.

Carlsmith, J. M., & Gross, A. E. Some effects of guilt on compliance. *Journal of Personality and Social Psychology*, 1969, **11**, 232–239.

Carroll, E. I. *The face of emotion*. New York: Appleton, 1971.

Cartwright, D. S. The nature of gangs. In D. S. Cartwright, B. Tomson, & H. Schwartz (Eds.), *Gang delinquency*. Monterey, Calif.: Brooks/Cole, 1975.

Carver, C. S., & Scheier, M. F. Self-focusing effects of dispositional self-consciousness, mirror presence, and audience presence. *Journal of Personality and Social Psychology*, 1978, **36**, 324–332.

Carver, C. S., & Scheier, M. F. *Attention and self-regulation*. New York: Springer-Verlag, 1981.

Cash, T. F. Physical attractiveness: An annotated bibliography of theory and research in the behavioral sciences (Ms. 2370). *Catalog of Selected Documents in Psychology*, 1981, **11**, 83.

Cash, T. F., Begley, P. J., McGown, D. A., & Weise, B. C. When counselors are heard but not seen: Initial impact of physical attractiveness. *Journal of Counseling Psychology*, 1975, **22**, 273–279.

Cash, T. F., Gillen, B., & Burns, D. S. Sexism and beautyism in personnel consultant decision making. *Journal of Applied Psychology*, 1977, **62**, 301–310.

Cass, R. C., & Edney, J. J. The commons dilemma: A simulation testing the effects of resource visibility and territorial division. *Human Ecology*, 1978, **6**, 371–386.

Cavior, N., & Boblett, P. Physical attractiveness of dating versus married couples. *Proceedings of the 80th Annual Convention of the American Psychological Association*, 1972, **7**, 175–176.

Cavoukian, A. Eyewitness testimony: The ineffectiveness of discrediting information. Paper presented at the American Psychological Association convention, 1980.

Cavoukian, A., & Doob, A. N. The effects of a judge's charge and subsequent re-charge on judgments of guilt. *Basic and Applied Social Psychology*, 1980, **1**, 103–114.

CBS News/New York Times. Poll on sex-role norms, October 1977. Reported in *Public Opinion*, January–February 1979, p. 37.

CBS News/New York Times. Survey, February 16–19, 1978. Reported in *Public Opinion*, September–October 1978, p. 37.

Chaiken, S. Communicator physical attractiveness and persuasion. *Journal of Personality and Social Psychology*, 1979, **37**, 1387–1397.

Chaiken, S. Heuristic versus systematic information processing and the use of source versus message cues in persuasion. *Journal of Personality and Social Psychology*, 1980, **39**, 752–766.

Chaiken, S., & Baldwin, M. W. Affective-cognitive consistency and the effect of salient behavioral information on the self-perception of attitudes. *Journal of Personality and Social Psychology*, 1981, **41**, 1–12.

Chaiken, S., & Eagly, A. H. Communication modality as a determinant of message persuasiveness and message comprehensibility. *Journal of Personality and Social Psychology*, 1978, **34**, 605–614.

Chaikin, A. L., & Derlega, V. J. Nonverbal mediators of expectancy effects in black and white children. *Journal of Personality and Social Psychology*, 1979, **37**, 897–912.

Chance, J. E., & Goldstein, A. G. Depth of processing in response to own- and other-race faces. *Personality and Social Psychology Bulletin*, 1981, **7**, 475–480.

Chapman, L. J., & Chapman, J. P. Genesis of popular but erroneous psychodiagnostic observations. *Journal of Abnormal Psychology*, 1969, **74**, 272–280.

Chapman, L. J., & Chapman, J. P. Test results are what you think they are. *Psychology Today*, November 1971, pp. 18–22, 106–107.

Check, J., & Malamuth, N. Can there be positive effects of participation in pornography experiments? *Journal of Sex Research*, 1983, in press.

Chen, S. C. Social modification of the activity of ants in nest-building. *Physiological Zoology*, 1937, **10**, 420–436.

Chertkoff, J. M. Sociopsychological views on sequential effects in coalition formation. *merican Behavioral Scientist*, 1975, **18**, 451–471.

Chesterfield, Lord. *Letters*.

Chickering, A. W., & McCormick, J. Personality development and the college experience. *Research in Higher Education*, 1973, No. 1, 62–64.

Chobot, D. S., Goldberg, P. A., Abramson, L. M., & Abramson, P. R. Prejudice against women: A replication and extension. *Psychological Reports*, 1974, **35**, 478.

Christian, J. J., Flyger, V., & Davis, D. E. Factors in the mass mortality of a herd of sika deer, *Cervus Nippon*. *Chesapeake Science*, 1960, **1**, 79–95.

Cialdini, R. B., & Ascani, K. Test of a concession procedure for inducing verbal, behavioral and further compliance with a request to give blood. *Journal of Applied Psychology*, 1976, **61**, 295–300.

Cialdini, R. B., Bickman, L., & Cacioppo, J. T. An example of consumeristic social psychology: Bargaining tough in the new car showroom. *Journal of Applied Social Psychology*, 1979, **9**, 115–126.

Cialdini, R. B., Cacioppo, J. T., Bassett, R., & Miller, J. A. Low-ball procedure for producing compliance: Commitment then cost. *Journal of Personality and Social Psychology*, 1978, **36**, 463–476.

Cialdini, R. B., Darby, B. L., & Vincent, J. E. Transgression and altruism: A case for hedonism. *Journal of Experimental Social Psychology*, 1973, **9**, 502–516.

Cialdini, R. B., & Kenrick, D. T. Altruism as hedonism: A social development perspective on the relationship of negative mood state and helping. *Journal of Personality and Social Psychology*, 1976, **34**, 907–914.

Cialdini, R. B., Kenrick, D. T., & Baumann, D. J. Effects of mood on prosocial behavior in children and adults. In N. Eisenberg-Berg (Ed.), *The development of prosocial behavior*. New York: Academic Press, 1981.

Cialdini, R. B., & Richardson, K. D. Two indirect tactics of image management: Basking and blasting. *Journal of Personality and Social Psychology*, 1980, **39**, 406–415.

Cialdini, R. B., & Schroeder, D. A. Increasing compliance by legitimizing paltry contributions: When even a penny helps. *Journal of Personality and Social Psychology*, 1976, **34**, 599–604.

Cialdini, R. B., Vincent, J. E., Lewis, S. K., Catalan, J., Wheeler, D., & Danby, B. L. Reciprocal concessions procedure for inducing compliance: The door-in-the-face technique. *Journal of Personality and Social Psychology*, 1975, **31**, 206–215.

Cicero. *De Finibus*. Book iii, chap. 9, sec. 31.

Clark, K., & Clark, M. Racial identification and preference in Negro children. In T. M. Newcomb & E. L. Hartley (Eds.), *Readings in social psychology*. New York: Holt, 1947.

Clark, M. S. Noncomparability of benefits given and received: A cue to the existence of friendship. *Social Psychology Quarterly*, 1981, **44**, 375–381.

Clark, M. S., & Mills, J. Interpersonal attraction in exchange and communal relationships. *Journal of Personality and Social Psychology*, 1979, **37**, 12–24.

Clark, R. D., III. Effects of sex and race on helping behavior in a nonreactive setting. *Representative Research in Social Psychology*, 1974, **5**, 1–6.

Clark, R. D., III. The effects of reinforcement, punishment and dependency on helping behavior. *Personality and Social Psychology Bulletin*, 1975, **1**, 596–599.

Clarke, A. C. An examination of the operation of residual propinquity as a factor in mate selection. *American Sociological Review*, 1952, **27**, 17–22.

Cleghorn, R. ABC News, meet the Literary Digest. *Detroit Free Press*, October 31, 1980.

Clifford, M. M., & Walster, E. H. The effect of

physical attractiveness on teacher expectation. *Sociology of Education*, 1973, **46**, 248–258.

Cline, M. E., Holmes, D. S., & Werner, J. C. Evaluations of the work of men and women as a function of the sex of the judge and type of work. *Journal of Applied Social Psychology*, 1977, **7**, 89–93.

Cline, V. B., Croft, R. G., & Courrier, S. Desensitization of children to television violence. *Journal of Personality and Social Psychology*, 1973, **27**, 360–365.

Clore, G. L., Bray, R. M., Itkin, S. M., & Murphy, P. Interracial attitudes and behavior at a summer camp. *Journal of Personality and Social Psychology*, 1978, **36**, 107–116.

Clore, G. L., Wiggins, N. H., & Itkin, G. Gain and loss in attraction: Attributions from nonverbal behavior. *Journal of Personality and Social Psychology*, 1975, **31**, 706–712.

Coates, B., Pusser, H. E., & Goodman, I. The influence of "Sesame Street" and "Mister Rogers' Neighborhood" on children's social behavior in the preschool. *Child Development*, 1976, **47**, 138–144.

Cocozza, J. J., & Steadman, H. J. Prediction in psychiatry: An example of misplaced confidence in experts. *Social Problems*, 1978, **25**, 265–276.

Codol, J.-P. On the so-called superior conformity of the self behavior: Twenty experimental investigations. *European Journal of Social Psychology*, 1976, **5**, 457–501.

Cohen, C. E. Person categories and social perception: Testing some boundaries of the processing effects of prior knowledge. *Journal of Personality and Social Psychology*, 1981, **40**, 441–452.

Cohen, D. Familiar faces at the British psychology society meeting. *APA Monitor*, March 1980, p. 13.

Cohen, E. G. Design and redesign of the desegregated school: Problems of status, power and conflict. In W. G. Stephan & J. R. Feagin (Eds.), *School desegregation: Past, present, and future*. New York: Plenum Press, 1980. (a)

Cohen, E. G. A multi-ability approach to the integrated classroom. Paper presented at the American Psychological Association convention, 1980. (b)

Cohen, S. Training to understand TV advertising: Effects and some policy implications. Paper presented at the American Psychological Association convention, 1980.

Cohen, S., Evans, G., Krantz, D., & Stokols, D. Physiological, motivational, and cognitive effects of aircraft noise on children: Moving from the laboratory to the field. *American Psychologist*, 1980, **35**, 231–243.

Cole, D. L. Psychology as a liberating art. *Teaching of Psychology*, 1982, **9**, 23–26.

Coleman, J. S. *Community conflict*. New York: Free Press, 1957.

Coles, R. Shrinking history. *New York Review of Books*, Part I, February 22, 1973, pp. 15–21; Part II, March 8, 1973, pp. 25–29.

College Board. *Student descriptive questionnaire*, 1976-1977 data. Princeton, N.J.: Educational Testing Service.

Collins, B. E., & Hoyt, M. F. Personal responsibility-for-consequences: An integration and extension of the forced compliance literature. *Journal of Experimental Social Psychology*, 1972, **8**, 558–593.

Comstock, G., Chaffee, S., Katzman, N., McCombs, M., & Roberts, D. *Television and human behavior*. New York: Columbia University Press, 1978.

Condran, J. G. Changes in white attitudes toward blacks: 1963–1977. *Public Opinion Quarterly*, 1979, **43**, 463–476.

Condry, J., & Condry, S. Sex differences: A study in the eye of the beholder. *Child Development*, 1976, **47**, 812–819.

Context, February 1, 1970, p. 1.

Conway, F., & Siegelman, J. *Snapping: America's epidemic of sudden personality change*. New York: Delta Books, 1979.

Cook, S. W. Opportunities for future social science contributions to school desegregation. Paper presented at the American Psychological Association convention, 1975.

Cook, S. W. Interpersonal and attitudinal outcomes in cooperating interracial groups. *Journal of Research and Development in Education*, 1978, **12**, 97–113.

Cook, S. W. Social science and school desegregation: Did we mislead the Supreme Court? *Personality and Social Psychology Bulletin*, 1979, **5**, 420–437.

Cook, S. W. Unresolved issues of cooperative learning. Paper presented at the American Psychological Association convention, 1980.

Cook, T. D., & Flay, B. R. The persistence of experimentally induced attitude change. In L. Berkowitz (Ed.), *Advances in experimental social psychology.* Vol. 11. New York: Academic Press, 1978.

Cooper, H. M. Statistically combining independent studies: A meta-analysis of sex differences in conformity research. *Journal of Personality and Social Psychology*, 1979, **37**, 131–146.

Cosby, P. C. Self-disclosure: A literature review. *Psychological Bulletin*, 1973, **79**, 73–91.

Cotton, J. L. Ambient temperature and violent crime. Paper presented at the Midwestern Psychological Association convention, 1981.

Cottrell, N. B., Wack, D. L., Sekerak, G. J., & Rittle, R. M. Social facilitation of dominant responses by the presence of an audience and the mere presence of others. *Journal of Personality and Social Psychology*, 1968, **9**, 245–250.

Cousins, N. The taxpayers revolt: Act two. *Saturday Review*, September 16, 1978, p. 56.

Cowan, C., Thompson, W., & Ellsworth, P. C. The effects of death qualification on jurors' predisposition to convict and on the quality of deliberation. *Law and Human Behavior*, 1982, in press.

Craik, F. I. M., & Tulving, E. Depth of processing and the retention of words in episodic memory. *Journal of Experimental Psychology*, 1975, **104**, 268–294.

Crano, W. D., & Mellon, P. M. Causal influence of teachers' expectations on children's academic performance: A cross-lagged panel analysis. *Journal of Educational Psychology*, 1978, **70**, 39–49.

Crawford, T. J. Sermons on racial tolerance and the parish neighborhood context. *Journal of Applied Social Psychology*, 1974, **4**, 1–23.

Crespi, I. Attitude measurement, theory, and prediction. *Public Opinion Quarterly*, 1977, **41**, 285–294.

Crocker, J. Judgment of covariation by social perceivors. *Psychological Bulletin*, 1981, **90**, 272–292.

Crocker, J., Hannah, D. B., & Weber, R. Personal memory and causal attributions. *Journal of Personality and Social Psychology*, 1982, in press.

Crosby, F. A model of egoistical relative deprivation. *Psychological Review*, 1976, **83**, 85–113.

Crosby, F., Bromley, S., & Saxe, L. Recent unobtrusive studies of black and white discrimination and prejudice: A literature review. *Psychological Bulletin*, 1980, **87**, 546–563.

Crosby, F., & Nyquist, L. The female register: An empirical study of Lakoff's hypotheses. *Language in Society*, 1977, **6**, 313–322.

Cross, J. F., & Cross, J. Age, sex, race, and the perception of facial beauty. *Developmental Psychology*, 1971, **5**, 433–439.

Cross, P. Not *can* but *will* college teaching be improved? *New Directions for Higher Education*, Spring 1977, No. 17, pp. 1–15.

Crouse, B. B., & Mehrabian, A. Affiliation of opposite-sexed strangers. *Journal of Research in Personality*, 1977, **11**, 38–47.

Crutchfield, R. A. Conformity and character. *American Psychologist*, 1955, **10**, 191–198.

Cunningham, J. D. Self-disclosure intimacy: Sex, sex-of-target, cross-national, and generational differences. *Personality and Social Psychology Bulletin*, 1981, **7**, 314–319.

Cunningham, J. D., Starr, P. A., & Kanouse, D. E. Self as actor, active observer, and passive observer: Implications for causal attributions. *Journal of Personality and Social Psychology*, 1979, **37**, 1146–1152.

Cunningham, M. R. Weather, mood, and helping behavior: Quasi experiments with the sunshine Samaritan. *Journal of Personality and Social Psychology*, 1979, **37**, 1947–1956.

Cunningham, M. R., Steinberg, J., & Grev, R. Wanting to and having to help: Separate motivations for positive mood and guilt-induced helping. *Journal of Personality and Social Psychology*, 1980, **38**, 181–192.

Curry, T. J., & Emerson, R. M. Balance theory: A theory of interpersonal attraction? *Sociometry*, 1970, **33**, 216–238.

Dabbs, J. M., & Janis, I. L. Why does eating while reading facilitate opinion change? An experimental inquiry. *Journal of Experimental Social Psychology*, 1965, **1**, 133–144.

Dalto, C. A., Ajzen, I., & Kaplan, K. J. Self-disclosure and attraction: Effects of intimacy and desirability on beliefs and attitudes. *Journal of Research in Personality*, 1979, **13**, 127–138.

Darley, J. M., & Batson, C. D. From Jerusalem to Jericho: A study of situational and dispositional variables in helping behavior. *Journal of Personality and Social Psychology*, 1973, **27**, 100–108.

Darley, J. M., & Berscheid, E. Increased liking as a result of the anticipation of personal contact. *Human Relations*, 1967, **20**, 29–40.

Darley, J. M., & Gross, P. H. A hypothesis-conforming bias in labelling effects. *Journal of Personality and Social Psychology*, 1983, in press.

Darley, J. M., & Latané, B. Bystander intervention in emergencies: Diffusion of responsibility. *Journal of Personality and Social Psychology*, 1968, **8** 377–383.

Darley, J. M., & Latané, B. When will people help in a crisis? *Psychology Today*, December 1968, pp. 54–57, 70–71.

Darley, J. M., Seligman, C., & Becker, L. J. The lesson of twin rivers: Feedback works. *Psychology Today*, April 1979, pp. 16, 23–24.

Darley, J. M., Teger, A. I., & Lewis, L. D. Do groups always inhibit individuals' response to potential emergencies? *Journal of Personality and Social Psychology*, 1973, **26**, 395–399.

Darley, S., & Cooper, J. Cognitive consequences of forced non-compliance. *Journal of Personality and Social Psychology*, 1972, **24**, 321–326.

Darlington, R. B., & Macker, C. E. Displacement of guilt-produced altruistic behavior. *Journal of Personality and Social Psychology*, 1966, **4**, 442–443.

Darrow, C. (1933), cited by E. H. Sutherland & D. R. Cressy, *Principles of criminology*. Philadelphia: Lippincott, 1966, p. 442.

Dashiell, J. F. An experimental analysis of some group effects. *Journal of Abnormal and Social Psychology*, 1930, **25**, 190–199.

Davis, J. D. When boy meets girl: Sex roles and the negotiation of intimacy in an acquaintance exercise. *Journal of Personality and Social Psychology*, 1978, **36**, 684–692.

Davis, J. H., Holt, R. W., Spitzer, C. E., & Stasser, G. The effects of consensus requirements and multiple decisions on mock juror verdict preferences. *Journal of Experimental Social Psychology*, 1981, **17**, 1–15.

Davis, J. H., Kerr, N. L., Atkin, R. S., Holt, R., & Meek, D. The decision processes of 6- and 12-person mock juries assigned unanimous and two-thirds majority rules. *Journal of Personality and Social Psychology*, 1975, **32**, 1–14.

Davis, J. H., Kerr, N. L., Strasser, G., Meek, D., & Holt, R. Victim consequences, sentence severity, and decision process in mock juries. *Organizational Behavior and Human Performance*, 1977, **18**, 346–365.

Davis, K. E., & Jones, E. E. Changes in interpersonal perception as a means of reducing cognitive dissonance. *Journal of Abnormal and Social Psychology*, 1960, **61**, 402–410.

Davis, M. H. The case for attributional egotism. Paper presented at the American Psychological Association convention, 1979.

Davis, M. H., & Stephan, W. G. Attributions for exam performance. *Journal of Applied Social Psychology*, 1980, **10**, 235–248.

Dawes, R. M. Shallow psychology. In J. S. Carroll & J. W. Payne (Eds.), *Cognition and social behavior*. Hillsdale, N.J.: Lawrence Erlbaum, 1976.

Dawes, R. M. You can't systematize human judgment: Dyslexia. In R. A. Shweder (Ed.), *New directions for methodology of social and behavioral science: Fallible judgment in behavioral research*. San Francisco: Jossey-Bass, 1980.

Dawes, R. M. Social dilemmas. *Annual Review of Psychology*, 1980, **31**, 169–193.

Dawes, R. M., McTavish, J., & Shaklee, H. Behavior, communication, and assumptions about other people's behavior in a commons dilemma situation. *Journal of Personality and Social Psychology*, 1977, **35**, 1–11.

Dawkins, R. *The selfish gene*. New York: Oxford University Press, 1976.

Deaux, K. *The behavior of men and women*. Monterey, Calif.: Brooks/Cole, 1976.

Deaux, K., & Emswiller, T. Explanations of successful performance on sex-linked tasks: What is skill for the male is luck for the female. *Journal of Personality and Social Psychology*, 1974, **29**, 80–85.

Deci, E. L. *The psychology of self-determination*. Lexington, Mass.: Lexington Books, 1980.

Deci, E. L., Nezlek, J., & Sheinman, L. Characteristics of the rewarder and intrinsics of motivation of the rewardee. *Journal of Personality and Social Psychology*, 1981, **40**, 1–10.

Deci, E. L., & Ryan, R. M. The empirical exploration of intrinsic motivational processes. In L. Berkowitz (Ed.), *Advances in experimental social psychology* (Vol. 13). New York: Academic Press, 1980.

Deffenbacher, K. A. Eyewitness accuracy and confidence: Can we infer anything about their relationship? *Law and Human Behavior*, 1980, **4**, 243–260.

DeJong, W. An examination of self-perception mediation of the foot-in-the-door effect. *Journal of Personality and Social Psychology*, 1979, **37**, 2221–2239.

DeJong, W. Consensus information and the foot-in-the door effect. *Personality and Social Psychology Bulletin*, 1981, 7, 423–430.

Delgado, J. In M. Pines, *The brain changers.* New York: Harcourt Brace Jovanovich, 1973.

Dembroski, T. M., Lasater, T. M., & Ramirez, A. Communicator similarity, fear arousing communications, and compliance with health care recommendations. *Journal of Applied Social Psychology*, 1978, **8**, 254–269.

Dengerink, H. A., & Myers, J. D. Three effects of failure and depression on subsequent aggression. *Journal of Personality and Social Psychology*, 1977, **35**, 88–96.

Denmark, F. L. The psychology of women: An overview of an emerging field. *Personality and Social Psychology Bulletin*, 1977, **3**, 356–367.

Dermer, M., Cohen, S. J., Jacobsen, E., & Anderson, E. A. Evaluative judgments of aspects of life as a function of vicarious exposure to hedonic extremes. *Journal of Personality and Social Psychology*, 1979, **37**, 247–260.

Dermer, M., & Pyszczynski, T. A. Effects of erotica upon men's loving and liking responses for women they love. *Journal of Personality and Social Psychology*, 1978, **36**, 1302–1309.

Dermer, M., & Thiel, D. L. When beauty may fail. *Journal of Personality and Social Psychology*, 1975, **31**, 1168–1176.

Desor, J. A. Toward a psychological theory of crowding. *Journal of Personality and Social Psychology*, 1972, **21**, 79–83.

Deutsch, M. Social psychological perspectives on distributive justice. Unpublished manuscript, Teachers College, Columbia University, 1977.

Deutsch, M. Fifty years of conflict. In L. Festinger (Ed.), *Retrospectives on social psychology.* New York: Oxford University Press, 1980.

Deutsch, M., & Collins, M. E. *Interracial housing: A psychological evaluation of a social experiment.* Minneapolis: University of Minnesota Press, 1951.

Deutsch, M., & Gerard, H. B. A study of normative and informational social influence upon individual judgment. *Journal of Abnormal and Social Psychology*, 1955, **51**, 629–636.

Deutsch, M., & Krauss, R. M. The effect of threat upon interpersonal bargaining. *Journal of Abnormal and Social Psychology*, 1960, **61**, 181–189.

de Vaux, R. *Ancient Israel* (Vol. 2): *Religious institutions.* New York: McGraw-Hill, 1965.

DeVries, D. L., & Slavin, R. E. Teams-games-tournaments (TGT): Review of ten classroom experiments. *Journal of Research and Development in Education*, 1978, **12**, 28–38.

Diaconis, P. Statistical problems in ESP research. *Science*, 1978, **201**, 131–136. Quoted from H. H. Nininger, *Our stone-pelted earth.* Boston: Houghton Mifflin, 1933.

Diener, E. Effects of prior destructive behavior, anonymity, and group presence on deindividuation and aggression. *Journal of Personality and Social Psychology*, 1976, **33**, 497–507.

Diener, E. Deindividuation, self-awareness, and disinhibition. *Journal of Personality and Social Psychology*, 1979, **37**, 1160–1171.

Diener, E., & Crandall, R. An evaluation of the Jamaican anticrime program. *Journal of Applied Social Psychology*, 1979, **9**, 135–146.

Diener, E., Fraser, S. C., Beaman, A. L., & Kelem, R. T. Effects of deindividuation on variables on stealing among Halloween trick-or-treaters. *Journal of Personality and Social Psychology*, 1976, **33**, 178–183.

Diener, E., Lusk, R., DeFour, D., & Flax, R. Deindividuation: Effects of group size, density, number of observers, and group member similarity on self-consciousness, and disinhibited behavior. *Journal of Personality and Social Psychology*, 1980, **39**, 449–459.

Diener, E., & Wallbom, M. Effects of self-awareness on antinormative behavior. *Journal of Research in Personality*, 1976, **10**, 107–111.

Dillehay, R. C., & Nietzel, M. T. Constructing a science of jury behavior. In L. Wheeler (Ed.), *Review of personality and social psychology* (Vol. 1.). Beverly Hills, Calif.: Sage Publications, 1980.

Dion, K. K. Physical attractiveness and evaluations of children's transgressions. *Journal of Personality and Social Psychology*, 1972, **24**, 207–213.

Dion, K. K. Young children's stereotyping of facial attractiveness. *Developmental Psychology*, 1973, **9**, 183–188.

Dion, K. K. Physical attractiveness and interpersonal attraction. In M. Cook & G. Wilson (Eds.), *Love and attraction.* New York: Pergamon Press, 1979.

Dion, K. K., & Berscheid, E. Physical attractiveness and peer perception among children. *Sociometry*, 1974, **37**, 1–12.

Dion, K. K., Berscheid, E., & Walster, E. What is beautiful is good. *Journal of Personality and Social Psychology*, 1972, **24**, 285–290.

Dion, K. K., & Dion, K. L. Defensiveness, intimacy, and heterosexual attraction. *Journal of Research in Personality*, 1978, **12**, 479–487.

Dion, K. K., & Stein, S. Physical attractiveness and interpersonal influence. *Journal of Experimental Social Psychology*, 1978, **14**, 97–109.

Dion, K. L. Intergroup conflict and intra-group cohesiveness. In W. G. Austin, & S. Worchel (Eds.), *The social psychology of intergroup relations*. Monterey, Calif.: Brooks/Cole, 1979.

Doise, W. Intergroup relations and polarization of individual and collective judgments. *Journal of Personality and Social Psychology*, 1969, **12**, 136–143.

Dollard, J., Doob, L., Miller, N., Mowrer, O. H., & Sears, R. R. *Frustration and aggression*. New Haven, Conn.: Yale University Press, 1939.

Doms, M., & Van Avarmaet, E. Majority influence, minority influence and conversion behavior: A replication. *Journal of Experimental Social Psychology*, 1980, **16**, 283–292.

Donnerstein, E. Aggressive erotica and violence against women. *Journal of Personality and Social Psychology*, 1980, **39**, 269–277.

Donnerstein, E., & Berkowitz, L. Victim reactions in aggressive erotic films as a factor in violence against women. *Journal of Personality and Social Psychology*, 1981, **41**, 710–724.

Donnerstein, E., Donnerstein, M., & Evans, R. Erotic stimuli and aggression: Facilitation or inhibition. *Journal of Personality and Social Psychology*, 1975, **32**, 237–244.

Donnerstein, E., & Malamuth, N. The effects of aggressive-erotic mass media stimuli. In L. Berkowitz (Ed.), *Advances in experimental social psychology* (Vol. 15). New York: Academic Press, 1982.

Donnerstein, M., & Donnerstein, E. Modeling in the control of interracial aggression: The problem of generality. *Journal of Personality*, 1977, **45**, 100–116.

Doob, A. N., & Kirshenbaum, H. M. Bias in police lineups—partial remembering. *Journal of Police Science and Administration*, 1973, **1**, 287–293.

Dooling, D. J., & Lachman, R. Effects of comprehension on retention of prose. *Journal of Experimental Psychology*, 1971, **88**, 216–222.

Douglass, F. *Narrative of the life of Fredrick Douglass, an American slave: Written by himself* (B. Quarles, Ed.). Cambridge, Mass.: Harvard University Press, 1960.

Drabman, R. S., & Thomas, M. H. Does media violence increase children's toleration of real-life aggression? *Developmental Psychology*, 1974, **10**, 418–421.

Drabman, R. S., & Thomas, M. H. Does TV violence breed indifference? *Journal of Communications*, 1975, **25**(4), 86–89.

Drabman, R. S., & Thomas, M. H. Does watching violence on television cause apathy? *Pediatrics*, 1976, **57**, 329–331.

Drabman, R. S., & Thomas, M. H. Children's imitation of aggressive and prosocial behavior when viewing alone and in pairs. *Journal of Communication*, 1977, **27**(3), 199–205.

Duncan, B. L. Differential social perception and attribution of intergroup violence: Testing the lower limits of stereotyping of blacks. *Journal of Personality and Social Psychology*, 1976, **34**, 590–598.

Dutton, D. G. Reactions of restaurateurs to blacks and whites violating restaurant dress regulations. *Canadian Journal of Behavioural Science*, 1971, **3**, 298–302.

Dutton, D. G. Reverse discrimination: The relationship of amount of perceived discrimination toward a minority group on the behavior of majority group members. *Canadian Journal of Behavioural Science*, 1973, 5, 34–45.

Dutton, D. G., & Aron, A. P. Some evidence for heightened sexual attraction under conditions of high anxiety. *Journal of Personality and Social Psychology*, 1974, **30**, 510–517.

Dutton, D. G., & Lake, R. A. Threat of own prejudice and reverse discrimination in interracial situations. *Journal of Personality and Social Psychology*, 1973, **28**, 94–100.

Duval, S. Conformity on a visual task as a function of personal novelty on attitudinal dimensions and being reminded of the object status of self. *Journal of Experimental Social Psychology*, 1976, **12**, 87–98.

Duval, S., Duval, V. H., & Neely, R. Self-focus, felt responsibility, and helping behavior. *Journal of Personality and Social Psychology*, 1979, **37**, 1769– 1778.

Duval, S., & Wicklund, R. A. *A theory of objective self-awareness*. New York: Academic Press, 1972.

Eagly, A. H., & Carli, L. L. Sex of researcher and sex-typed communications as determinants of sex differences in influenceability: A meta-analysis of social influence studies. *Psychological Bulletin*, 1981, **90**, 1–20.

Eagly, A. H., & Himmelfarb, S. Attitudes and opinions. *Annual Review of Psychology*, 1978, **29**, 517–554.

Eagly, A. H., Wood, W., & Chaiken, S. Causal inferences about communicators and their effect on opinion change. *Journal of Personality and Social Psychology*, 1978, **36**, 424–435.

Eagly, A. H., Wood, W., & Fishbaugh, L. Sex differences in conformity: Surveillance by the group as a determinant of male nonconformity. *Journal of Personality and Social Psychology*, 1981, **40**, 384–394.

Eakins, B. W., & Eakins, R. G. *Sex differences in human communication*. Boston: Houghton Mifflin, 1978.

Ebbesen, E. B., Duncan, B., & Konecni, V. J. Effects of content of verbal aggression on future verbal aggression: A field experiment. *Journal of Experimental Social Psychology*, 1975, **11**, 192–204.

Edney, J. J. Free riders en route to disaster. *Psychology Today*, August, 1979, pp. 80–87, 102. (a)

Edney, J. J. The nuts game: A concise commons dilemma analog. *Environmental Psychology and Nonverbal Behavior*, 1979, **3**, 252–254. (b)

Edney, J. J. The commons problem: Alternative perspectives. *American Psychologist*, 1980, **35**, 131–150.

Edney, J. J., & Harper, C. S. The commons dilemma: A review of contributions from psychology. *Environmental Management*, 1978, **2**, 491–507.

Efran, M. G. The effect of physical appearance on the judgment of guilt, interpersonal attraction, and severity of recommended punishment in a simulated jury task. *Journal of Research in Personality*, 1974, **8**, 45–54.

Ehrhardt, A. A., & Meyer-Bahlburg, H. F. L. Effects of prenatal sex hormones on gender-related behavior. *Science*, 1980, **211**, 1312–1318.

Eibl-Eibesfeldt, I. *The biology of peace and war: Men, animals, and aggression*. New York: Viking Press, 1979.

Einhorn, H. J., & Hogarth, R. M. Confidence in judgment: Persistence of the illusion of validity. *Psychological Review*, 1978, **85**, 394–416.

Eisenger, R., & Mills, J. Perception of the sincerity and competence of a communicator as a function of the extremity of his position. *Journal of Experimental Social Psychology*, 1968, **4**, 224–232.

Ekman, P. *The face of man: Expressions of universal emotions in a New Guinea village*. New York: Garland STPM Press, 1980.

Elashoff, J. R., & Snow, R. E. *Pygmalion reconsidered*. Worthington, Ohio: Charles A. Jones, 1971.

Elder, G. H., Jr. Appearance and education in marriage mobility. *American Sociological Review*, 1969, **34**, 519–533.

Eldersveld, S. J., & Dodge, R. W. Personal contact or mail propaganda? An experiment in voting turnout and attitude change. In D. Katz, D. Cartwright, S. Eldersveld, & A. M. Lee (Eds.), *Public opinion and propaganda*. New York: Dryden Press, 1954.

Eliot, T. S. "The Hollow Men." In *The Complete Poems and Plays, 1909–1950*. New York: Harcourt Brace and Company, 1958.

Elman, D., & Killebrew, T. J. Incentives and seat belts: Changing a resistant behavior through extrinsic motivation. *Journal of Applied Social Psychology*, 1978, **8**, 72–83.

Emswiller, T., Deaux, K., & Willits, J. E. Similarity, sex, and requests for small favors. *Journal of Applied Social Psychology*, 1971, **1**, 284–291.

Epstein, J. F., O'Neal, E. C., & Jones, K. J. Prior experience with firearms can mitigate the weapons effect. Paper presented at the American Psychological Association convention, 1980.

Epstein, S. The stability of behavior: II. Implications for psychological research. *American Psychologist*, 1980, **35**, 790–806.

Epstein, Y. M., Krupat, E., & Obudho, C. Clean is beautiful: Identification and preference as a function of race and cleanliness. *Journal of Social Issues*, 1976, **32**(2), 109–118.

Epstein, Y. M., Woolfolk, R. L., & Lehrer, P. M. Physiological, cognitive, and nonverbal responses to repeated exposure to crowding. *Journal of Applied Social Psychology*, 1981, **11**, 1–13.

Erickson, B., Holmes, J. G., Frey, R., Walker, L., & Thibaut, J. Functions of a third party in the resolution of conflict: The role of a judge in pretrial conferences. *Journal of Personality and Social Psychology*, 1974, **30**, 296–306.

Erickson, B., Lind, E. A., Johnson, B. C., & O'Barr, W. M. Speech style and impression formation in a court setting: The effects of powerful and powerless speech. *Journal of Experimental Social Psychology*, 1978, **14**, 266–279.

Ericsson, K. A., & Simon, H. A. Verbal reports as data. *Psychological Reviews*, 1980, **87**, 215–217.

Eron, L. D. Prescription for reduction of aggression. *American Psychologist*, 1980, **35**, 244–252.

Eron, L. D. Parent-child interaction, television violence, and aggression of children. *American Psychologist*, 1981, **37**, 197–211.

Eron, L. D., & Huesmann, L. R. Adolescent aggression and television. *Annals of the New York Academy of Sciences*, 1980, **347**, 319–331.

Erskine, H. The polls: Women's role. *Public Opinion Quarterly*, 1971, **35**, 275–290.

Etaugh, C., & Rose, S. Adolescents' sex bias in the evaluation of performance. *Developmental Psychology*, 1975, **11**, 663–664.

Etaugh, C., & Sanders, S. Evaluation of performance as a function of status and sex variables. *Journal of Social Psychology*, 1974, **94**, 237–241.

Etzioni, A. The Kennedy experiment. *The Western Political Quarterly*, 1967, **20**, 361–380.

Etzioni, A. Human beings are not very easy to change after all. *Saturday Review*, June 3, 1972, 45–47.

European Economic Community Commission. Survey, October–November, 1977. Reported in *Public Opinion*, February–March 1980, p. 37.

Evans, G. W. Human spatial behavior: The arousal model. In A. Baum & Y. M. Epstein (Eds.), *Human response to crowding*. Hillsdale, N.J.: Lawrence Erlbaum, 1978.

Evans, G. W. Behavioral and physiological consequences of crowding in humans. *Journal of Applied Social Psychology*, 1979, **9**, 27–46.

Evans, R. I., Rozelle, R. M., Maxwell, S. E., Raines, B. E., Dill, C. A., Guthrie, T. J., Henderson, A. H., & Hill, P. C. Social modeling films to deter smoking in adolescents: Results of a three year field investigation. *Journal of Applied Psychology*, 1981, **66**, 399–414.

Falbo, T. Relationships between sex, sex role, and social influence. *Psychology of Women Quarterly*, 1977, **2**, 62–72.

Falbo, T. PAQ types and power strategies used in intimate relationships. *Psychology of Women Quarterly*, 1982, **6**, in press.

Falbo, T., & Peplau, L. A. Power strategies in intimate relationships. *Journal of Personality and Social Psychology*, 1980, **38**, 618–628.

Faranda, J. A., Kaminski, J. A. & Giza, B. K. An assessment of attitudes toward women with the bogus pipeline. Paper presented at the American Psychological Association convention, 1979.

Farley, R., Schuman, H., Bianchi, S., Colasanto, D., & Hatchett, S. Chocolate city, vanilla suburbs: Will the trend toward racially separate communities continue? *Social Science Research*, 1978, **7**, 319–344.

Farquhar, J. W., Maccoby, N., Wood, P. D., Alexander, J. K., Breitrose, H., Brown, B. W., Jr., Haskell, W. L., McAlister, A. L., Meyer, A. J., Nash, J. D., & Stern, M. P. Community education for cardiovascular health. *Lancet*, June 4, 1977, 1192–1195.

Fazio, R. H. On the self-perception explanation of the overjustification effect: The role of the salience of initial attitude. *Journal of Experimental Social Psychology*, 1981, **17**, 417–426.

Fazio, R. H., Effrein, E. A., & Falender, V. J. Self-perceptions following social interaction. *Journal of Personality and Social Psychology*, 1981, **41**, 232–242.

Fazio, R. H., & Zanna, M. P. Direct experience and attitude-behavior consistency. In L. Berkowitz (Ed.), *Advances in experimental social psychology*, Vol. 14. New York: Academic Press, 1981.

Fazio, R. H., Zanna, M. P., & Cooper, J. Dissonance versus self-perception: An integrative view of each theory's proper domain of application. *Journal of Experimental Social Psychology*, 1977, **13**, 464–479.

Fazio, R. H., Zanna, M. P., & Cooper, J. On the relationship of data to theory: A reply to Ronis and Greenwald. *Journal of Experimental Social Psychology*, 1979, **15**, 70–76.

Feierabend, I., & Feierabend, R. Conflict, crisis, and collision: A study of international stability. *Psychology Today*, May 1968, pp. 26–32, 69–70.

Feierabend, I., & Feierabend, R. Systemic conditions of political aggression: An application of frustration-aggression theory. In I. K. Feierabend, R. L. Feierabend, & T. R. Gurr (Eds.), *Anger, violence, and politics: Theories and research*. Englewood Cliffs, N.J.: Prentice Hall, 1972.

Feldman, K. A., & Newcomb, T. M. *The impact of college on students*. San Francisco: Jossey-Bass, 1969.

Feldman, R. S. & Prohaska, T. The student as Pygamalion: Effect of student expectation on the teacher. *Journal of Educational Psychology*, 1979, **71**, 485–493.

Feldman, R. S., & Theiss, A. J. The teacher and student as Pygmalions: Joint effects of teacher and student expectations. *Journal of Educational Psychology*, 1982, **74**, 217–223.

Feldman-Summers, S., & Kiesler, S. B. Those who are number two try harder: The effect of sex on attributions of causality. *Journal of Personality and Social Psychology*, 1974, **30**, 846–855.

Feller, W. *An introduction to probablility theory and its applications* (Vol. 1). New York: Wiley, 1968. Cited by B. Fischhoff in For those condemned to study the past: Reflections on historical judgment. In R. A. Shweder (Ed.) *New directions for methodology of social and behavioral science*. San Francisco: Jossey-Bass, 1980.

Felson, R. B. Ambiguity and bias in the self-concept. *Social Psychology Quarterly*, 1981, **44**, 64–69.

Felson, R. B., & Bohrnstedt, G. W. Are the good beautiful or the beautiful good? The relationship between children's perceptions of ability and perceptions of physical attractiveness. *Social Psychology Quarterly*, 1979, **42**, 386–392.

Fenigstein, A., & Carver, C. S. Self-focusing effects of heartbeat feedback. *Journal of Personality and Social Psychology*, 1978, **36**, 1241–1250.

Fernandez-Collado, C., & Greenberg, B. S., with Korzenny, F., & Atkin, C. K. Sexual intimacy and drug use in TV series. *Journal of Communication*, 1978, **28**(3), 30–37.

Fersch, E. A., Jr. *Psychology and psychiatry in courts and corrections*. New York: Wiley, 1980.

Feshbach, N. D. The child as "psychologist" and "economist": Two curricula. Paper presented at the American Psychological Association convention, 1980.

Feshbach, N. D., & Feshbach, S. Empathy training and the regulation of aggression: Potentialities and limitations. Paper presented at the Western Psychological Association convention, 1981.

Feshbach, S. Aggression. In P. H. Mussen (Ed.), *Carmichael's manual of child psychology* (Vol. 3). New York: Wiley, 1970.

Feshbach, S. Television advertising and children: Policy issues and alternatives. Paper presented at the American Psychological Association convention, 1980.

Festinger, L. A theory of social comparison processes. *Human Relations*, 1954,7, 117–140.

Festinger, L. Behavioral support for opinion change. *Public Opinion Quarterly*, 1964, **28**, 404–417.

Festinger, L. Looking backward. In L. Festinger (Ed.), *Retrospections on social psychology*. New York: Oxford University Press, 1980.

Festinger, L. & Carlsmith, J. M. Cognitive consequences of forced compliance. *Journal of Abnormal and Social Psychology*, 1959, **58**, 203–210.

Festinger, L. & Maccoby, N. On resistance to persuasive communications. *Journal of Abnormal and Social Psychology*, 1964, **68**, 359–366.

Festinger, L., Pepitone, A., & Newcomb, T. Some consequences of deindividuation in a group. *Journal of Abnormal and Social Psychology*, 1952, **47**, 382–389.

Festinger, L., Schachter, S., & Back, K. *Social pressures in informal groups: A study of human factors in housing*. New York: Harper & Bros., 1950.

Feynman, R. *The character of physical law*. Cambridge, Mass.: MIT Press, 1967.

Fichter, J. *America's forgotten priests: What are they saying?* New York: Harper, 1968.

Fiedler, F. W. Leadership effectiveness. *American Behavioral Scientist*, 1981, **24**, 619–632.

Fields, J. M., & Schuman, H. Public beliefs about the beliefs of the public. *Public Opinion Quarterly*, 1976, **40**, 427–448.

Fincham, F. D. & Jaspars, J. M. Attribution of responsibility: From man the scientist to man as lawyer. In L. Berkowitz (Ed.), *Advances in Experimental Social Psychology* (Vol. 13.) New York: Academic Press, 1980.

Fischhoff, B. Perceived informativeness of facts. *Journal of Experimental Psychology: Human Perception and Performance*, 1977, **3**, 349–358.

Fischhoff, B. Debiasing. In D. Kahneman, P. Slovic, & A. Tversky (Eds.), *Judgment under uncertainty: Heuristics and biases*. New York: Cambridge University Press, 1982.

Fischhoff, B., & Beyth, R. "I knew it would happen": Remembered probabilities of once-future things. *Organizational Behavior and Human Performance*, 1975, **13**, 1–16.

Fischhoff, B., Slovic, P., & Lichtenstein, S. Knowing with certainty: The appropriateness of extreme confidence. *Journal of Experimental Psychology: Human Perception and Performance*, 1977, **3**, 552–564.

Fishbein, D., & Thelen, M. H. Husband-wife similarity and marital satisfaction: A different approach. Paper presented at the Midwestern Psychological Association convention, 1981. (a)

Fishbein, D., & Thelen, M. H. Psychological factors in mate selection and marital satisfaction: A review (Ms. 2374). *Catalog of Selected Documents in Psychology*, 1981, **11**, 84. (b)

Fishbein, M., & Ajzen, I. Attitudes toward objects as predictive of single and multiple behavioral criteria. *Psychological Review*, 1974, **81**, 59–74.

Fisher, G. H. Ambiguity of form: Old and new. *Perception and Psychophysics*, 1968, **4**, 189–192.

Fishman, D. B., & Loftus, E. F. Expert psychological testimony on eyewitness identification. *Law and Psychology Review*, 1978, **4**, 87–103.

Fishman, P. M. What do couples talk about when they're alone? In D. Butturff & E. L. Epstein (Eds.), *Women's language and style*. Akron, Ohio: University of Akron Press, 1978.

Fiske, D. W. When are verbal reports veridical? In R. A. Shweder (Ed.), *New directions for methodology of social and behavioral science: Fallible judgment in behavioral research*. San Francisco: Jossey-Bass, 1980.

Fiske, S. T. Social cognition and affect. In J. H. Harvey (Ed.), *Cognition, social behavior, and the environment*. Hillsdale, N.J.: Lawrence Erlbaum, 1980.

Fitzpatrick, A. R., & Eagly, A. H. Anticipatory belief polarization as a function of the expertise of a discussion partner. *Personality and Social Psychology Bulletin*, 1981, **7**, 636–642.

Flaherty, J. F., & Dusek, J. B. An investigation of the relationship between psychological androgyny and components of self-concept. *Journal of Personality and Social Psychology*, 1980, **38**, 984–992.

Flowers, M. L. A laboratory test of some implications of Janis's groupthink hypotheses. *Journal of Personality and Social Psychology*, 1977, **35**, 888–896.

Foa, U. G., & Foa, E. B. *Resource theory of social exchange*. Morristown, N.J.: General Learning Press, 1975.

Foley, L. A. Personality and situational influences on changes in prejudice: A replication of Cook's railroad game in a prison setting. *Journal of Personality and Social Psychology*, 1976, **34**, 846–856.

Fonberg, E. Physiological mechanisms of emotional and instrumental aggression. In S. Feshbach & A. Fraczek (Eds.), *Aggression and behavior change*. New York: Praeger, 1979.

Forer, B. R. The fallacy of personal validation: A classroom demonstration of gullibility. *Journal of Abnormal and Social Psychology*, 1949, **44**, 118–123.

Form, W. H., & Nosow, S. *Community in disaster*. New York: Harper, 1958.

Forsyth, D. R., Berger, R. E., & Mitchell, T. The effects of self-serving vs. other-serving claims of responsibility on attraction and attribution in groups. *Social Psychology Quarterly*, 1981, **44**, 59–64.

Forward, J. R., & Williams, J. R. Internal-external control and black militancy. *Journal of Social Issues*, 1970, **26**(1), 75–92.

Foss, R. D. The role of social influence in blood donation. Paper presented at the American Psychological Association convention, 1978.

Foss, R. D. Structural effects in simulated jury decision making. *Journal of Personality and Social Psychology*, 1981, **40**, 1053–1062.

Foss, R. D., & Dempsey, C. B. Blood donation and the foot-in-the-door technique: A limiting case. *Journal of Personality and Social Psychology*, 1979, **37**, 580–590.

Foulke, E., & Sticht, T. G. Review of research on the intelligibility and comprehension of accelerated speech. *Psychological Bulletin*, 1969, **72**, 50–62.

Francis, W. D., & Schofield, J. W. The impact of race on interaction in a desegregated school. *Journal of Educational Psychology*, 1982, in press.

Frankel, A., & Snyder, M. L. Poor performance following unsolvable problems: Learned helplessness or egotism? *Journal of Personality and Social Psychology*, 1978, **36**, 1415–1423.

Franklin, B. J. Victim characteristics and helping behavior in a rural southern setting. *Journal of Social Psychology*, 1974, **93**, 93–100.

Freedman, J. L. Long-term behavioral effects of cognitive dissonance. *Journal of Experimental Social Psychology*, 1965, **1**, 145–155.

Freedman, J. L. *Crowding and behavior*. New York: Viking Press, 1975.

Freedman, J. L. Reconciling apparent differences between the responses of humans and other animals to crowding. *Psychological Review*, 1979, **86**, 80–85.

Freedman, J. L., Birsky, J., & Cavoukian, A. Environmental determinants of behavioral contagion: Density and number. *Basic and Applied Social Psychology*, 1980, **1**, 155–161.

Freedman, J. L., & Fraser, S. C. Compliance without pressure: The foot-in-the-door technique. *Journal of Personality and Social Psychology*, 1966, **4**, 195–202.

Freedman, J. L., Heshka, S., & Levy, A. Population density and pathology: Is there a relationship? *Journal of Experimental Social Psychology*, 1975, **11**, 539–552.

Freedman, J. L., & Perlick, D. Crowding, contagion, and laughter. *Journal of Experimental Social Psychology*, 1979, **15**, 295–303.

Freedman, J. L., & Sears, D. O. Warning, distraction, and resistance to influence. *Journal of Personality and Social Psychology*, 1965, **1**, 262–266.

Fried, R., & Berkowitz, L. Music hath charms . . . and can influence helpfulness. *Journal of Applied Social Psychology*, 1979, **9**, 199–208.

Friedrich, L. K., & Stein, A. H. Aggressive and prosocial television programs and the natural behavior of preschool children. *Monographs of the Society for Research in Child Development*, 1973, **38**(4, Serial No. 151).

Friedrich, L. K., & Stein, A. H. Prosocial television and young children: The effects of verbal labeling and role playing on learning and behavior. *Child Development*, 1975, **46**, 27–38.

Friend, P., Kalin, R., & Giles, H. Sex bias in the evaluation of journal articles: Sexism in England. *British Journal of Social and Clinical Psychology*, 1979, **18**, 77–78.

Frieze, I. H., Bar-Tal, D., & Carroll, J. S. (Eds.). *New approaches to social problems: Applications of attribution theory*. San Francisco: Jossey-Bass, 1979.

Frieze, I. H., & Knoble, J. The effects of alcohol on marital violence. Paper presented at the American Psychological Association convention, 1980.

Frieze, I. H., Parsons, J. E., Johnson, P. B., Ruble, D. N., & Zellman, G. L. *Women and sex roles: A social psychological perspective*. New York: W. W. Norton, 1978.

Frodi, A. Experimental and physiological responses associated with anger and aggression in women and men. *Journal of Research in Personality*, 1978, **12**, 335–349.

Frodi, A., Macaulay, J., & Thome, P. R. Are women always less aggressive than men? A review of the experimental literature. *Psychology Bulletin*, 1977, **84**, 634–660.

Froming, W. J., Walker, G. R., & Lopyan, K. J. Public and private self-awareness: When personal attitudes conflict with societal expectations. *Journal of Experimental Social Psychology*, 1982, **18**, in press.

Fulbright, J. W. United Press International, April 5, 1971. Cited by A. C. Elms, *Social psychology and social reliance*. Boston: Little, Brown, 1972.

Funder, D. C. On seeing ourselves as others see us: Self-other agreement and discrepancy in personality ratings. *Journal of Personality*, 1980, **48**, 473–493.

Furst, C. J., Burnam, M. A., & Kocel, K. M. Life stressors and romantic affiliation. Paper presented at the Western Psychological Association convention, 1980.

Gaebelein, J. W., & Mander, A. Consequences for targets of aggression as a function of aggressor and instigator roles: Three experiments. *Personality and Social Psychology Bulletin*, 1978, **4**, 465–468.

Gaertner, S. L. Helping behavior and racial discrimination among liberals and conservatives. *Journal of Personality and Social Psychology*, 1973, **25**, 335–341.

Gaertner, S. L. The role of racial attitudes in helping behavior. *Journal of Social Psychology*, 1975, **97**, 95–101.

Gaertner, S. L., & Bickman, L. Effects of race on the elicitation of helping behavior. *Journal of Personality and Social Psychology*, 1971, **20**, 218–222.

Gaertner, S. L., & Dovidio, J. F. The subtlety of white racism, arousal, and helping behavior. *Journal of Personality and Social Psychology*, 1977, **35**, 691–707.

Gager, N., & Schurr, C. *Sexual assault: Confronting rape in America*. New York: Grosset and Dunlap, 1976.

Galizio, M., & Hendrick, C. Effect of musical accompaniment on attitude: The guitar as a prop for persuasion. *Journal of Applied Social Psychology*, 1972, **2**, 350–359.

Gallup, G. H. *The Gallup poll: Public opinion 1935–1971* (Vol. 3). New York: Random House, 1972. pp. 551, 1716.

Gallup, G. H. *The Gallup poll: Public opinion 1972–1977* (Vol. 4). Wilmington, Del.: Scholarly Resources, Inc., 1978.

Gallup Opinion Index. Political, social and economic trends, No. 155, June 1978, pp. 1–5.

Gallup Opinion Index. No. 183, December 1980, p. 75.

Gallup poll, June 15, 1978. Reported in Princeton Religion Research Center, *Emerging Trends*, undated, **1**(3).

Gallup poll. December 5–8, 1980. Reported in *Public Opinion*, April–May 1981, p. 38.

Gallup poll. February 14–23, 1981. Reported in *Newsweek* March 9, 1981.

Gallup poll. Equal rights amendment. Reported by NBC *Today Show*, December 4, 1981.

Gamson, W. A., Fireman, B., & Rytina, S. *Encounters with unjust authority*. Homewood, Ill.: Dorsey Press, 1982.

Garbarino, J., & Bronfenbrenner, U. The socialization of moral judgment and behavior in cross-cultural perspective. In T. Lickona (Ed.), *Moral development and behavior: Theory, research, and social issues*. New York: Holt, Rinehart and Winston, 1976.

Gardner, M. *Fads and fallacies in the name of science*. New York: Dover, 1957. Cited by E. Hilgard in *Divided* *consciousness: Multiple controls in human thought and action*. New York: Wiley, 1977.

Gaskie, M. F. Toward workability of the workplace. *Architectural Record*, mid-August 1980, pp. 70–75.

Gastorf, J. W., Suls, J., & Sanders, G. S. Type A coronary-prone behavior pattern and social facilitation. *Journal of Personality and Social Psychology*, 1980, **8**, 773–780.

Gates, M. F., & Allee, W. C. Conditioned behavior of isolated and grouped cockroaches on a simple maze. *Journal of Comparative Psychology*, 1933, **15**, 331–358.

Gazzaniga, M. The split brain in man. In R. Held & W. Richards (Eds.), *Perception: Mechanisms and models*. San Francisco: W. H. Freeman, 1972.

Geen, R. G. The effects of being observed on performance. In P. B. Paulus (Ed.), *Psychology of group influence*. Hillsdale, N.J.: Lawrence Erlbaum, 1980.

Geen, R. G. Evaluation apprehension and social facilitation: A reply to Sanders. *Journal of Experimental Social Psychology*, 1981, **17**, 252–256.

Geen, R. G., & Quanty, M. B. The catharsis of aggression: An evaluation of a hypothesis. In L. Berkowitz (Ed.), *Advances in experimental social psychology* (Vol. 10). New York: Academic Press, 1977.

Geen, R. G., Rakosky, J. J., & Pigg, R. Awareness of arousal and its relation to aggression. *British Journal of Social and Clinical Psychology*, 1972, **11**, 115–121.

Geis, F. L., Brown, V., Jennings (Walstedt), J., & Porter, N. Do stereotyped TV commercials depress women's achievement aspirations? *Sex Roles*, 1982, in press.

Gerard, H. B., & Mathewson, G. C. The effects of severity of initiation on liking for a group: A replication. *Journal of Experimental Social Psychology*, 1966, **2**, 278–287.

Gerard, H. B., Wilhelmy, R. A., & Conolley, E. S. Conformity and group size. *Journal of Personality and Social Psychology*, 1968, **8**, 79–82.

Gerbasi, K. C., Zuckerman, M., & Reis, H. T. Justice needs a new blindfold: A review of mock jury research. *Psychological Bulletin*, 1977, **84**, 323–345.

Gerbner, G. Television: The American schoolchild's national curriculum day in and day out. *PTA Today*, April 1981, pp. 3–5.

Gerbner, G., Gross, L., Signorielli, N., Morgan, M., & Jackson-Beeck, M. The demonstration of power: Violence profile No. 10. *Journal of Communication*, 1979, **29**(3), 177–196.

Gerbner, G., Gross, L., Signorielli, N., & Morgan, M. Television, violence, victimization, and power. *American Behavioral Scientist*, 1980, **23**, 705–716.

Gergen, K. J., Gergen, M. M., & Meter, K. Individual orientations to prosocial behavior. *Journal of Social Issues*, 1972, **28**(3), 105–130.

Gergen, K. J., Gergen, M. M., & Barton, W. N. Deviance in the dark. *Psychology Today*, October 1973, pp. 129–130.

Gibbons, F. X. Sexual standards and reactions to pornography: Enhancing behavioral consistency through self-focused attention. *Journal of Personality and Social Psychology*, 1978, **36**, 976–987.

Gilbert, S. J. Another look at the Milgram obedience studies: The role of the graduated series of shocks. *Personality and Social Psychology Bulletin*, 1981, **7**, 690–695.

Gillis, J. S., & Avis, W. E. The male-taller norm in mate selection. *Personality and Social Psychology Bulletin*, 1980, **6**, 396–401.

Gilkey, L. *Shantung compound*. New York: Harper & Row, 1966.

Gilmor, T. M. Locus of control as a mediator of adaptive behaviour in children and adolescents. *Canadian Psychological Review*, 1978, **19**, 1–26.

Gilmor, T. M., & Reid, D. W. Locus of control and causal attribution for positive and negative outcomes on university examinations. *Journal of Research in Personality*, 1979, **13**, 154–160.

Gilovich, T. Seeing the past in the present: The effect of associations to familiar events on judgments and decisions. *Journal of Personality and Social Psychology*, 1981, **40**, 797–808.

Ginsburg, B., & Allee, W. C. Some effects of conditioning on social dominance and subordination in inbred strains of mice. *Physiological Zoology*, 1942, **15**, 485–506.

Glass, D. C. Changes in liking as a means of reducing cognitive discrepancies between self-esteem and aggression. *Journal of Personality*, 1964, **32**, 531–549.

Glass, D. C., & Singer, J. E. *Urban stress*. New York: Academic Press, 1972.

Glassman, J. B., Burkhart, B. R., Grant, R. D., & Vallery, G. G. Density, expectation and extended task performance: An experiment in the natural environment. *Environment and Behavior*, 1978, **10**, 299–315.

Gleason, J. M., & Harris, V. A. Group discussion

and defendant's socio-economic status as determinants of judgments by simulated jurors. *Journal of Applied Social Psychology*, 1976, **6**, 186–191.

Glenn, N. D. Aging and attitudinal stability. In O. G. Brim, Jr. & J. Kagan (Eds.), *Constancy and change in human development*. Cambridge, Mass.: Harvard University Press, 1980.

Glenn, N. D. Personal communication, 1981.

Gmelch, G. Baseball magic. *Human Nature*, August 1978, pp. 32–39.

Goethals, G. R., & Nelson, E. R. Similarity in the influence process: The belief-value distinction. *Journal of Personality and Social Psychology*, 1973, **25**, 117–122.

Goethals, G. R., & Reckman, R. F. The perception of consistency in attitudes. *Journal of Experimental Social Psychology*, 1973, **9**, 491–501.

Goethals, G. R., & Zanna, M. P. The role of social comparison in choice shifts. *Journal of Personality and Social Psychology*, 1979, **37**, 1469–1476.

Goffman, E. On cooling the mark out: Some aspects of adaptation to failure. *Psychiatry*, 1952, **15**, 451–463.

Goffman, E. *Interaction ritual*. Garden City, N.Y.: Doubleday Anchor, 1967.

Gold, A. R. Reactions to work by authors differing in sex and achievement (Unpublished doctoral dissertation, Columbia University, 1972). (University Microfilms No. 72-31, 210.)

Goldberg, L. R. Simple models or simple processes? Some research on clinical judgments. *American Psychologist*, 1968, **23**, 483–496.

Goldberg, M. E., & Gorn, G. J. Television's impact on preferences for non-white playmates: Canadian Sesame Street inserts. *Journal of Broadcasting*, 1979, **23**, 27–32.

Goldberg, P. Are women prejudiced against women? *Transaction*. April 1968, pp. 28–30.

Golding, W. *Lord of the flies*. New York: Coward-McCann, 1962.

Goldman, C. An examination of social facilitation. Unpublished manuscript, University of Michigan, 1967. Cited by R. B. Zajonc in Compresence, in P. B. Paulus (Ed.), *Psychology of group influence*. Hillsdale, N.J.: Lawrence Erlbaum, 1980.

Goldman, W., & Lewis, P. Beautiful is good: Evidence that the physically attractive are more socially skillful. *Journal of Experimental Social Psychology*, 1977, **13**, 125–130.

Goldstein, A. P., Garr, E. G., Davidson, W. S., II, & Wehr, P. *In response to aggression: Methods of control and prosocial alternatives*. Elmsford, N.Y.: Pergamon Press, 1981.

Goldstein, J. H. *Social psychology*. New York: Academic Press, 1980.

Goldstein, J. H., & Arms, R. L. Effects of observing athletic contests on hostility. *Sociometry*, 1971, **34**, 83–90.

Goldstein, M., & Davis, E. E. Race and belief: A further analysis of the social determinants of behavioral intentions. *Journal of Personality and Social Psychology*, 1972, **22**, 346–355.

Gollwitzer, P. M., Earle, W. B., & Stephan, W. G. Affect as a determinant of egotism: Residual excitation and performance attributions. *Journal of Personality and Social Psychology*, in press.

Gonzalez, A. E. J., & Cooper, J. What to do with leftover dissonance: Blame it on the lights. Unpublished manuscript, Princeton University, 1975.

Gorsuch, R. L. Religion as a significant predictor of important human behavior. In W. J. Donaldson, Jr. (Ed.), *Research in Mental Health and Religious Behavior*, Psychological Studies Institute, 1976.

Gorsuch, R. L., & Aleshire, D. Christian faith and ethnic prejudice: A review and interpretation of research. *Journal for the Scientific Study of Religion*, 1974, **13**, 281–307.

Gottlieb, J., & Carver, C. S. Anticipation of future interaction and the bystander effect. *Journal of Experimental Social Psychology*, 1980, **16**, 253–260.

Gould, L. X. *Ms.*, May 1980, pp. 61–64.

Gould, R., Brounstein, P. J., & Sigall, H. Attributing ability to an opponent: Public aggrandizement and private denigration. *Sociometry*, 1977, **40**, 254–261.

Gouldner, A. W. The norm of reciprocity: A preliminary statement. *American Sociological Review*, 1960, **25**, 161–178.

Graziano, W., Brothen, T., & Berscheid, E. Height and attraction: Do men and women see eye-to-eye? *Journal of Personality*, 1978, **46**, 128–145.

Greeley, A. M. *The sociology of the paranormal: A reconnaissance*. Beverly Hills: Sage, 1975.

Greeley, A. M. Pop psychology and the Gospel. *Theology Today*, 1976, **23**, 224–231.

Greeley, A. M., & Sheatsley, P. B. The acceptance of desegregation continues to advance. *Scientific American*, 1971, **225**(6), 13–19. (a)

Greeley, A. M., & Sheatsley, P. B. Attitudes toward racial integration. *Scientific American*, 1971, **225**(6), 13–19. (b)

Green, S. K., & Gross, A. E. Self-serving biases in implicit evaluations. *Personality and Social Psychology Bulletin*, 1979, **5**, 214–217.

Greenberg, J. Group vs. individual equity judgments: Is there a polarization effect? *Journal of Experimental Social Psychology*, 1979, **15**, 504–512.

Greenberg, J. Attentional focus and locus of performance causality as determinants of equity behavior. *Journal of Personality and Social Psychology*, 1980, **38**, 579–585.

Greenberg, J., Pyszczynski, T., & Solomon, S. The self-serving bias: Beyond self-presentation. *Journal of Experimental Social Psychology*, 1982, **18**, 56–67.

Greenwald, A. G. Cognitive learning, cognitive response to persuasion, and attitude change. In A. G. Greenwald, T. C. Brock, & T. M. Ostrom (Eds.), *Psychological foundations of attitudes*. New York: Academic Press, 1968.

Greenwald, A. G. On the inconclusiveness of crucial cognitive tests of dissonance versus self-perception theories. *Journal of Experimental Social Psychology*, 1975, **11**, 490–499.

Greenwald, A. G. The totalitarian ego: Fabrication and revision of personal history. *American Psychologist*, 1980, **35**, 603–618.

Griffitt, W. Environmental effects on interpersonal affective behavior: Ambient effective temperature and attraction. *Journal of Personality and Social Psychology*, 1970, **15**, 240–244.

Griffitt, W., & Jackson, T. Simulated jury decisions: The influence of jury-defendant attitude similarity-dissimilarity. *Social Behavior and Personality*, 1973, **1**, 1–7.

Griffitt, W., & Veitch, R. Hot and crowded: Influences of population density and temperature on interpersonal affective behavior. *Journal of Personality and Social Psychology*, 1971, **17**, 92–98.

Griffitt, W., & Veitch, R. Preacquaintance attitude similarity and attraction revisited: Ten days in a fall-out shelter. *Sociometry*, 1974, **37**, 163–173.

Grofman, B. The slippery slope: Jury size and jury verdict requirements—legal and social science approaches. In B. H. Raven (Ed.), *Policy studies review annual* (Vol. 4). Beverly Hills, Calif.: Sage Publications, 1980.

Gross, A. E., & Crofton, C. What is good is beautiful. *Sociometry*, 1977, **40**, 85–90.

Grube, J. W., Kleinhesselink, R. R., & Kearney, K. A. Male self-acceptance and attraction toward women. *Personality and Social Psychology Bulletin*, 1982, **8**, 107–112.

Gruder, C. L. Choice of comparison persons in evaluating oneself. In J. M. Suls & R. L. Miller (Eds.), *Social comparison processes*. Washington: Hemisphere Publishing, 1977.

Gruder, C. L., Cook, T. D., Hennigan, K. M., Flay, B., Alessis, C., & Kalamaj, J. Empirical tests of the absolute sleeper effect predicted from the discounting cue hypothesis. *Journal of Personality and Social Psychology*, 1978, **36**, 1061–1074.

Gruder, C. L., Romer, D., & Korth, B. Dependency and fault as determinants of helping. *Journal of Experimental Social Psychology*, 1978, **14**, 227–335.

Grunberger, R. *The 12-year Reich: A social history of Nazi Germany 1933–1945*. New York: Holt, Rinehart & Winston, 1971.

Grush, J. E. Attitude formation and mere exposure phenomena: A nonartifactual explanation of empirical findings. *Journal of Personality and Social Psychology*, 1976, **33**, 281–290.

Grush, J. E. A summary review of mediating explanations of exposure phenomena. *Personality and Social Psychology Bulletin*, 1979, **5**, 154–159.

Grush, J. E. Impact of candidate expenditures, regionality, and prior outcomes on the 1976 Democratic presidential primaries. *Journal of Personality and Social Psychology*, 1980, **38**, 337–347.

Grush, J. E., McKeough, K. L., & Ahlering, R. F. Extrapolating laboratory exposure research to actual political elections. *Journal of Personality and Social Psychology*, 1978, **36**, 257–270.

Gurr, T. R. The calculus of civil conflict. *Journal of Social Issues*, 1972, **28**(1), 27–47.

Gutierres, S. E., & Kenrick, D. T. Effects of physical attractiveness of stimulus photos on own self esteem. Paper presented at the Western Psychological Association convention, 1979.

Gutmann, D. L. Parenthood, key to comparative study of the life cycle. In N. Datan & L. Ginsberg (Eds.), *Life span developmental psychology: Normative life crises*. New York: Academic Press, 1975.

Haan, N. Two moralities in action contexts: Relationships to thought, ego regulation, and development. *Journal of Personality and Social Psychology*, 1978, **36**, 286–305.

Haas, A. Male and female spoken language differences: Stereotypes and evidence. *Psychological Bulletin*, 1979, **86**, 616–626.

Hacker, H. M. Women as a minority group. *Social Forces*, 1951, **30**, 60–69.

Hadden, J. K. *The gathering storm in the churches.* Garden City, N.Y.: Doubleday, 1969.

Hall, C. S. The incredible Freud. *Contemporary Psychology*, 1978, **23**, 38–39.

Hall, J. A. Gender effects in decoding nonverbal cues. *Psychological Bulletin*, 1978, **85**, 845–857.

Hamblin, R. L., Buckholdt, D., Bushell, D., Ellis, D., & Ferritor, D. Changing the game from get the teacher to learn. *Trans-action*, January 1969, pp. 20–25, 28–31.

Hamill, R., Wilson, T. D., & Nisbett, R. E. Insensitivity to sample bias: Generalizing from atypical cases. *Journal of Personality and Social Psychology*, 1980, **39**, 578–589.

Hamilton, D. L. Stereotype activation and social information processing. Paper presented at the American Psychological Association convention, 1981.

Hamilton, D. L., & Bishop, G. D. Attitudinal and behavioral effects of initial integration of white suburban neighborhoods. *Journal of Social Issues*, 1976, **32**(2), 47–67.

Hamilton, D. L., & Gifford, R. K. Illusory correlation in interpersonal perception: A cognitive basis of stereotypic judgments. *Journal of Experimental Social Psychology*, 1976, **12**, 392–407.

Hamilton, D. L., & Rose, T. L. Illusory correlation and the maintenance of stereotypic beliefs. *Journal of Personality and Social Psychology*, 1980, **39**, 832–845.

Hamilton, D. L., & Zanna, M. P. Differential weighting of favorable and unfavorable attributes in impressions of personality. *Journal of Experimental Research in Personality*, 1972, **6**, 204–212.

Hamilton, V. L. Intuitive psychologist or intuitive lawyer? Alternative models of the attribution process. *Journal of Personality and Social Psychology*, 1980, **39**, 767–772.

Hans, V. P. Evaluating the jury: A case study of the uses of research in policy formation. In R. Roesch & R. Corrado (Eds.), *Evaluation and criminal justice policy*. Beverly Hills, Calif.: Sage Publications, 1981.

Hans, V. P., & Vidmar, N. Jury selection. In N. L. Kerr & R. M. Bray (Eds.), *The psychology of the courtroom*. New York: Academic Press, 1981.

Hansel, C. E. M. *ESP and parapsychology: A critical reevaluation*. Buffalo, N.Y.: Prometheus Books, 1980.

Hardin, G. The tragedy of the commons. *Science*, 1968, **162**, 1243–1248.

Harkins, S. G. Effects of task difficulty and task responsibility on social loafing. Presentation to the First International Conference on Social Processes in Small Groups, Kill Devil Hills, North Carolina, 1981.

Harkins, S. G., & Latané, B. Population and political participation. Paper presented at the American Psychological Association convention, 1980.

Harkins, S. G., Latané, B., & Williams, K. Social loafing: Allocating effort or taking it easy? *Journal of Experimental Social Psychology*, 1980, **16**, 457–465.

Harkins, S. G., & Petty, R. E. Effects of source magnification of cognitive effort on attitudes: An information-processing view. *Journal of Personality and Social Psychology*, 1981, **40**, 401–413. (a)

Harkins, S. G., & Petty, R. E. The multiple source effect in persuasion: The effects of distraction. *Personality and Social Psychology Bulletin*, 1981, **7**, 627–635. (b)

Harris, L. J. Sex differences in spatial ability: Possible environmental, genetic, and neurological factors. In M. Kinsbourne (Ed.), *Asymmetrical function of the brain*. Cambridge: Cambridge University Press, 1978, pp. 405–522.

Harris, L. J. Variances and anomalies. *Science*, 1979, **206**, 50–52.

Harris, T. G. Introduction to E. H. Walster and G. W. Walster, *A new look at love*. Reading, Mass.: Addison-Wesley, 1978.

Harrison, A. A. Mere exposure. In L. Berkowitz (Ed.), *Advances in experimental social psychology* (Vol. 10). New York: Academic Press, 1977, pp. 39–83.

Harvey, J. H., Town, J. P., & Yarkin, K. L. How fundamental is the fundamental attribution error? *Journal of Personality and Social Psychology*, 1981, **40**, 346–349.

Harvey, J. H., & Weary, G. *Perspectives on attributional process*. Dubuque, Iowa: W. C. Brown, 1981.

Hastorf, A., & Cantril, H. They saw a game: A case study. *Journal of Abnormal and Social Psychology*, 1954, **49**, 129–134.

Hatfield, E. See also E. Walster (Hatfield).

Hatfield, E., Walster, G. W., & Traupmann, J. Equity and premarital sex. In M. Cook and G. Wilson (Eds.), *Love and attraction*. New York: Pergamon Press, 1979.

Hatfield, M. O. On neighborhood government. Statement to the Platform Committee, Republican National Convention, 1972.

Hatfield, M. O. Neighborhood government act of 1975. *Congressional Record*, October 1, 1975, **121**, No. 146, p. 30.

Hatvany, N., & Strack, F. The impact of a discredited key witness. *Journal of Applied Social Psychology*, 1980, **10**, 490–509.

Hearold, S. L. Meta-analysis of the effects of television on social behavior. Paper presented at the American Educational Research Association convention, 1979.

Heider, F. *The psychology of interpersonal relations.* New York: Wiley, 1980.

Heilman, M. E. Oppositional behavior as a function of influence attempt intensity and retaliation threat. *Journal of Personality and Social Psychology*, 1976, **33**, 574–578.

Hellman, P. *Avenue of the righteous of nations.* New York: Atheneum, 1980.

Helmreich, R. L., Spence, J. T., & Holahan, C. K. Psychological androgyny and sex role flexibility: A test of two hypotheses. *Journal of Personality and Social Psychology*, 1979, **37**, 1631–1644.

Hemsley, G. D., & Doob, A. N. The effect of looking behavior on perceptions of a communicator's credibility. *Journal of Applied Social Psychology*, 1978, **8**, 136–144.

Hendrick, S. S. Self-disclosure and marital satisfaction. *Journal of Personality and Social Psychology*, 1981, **40**, 1150–1159.

Henley, N. *Body politics: Power, sex, and nonverbal communication.* Englewood Cliffs, N.J.: Prentice-Hall, 1977.

Hennigan, K. M., Del Rosario, M. L., Heath, L., Cook, T. D., Wharton, J. D., & Calder, B. J. Impact of the introduction of television of crime in the United States: Empirical findings and theoretical implications. *Journal of Personality and Social Psychology*, 1982, **42**, 461–477.

Henslin, M. Craps and magic. *American Journal of Sociology*, 1967, **73**, 316–330.

Heradstveit, D. *The Arab-Israeli conflict: Psychological obstacles to peace* (Vol. 28). Oslo, Norway: Universitetsforlaget, 1979. Distributed by Columbia University Press. Reviewed by R. K. White, *Contemporary Psychology*, 1980, **25**, 11–12.

Hesselink, A. Unpublished analysis of American magazine descriptions of the Japanese, 1943–1945 versus 1953–1955, Hope College, Holland, Michigan, 1973.

Higbee, K. L., Millard, R. J., & Folkman, J. R. Social psychology research during the 1970s: Predominance of experimentation and college students. *Personality and Social Psychology Bulletin*, 1982, **8**, 180–183.

Higgins, E. T., & Rholes, W. S. Saying is believing: Effects of message modification on memory and liking for the person described. *Journal of Experimental Social Psychology*, 1978, **14**, 363–378.

Higgins, S. Subject age as a factor in female prejudice against females. Unpublished manuscript, Western Illinois University, 1973.

Hilgard, E. R. *Divided consciousness: Multiple controls in human thought and action.* New York: Wiley, 1977.

Hilgard, E. R., & Loftus, E. F. Effective interrogation of the eyewitness. *International Journal of Clinical and Experimental Hypnosis*, 1979, **27**, 342–357.

Hill, G. W. Group versus individual performance: Are N + 1 heads better than one? *Psychological Bulletin*, 1982, **91**, 517–539.

Hill, W. F. Effects of mere exposure on preferences in nonhuman animals. *Psychological Bulletin*, 1978, **85**, 1177–1198.

Hirt, E. R., & Kimble, C. E. The home-field advantage in sports: Differences and correlates. Paper presented at the Midwestern Psychological Association convention, 1981.

Hodges, B. H. Effect of valence on relative weighting in impression formation. *Journal of Personality and Social Psychology*, 1974, **30**, 378–381.

Hodgson, B. War and peace in Northern Ireland. *National Geographic*, 1981, **159**(4), 470–499.

Hoffman, L. W. Changes in family roles, socialization, and sex differences. *American Psychologist*, 1977, **32**, 644–657.

Hoffman, M. L. Sex differences in empathy and related behaviors. *Psychological Bulletin*, 1977, **84**, 712–722.

Hoffman, M. L. Is altruism part of human nature? *Journal of Personality and Social Psychology*, 1981, **40**, 121–137.

Hokanson, J. E., & Burgess, M. The effects of frustration and anxiety on overt aggression. *Journal of Abnormal and Social Psychology*, 1962, **65**, 232–237. (a)

Hokanson, J. E., & Burgess, M. The effects of three types of aggression on vascular processes. *Journal of Abnormal and Social Psychology*, 1962, **64**, 446–449. (b)

Hokanson, J. E., Burgess, M., & Cohen, M. F. Effects of displaced aggression on systolic blood pressure. *Journal of Abnormal and Social Psychology*, 1963, **67**, 214–218.

Hokanson, J. E., & Edelman, R. Effects of three social responses on vascular processes. *Journal of Personality and Social Psychology*, 1966, **3**, 442–447.

Hokanson, J. E., & Shetler, S. The effect of overt aggression on physiological arousal. *Journal of Abnormal and Social Psychology*, 1961, **63**, 446–448.

Hollander, E. P. Conformity, status, and idiosyncrasy credit. *Psychological Review*, 1958, **65**, 117– 127.

Holmes, O. W. Law in science and science in law. *Harvard Law Review*, 1889, **12**, 443. Cited by W. N. Brooks and A. N. Doob. Justice and the jury. *Journal of Social Issues*, 1975, **31**, 171–182.

Hornstein, H. *Cruelty and kindness*. Englewood Cliffs, N.J.: Prentice-Hall, 1976.

Hosch, H. M., Beck, E. L., & McIntyre, P. Influence of expert testimony regarding eyewitness accuracy on jury decisions. *Law and Human Behavior*, 1980, **4**, 287–296.

Houlden, P., LaTour, S., Walker, L., & Thibaut, J. Preference for modes of dispute resolution as a function of process and decision control. *Journal of Experimental Social Psychology*, 1978, **14**, 13–30.

House, R. A 1976 theory of charismatic leadership. In J. G. Hunt, & L. Larson (Eds.), *Leadership: The cutting edge*. Carbondale, Ill.: Southern Illinois Press, 1977.

Hovland, C. I., Lumsdaine, A. A., & Sheffield, F. D. *Experiments on mass communication. Studies in social psychology in World War II* (Vol. III). Princeton, N.J.: Princeton University Press, 1949.

Hovland, C. I., & Sears, R. Minor studies of aggression: Correlation of lynchings with economic indices. *Journal of Psychology*, 1940, **9**, 301–310.

Howard, J. W., & Rothbart, M. Social categorization and memory for in-group and out-group behavior. *Journal of Personality and Social Psychology*, 1980, **38**, 301–310.

Huesmann, L. R. Television violence and aggressive behavior. In D. Pearl & L. Bouthilet (Eds.), *Television and behavior: Ten years of scientific progress and implications for the 80's*. Washington, D.C.: Superintendent of Documents, U.S. Government Printing Office, 1982.

Hull, J. G. A self-awareness model of the causes and effects of alcohol consumption. *Journal of Abnormal Psychology*, 1981, **90**, 586–600.

Hull, J. G., Levenson, R. W., Young, R. D., & Sher, K. J. The self-awareness reducing effects of alcohol consumption. *Journal of Personality and Social Psychology*, 1982, in press.

Hunt, P. J., & Hillery, J. M. Social facilitation in a location setting: An examination of the effects over learning trials. *Journal of Experimental Social Psychology*, 1973, **9**, 563–571.

Huston, T. L. Ambiguity of acceptance, social desirability, and dating choice. *Journal of Experimental Social Psychology*, 1973, **9**, 32–42.

Huston, T. L., Ruggiero, M., Conner, R., & Geis, G. Bystander intervention into crime: A study based on naturally-occurring episodes. *Social Psychology Quarterly*, 1981, **44**, 14–23.

Hyman, H. H., & Sheatsley, P. B. Attitudes toward desegregation. *Scientific American*, 1956, **195**(6), 35–39, and 1964, **211**(1), 16–23.

Hyman, R. The psychic reading. In T. A. Sebeok & R. Rosenthal (Eds.), *The Clever Hans phenomenon: Communication with horses, whales, apes, and people. Annals of the New York Academy of Sciences* (Vol. 364). New York: New York Academy of Sciences, 1981.

Hyman, R. Cold reading: How to convince strangers that you know all about them. In K. Frazier (Ed.), *Paranormal borderlands of science*. Buffalo, N.Y.: Prometheus Books, 1981.

Ickes, W. On disconfirming our perceptions of others. Paper presented at the American Psychological Association convention, 1980.

Ickes, W. Sex role influences in dyadic interaction: A theoretical model. In C. Mayo & N. Henley (Eds.), *Gender and nonverbal behavior*. New York: Springer-Verlag, 1981.

Ickes, W. A basic paradigm for the study of personality, roles, and social behavior. In W. Ickes & E. S. Knowles (Eds.), *Personality, roles, and social behavior*. New York: Springer-Verlag, 1982.

Ickes, W. Attributional styles and the self-concept. In L. Y. Abramson (Ed.), *Attributional process and clinical psychology*. New York: Guilford Press, in press.

Ickes, W., & Barnes, R. D. Boys and girls together—and alienated: On enacting stereotyped sex roles in mixed-sex dyads. *Journal of Personality and Social Psychology*, 1978, **36**, 669–683.

Ickes, W., & Layden, M. A. Attributional styles. In J. H. Harvey, W. Ickes, & R. F. Kidd (Eds.), *New directions in attribution research* (Vol. 2). Hillsdale, N.J.: Lawrence Erlbaum, 1978.

Ickes, W., Layden, M. A., & Barnes, R. D. Objective self-awareness and individuation: An empirical link. *Journal of Personality*, 1978, **46**, 146–161.

Ickes, W., Patterson, M. L., Rajecki, D. W., & Tanford, S. Behavioral and cognitive consequences of reciprocal versus compensatory responses to preinteraction expectancies. *Social Cognition*, 1982, **1**, 160–190.

Ingham, A. G., Levinger, G., Graves, J., & Peckham, V. The Ringelmann effect: Studies of group size and group performance. *Journal of Experimental Social Psychology*, 1974, **10**, 371–384.

Insko, C. A., & Wilson, M. Interpersonal attraction as a function of social interaction. *Journal of Personality and Social Psychology*, 1977, **35**, 903–911.

Isen, A. M. Success, failure, attention, and reaction to others: The warm glow of success. *Journal of Personality and Social Psychology*, 1970, **15**, 294–301.

Isen, A. M., Clark, M., & Schwartz, M. F. Duration of the effect of good mood on helping: Footprints on the sands of time. *Journal of Personality and Social Psychology*, 1976, **34**, 385–393.

Isen, A. M., Horn, N., & Rosenhan, D. L. Effects of success and failure on children's generosity. *Journal of Personality and Social Psychology*, 1973, **27**, 239–247.

Isen, A. M., & Levin, P. F. Effect of feeling good on helping: Cookies and kindness. *Journal of Personality and Social Psychology*, 1972, **21**, 384–388.

Isen, A. M., Shalker, T. E., Clark, M., & Karp, L. Affect, accessibility of material in memory, and behavior: A cognitive loop. *Journal of Personality and Social Psychology*, 1978, **36**, 1–12.

ISR Newsletter. Institute for Social Research, University of Michigan, 1975, **3**(4), 4–7.

Izard, C. E. *The Face of Emotion*. New York: Appleton, 1971.

Jackman, M. R., & Senter, M. S. Beliefs about race, gender, and social class different, therefore unequal: Beliefs about trait differences between groups of unequal status. In D. J. Treiman & R. V. Robinson (Eds.), *Research in stratification and mobility* (Vol. 2). Greenwich, Conn.: JAI Press, 1981.

Jackson, D. J., & Huston, T. L. Physical attractiveness and assertiveness. *Journal of Social Psychology*, 1975, **96**, 79–84.

Jackson, J. Column in syndicated newspapers, July 19, 1981.

Jackson, J. M., & Latané, B. All alone in front of all those people: Stage fright as a function of number and type of co-performers and audience. *Journal of Personality and Social Psychology*, 1981, **40**, 73–85.

Jacobs, R. C., & Campbell, D. T. The perpetuation of an arbitrary tradition through several generations of a laboratory microculture. *Journal of Abnormal and Social Psychology*, 1961, **62**, 649–658.

Jaffe, Y., Shapir, N., & Yinon, Y. Aggression and its escalation. *Journal of Cross-Cultural Psychology*, 1981, **12**, 21–36.

Jaffe, Y., & Yinon, Y. Retaliatory aggression in individuals and groups. *European Journal of Social Psychology*, 1979, **9**, 177–186.

James, W. *Talks to teachers on psychology: And to students on some of life's ideals*. New York: Holt, 1922, p. 33. (Originally published, 1899.) Cited by W. J. McKeachie, Psychology in America's bicentennial year. *American Psychologist*, 1976, **31**, 819–833.

James, W. *The varieties of religious experience*. New York: Mentor Books, 1958. (Originally published, 1902.)

Janis, I. Groupthink. *Psychology Today*, November 1971, pp. 43–46.

Janis, I. L. *Victims of groupthink*. Boston: Houghton Mifflin, 1982.

Janis, I. L. (a) Counteracting the adverse effects of concurrence-seeking in policy-planning groups: Theory and research perspectives. In H. Brandstätter, J. H. Davis, & G. Stocker-Kreichgauer (Eds.), *Group decision making*. New York: Academic Press, 1982.

Janis, I. L., Kaye, D., & Kirschner, P. (b) Facilitating effects of eating-while-reading on responsiveness to persuasive communications. *Journal of Personality and Social Psychology*, 1965, **1**, 181–186.

Janis, I. L., & Mann, L. Effectiveness of emotional role-playing in modifying smoking habits and attitudes. *Journal of Experimental Research in Personality*, 1965, **1**, 84–90.

Janis, I. L., & Mann, L. *Decision-making: A psychological analysis of conflict, choice and commitment*. New York: Free Press, 1977.

Jeffery, R. The psychologist as an expert witness on the issue of insanity. *American Psychologist*, 1964, **19**, 838–843.

Jellison, J. M., & Green, J. A self-presentation approach to the fundamental attribution error: The norm of internality. *Journal of Personality and Social Psychology*, 1981, **40**, 643–649.

Jencks, C. *Who gets ahead? The determinants of economic success in America*. New York: Basic Books, 1979.

Jennings, D. L., Amabile, T. M., & Ross, L. Informal covariation assessment: Data-based vs theory-based judgments. In D. Kahneman, P. Slovic, & A. Tversky (Eds.), *Judgment under uncertainty: Heuristics and biases.* New York: Cambridge University Press, 1982.

Jennings, D. L., Lepper, M. R., & Ross, L. Persistence of impressions of personal persuasiveness: Perseverance of erroneous self-assessments outside the debriefing paradigm. *Personality and Social Psychology Bulletin*, 1981, **7**, 257–262.

Jennings (Walstedt), J., Geis, F. L., & Brown, V. Influence of television commercials on women's self-confidence and independent judgment. *Journal of Personality and Social Psychology*, 1980, **38**, 203–210.

Jervis, R. Hypotheses on misperception. In M. Halperin & A. Kanter (Eds.), *Readings in American foreign policy*. Boston: Little, Brown, 1973.

Johnson, D. W., & Johnson, R. T. *Learning together and alone*. Englewood Cliffs, N.J.: Prentice-Hall, 1975.

Johnson, D. W., Maruyama, G., Johnson, R., Nelson, D., & Skon, L. Effects of cooperative, competitive, and individualistic goal structures on achievement: A meta-analysis. *Psychological Bulletin*, 1981, **89**, 47–62.

Johnson, N., Horton, R. W., & Santogrossi, D. A. Mitigating the impact of televised violence. Paper presented at the American Psychological Association convention, 1978.

Johnson, N. R., Stemler, J. G., & Hunter, D. Crowd behavior as risky shift: A laboratory experiment. *Sociometry*, 1977, **40**, 183–187.

Johnson, R. D., & Downing, L. J. Deindividuation and valence of cues: Effects of prosocial and antisocial behavior. *Journal of Personality and Social Psychology*, 1979, **37**, 1532–1538.

Johnson, R. N. *Aggression in man and animals*. Philadelphia: W. B. Saunders, 1972.

Johnston, J., Ettema, J., & Davidson, T. *An evaluation of FREESTYLE: A television series to reduce sex-role stereotypes*. Ann Arbor: Institute for Social Research, University of Michigan, 1980.

Jones, E. E. *Ingratiation*. New York: Appleton-Century-Crofts, 1964.

Jones, E. E. How do people perceive the causes of behavior? *American Scientist*, 1976, **64**, 300–305.

Jones, E. E. The rocky road from acts to dispositions. *American Psychologist*, 1979, **34**, 107–117.

Jones, E. E., & Berglas, S. Control of attributions about the self through self-handicapping strategies: The appeal of alcohol and the role of underachievement. *Personality and Social Psychology*, 1978, **4**, 200–206.

Jones, E. E., & Davis, K. E. From acts to dispositions: The attribution process in person perception. In L. Berkowitz (Ed.), *Advances in experimental social psychology* (Vol. 2). New York: Academic Press, 1965.

Jones, E. E., & Harris, V. A. The attribution of attitudes. *Journal of Experimental Social Psychology*, 1967, **3**, 2–24.

Jones, E. E., & Nisbett, R. E. *The actor and the observer: Divergent perceptions of the causes of behavior.* Morristown, N.J.: General Learning Press, 1971.

Jones, E. E., Rhodewalt, F., Berglas, S., & Skeleton, J. A. Effects of strategic self-presentation on subsequent self-esteem. *Journal of Personality and Social Psychology*, 1981, **41**, 407–421.

Jones, E. E., Riggs, J. M., & Quattrone, G. Observer bias in the attitude attribution paradigm: Effect of time and information order. *Journal of Personality*, 1979, **37**, 1230–1238.

Jones, E. E., Rock, L., Shaver, K. G., Goethals, G. R., & Ward, L. M. Pattern of performance and ability attribution: An unexpected primacy effect. *Journal of Personality and Social Psychology*, 1968, **10**, 317–340.

Jones, E. E., & Sigall, H. The bogus pipeline: A new paradigm for measuring affect and attitude. *Psychological Bulletin*, 1971, **76**, 349–364.

Jones, E. E., Wood, G. C., & Quattrone, G. A. Perceived variability of personal characteristics of in-groups and out-groups: The role of knowledge and evaluation. *Personality and Social Psychology Bulletin*, 1981, **7**, 523–528.

Jones, R. A., & Brehm, J. W. Persuasiveness of one- and two-sided communications as a function of awareness there are two sides. *Journal of Experimental Social Psychology*, 1970, **6**, 47–56.

Jones, W. H. Characteristics of occult believers. Paper presented at the American Psychological Association convention, 1980. (a)

Jones, W. H. Teaching anomalistics. Paper presented at the American Psychological Association convention, 1980. (b)

Jones, W. H., Russell, D. W., & Nickel, T. W. Belief in the paranormal scale: An objective instrument to measure belief in magical phenomena and causes (Ms. No. 1577). *JSAS Catalog of Selected Documents in Psychology*, 1977, **7**, 100.

Jorgenson, D. O., & Papciak, A. S. The effects of communication, resource feedback, and identifiability on behavior in a simulated commons. *Journal of Experimental Social Psychology*, 1981, **17**, 373–385.

Jourard, S. M. *The transparent self*. Princeton, N.J.: Van Nostrand, 1964.

Kahle, L. R. *Attitudes, attributes and adaptation*. London: Pergamon Press, 1983.

Kahle, L. R., & Berman, J. Attitudes cause behaviors: A cross-lagged panel analysis. *Journal of Personality and Social Psychology*, 1979, **37**, 315–321.

Kahn, A., Nelson, R. E., & Gaeddert, W. P. Sex of subject and sex composition of the group as determinants of reward allocations. *Journal of Personality and Social Psychology*, 1980, **38**, 737–750.

Kahn, M. W. The effect of severe defeat at various age levels on the aggressive behavior of mice. *Journal of Genetic Psychology*, 1951, **79**, 117–130.

Kahneman, D., Slovic, P., & Tversky, A. (Eds.). *Judgment under uncertainty: Heuristics and biases*. N.Y.: Cambridge University Press, 1982.

Kahneman, D., & Tversky, A. Subjective probability: A judgment of representativeness. *Cognitive Psychology*, 1972, **3**, 430–454.

Kahneman, D., & Tversky, A. On the psychology of prediction. *Psychological Review*, 1973, **80**, 237–251.

Kahneman, D., & Tversky, A. Intuitive prediction: Biases and corrective procedures. *Management Science*, 1979, **12**, 313–327.

Kalick, S. M. *Plastic surgery, physical appearance, and person perception*. Unpublished doctoral dissertation, Harvard University, 1977. Cited by E. Berscheid in An overview of the psychological effects of physical attractiveness and some comments upon the psychological effects of knowledge of the effects of physical attractiveness. In W. Lucker, K. Ribbens, & J. A. McNamera (Eds.), *Logical aspects of facial form* (craniofacial growth series). Ann Arbor: University of Michigan Press, 1981.

Kalven, H., Jr., & Zeisel, H. *The American jury*. Chicago: University of Chicago Press, 1966.

Kandel, D. B. Similarity in real-life adolescent friendship pairs. *Journal of Personality and Social Psychology*, 1978, **36**, 306–312.

Kaplan, M. F., & Anderson, N. H. Information integration theory and reinforcement theory as approaches to interpersonal attraction. *Journal of Personality and Social Psychology*, 1973, **28**, 301–312.

Kaplan, M. F., & Schersching, C. Reducing juror bias: An experimental approach. In P. D. Lipsitt & B. D. Sales (Eds.), *New directions in psycholegal research*. New York: Van Nostrand Reinhold, 1980, pp. 149–170.

Karabenick, S. A., Lerner, R. M., & Beecher, M. D. Relation of political affiliation to helping behavior on election day, November 7, 1972. *Journal of Social Psychology*, 1973, **91**, 223–227.

Karlin, R., Epstein, Y., & Aiello, J. Strategies for the investigation of crowding. In A. Esser & B. Greenbie (Eds.), *Design for communality and privacy*. New York: Plenum, 1978.

Karlin, R. A., Rosen, L. S., & Epstein, Y. M. Three into two doesn't go: A follow-up on the effects of overcrowded dormitory rooms. *Personality and Social Psychology Bulletin*, 1979, **5**, 391–395.

Karlins, M., Coffman, T. L., & Walters, G. On the fading of social stereotypes: Studies in three generations of college students. *Journal of Personality and Social Psychology*, 1969, **13**, 1–17.

Kassin, S. M. Consensus information, prediction, and causal attribution: A review of the literature and issues. *Journal of Personality and Social Psychology*, 1979, **37**, 1966–1981.

Kassin, S. M., & Wrightsman, L. S. On the requirements of proof: The timing of judicial instruction and mock juror verdicts. *Journal of Personality and Social Psychology*, 1979, **37**, 1877–1887.

Katz, A. M., & Hill, R. Residential propinquity and marital selection: A review of theory, method, and fact. *Marriage and Family Living*, 1958, **20**, 237–335.

Katz, E. The two-step flow of communication: An up-to-date report on a hypothesis. *Public Opinion Quarterly*, 1957, **21**, 61–78.

Katz, I., Cohen, S., & Glass, D. Some determinants of cross-racial helping behavior. *Journal of Personality and Social Psychology*, 1975, **32**, 964–970.

Katz, L. S., & Reid, J. F. Expert testimony on the fallibility of eyewitness identification. *Criminal Justice Journal*, 1977, **1**, 177–206.

Katzev, R., Edelsack, L., Steinmetz, G., & Walker, T. The effect of reprimanding transgressions on subsequent helping behavior: Two field experiments. *Personality and Social Psychology Bulletin*, 1978, **4**, 126–129.

Keating, C. F., Mazur, A., Segall, M. H., Cysneiros, P. G., Divale, W. T., Kilbride, J. E., Komin, S., Leahy, P., Thurman, B., & Wirsing, R. Culture and the perception of social dominance from facial expression. *Journal of Personality and Social Psychology*, 1981, **40**, 615–626.

Keating, J. P., & Brock, T. C. Acceptance of persuasion and the inhibition of counterargumentation under various distraction tasks. *Journal of Experimental Social Psychology*, 1974, **10**, 301–309.

Kelley, H. H. Attribution in social interaction. In E. E. Jones, D. E. Kanouse, H. H. Kelley, R. E. Nisbett, S. Valins, & B. Weiner (Eds.), *Attribution: Perceiving the causes of behavior*. Morristown, N.J.: General Learning Press, 1972.

Kelley, H. H. The process of causal attribution. *American Psychologist*, 1973, **28**, 107–128.

Kelley, H. H. *Personal relationships: Their structures and processes*. Hillsdale, N.J.: Lawrence Erlbaum, 1979.

Kelley, H. H., & Stahelski, A. J. The social interaction basis of cooperators' and competitors' beliefs about others. *Journal of Personality and Social Psychology*, 1970, **16**, 66–91.

Kelman, H. C. (Ed.). *International behavior: A social psychological anaylsis*. New York: Holt, Rinehart and Winston, 1965.

Kelman, H. C., & Cohen, S. P. Reduction of international conflict: An interactional approach. In W. G. Austin and S. Worchel, *The social psychology of intergroup relations*. Monterey, Calif.: Brooks/Cole, 1979.

Kennedy, J. F. *Profiles in courage*. New York: Harper, 1956.

Kenny, D. A., & Nasby, W. Splitting the reciprocity correlation. *Journal of Personality and Social Psychology*, 1980, **38**, 249–256.

Kenrick, D. T., Baumann, D. J., & Cialdini, R. B. A step in the socialization of altruism as hedonism: Effects of negative mood on children's generosity under public and private conditions. *Journal of Personality and Social Psychology*, 1979, **37**, 747–755.

Kenrick, D. T., & Cialdini, R. B. Romantic attraction: Misattribution versus reinforcement explanations. *Journal of Personality and Social Psychology*, 1977, **35**, 381–391.

Kenrick, D. T., Cialdini, R. B., & Linder, D. E. Misattribution under fear-producing circumstances: Four failures to replicate. *Personality and Social Psychology Bulletin*, 1979, **5**, 329–334.

Kenrick, D. T., & Gutierres, S. E. Contrast effects and judgments of physical attractiveness: When beauty becomes a social problem. *Journal of Personality and Social Psychology*, 1980, **38**, 131–140.

Kerr, N. L. Beautiful and blameless: Effects of victim attractiveness and responsibility on mock jurors' verdicts. *Personality and Social Psychology Bulletin*, 1978, **4**, 479–482. (a)

Kerr, N. L. Severity of prescribed penalty and mock jurors' verdicts. *Journal of Personality and Social Psychology*, 1978, **36**, 1431–1442. (b)

Kerr, N. L. Effects of prior juror experience on juror behavior. *Basic and Applied Social Psychology*, 1981, **2**, 175–193.

Kerr, N. L., Atkin, R. S., Stasser, G., Meek, D., Holt, R. W., & Davis, J. H. Guilt beyond a reasonable doubt: Effects of concept definition and assigned decision rule on the judgments of mock jurors. *Journal of Personality and Social Psychology*, 1976, **34**, 282–294.

Kerr, N. L., & Bruun, S. E. Ringelmann revisited: Alternative explanations for the social loafing effect. *Personality and Social Psychology Bulletin*, 1981, **7**, 224–231.

Khrushchev, N. Quoted in *Time*, June 23, 1980, p. 65.

Kidd, J. B., & Morgan, J. R. A predictive informations system for management. *Operational Research Quarterly*, 1969, **20**, 149–170.

Kidd, R. F., & Berkowitz, L. Effect of dissonance arousal on helpfulness. *Journal of Personality and Social Psychology*, 1976, **33**, 613–622.

Kiesler, C. A. *The psychology of commitment: Experiments linking behavior to belief*. New York: Academic Press, 1971.

Kiesler, C. A., & Kiesler, S. B. Role of forewarning in persuasive communications. *Journal of Abnormal and Social Psychology*, 1964, **68**, 547–549.

Kiesler, C. A., & Kiesler, S. B. *Conformity*. Reading, Mass.: Addison-Wesley, 1969.

Kiesler, C. A., & Pallak, M. S. Minority influence: The effect of majority reactionaries and defectors, and minority and majority compromisers, upon majority opinion and attraction. *European Journal of Social Psychology*, 1975, **5**, 237–256.

Kiesler, C. A., & Pallak, M. S. Arousal properties of dissonance manipulations. *Psychological Bulletin*, 1976, **83**, 1014–1025.

Kiesler, S. B., & Baral, R. L. The search for a romantic partner: The effects of self-esteem and physical attractiveness on romantic behavior. In K. Gergen & D. Marlowe (Eds.), *Personality and Social Behavior*. Reading, Mass.: Addison-Wesley, 1970.

Kimble, C. E., Fitz, D., & Onorad, J. R. Effectiveness of counteraggression strategies in reducing interactive aggression by males. *Journal of Personality and Social Psychology*, 1977, **35**, 272–278.

Kimble, C. E., Yoshikawa, J. C., & Zehr, H. D. Vocal and verbal assertiveness in same-sex and mixed-sex groups. *Journal of Personality and Social Psychology*, 1981, **40**, 1047–1054.

Kimmel, M. J., Pruitt, D. G., Magenau, J. M., Konar-Goldband, E., & Carnevale, P. J. D. Effects of trust, aspiration, and gender on negotiation tactics. *Journal of Personality and Social Psychology*, 1980, **38**, 9–22.

Kinder, D. R., & Sears, D. O. Prejudice and politics: Symbolic racism versus racial threats to the good life. *Journal of Personality and Social Psychology*, 1981, **40**, 414–431.

Kirkpatrick, J. Speech to National Conservative Political Action Conference, March 21, 1981.

Kirmeyer, S. L. Urban density and pathology: A review of research. *Environment and Behavior*, 1978, **10**, 257–269.

Klaas, E. T. Psychological effects of immoral actions: The experimental evidence. *Psychological Bulletin*, 1978, **85**, 756–771.

Kleck, R. E., & Strenta, A. Perceptions of the impact of negatively valued physical characteristics on social interaction. *Journal of Personality and Social Psychology*, 1980, **5**, 861–873.

Klein, H. M., & Willerman, L. Psychological masculinity and femininity and typical maximal dominance expression in women. *Journal of Personality and Social Psychology*, 1979, **37**, 2059–2070.

Kleinke, C. L. Compliance to requests made by gazing and touching experimenters in field settings. *Journal of Experimental Social Psychology*, 1977, **13**, 218–223.

Kleinke, C. L., & Walton, J. H. Influence of reinforced smiling on affective responses in an interview. *Journal of Personality and Social Psychology*, 1982, **42**, 557–565.

Klopfer, P. M. Influence of social interaction on learning rates in birds. *Science*, 1958, **128**, 903– 904.

Knight, J. A., & Vallacher, R. R. Interpersonal engagement in social perception: The consequences of getting into the action. *Journal of Personality and Social Psychology*, 1981, **40**, 990–999.

Knight, P. A., & Weiss, H. M. Benefits of suffering: Communicator suffering, benefiting, and influence. Paper presented at the American Psychological Association convention, 1980.

Knox, R. E., & Inkster, J. A. Postdecision dissonance at post-time. *Journal of Personality and Social Psychology*, 1968, **8**, 319–323.

Knudson, R. M., Sommers, A. A., & Golding, S. L. Interpersonal perception and mode of resolution in marital conflict. *Journal of Personality and Social Psychology*, 1980, **38**, 751–763.

Kohlberg, L. The philosophy of moral development: Essays in moral development (Vol. I). New York: Harper & Row, 1981.

Kolata, G. B. Math and sex: Are girls born with less ability? *Science*, 1980, **210**, 1234–1235.

Konecni, V. J. Some effects of guilt on compliance: A field replication. *Journal of Personality and Social Psychology*, 1972, **23**, 30–32.

Koocher, G. P. Bathroom behavior and human dignity. *Journal of Personality and Social Psychology*, 1977, **35**, 120–121.

Korabik, K. Changes in physical attractiveness and interpersonal attraction. *Basic and Applied Social Psychology*, 1981, **2**, 59–66.

Koriat, A., Lichtenstein, S., & Fischhoff, B. Reasons for confidence. *Journal of Experimental Psychology: Human Learning and Memory*, 1980, **6**, 107–118.

Korte, C. Urban-nonurban differences in social behavior and social psychological models of urban impact. *Journal of Social Issues*, 1980, **36**, 29–51.

Kraut, R. E. Effects of social labeling on giving to charity. *Journal of Experimental Social Psychology*, 1973, **9**, 551–562.

Kraut, R. E., & Poe, D. Behavioral roots of person perception: The deception judgments of customs inspectors and laymen. *Journal of Personality and Social Psychology*, 1980, **39**, 784–798.

Krebs, D. Altruism—An examination of the concept and a review of the literature. *Psychological Bulletin*, 1970, **73**, 258–302.

Krebs, D. Empathy and altruism. *Journal of Personality and Social Psychology*, 1975, **32**, 1134–1146.

Krebs, D., & Adinolfi, A. A. Physical attractiveness, social relations, and personality style. *Journal of Personality and Social Psychology*, 1975, **31**, 245–253.

Krech, D., Crutchfield, R. A., & Ballachey, E. I. *Individual in society*. New York: McGraw-Hill, 1962.

Kuiper, N. A. Depression and causal attributions for success and failure. *Journal of Personality and Social Psychology*, 1978, **36**, 236–246.

Kulka, R. A., & Colten, M. E. The relative salience of major life roles among adult Americans. Paper presented at the American Psychological Association convention, 1980.

Kunst-Wilson, W. R., & Zajonc, R. B. Affective discrimination of stimuli that cannot be recognized. *Science*, 1980, **207**, 557–558.

Kuo, Z. Y. The genesis of the cat's response to the rat. *Journal of Comparative Psychology*, 1930, **11**, 1–35.

Lagerspetz, K. Modification of aggressiveness in mice. In S. Feshbach & A. Fraczek (Eds.), *Aggression in behavior change*. New York: Praeger, 1979.

Laird, J. D. Self-attribution of emotion: The effects of expressive behavior on the quality of emotional experience. *Journal of Personality and Social Psychology*, 1974, **29**, 475–486.

Lakoff, R. T. Language and sexual identity. *Semiotica*, 1977, **19**, 119–130.

Lamal, P. A. College student common beliefs about psychology. *Teaching of Psychology*, 1979, **6**, 155–158.

Lamb, T. A. Nonverbal and paraverbal control in dyads and triads: Sex or power differences? *Social Psychology Quarterly*, 1981, **44**, 49–53.

Landers, A. Column in syndicated newspapers. April 8, 1969. Cited by L. Berkowitz in The case for bottling up rage. *Psychology Today*, September 1973, pp. 24–31.

Landy, D., & Sigall, H. Beauty is talent: Task evaluation as a function of the performer's physical attractiveness. *Journal of Personality and Social Psychology*, 1974, **29**, 299–304.

Langer, E. J. The psychology of chance. *Journal for the Theory of Social Behavior*, 1977, **7**, 185–208.

Langer, E. J., & Benevento, A. Self-induced dependence. *Journal of Personality and Social Psychology*, 1978, **36**, 886–893.

Langer, E. J., Blank, A., & Chanowitz, B. The mindlessness of ostensibly thoughtful action: The role of "placebic" information in interpersonal interaction. *Journal of Personality and Social Psychology*, 1978, **36**, 635–642.

Langer, E. J., & Imber, L. The role of mindlessness in the perception of deviance. *Journal of Personality and Social Psychology*, 1980, **39**, 360–367.

Langer, E. J., Janis, I. L., & Wofer, J. A. Reduction of psychological stress in surgical patients. *Journal of Experimental Social Psychology*, 1975, **11**, 155–165.

Langer, E. J., & Rodin, J. The effects of choice and enhanced personal responsibility for the aged: A field experiment in an institutional setting. *Journal of Personality and Social Psychology*, 1976, **34**, 191–198.

Langer, E. J., & Roth, J. Heads I win, tails it's chance: The illusion of control as a function of the sequence of outcomes in a purely chance task. *Journal of Personality and Social Psychology*, 1975, **32**, 951–955.

Langlois, J. H., & Stephan, C. W. Beauty and the beast: The role of physical attractiveness in the development of peer relations and social behavior. In S. S. Brehm, S. M. Kassin, & F. X. Gibbons (Eds.), *Developmental social psychology*. New York: Oxford University Press, 1981.

Lansing, J. B., Marans, R. W., & Zehner, R. G. *Planned residential environments*. Ann Arbor, Mich.: Institute for Social Research, University of Michigan, 1970.

Lanzetta, J. T. Group behavior under stress. *Human Relations*, 1955, **8**, 29–53.

Lanzetta, J. T., Cartwright-Smith, J., & Kleck, R. E. Effects of nonverbal dissimulation in emotional experience and autonomic arousal. *Journal of Personality and Social Psychology*, 1976, **33**, 354–370.

La Rochefoucauld. *Maxims*, 1665. Translated by J. Heard, 1917. Boston: International Pocket Library, 1965.

Larsen, K. Conformity in the Asch experiment. *Journal of Social Psychology*, 1974, **94**, 303–304.

Larwood, L. Swine flu: A field study of self-serving biases. *Journal of Applied Social Psychology*, 1978, **18**, 283–289.

Larwood, L., & Whittaker, W. Managerial myopia: Self-serving biases in organizational planning. *Journal of Applied Psychology*, 1977, **62**, 194–198.

Latané, B. The psychology of social impact. *American Psychologist*, 1981, **36**, 343–356.

Latané, B., & Darley, J. M. Group inhibition of bystander intervention in emergencies. *Journal of Personality and Social Psychology*, 1968, **10**, 215–221.

Latané, B., & Darley, J. M. *The unresponsive bystander: Why doesn't he help?* New York: Appleton-Century-Crofts, 1970.

Latané, B., & Nida, S. Ten years of research on group size and helping. *Psychological Bulletin*, 1981, **89**, 308–324.

Latané, B., & Rodin, J. A lady in distress: Inhibiting effects of friends and strangers on bystander intervention. *Journal of Experimental Social Psychology,* 1969, **5**, 189–202.

Latané, B., Williams, K., & Harkins, S. Many hands make light the work: The causes and consequences of social loafing. *Journal of Personality and Social Psychology,* 1979, **37**, 822–832.

Latané, B., & Wolf, S. The social impact of majorities and minorities. *Psychological Review,* 1981, **88**, 438–453.

Lau, R. R., & Russell, D. Attributions in the sports pages. *Journal of Personality and Social Psychology,* 1980, **39**, 29–38.

Laughlin, P. R. Social combination processes of cooperative problem-solving groups on verbal intellective tasks. In M. Fishbein (Ed.), *Progress in social psychology.* Hillsdale, N.J.: Lawrence Erlbaum, 1980.

Laughlin, P. R., & Adamopoulos, J. Social combination processes and individual learning for six-person cooperative groups on an intellective task. *Journal of Personality and Social Psychology,* 1980, **38**, 941–947.

Lee, M. T., & Ofshe, R. The impact of behavioral style and status characteristics on social influence: A test of two competing theories. *Social Psychology Quarterly,* 1981, **44**, 73–82.

Lefkowitz, M. M., Blake, R. R., & Mouton, J. S. Status factors in pedestrian violation of traffic signals. *Journal of Abnormal and Social Psychology,* 1955, **51**, 704–706.

Lefkowitz, M. M., Eron, L. D., Walder, L. O., & Huesmann, L. R. *Growing up to be violent.* New York: Pergamon, 1976.

Leippe, M. R. Effects of integrative and memorial cognitive processes on the correspondence of eyewitness accuracy and confidence. *Law and Human Behavior,* 1980, **4**, 261–274.

Lenihan, K. J. Perceived climates as a barrier to housing desegregation. Unpublished manuscript, Bureau of Applied Social Research, Columbia University, 1965.

Leon, D. *The Kibbutz: A new way of life.* London: Pergamon Press, 1969. Cited by B. Latané, K. Williams, & S. Harkins in Many hands make light the work: The causes and consequences of social loafing. *Journal of Personality and Social Psychology,* 1979, **37**, 822–832.

Lepper, M. R. & Greene, D. (Eds.). *The hidden costs of reward.* Hillsdale, N.J.: Lawrence Erlbaum, 1979.

Lerner, M. J. *The belief in a just world: A fundamental delusion.* New York: Plenum, 1980.

Lerner, M. J., & Miller, D. T. Just world research and the attribution process: Looking back and ahead. *Psychological Bulletin,* 1978, **85**, 1030–1051.

Lerner, M. J., & Simmons, C. H. Observer's reaction to the "innocent victim": Compassion or rejection? *Journal of Personality and Social Psychology,* 1966, **4**, 203–210.

Lerner, R. M., & Frank, P. Relation of race and sex to supermarket helping behavior. *Journal of Social Psychology,* 1974, **94**, 201–203.

Levenson, H., Burford, B., Bonno, B., & Davis, L. Are women still prejudiced against women? A replication and extention of Goldberg's study. *Journal of Psychology,* 1975, **89**, 65–71.

Leventhal, G. S. The distribution of rewards and resources in groups and organizations. In L. Berkowitz & E. Walster (Hatfield) (Eds.), *Advances in experimental social psychology* (Vol. 9). New York: Academic Press, 1976.

Leventhal, H. Findings and theory in the study of fear communications. In L. Berkowitz (Ed.), *Advances in experimental social psychology* (Vol. 5). New York: Academic Press, 1970.

Leventhal, H. Toward a comprehensive theory of emotion. In L. Berkowitz (Ed.), *Advances in experimental social psychology* (Vol. 13). New York: Academic Press, 1980.

Levine, D. W., O'Neal, E. C., Garwood, S. G., & McDonald, P. J. Classroom ecology: The effects of seating position on grades and participation. *Personality and Social Psychology Bulletin,* 1980, **6**, 409–412.

Levine, J. M. Reaction to opinion deviance in small groups. In P. B. Paulus, *Psychology of group influence.* Hillsdale, N.J.: Lawrence Erlbaum, 1980.

Levine, R., & Uleman, J. S. Perceived locus of control, chronic self-esteem, and attributions to success and failure. *Personality and Social Psychology Bulletin,* 1979, **5**, 69–72.

Levy, J. Colloquium address, Hope College, Holland, Michigan, March 1978.

Levy, J., Trevarthen, C., & Sperry, R. W. Perception of bilateral chimeric figures following hemispheric deconnexion. *Brain,* 1972, **95**, 61–78.

Lewinsohn, P. M., Mischel, W., Chapline, W., & Barton, R. Social competence and depression: The role of illusory self-perceptions. *Journal of Abnormal Psychology,* 1980, **89**, 203–212.

Lewis, C. S. *Mere Christianity*. New York: Macmillan, 1960.

Lewis, C. S. *The horse and his boy*. New York: Collier Books, 1974.

Leyens, J. P., Camino, L., Parke, R. D., & Berkowitz, L. Effects of movie violence on aggression in a field setting as a function of group dominance and cohesion. *Journal of Personality and Social Psychology*, 1975, **32**, 346–360.

Lichtenbert, P., & Norton, D. G. *Cognitive and mental development in the first five years of life: A review of recent research*. Bethesda, Md. National Institute of Mental Health, 1970.

Lichtenstein, S., & Fischhoff, B. Training for calibration. *Organizational Behavior and Human Performance*, 1980, **26**, 149–171.

Lieberman, S. The effects of changes in roles on the attitudes of role occupants. *Human Relations*, 1956, **9**, 385–402.

Liebert, R. M., & Baron, R. A. Some immediate effects of televised violence on children's behavior. *Developmental Psychology*, 1972, **6**, 469–475.

Lindsay, R. C. L., Wells, G. L., & Rumpel, C. H. Can people detect eyewitness-identification accuracy within and across situations? *Journal of Applied Psychology*, 1981, **66**, 79–89.

Lindskold, S. Trust development, the GRIT proposal, and the effects of conciliatory acts on conflict and cooperation. *Psychological Bulletin*, 1978, **85**, 772–793.

Lindskold, S. Conciliation with simultaneous or sequential interaction: Variations in trustworthiness and vulnerability in the prisoner's dilemma. *Journal of Conflict Resolution*, 1979, **23**, 704–714.

Lindskold, S. (a) Managing conflict through announced conciliatory initiatives backed with retaliatory capability. In W. G. Austin and S. Worchel (Eds.), *The social psychology of intergroup relations*. Monterey, Calif.: Brooks/Cole, 1979.

Lindskold, S. (b) The laboratory evaluation of GRIT: Trust, cooperation, aversion to using conciliation. Paper presented at the American Association for the Advancement of Science convention, 1981.

Lindskold, S., & Aronoff, J. R. Conciliatory strategies and relative power. *Journal of Experimental Social Psychology*, 1980, **16**, 187–198.

Lindskold, S., Bennett, R., & Wayner, M. Retaliation level as a foundation for subsequent conciliation. *Behavioral Science*, 1976, **21**, 13–18.

Lindskold, S., & Collins, M. G. Inducing cooperation by groups and individuals. *Journal of Conflict Resolution*, 1978, **22**, 679–690.

Lindskold, S., & Finch, M. L. Styles of announcing conciliation. *Journal of Conflict Resolution*, 1981, **25**, 145–155.

Lindskold, S., & Propst, L. R. Deindividuation, self-awareness, and impression management. In J. T. Tedeschi (Ed.), *Impression management theory and social psychological research*. New York: Academic Press, 1981.

Lindskold, S., Walters, P. S., Koutsourais, H., & Shayo, R. Cooperators, competitors, and response to GRIT. Unpublished manuscript, Ohio University, 1981.

Linsenmeier, J. A. W., & Wortman, C. B. Attitudes toward workers and toward their work: More evidence that sex makes a difference. *Journal of Applied Social Psychology*, 1979, **9**, 326–334.

Lipset, S. M. University students and politics in underdeveloped countries. *Comparative Education Review*, 1966, **10**, 132–162.

Lipton, J. P. On the psychology of eyewitness testimony. *Journal of Applied Psychology*, 1977, **62**, 90–95.

Locksley, A., Borgida, E., Brekke, N., & Hepburn, C. Sex stereotypes and social judgment. *Journal of Personality and Social Psychology*, 1980, **39**, 821–831.

Locksley, A., Hepburn, C., & Ortiz, V. Social stereotypes and judgments of invididuals: An instance of the base-rate fallacy. *Journal of Experimental Social Psychology*, 1982, **18**, 23–42.

Locksley, A., Ortiz, V., & Hepburn, C. Social categorization and discriminatory behavior: Extinguishing the minimal intergroup discrimination effect. *Journal of Personality and Social Psychology*, 1980, **39**, 773–783.

Lofland, J., & Stark, R. Becoming a world-saver: A theory of conversion to a deviant perspective. *American Sociological Review*, 1965, **30**, 862–864.

Loftus, E. F. Reconstructing memory: The incredible eyewitness. *Psychology Today*, December 1974, pp. 117–119.

Loftus, E. F. *Eyewitness testimony*. Cambridge, Mass.: Harvard University Press, 1979. (a)

Loftus, E. F. The malleability of human memory. *American Scientist*, 1979, **67**, 312–320. (b)

Loftus, E. F. Impact of expert psychological testimony on the unreliability of eyewitness identification. *Journal of Applied Psychology*, 1980, **65**, 9–15. (a)

Loftus, E. F. *Memories are made of this: New insights*

into the workings of human memory. Reading, Mass.: Addison-Wesley, 1980. (b)

Loftus, E. F. & Loftus, G. R. On the permanence of stored information in the human brain. *American Psychologist*, 1980, **35**, 409–420.

Loftus, E. F., Miller, D. G., & Burns, H. J. Semantic integration of verbal information into a visual memory. *Journal of Experimental Psychology: Human Learning and Memory*, 1978, **4**, 19–31.

Loftus, E. F., & Palmer, J. C. Reconstruction of automobile destruction: An example of the interaction between language and memory. *Journal of Verbal Learning and Verbal Behavior*, 1973, **13**, 585–589.

Loftus, E. F., & Zanni, G. Eyewitness testimony: The influence of the wording of a question. *Bulletin of the Psychonomic Society*, 1975, **5**, 86–88.

Lombardo, J. P., Weiss, R. F., & Buchanan, W. Reinforcing and attracting functions of yielding. *Journal of Personality and Social Psychology*, 1972, **21**, 359–368.

London, P. The rescuers: Motivational hypotheses about Christians who saved Jews from the Nazis. In J. Macaulay & L. Berkowitz (Eds.), *Altruism and helping behavior*. New York: Academic Press, 1970.

Loo, C. Chinatown: Crowding and mental health. Paper presented at the American Psychological Association convention, 1980.

Lord, C. G., Ross, L., & Lepper, M. Biased assimilation and attitude polarization: The effects of prior theories on subsequently considered evidence. *Journal of Personality and Social Psychology*, 1979, **37**, 2098–2109.

Lorenz, K. *On aggression*. New York: Bantam Books, 1976.

Lott, A. J., & Lott, B. E. Group cohesiveness, communication level, and conformity. *Journal of Abnormal and Social Psychology*, 1961, **62**, 408–412.

Lott, A. J., & Lott, B. E. The role of reward in the formation of positive interpersonal attitudes. In T. Huston (Ed.), *Foundations of interpersonal attraction*. New York: Academic Press, 1974.

Louis Harris & Associates (with analysis by Simon, W., & Miller, P.) *The Playboy report on American men*. Chicago: Playboy, 1979.

Lowe, C. A., & Goldstein, J. W. Reciprocal liking and attributions of ability: Mediating effects of perceived intent and personal involvement. *Journal of Personality and Social Psychology*, 1970, **16**, 291–297.

Lowry, D. T., Love, G., & Kirby, M. Sex on the soap operas: Patterns of intimacy. *Journal of Communication*, 1981, **31**(3), 90–96.

Loy, J. W., & Andrews, D. S. They also saw a game: A replication of a case study. *Replications in Social Psychology*, 1981, **1**(2), 45–59.

Lubinski, D., Tellegen, A., & Butcher, J. M. The relationship between androgyny and subjective indicators of emotional well-being. *Journal of Personality and Social Psychology*, 1981, **40**, 722–730.

Lumsdaine, A. A., & Janis, I. L. Resistance to "counter-propaganda" produced by one-sided and two-sided "propaganda" presentations. *Public Opinion Quarterly*, 1953, **17**, 311–318.

MacArthur, D. Quoted in J. D. Frank's statement on psychological aspects of international relations before a hearing of the Committee on Foreign Relations, United States Senate, May 25, 1966. Reprinted in D. E. Linder (Ed.), *Psychological dimensions of social interaction: Readings and perspectives*. Reading, Mass.: Addison-Wesley, 1973.

Maccoby, E. E. *Social development*. New York: Harcourt Brace Jovanovich, 1980.

Maccoby, E. E., & Jacklin, C. N. *The psychology of sex differences*. Stanford, Calif.: Stanford University Press, 1974.

Maccoby, N. Promoting positive health behaviors in adults. In L. A. Bond & J. C. Rosen (Eds.), *Competence and coping during adulthood*. Hanover, N.H.: University Press of New England, 1980.

Maccoby, N., & Alexander, J. Use of media in lifestyle programs. In P. O. Davidson & S. M. Davidson (Eds.), *Behavioral medicine: Changing health lifestyles*. New York: Brunner/Mazel, 1980.

MacDonald, A. P. Internal-external locus of control. In J. P. Robinson & R. P. Shaver (Eds.), *Measures of social psychological attitudes*. Ann Arbor: Institute for Social Research, 1973.

MacKay, J. L. Selfhood: Comment on Brewster Smith. *American Psychologist*, 1980, **35**, 106–107.

MacLachlan, J. What people really think of fast talkers. *Psychology Today*, November 1979, pp. 113–117.

MacLachlan, J., & La Barbera, P. Time compressed TV commercials. *Journal of Advertising Research*, August, 1978, **18**, 11–15.

MacLachlan, J., & Siegel, M. H. Reducing the costs of TV commercials by use of time compressions. *Journal of Marketing Research*, 1980, **17**, 52–57.

Maddux, J. E., & Rogers, R. W. Effects of source expertness, physical attractiveness, and supporting arguments on persuasion: A case of brains over beauty. *Journal of Personality and Social Psychology*, 1980, **39**, 235–244.

Malamuth, N. M. Rape fantasies as a function of exposure to violent sexual stimuli. *Archives of Sexual Behavior*, 1981, **10**, 33–47.

Malamuth, N. M. Rape proclivity among males. *Journal of Social Issues*, **37**(4), 138–157.

Malamuth, N. M., & Check, J. V. P. The effects of media exposure on acceptance of violence against women: A field experiment. *Journal of Research in Personality*, 1981, **15**, 436–446.

Malamuth, N. M., Haber, S., & Feshbach, S. Testing hypotheses regarding rape: Exposure to sexual violence, sex differences, and the "normality" of rapists. *Journal of Research in Personality*, 1980, **14**, 121–137.

Malamuth, N. M., Heim, M., & Feshbach, S. Sexual responsiveness of college students to rape depictions: Inhibitory and disinhibitory effects. *Journal of Personality and Social Psychology*, 1980, **38**, 399–408.

Malamuth, N. M., & Spinner, R. A. A longitudinal content analysis of sexual violence in the best-selling erotic magazines. *Journal of Sex Research*, 1980, **16**, 226–237.

Malkiel, B. G. *A random walk down Wall Street*. New York: W. W. Norton, 1975.

Malpass, R. S., & Kravitz, J. Recognition for faces of own and other race. *Journal of Personality and Social Psychology*, 1969, **13**, 330–334.

Manes, A. L., & Melnyk, P. Televised models of female achievement. *Journal of Applied Social Psychology*, 1974, **4**, 365–374.

Manis, M. Cognitive social psychology. *Personality and Social Psychology Bulletin*, 1977, **3**, 550–566.

Manis, M., Avis, N. E., & Cardoze, S. Reply to Bar-Hillel and Fischhoff. *Journal of Personality and Social Psychology*, 1981, **41**, 681–683.

Manis, M., Cornell, S. D., & Moore, J. C. Transmission of attitude-relevant information through a communication chain. *Journal of Personality and Social Psychology*, 1974, **30**, 81–94.

Manis, M., Dovalina I., Avis, N. E., & Cardoze, S. Base-rates *can* affect individual predictions. *Journal of Personality and Social Psychology*, 1980, **38**, 231–248.

Mann, L. The baiting crowd in episodes of threatened suicide. *Journal of Personality and Social Psychology*, 1981, **41**, 703–709.

Mann, L., & Janis, I. L. A follow-up study on the long-term effects of emotional role playing. *Journal of Personality and Social Psychology*, 1968, **8**, 339– 342.

Mantell, D. M. The potential for violence in Germany. *Journal of Social Issues*, 1971, **27**(4), 101–112.

Marcus, S. Review of *Obedience to authority*. New York Times Book Review, January 13, 1974, pp. 1–2.

Marks, D., & Kammann, R. *The psychology of the psychic*. Buffalo, N.Y.: Prometheus, 1980.

Marks, G., Miller, N., & Maruyama, G. Effect of targets' physical attractiveness on assumptions of similarity. *Journal of Personality and Social Psychology*, 1981, **41**, 198–206.

Marks, G., Miller, N., & Maruyama, G. The effect of physical attractiveness on assumptions of similarity. *Journal of Personality and Social Psychology*, 1981, **41**, 198–206.

Markus, H. The effect of mere presence on social facilitation: An unobtrusive test. *Journal of Experimental Social Psychology*, 1978, **14**, 389–397.

Marler, P. Aggression and its control in animal society. Presentation to the American Psychological Association convention, 1974.

Marshall, D. S., & Suggs, R. C. (Eds.). *Human sexual behavior: Variations in the ethnographic spectrum*. New York: Basic Books, 1971.

Martin, J. Relative deprivation: A theory of distributive injustice for an era of shrinking resources. In *Research in organizational behavior* (Vol. 3). Greenwich, Conn: JAI Press, 1980.

Martin, J. Stories and scripts in organizational settings. In A. Hastorf & A. Isen (Eds.), *Cognitive Social Psychology*. New York: Elsevier-North Holland, Inc., 1982.

Marty, M. E. Watch your language. *Context*, April 15, 1982, p. 6.

Maruyama, G., & Miller, N. Physical attractiveness and personality. In B. A. Maher & W. B. Maher (Eds.), *Progress in Experimental Personality Research*. New York: Academic Press, 1981.

Maruyama, G., & Miller, N. Physical attractiveness, race, and essay evaluation. *Personality and Social Psychology Bulletin*, 1980, **6**, 384–390.

Maruyama, G., Rubin, R. A., & Kingsbury, G. Self-esteem and educational achievement: Independent constructs with a common cause? *Journal of Personality and Social Psychology*, 1981, **40**, 962–975.

Marvelle, K., & Green, S. Physical attractiveness

and sex bias in hiring decisions for two types of jobs. *Journal of the National Association of Women Deans, Administrators, and Counselors*, 1980, **44**(1), 3–6.

Maslach, C. The client role in staff burn-out. *Journal of Social Issues*, 1978, **34**(4), 111–124.

Maslach, C., & Jackson, S. E. Burned-out cops and their families. *Psychology Today*, May 1979, pp. 59–62.

Maslow, B. G. (Ed.). *Abraham H. Maslow: A memorial volume*. Monterey, Calif.: Brooks/Cole, 1972.

Maslow, A. H., & Mintz, N. L. Effects of esthetic surroundings: I. Initial effects of three esthetic conditions upon perceiving "energy" and "well-being" in faces. *Journal of Psychology*, 1956, **41**, 247–254.

Mathes, E. The effects of physical attractiveness and anxiety on heterosexual attraction over a series of five encounters. *Journal of Marriage and the Family*, 1975, **37**, 769–774.

Mayer, F. S., Duval, S., & Duval, V. H. An attributional analysis of commitment. *Journal of Personality and Social Psychology*, 1980, **39**, 1072–1080.

McAlister, A. L., Perry, C., & Maccoby, N. Adolescent smoking: Onset and prevention. *Pediatrics*, 1979, **63**, 650–658.

McAlister, A., Perry, C., Killen, J., Slinkard, L. A., & Maccoby, N. Pilot study of smoking, alcohol and drug abuse prevention. *American Journal of Public Health*, 1980, **70**, 719–721.

McAndrew, F. T. Pattern of performance and attributions of ability and gender. *Personality and Social Psychology Bulletin*, 1981, **7**, 583–587.

McArthur, L. A. The how and what of why: Some determinants and consequences of causal attribution. *Journal of Personality and Social Psychology*, 1972, **22**, 171–193.

McArthur, L. Z., & Friedman, S. A. Illusory correlation in impression formation: Variations in the shared distinctiveness effect as a function of the distinctive person's age, race, and sex. *Journal of Personality and Social Psychology*, 1980, **39**, 615–624.

McBurney, D. H. Persistence of parapsychology. Paper presented at the American Psychological Association convention, 1980.

McCain, G., Cox, C., & Paulus, P. B. The relationship between crowding and manifestations of illness in prison settings. In D. J. Osborne et al. (Eds.), *Research in psychology and medicine* (Vol. II). New York: Academic Press, 1981.

McCarthy, D. P., & Saegert, S. Residential density, social overload, and social withdrawal. In J. R. Aiello & A. Baum (Eds.), *Residential crowding and design*. New York: Plenum Press, 1979.

McCarthy, J. F., & Kelly, B. R. Aggressive behavior and its effect on performance over time in ice hockey athletes: An archival study. *International Journal of Sport Psychology*, 1978, **9**, 90–96.(a)

McCarthy, J. F., & Kelly, B. R. Aggression, performance variables, and anger self-report in ice hockey players. *Journal of Psychology*, 1978, **99**, 97–101. (b)

McCauley, C., & Stitt, C. L. An individual and quantitative measure of stereotypes. *Journal of Personality and Social Psychology*, 1978, **36**, 929–940.

McClelland, L., & Cook, S. W. Energy conservation effects of continuous in-home feedback in all-electric homes. *Journal of Environmental Systems*, 1979–1980, **9**, 169–173. (a)

McClelland, L., & Cook, S. W. Promoting energy conservation in mastered-metered apartments through group financial incentives. *Journal of Applied Social Psychology*, 1980, **10**, 20–31. (b)

McClintock, C. B., Spaulding, C. B., & Turner, H. A. Political orientations of academically affiliated psychologists. *American Psychologist*, 1965, **20**, 211–221.

McConahay, J. B. The effects of school desegregation upon student racial attitudes and behavior: A critical review of the literature and a prolegomenon to future research. *Law and Contemporary Problems*, 1978, **42**, 77–107.

McConahay, J. B. Reducing racial prejudice in desegregated schools. In W. D. Hawley (Ed.), *Effective school desegregation*. Beverly Hills, Calif.: Sage, 1981.

McConahay, J. B. Self-interest versus racial attitudes as correlates of anti-busing attitudes in Louisville: Is it the buses or the blacks? *Journal of Politics*, 1982, in press.

McConahay, J. B., Hardee, B. B., & Batts, V. Has racism declined in America? It depends upon who is asking and what is asked. *Journal of Conflict Resolution*, 1981, **25**(4), 563–579.

McCullough, J. L., & Ostrom, T. M. Repetition of highly similar messages and attitude change. *Journal of Applied Psychology*, 1974, **59**, 395–397.

McGillis, D. Biases and jury decision making. In I. H. Frieze, D. Bar-Tal, & J. S. Carroll, *New approaches to social problems*. San Francisco: Jossey-Bass, 1979.

McGlone, J. Sex differences in human brain asymmetry: A critical survey (with 33 commentaries by other investigators). *Behavioral and Brain Sciences,* 1980, **3**, 215–264.

McGuinness, D., & Pribram, K. The origins of sensory bias in the development of gender differences in perception and cognition. In M. Bortner (Ed.), *Cognitive growth and development: Essays in honor of Herbert G. Birch.* New York: Brunner/Mazel, 1978. Cited by D. Goleman in Special abilities of the sexes: Do they begin in the brain? *Psychology Today*, November 1978, pp. 48–59, 120.

McGuire, W. J. Inducing resistance to persuasion: Some contemporary approaches. In L. Berkowitz (Ed.), *Advances in experimental social psychology* (Vol. 1). New York: Academic Press, 1964.

McGuire, W. J. Personality and susceptibility to social influence. In E. F. Borgatta & W. W. Lambert (Eds.), *Handbook of personality theory and research.* Chicago: Rand-McNally, 1968.

McGuire, W. J. The yin and yang of progress in social psychology: Seven koan. *Journal of Personality and Social Psychology,* 1973, **26**, 446–456.

McGuire, W. J. An information-processing model of advertising effectiveness. In H. L. Davis & A. J. Silk (Eds.), *Behavioral and management sciences in marketing.* New York: Ronald Press, 1978.

McGuire, W. J., McGuire, C. V., Child, P., & Fujioka, T. Salience of ethnicity in the spontaneous self-concept as a function of one's ethnic distinctiveness in the social environment. *Journal of Personality and Social Psychology,* 1978, **36**, 511–520.

McGuire, W. J., McGuire, C. V., & Winton, W. Effects of household sex composition on the salience of one's gender in the spontaneous self-concept. *Journal of Experimental Social Psychology,* 1979, **15**, 77–90.

McGuire, W. J., & Padawer-Singer, A. Trait salience in the spontaneous self-concept. *Journal of Personality and Social Psychology,* 1978, **33**, 743–754.

McMillen, D. L., & Austin, J. B. Effect of positive feedback on compliance following transgression. *Psychonomic Science,* 1971, **24**, 59–61.

McMillen, D. L., Sanders, D. Y., & Solomon, G. S. Self-esteem, attentiveness, and helping behavior. *Personality and Social Psychology Bulletin,* 1977, **3**, 257–261.

McNeel, S. P. Tripling up: Perceptions and effects of dormitory crowding. Paper presented at the American Psychological Association convention, 1980.

Mead, M. *Sex and temperament in three primitive societies.* New York: Morrow, 1935.

Medalia, N. Z., & Larsen, O. N. Diffusion and belief in a collective delusion: The Seattle windshield pitting epidemic. *American Sociological Review,* 1958, **23**, 180–186.

Meece, J. L., Parsons, J. E., Kaczala, C. M., Goff, S. B., & Futterman, R. Sex differences in math achievement: Toward a model of academic choice. *Psychological Bulletin,* 1982, **91**, 324–348.

Meehl, P. E. *Clinical vs. statistical prediction: A theoretical analysis and a review of evidence.* Minneapolis: University of Minnesota Press, 1954.

Meehl, P. E. Wanted—A good cookbook. *American Psychologist,* 1956, **11**, 262–272.

Mehrabian, A., & Diamond, S. G. Effects of furniture arrangement, props, and personality on social interaction. *Journal of Personality and Social Psychology,* 1971, **20**, 18–30.

Menninger, K. The crime of punishment. *Saturday Review,* September 7, 1968, pp. 21–24.

Merton, R. K., & Kitt, A. S. Contributions to the theory of reference group behavior. In R. K. Merton & P. F. Lazarsfeld (Eds.), *Continuities in social research: Studies in the scope and method of the American soldier.* Glencoe, Ill.: Free Press, 1950.

Messe, L. A., & Sivacek, J. M. Predictions of others' responses in a mixed-motive game: Self-justification or false consensus? *Journal of Personality and Social Psychology,* 1979, **37**, 602–607.

Messick, D. M., & Sentis, K. P. Fairness and preference. *Journal of Experimental Social Psychology,* 1979, **15**, 418–434.

Mewborn, C. R., & Rogers, R. W. Effects of threatening and reassuring components of fear appeals on physiological and verbal measures of emotion and attitudes. *Journal of Experimental Social Psychology,* 1979, **15**, 242–253.

Meyer, D. S. *The winning candidate: How to defeat your political candidate.* New York: Heinemann, 1966. Cited by P. Suedfeld, D. Rank, and R. Borre in Frequency of exposure and evaluation of candidates and campaign speeches. *Journal of Applied Social Psychology,* 1975, 5, 118–126.

Meyer, J. P., & Mulherin, A. From attribution to helping: An analysis of the mediating effects of affect and expectancy. *Journal of Personality and Social Psychology,* 1980, **39**, 201–210.

Michaels, J. W., Blommel, J. M., Brocato, R. M., Linkous, R. A., & Rowe, J. S. Social facilitation and inhibition in a natural setting. *Replications in Social Psychology*, 1982, 2, 21–24.

Middlemist, R. D., Knowles, E. S., & Matter, C. F. Personal space invasions in the lavatory: Suggestive evidence for arousal. *Journal of Personality and Social Psychology*, 1976, **33**, 541–546.

Middlemist, R. D., Knowles, E. S., & Matter, C. F. What to do and what to report: A reply to Koocher. *Journal of Personality and Social Psychology*, 1977, **35**, 122–124.

Middleton, T. H. Boys and girls together. *Saturday Review*, May 1980, p. 26.

Miell, D., Duck, S., & La Gaipa, J. Interactive effects of sex and timing in self disclosure. *British Journal of Social and Clinical Psychology*, 1979, **18**, 355–362.

Milgram, S. Nationality and conformity. *Scientific American*, December 1961, pp. 45–51.

Milgram, S. Some conditions of obedience and disobedience to authority. *Human Relations*, 1965, **18**, 57–76.

Milgram, S. The experience of living in cities: A psychological analysis. In F. F. Korten, S. W. Cook, & J. I. Lacey (Eds.), *Psychology and the problems of society*. Washington, D.C.: American Psychological Association, 1970.

Milgram, S. *Obedience to authority*. New York: Harper and Row, 1974.

Milgram, S. *The individual in a social world*. Reading, Mass: Addison-Wesley, 1977.

Milgram, S., Bickman, L., & Berkowitz, L. Note on the drawing power of crowds of different size. *Journal of Personality and Social Psychology*, 1969, **13**, 79–82.

Miller, A. G., Gillen, B., Schenker, C., & Radlove, S. Perception of obedience to authority. *Proceedings of the 81st annual convention of the American Psychological Association*, 1973, **8**, 127–128.

Miller, A. G., Hinkle, S. W., Pliske, D., & Pliske, R. M. Reactions to the Patricia Hearst case: An attributional perspective. *Psychological Reports*, 1977, **41**, 683–695.

Miller, A. G., Jones, E. E., & Hinkle, S. A robust attribution error in the personality domain. *Journal of Experimental Social Psychology*, 1981, **17**, 587–600.

Miller, C. E., & Anderson, P. D. Group decision rules and the rejection of deviates. *Social Psychology Quarterly*, 1979, **42**, 354–363.

Miller, D. T. Ego involvement and attributions for success and failure. *Journal of Personality and Social Psychology*, 1976, **34**, 901–906.

Miller, D. T. Altruism and threat to a belief in a just world. *Journal of Experimental Social Psychology*, 1977, **13**, 113–124.

Miller, F. D., Smith, E. R., & Uleman, J. Measurement and interpretation of situational and dispositional attributions. *Journal of Experimental Social Psychology*, 1981, **17**, 80–95.

Miller, G. R., Bender, D., Florence, T., & Nicholson, H. Real versus reel: What's the difference? *Journal of Communication*, 1974, **21**(3), 99–111.

Miller, G. R., & Fontes, N. E. Trial by videotape. *Psychology Today*, May 1979, pp. 92–100, 112. (a)

Miller, G. R., & Fontes, N. E. *Videotape on trial: A view from the jury box*. Beverly Hills, Calif.: Sage Publications, 1979. (b)

Miller, N. E. The frustration-aggression hypothesis. *Psychological Review*, 1941, **48**, 337–342.

Miller, N., & Campbell, D. T. Recency and primacy in persuasion as a function of the timing of speeches and measurements. *Journal of Abnormal and Social Psychology*, 1959, **59**, 1–9.

Miller, N., Maruyama, G., Beaber, R. J., & Valone, K. Speed of speech and persuasion. *Journal of Personality and Social Psychology*, 1976, **34**, 615–624.

Miller, N. E., & Bugelski, R. Minor studies of aggression: II. The influence of frustrations imposed by the in-group on attitudes expressed toward out-groups. *Journal of Psychology*, 1948, **25**, 437–442.

Millett, K. The shame is over. *Ms.*, January 1975, pp. 26–29.

Millett, K. *The basement: Meditations on human sacrifice*. New York: Simon and Schuster, 1979.

Mills, J., & Clark, M. S. Exchange and communal relationships. In L. Wheeler (Ed.), *Review of personality and social psychology* (Vol. III). Beverly Hills, Calif.: Sage, 1982.

Mims, P. R., Hartnett, J. J., & Nay, W. R. Interpersonal attraction and help volunteering as a function of physical attractiveness. *Journal of Psychology*, 1975, **89**, 125–131.

Minard, R. D. Race relationships in the Pocohontas coal field. *Journal of Social Issues*, 1952, **8**(1), 29–44.

Mintz, A. A re-examination of correlations between

lynchings and economic indices. *Journal of Abnormal and Social Psychology*, 1946, **41**, 154–160.

Mischel, H. N. Sex bias in the evaluation of professional achievements. *Journal of Educational Psychology*, 1974, **66**, 157–166.

Mischel, W. *Personality and assessment*. New York: Wiley, 1968.

Mita, T. H., Dermer, M., & Knight, J. Reversed facial images and the mere-exposure hypothesis. *Journal of Personality and Social Psychology*, 1977, **35**, 597–601.

Money, J., & Ehrhardt, A. A. *Man and woman, boy and girl: The differentiation and dimorphism of gender identity from conception to maturity*. Baltimore: Johns Hopkins University Press, 1972.

Money, J., Hampson, J. G., & Hampson, J. L. Imprinting and the establishment of gender role. *A.M.A. Archives of Neurology and Psychiatry*, 1957, **77**, 333–336.

Monge, P. T., & Kirste, K. K. Measuring proximity in human organization. *Social Psychology Quarterly*, 1980, **43**, 110–115.

Monson, T. C., & Snyder, M. Actors, observers, and the attribution process: Toward a reconceptualization. *Journal of Experimental Social Psychology*, 1977, **13**, 89–111.

Monson, T. C., Tanke, E. D., & Lund, J. Determinants of social perception in a naturalistic setting. *Journal of Research in Personality*, 1980, **14**, 104–120.

Moody, K. *Growing up on television: The TV effect*. New York: Times Books, 1980.

Moore, B. S., Underwood, B., & Rosenhan, D. L. Affect and altruism. *Developmental Psychology*, 1973, **8**, 99–104.

Moore, D. L., & Baron, R. S. Social facilitation: A physiological analysis. In J. T. Cacioppo & R. Petty (Eds.), *Social psychophysiology*. New York: Guilford Press, 1983.

Moran, G., & Comfort, C. Scientific juror selection: Sex as a moderator of demographic and personality predictors of impaneled felony juror behavior. *Journal of Personality and Social Psychology*, 1982, in press.

Moreland, R. L., & Zajonc, R. B. Is stimulus recognition a necessary condition for the occurrence of exposure effects? *Science*, 1980, **207**, 557–558.

Morgan, D. L., & Alwin, D. F. When less is more: School size and student social participation. *Social Psychology Quarterly*, 1980, **43**, 241–252.

Morris, S. Belief in ESP: Effects of dehoaxing. *Skeptical Inquirer*, 1980, **4**(3), 18–31. (a)

Morris, S. Interview, James Randi. *Omni*, April 1980, pp. 76–78, 104–108. (b)

Morris, W. N., & Miller, R. S. The effects of consensus-breaking and consensus-preempting partners on reduction of conformity. *Journal of Experimental Social Psychology*, 1975, **11**, 215–223.

Morse, S. J., Gergen, K. J., Peele, S., & van Ryneveld, J. Reactions to receiving expected and unexpected help from a person who violates or does not violate a norm. *Journal of Experimental Social Psychology*, 1977, **13**, 397–402.

Morse, S. J., & Gruzen, J. The eye of the beholder: A neglected variable in the study of physical attractiveness. *Journal of Personality*, 1976, **44**, 209–225.

Moscovici, S., Lage, S., & Naffrechoux, M. Influence on a consistent minority on the responses of a majority in a color perception task. *Sociometry*, 1969, **32**, 365–380.

Moscovici, S., & Personnaz, B. Studies in social influence: V. Minority influence and conversion behavior in a perceptual task. *Journal of Experimental Social Psychology*, 1980, **16**, 270–282.

Moscovici, S., & Zavalloni, M. The group as a polarizer of attitudes. *Journal of Personality and Social Psychology*, 1969, **12**, 124–135.

Mossip, C. E. Hemispheric specialization as seen in children's perception of faces. Paper presented at the Eastern Psychological Association convention, 1979. Cited by R. K. Unger in Toward a redefinition of sex and gender. *American Psychologist*, 1979, **34**, 1085–1094.

Moyer, K. E. *The psychobiology of aggression*. New York: Harper & Row, 1976.

Moynihan, D. P. Social science and the courts. *Public Interest*, 1979, **54**, 12–31.

Murdock, G. P. Comparative data on the division of labor by sex. *Social Forces*, 1935, **15**, 551–553.

Murdock, G. P. The common denominator of cultures. In R. Linton (Ed.), *The science of man and the world crisis*. New York: Columbia University Press, 1945.

Murray, H. A., & Wheeler, D. R. A note on the possible clairvoyance of dreams. *Journal of Psychology*, 1937, **3**, 309–313.

Murray, J. P. *Television and youth: 25 years of research* *and controversy*. Boys Town, Neb.: The Boys Town Center for the Study of Youth Development, 1980.

Murray, J. P., & Kippax, S. From the early window to the late night show: International trends in the study of television's impact on children and adults. In L. Berkowitz (Ed.), *Advances in experimental social psychology* (Vol. 12). New York: Academic Press, 1979.

Murstein, B. I. Physical attractiveness and marital choice. *Journal of Personality and Social Psychology*, 1972, **22**, 8–12.

Murstein, B. I. *Who will marry whom*. New York: Springer, 1976.

Murstein, B. I., & Christy, P. Physical attractiveness and marriage adjustment in middle-aged couples. *Journal of Personality and Social Psychology*, 1976, **34**, 537–542.

Muson, H. Teenage violence and the telly. *Psychology Today*, March 1978, pp. 50–54.

Mussen, P. H. Early sex-role development. In D. A. Goslin (Ed.), *Handbook of socialization theory and research*. Chicago: Rand McNally, 1969.

Myers, D. G. Enhancement of initial risk tendencies in social situations (Unpublished doctoral dissertation, University of Iowa, 1967). (University Microfilms No. 68-958.)

Myers, D. G. Polarizing effects of social comparison. *Journal of Experimental Social Psychology*, 1978, **14**, 554–563.

Myers, D. G., & Bach, P. J. Group discussion effects on conflict behavior and self-justification. *Psychological Reports*, 1976, **38**, 135–140.

Myers, D. G., & Bishop, G. D. Discussion effects on racial attitudes. *Science*, 1970, **169**, 778–789.

Nance, J. *The gentle Tasaday: A stone age people in the Philippine rain forest*. New York: Harcourt Brace Jovanovich, 1975.

Napolitan, D. A., & Goethals, G. R. The attribution of friendliness. *Journal of Experimental Social Psychology*, 1979, **15**, 105–113.

National Commission on the Causes and Prevention of Violence. *To establish justice, insure domestic tranquility*. Washington, D.C.: U.S. Government Printing Offices, 1969.

National Enquirer. February 7, 1978, p. 1.

National Institute of Mental Health. *Television and Behavior: Ten Years of Scientific Progress and Implications for the Eighties*, 1982.

National Opinion Research Center. *General social surveys, 1972–1980: Cumulative codebook*. Storrs, Conn.: Roper Public Opinion Research Center, University of Connecticut, 1980.

NBC News. April 20, 1977. (a)

NBC News Poll. November 29–30, 1977. Cited by *Public Opinion*, January–February 1979, p. 36. (b)

Neisser, U. *Cognition and reality: Principles and implications of cognitive psychology*. San Francisco: Freeman, 1976.

Nemeth, C. Interactions between jurors as a function of majority vs. unanimity decision rules. *Journal of Applied Social Psychology*, 1977, **7**, 38–56.

Nemeth, C. The role of an active minority in intergroup relations. In W. G. Austin and S. Worchel (Eds.), *The social psychology of intergroup relations*. Monterey, Calif.: Brooks/Cole, 1979.

Nemeth, C., & Wachtler, J. Creating the perceptions of consistency and confidence: A necessary condition for minority influence. *Sociometry*, 1974, **37**, 529– 540.

Newcomb, T. M. *The acquaintance process*. New York: Holt, Rinehart and Winston, 1961.

Newman, H. M., & Langer, E. J. Post-divorce adaptation and the attribution of responsibility. *Sex Roles*, 1981, **7**, 223–231.

Newman, J., & McCauley, C. Eye contact with strangers in city, suburb, and small town. *Environment and Behavior*, 1977, **9**, 547–558.

Newman, O. *Defensible space*. New York: Macmillan, 1972.

Newman, O. *Architectural design for crime prevention*. Government Printing Office: U.S. Department of Justice, 1973.

Newsweek. May 19, 1980, p. 72.

Newsweek. March 2, 1981, p. 38; March 9, 1981, p. 28.

Newtson, D., & Czerlinsky, T. Adjustment of attitude communications for contrasts by extreme audiences. *Journal of Personality and Social Psychology*, 1974, **30**, 829–837.

Nias, D. K. B. Marital choice: Matching or complementation? In M. Cook and G. Wilson (Eds.), *Love and attraction*. Oxford: Pergamon, 1979.

Nicosia, G. J., Hyman, D., Karlin, R. A., Epstein, Y. M., & Aiello, J. R. Effects of bodily contact on reactions to crowding. *Journal of Applied Social Psychology*, 1979, **9**, 508–523.

Nida, S. A., & Williams, J. E. Sex-stereotyped traits,

physical attractiveness, and interpersonal attraction. *Psychological Reports*, 1977, **41**, 1311– 1322.

Nielsen Co., A. C. 1981 data cited by *U.S. News & World Report*, Aug. 2, 1982, p. 29.

Nisbett, R. E. The trait construct in lay and professional psychology. In L. Festinger (Ed.), *Retrospections on social psychology*. New York: Oxford University Press, 1980.

Nisbett, R. E., & Bellows, N. Verbal reports about causal influences on social judgments: Private access versus public theories. *Journal of Personality and Social Psychology*, 1977, **35**, 613–624.

Nisbett, R. E., Borgida, E., Crandall, R., & Reed, H. Popular induction: Information is not necessarily informative. In J. S. Carroll and J. W. Payne (Eds.), *Cognition and social behavior*. Hillsdale, N.J.: Lawrence Erlbaum, 1976.

Nisbett, R. E., & Ross, L. *Human inference: Strategies and shortcomings of social judgment*. Englewood Cliffs, N.J.: Prentice-Hall, 1980.

Nisbett, R. E., & Schachter, S. Cognitive manipulation of pain. *Journal of Experimental Social Psychology*, 1966, **2**, 227–236.

Nisbett, R. E., & Wilson, T. D. Telling more than we can know: Verbal reports on mental process. *Psychological Review*, 1977, **84**, 231–259.

Nisbett, R. E., Zukier, H., & Lemley, R. E. The dilution effect: Nondiagnostic information weakens the implications of diagnostic information. Cognitive Psychology, *1981*, **13**, 248–277.

O'Dea, T. F. Sects and cults. In D. L. Sills (Ed.), *International encyclopedia of the social sciences* (Vol. 14). New York: Macmillan, 1968.

O'Donnell, W. J., & O'Donnell, K. J. Update: Sex-role messages in TV commercials. *Journal of Communication*, 1978, **28**(1), 156–158.

O'Gorman, H. J., & Garry, S. L. Pluralistic ignorance—a replication and extension. *Public Opinion Quarterly*, 1976, **40**, 449–458.

O'Leary, M. R., & Dengerink, H. A. Aggression as a function of the intensity and pattern of attack. *Journal of Experimental Research in Personality*, 1973, **7**, 61–70.

O'Leary, V. E., & Donoghue, J. M. Latitudes of masculinity: Reactions to sex-role deviance in men. *Journal of Social Issues*, 1978, **34**, 17–28.

Olsen, M. E. Consumers' attitudes toward energy conservation. *Journal of Social Issues*, 1981, **37**(2), 108–131.

Olson, J. M., & Zanna, M. P. Promoting physical activity: A social psychological perspective. Report prepared for the Ministry of Culture and Recreation, Sports and Fitness Branch, 77 Bloor St. West, 8th Floor, Toronto, Ontario M7A 2R9, November 1981.

Olweus, D. Stability of aggressive reaction patterns in males: A review. *Psychological Bulletin*, 1979, **86**, 852–875.

Osgood, C. E. *An alternative to war or surrender*. Urbana, Ill.: University of Illinois Press, 1962.

Osgood, C. E. Statement on psychological aspects of international relations. Committee on Foreign Relations, United States Senate, May 25, 1966. Reprinted in D. G. Linder (Ed.), *Psychological dimensions of social interaction*. Reading, Mass.: Addison-Wesley, 1973.

Osgood, C. E. GRIT: A strategy for survival in mankind's nuclear age? Paper presented at the Pugwash Conference on New Directions in Disarmament, Racine, Wis. 1980.

Oskamp, S. Effects of programmed strategies on cooperation in the prisoner's dilemma and other mixed-motive games. *Journal of Conflict Resolution*, 1971, **15**, 225–229.

Osterhouse, R. A., & Brock, T. C. Distraction increases yielding to propaganda by inhibiting counterarguing. *Journal of Personality and Social Psychology*, 1970, **15**, 344–358.

Owens, G., & Ford, J. G. Further consideration of the "what is good is beautiful" finding. *Social Psychology*, 1978, **41**, 73–75.

Pagano, M. R., & Taylor, S. P. The initiation of attack as a function of alcohol dosage. Paper presented at the Midwestern Psychological Association convention, 1981.

Page, M. M., & Scheidt, R. J. The elusive weapons effect: Demand awareness, evaluation apprehension, and slightly sophisticated subjects. *Journal of Personality and Social Psychology*, 1971, **20**, 304–318.

Pallak, M. S., Cook, D. A., & Sullivan, J. J. Commitment and energy conservation. In L. Bickman (Ed.), *Applied Social Psychology Annual* (Vol. 1). Beverly Hills, Calif.: Sage Publications, 1980.

Pallak, M. S., Mueller, M., Dollar, K., & Pallak, J. Effect of commitment on responsiveness to an extreme consonant communication. *Journal of Personality and Social Psychology*, 1972, **23**, 429–436.

Palmer, E. L., & Dorr, A. (Eds.). *Children and the faces of television: Teaching, violence, selling*. New York: Academic Press, 1980.

Paloutzian, R. Pro-ecology behavior: Three field experiments on litter pickup. Paper presented at the Western Psychological Association convention, 1979.

Panek, P. E., Deitchman, R., Burkholder, J. H., Speroff, T., & Haude, R. H. Evaluation of feminine professional competence as a function of level of accomplishment. *Psychological Reports*, 1976, **38**, 875–880.

Parke, R. D. Rules, roles, and resistance to deviation: Recent advances in punishment, discipline, and self-control. In A. Pick (Ed.), *Symposia of Child Psychology* (Vol. 8). Minneapolis: University of Minnesota Press, 1974.

Parke, R. D., Berkowitz, L., Leyens, J. P., West, S. G., & Sebastian, J. Some effects of violent and nonviolent movies on the behavior of juvenile delinquents. In L. Berkowitz (Ed.), *Advances in experimental social psychology* (Vol. 10). New York: Academic Press, 1977.

Partridge, A., & Eldridge, C. *The second circuit sentencing study: A report to the judges of the second circuit.* Washington, D.C.: Federal Judicial Center, 1974. Cited by M. J. Saks and R. Hastie in *Social psychology in court*. New York: Van Nostrand Reinhold, 1978.

Patterson, G. R., Littman, R. A., & Bricker, W. Assertive behavior in children: A step toward a theory of aggression. *Monographs of the Society for Research in Child Development* (Serial No. 113), 1967, **32**, 5.

Patterson, M. L. An arousal model of interpersonal crowding. *Psychological Review*, 1976, **83**, 235–245.

Patterson, T. E. The role of the mass media in presidential campaigns: The lessons of the 1976 election. *Items*, 1980, **34**, 25–30. Social Science Research Council, 605 Third Avenue, New York, N.Y. 10016.

Patton, G. S., Jr. *War as I knew it*. Boston: Houghton Mifflin, 1949.

Pauling, L. Quoted by Etzioni, A. *The hard way to peace: A new strategy*. New York: Collier, 1962.

Paulus, P., McCain, G., & Cox, V. Prison standards: Some pertinent data on crowding. *Federal Probation*, 1981, **45**(4), 48–54.

Peck, T. When women evaluate women, nothing succeeds like success: The differential effects of status upon evaluations of male and female professional ability. *Sex Roles*, 1978, **4**, 205–213.

Peevers, B. H. Androgyny on the TV screen? An analysis of sex-role portrayal. *Sex Roles*, 1979, **5**, 797–809.

Pendleton, M., & Batson, C. D. Self-presentation and the door-in-the-face technique for inducing compliance. *Personality and Social Psychology Bulletin*, 1979, **5**, 77–81.

Pennebaker, J. W., & Lightner, J. M. Competition of internal and external information in an exercise setting. *Journal of Personality and Social Psychology*, 1980, **39**, 165–174.

Penner, L. A., Dertke, M. C., & Achenbach, C. J. The "flash" system: A field study of altruism. *Journal of Applied Social Psychology*, 1973, **3**, 362–370.

Penrod, S. Research summary from study of attorney and scientific jury selection models. Unpublished manuscript, University of Wisconsin, 1981.

Perloff, R. M., & Brock, T. C. ". . . And thinking makes it so": Cognitive responses to persuasion. In M. E. Roloff & G. R. Miller (Eds.), *Persuasion: New directions in theory and research*. Beverly Hills: Sage Publications, 1980.

Perls, F. S. *Ego, hunger and aggression: The beginning of Gestalt therapy*. Random House, 1969. Cited by Berkowitz in The case for bottling up rage. *Psychology Today*, July 1973, pp. 24–30.

Perrin, S., & Spencer, C. The Asch effect—a child of its time? *Bulletin of the British Psychology Society*, 1980, **32**, 405–406.

Perry, D. G., & Bussey, K. The social learning theory of sex differences: Imitation is alive and well. *Journal of Personality and Social Psychology*, 1979, **37**, 1699–1712.

Pessin, J. The comparative effects of social and mechanical stimulation on memorizing. *American Journal of Psychology*, 1933, **45**, 263–270.

Pessin, J., & Husband, R. W. Effects of social stimulation on human maze learning. *Journal of Abnormal and Social Psychology*, 1933, **28**, 148–154.

Peter, L. J., & Hull, R. *The Peter principle: Why things always go wrong*. New York: Morrow, 1969.

Peterson, C. Attribution in the sports page: An archival investigation of the covariation hypothesis. *Social Psychology Quarterly*, 1980, **43**, 136–141.

Peterson, C., Schwartz, S. M., & Seligman, M. E.

P. Self-blame and depressive symptoms. *Journal of Personality and Social Psychology*, 1981, **41**, 253–259.

Peterson, J. L., & Zill, N. Television viewing in the United States and children's intellectual, social, and emotional development. *Television and Children*, 1981, 2(2), 21–28.

Pettigrew, T. F. Personality and sociocultural factors in intergroup attitudes: A cross-national comparison. *Journal of Conflict Resolution*, 1958, **2**, 29–42.

Pettigrew, T. F. Racially separate or together? *Journal of Social Issues*, 1969, **25**, 43–69.

Pettigrew, T. F. Three issues in ethnicity: Boundaries, deprivations, and perceptions. In J. M. Yinger & S. J. Cutler (Eds.), *Major social issues: A multidisciplinary view*. New York: Free Press, 1978.

Pettigrew, T. F. The ultimate attribution error: Extending Allport's cognitive analysis of prejudice. *Personality and Social Psychology Bulletin*, 1979, **5**, 461–476.

Pettigrew, T. F. Prejudice. In S. Thernstrom et al. (Eds.), *Harvard encyclopedia of American ethnic groups*. Cambridge, Mass.: Harvard University Press, 1980.

Petty, R. E., & Brock, T. C. Effects of "Barnum" personality assessments on cognitive behavior. *Journal of Consulting and Clinical Psychology*, 1979, **47**, 201–203.

Petty, R. E., & Cacioppo, J. T. Forewarning cognitive responding, and resistance to persuasion. *Journal of Personality and Social Psychology*, 1977, **35**, 645–655.

Petty, R. E., & Cacioppo, J. T. Effects of forewarning of persuasive intent and involvement on cognitive response and persuasion. *Personality and Social Psychology Bulletin*, 1979, **5**, 173–176. (a)

Petty, R. E., & Cacioppo, J. T. Issue involvement can increase or decrease persuasion by enhancing message-relevant cognitive responses. *Journal of Personality and Social Psychology*, 1979, **37**, 1915–1926. (b)

Petty, R. E., Cacioppo, J. T., & Goldman, R. Personal involvement as a determinant of argument-based persuasion. *Journal of Personality and Social Psychology*, 1981, **41**, 847–855.

Petty, R. E., Cacioppo, J. T., & Heesacker, M. Effects of rhetorical questions on persuasion: A cognitive response analysis. *Journal of Personality and Social Psychology*, 1981, **40**, 432–440.

Petty, R. E., Harkins, S. G., & Williams, K. D. The effects of group diffusion of cognitive effort on attitudes: An information processing approach. *Journal of Personality and Social Psychology*, 1980, **38**, 81–92.

Petty, R. E., Ostrom, T. M., & Brock, T. C. (Eds.), *Cognitive responses in persuasion*. Hillsdale, N.J.: Lawrence Erlbaum, 1981.

Petty, R. E., Wells, G. L., & Brock, T. C. Distraction can enhance or reduce yielding to propaganda: Thought disruption versus effort justification. *Journal of Personality and Social Psychology*, 1976, **34**, 874–884.

Phares, E. J. *Locus of control in personality*. Morristown, N.J.: General Learning Press, 1976.

Pheterson, G. I. Female prejudice against men. Unpublished manuscript, Connecticut College, 1969. Cited by G. I. Pheterson, S. B. Kiesler, & P. A. Goldberg in Evaluation of the performance of women as a function of their sex, achievement, and personal history. *Journal of Personality and Social Psychology*, 1971, **19**, 114–118.

Pheterson, G. I., Kiesler, S. B., & Goldberg, P. A. Evaluation of the performance of women as a function of their sex, achievement, and personal history. *Journal of Personality and Social Psychology*, 1971, **19**, 114–118.

Phillips, D. P. The influence of suggestion on suicide: Substantive and theoretical implications of the Werther effect. *American Sociological Review*, 1974, **39**, 340–354.

Phillips, D. P. Motor vehicle fatalities increase just after publicized suicide stories. *Science*, 1977, **196**, 1464–1465.

Phillips, D. P. Airplane accident fatalities increase just after newspaper stories about murder and suicide. *Science*, 1978, **201**, 748–750.

Phillips, D. P. Suicide, motor vehicle fatalities, and the mass media: Evidence toward a theory of suggestion. *American Journal of Sociology*, 1979, **84**, 1150–1174.

Piaget, J. *The moral development of the child*. New York: Free Press, 1948.

Piliavin, I. M., Rodin, J., & Piliavin, J. A. Good Samaritanism: An underground phenomenon. *Journal of Personality and Social Psychology*, 1969, **13**, 289–299.

Piliavin, J. A., Evans, D. E., & Callero, P. Learning to "Give to unnamed strangers": The process of commitment to regular blood donation. In E. Staub, D. Bar-Tal, J. Karylowski, & J. Reykawski (Eds.), *The Development and Maintenance of Prosocial Behavior: International Perspectives*. New York: Plenum, 1982.

Piliavin, J. A., & Piliavin, I. M. The Good Samaritan: Why *does* he help? Unpublished manuscript, University of Wisconsin, 1973.

Pleck, J. Changing patterns of work and family roles.

Working paper no. 81, Wellesley College, Center for Research on Women, Wellesley, Mass. 02181, 1981.

Pliner, P., Hart, H., Kohl, J., & Saari, D. Compliance without pressure: Some further data on the foot-in-the-door technique. *Journal of Experimental Social Psychology*, 1974, **10**, 17–22.

Pomazal, R. J., & Clore, G. L. Helping on the highway: The effects of dependency and sex. *Journal of Applied Social Psychology*, 1973, **3**, 150–164.

Porter, N. P., & Geis, F. L. Women and nonverbal leadership cues: When seeing is not believing. In C. Mayo & N. M. Henley (Eds.), *Gender and nonverbal behavior*. New York: Springer-Verlag, 1981.

Prentice-Dunn, S., & Rogers, R. W. Effects of deindividuating situational cues and aggressive models on subjective deindividuation and aggression. *Journal of Personality and Social Psychology*, 1980, **39**, 104–113.

Price, G. H., Dabbs, J. M., Jr., Clower, B. J., & Resin, R. P. At first glance—Or, is physical attractiveness more than skin deep? Paper presented at the Eastern Psychological Association convention, 1974. Cited by K. L. Dion & K. K. Dion. Personality and behavioral correlates of romantic love. In M. Cook & G. Wilson (Eds.), *Love and attraction*. Oxford: Pergamon, 1979.

Price, R. H., & Bouffard, D. L. Behavioral appropriateness and situational constraint as dimensions of social behavior. *Journal of Personality and Social Psychology*, 1974, **30**, 579–586.

Price, R. A., & Vandenberg, S. G. Matching for physical attractiveness in married couples. *Personality and Social Psychology Bulletin*, 1979, 5, 398–399.

Propst, R., Adams, J., & Propst, C. *The Senator Hatfield office innovation project*. Ann Arbor, Mich.: Herman Miller Research Corp., 3971 South Research Park Drive, 1977.

Pruitt, D. G. Kissinger as a traditional mediator with power. In J. Z. Rubin (Ed.), *Dynamics of third party intervention: Kissinger in the Middle East*. New York: Praeger, 1981. (a)

Pruitt, D. G. *Negotiation behavior*. New York: Academic Press, 1981. (b)

Pruitt, D. G., & Kimmel, M. J. Twenty years of experimental gaming: Critique, synthesis, and suggestions for the future. *Annual Review of Psychology*, 1977, **28**, 363–392.

Pruitt, D. G., & Lewis, S. A. Development of integrative solutions in bilateral negotiation. *Journal of Personality and Social Psychology*, 1975, **31**, 621–633.

Pruitt, D. G., & Lewis, S. A. The psychology of integrative bargaining. In D. Druckman (Ed.), *Negotiations: A social-psychological analysis*. New York: Halsted, 1977.

Quattrone, G. A. Overattribution and unit formation: When behavior engulfs the person. *Journal of Personality and Social Psychology*, 1982, **42**, 593–607.

Quattrone, G. A., & Jones, E. E. The perception of variability within in-groups and out-groups: Implications for the law of small numbers. *Journal of Personality and Social Psychology*, 1980, **38**, 141–152.

Randi, J. *Flim-flam*. New York: Crowell, 1980.

Randi, J. Personal communication. 1981.

Rapoport, A. *Fights, games, and debates*. Ann Arbor: University of Michigan Press, 1980.

Raven, B. H. The Nixon group. *Journal of Social Issues*, 1974, **30**(4), 297–320.

RCAgenda. November–December 1979, p. 11. 475 Riverside Drive, New York, N.Y. 10027.

Regan, D. T., & Cheng, J. B. Distraction and attitude change: A resolution. *Journal of Experimental Social Psychology*, 1973, **9**, 138–147.

Regan, D. T., & Fazio, R. On the consistency between attitudes and behavior: Look to the method of attitude formation. *Journal of Experimenal Social Psychology*, 1977, **13**, 28–45.

Regan, D. T., Williams, M., & Sparling, S. Voluntary expiation of guilt: A field experiment. *Journal of Personality and Social Psychology*, 1972, **24**, 42–45.

Regan, J. W. Guilt, perceived injustice, and altruistic behavior. *Journal of Personality and Social Psychology*, 1971, **18**, 124–132.

Reichner, R. F. Differential responses to being ignored: The effects of architectural design and social density on interpersonal behavior. *Journal of Applied Social Psychology*, 1979, **9**, 13–26.

Reik, T. *A psychologist looks at love*. New York: Farrar and Rinehart, 1944.

Reilly, M. E. A case study of role conflict: Roman Catholic priests. *Human Relations*, 1978, **31**, 77–90.

Reingen, P. H., & Kernam, J. B. Compliance with an interview request: A foot-in-the-door, self-perception interpretation. *Journal of Marketing Research*, 1977, **14**, 365–369.

Reinisch, M. Prenatal exposure to synthetic progestins increases potential for aggression in humans. *Science*, 1981, **211**, 1171–1172.

Reis, H. T., & Jackson, L. A. Sex differences in reward allocation: Subjects, partners, and tasks. *Journal of Personality and Social Psychology*, 1981, **40**, 465–478.

Reis, H. T., Nezlek, J., & Wheeler, L. Physical attractiveness in social interaction. *Journal of Personality and Social Psychology*, 1980, **38**, 604– 617.

Reitzes, D. C. The role of organizational structures: Union versus neighborhood in a tension situation. *Journal of Social Issues*, 1953, **9**(1), 37–44.

Renaud, H., & Estess, F. Life history interviews with one hundred normal American males: "Pathogenecity" of childhood. *American Journal of Orthopsychiatry*, 1961, **31**, 786–802.

Reston, J. Proxmire on love. *New York Times*, March 14, 1975.

Reychler, L. The effectiveness of a pacifist strategy in conflict resolution. *Journal of Conflict Resolution*, 1979, **23**, 228–260.

Reyes, R. M., Thompson, W. C., & Bower, G. H. Judgmental biases resulting from differing availabilities on arguments. *Journal of Personality and Social Psychology*, 1980, **39**, 2–12.

Rhine, R. J., & Severance, L. J. Ego-involvement, discrepancy, source credibility, and attitude change. *Journal of Personality and Social Psychology*, 1970, **16**, 175–190.

Rhodewalt, F., & Comer, R. Induced-compliance attitude change: Once more with feeling. *Journal of Experimental Social Psychology*, 1979, **15**, 35–47.

Rholes, F. H., Jr. Thermal comfort and strategies for energy conservation. *Journal of Social Issues*, 1981, **37**(2), 132–149.

Rianoshek, R. A comment on Sampson's psychology and the American ideal. *Journal of Personality and Social Psychology*, 1980, **38**, 105–107.

Rice, M. E., & Grusec, J. E. Saying and doing: Effects on observer performance. *Journal of Personality and Social Psychology*, 1975, **32**, 584–593.

Richardson, D. C., Bernstein, S., & Taylor, S. P. The effect of situational contingencies on female retaliative behavior. *Journal of Personality and Social Psychology*, 1979, **37**, 2044–2048.

Richardson, L. F. Generalized foreign policy. *British Journal of Psychology Monographs Supplements*, 1969, **23**. Cited by A. Rapoport in *Fights, games, and debates*. Ann Arbor: University of Michigan Press, 1960, p. 15.

Richman, A. The polls: Public attitudes toward the energy crisis. *Public Opinion Quarterly*, 1979, **43**, 576–585.

Riess, M., Rosenfeld, P., Melburg, V., & Tedeschi, J. T. Self-serving attributions: Biased private perceptions and distorted public descriptions. *Journal of Personality and Social Psychology*, 1981, **41**, 224–231.

Riordan, C. A. Effects of admission of influence on attributions and attraction. Paper presented at the American Psychological Association convention, 1980.

Riordan, C. A., & Ruggiero, J. Producing equal-status interracial interaction: A replication. *Social Psychology Quarterly*, 1980, **43**, 131–136.

Rittle, R. M. Changes in helping behavior: Self-versus situational perceptions as mediators of the foot-in-the-door effect. *Personality and Social Psychology Bulletin*, 1981, **7**, 431–437.

Robertson, I. *Sociology*. New York: Worth Publishers, 1977.

Robinson, C. L., Lockard, J. S., & Adams, R. M. Who looks at a baby in public. *Ethology and Sociobiology*, 1979, **1**, 87–91.

Robinson, J. P. Television's impact on everyday life: Some cross-national evidence. In E. A. Rubinstein, G. A. Comstock, & J. P. Murray (Eds.), *Television and social behavior* (Vol. 4): *Television in day-to-day life: Patterns of use*. Washington, D.C.: Government Printing Office, 1972.

Robison, A. J. Opinion change as a function of the communicator's sex. Unpublished manuscript, Western Illinois University, 1972.

Rochon, J. *An evaluation of the seat belt education campaign*. Ottawa: Department of Transport, 1977. Cited by J. M. Olson & M. Zanna, Promoting physical activity: A social psychological perspective. Report prepared for the Ministry of Culture and Recreation, Sports and Fitness Branch, 77 Bloor St. West, 8th Floor, Toronto, Ontario M7A 2R9, November 1981.

Rodin, J. Density, perceived choice, and response to controllable and uncontrollable outcomes. *Journal of Experimental Social Psychology*, 1976, **12**, 564–578.

Rodin, J., & Langer, E. J. Long-term effects of a control-relevant intervention with the institutionalized aged. *Journal of Personality and Social Psychology*, 1977, **35**, 897–902.

Rodin, J., Solomon, S. K., & Metcalf, J. Role of control in mediating perceptions of density. *Journal of Personality and Social Psychology*, 1978, **36**, 988–999.

Rogers, C. R. Reinhold Niebuhr's *The self and the dramas of history*: A criticism. *Pastoral Psychology*, 1958, **9**, 15–17.

Rogers, R. W., & Mewborn, C. R. Fear appeals and attitude change: Effects of a threat's noxiousness, probability of occurrence, and the efficacy of coping responses. *Journal of Personality and Social Psychology*, 1976, **34**, 54–61.

Rogers, R. W., & Prentice-Dunn, S. Deindividuation and anger-mediated interracial aggression: Unmasking regressive racism. *Journal of Personality and Social Psychology*, 1981, **41**, 63–73.

Rohrer, J. H., Baron, S. H., Hoffman, E. L., & Swander, D. V. The stability of autokinetic judgments. *Journal of Abnormal and Social Psychology*, 1954, **49**, 595–597.

Rokeach, M. *Beliefs, attitudes, and values*. San Francisco: Jossey-Bass, 1968.

Rokeach, M., & Mezei, L. Race and shared beliefs as factors in social choice. *Science*, 1966, **151**, 167– 172.

Root, L. Designers modify the open house to meet complaints of workers. *Wall Street Journal*, November 5, 1980, p. 29.

Roper Organization. *The 1980 Virginia Slims American women's poll* (conducted in late 1979). (Published by Philip Morris USA, undated.)

Rose, T. L., & Hamilton, D. L. Stereotypes as schemata. Paper presented at the Western Psychological Association convention, 1979.

Rosenberg, L. A. Group size, prior experience and conformity. *Journal of Abnormal and Social Psychology*, 1961, **63**, 436–437.

Rosenfeld, D. The relationship between self-esteem and egotism in males and females. Unpublished manuscript, Southern Methodist University, 1979.

Rosenfeld, D., Folger, R., & Adelman, H. F. When rewards reflect competence: A qualification of the overjustification effect. *Journal of Personality and Social Psychology*, 1980, **39**, 368–376.

Rosenhan, D. L. The natural socialization of altruistic autonomy. In J. Macaulay & L. Berkowitz (Eds.), *Altruism and helping behavior*. New York: Academic Press, 1970.

Rosenhan, D. L. On being sane in insane places. *Science*, 1973, **179**, 250–258.

Rosenhan, D. L., Salovey, P., & Hargis, K. The joys of helping: Focus of attention mediates the impact of positive affect on altruism. *Journal of Personality and Social Psychology*, 1981, **40**, 899–905.

Rosenhan, D. L., Underwood, B., & Moore, B. Affect moderates self-gratification and altruism. *Journal of Personality and Social Psychology*, 1974, **30**, 546–553.

Rosenkrantz, P. S., Vogel, S. R., Bee, H., Broverman, I. K., & Broverman, D. M. Sex-role stereotypes and self-concepts in college students. *Journal of Consulting and Clinical Psychology*, 1968, **32**, 287–295.

Rosenthal, R. *Experimenter effects in behavioral research*. New York: Appleton-Century-Crofts, 1966.

Rosenthal, R. The Pygmalion effect lives. *Psychology Today*, September 1973, pp. 56–63.

Rosenthal, R., & DePaulo, B. M. Sex differences in eavesdropping on nonverbal cues. *Journal of Personality and Social Psychology*, 1979, **37**, 273–285.

Rosenthal, R., Hall, J. A., Archer, D., DiMatteo, M. R., & Rogers, P. L. The PONS test: Measuring sensitivity to nonverbal cues. In S. Weitz (Ed.), *Nonverbal communication* (2d ed). New York: Oxford University Press, 1979.

Rosenthal, R., & Jacobson, L. *Pygmalion in the classroom: Teacher expectation and pupils' intellectual development*. New York: Holt, Rinehart, & Winston, 1968.

Rosenthal, R., & Rubin, D. B. Interpersonal expectancy effects: The first 345 studies. *Behavioral and Brain Sciences*, 1978, **2**, 377–415.

Rosenzweig, M. R. Cognitive dissonance. *American Psychologist*, 1972, **27**, 769.

Ross, C. Rejected. *New West*, February 12, 1979, pp. 39–43.

Ross, L. D. The intuitive psychologist and his shortcomings: Distortions in the attribution process. In L. Berkowitz (Ed.), *Advances in experimental social psychology* (Vol. 10). New York: Academic Press, 1977.

Ross, L. D. The "intuitive scientist" formulation and its developmental implications. In J. H. Havell & L. Ross (Eds.), *Social cognitive development: Frontiers and possible futures*. Cambridge, England: Cambridge University Press, 1981.

Ross, L. D., Amabile, T. M., & Steinmetz, J. L. Social roles, social control, and biases in social-perception processes. *Journal of Personality and Social Psychology*, 1977, **35**, 485–494.

Ross, L. D., & Anderson, C. A. Shortcomings in the Attribution process: On the origins and maintenance of erroneous social assessments. In D. Kahneman, P. Slovic, & A. Tversky, (Eds.), *Judgment under uncertainty: Heuristics and biases*. New York: Cambridge University Press, 1982.

Ross, L. D., & Lepper, M. R. The perseverance of beliefs: Empirical and normative considerations. In R. A. Shweder (Ed.), *New directions for methodology of behavioral science: Fallible judgment in behavioral research*. San Francisco: Jossey-Bass, 1980.

Ross, L. D., Lepper, M. R., Strack, F., & Steinmetz, J. Social explanation and social expectation: Effects of real and hypothetical explanations on subjective likelihood. *Journal of Personality and Social Psychology*, 1977, **35**, 817–829.

Ross, L. D., Turiel, E., Josephson, J., & Lepper, M. R. Developmental perspectives on the fundamental attribution error. Unpublished manuscript, Stanford University, 1978.

Ross, M., & Lumsden, A. Attributions of responsibility in sport settings: It's not how you play the game, but whether you win or lose. In H. H. Kelley, H. Hiebsch, H. Brandstätter, (Ed.), *Proceedings of the XXII International Congress of Psychology*. Amsterdam: North Holland Publishing Co., in press.

Ross, M., McFarland, C., & Fletcher, G. J. O. The effect of attitude on the recall of personal histories. *Journal of Personality and Social Psychology*, 1981, **40**, 627–634.

Ross, M., & Sicoly, F. Egocentric biases in availability and attribution. *Journal of Personality and Social Psychology*, 1979, **37**, 322–336.

Ross, M., Thibaut, J., & Evenbeck, S. Some determinants of the intensity of social protest. *Journal of Experimental Social Psychology*, 1971, **7**, 401–418.

Rossi, A. The biosocial side of parenthood. *Human Nature*, June 1978, pp. 72–79.

Rothbart, M., & Birrell, P. Attitude and the Perception of faces. *Journal of Research Personality*, 1977, **11**, 209–215.

Rothbart, M., Evans, M., & Fulero, S. Recall for confirming events: Memory processes and the maintenance of social stereotypes. *Journal of Experimental Social Psychology*, 1979, **15**, 343–355.

Rothbart, M., Fulero, S., Jensen, C., Howard, J., & Birrell, P. From individual to group impressions: Availability heuristics in stereotype formation. *Journal of Experimental Social Psychology*, 1978, **14**, 237–255.

Rotter, J. Internal-external locus of control scale. In J. P. Robinson & R. P. Shaver (Eds.), *Measures of social psychological attitudes*. Ann Arbor: Institute for Social Research, 1973.

Rubin, J. Z. Experimental research on third-party intervention in conflict: Toward some generalizations. *Psychological Bulletin*, 1980, **87**, 379–391.

Rubin, J. Z. (Ed). *Third party intervention in conflict: Kissinger in the Middle East*. New York: Praeger, 1981.

Rubin, J. Z., Provenzano, F. J., & Luria, Z. The eye of the beholder: Parents' views on sex of newborns. *American Journal of Orthopsychiatry*, 1974, **44**, 512–519.

Rubin, R. B. Ideal traits and terms of address for male and female college professors. *Journal of Personality and Social Psychology*, 1981, **41**, 966–974.

Rubin, R. T., Reinisch, J. M., & Haskett, R. F. Postnatal gonadal steroid effects on human behavior. *Science*, 1980, **211**, 1318–1324.

Rubin, Z. Measurement of romantic love. *Journal of Personality and Social Psychology*, 1970, **16**, 265–273.

Rubin, Z. *Liking and loving: An invitation to social psychology*. New York: Holt, Rinehart, and Winston, 1973.

Rubin, Z., Hill, C. T., Peplau, L. A., & Dunkel-Schetter, C. Self-disclosure in dating couples: Sex roles and the ethic of openness. *Journal of Marriage and Family*, 1980, **42**, 305–317.

Ruble, D. N., Feldman, S. N., Higgins, E. T., & Karlovac, M. Locus of causality and the use of information in the development of causal attributions. *Journal of Personality*, 1979, **47**, 595–614.

Ruff, C., Associates. The office of the 80's: Designing for people and productivity. *Fortune*, June 2, 1980 (unnumbered insert).

Runyan, W. M. Why did Van Gogh cut off his ear? The problem of alternative explanations in psychobiography. *Journal of Personality and Social Psychology*, 1981, **40**, 1070–1077.

Rusbutt, C. E. Commitment and satisfaction in romantic associations: A test of the investment model. *Journal of Experimental Social Psychology*, 1980, **16**, 172–186.

Rushton, J. P. Generosity in children: Immediate and long-term effects of modeling, preaching, and moral judgment. *Journal of Personality and Social Psychology*, 1975, **31**, 459–466.

Rushton, J. P. Socialization and the altruistic behavior of children. *Psychological Bulletin*, 1976, **83**, 898–913.

Rushton, J. P. The effects of prosocial television and film material on the behavior of viewers. In L. Berkowitz (Ed.), *Advances in experimental social psychology* (Vol. 12). New York: Academic Press, 1979.

Rushton, J. P. *Altruism, socialization, and society*. Englewood Cliffs, N.J.: Prentice-Hall, 1980.

Rushton, J. P., & Campbell, A. C. Modeling, vicarious reinforcement and extraversion on blood donating in adults: Immediate and long-term effects. *European Journal of Social Psychology*, 1977, **7**, 297–306.

Russell, D., & Jones, W. H. Superstition fails: Reactions to disconfirmation of paranormal beliefs. *Personality and Social Psychology Bulletin*, 1980, **6**, 83–88.

Sabini, J., & Silver, M. *Moralities of everyday life*. New York: Oxford University Press, 1982.

Saegert, S., Swap, W., & Zajonc, R. B. Exposure, context, and interpersonal attraction. *Journal of Personality and Social Psychology*, 1973, **25**, 234–242.

Sagar, H. A., & Schofield, J. W. Integrating the desegregated school: Perspectives, practices and possibilities. In M. Wax (Ed.), *Comparative studies in interracial education*. Washington, D.C.: Government Printing Office, 1980. (a)

Sagar, H. A., & Schofield, J. W. Race and gender barriers: Preadolescent peer behavior in academic classrooms. Paper presented at the American Psychological Association convention, 1980. (b)

Sagar, H. A., & Schofield, J. W. Racial and behavioral cues in black and white children's perceptions of ambiguously aggressive acts. *Journal of Personality and Social Psychology*, 1980, **39**, 590–598. (c)

Saks, M. J. Ignorance of science is no excuse. *Trial*, 1974, **10**(6), 18–20.

Saks, M. J. *Jury verdicts*. Lexington, Mass.: Heath, 1977.

Saks, M. J., & Hastie, R. *Social psychology in court*. New York: Van Nostrand Reinhold, 1978.

Sakurai, M. M. Small group cohesiveness and detrimental conformity. *Sociometry*, 1975, **38**, 340–357.

Sales, S. M. Economic threat as a determinant of conversion rates in authoritarian and nonauthoritarian churches. *Journal of Personality and Social Psychology*, 1972, **23**, 420–428.

Saltzstein, H. D., & Sandberg, L. Indirect social influence: Change in judgmental process or anticipatory conformity. *Journal of Experimental Social Psychology*, 1979, **15**, 209–216.

Sampson, E. E. On justice as equality. *Journal of Social Issues*, 1975, **31**(3), 45–64.

Sampson, E. E. Psychology and the American ideal. *Journal of Personality and Social Psychology*, 1977, **35**, 767–782.

Sanders, C. Nation's new hero is a beer-bellied bigot with 60 million fans. *Ebony*, June 1972, pp. 187–192. Cited by J. C. Brigham in Verbal aggression and ethnic humor: What is their effect? In J. C. Brigham & L. S. Wrightsman (Eds.), *Contemporary issues in social psychology* (3d ed). Monterey, Calif.: Brooks/ Cole, 1977.

Sanders, G. S. Driven by distraction: An integrative review of social facilitation and theory and research. *Journal of Experimental Social Psychology*, 1981, **17**, 227–251. (a)

Sanders, G. S. Toward a comprehensive account of social facilitation: Distraction/conflict does not mean theoretical conflict. *Journal of Experimental Social Psychology*, 1981, **17**, 262–265. (b)

Sanders, G. S., & Baron, R. S. The motivating effects of distraction on task performance. *Journal of Personality and Social Psychology*, 1975, **32**, 956–963.

Sanders, G. S., & Baron, R. S. Is social comparison irrelevant for producing choice shifts? *Journal of Experimental Social Psychology*, 1977, **13**, 303–314.

Sanders, G. S., Baron, R. S., & Moore, D. L. Distraction and social comparison as mediators of social facilitation effects. *Journal of Experimental Social Psychology*, 1978, **14**, 291–303.

Santee, R. T., & Maslach, C. To agree or not to agree: Personal dissent amid social pressure to conform. *Journal of Personality and Social Psychology*, 1982, **42**, 690–700.

Sasfy, J., & Okun, M. Form of evaluation and audience expertness as joint determinants of audience effects. *Journal of Experimental Social Psychology*, 1974, **10**, 461–467.

Saturday Review. April 1, 1978, p. 42.

Saunders, D. M., Vidmar, N., & Hewitt, E. Eyewitness testimony and the discrediting effect.

In B. Clifford & S. Lloyd-Bostock (Eds.), *Eyewitness Identification*. London: Wiley, 1982.

Sawyer, J. Measurement *and* prediction, clinical *and* statistical. *Psychological Bulletin*, 1966, **66**, 178–200.

Scanlan, T. K., & Passer, M. W. Self-serving biases in the competitive sport setting: An attributional dilemma. *Journal of Sport Psychology*, 1980, **2**, 124–136.

Schachter, S. Deviation, rejection and communication. *Journal of Abnormal and Social Psychology*, 1951, **46**, 190–207.

Schachter, S., & Singer, J. E. Cognitive, social and physiological determinants of emotional state. *Psychological Review*, 1962, **69**, 379–399.

Schafer, R. B., & Keith, P. M. Equity and depression among married couples. *Social Psychology Quarterly*, 1980, **43**, 430–435.

Schaffner, P. E., Wandersman, A., & Stang, D. Candidate name exposure and voting: Two field studies. *Basic and Applied Social Psychology*, 1981, **2**, 195–203.

Scheier, M. F. The effects of public and private self-consciousness on the public expression of personal beliefs. *Journal of Personality and Social Psychology*, 1980, **39**, 514–521.

Schein, E. H. The Chinese indoctrination program for prisoners of war: A study of attempted brainwashing. *Psychiatry*, 1956, **19**, 149–172.

Schiffenbauer, A. I., Brown, J. E., Perry, P. L., Schulack, L. K., & Zanzola, A. M. The relationship between density and crowding: Some architectural modifiers. *Environment and Behavior*, 1977, **9**, 3–14.

Schiffenbauer, A., & Schiavo, R. S. Physical distance and attraction: An intensification effect. *Journal of Experimental Social Psychology*, 1976, **12**, 274–282.

Schlenker, B. R. Egocentric perceptions in cooperative groups: A conceptualization and research review. Final Report, Office of Naval Research Grant NR 170-797, 1976.

Schlenker, B. R. *Impression management: The self-concept, social identity, and interpersonal relations*. Belmont, Calif.: Brooks/Cole, 1980.

Schlenker, B. R., & Leary, M. R. Audiences' reactions to self-enhancing, self-denigrating, and accurate self-presentations. *Journal of Experimental Social Psychology*, 1982, **18**, 89–104.

Schlenker, B. R., & Miller, R. S. Group cohesiveness as a determinant of egocentric perceptions in cooperative groups. *Human Relations*, 1977, **30**, 1039–1055. (a)

Schlenker, B. R., & Miller, R. S. Egocentrism in groups: Self-serving biases or logical information processing? *Journal of Personality and Social Psychology*, 1977, **35**, 755–764. (b)

Schlenker, B. R., Miller, R. S., Leary, M. R., & McGown, N. E. Group performance and interpersonal evaluations as determinants of egotistical attributions in groups. *Journal of Personality*, 1979, **47**, 575–594.

Schlesinger, A. M., Jr. *A thousand days*. Boston: Houghton Mifflin, 1965. Cited by I. L. Janis in *Victims of groupthink*. Boston: Houghton Mifflin, 1972, p. 40.

Schmidt, D. E., & Keating, J. P. Human crowding and personal control: An integration of the research. *Psychological Bulletin*, 1979, **86**, 680–700.

Schmidt, G. Male-female differences in sexual arousal and behavior during and after exposure to sexually explicit stimuli. *Archives of Sexual Behavior*, 1975, **4**, 353–364.

Schmutte, G. T., & Taylor, S. P. Physical aggression as a function of alcohol and pain feedback. *Journal of Social Psychology*, 1980, **110**, 235–244.

Schofield, J. W. Complementary and conflicting identities: Images and interaction in an interracial school. In S. Asher & J. Gottman (Eds.), *The development of children's friendships: Description and intervention*. Cambridge, England: Cambridge University Press, 1981.

Schofield, J. W., & Sagar, H. A. Peer interaction patterns in an integrated middle school. *Sociometry*, 1977, **40**, 130–138.

Schulman, A. I. Memory for words recently classified. *Memory and cognition*, 1974, **2**, 47–52.

Schulz, R., & Hanusa, B. H. Experimental social gerontology: A social psychological perspective. *Journal of Social Issues*, 1980, **36**(2), 30–46.

Schulz, J. W., & Pruitt, D. G. The effects of mutual concern on joint welfare. *Journal of Experimental Social Psychology*, 1978, **14**, 480–492.

Schwartz, S. H. Elicitation of moral obligation and self-sacrificing behavior: An experimental study of volunteering to be a bone marrow donor. *Journal of Personality and Social Psychology*, 1970, **15**, 283–293.

Schwartz, S. H. The justice of need and the activation of humanitarian norms. *Journal of Social Issues*, 1975, **31**(3), 111–136.

Schwartz, S. H., & Ames, R. E. Positive and negative

referent others as sources of influence: A case of helping. *Sociometry*, 1977, **40**, 12–21.

Schwartz, S. H., & Gottlieb, A. Participants' post-experimental reactions and the ethics of bystander research. *Journal of Experimental Social Psychology*, 1981, **17**, 396–407.

Schwartz, T. Pollsters denounce ABC's debate survey. *New York Times*, October 30, 1980, p. B19.

Schwebel, A. I., & Cherlin, D. L. Physical and social distance in teacher-pupil relationships. *Journal of Educational Psychology*, 1972, **63**, 543–550.

Scott, J. P. *Aggression*. Chicago: University of Chicago Press, 1958.

Scott, J. P., & Marston, M. V. Nonadaptive behavior resulting from a series of defeats in fighting mice. *Journal of Abnormal and Social Psychology*, 1953, **48**, 417–428.

Scully, M. G. Faculty members liberal on politics, found conservative on academic issues. *Chronicle of Higher Education*, April 6, 1970, pp. 1, 4–5.

Sears, D. O. Life stage effects upon attitude change, especially among the elderly. Manuscript prepared for Workshop on the Elderly of the Future, Committee on Aging, National Research Council, May 3–5, 1979, Annapolis, Md.

Sears, D. O., Hensler, C. P., & Speer, L. K. Whites' opposition to "busing": Self-interest or symbolic politics? *American Political Science Review*, 1979, **73**, 369–384.

Seaver, W. B., & Patterson, A. H. Decreasing fuel-oil consumption through feedback and social commendation. *Journal of Applied Behavior Analysis*, 1976, **9**, 147–152.

Sechrest, L. Personality. In M. R. Rosenzweig & L. W. Porter (Eds.), *Annual review of psychology*, 1976, **27**, 1–27.

Selby, J. W., Calhoun, L. G., & Brock, T. A. Sex differences in the social perception of rape victims. *Personality and Social Psychology Bulletin*, 1977, **3**, 412–415.

Seligman, C., Fazio, R. H., & Zanna, M. P. Effects of salience of extrinsic rewards on liking and loving. *Journal of Personality and Social Psychology*, 1980, **38**, 453–460.

Seligman, C., Kriss, M., Darley, J. M., Fazio, R. H., Becker, L. J., & Pryor, J. B. Predicting summer energy consumption from homeowners' attitudes. *Journal of Applied Social Psychology*, 1979, **9**, 70–90.

Seligman, C., Paschall, N., & Takata, G. Effects of physical attractiveness on attribution of responsibility. *Canadian Journal of Behavioural Science*, 1974, **6**, 290–296.

Seligman, M. E. P. *Helplessness: On depression, development and death*. San Francisco: W. H. Freeman, 1975.

Seligman, M. E. P. Submissive death: Giving up on life. *Psychology Today*, May 1977, pp. 80–85.

Seta, J. J. The impact of comparison processes on coactors' task performance. *Journal of Personality and Social Psychology*, 1982, **42**, 281–291.

Shakespeare, W. *A midsummer night's dream*. Act II, Scene 2, l. 115.

Shaklee, H., & Fischhoff, B. Limited minds and multiple causes: Discounting in multi-causal attributions. Unpublished manuscript, University of Iowa, 1977.

Sharan, S., & Sharan, Y. *Small group teaching*. Englewood Cliffs, N. J.: Educational Technology, 1976.

Shaver, K. G. Defensive attribution: Effects of severity and relevance on the responsibility assigned for an accident. *Journal of Personality and Social Psychology*, 1970, **14**, 101–113.

Shavit, H., & Shouval, R. Self-esteem and cognitive consistency effects on self-other evaluation. *Journal of Experimental Social Psychology*, 1980, **16**, 417–425.

Shaw, G. B. (1891) The quintessence of Ibsenism. In D. H. Lawrence (Ed.), *Selected non-dramatic writings of Bernard Shaw*. Boston: Houghton Mifflin (undated). Cited by C. Tavris & C. Offir in *The longest war: Sex differences in perspective*. New York: Harcourt Brace Jovanovich, 1977.

Shaw, M. E. *Group dynamics: The psychology of small group behavior*. New York: McGraw Hill, 1981.

Sheppard, B. H., & Vidmar, N. Adversary pretrial procedures and testimonial evidence: Effects of lawyer's role and machiavellianism. *Journal of Personality and Social Psychology*, 1980, **39**, 320–332.

Sherif, C. W. Comment on ethical issues in Malamuth, Heim, and Feshbach's "Sexual Responsiveness of college students to rape depictions: Inhibitory and disinhibitory effects." *Journal of Personality and Social Psychology*, 1980, **38**, 409–412.

Sherif, M. An experimental approach to the study of attitudes. *Sociometry*, 1937, **1**, 90–98.

Sherif, M. *In common predicament: Social psychology*

of intergroup conflict and cooperation. Boston: Houghton Mifflin, 1966.

Sherif, M., & Sherif, C. W. *Social psychology*. New York: Harper & Row, 1969.

Sherman, J. A. *Sex-related cognitive differences*. Springfield, Ill.: Charles C Thomas, 1978.

Sherman, S. J. On the self-erasing nature of errors of prediction. *Journal of Personality and Social Psychology*, 1980, **39**, 211–221.

Sherman, S. J., & Gorkin, L. Attitude bolstering when behavior is inconsistent with central attitudes. *Journal of Experimental Social Psychology*, 1980, **16**, 388–403.

Sherman, S. J., Presson, C. C., Chassin, L., Bensenberg, M., Corty, E., & Olshavsky, R. Direct experience and the predictability of smoking intentions in adolescents. *Personality and Social Psychology Bulletin*, 1983, in press.

Sherrod, D. R. Crowding, perceived control, and behavioral aftereffects. *Journal of Applied Social Psychology*, 1974, **4**, 171–186.

Sherrod, D. R., Armstrong, D., Hewitt, J., Madonia, B., Speno, S., & Teruya, D. Environmental attention, affect, and altruism. *Journal of Applied Social Psychology*, 1977, **7**, 359–371.

Short, J. F., Jr. (Ed.). *Gang delinquency and delinquent subcultures*. New York: Harper & Row, 1969.

Shouval, R., Venaki, S. K., Bronfenbrenner, U., Devereus, E. C., & Kiely, E. Anomalous reactions to social pressure of Israeli and Soviet children raised in family versus collective settings. *Journal of Personality and Social Psychology*, 1975, **32**, 477–489.

Shrauger, J. S. Responses to evaluation as a function of initial self-perceptions. *Psychological Bulletin*, 1975, **82**, 581–596.

Shubik, M. The dollar auction game: A paradox in noncooperating behavior and escalation. *Journal of Conflict Resolution*, 1971, **15**, 109–111.

Shure, G. H., Meeker, R. J., & Hansford, E. A. The effectiveness of pacifist strategies in bargaining games. *Journal of Conflict Resolution*, 1965, **9**(1), 106–117.

Sigall, H. Effects of competence and consensual validation on a communicator's liking for the audience. *Journal of Personality and Social Psychology*, 1970, **16**, 252–258.

Sigall, H., & Ostrove, N. Beautiful but dangerous: Effects of offender attractiveness and nature of the crime on juridic judgment. *Journal of Personality and Social Psychology*, 1975, **31**, 410–414.

Sigall, H., & Page, R. Current stereotypes: A little fading, a little faking. *Journal of Personality and Social Psychology*, 1971, **18**, 247–255.

Sillars, A. Applications of attribution theory to problems in interpersonal conflict resolution. In J. H. Harvey, W. Ickes, & R. F. Kidd (Eds.), *New directions in attribution research*. Hillsdale, N.J.: Lawrence Erlbaum, 1981.

Silver, L. B., Dublin, C. C., & Lourie, R. S. Does violence breed violence? Contributions from a study of the child abuse syndrome. *American Journal of Psychiatry*, 1969, **126**, 404–407.

Silver, M., & Geller, D. On the irrelevance of evil: The organization and individual action. *Journal of Social Issues*, 1978, **34**, 125–136.

Silverman, B. I. Consequences, racial discrimination, and the principle of belief congruence. *Journal of Personality and Social Psychology*, 1974, **29**, 497–508.

Silverman, L. T., Sprafkin, J. N., & Rubinstein, E. A. *Sex on television: A content analysis of the 1977-78 prime-time programs*. Stony Brook, N.Y.: Brookdale International Institute, 1978.

Silverman, L. T., Sprafkin, J. N., & Rubinstein, E. A. Physical contact and sexual behavior on prime-time TV. *Journal of Communication*, 1979, **29**, 33–43.

Simon, H. A. *Models of man: Social and rational*. New York: Wiley, 1957.

Simon, P. Interview in *Wittenburg Door*, June–July 1980, p. 20.

Singer, B., & Benassi, V. A. Fooling some of the people all of the time. *Skeptical Inquirer*, 1980–81, **5**(2), 17–24.

Singer, D. G., & Singer, J. L. Is human imagination going down the tube? *Chronicle of Higher Education*, April 23, 1979, p. 56.

Singer, M. Cults and cult members. Address to the American Psychological Association convention, 1979. (a)

Singer, M. Interviewed by M. Freeman. Of cults and communication: A conversation with Margaret Singer. *APA Monitor*, July–August 1979, pp. 6–7. (b)

Sissons, M. Race, sex, and helping behaviour. *British Journal of Social Psychology*, 1981, **20**, 285–292.

Skinner, B. F. Superstition in the pigeon. *Journal of Experimental Psychology*, 1948, **38**, 168–172.

Skinner, B. F. *Beyond freedom and dignity*. New York: Knopf, 1971.

Skotko, V. P. The relation between interpersonal attraction and measures of self-disclosure. *Journal of Social Psychology*, 1980, **112**, 311–312.

Skrypnek, B. J., & Snyder, M. On the self-perpetuating nature of stereotypes about women and men. *Journal of Experimental Social Psychology*, 1982, **18**, 277–291.

Slavin, R. E. Cooperative learning and desegregation. Paper presented at the American Psychological Association convention, 1980.

Slavin, R. E., & Madden, N. A. School practices that improve race relations. *American Educational Research Journal*, 1979, **16**, 169–180.

Slovic, P. From Shakespeare to Simon: Speculations—and some evidence—about man's ability to process information. *Oregon Research Institute Research Bulletin*, 1972, **12**(2).

Slovic, P., & Fischhoff, B. On the psychology of experimental surprises. *Journal of Experimental Psychology: Human Perception and Performance*, 1977, **3**, 544–551.

Small, K. H., & Peterson, J. The divergent perceptions of actors and observers. *Journal of Social Psychology*, 1981, **113**, 123–132.

Smedley, J. W., & Bayton, J. A. Evaluative race-class stereotypes by race and perceived class of subjects. *Journal of Personality and Social Psychology*, 1978, **36**, 530–535.

Smith, A. *The wealth of nations*. Book 1. Chicago: University of Chicago Press, 1976. (Originally published, 1776.)

Smith, D. E., Gier, J. A., & Willis, F. N. Interpersonal touch and compliance with a marketing request. *Basic and Applied Social Psychology*, 1982, **3**, 35–38.

Smith, E. E. Methods for changing consumer attitudes: A report of three experiments. Cited by P. G. Zimbardo, E. B. Ebbesen, & C. Maslach. *Influencing attitudes and changing behavior*. Reading, Mass.: Addison-Wesley, 1977.

Smith, E. R., & Miller F. D. Limits on perception of cognitive processes: A reply to Nisbett and Wilson. *Psychological Review*, **85**, 355–362.

Smith, H. *The Russians*. New York: Ballantine Books, 1976. Cited by B. Latané, K. Williams, and S. Harkins in Many hands make light the work. *Journal of Personality and Social Psychology*, 1979, **37**, 822–832.

Smith, H. W. Territorial spacing on a beach revisited: A cross-national exploration. *Social Psychology Quarterly*, 1981, **44**, 132–137.

Smith, M. B. Psychology and values. *Journal of Social Issues*, 1978, **34**, 181–199.

Smith, M. L. Sex bias in counseling and psychotherapy. *Psychological Bulletin*, 1980, **89**, 392–407.

Smith, T. W. Happiness: Time trends, seasonal variations, intersurvey differences, and other mysteries. *Social Psychology Quarterly*, 1979, **42**, 18–30.

Snyder, C. R. Why horoscopes are true: The effects of specificity on acceptance of astrological interpretations. *Journal of Clinical Psychology*, 1974, **30**, 577–580.

Snyder, C. R. The "illusion" of uniqueness. *Journal of Humanistic Psychology*, 1978, **18**, 33–41.

Snyder, C. R. The uniqueness mystique. *Psychology Today*, March 1980, pp. 86–90.

Snyder, C. R., & Fromkin, H. L. *Uniqueness: The human pursuit of difference*. New York: Plenum, 1980.

Snyder, C. R., & Newburg, C. L. The Barnum effect in a group setting. *Journal of Personality Assessment*, 1981, **45**, 622-629.

Snyder, C. R., Shenkel, R. J., & Lowery, C. R. Acceptance of personality interpretations: The "Barnum effect" and beyond. *Journal of Consulting and Clinical Psychology*, 1977, **45**, 104–114.

Snyder, M. On the nature of social knowledge. Paper presented at the Midwestern Psychological Association convention, 1978.

Snyder, M. Self-monitoring processes. In L. Berkowitz (Ed.), *Advances in experimental social psychology*. New York: Academic Press, 1979.

Snyder, M. Seek, and ye shall find: Testing hypotheses about other people. In E. T. Higgins, C. P. Herman, & M. P. Zanna (Eds.), *Social cognition: The Ontario symposium on personality and social psychology*. Hillsdale, N.J.: Lawrence Erlbaum, 1981. (a)

Snyder, M. On the influence of individuals on situations. In N. Cantor & J. F. Kihlstrom (Eds.), *Personality, cognition, and social interaction*. Hillsdale, N.J.: Lawrence Erlbaum, 1981. (b)

Snyder, M. When believing means doing: Creating links between attitudes and behavior. In M. Zanna, E. T. Higgins, & C. P. Herman (Eds.), *Consistency in social behavior: The Ontario symposium* (Vol. 2). Hillsdale, N.J.: Lawrence Erlbaum, 1982.

Snyder, M., & Campbell, B. Testing hypotheses about other people: The role of the hypothesis. *Personality and Social Psychology Bulletin*, 1980, **6**, 421–426.

Snyder, M., & Campbell, B. Self-monitoring: The self in action. In J. Suls (Ed.), *Psychological perspectives on the self*. Hillsdale, N.J.: Lawrence Erlbaum, 1982.

Snyder, M., Campbell, B., & Preston, E. Testing hypotheses about human nature: Assessing the accuracy of social stereotypes. *Social Cognition*, 1982, in press.

Snyder, M., & Cantor, N. Testing hypotheses about other people: The use of historical knowledge. *Journal of Experimental Social Psychology*, 1979, **15**, 330–342.

Snyder, M., & Cunningham, M. To comply or not comply: Testing the self-perception explanation of the "foot-in-the-door" phenomenon. *Journal of Personality and Social Psychology*, 1975, **31**, 64–67.

Snyder, M., & Gangestad, S. Hypothesis-testing processes. In J. H. Harvey, W. Ickes, & R. F. Kidd (Eds.), *New directions in attribution research*. Hillsdale, N.J.: Lawrence Erlbaum, 1981.

Snyder, M., Grether, J., & Keller, K. Staring and compliance: A field experiment on hitchhiking. *Journal of Applied Social Psychology*, 1974, **4**, 165–170.

Snyder, M., & Ickes, W. Personality and social behavior. In G. Lindzey & E. Aronson (Eds.), *Handbook of social psychology* (3d ed.). Reading, Mass.: Addison-Wesley, in press.

Snyder, M., & Kendzierski, D. Acting on one's attitudes: Procedure for linking attitude and behavior. *Journal of Experimental Social Psychology*, 1982, **18**, 165–183.

Snyder, M., & Skrypnek, B. J. Testing hypotheses about the self-assessments of job suitability. *Journal of Personality*, 1981, **49**, 193–210.

Snyder, M., & Swann, W. B., Jr. When actions reflect attitudes: The politics of impression management. *Journal of Personality and Social Psychology*, 1976, **34**, 1034–1042.

Snyder, M., & Swann, W. B., Jr. Behavioral confirmation in social interaction: From social perception to social reality. *Journal of Experimental Social Psychology*, 1978, **14**, 148–162. (a)

Snyder, M., & Swann, W. B., Jr. Hypothesis-testing processes in social interaction. *Journal of Personality and Social Psychology*, 1978, **36**, 1202–1212. (b)

Snyder, M., Tanke, E. D., & Berscheid, E. Social perception and interpersonal behavior: On the self-fulfilling nature of social stereotypes. *Journal of Personality and Social Psychology*, 1977, **35**, 656–666.

Snyder, M. L., & Frankel, A. Observer bias: A stringent test of behavior engulfing the field. *Journal of Personality and Social Psychology*, 1976, **34**, 857–864.

Snyder, M. L., Smoller, B., Strenta, A., & Frankel, A. A comparison of egotism, negativity and learned helplessness as explanations for poor performance after unsolvable problems. *Journal of Personality and Social Psychology*, 1981, **40**, 24–30.

Sohn, D. Critique of Cooper's meta-analytic assessment of the findings on sex differences in conformity behavior. *Journal of Personality and Social Psychology*, 1980, **39**, 1215–1221.

Solomon, H., & Solomon, L. Z. Effects of anonymity on helping in emergency situations. Paper presented at the Eastern Psychological Association convention, 1978.

Solomon, H., Solomon, L. Z., Arnone, M. M., Maur, B. J., Reda, R. M., & Rother, E. O. Anonymity and helping. *Journal of Social Psychology*, 1981, **113**, 37–43.

Solomon, L. Z., Solomon, H., & Stone, R. Helping as a function of number of bystanders and ambiguity of emergency. *Personality and Social Psychology Bulletin*, 1978, **4**, 318–321.

Sommer, R. Classroom ecology. *Journal of Applied Behavioral Science*, 1967, **3**, 489–503.

Sommer, R. *Personal space*. Englewood Cliffs, N.J.: Prentice-Hall, 1969.

Sommer, R., & Olsen, H. The soft classroom. *Environment and Behavior*, 1980, **5**, 3–16.

Sommer, R., & Ross, H. Social interaction on a geriatrics ward. *International Journal of Social Psychiatry*, 1958, **4**, 128–133.

Sorrentino, R. M., King, G., & Leo, G. The influence of the minority on perception: A note on a possible alternative explanation. *Journal of Experimental Social Psychology*, 1980, **16**, 293–301.

Sparacino, J., & Hansell, S. Physical attractiveness and academic performance: Beauty is not always talent. *Journal of Personality*, 1979, **47**, 449–469.

Speer, A. *Inside the Third Reich: Memoirs*. (R. Winston & C. Winston. trans.). New York: Avon Books, 1971.

Spence, J. T., Deaux, K., & Helmreich, R. L. Sex roles in contemporary American society. In G. Lindzey & E. Aronson (Eds.), *Handbook of Social Psychology* (3d ed.). Reading, Mass.: Addison-Wesley, in press.

Spiegel, H. W. *The growth of economic thought*. Durham, N.C.: Duke University Press, 1971.

Spivak, J. *Wall Street Journal*, June 6, 1979.

Sprafkin, J. N., & Silverman, L. T. Update: Physically intimate and sexual behavior on prime time television, 1978-79. *Journal of Communication*, 1981, **3**(1), 34–40.

Stark, R., & Bainbridge, W. S. Networks of faith:

Interpersonal bonds and recruitment to cults and sects. *American Journal of Sociology*, 1980, **85**, 1376–1395.

Stasser, G., Kerr, N. L., & Bray, R. M. The social psychology of jury deliberations: Structure, process, and product. In N. L. Kerr & R. M. Bray (Eds.), *The psychology of the courtroom*. New York: Academic Press, 1981.

Staub, E. To rear a prosocial child: Reasoning, learning by doing, and learning by teaching others. In D. J. DePalma & J. M. Foley (Eds.), *Moral development: Current theory and research*. Hillsdale, N.J.: Erlbaum, 1975.

Staub, E. *Positive social behavior and morality: Social and personal influences* (Vol. 1). New York: Academic Press, 1978.

Steele, C. M., Southwick, L. L., & Critchlow, B. Dissonance and alcohol: Drinking your troubles away. *Journal of Personality and Social Psychology*, 1981, **41**, 831-846.

Stein, A. H., & Friedrich, L. K. Television content and young children's behavior. In J. P. Murray, E. A. Rubinstein, & G. A. Comstock (Eds.), *Television and social learning*. Washington, D.C.: Government Printing Office, 1972.

Stein, D. D., Hardyck, J. A., & Smith, M. B. Race and belief: An open and shut case. *Journal of Personality and Social Psychology*, 1965, **1**, 281–289.

Stein, R. T., & Heller, T. An empirical analysis of the correlations between leadership status and participation rates reported in the literature. *Journal of Personality and Social Psychology*, 1979, **37**, 1993–2002.

Steiner, I. D. *Group process and productivity*. New York: Academic Press, 1972.

Steiner, I. D. Heuristic models of groupthink. In M. Brandstätter, J. H. Davis, & G. Stocker-Kreichgauer (Eds.), *Group decision making*. New York: Academic Press, 1982, pp. 503–524.

Stephan, W. G. School desegregation: An evaluation of predictions made in *Brown v. Board of Education. Psychological Bulletin*, 1978, **85**, 217–238.

Stephan, W. G., Bernstein, W. M., Stephan, C., & Davis, M. H. Attributions for achievement: Egotism vs. expectancy confirmation. *Social Psychology Quarterly*, 1979, **42**, 5–17.

Stephan, W. G., Berscheid, E., & Walster, E. Sexual arousal and heterosexual perception. *Journal of Personality and Social Psychology*, 1971, **20**, 93–101.

Stewart, J. E., II. Defendant's attractiveness as a factor in the outcome of criminal trials: An observational study. *Journal of Applied Social Psychology*, 1980, **10**, 348–361.

Stires, L. Classroom seating location, student grades, and attitudes: Environment or self-selection. *Environment and Behavior*, 1980, **12**, 241–254.

Stockdale, J. E. Crowding: Determinants and effects. In L. Berkowitz (Ed.), *Advances in experimental social psychology* (Vol. 11). New York: Academic Press, 1978.

Stokols, D. On the distinction between density and crowding: Some implications for future research. *Psychological Review*, 1972, **79**, 275–278.

Stokols, D. A typology of crowding experiences. In A. Baum & Y. M. Epstein (Eds.), *Human response to crowding*. Hillsdale, N.J.: Erlbaum, 1978, pp. 219–255.

Stoner, J. A. F. A comparison of individual and group decisions involving risk. Unpublished master's thesis, Massachusetts Institute of Technology, 1961. Cited by D. G. Marquis in Individual responsibility and group decisions involving risk. *Industrial Management Review*, 1962, **3**, 8–23.

Stoppard, J. M., & Kalin, R. Can gender stereotypes and sex-role conceptions be distinguished? *British Journal of Social and Clinical Psychology*, 1978, **17**, 211–217.

Storms, M. D. Videotape and the attribution process: Reversing actors' and observers' points of view. *Journal of Personality and Social Psychology*, 1973, **27**, 165–175.

Storms, M. D., & Thomas, G. C. Reactions to physical closeness. *Journal of Personality and Social Psychology*, 1977, **35**, 412–418.

Stouffer, S. A., Suchman, E. A., DeVinney, L. C., Star, S. A., & Williams, R. M., Jr. *The American soldier: Adjustment during Army life* (Vol. 1). Princeton, N.J.: Princeton University Press, 1949.

Strauss, M. A., & Gelles, R. J. *Behind closed doors: Violence in the American family*. New York: Anchor/Doubleday, 1980.

Strenta, A., & DeJong, W. The effect of a prosocial label on helping behavior. *Social Psychology Quarterly*, 1981, **44**, 142–147.

Stretch, R. H., & Figley, C. R. Beauty and the boast: Predictors of interpersonal attraction in a dating experiment. *Psychology, A Quarterly Journal of Human Behavior*, 1980, **17**, 34–43.

Strodbeck, F. L., & Mann, R. D. Sex-role differentiation in jury deliberations. *Sociometry*, 1956, **19**, 3–11.

Stroebe, W., Insko, C. A., Thompson, V. D., & Layton, B. D. Effects of physical attractiveness, attitude similarity, and sex on various aspects of interpersonal attraction. *Journal of Personality and Social Psychology*, 1971, **18**, 79–91.

Stroufe, R., Chaikin, A., Cook, R., & Freeman, V. The effects of physical attractiveness on honesty: A socially desirable response. *Personality and Social Psychology*, 1977, **3**, 59–62.

Strumpel, B. Economic life-styles, values, and subjective welfare. In B. Strumpel (Ed.), *Economic means for human needs*. Ann Arbor, Mich.: Institute for Social Research, University of Michigan, 1976.

Strunk, W., & White, E. B. *The elements of style*. New York: Macmillan, 1979.

Sue, S., Smith, R. E., & Caldwell, C. Effects of inadmissible evidence on the decisions of simulated jurors: A moral dilemma. *Journal of Applied Social Psychology*, 1973, **3**, 345–353.

Suedfeld, P., Rank, D., & Borrie, R. Frequency of exposure and evaluation of candidates and campaign speeches. *Journal of Applied Social Psychology*, 1975, **5**, 118–126.

Suls, J. M., & Tesch, F. Students' preferences for information about their test performance: A social comparison study. *Journal of Experimental Social Psychology*, 1978, **8**, 189–197.

Sun, M. Cancer institute passes first test in Senate. *Science*, 1981, **212**, 1122.

Sundstrom, E. Crowding as a sequential process: Review of research on the effects of population density on humans. In A. Baum & Y. M. Epstein (Eds.), *Human response to crowding*. Hillsdale, N.J.: Lawrence Erlbaum, 1978.

Sundstrom, E., & Sundstrom, M. G. *Workplaces: The psychology of the physical environment in organizations*. Monterey, Calif.: Brooks/Cole, 1983.

Surlin, S. H. Bigotry on the air and in life: The Archie Bunker case. *Public Telecommunications Review*, 1974, **2**(2), 34–41.

Svenson, O. Are we all less risky and more skillful than our fellow drivers? *Acta Psychologica*, 1981, **47**, 143–148.

Swafford, T. Quoted by L. Bogart. After the Surgeon General's report: Another look backward. In S. B. Withey & R. P. Abeles (Eds.), *Television and social behavior: Beyond violence and children*. Hillsdale, N.J.: Lawrence Erlbaum, 1980.

Swann, W. B., Jr., Giuliano, T., & Wegner, D. M. Where leading questions can lead: The power of conjecture in social interaction. *Journal of Personality and Social Psychology*, 1982, **42**, 1025–1035.

Swann, W. B., Jr., & Read, S. J. Acquiring self-knowledge: The search for feedback that fits. *Journal of Personality and Social Psychology*, 1981, **41**, 1119–1128. (a)

Swann, W. B., Jr., & Read, S. J. Self-verification processes: How we sustain our self-conceptions. *Journal of Experimental Social Psychology*, 1981, **17**, 351–372. (b)

Swap, W. C. Interpersonal attraction and repeated exposure to rewarders and punishers. *Personality and Social Psychology Bulletin*, 1977, **3**, 248–251.

Swedish Information Service. *Social change in Sweden*, No. 19, p. 5. September 1980. (Published by the Swedish Consulate General, 825 Third Avenue, New York, N.Y. 10022.)

Sweeney, J. An experimental investigation of the free rider problem. *Social Science Research*, 1973, **2**, 277–292.

Symons, D. (interviewed by S. Keen). Eros and alley cop. *Psychology Today*, February 1981, p. 54.

Szucko, J. J., & Kleinmuntz, B. Statistical versus clinical lie detection. *American Psychologist*, 1981, **36**, 488–496.

Tajfel, H. Experiments in intergroup discrimination. *Scientific American*, November 1970, pp. 96–102.

Tajfel, H. *Human groups and social categories: Studies in social psychology*. London: Cambridge University Press, 1981.

Tajfel, H. Social psychology of intergroup relations. *Annual Review of Psychology*, 1982, **33**, 1–39.

Tajfel, H., & Billig, M. Familiarity and categorization in intergroup behavior. *Journal of Experimental Social Psychology*, 1974, **10**, 159–170.

Tanke, E. D., & Tanke, T. J. Getting off a slippery slope: Social science in the judicial processes. *American Psychologist*, 1979, **34**, 1130–1138.

Tannenbaum, P. H., & Zillman, D. Emotional arousal in the facilitation of aggression through communication. In L. Berkowitz (Ed.), *Advances in experimental social psychology* (Vol. 8). New York: Academic Press, 1975.

Tapp, J. L. Psychological and policy perspectives on the law: Reflections on a decade. *Journal of Social Issues*, 1980, **36**(2), 165–192.

Tavris, C., & Offir, C. *The longest war: Sex differences in perspective.* New York: Harcourt Brace Jovanovich, 1977.

Taylor, D. A. Motivational bases. In G. J. Chelune (Ed.), *Self-disclosure: Origins, patterns, and implications of openness in interpersonal relationships.* San Francisco: Jossey-Bass, 1979.

Taylor, D. A. Effects of personalistic self-disclosure. *Personality and Social Psychology Bulletin*, 1981, **7**, 487–492.

Taylor, D. A., Gould, R. J., & Brounstein, P. J. Effects of personalistic self-disclosure. *Personality and Social Psychology Bulletin*, 1981, **7**, 487–492.

Taylor, D. G., Sheatsley, P. B., & Greeley, A. M. Attitudes toward racial integration. *Scientific American*, 1978, **238**(6), 42–49.

Taylor, D. M., & Doria, J. R. Self-serving and group-serving bias in attribution. *Journal of Social Psychology*, 1981, **113**, 201–211.

Taylor, R. B., De Soto, C. B., & Lieb, R. Sharing secrets: Disclosure and discretion in dyads and triads. *Journal of Personality and Social Psychology*, 1979, **37**, 1196–1203.

Taylor, S. E. Remarks at symposium on social psychology and medicine, American Psychological Association convention, 1979.

Taylor, S. E. A categorization approach to stereotyping. In D. L. Hamilton (Ed.), *Cognitive processes in stereotyping and intergroup behavior.* Hillsdale, N.J.: Lawrence Erlbaum, 1981.

Taylor, S. E., Crocker, J., Fiske, S. T., Sprinzen, M., & Winkler, J. D. The generalizability of salience effects. *Journal of Personality and Social Psychology*, 1979, **37**, 357–368.

Taylor, S. E., & Fiske, S. T. Salience, attention, and attribution: Top of the head phenomena. In L. Berkowitz (Ed.), *Advances in experimental social psychology* (Vol. 11). New York: Academic Press, 1978.

Taylor, S. E., Fiske, S. T., Etcoff, N. L., & Ruderman, A. J. Categorical and contextual bases of person memory and stereotyping. *Journal of Personality and Social Psychology*, 1978, **36**, 778–793.

Taylor, S. E., & Thompson, S. C. Stalking the elusive "vividness" effect. *Psychological Review*, 1982, **89**, 155–181.

Taylor, S. P., & Pisano, R. Physical aggression as a function of frustration and physical attack. *Journal of Social Psychology*, 1971, **84**, 261–267.

Taynor, J., & Deaux, K. When women are more deserving than men: Equity, attribution, and perceived sex differences. *Journal of Personality and Social Psychology*, 1973, **28**, 360–367.

Taynor, J., & Deaux, K. Equity and perceived sex differences: Role behavior as defined by the task, the mode, and the actor. *Journal of Personality and Social Psychology*, 1975, **32**, 381–390.

Tedeschi, J. T., Schlenker, B. R., & Bonoma, T. V. *Conflict, power, and games.* Chicago: Aldine, 1973.

Tedeschi, J. T. (Ed.). *Impression management theory and social psychological research.* New York: Academic Press, 1981.

Teger, A. I. *Too much invested to quit.* New York: Pergamon Press, 1980.

Telch, M. J., Killen, J. D., McAlister, A. L., Perry, C. L., & Maccoby, N. Long-term follow-up of a pilot project on smoking prevention with adolescents. Paper presented at the American Psychological Association convention, 1981.

Tennov, D. *Love and limerence: The experience of being in love.* New York: Stein and Day, 1979, p. 22.

Tesser, A. Self-generated attitude change. In L. Berkowitz (Ed.), *Advances in experimental social psychology* (Vol. 11). New York: Academic Press, 1978.

Tesser, A. Self-esteem maintenance in family dynamics. *Journal of Personality and Social Psychology*, 1980, **39**, 77–91.

Tesser, A., & Brodie, M. A note on the evaluation of a "computer date." *Psychonomic Science*, 1971, **23**, 300.

Tesser, A., Gatewood, R., & Driver, M. Some determinants of gratitude. *Journal of Personality and Social Psychology*, 1968, **9**, 233–236.

Tesser, A., Rosen, S., & Conlee, M. C. News valence and available recipient as determinants of news transmission. *Sociometry*, 1972, **35**, 619–628.

Tetlock, P. E. Explaining teacher explanations of pupil performance: A self-presentation interpretation. *Social Psychology Quarterly*, 1980, **43**, 283–290.

Tetlock, P. E. Integrative complexity and international conflict. Paper presented at the American Psychological Association convention, 1981. (a)

Tetlock, P. E. Pre- to post-election shifts in presidential rhetoric: Impression management or cognitive adjustment. *Journal of Personality and Social Psychology*, 1981, **41**, 207–212. (b)

Tetlock, P. E. Personality and isolationism: Content

analysis of senatorial speeches. *Journal of Personality and Social Psychology*, 1981, **41**, 737–743. (c)

Tetlock, P. E., & Levi, A. Attribution bias: On the inconclusiveness of the cognitive-motivation debate. *Journal of Experimental Social Psychology*, 1982, **18**, 68–88.

Thomas, A., Chess, S., & Birch, H. G. The origin of personality. *Scientific American*, August 1970, pp. 102–109.

Thomas, E. J., & Fink, C. F. Models of group problem solving. *Journal of Abnormal and Social Psychology*, 1961, **63**, 53–63.

Thomas, G. C., & Batson, C. D. Effect of helping under normative pressure on self-perceived altruism. *Social Psychology Quarterly*, 1981, **44**, 127–131.

Thomas, G. C., Batson, C. D., & Coke, J. S. Do Good Samaritans discourage helpfulness? Self-perceived altruism after exposure to highly helpful others. *Journal of Personality and Social Psychology*, 1981, **40**, 194–200.

Thomas, K. W., & Pondy, L. R. Toward an "intent" model of conflict management among principal parties. *Human Relations*, 1977, **30**, 1089–1102.

Thomas, L. Hubris in science? *Science*, 1978, **200**, 1459–1462.

Thomas, L. Quoted by J. L. Powell. Testimony before the Senate Subcommittee on Science, Technology and Space, April 22, 1981.

Thomas, M. H., & Drabman, R. S. Toleration of real-life aggression as a function of exposure to televised violence and age of subject. *Merrill-Palmer Quarterly*, 1975, **21**, 227–232.

Thomas, M. H., Horton, R. W., Lippincott, E. C., & Drabman, R. S. Desensitization to portrayals of real-life aggression as a function of exposure to television violence. *Journal of Personality and Social Psychology*, 1977, **35**, 450–458.

Thompson, S. C., & Kelley, H. H. Judgments of responsibility for activities in closed relationships. *Journal of Personality and Social Psychology*, 1981, **41**, 469–477.

Thompson, W. C., Cowan, C. L., & Rosenhan, D. L. Focus of attention mediates the impact of negative affect on altruism. *Journal of Personality and Social Psychology*, 1980, **38**, 291–300.

Thompson, W. C., Fong, G. T., & Rosenhan, D. L. Inadmissible evidence and juror verdicts. *Journal of Personality and Social Psychology, 1981*, **40**, 453–463.

Thorndike, R. L. Review of Pygmalion in the classroom. *American Educational Research Journal*, 1968, **5**, 708–711.

Thornton, A., & Freedman, D. Changes in the sex role attitudes of women, 1962–1977: Evidence from a panel study. *American Sociological Review*, 1979, **44**, 831–842.

Thune, E. S., Manderscheid, R. W., & Silbergeld, S. Status or sex roles as determinants of interaction patterns in small, mixed-sex groups. *Journal of Social Psychology*, 1980, **112**, 51–65.

Time. January 7, 1980. (a)

Time. January 14, 1980, p. 30. (b)

Time. May 5, 1980. (c)

Time. March 16, 1981, p. 31.

Toronto News, July 26, 1977.

Travis, L. E. The effect of a small audience upon eye-hand coordination. *Journal of Abnormal and Social Psychology*, 1925, **20**, 142–146.

Triandis, H. C. Some dimensions of intercultural variation and their implications for interpersonal behavior. Paper presented at the American Psychological Association convention, 1981.

Triplett, N. The dynamogenic factors in pacemaking and competition. *American Journal of Psychology*, 1898, **9**, 507–533.

Tuchman, G. The symbolic annihilation of women by the mass media. In G. Tuchman, A. K. Daniels, & J. Benet (Eds.), *Hearth and home: Images of women in the mass media*. New York: Oxford University Press, 1978.

Tumin, M. M. Readiness and resistance to desegregation: A social portrait of the hard core. *Social Forces*, 1958, **36**, 256–263.

Tversky, A., & Kahneman, D. Availability: A heuristic for judging frequency and probability. *Cognitive Psychology*, 1973, 5, 207–232.

Tversky, A., & Kahneman, D. Judgment under uncertainty: Heuristics and biases. *Science*, 1974, **185**, 1123–1131.

Tversky, A., & Kahneman, D. Causal schemas in judgments under uncertainty. In M. Fishbein (Ed.), *Progress in social psychology* (Vol. 1). Hillsdale, N.J.: Lawrence Erlbaum, 1980.

Tversky, A., & Kahneman, D. The framing of decisions and the psychology of choice. *Science*, 1981, **211**, 453–458.

TV Guide. January 26, 1977, pp. 5–10.

Twain, M. *Life on the Mississippi*, 1874.

Tyler, T. R., & Sears, D. O. Coming to like obnoxious people when we must live with them. *Journal of Personality and Social Psychology*, 1977, **35**, 200–211.

Ugwuegbu, C. E. Racial and evidential factors in juror attribution of legal responsibility. *Journal of Experimental Social Psychology*, 1979, **15**, 133–146.

Underwood, B., & Moore, B. Perspective-taking and altruism. *Psychological Bulletin*, 1982, **91**, 143–173.

Unger, R. K. Whom does helping help? Paper presented at the Eastern Psychological Association convention, April 1979. (a)

Unger, R. K. Toward a redefinition of sex and gender. *American Psychologist*, 1979, **34**, 1085–1094. (b)

UPI. September 23, 1967. Cited by P. G. Zimbardo, in The human choice: Individuation, reason, and order versus deindividuation, impulse, and chaos. In W. J. Arnold & D. Levine (Eds.), *Nebraska Symposium on Motivation*, 1969. Lincoln: University of Nebraska Press, 1970.

U.S. Commission on Obscenity and Pornography. *The report of the Commission on Obscenity and Pornography*. Washington, D.C.: Government Printing Office, 1970.

***U.S. Department of Commerce News*.** Bureau of Economic Analysis, May 3, 1981.

U.S. Department of Justice. *Sourcebook of criminal justice statistics*. Washington, D.C.: Government Printing Office, 1980.

U.S. Department of Labor. *Employment in perspective: Working women* (Report 647). Washington, D.C.: Bureau of Labor Statistics, 1981.

U.S. Supreme Court, Plessy V. Ferguson, 1896. Quoted by L. J. Severy, J. C. Brigham, & B. R. Schlenker, *A contemporary introduction to social psychology*. New York: McGraw-Hill, p. 126.

Valenstein, E. S. *Brain control*. New York: Wiley, 1973.

Van de Ven, A. H., & Delbecq, A. L. Nominal versus interacting group processes. *Academy of Management Journal*, 1971, **14**, 201–211.

Van Leeuwen, M. S. A cross-cultural examination of psychological differentiation in males and females. *International Journal of Psychology*, 1978, **13**, 87–122.

Vanneman, R. D., & Pettigrew, T. Race and relative deprivation in the urban United States. *Race*, 1972, **13**, 461–486.

Varela, J. A. *Psychological solutions to social problems*. New York: Academic Press, 1971.

Vaughan, K. B., & Lanzetta, J. T. The effect of modification of expressive displays on vicarious emotional arousal. *Journal of Experimental Social Psychology*, 1981, **17**, 16–30.

Veitch, R., DeWood, R., & Bosko, K. Radio news broadcasts: Their effects on interpersonal helping. *Sociometry*, 1977, **40**, 383–386.

Veitch, R., & Griffitt, W. Good news—bad news: Affective and interpersonal effects. *Journal of Applied Social Psychology*, 1976, **6**, 69–75.

Verbrugge, L. M., & Taylor, R. B. Consequences of population density and size. *Urban Affairs Quarterly*, 1980, **16**, 135–160.

Vidmar, N. The other issues in jury simulation research. *Law and Human Behavior*, 1979, **3**, 95–106.

Vidmar, N., & Rokeach, M. Archie Bunker's bigotry: A study in selective perception and exposure. *Journal of Communication*, 1974, **24**(1), 36–47.

von Baeyer, C. L., Sherk, D. L., & Zanna, M. P. Impression management in the job interview: When the female applicant meets the male (chauvinist) interviewer. *Personality and Social Psychology Bulletin*, 1981, **7**, 45–51.

Vreeland, R. Is it true what they say about Harvard boys? *Psychology Today*, January 1972, pp. 65–68.

Wachtler, J., & Counselman, E. When increasing liking for a communicator decreases opinion change: An attribution analysis of attractiveness. *Journal of Experimental Social Psychology*, 1981, **17**, 386–395.

Walden, T. A., Nelson, P. A., & Smith, D. E. Crowding, privacy, and coping. *Environment and Behavior*, 1981, **13**, 205–224.

Walker, E. H. Matching bits with the computer. *Psychology Today*, June 1981, p. 108.

Walker, M., Harriman, S., & Costello, S. The influence of appearance on compliance with a request. *Journal of Social Psychology*, 1980, **112**, 159–160.

Wallace, M. *New York Times*, November 25, 1969.

Wallies, R. V. Success information as a factor in female evaluation of males and females. Unpublished manuscript, Western Illinois University, 1973.

Wallston, B. S. What are the questions in psychology

of women? A feminist approach to research. *Psychology of Women Quarterly*, 1981, **5**, 597–617.

Walster (Hatfield), E. The effect of self-esteem on romantic liking. *Journal of Experimental Social Psychology*, 1965, **1**, 184–197.

Walster (Hatfield), E., Aronson, V., Abrahams, D., & Rottman, L. Importance of physical attractiveness in dating behavior. *Journal of Personality and Social Psychology*, 1966, **4**, 508–516.

Walster (Hatfield), E., & Festinger, L. The effectiveness of "overheard" persuasive communications. *Journal of Abnormal and Social Psychology*, 1962, **65**, 395–402.

Walster (Hatfield), E., & Walster, G. W. *A new look at love*. Reading, Mass.: Addison-Wesley, 1978.

Walster (Hatfield), E., Walster, G. W., & Berscheid, E. *Equity: Theory and research*. Boston: Allyn and Bacon, 1978.

Wanderer, Z. W. Validity of clinical judgments on human figure drawings. *Journal of Consulting and Clinical Psychology*, 1969, **33**, 143–150.

Ward, C. Differential evaluation of male and female expertise: Prejudice against women? *British Journal of Social and Clinical Psychology*, 1979, **18**, 65–69.

Ward, C. Prejudice against women: Who, when, and why? *Sex roles*, 1971, **7**, 163–171.

Ward, W. C., & Jenkins, H. M. The display of information and the judgment of contingency. *Canadian Journal of Psychology*, 1965, **19**, 231–241.

Warnick, D. H., & Sanders, G. S. The effects of group discussion on eyewitness accuracy. *Journal of Applied Social Psychology*, 1980, **10**, 249–259.

Wason, P. C. On the failure to eliminate hypotheses in a conceptual task. *Quarterly Journal of Experimental Psychology*, 1960, **12**, 129–140.

Watson, C. R. Blacks don't need 'black leaders.' *Newsweek*, November 30, 1981, p. 25.

Watson, R. I., Jr. Investigation into deindividuation using a cross-cultural survey technique. *Journal of Personality and Social Psychology*, 1973, **25**, 342–345.

Watts, W. A. Relative persistence of opinion change induced by active compared to passive participation. *Journal of Personality and Social Psychology*, 1967, 5, 4–15.

Wax, S. L. A survey of restrictive advertising and discrimination by summer reports in the province of Ontario. Canadian Jewish Congress. *Information and Comment*, 1948, **7**, 10–13. Cited by G. W. Allport in *The nature of prejudice*. Garden City, N.Y.: Doubleday Anchor Books, 1958, p. 5.

Weary, G. Self-serving attributional biases and concern over public defensibility of causal judgments. Paper presented at the Midwestern Psychological Association convention, 1980.

Weary, G., Harvey, J. H., Schwieger, P., Olson, C. T., Perloff, R., & Pritchard, S. Self-presentation and the moderation of self-serving biases. *Social Cognition*, 1982, **1**, 140–159.

Weatherley, D. Anti-Semitism and the expression of fantasy aggression. *Journal of Abnormal and Social Psychology*, 1961, **62**, 454–457.

Wehr, P. *Conflict regulation*. Boulder, Colo.: Westview Press, 1979.

Weigel, R. H., & Loomis, J. W. Televised models of female achievement revisited: Some progress. *Journal of Applied Social Psychology*, 1981, **11**, 58–63.

Weigel, R. H., Loomis, J. W., & Soja, M. J. Race relations on prime time television. *Journal of Personality and Social Psychology*, 1980, **39**, 884–893.

Weinberg, H. I., & Baron, R. S. The discredible eyewitness. *Personality and Social Psychology Bulletin*, 1982, **8**, 60–67.

Weiner, B. A cognitive (attribution)—emotion— action model of motivated behavior: An analysis of judgments of help-giving. *Journal of Personality and Social Psychology*, 1980, **39**, 186–200.

Weiner, B. The emotional consequences of causal ascriptions. Unpublished manuscript, UCLA, 1981.

Weinstein, N. D. Unrealistic optimism about future life events. *Journal of Personality and Social Psychology*, 1980, **39**, 806–820.

Weinstein, N. D., & Lachendro, E. Egocentrism and unrealistic optimism about the future. *Personality and Social Psychology Bulletin*, 1982, in press.

Weiss, J., & Brown, P. Self-insight error in the explanation of mood. Unpublished manuscript, Harvard University, 1976.

Weiten, W. The attraction-leniency effect in jury research: An examination of external validity. *Journal of Applied Social Psychology*, 1980, **10**, 340–347.

Welch, R. L., Huston-Stein, A., Wright, J. C., & Plehal, R. Subtle sex-role cues in children's commercials. *Journal of Communication*, 1979, **29**(3), 202–209.

Wells, G. L., Ferguson, T. J., & Lindsay, R. C. L. The tractability of eyewitness confidence and its implications for triers of fact. *Journal of Applied Psychology*, 1981, **66**, 688–696.

Wells, G. L., & Leippe, M. R. How do triers of fact enter the accuracy of eyewitness identification? Memory for peripheral detail can be misleading. *Journal of Applied Psychology*, 1981, **66**, 682–687.

Wells, G. L., Lindsay, R. C. L., & Ferguson, T. Accuracy, confidence, and juror perceptions in eyewitness identification. *Journal of Applied Psychology*, 1979, **64**, 440–448.

Wells, G. L., Lindsay, R. C. L., & Tousignant, J. P. Effects of expert psychological advice on human performance in judging the validity of eyewitness testimony. *Law and Human Behavior*, 1980, **4**, 275–285.

Wells, G. L., & Petty, R. E. The effects of overt head movements on persuasion: Compatibility and incompatibility of responses. *Basic and Applied Social Psychology*, 1980, **1**, 219–230.

West, C. Why can't a woman be more like a man? *Sociology of Work and Occupation*, 1982, **9**, 5–29.

West, S. G., & Brown, T. J. Physical attractiveness, the severity of the emergency and helping: A field experiment and interpersonal simulation. *Journal of Experimental Social Psychology*, 1975, **11**, 531–538.

West, S. G., Gunn, S. P., & Chernicky, P. Ubiquitous Watergate: An attributional analysis. *Journal of Personality and Social Psychology*, 1975, **32**, 55–65.

West, S. G., Whitney, G., & Schnedler, R. Helping a motorist in distress: The effects of sex, race, and neighborhood. *Journal of Personality and Social Psychology*, 1975, **31**, 691–698.

Weyant, J. M. Effects of mood states, costs, and benefits on helping. *Journal of Personality and Social Psychology*, 1978, **36**, 1169–1176.

White, G. L. Physical attractiveness and courtship progress. *Journal of Personality and Social Psychology*, 1980, **39**, 660–668.

White, G. L., Fishbein, S., & Rutsein, J. Passionate love and the misattribution of arousal. *Journal of Personality and Social Psychology*, 1981, **41**, 56–62.

White, P. Limitations in verbal reports of internal events: A refutation of Nisbett and Wilson and of Bem. *Psychological Review*, 1980, **87**, 105–112.

White, R. K. Three not-so-obvious contributions of psychology to peace. *Journal of Social Issues*, 1969, **25**(4), 23–39.

White, R. K. Selective inattention. *Psychology Today*, November 1971, pp. 47–50, 78–84.

White, R. K. Misperception in the Arab-Israeli conflict. *Journal of Social Issues*, 1977, **33**(1), 190–221.

Whitley, B. E., Jr. Sex roles and psychotherapy: A current appraisal. *Psychological Bulletin*, 1979, **86**, 1309–1321.

Whitley, B. E., Jr. Sex-role orientation and psychological well-being: Two meta-analyses. Paper presented at the Eastern Psychological Association convention, 1982.

Whitman, R. M., Kramer, M., & Baldridge, B. Which dream does the patient tell? *Archives of General Psychology*, 1963, **8**, 277–282.

Whittaker, J. O., & Meade, R. D. Social pressure in the modification and distortion of judgment: A cross-cultural study. *International Journal of Psychology*, 1967, **2**, 109–113.

Wichman, H., & Healy, V. In their own spaces: Student built lofts in dormitory rooms. Paper presented at the American Psychological Association convention, 1979.

Wicker, A. W. Attitudes versus actions: The relationship of verbal and overt behavioral responses to attitude objects. *Journal of Social Issues*, 1969, **25**, 41–78.

Wicker, A. W. An examination of the "other variables" explanation of attitude-behavior inconsistency. *Journal of Personality and Social Psychology*, 1971, **19**, 18–30.

Wicker, A. W. Ecological psychology: Some recent and prospective developments. *American Psychologist*, 1979, **34**, 755–765.

Wicklund, R. A. The influence of self-awareness on human behavior. *American Scientist*, 1979, **67**, 187–193.

Wicklund, R. A., & Brehm, J. W. *Perspectives on cognitive dissonance*. Hillsdale, N.J.: Lawrence Erlbaum, 1976.

Wilder, D. A. Perception of groups, size of opposition, and social influence. *Journal of Experimental Social Psychology*, 1977, **13**, 253–268.

Wilder, D. A. Perceiving persons as a group: Effects on attributions of causality and beliefs. *Social Psychology*, 1978, **41**, 13–23.

Wilder, D. A. Perceiving persons as a group: Categorization and intergroup relations. In D. L. Hamilton (Ed.), *Cognitive processes in stereotyping and intergroup behavior*. Hillsdale, N.J.: Lawrence Erlbaum, 1981.

Wiley, M. G., Crittenden, K. S., & Birg, L. D. Why

a rejection? Causal attribution of a career achievement event. *Social Psychology Quarterly*, 1979, **42**, 214–222.

Wilke, H., & Lanzetta, J. T. The obligation to help: The effects of amount of prior help on subsequent helping behavior. *Journal of Experimental Social Psychology*, 1970, **6**, 488–493.

Williams, K. D. The effects of group cohesion on social loafing. Paper presented at the Midwestern Psychological Association convention, 1981.

Williams, K. D., Harkins, S., & Latané, B. Identifiability as a deterrent to social loafing: Two cheering experiments. *Journal of Personality and Social Psychology*, 1981, **40**, 303–311.

Williams, R. M., Jr. Relative deprivation. In L. Coser (Ed.), *The idea of social structure: Papers in honor of Robert K. Merton*. New York: Harcourt Brace Jovanovich, 1975.

Willis, F. N., & Hamm, H. K. The use of interpersonal touch in securing compliance. *Journal of Nonverbal Behavior*, 1980, 5, 49–55.

Wills, T. A. Perceptions of clients by professional helpers. *Psychological Bulletin*, 1978, **85**, 968–1000.

Wills, T. A. Downward comparison principles in social psychology. *Psychological Bulletin*, 1981, **90**, 245–271.

Wilson, D. W. Is helping a laughing matter? *Psychology*, 1981, **18**, 6–9.

Wilson, D. W., & Donnerstein, E. Anonymity and interracial helping. Paper presented at the Southwestern Psychological Association convention, 1979.

Wilson, E. O. *On human nature*. Cambridge, Mass.: Harvard University Press, 1978.

Wilson, R. C., Gaft, J. G., Dienst, E. R., Wood, L., & Bavry, J. L. *College professors and their impact on students*. New York: Wiley, 1975.

Wilson, T. D., & Lassiter, G. D. Increasing intrinsic interest with superfluous extrinsic constraints. *Journal of Personality and Social Psychology*, 1982, **42**, 811–819.

Wilson, W. R. Feeling more than we can know: Exposure effects without learning. *Journal of Personality and Social Psychology*, 1979, **37**, 811–821.

Winch, R. F. *Mate selection: A study of complementary needs*. New York: Harper & Row, 1958.

Winkler, J., & Taylor, S. Unpublished study reported by J. D. Winkler, S. E. Taylor, R. F. Tebbets, J. B. Jemmott III, & J. Johnson in Information types, cognitive heuristics, and political persuasion. Paper presented at the American Psychological Association convention, 1979.

Winter, F. W. A laboratory experiment of individual attitude response to advertising exposure. *Journal of Marketing Research*, 1973, **10**, 130–140.

Wirth, L. Cited by J. P. Wogaman in *The great economic debate*. Philadelphia: Westminster Press, 1977, p. 29.

Wispe, L. G., & Freshley, H. B. Race, sex, and sympathetic helping behavior: The broken bag caper. *Journal of Personality and Social Psychology*, 1971, **17**, 59–65.

Wittig, M. A., & Petersen, A. C. (Eds.). *Sex-related differences in cognitive functioning: Developmental issues*. New York: Academic Press, 1979.

Wixon, D. R., & Laird, J. D. Awareness and attitude change in the forced-compliance paradigm: The importance of when. *Journal of Personality and Social Psychology*, 1976, **34**, 376–384.

Wolf, S., & Montgomery, D. A. Effects of inadmissible evidence and level of judicial admonishment to disregard on the judgments of mock jurors. *Journal of Applied Social Psychology*, 1977, 7, 205–219.

Wolfgang, M. E., & Ferracuti, F. *The subculture of violence*. London: Tavistock, 1967.

Wolosin, R. J., Sherman, S. J., & Mynatt, C. R. When self-interest and altruism conflict. *Journal of Personality and Social Psychology*, 1975, **32**, 752–760.

Women on Words and Images. *Dick and Jane as victims: Sex stereotyping in children's readers*. Princeton: 1972. Cited by C. Tavris & C. Offir in *The longest war: Sex differences in perspective*. New York: Harcourt Brace Jovanovich, 1977, p. 177.

Women's Campaign Fund. 1981. 1725 I Street N.W., Washington, D.C. 20006.

Wood, G. The knew-it-all-along effect. *Journal of Experimental Psychology: Human Perception and Performance*, 1979, **4**, 345–353.

Wood, W., & Eagly, A. H. Stages in the analysis of persuasive messages: The role of causal attributions and message comprehension. *Journal of Personality and Social Psychology*, 1981, **40**, 246–259.

Worchel, S., & Andreoli, V. Facilitation of social interaction through deindividuation of the target. *Journal of Personality and Social Psychology*, 1978, **36**, 549–556.

Worchel, S., Andreoli, V. A., & Folger, R. Intergroup cooperation and intergroup attraction: The effect of previous interaction and outcome of combined effort. *Journal of Experimental Social Psychology*, 1977, **13**, 131–140.

Worchel, S., Axsom, D., Ferris, F., Samah, G., & Schweitzer, S. Deterrents of the effect of intergroup cooperation on intergroup attraction. *Journal of Conflict Resolution*, 1978, **22**, 429–439.

Worchel, S., & Norvell, N. Effect of perceived environmental conditions during cooperation on intergroup attraction. *Journal of Personality and Social Psychology*, 1980, **38**, 764–772.

Worchel, S., & Yohai, S. M. L. The role of attribution in the experience of crowding. *Journal of Experimental Social Psychology*, 1979, **15**, 91–104.

Word, C. O., Zanna, M. P., & Cooper, J. The nonverbal mediation of self-fulfilling prophecies in interracial interaction. *Journal of Experimental Social Psychology*, 1974, **10**, 109–120.

Workman, E. A., & Williams, R. L. Effects of extrinsic rewards on intrinsic motivation in the classroom. *Journal of School Psychology*, 1980, **18**, 141–147.

Wright, P., & Rip, P. D. Retrospective reports on the causes of decisions. *Journal of Personality and Social Psychology*, 1981, **40**, 601–614.

Wrightsman, L. The American trial jury on trial: Empirical evidence and procedural modifications. *Journal of Social Issues*, 1978, **34**, 137–164.

Wylie, R. C. *The self-concept* (Vol. 2): *Theory and research on selected topics*. Lincoln, Neb.: University of Nebraska Press, 1979.

Yancey, W. L. Architecture, interaction, and social control: The case of a large-scale public housing project. *Environment and Behavior*, 1971, **3**, 3–21.

Yankelovich, Skelly, & White. Surveys conducted for the American Council of Life Insurance, 1973–1978. Reported in *Public Opinion*, December–January 1980, p. 34.

Yinon, Y., & Bizman, A. Noise, success, and failure as determinants of helping behavior. *Personality and Social Psychology Bulletin*, 1980, **6**, 125–130.

Yinon, Y., Jaffe, Y., & Feshbach, S. Risky aggression in individuals and groups. *Journal of Personality and Social Psychology*, 1975, **31**, 808–815.

Young, P. National Center for Health Statistics data cited in Newhouse News Service release, *Grand Rapids Press*, March 7, 1982.

Young, W. R. There's a girl on the tracks! *Reader's Digest*, February 1977, pp. 91–95.

Younger, J. C., & Doob, A. N. Attribution and aggression: The misattribution of anger. *Journal of Research in Personality*, 1978, **12**, 164–171.

Younger, J. C., Walker, L., & Arrowood, J. A. Postdecision dissonance at the fair. *Personality and Social Psychology Bulletin*, 1977, **3**, 284–287.

Yuchtman (Yaar), E. Effects of social-psychological factors on subjective economic welfare. In B. Strumpel (Ed.), *Economic means for human needs*. Ann Arbor: Institute for Social Research, University of Michigan, 1976.

Yukl, G. Effects of the opponent's initial offer, concession magnitude, and concession frequency on bargaining behavior. *Journal of Personality and Social Psychology*, 1974, **30**, 323–335.

Zabelka, G. I was told it was necessary. *Sojourners*, August 1980, pp. 12–15. (Interview by C. C. McCarthy.)

Zajonc, R. B. Social facilitation. *Science*, 1965, **149**, 269–274.

Zajonc, R. B. Attitudinal effects of mere exposure. *Journal of Personality and Social Psychology*, 1968, **9**, Monograph Suppl. No. 2, part 2.

Zajonc, R. B. Brainwash: Familiarity breeds comfort. *Psychology Today*, February 1970, pp. 32–35, 60–62.

Zajonc, R. B. Feeling and thinking: Preferences need no inferences. *American Psychologist*, 1980, **35**, 151–175.

Zajonc, R. B., & Sales, S. M. Social facilitation of dominant and subordinate responses. *Journal of Experimental Social Psychology*, 1966, **2**, 160–168.

Zander, A. Students' criteria of satisfaction in a classroom committee project. *Human Relations*, 1969, **22**, 195–207.

Zanna, M. P., Klosson, E. C., & Darley, J. M. How television news viewers deal with facts that contradict their beliefs: A consistency and attribution analysis. *Journal of Applied Social Psychology*, 1976, **6**, 159–176.

Zanna, M. P., Olson, J. M., & Fazio, R. H. Attitude-behavior consistency: An individual difference perspective. *Journal of Personality and Social Psychology*, 1980, **38**, 432–440.

Zanna, M. P., Olson, J. M., & Fazio, R. H. Self-perception and attitude-behavior consistency. *Personality and Social Psychology Bulletin*, 1981, **7**, 252–256.

Zanna, M. P., & Pack, S. J. On the self-fulfilling nature of apparent sex differences in behavior. *Journal of Experimental Social Psychology*, 1975, **11**, 583–591.

Zeiler, M. D. Superstitious behavior in children: An experimental analysis. In H. W. Reese (Ed.), *Advances in child development and behavior* (Vol. 7). New York: Academic Press, 1972.

Zeisel, H., & Diamond, S. S. The jury selection in the Mitchell-Stans conspiracy trial. *American Bar Foundation Research Journal*, 1976, **1**, 151–174 (see p. 167). Cited by L. Wrightsman, The American trial jury on trial: Empirical evidence and procedural modifications. *Journal of Social Issues*, 1978, **34**, 137–164.

Zillman, D. *Hostility and aggression*. Hillsdale, N.J.: Lawrence Erlbaum, 1979.

Zillmann, D., & Bryant, J. Effect of residual excitation on the emotional response to provocation and delayed aggressive behavior. *Journal of Personality and Social Psychology*, 1974, **30**, 782–791.

Zillmann, D., Katcher, A. H., & Milavsky, B. Excitation transfer from physical exercise to subsequent aggressive behavior. *Journal of Experimental Social Psychology*, 1972, **8**, 247–259.

Zimbardo, P. G. The human choice: Individuation, reason, and order versus deindividuation, impulse, and chaos. In W. J. Arnold & D. Levine (Eds.), *Nebraska Symposium on Motivation, 1969*. Lincoln: University of Nebraska Press, 1970.

Zimbardo, P. G. *The psychological power and pathology of imprisonment*. A statement prepared for the U.S. House of Representatives Committee on the Judiciary, Subcommittee No. 3: Hearings on Prison Reform, San Francisco, Calif.: October 25, 1971.

Zimbardo, P. G. Pathology of imprisonment. *Trans-action/Society*, April 1972, pp. 4–8. (a)

Zimbardo, P. G. The Stanford prison experiment. 1972. A slide/tape presentation produced by Philip G. Zimbardo, Inc., P.O. Box 4395, Stanford, Calif. 94305. (b)

Zimbardo, P. G., Ebbesen, E. B., & Maslach, C. *Influencing attitudes and changing behavior*. Reading, Mass.: Addison-Wesley, 1977.

Zimbardo, P. G., Haney, C., & Banks, W. C. A Pirandellian prison. *New York Times Magazine*, April 8, 1973, pp. 38–60.

Zimmerman, D. H., & West, C. Sex roles, interruptions and silences in conversation. In B. Thorne & N. M. Henley (Eds.), *Language and Sex: Difference and dominance*. Rowley, Mass.: Newbury House Publishers, 1975.

Zuckerman, M. Attribution of success and failure revisited, or: The motivational bias is alive and well in attribution theory. *Journal of Personality*, 1979, **47**, 245–287.

Zukier, H. A. The dilution effect: Role of the correlation and the dispersion of predictor variables in the use of nondiagnostic information. *Journal of Personality and Social Psychology*, 1982, in press.

Zusne, L., & Jones, W. H. *Anomalistic psychology: A case study of extraordinary phenomena of behavior and experience*. Hillsdale, N.J.: Lawrence Erlbaum, 1981.

Acknowledgments

Fig. 8-3 from Aronson, Turner and Carlsmith, "Communicator credibility and communication discrepancy as determinants of opinion change." *Journal of Abnormal and Social Psychology*, 1963, 67, 31–36. © 1963 American Psychological Association.

Fig. 7-2 from Asch, "Studies of independence and conformity: A minority of one against a unanimous majority." *Psychological Monographs*, 1956, 70, No. 9, Whole No. 416.

Fig. 15-4 from Baum and Davis: "Reducing stress of high density living: An accelerated intervention." *Journal of Personality and Social Psychology*, 1980, 38, 471–481.

Fig. 15-3 from Baum and Valins, *Architecture and Social Behavior*: Hillsdale, New Jersey: Erlbaum, 1977, p. 21. Reprinted with permission of authors and publisher.

Fig. 15-5 from Becker, Seligman and Darley: "Psychological strategies to reduce energy consumption: Project summary report." The Center for Energy and Environment Studies, Princeton University, 1979. Reprinted by permission of John M. Darley and Clive Seligman.

Fig. 6-8A and 6-8B from Bell, Fisher, and Loomis: *Environmental Psychology*. Reprinted by permission of CBS Saunders College Publishing, 1978.

Box 6-2 from "Personality development in males and females: The influence of differential socialization." Excerpted from Master Lecture of J. Block presented at American Psychological Association, 1979.

Fig. 8-7 adapted from *Competence and Coping During Adulthood* edited by Lynne A. Bond and James Rosen, by permission of University Press of New England, © 1980 by the Vermont Conference on the Primary Prevention of Psychopathology.

Box 9-2 adapted from Janis in Brandsatter, Davis, and Stocker-Kreichgauer (eds.): *Contemporary Problems in Group Decision Making*. New York, Academic Press, in press.

Citation for use in Ch. 12, p. 434 from Burstein, Doughtie, and Raphaeli: "Contrastive vignette techniques: An indirect methodology designed to address reactive social attitude measurement." from *Journal of Applied Social Psychology*, 1980, V. 10(2), pp. 147–165. Permission granted by V. H. Winston and Sons.

Fig. 10-6 from Carlsmith and Anderson. "Ambient temperature and the occurance of collective violence: A new analysis." *Journal of Personality and Social Psychology*, 1979, 37, 337–344.

Fig. 8-8 from Chaiken and Eagly: "Communication modality as a determinant of message persuasiveness and message comprehensibility." *Journal of Personality and Social Psychology*. 1978, 34, 605–614.

Fig. 6-1 from Condry and Condry, "Sex differences: A Study in the eye of the beholder." *Child Development*, 1976, 47, p. 812–819. © The Society for Research in Child Development, Inc.

Fig. 7-3 from Crutchfield, "Conformity and character." *American Psychologist*, 1955, 10, 191–198.

Citation for use in Ch. 5, p. 163 from Dawes: "Shallow Psychology" in Carroll and Payne (eds.) *Cognition and Social Behavior*, Hillsdale, NJ: Erlbaum, 1976, p. 1–11. Reprinted by permission of authors and publisher.

Fig. 8-6 from H. L. Davis and Silk (eds.) *Behaviorial and Management Science in Marketing*, New York: Ronald Press, 1978, pp. 156–180.

Fig. 10-2 from Dollard et al.: *Frustration and Aggression*. New Haven: Yale University Press, 1939 and Miller: "The frustration-aggression hypothesis," *Psychological Review*, 1941, 48, 337–342. Reprinted by permission of Yale University Press.

Fig. 10-9 from Donnerstein: "Aggression: Erotica and violence against women." *Journal of Personality and Social Psychology*, 1980, 39, 269–277.

Fig. 10-8 from Donnerstein, Donnerstein, and Evans: "Erotic stimuli and aggression: Facilitation or inhibition." *Journal of Personality and Social Psychology*, 1975, 32, 237–244.

Fig. 12-3 from Farley et al: "Chocolate city, vanilla suburbs: Will the trend toward racially separate communities continue?" *Social Science Research*, 1978, p. 319–344. With permission of Academic Press.

Box 7-3 reprinted by permission of Farrar, Straus and Giroux, Inc. Excerpt from *A Wrinkle In Time* by Madeleine L'Engle. Copyright © 1962 by Madeleine L'Engle Franklin.

Fig. 13-1 reprinted from Festinger, Schachter, and Back from *Social Pressures in Informal Groups* with permission of Stanford University Press © 1950 by Festinger, Schachter and Back. Renewed 1978.

Fig. 7-6 from Garbarino and Bronfenbrenner. "The socialization of moral judgement and behavior in cross-cultural perspective" in T. Likona (ed.) *Moral Development and Behavior: Theory Research and Social Issues*. New York: Holt, Rinehart and Winston, 1976.

Fig. 12-5 reprinted from General Social Surveys, 1972–1980. Cumulative Codebook, Storrs, CT. Roper Public Opinion Research Center, University of Connecticut 1980; data taken from *Public Opinion*, © by American Enterprise Institute.

Fig. 12-1 General social surveys, 1972–80. Cumulative codebook, Storrs, CT. Roper Public Opinion Research Center, University of Connecticut, 1980.

Fig. 10.3 from Gurr: "The calculus of Civil Conflict," *Journal of Social Issues*, 1972, 28(1), 27–47. Reprinted by permission of Plenum Publishing Corp.

Box 10-2 from *A Preface to History* by Gustavson. Copyright © 1955 by Gustavson. Used with the permission of McGraw-Hill Book Co.

Fig. 8-4: Hovland, Lamsdaine and Sheffield. *Experiments on Mass Communication: Studies on Social Psychology in WWII*, Vol. III. Princeton, New Jersey, Princeton University Press 1949.

Table 6-1 from Henley: *Body Politics: Power, Sex, and Nonverbal Communication*. Englewood Cliffs, New Jersey: Prentice-Hall, 1977, p. 181. © 1977 by Prentice-Hall, Inc.

Box 2-1: Ray Hyman "Cold reading: How to convince strangers that you know all about them," in *Paranormal Borderlands of Science*, eds. K. Frazier (Buffalo, NY: Prometheus Books, 1981), p. 86.

Fig. 6-5 from Ickes and Barnes: "Boys and girls together—and alienated. On enacting sex roles in mixed sex dyads." *Journal of Personality and Social Psychology*, 1978, 36, 669–683. © 1978 American Psychological Association.

Fig. 11-3 from Isen, Clark and Schwartz, "Duration of the effect of good mood on helping: Footprints on the sands of time." *Journal of Personality and Social Psychology*, 1973, 27, 239–247.

Fig. 10-10 from Jaffee, Shapir, and Yinon: "Retaliatory aggression in individuals and groups." *European Journal of Social Psychology*, 1979, 9, p. 177–186. © 1981 Jaffee, Shapir, and Yinon. Reprinted by permission of John Wiley and Sons, Ltd.

Fig. 8-1 from Janis, Kaye, and Kirschner: "Facilitating effects of eating-while-reading on responsiveness of persuasive communications." *Journal of Personality and Social Psychology* 1965, 1, 181–186. © 1965 American Psychological Association.

Fig. 9-8 from Janis and Mann: *Decision Making: A Psychological Analysis of Conflict, Choice and Commitment.*, p. 132. © 1977 by The Free Press, a Division of Macmillan Publishing Co., Inc.

Fig. 3-1 from Jones and Harris: "The Attribution of

Attitudes." *Journal of Experimental Social Psychology*, 1967, 3, 1–24.

Fig. 11-2 from Latané and Darley: *The Unresponsive Bystander: Why Doesn't He Help?* New York: Appleton-Century-Crofts, 1970.

Fig. 11-1 from Latané and Darley: "Group inhibition of bystander intervention in emergencies," *Journal of Personality and Social Psychology*, 1968, 10, 215–221.

Citation for permission to use in Chapter 11 from Latané and Darley: *The Unresponsive Bystander: Why Doesn't He Help?* New York: Appleton-Century-Crofts, 1970.

Fig. 2-2 from Lieberman, "The effects of changes in roles on the attitudes of role occupants," *Human Relations*, 1956, 9, 385–402. Reprinted by permission of Plenum Publishing Corp.

Fig. 10-5 from Loch (ed.) *Psychology of Crime and Criminal Justice*. New York: Holt, Rinehart and Winston, 1979, p. 198–236.

Fig. 16-4 from Loftus: *Eyewitness Testimony*. Cambridge, MA: Harvard University Press. 1979.

Fig. 16-2 from Loftus: "The malleability of human memory." *American Scientist*, 1979. 67, 312–320.

Citation for use in Ch. 4, p. 126 reprinted by permission of Joanne Martin, from Martin, Patterson, and Price. "The effects of level of abstraction of a script on accuracy of recall." Paper presented to Western Psychological Association Convention, 1979.

Figs. 8-9 and 8-10 reprinted by permission of Alfred McAlister from McAlister et al: "Long-term follow-up of a pilot project on smoking prevention with adolescents." Paper presented to the American Psychological Association Convention, 1981.

Fig. 7-4 from Milgram, Bickman, and Berkowitz: "Note on the drawing power of crowds of different size." *Journal of Personality and Social Psychology*, 1969, 13, 79–82, © 1969 American Psychological Association.

Fig. 7-3 data from Tables 1 and 2 in *Obedience to Authority: An Experimental View* by Stanley Milgram. Reprinted by permission of Harper & Row Publishers, Inc.

Box 7-1 citation from p. 56 of *Obedience to Authority: An Experimental View* by Stanley Milgram. Reprinted by permission of Harper & Row Publishers, Inc.

Fig. 9-6 from "Discussion Effects on Social Attitudes Science," by Myers and Bishop, *Science*, Vol. 169, pp. 778–789. August 1970 © by the American Association for the Advancement of Science.

Fig. 9-7 from Myers: "Polarizing effects of social comparison." *Journal of Experimental Social Psychology*. 1978, 14, 554–563.

Fig. 15-2 adapted from Joseph Newman and Clark McCauley, "Eye contact with strangers in city, suburb, and small town," *Environment and Behavior*, Vol. 9, No. 4, p. 552 © 1977 Sage Publications, Inc., with permission of the publisher and authors.

Box 6-3: © 1979 by The New York Times Co. Reprinted by permission.

Box 12-3: © 1976 by The New York Times Co. Reprinted by permission.

Box 4-6: © 1981 by The New York Times Co. Reprinted by permission.

Fig. 3-2 from Nisbett and Ross: *Human Inference*, Prentice-Hall, 1980, p. 84. Copyright © by the American Psychological Association. Adapted by permission of the author.

Citation for permission to use in Ch. 4, p. 121 from Nisbett, Zukler, and Lemley: "The dilution effect: non-diagnostic information." *Cognitive Psychology*, in press 1982. Vol. 13. Pp. 248–277.

Fig. 6-3 reprinted by permission of *Public Opinion*. February/March, 1980, p. 37. © 1980 by The Trustees of Columbia University. From Survey by the European Economic Commission.

Fig. 6-4 from CBS/The New York Times Poll, October, 1977. Reprinted by permission of *Public Opinion*, September/October, 1978, p. 37. © 1978 by Trustees of Columbia University.

Box 3-1 from Robinson and Shaver (eds.), "Measures of social psychological attitudes." Ann Arbor: Institute for Social Research. 1973. Pp. 227–234. © 1973 by the American Psychological Association. Reprinted/adapted by permission of the author.

Fig. 12-2 from Rogers and Prentice-Dunn, "Deindividuation and anger-mediated interracial aggression: Unmasking regressive racism." *Journal of Personality and Social Psychology*, 1981, 41, 63–73.

Box 6-1 from "Non-role dating" by John and Letha Scanzoni. Reprinted by permission of *"The Other Side,"* 300, Philadelphia, PA 19144. © 1982.

Citation for permission to use in Ch. 2, p. 56 from Schein: "The Chinese indocrination program for prisoners of war. A study of attempted 'brainwashing'." *Psychiatry*, 1956, 19, 149–172.

Fig. 15-1 from Schmidt and Keating: "Human crowding and personal control: On integration of the research." *Psychological Bulletin*, 1979, 86, 680–700. Copyright © 1979 American Psychological Association.

Fig. 7-1 from p. 209 of *Social Psychology* by Muzafer Sherif and Carolyn Sherif. © 1969 by Sherif.

Fig. 14-3 taken from Sherif: *In Common Predicament: Social Psychology of Intergroup Conflict and Cooperation*. Boston: Houghton Mifflin Company. Reprinted by permission of Houghton Mifflin Company.

Citation in Ch. 9 p. 322 reprinted by permission of Macmillan Publishing Co, Inc. from *Inside the Third Reich* by Albert Speer (Translation: Copyright © 1979 by Macmillan Publishing Company, Inc.)

Box 1-1 from Tversky-Kahnman: "The framing of decisions and the psychology of choice," *Science*, Vol. 211. Pp. 453–458, 1981. © 1981.

Box 11-1 reprinted by permission of United Press International.

Box 13-1 reprinted by permission of United Press International.

Citation for permission to use in Chapter 9, p. 324 from Van de Ven-Delbecq: "Nominal versus interacting group processes." *Academy of Management Journal*, 1971, 14, 201–211.

Citation for use in Ch. 12, p. 420 from Wax: "A survey of restrictive advertising and discrimination by summer resorts in the provinces of Ontario." Canadian Jewish Congress: Information and Comment, 1948, 7, 10–13. Cited from Allport: *The Nature of Prejudice*, © 1958. Reprinted with permission of Addison-Wesley, Reading, MA. P. 5.

Fig. 6-2 reprinted by permission of Women's Campaign Fund.

Fig. 13-2 from Zajonc, "Attitudinal effects of mere exposure." *Journal of Personality and Social Psychology*, 1968. *Monograph Supplement* No. 2, Part 2. © 1968 by the American Psychological Association.

Fig. 9-1 from Zajonc and Scales: "Social interaction of dominant and subordinate responses." From *Journal of Experimental Social Psychology*, 1966, 2, 160–168.

Citation for permission to use in Ch. 6, p. 171 from Philip Zimbardo "The Psychological Power and Pathology of Imprisonment." A statement prepared for the United States House of Representatives.

NAME INDEX

SUBJECT INDEX